# THE GUIDE
## TO THE
# ARCHITECTURE
## OF
# PARIS

OTHER BOOKS BY NORVAL WHITE

*The Architecture Book*
*New York: A Physical History*

BY NORVAL WHITE AND ELLIOT WILLENSKY

*AIA Guide to New York City*

# THE
# GUIDE
## TO THE
# ARCHITECTURE
## OF
# PARIS

NORVAL WHITE

CHARLES SCRIBNER'S SONS
NEW YORK

MAXWELL MACMILLAN INTERNATIONAL
NEW YORK   OXFORD   SINGAPORE   SYDNEY

Charles Scribner's Sons
Macmillan Publishing Company
866 Third Avenue, New York, NY 10022

Macmillan Publishing Company is part of the
Maxwell Communication Group of Companies.

Library of Congress Cataloging-in-Publication Data

White, Norval, 1926–
    The guide to the architecture of Paris / Norval White.
        p.   cm.
    Includes index.
    ISBN 0-684-19293-4
    1. Paris (France)—Description—1975– —Tours.  2. Walking—France—
Paris—Guide-books.   3.   Architecture—France—Paris—Guide-books.   4.
Paris (France)—Buildings, structures, etc.—Guide-books.  5. Architects—
France—Paris—Indexes.   6. Paris (France)—Maps, Tourist.  I. Title.
    DC708.W49   1991
    914.4'3604839—dc20                                                      90-45141
                                                                                CIP

Design by ROBERT BULL DESIGN

Macmillan books are available at special discounts for bulk purchases for sales promotions, premiums, fund-raising, or educational use. For details, contact:
    Special Sales Director
    Macmillan Publishing Company
    866 Third Avenue
    New York, NY 10022

10   9   8   7   6   5   4   3   2   1

Printed in the United States of America

To Elliot Willensky
1933–1990
a gentle man
a noble gadfly
friend, colleague in architecture, sometime coauthor

Paris is the greatest temple ever built to material joys and the lust of the eyes.

**Henry James**

•

Mrs. Allonby: They say, Lady Hunstanton, that when good Americans die they go to Paris.

Lady Hunstanton: Indeed? And when bad Americans die, where do they go to?

Lord Illingworth: Oh, they go to America.

**Oscar Wilde in *A Woman of No Importance***

•

The last time I see Paris will be on the day I die. The city was inexhaustible, and so is its memory.

**Elliot Paul in *The Last Time I Saw Paris***

•

If you are lucky enough to have lived in Paris as a young man, then wherever you go for the rest of your life, it stays with you, for Paris is a moveable feast.

**Ernest Hemingway in *A Moveable Feast***

# CONTENTS

•

Names of architects of particular interest (whether for deserved fame or notoriety) are set **boldface** in each stream of contents. The buildings and architects listed are merely highlights of the walking tour cited, and there are many intervening buildings between and beyond those noted. Though all architects concerned with a particular building are listed in the entry itself, the following section frequently lists only the principal architect *or* the first of a sequence of names followed by *et al.* to indicate peers participating. In medieval and other early architecture, where there is no known architect, later architects who completed, modified, or restored the building may be cited. Sometimes tours overlap into contiguous arrondissements, as the natural neighborhoods and paths for strolling do not respect political boundaries.

•

# 1

## FIRST
## ARRONDISSEMENT
### SOUTH 1
#### PLACE DE LA CONCORDE TO THE LOUVRE

Place de la Concorde, Les Palais de Gabriel: **Jacques-Ange Gabriel** and **Jacques-Ignace Hittorf;** Jeu de Paume; rue Saint-Florentin; Aux Trois Quartiers: **Louis Faure-Dujarric;** rue Saint-Honoré; Eglise Polonaise: **Charles Errard;** place Vendôme: **Jules Hardouin-Mansart;** Eglise Saint-Roch: **Jacques Lemercier;** Comédie Française: **Victor Louis;** Bibliothèque Nationale: **Pierre Le Muet** and **Henri Labrouste;** Eglise Notre-Dame-des-Victoires: **Pierre Le Muet;** place des Victoires: **Jules Hardouin-Mansart;** Jardin du Palais-Royal: **Victor Louis;** Galerie Véro-Dodat: **Constant Protain;** l'Oratoire du Louvre: **Clément II Métezeau;** Eglise Saint-Germain-l'Auxerrois: **Victor Baltard;** Louvre: **Pierre Lescot, Jacques Lemercier, Louis Le Vau, Claude Perrault, Hector Lefuel, Percier et Fontaine,** and **I. M. Pei;** Palais Royal: **Jacques Lemercier**

# 2

## FIRST AND FOURTH
## ARRONDISSEMENTS
### ISLANDS IN THE RIVER 15
#### PONT DE SULLY TO SQUARE DU VERT GALANT

Hôtel Lambert: **Louis Le Vau;** Arcade de l'Hôtel Bretonvilliers: **Jean Androuet du Cerceau;** Hôtel Lauzun: **Louis Le Vau;** quai

d'Anjou; Eglise Saint-Louis-en-l'Ile: **Louis Le Vau;** quai de Béthune;
quai d'Orléans; quai de Bourbon; Hôtel Le Charron: **Sébastien
Bruand;** les Déportées: **Georges-Henri Pingusson;** Cathédrale
Notre-Dame de Paris: **Pierre de Montreuil,** then **Eugène
Viollet-le-Duc;** pont d'Arcole: **Alphonse Oudry;** Sainte-Chapelle:
**Pierre de Montreuil,** then **Eugène Viollet-le-Duc;** La Conciergerie;
quai des Orfèvres: **Henri Sauvage;** place Dauphine;
square du Vert Galant

# 3

## FIRST AND SECOND
## ARRONDISSEMENTS
### SOUTHEAST  23
#### BOURSE DU COMMERCE, LES HALLES, AND ENVIRONS

Bourse du Commerce: **Nicolas Lecamus de Mézières** and
**François-Joseph Bélanger;** Hôtel Thoinard de Vougy: **Germain
Boffrand;** rue Jean-Jacques-Rousseau; passage du Grand Cerf; passage
du Bourg-l'Abbé: **Lusson** and **Paul Blondel;** Tour de Jean sans Peur;
Eglise Saint-Leu/Saint-Gilles: **Charles de Wailly** and **Victor Baltard;**
Fontaine des Innocents: **Jean Goujon;** Café Costès: **Philippe Starck;**
Forum des Halles: **Jean Willerval, Claude Vasconi,** and **Georges
Pancreac'h;** Jardin des Halles: **Louis Arrètche;** Les Halles
Souterraines: **Paul Chemetov;** Eglise Saint-Eustache: **Pierre
Lemercier, Charles David, François Petit,** and **Mansart de Jouy;**
La Samaritaine: **Frantz Jourdain** and **Henri Sauvage**

# 4

## SECOND
## ARRONDISSEMENT
### NORTH  30
#### PORTE SAINT-DENIS TO PLACE DES VICTOIRES

Porte Saint-Denis: **Nicolas-François Blondel;** Eglise
Notre-Dame-de-Bonne-Nouvelle: **Hippolyte Godde;** passage du Caire;
Félix Potin: **Charles Le Maresquier;** 118, rue Réaumur: **Charles J.
Guiral de Montarnal;** 124, rue Réaumur: **Georges Chédanne;**
Théâtre des Variétés; passage des Panoramas; 8-10, rue Saint-Marc:
**Henri Sauvage;** Palais de la Bourse: **Alexandre-Théodore
Brongniart;** Le Vaudeville; rue des Colonnes; Crédit Lyonnais: **André
Narjoux;** Fontaine Gaillon: **Ludovico Visconti;** passage Choiseul

# 5

## THIRD
## ARRONDISSEMENT
### NORTH  37
#### SAINT-DENIS-DU-SACREMENT TO SAINTE-ELISABETH

Eglise Saint-Denis-du-Sacrement: **Hippolyte Godde;** rue
Vieille-du-Temple; rue de Saintonge; Hôtel de Tallard: **Pierre Bullet;**
rue Charlot; 10, rue de Bretagne: **Hector Guimard;** rue des
Filles-du-Calvaire; Fontaine Boucherat: **Jean Beausire;** Mairie; Marché

François-Hippolyte Destailleur; Musée Grévin: Eugène-Alfred Hénard; passage des Princes; Maison Dorée: Victor Lemaire and Pierre Dufau; Salle Favart: Stanislas-Louis Bernier; Crédit Lyonnais: William Bouwens van der Boijen, André Narjoux, Victor Laloux, and Gustave Eiffel; Cinéma Gaumont-Opéra: Charles Le Maresquier; Cinéma Paramount-Opéra: Auguste Magne

Cinéma Rex: Auguste Bluysen and John Eberson; Banque National de Paris: Edouard-Jules Corroyer; Eglise Saint-Eugène-Sainte-Cécile: Louis-Auguste Boileau; Folies Bergère: Pico; Hôtel de Botterel-Quintin: Pérard de Montreuil and Sébastien-Jean Duboisterf; Hôtels Titon and de Goix: Jean-Charles Delafosse; Hôtel du Marquis de Thoix: Munster

Place de la République; Canal Saint-Martin; passerelle de la Douane; Groupe Scolaire: Lionel and Daniel Brandon; Gymnase Jenmapes: Antoine Grumbach; 100,000 Chemises: Charles J. Guiral de Montarnal; Gare de l'Est: François-Alexandre Duquesney; Gare du Nord: Jacques-Ignace Hittorf; Hôpital Lariboisière: Gauthier; Cinéma Louxor: Ripey; Eglise Saint-Vincent-de-Paul: Jean-Baptiste Lepère and Jacques-Ignace Hittorf; boulevard Magenta; Marché Saint-Quentin; Eglise Saint-Laurent: Simon-Claude Constant-Dufeux; Faïenceries de Choisy: G. Jacobin and Ernest Brunnarius; Mairie: Jean-Eugène Rouyer; Hôtel Goûthière: Joseph Métivier; Restaurant Chez Julien; Porte Saint-Denis: Nicolas-François Blondel; Porte Saint-Martin: Pierre Bullet

Avenue de la République; 31, rue Saint-Ambroise: Mario Heymann and Roger Anger; 25, rue Saint-Ambroise: Louis Miquel and Georges Maurios; Direction de l'Eau: Christian de Portzamparc; rue de la Roquette; rue de Charonne; avenue Philippe-Auguste

avenue d'Italie: **Vittorio Mazzucconi;** Les Palmes d'Italie: **Michel Bourdeau;** tour Super-Italie: **Maurice Novarina;** boulevards des Maréchaux; Stade Sébastien-Charléty: **Henri Gaudin;** rue Küss/Groupe Scolaire: **Roger-Henri Expert;** Cité Florale; Eglise Sainte-Anne-de-la-Maison-Blanche: **Prosper Bobin;** Petite Alsace: **Jean Walter;** Lycée Estienne: **Mansot** and **Dammartin;** Le Métro Aérien: **Jean-Camille Formigé**

# 34

## FOURTEENTH
## ARRONDISSEMENT
### EAST   243
#### PLACE DENFERT-ROCHEREAU TO
#### SAINT-PIERRE-DE-MONTROUGE AND BACK

Place Denfert-Rochereau; Barrière d'Enfer: **Claude-Nicolas Ledoux;** Les Catacombes; Lion de Belfort: **Frédéric-Auguste Bartholdi;** Observatoire de Paris: **Claude Perrault;** Ecole Spécial d'Architecture: **Cuno Brullman** and **Arno Fougeras-Lavergnolle;** 11, rue Schoelcher: **Gauthier et Gauthier;** Cimetière Montparnasse; Logements, 3, rue Lalande: **Thierry Gruber;** 7, rue Danville: **Henri Sauvage;** Annexe/Mairie: **Georges Sébille;** Eglise Saint-Pierre-de-Montrouge: **Joseph Vaudremer;** Villa Adrienne; La Rouchefoucauld: **Jacques-Denis Antoine**

# 35

## FOURTEENTH
## ARRONDISSEMENT
### WEST   251
#### GARE MONTPARNASSE TO
#### PORTE DE VANVES

Tour Montparnasse: **Eugène Baudouin et al.;** place de Catalogne; Les Colonnes et l'Amphithéâtre: **Ricardo Bofill;** Eglise Notre-Dame-du-Travail: **Jules Astruc;** rue de l'Ouest: **Antoine Grumbach et al.;** HBM, 156, rue Raymond-Losserand: **Maurice Peyret-Dortail;** Villa Léone; 9-19, rue Louis-Morard: **Henri Robert;** avenue du Général-Maistre

# 36

## FOURTEENTH
## ARRONDISSEMENT
### SOUTH   257
#### CITE UNIVERSITAIRE, PARC DE MONTSOURIS,
#### AND THEIR SURROUNDS

**Le Corbusier, Lucio Costa, Willem Dudok, Louis-Hippolyte Boileau, Marc Solotareff, André Lurçat, Raymond Fischer, Auguste Perret, Jacques Bonnier, Jean Delechette, Paul Huillard, Louis Süe, Lenin**

Besnard; Immeuble/Sébastien-Mercier/Léontine: **Pol Abraham;** 25, rue Cévennes: **Gérard Thurnauer;** rond-point Saint-Charles: **Charles and Henri Delacroix;** Canal Plus: **Richard Meier;** rue Cauchy; boulevard Victor; "Paquebot"-Immeuble: **Pierre Patout;** Ministère de la Marine: **Auguste Perret;** Parc André-Citroën: **Patrick Berger et al.**

# 41
## SIXTEENTH
## ARRONDISSEMENT
### AUTEUIL  296
#### PLACE D'AUTEUIL TO RUE MALLET-STEVENS

Eglise Notre-Dame-d'Auteuil: **Joseph Vaudremer;** Chapelle Sainte-Bernadette: **Hulot** and **Busse;** square Henri-Paté, **Pierre Patout;** Logements: **Joachim Richard, Jean Ginsberg, François Heep, Berthold Lubetkin, Hector Guimard, Bernard Reichen, Philippe Robert, Henri Sauvage, Pol Abraham, Le Corbusier,** and **Robert Mallet-Stevens.**

# 42
## SIXTEENTH
## ARRONDISSEMENT
### CHAILLOT  306
#### PALAIS DE CHAILLOT TO CIMETIERE DE PASSY

Palais de Chaillot: **Jacques Carlu, Léon Azéma,** and **Louis-Hippolyte Boileau;** Musée Guimet; Palais Galliera: **Louis Ginain;** Eglise Saint-Pierre-de-Chaillot: **Emile Bois;** Musée d'Art Moderne de la Ville de Paris/Palais de Tokio: **Alfred Aubert et al.;** Conseil Economique et Social: **Auguste Perret;** 25 bis, rue Franklin: **Auguste and Gustave Perret;** 17, rue Franklin: **Marcel and Robert Hennequet;** 39, rue Scheffer: **Ernest Herscher;** Cimetière de Passy entrance: **René Berger**

# 43
## SIXTEENTH
## ARRONDISSEMENT
### VICTOR HUGO  315
#### PLACE VICTOR-HUGO THROUGH PASSY AND BACK

Place Victor Hugo; 50, avenue Victor-Hugo. **Charles Plumet;** Restaurant Prunier Traktir: **Louis-Hippolyte Boileau;** 58 bis, avenue Foch: **Alfred Fasquelle;** 53, avenue Foch: **Charles Abella;** Musée d'Ennery; 27, villa Saïd: **Auguste Perret;** Métro Dauphine: **Hector Guimard;** St. James Club: **Alfred Aldrophe;** Institut Supérieur de Gestion: **William Bouwens van der Boijen;** Logements: **Michel Roux-Spitz, Jean Walter,** and **Charles Thomas;** Mairie: **Godeboeuf;** Cinéma Victor-Hugo: **Jean Charaval** and **Marcel Mélendes;** Hôtel Pauilhac: **Charles Letrosne;** Caserne des Sapeurs/Pompiers: **Robert Mallet-Stevens;** Cité Commercial d'Argentine: **Henri Sauvage**

Weisengrün et al.; Eglise Saint-Jean-Baptiste-de-Belleville: **Lassus;** Parc de Belleville: **François Debulois;** passage Plantin; 100, boulevard de Belleville: **Frédéric Borel;** Odoul et Cie.: **Eugène Beaudouin** and **Marcel Lods;** Hôpital Saint-Louis: **Claude Vellefaux;** L'Egalitaire: **Raphaël Loiseau**

# 54

## NINETEENTH ARRONDISSEMENT
### BUTTES-CHAUMONT  394
PARC DES BUTTES-CHAUMONT AND ENVIRONS TO THE NORTHWEST

Parc des Buttes-Chaumont: **Alphonse Alphand, Pierre Barrillet-Deschamps** and **Gabriel Davioud;** Eglise Saint-Serge: **Staletzky;** Mairie: **Gabriel Davioud;** Eglise Notre-Dame-des-Buttes-Chaumont: **D. Honegger;** Piscine Pailleron: **Lucien Pollet;** Marché Secrétan: **Victor Baltard;** PCF Headquarters: **Oscar Niemayer**

# 55

## NINETEENTH ARRONDISSEMENT
### ROTONDE-BASSIN  400
STALINGRAD TO STALINGRAD

Rotonde de la Villette: **Claude-Nicolas Ledoux;** Bassin de la Villette: **Bernard Huet;** Métro Aérien: **Fulgence Bienvenue** and **Jean-Camille Formigé,** Conservatoire de Musique XIXe: **Fernand Pouillon:** 64, quai de la Loire: **Edith Girard;** College Tandou: **Henri Gaudin;** Gymnase and bains-douches: **Charles Gauthier** and **Charles Narjoux;** pont Levant de la Villette: **Five-Lilles;** Eglise Saint-Jacques-Saint-Christophe: **Pierre-Eugène Lequeux;** 23, quai de l'Oise: **Claude Vasconi;** rue de Flandre; former Entrepôts/Galerie Barbès: **Christian Maisonhaute** and **Jacques Lévy;** Hôtel Industriel: **Jean-Paul Viguier** and **Jean-François Jodry;** Logements/rue Mathis: **Jean-Pierre Buffi;** Les Orgues de Flandre: **Martin van Treeck;** Ateliers/passage de Flandre: **Yves Lion** and **François Leclercq;** Eglise Notre-Dame-des-Foyers

# 56

## NINETEENTH ARRONDISSEMENT
### VILLETTE  408
PORTE DE LA VILLETTE TO PARC DES BUTTES-CHAUMONT

113, boulevard MacDonald: **P. Enault;** Maison de la Villette; Villette Nord: **Gérard Thurnauer;** Cité des Sciences et de l'Industrie: **Adrian Fainsilber;** Les Folies: **Bernard Tschumi;** Le Jardin des Bambous: **Alexandre Chemetov;** La Grande Halle: **Jules de Mérindol, Bernard Reichen,** and **Philippe Robert;** Bureau de Poste: **Jacques Debat-Ponsan;** Logements/190, avenue Jean-Jaurès: **Aldo Rossi;** Cité de la Musique: **Christian de Portzamparc;** ZAC Manin-Jaurès:

# ACKNOWLEDGMENTS

First and foremost, Catherine Lobstein did basic research, collected information from libraries and periodicals, contributed ideas and content, and read the manuscript in its various forms. The book could not have attained its final extent and quality without her.

The Lobstein family put up with the occupation of their study-mezzanine at Saint-Amand-de-Vergt (Dordogne) for two long summers of writing, a peaceful place where the research of Paris was translated into the final manuscript.

At Charles Scribner's Sons, Erika Goldman provided concerned support with the aid of her associates. Joel Honig performed virtuoso copy editing far beyond the normal services of his profession. His sleek improvements of my translations are a delight. Janet Tingey's art direction and Robert Bull's maps are elegant in both the aesthetic and mathematical senses. And Carole McCurdy's indefatigable cross-checking has made perfection, though elusive and impossible, nearer and closer.

Two others who helped substantially were François Moulignat in Paris and Tom Knight in New York.

# NOTES TO THE READER

This book is written from an American point of view, and, indeed, Americans have always been the greatest fans of Paris, perhaps even greater than the French themselves. Myriad artists and writers have lived and worked here, leaving marks that have had a greater impact on America than on France, although much of their work has become integrated into overall French cultural history. Here one remembers Henry Miller, Gertrude Stein, Ernest Hemingway, and F. Scott Fitzgerald; and in the visual arts Alexander Calder, James McNeill Whistler, and John Singer Sargent.

As for architects, Jefferson had come to Paris not only as a politician but also to work with Clérisseau. He was followed by Charles Bulfinch, Richard Morris Hunt, H. H. Richardson, Louis Sullivan, Bernard Maybeck, Raymond Hood, and countless others who not only absorbed the newly professional education available at the Ecole des Beaux-Arts (Hunt was first there in 1846) but also *lived* in this elegant urban complex called Paris, learning from its built architecture. Perhaps the view from America's polyglot culture, where this disciplined evolution of both urban design and architecture was especially savored, could open expatriates' eyes to what resident Parisians could not see, whether laypersons or professionals, for overfamiliarity sometimes blurs vision. Conversely, such is surely the case for French observers of America, from de Tocqueville to Le Corbusier.

This is a guide to the architectural elements of *all* Paris in *all* periods of its history, from the more obvious buildings of the central city to the monuments, nooks, and crannies of the outer arrondissements. It is by no means dispassionate; architecture evokes strong feelings and heady dispute. But the opinions stated here are intended more to open discussion than to end it. Only by taking its own stand can the Guide arouse the traveler's attention. The opinions are held with conviction—but relish your own.

This is a guide for the pedestrian and transit user: everything can be seen either just by walking or by walking from and to Métro and bus stops. Touring by car is frenetic and dangerous to the driver trying to see architectural form and detail. Parking is difficult and sometimes just not available. But at the pace of a *flâneur* (stroller) one savors the detail, the texture of architecture. For a survey of the general territory in advance of detailed walking tours, tour buses and boats along the Seine are available, but the city buses are cheaper and perhaps more fun. The city's fabric can be appreciated by walking at leisure, stopping at a café or two to study the neighborhood while stationary.

As you explore along the tour routes, you will find buildings of "your own," many with entrance doors or *portes cochères* where you can buzz into the interior world that is so much a part of Paris. Sometimes you will discover an earlier period's architecture that backs up and/or surrounds the courtyard; this inner world, however, is becoming less and less accessible for reasons of general security. Here a code is punched into an electronic locking system, a code known only by those resident (and their friends or clients who are "honored" with it). This sad circumstance makes much of the urban fabric and texture visible only from eyries such as the Eiffel Tower, where the inner gardens and secret architecture can be distantly enjoyed.

## ORGANIZATION

The guide is divided into fifty-eight walking tours that explore all twenty arrondissements, some more intensely than others, but with the intent of familiarizing the reader with the whole of Paris rather than with that limited list of monuments both ancient and modern which is usually presented. As the survey is organized geographically, rather than by stylistic or historical groupings, one can enjoy the city's intermingled history where, for example, a Roman ruin and a late Gothic house stand across the street from an elegant *Art Moderne* café (the Thermes de Cluny, Hôtel de Cluny, and Café de Cluny). Such contrasts are the essence of what makes Paris rich architecturally, for they are the elegant substructure supporting the discipline of an urbanistically organized city. The typical vision of Paris—one of avenues, boulevards, and *places,* of the stroller out to see and be seen—is grand. But along those boulevards, and within those *places,* is a spectrum of an architecture that is mostly understated in form but frequently rich in personal stylistic detail from many periods. The architecture of *immeubles* (apartment houses) dominates it all, from the early experiments of the time of Louis XVI, the Empire, the Restoration, and Louis Philippe, through the vast constructions of Baron Haussmann that permeate the city, to the modern experiments of Art Nouveau, Art Deco, and those unique individual works by Lavirotte, Guimard, Le Corbusier, and Mallet-Stevens.

The index lists all architects whose works appear in this book, so that you may search for your favorites; and it gives their dates of birth and death where these could be found. Families of architects—and also architects with merely the same name—can be separated by the time or times in which they lived: the multiples of those named Blondel, Androuet du Cerceau, Delacroix, Boileau, Jourdain, et al.

## MAPS

Each walking tour is described on a specially designed map that delineates the route to be followed. **Numbers shown are the (street, avenue, or boulevard) house numbers.** For those in search of a particular building, this cartographic location together with the descriptive location given in the entry (citing the streets flanking the block) should make it simple to find.

## ENTRIES AND THE STAR SYSTEM

Each entry is preceded by a bracketed number and is identified by name in **boldface** type. The first number indicates the arrondissement, the letter indicates the section of the arrondissement, and the second number is that of the entry itself. Thus **[4s-21.]** defines the 4th arrondissement/south and entry 21; and **[16a-6.]** refers to the 16th arrondissement's Auteuil and entry 6.

For buildings with no name, the address is also included in boldface, as part of the basic identification. A named building is followed by its address, the names of boundary streets, the designer's (or designers') name(s), and finally the date of completion (or projected completion). When no other title follows a designer's name, one can assume that title is architect. Some dates may differ from those listed in other sources, since "the date" of a building may refer to completion, dedication, or use. Don't despair, for the difference of a year or two or three is trivial in a city with two thousand years under its belt.

The stars are not necessarily an indication of absolute quality but, rather, of importance and priority:

★★★★ If your time is limited, this is an absolute must. Worthy of a visit even if you will never see more than ten buildings in Paris.
★★★ Don't miss it if you are still strong enough: it is worth seeing without ever taking any "tour."
★★ If you are within one arrondissement's distance, track it down.
★ If you are taking a tour, it is a highlight worth noting.
**NO** ★ If time is limited, skip it in favor of starred buildings.

Buildings without stars are frequently distinguished—and even beautiful—but are mostly of a category with numerous examples. You will see dozens of equal quality, which is one of the joys of Paris. Certainly, housing of the 17th and 18th centuries, as well as endless streets of wonderful Haussmannian and post-Haussmannian architecture, are rich and often visually extravagant. Few of these are starred, for you will pass by scores of them. Opinions about absolute quality are reserved for the text, and therefore you may find a starred building praised or perhaps even damned with faint praise.

## HAUSSMANNIAN BOULEVARDS

Many avenues and boulevards were cut through in the 1860s under Baron Georges-Eugène Haussmann, appointed prefect of Paris in 1853 by the newly proclaimed Emperor Napoléon III. The reasons were multiple. Much literature dwells on the emperor's need to open up Paris from its then largely medieval structure of narrow and winding streets, where revolutionaries could gather and retreat from the army. This was partly true, and wide boulevards offered vistas for rifle fire and cannonballs. But for his reign the emperor also wanted a grand city that functioned well: boulevards for fast and easy circulation that offered grandeur of movement between major monuments, as well as a system of transport that followed them (the omnibuses, first horse-drawn), sewers that drained them, aqueducts that watered them, and parks that blossomed among them, for Napoléon had become a great fan of the Romantic park during his London exile.

The purest of these originals, complete with the buildings that formed them, are the boulevard Haussmann itself, particularly between rue du Faubourg-Saint-Honoré and place Saint-Augustin, and the avenue de l'Opéra. The former demonstrates that the unaltered original, all built at one time, can bring monotony to the street, here happily punctured by the grand Hôtel Jacquemart-André. Haussmannian streets, where time for architectural evolution was allowed, where individually designed buildings flanked the new cut, often supply a spectrum of architecture much richer and more fascinating—boulevard Raspail, for example.

## MORE ON WALKING TOURS

The walking tours are organized by geographical areas of proximate architectural interest. Each tour lies mostly within one of the twenty arrondissements but frequently overlaps into a neighbor or neighbors, where development has occurred at a line or nexus despite political divisions (modern Montparnasse, shared by the 6th, 14th, and 15th arrondissements), or where existing villages were intentionally split by Napoléon III to limit their revolutionary ardor (Belleville, shared by the 10th, 11th, 19th, and 20th arrondissements).

## HOUSE NUMBERING

House numbering for streets, boulevards, and avenues that parallel (more or less) the Seine follows that movement: numbers rising with the flow, with even *(pair)* on the right and odd *(impair)* on the left. Streets perpendicular to the Seine start their numbering at the river; facing away from the river, even is on the right, odd on the left. Because numbers were organized not block by block but, rather, as the city grew, the result creates two problems for the traveler. First, successive numbers on opposite sides of the street are often very distant from each other; 237, rue Saint-Honoré, for example, is across from No. 360. Second, as lots were infilled between existing buildings already numbered, or when a building was split in two, no number was available, and the new entrance was designated by adding *bis* or *ter* to the lower number; *bis* means literally "again," so that 21 bis is 21 again. When a third building sneaks in, it becomes 21 ter, or 21 thrice.

# WALLS AND GROWTH

At the end of the 3rd century B.C. a small Gallic trading town was established on the **Ile de la Cité,** within the seemingly safe embrace of the river Seine. This natural moat did not, however, save it from the power of Rome: Julius Caesar's legions crushed those of Vercingétorix in 52 B.C., and the town, named Lutetia to simulate the phonetic name of the Gauls, thence grew as a Roman colonial outpost at Gaul's crossroads. The main trade route from the Mediterranean to Northern Europe passed over the footprints of what are now the right bank's **rue Saint-Martin** and the left bank's **rue Saint-Jacques.** Under Roman rule and protection, the island's citizens expanded across the river's south arm to the **left bank,** particularly on and around the **Montagne Sainte Geneviève,** and that organized (and literally civilized) Roman town has left substantial traces at the **Thermes (baths) de Cluny** and the **Arènes de Lutèce.** Roman power stabilized and protected the community without need for walls.

As Roman power declined and the security such power provided vanished with it, the islanders erected walls around the Ile de la Cité in the late 3rd century A.D. Along five succeeding perimeters, walls have defined the edges of the city defensively, politically, economically, and urbanistically— five concentric rings that still express sequential stages of development, and still mostly mark lines of activity: Here were the walls of Philippe Auguste, of Charles V, of Louis XIII, of the Fermiers Généraux, of Adolphe Thiers. And here are the **Grands Boulevards,** the **Boulevards Extérieurs,** the **Boulevards des Maréchaux,** and the **Périphérique,** all linear voids of travel where the solid ranks of parapets and bastions once stood.

The wall of Philippe-Auguste (1180) has left remnants that can be savored in what are now apparently random places. This most ancient of remnant wall sites can be seen behind **Eglise Saint-Paul** and the **Lycée Charlemagne** along the **rue des Jardins-Saint-Paul** (see **[4s-25.]**); and along the **rue des Francs-Bourgeois** opposite the **Hôtel de Soubise** (a tower-bastion, see **[3/4m-29.]**). Later urban events have obliterated its linear impact, leaving isolated lines and points harbored for their venerability.

The walls from Charles V (1370) to Louis XIII (1630s) are remembered, on the other hand, as a clear and continuous swath (the latter wall being an extension and elaboration of the former). The 14th-century works of Charles were anchored at the east by the bastion of the **Bastille** that, later elevated to fort status, and then prison, became, in its destruction, a revolutionary symbol. The west anchor was the **Old Louvre,** a square court-yarded donjon one quarter the size of the much later, and still extant (16th–17th centuries), **Cour Carrée.** After expansion of the Louvre along the Seine, and construction of the **Tuileries Palace** for Catherine de' Medici, the wall was extended to embrace not only the palaces proper, but the **Tuileries Gardens.** This extension and the concurrent modification and modernization of Charles V's original wall (warfare was becoming technologically sophisticated) were completed under Louis XIII. Louis XIV, victorious in battle, and secured thereby from fear of attack, made the grand gesture of demolishing his father's recently extended and modernized walls, leaving a wide swath for development: a boulevard, grandly planted with trees for the carriages of the elegant and the strolling of the precocious *boulevardier. A boulevard,* by definition, is the service road of a fortification. Here the same literal way became the service road of fashion, to be embraced by theaters, cafés, restaurants of style, as the **grands boulevards:** now the boulevards de la Madeleine, des Capucines, des Italiens, Montmartre, Poissonnière, de Bonne Nouvelle, Saint-Denis, Saint-Martin, du Temple, des Filles du Calvaire, and Beaumarchais. The fortified line of hefty and dour solids now served as a frivolous social void. And here today cafés, cinémas, and the **Palais Garnier** (old opera) maintain similar, but more mundane spirits.

The Fermiers Généraux were the forty nobles who served as import tax collectors for the king on goods and produce entering Paris. In 1784–1789 they erected a wall, punctuated by fifty-two gates, each honored with an elegant toll station designed by **Claude-Nicolas Ledoux.** The Farmer-Generals, of course, received commissions for services, and hence their wall was a capital investment toward future profits. Instantly the object of hate (which circumventing smugglers laddered over and tunneled under), the wall became a symbol of oppression for the Revolution. Short-lived, and erected against only France's own citizens, the wall disappeared in a few decades, Ledoux's works and all, except for those at place Denfert-Rochereau (**Barrière d'Enfer [14e-1.]**), and place de la Nation (**Barrière du Trône [20s-10.]**), both toll stations; that at place de Stalingrad (**Rotonde de la Villette [19r-1.]**), administrative offices; and the **Rotonde de Chartres** at the Parc Monceau **[17m-50.]** (viewing pavilion for the Duc d'Orléans). The line of the wall can be experienced on the Métro Aérien (the elevated portions of what is largely a subway), on the left bank between **Charles de Gaulle/Etoile** and **Nation** (line 6); and similarly on the right bank from **Porte Dauphine** via **Charles de Gaulle/Etoile** to **Nation** (line 2).

The last, largest, and least effective wall (1841–1845) was that of Adolphe Thiers, writer and politician, foreign minister and president of the council under Louis-Philippe (he was later the first president of the Third Republic). A swath ranging from 1,200 to 1,350 feet wide (380 to 435 meters) was marked by the wall proper and its service boulevards, and fronted with an apron of land, the *zone non aedificandi,* where building was prohibited, ostensibly to leave the field of fire open to cannons mounted on the walls. Of course its first and only test failed in the Franco-Prussian war of 1871, where the Thiers wall was easily bypassed (forebodings of the Maginot line in 1940). The wall and its surrounds, a national property, were ceded in sequential sections to the city of Paris. The wall's footprint became the **Boulevards des Maréchaux** that formed the first perimeter ring around Paris; in the 1920s and 1930s, here rose the renowned red belt of social housing (the wall was slowly demolished between 1919 and 1932 and the housing that sprung up was popularly called the "red" belt because it housed left-wing workers, largely in red brick!). Later the *zone non aedificandi* provided space for sports, stadia, lycées, some housing, and the **périphérique.**

In sum, Paris reads as a symbolic tree, annual rings of growth marked by walls and the voids of activity that have replaced them.

# GLOSSARY

Words from the French that have been adopted into the English language are set in roman type. Where the meaning in English may be substantially different, however, French words are indicated in italics, even where an identical spelling occurs in English.

## A

abattoir  Slaughterhouse.

*abreuvoir*  Drinking trough for horses and, hence, a place where they are stabled.

*accueil*  A place of reception.

aisle  *Nef* in French (strictly speaking, *nef latérale*), but both nave and aisles are commonly referred to as *nefs*.

ambulatory  The walk-around space circumventing the chancel and altar space of a church, off of which are frequently radiating chapels.

*aménagement*  Interior arrangements and furnishings; arrangement of buildings, as in a master plan.

anthemion  A Greek ornament composed of stylized honeysuckle and used in Greek Revival and neo-Grec decoration.

apse  The exedral space of a church or its chancel, usually a semicircle in plan.

arched corbel table  A series of small, decorative arches at the cornice line of a Romanesque, or neo-Romanesque church; originally Lombardic.

architrave  The chief beam of a Classical or neo-Classical entablature, spanning directly above and between columns and, in turn, supporting frieze and cornice.

arrondissement  The subdivision of a French city, analogous to a borough or ward in England or America.

Arts and Crafts  An English term referring to the resurgence of, particularly, wood craftsmanship in the 1870s.

Art Deco *(Art Décoratif)*  The geometric and quasi-cubistic architecture that was the signature of the Exposition des Arts Décoratifs of 1925 in Paris, more apparent in detail than in overall form.

Art Moderne  The mostly white, streamlined, and/or stripped neo-Classical architecture from the Paris international exposition of 1937. Its use of sinuous stucco and chromium made one think that buildings might wish to travel at the speed of aircraft.

Art Nouveau  When Samuel Bing opened his shop *Art Nouveau* in Paris (1898), little did he know that the sinuous style that we have inherited would be so named: vegetative ornament that not only became the surface decoration of the then "modern" architecture but also contributed to form, particularly in the Métro entrances of Hector Guimard.

atelier  The studio or workshop of an artisan, architect, painter, or sculptor.

atlantes  The masculine counterparts of caryatids, those ladies who support the porch of the Erechtheum, on the Acropolis.

atrium  Originally the forecourt of an Early Christian church, or the inner court of a Roman house, open to the sky, the term now refers to both covered and uncovered communal public spaces.

*auberge*  Inn.

## B

*bains-douches*  Municipal shower baths that, in a pre–World War II society of limited plumbing, were sometimes also a joyous architectural event.

baldachino A structured canopy over the altar, evolved from the ciborium of the early Christian church. The most noted is that of Saint Peter's in Rome, by Bernini.

Baroque The late Renaissance of the 17th century in Italy that now, in retrospect, seems to have had a greater impact on Paris than was formerly thought.

barrel vault A continuous round arch *(voûte en berceau)*.

*barrières* Ledoux's fifty-two wondrous tollgates, which were the punctuating glories of the 1780s wall built by the Fermiers Généraux.

basilica Originally the building for a Roman lawcourt, where a central nave rose, with clerestories, above side aisles. The word later came to mean any major (in size) Catholic church that was not a cathedral.

bas-relief A sculpted plane that has subtle or modest projections.

bastion The part of a fortification that projects outward, allowing defenders to look back on invaders attacking adjacent walls.

batter The tapering back of a wall, giving it a receding upward slope and providing stability, as if it were a continuous buttress.

Bauhaus The school run sequentially by Van de Velde, Gropius, and Mies van der Rohe and last located at Berlin. It was at the Bauhaus that the machine aesthetic became a central ideology, although the objects created were made mostly by hand.

bay A structural set, composed of columns and beams or piers or vaults. It is one of a group of such sets; each added unit makes another bay.

bay window A projecting volume that gives perspective to the occupant up and down the street. In French the term is *bow window,* although in American usage that means a bellied rather than polygonal shape.

Beaux Arts Founded in 1648, the Ecole des Beaux-Arts merged with the Académie d'Architecture in 1793 to create a state-run school of architecture where archaeological reconstructions and fantasies generated the grandiloquent and wonderful architecture such as at the Palais Garnier. Ornate and classical, it placed special emphasis on the manipulation of vast crowds, vying for a pompous social life.

*beffroi* A bell tower, Italian style.

*Belle Epoque* Around 1900, used mostly in terms of interiors; the equivalent of Edwardian in Britain.

belvedere An architectural spot with a fine view, which can become a lovely object in its own right.

*béton armé* Reinforced concrete.

*bibliothèque* Library in the grand sense, not your spare bedroom.

*bis* "Again," as in the address 10 bis. Used where the original number 10 is next door, and no other numbers are available.

bistro(t) What would be a pub in England.

*bon marché* Inexpensive.

bollard A finial of iron, or a block of stone or concrete that limits vehicular access while allowing pedestrians to pass.

*borne* Milestone (but in kilometers, of course) or a boundary stone.

*boule* A ball or sphere, but also a game of steel balls that forms a popular form of urban bowling.

boulevard Technically the service road of a city's fortified walls. In Paris, this is largely true with the named boulevards within the sequential walls of Philippe Auguste, Charles V, Louis XIII, the Fermiers Généraux, and the walls of Thiers. However other Haussmannian routes sneaked in to grasp honor from the title: Richard-Lenoir, Voltaire, et al. The boulevards des Maréchaux line the service road of the 1841–45 Wall of Thiers.

*bourse* Stock exchange (alternately, purse, prize, grant, scholarship).

bow window The French use these English words for what we call a bay window; in American usage it is a bellied or curved version of a bay window, as at Louisburg Square in Boston.

*branché* Plugged in—and therefore trendy.

brasserie Technically a brewery but, in Paris, a modest bar and restaurant with a limited menu.

*brise-soleil* An architectural sunshade.

broken pediments  Pediments broken apart explosively as in Baroque and neo-Baroque architecture.

brutalism  The reinforced-concrete architecture of, primarily, 1960s Britain, where bold and brutal form and texture were drawn from the late work of Le Corbusier, such as the monastery of La Tourette.

*buffet d'orgue*  The cabinetry that contains an organ's pipes. In the 18th century it was frequently a major architectural conception in itself.

butte  A prominent hill or knoll.

buttress  The reinforcing element of a wall (French: *contrefort*) that in Gothic architecture became "flying," reinforcing from a distant mass of masonry by means of an arch.

Byzantine  Architecture pertaining to the Eastern Roman Empire, centered at Constantinople (Byzantium), cresting in the 530s at the church of Hagia Sophia.

# C

*cabinet*  A small room or office.

*caisse d'épargne*  Savings bank.

*calcaire*  Limestone.

campanile  A freestanding bell tower in the Italian manner.

capital  The "head" of a column, supporting in Classical and neo-Classical architecture the entablature.

*carré*  Square, as in the Cour Carrée of the Louvre.

*carrière*  Quarry.

*cartouche*  Ornamental insignia or escutcheon.

caryatid  A sculpted female figure supporting a column, pier, or pilaster.

cast iron  (French: *fonte*) the hard and brittle iron that can be cast in molds; it is good for columns with a vertical load, impossible for beams, which would crack in bending. For the latter *wrought* iron was used.

catacomb  A subterranean cemetery, with recesses to contain tombs; in Paris, just the removed bones from surface cemeteries.

cathedral  The principal church of a bishop, where his chair (cathedra) sits behind the altar. The word does not necessarily connote size or grandeur.

cavetto cornice  The Egyptians of the third millenium B.C. wove their plaited cornices in a curve that projected outward, a style that was picked up in temple stonework. In the early 1800s, particularly after Napoléon's Egyptian conquests, this was imitated in various Parisian buildings.

*chantier*  Workplace or work site.

Charles V  The wall that gave its site to Louis XIV's Grands Boulevards was that of Charles, extended to the west by Louis XIII.

charnel house  A building that serves as a repository for bodies and bones.

château  Literally a castle, but applied in French to grand unfortified country houses that would not be castles in English.

*château d'eau*  Water tower.

*chemin de fer*  Railroad (literally "iron road").

chevet  The east end of a Gothic church with its radiating chapels.

choir  Where the choir sits and, therefore, the area within the chancel around the altar.

*cité*  The ancient center of a city, as in the Ile de la Cité in Paris; but also applied to housing complexes that contain their own internal street system.

*classé*  Designating a monument: *classement parmi les monuments historiques.*

classic  Of recognized value, serving as a standard of excellence.

Classical  Relating to the architecture of ancient Greece and Rome and its derivatives: Renaissance, Baroque, neo-Classical, etc.

clerestory  The portion of the nave that rises above the side aisles of a church, with its principal glass—stained in medieval times, sometimes clear in the 18th century.

*cloche*  Bell, or a bell-shaped woman's hat.

*clocher*  Bell tower, or steeple.

*cloître* Cloister.

coffer Deeply recessed and highly ornamented soffit or ceiling elements that suggest a lavishly gilt and polychromed tripe. The Pantheon in Rome has the best-known example.

*collège* School, at a grammar or high school level, unlike the American or English college.

*colline* Hill.

*colombage* Half-timbering.

column A relatively slender vertical support. A French *colonne* must be round, but an English column need not be.

*comble* The attic or, better still, the "hat" of an immeuble. Here were the garrets for servants and students, within what was originally a form codified by Mansart senior (François) for châteaux, and hence the mansard roof.

Composite The order of ancient architecture in which the scrollwork of Ionic is crossbred with the acanthus leaves of Corinthian.

concierge The doorkeeper in a Parisian apartment house or hotel.

*concours* A design competition for an architectural commission.

*concours de façades* With the new law of 1892 allowing projections from a facade to "enrich" its architecture (a reaction to dour Hausmannianism), the city held competitions for the best facade, the winners receiving medals (gold for the architect, bronze for the owner; but the latter also received a tax abatement).

conoid A vaulted surface connecting a straight line at one end to an arc at the other.

console The vertically disposed brackets that support a ceiling, cornice, or balcony in Classical, Renaissance, and neo-Classical architecture.

constructivism Originally a movement that spread from Russia in the 1920s, this has been escalated in the late 1980s into deconstructivism, a mostly pseudointellectual posture of architects trying to make noise in a self-advertising way.

corbel Masonry that steps out from a vertical surface in courses to support a load from above.

Corinthian The order of ancient Greece and Rome that flaunts acanthus leaves on its capital.

*corps de logis* The main building of an *hôtel particulier.* On the street: an entry portal and pavilion. Within: the *corps de logis* housed the *patron.*

Cor-Ten Self-rusting steel that ultimately attains a dark brown matte patina.

*coupole* A small dome.

*cour* Court, of a prince or a building.

*couvent* Convent or monastery.

*crèche* Day-care center; originally a crib or manger.

*crépi* Rough French stucco on masonry.

cubism The movement of the first years of the 20th century led by painters: Braque, Picasso, Léger et al.

# D

dentils The toothy blocks under the cornice of a Greco-Roman or Renaissance entablature. They are reminiscent of wood joinery in earlier temples, from which Greek architecture in marble was derived.

*dépouillé* Stripped, skinned, denuded.

distyle in antis Two columns flanked by two blank walls.

Doric The austere and elegant set of parts (called an "order") developed in the 6th and 5th centuries B.C. in Greek architecture.

*dortoir* Dormitory.

# E

early Christian The architecture of the early Christian church, derived from the Roman basilica, or lawcourt. A high central nave rises over the aisles, bringing clerestory lighting into the main space. In Paris it is really neo-Early Christian.

Eastlakian Charles Eastlake (1836–1906), English architect, writer, and furniture designer, influenced works in many countries with his complex, eclectic, and arbitrary form and detail in furniture and cabinetry.

*échevin* A municipal magistrate.

echinus The round molding forming the bell of the capital in the Greek Doric order.

eclectic The borrowing of assorted historical styles and stylistic details for a single building.

EDF/GDF Electricité de France/Gaz de France, the Parisian utility companies (and for all of France).

Empire The architecture and, particularly, furniture of the time of Emperor Napoléon I (1804–1814).

entablature The set of roof parts supported by columns in a Classical or neo-Classical building: architrave, or first beam; frieze; and cornice.

entasis The slight swelling of a Classical column that reinforces the visual impression of strength. The best (i.e., the Parthenon) is so subtle that one is aware of it only after conscious intellectual effort.

*entrepôt* Warehouse.

*entresol* Mezzanine, or low floor between the ground floor *(rez-de-chaussée)* and the first (French) floor.

*étage* Floor or story. The *premier étage* is the floor that is one flight *up*. If there is an *entresol*, it may be *two* flights up. But, in a two-story building, the first floor may be called simply *l'étage.*

exedra A large semicircular alcove, or annex, to a central space, particularly in Classical or neo-Classical architecture.

# F

fasces A bundle of rods surrounding an ax with a projecting blade that was borne before ancient Roman magistrates as a badge of authority.

*faubourg* A suburb of the center city and, later, the near suburbs of Paris, beyond which is the *banlieue.* In Parisian history, the streets marked *faubourg* (as in Saint-Honoré) are the continuations of downtown beyond the *grands boulevards* of Louis XIV, and hence, the former walls of Charles V/Louis III.

*fer* Iron.

Fermiers Généraux Those forty agents of the king who collected taxes, taking a commission. Notorious particularly because of their wall, built in the 1780s by Ledoux.

festoon A pendant wreath; also describes any exuberant decoration.

flamboyant Flaming or flashy; when applied to the medieval it refers to the late and elaborated Gothic such as the north tower of Chartres.

*flâneur* Stroller.

*flèche* Arrow; also, a slender spire like that over the crossing of Notre Dame.

*folie* Whimsical building; folly; country house.

*fonctionnaire* Civil servant.

*fossé* A trench or ditch and, at grand scale, the kind of dry moat that surrounded the Charles V/Louis XIII wall on the site of the present Grands Boulevards.

*foyer* Lobby, but also a home or hostel: a *foyer pour les personnes âgées* is a home for the elderly.

fresco A water-based painting on fresh plaster.

frieze A Classical element of an entablature (cf. architrave and cornice), but also, more freely, a band of painted and/or sculpted decoration across a facade.

*fronton* Pediment.

# G

*gabarit*  The envelope and/or profile of a building that determines its relationship to the street and its neighbors. The *gabarit* of Parisian boulevard architecture determined a cornice at 17.54 meters (six floors), or 57′6″, surmounted by a receding *comble* (attic/roof volume) that contained two or three levels.

galleria  From the Italian: a glass-roofed street; see also *verrière*.

*garde-corps*  A balcony railing, or one where the window opening goes down to the floor.

*garde-fou*  The railing at a typical French window, where the sill is a foot or more off the floor. *Fou* means crazy or, more mildly, foolish.

*garde-manger*  A larder or cupboard. Typically, a compartment under the kitchen window, vented to the outside, where fresh food is kept cool but not refrigerated.

*garde-meuble*  Furniture warehouse, especially the royal one for the Bourbons.

*gare*  A station for trains, as in *Gare* du Nord, or planes, as the *aérogare* at Roissy/Charles de Gaulle.

Georgian  Of the Georges, those imported German kings of England who were in charge when the best of English urban design was around (late 18th and early 19th centuries). Simple but elegant brick-and-limestone.

Gothic  Late medieval architecture, pejoratively named after the "pagan" Ostrogoths and Visigoths by the disapproving 18th century. Aside from superficial detail and mannerisms (the pointed arch, ribs, bosses, finials, and so forth), Gothic is a structuralist's dream.

*gradins*  Steps or tiers; also receding stepped terraces in buildings such as Sauvage's *immeubles à gradins*.

*grand magasin*  Department store.

*grand standing*  For the arriviste, *immeubles* (apartment houses) of luxury. Usually more akin in spirit to Hollywood than to the boulevard architecture of Haussmann et Cie.

Greek Revival  The Greeks were revived for both archaeological and political honors (the 1820s revolution liberating them from Turkey). From the 1820s through the 1840s buildings were "decorated" with Greek details.

*grès*  Literally earthenware pottery, or sandstone, but in the late 19th and early 20th centuries it referred to the glazed tilework of artisans such as Bigot.

*grille*  A fence of iron bars surrounding a park or shielding an entry courtyard.

gusset  A plate or bracket that reinforces a connection, say, of a steel column and beam.


# H

*halle*  Market.

Haussmann  Baron Georges-Eugène Haussman was appointed prefect of Paris under Napoléon III, a position that gave him, in concert with Napoléon, dictatorial powers to reshape the city. See "Note to the Reader."

HBM  Habitation à Bon Marché, or inexpensive housing, developed privately in the late 19th century, but a public enterprise after 1913 in Paris. The competitions of that year engendered the first experimental social housing in France.

Henri IV  Protestant turned Catholic, Henri IV (King, 1589–1610) was the first great Parisian patron of urbanism: place des Vosges, place Dauphine, and the quadrupled Cour Carrée of the Louvre.

HLM  Habitation à Loyer Modérée. The successor program to the HBMs, post–World War II, that often inserted dissonant skyscrapers into the old urban texture of Paris, destroying the scale and context.

*hôtel de ville*  Town hall.
*hôtel particulier*  Grand town house, equivalent to the Italian palazzo.
*huisserie*  Entrance doorframe or window frame.


# I


iconostasis  The ornamental screen separating the priests and population of
    an Orthodox church.
*îlot*  Block of housing.
imbricated  Overlapping in concert, as with fish scales or shingles.
*immeuble*  Any building and its property, but commonly used for apartment
    house, technically an *immeuble de rapport*, or investment rental property.
*impasse*  Cul-de-sac, dead-end street.
Ionic  The elegant voluted order of Greek architecture. Its capitals are
    sometimes compared to ram's horns.


# J


*Jésuitique*  What the French termed Baroque architecture before they ac-
    cepted the latter word for their own 17th-century works, such as Val-
    de-Grâce. The Jesuits of Rome, of course, were the instigators of
    melodramatic architecture in a counterattack against the Protestant Ref-
    ormation.
*jeu de paume*  Tennis court.
*jubé*  A rood screen that separates the chancel of a church from the nave,
    often topped by a crucifix.
Jugendstil  German Art Nouveau, but with a more geometric and austere
    quality.


# L


*librairie*  Bookstore.
lintel  A horizontal architectural member spanning an opening (door, win-
    dow) and carrying the superposed load of masonry.
*logements sociaux*  Public housing, as HBMs and HLMs.
Louis XIII  In the 1630s Louis XIII extended the wall of Charles V to
    embrace the Tuileries and its gardens.
Louis XIV  After living in the Tuileries (1667–1678), Louis XIV left Paris
    for Saint-Germain-en-Laye (1678–1682) and then moved on to Ver-
    sailles for the remaining thirty-three years of his reign. Shunning Paris
    as a royal residence, he was nevertheless a patron of urbanism: the Cour
    Carrée, in its expanded form, was completed by Le Vau; but more
    important, beginning in 1670 he had the wall of Charles V/Louis XIII
    demolished and replaced by the Grands Boulevards.
Louis-Philippe  La Colonne de Juillet remembers the July Revolution, which
    put Louis-Philippe in power in 1830.
*lucarne*  Dormer window; sometimes a skylight.
*lycée*  School, particularly high school.


# M


*mairie*  Town hall for, particularly, the *maire* of each of the twenty Parisian
    arrondissements.
*maisonnette*  A small house, but in Paris it is an apartment within an *immeu-
    ble* that comprises two floors and is entered from street level.
Mannerist  Late Renaissance art and architecture; exaggerated and some-
    times affected but a preview of the Baroque. cf. Michelangelo.
mansard  An adjective referring to François Mansart (1598–1666), whose

steeply pitched roofs were brought to a high art form at such châteaux as Blois and Maisons-Laffitte. A pitch only 10–20 degrees off the vertical rose to a nearly flat roof atop it all.

*marais* A marsh or swamp. The Marais of Paris, in the 3rd and 4th arrondissements, was not infilled until the 16th century, to make way for the *hôtels particuliers* of the nobility seeking to be near the court at the Hôtel de Tournelles, favorite of Charles IX and Henri II.

marquise Entrance canopy and, particularly, the metal-and-glass ones of the 19th and early 20th centuries.

mastaba The battered (sloping-walled) tombs of early Egyptian nobility subordinate to the pyramids that they surrounded (cf. Gizeh, 2750 B.C.).

medieval Of the Middle Ages, a murky period from the fall of Rome (Gibbon's term) around A.D. 400 to the Renaissance of art and humanism in the 15th century in Italy, in the 16th in France.

metopes The sculptured space between triglyphs in a Classical Greek frieze.

Métropolitain The subway (trainway) of Paris—even when it runs on elevated tracks.

*meulière* A volcanic stone, sometimes referred to as "Versailles" and usually (but not always) laid in a random fashion.

*mitoyen* Mean, middle, or intermediate; hence, a *mur mitoyen* is a party wall.

*moderne* Modern, but more specifically applied to the architecture of the 1930s, as in Art Moderne.

modern style An imprecise description of the architecture produced during those struggling years from the late 1920s to World War II. One would never speak of Le Corbusier or Mallet-Stevens as being of the modern style; rather, these are the works of Roux-Spitz, et al.

modillion A horizontal ornamental bracket, usually in the form of a scroll, supporting a cornice, balcony, or other projection.

module A unit meant to be used as a measure but, more important, a prebuilt part of a building: a brick, for example, is a module.

mullion The major support member between adjacent panels of glass, or doors, or window sash, as in the aluminum posts separating glass sheets in a storefront, or the stone ribs separating lead-glazed areas in a Gothic church.

muntin The small bar separating panes of glass within a sash (that assembly of glass, muntins, and frames that is an operable piece or set), as in a French window or door.

# N

naiad A mythological nymph living in and giving life to fresh waters: lakes, rivers, springs, canals, fountains.

Napoléon I Napoléon (first consul, 1799–1804; emperor, 1804–1814) had more architectural ambition than product, but he started the Arc de Triomphe and continued what was to become La Madeleine, both completed a generation later. His favorite architects, Percier and Fontaine, erected the Arc de Triomphe du Carrousel, and extended the Tuileries with an arm along the rue de Rivoli back toward the Louvre. A palace for the king of Rome (his son) was to have been erected at the Trocadéro, and that hill was leveled in preparation for that event.

Napoléon III (president, 1848–1852; emperor, 1852–1870). Nephew of Napoléon I, this Bonaparte did for Paris what his uncle had done for glory. Appointing Baron Eugène Haussmann prefect in 1853, he reshaped Paris with myriad grand avenues, great sewers and aqueducts, a transportation system of omnibuses, and twenty-four parks of remarkable brilliance, such as Buttes-Chaumont, Monceau, and Montsouris.

nave The people's place, as the chancel is the place of God's symbols and his priests, and the transepts (or crossarms of the church) are the place of monks and brothers. The nave rises above the aisles of a Gothic church, bringing in stained light. Its ribbed structure's shell reminded its namers of a ship (Latin: *navis*): an inside-out, upside-down, religious ship bottomed to the sky and heavens.

*nef* Aisle *or* nave.

neo-Grec The late-19th-century re-revival of Greek detail.

non aedificandi The area in front of the Thiers wall of 1845 where there could be no buildings; an open field for clear gunfire at the approaching enemy.

*nouille* Noodle. It refers in architecture to the sinuous exaggerations of Art Nouveau.

# O

obelisk A land finial, a slightly tapered, square shaft, crowned by drastic beveling to form a pyramidal tip. Carved with hieroglyphics, monolithic granite obelisks punctuated the ground plane of temples.

octastyle With eight columns; *okta:* eight, *stylos:* column.

*octroi* Toll or tollhouse; originally a grant or concession.

oculus Eye or eyelike; a round window.

*oeil-de-boeuf* A circular or oval window.

*ogive* The French word for a pointed arch and the Gothic architecture that used it.

*orangerie* An orangehouse (or green and orangehouse!) for growing oranges in northern climates, usually walled and roofed in orthodox fashion and glazed to the south.

order Those kits of parts which formed the ancient Classical vocabulary of architecture and then, in modified form, that of Renaissance, Baroque, 18th-century, Greek Revival, Beaux Arts, and what-have-you architecture. Orders include base, column, capital, and entablature; Doric, Ionic, Corinthian, and Composite are the hierarchy.

organic In architecture, the search for a natural relationship with the animal and vegetable worlds, as opposed to the crisp orthogonal mathematical world. Frank Lloyd Wright averred that his works were organic.

oriel A small bay window to view the terrain.

# P

*palais* A palace, usually for a king, but the Palais de Justice extended its meaning to include the law.

palazzo *Hôtel particulier,* or grand town house

Palladian After the Italian architect Andrea Palladio (1508–1580), author of *I quattro libri dell'architectura* (1570), which influenced French architects, particularly with the Palladian window, an arched opening flanked by rectangular windows that rose to the spring of the arch.

*pan coupé* The truncated corner of a building that tapers to the intersection of two converging streets.

*pan de bois* Half-timbering; also known as *colombage.*

*paquebot* Ocean liner, or packet boat. Here the streamlined and tubular-railed imagery of such liners is transferred to the vocabulary of building.

*parapluie* Umbrella. Napoléan III called the glass train sheds (Gare du Nord, etc.) the parapluies of Paris.

*parterre* An ornamental garden having low patterned foliage with paths between the beds.

*parvis* The open space or *place* in front of a church, as at Notre Dame.

*passage* A narrow street; in Paris the more famous are those covered with glass *(verrières),* which brought elegance to shopping at the end of the 18th and beginning of the 19th centuries. (There are also uncovered *passages* in Paris.)

pediment Originally the triangular gabled end of a temple front, pediments became decorative parts for Renaissance architecture, crowning windows, tombs, and sculptural compositions. Later their form, with Baroque showmanship, was fractured, broken open.

pendentives The spherical segments that serve as structural and visual transitions between a dome and the rectangular space that supports it.

pergola A formal arbor covering a walk, with columns supporting light beams (joists) that may be entwined with vines, pendant with grapes or flowers, or just an architectural breaking of the sun.

*persiennes* Folding shutters, mostly steel, that shield the Parisian from noise and light and perhaps offer security against intruders. They nest in the reveals of Haussmannian masonry.

Philippe-Auguste The second, or post-Roman, wall was that of Philippe-Auguste. Mostly disappeared.

pier A fat support that may be merely large, or an assembly of articulated colonnettes, as in the pier in a Gothic or neo-Gothic nave.

*pierre de taille* Cut stone, and that mostly limestone or *calcaire* from the *carrières de Paris*. To be *pierre de taille* was to be upper class, as the rubble stone *(meulière)* was for the rabble.

*pignon* Gable.

pilaster The flat remembrance of a column that articulates a wall and frequently repeats the rhythm and parts of an adjacent colonnade. Usually decorative and nonstructural.

*pilier* A column that is not round, as distinct from one that is *(colonne)*. In English columns are freestanding elements of support, regardless of shape.

*pilotis* Pilings which Le Corbusier brought out of the ground at the Pavillon Suisse, raising the building so that pedestrian traffic could pass underneath.

*piscine* Swimming pool.

*poivrière* Pepper mill, and hence the round towers of 19th-century Haussmannian corners.

*place* Square in English, *piazza* in Italian. The French version is sometimes hard, without trees, as in place des Victoires or place Vendôme; sometimes with a central garden, as in place des Vosges.

PoMo Post Modern, that liberated architecture of the 1980s which allows a recycling of historical form in opposition to the abstract purity of "modern" architecture. The American Robert Venturi is its guru, and much of the infill housing (HLMs) of Paris uses its sometime neo-Classical parts to enliven their bland blocks.

*pompier* A fireman, and also the *pompous* and extravagant turn-of-the-century style in both painting and architecture, when more was more.

*porte* Door and, at the scale of the city, the entrance gates through the walls of Paris, now recalled as vestigial verbal symbols except at the Portes Saint-Denis and Saint-Martin, where one is greeted by triumphal arches (without walls).

porte cochère Carriage entrance, and in a Parisian *hôtel*, the grand double doors that lead to the courtyard, within which is set a smaller door for people.

Post Modern See PoMo.

*poubelle* Garbage can. Eugène-René Poubelle, prefect of Paris from 1883 to 1896, decreed the use of garbage cans, which were derisively named in his honor.

prêt-à-porter Ready-to-wear clothing.

*prévôt des marchands* Provost, or head of the Parisian guilds.

PTT *Poste, Téléphone, Télégraphe* in a more leisurely era; the state-run network now supervises *Postes, Télécommunications,* and *Télédiffusion.*

putti Figures of infant boys in Renaissance art.

# Q

*quai* Quay, wharf, or embankment.

quoin Corner stones of a building that visually, if not structurally, anchor it; usually articulated and rusticated.

# R

*rampe*  Railing of a stair; banister.

RATP  Régie Autonome des Transports Parisiens, the parent organization that oversees the Métro and bus systems. The RER (supersubway) is independent.

refectory  Dining hall of a monastic or collegial establishment.

*regard*  Look, regard; and here also a place for looking into (inspecting) the water supply system.

*Régence*  Regency, as in that of Anne of Austria for her son Louis XIV before his majority in 1661; or the duc d'Orléans for Louis XV (1715–1723). The latter gave rise to the style Régence.

*relais*  A relay station, as at an inn on a route to somewhere, where horses were changed and provisions supplied. It can be applied to a good restaurant that is quite static.

Renaissance  The flowering of humanism in literature, painting, sculpture, and architecture in the early 15th century in Italy. Here personal architectural creativity blossomed after the relative anonymity of the Middle Ages, and neo-Classicism, identified with the independent human spirit, became the idiom.

*Restauration*  The restoration of King Louis XVIII to the throne in 1815, after the Republic, Directory, Consulate, and Empire.

*retardataire*  Retarded, as in an architectural style used long after its fashion has waned elsewhere: the Hôtel de Cluny is retardataire, a Gothic house completed in 1498 at the dawn of the Renaissance.

reveal (n.)  The side, or cheek, of a window or door opening, that *reveals* the encompassing walls.

*rez-de-chaussée*  The ground floor, from which the *premier étage*, sometimes simply called *l'étage*, is one flight up. Literally, "road-level."

rococo  Popularly used to describe the ornate and romantic interior decoration of the mid-18th century, particularly in France. It brings to mind the painted cherubs, milkmaids, and cotton clouds of Boucher and Fragonard.

Romanesque  "Roman" in its use of arch and column, Romanesque is the Christian architecture of western Europe (as opposed to the Byzantine east), from the 10th through 12th centuries in particular. The Romanesque arch is round, and so were its vaults, limiting the structure's height in contrast to the later Gothic but rendering it monumental in contrast to a timber-roofed basilica.

*rondelle*  Ring of stone, a sculptor's calcaire doughnut.

*rond-point*  A traffic circle.

*rotonde*  Rotunda: a round building, usually covered by a dome.

rusticated  An odd phrase for urbanity in architecture: the opposite of rural or rustic. It describes incised articulating joints in Renaissance stonework that in Italy became monumental and in France were relatively timid.

# S

*saillie*  A projection or overhang from a building.

*salle*  A room, but it can also be a *grande salle*, such as a concert hall: Salle Pleyel.

sash  A movable window, part or whole, as in the two-sash that forms the inswinging French window (or door), or double-hung up-and-down-sliding sash.

SNCF  Société Nationale des Chemins de Fer, or French national railroad company.

soffit  The underside of an architectural part, as the soffit of a balcony.

space frame  A three-dimensional truss, drawn from the structural geometry of Buckminster Fuller or Alexander Graham Bell.

spandrel  The space between the window head of one floor and the window sill of the floor above, whether masonry or a panel. In traditional architecture it is the triangular space between two adjacent arches.

*square* An urban park in the English sense (e.g., Bedford Square) and sometimes a cul-de-sac embraced by buildings.

stele The memorial finial or slab set in the ground that remembers persons, places, or events. A tombstone is a stele, as are the Druidic remains of Stonehenge.

Stick Style Wood members (sticks) articulate a usually asymmetrical architecture in a structural expression inspired by neo-Gothicism.

strapwork Wrought-iron decorative structure in sinuous flat bands.

*surélévation* Extra stories added to an existing building.

swag Pendant decoration hanging between two points. See also festoon.

## T

*tardif* The stretched-out and sluggish end of a style, as in Haussmannian-*tardif*, which becomes more elaborate.

temper The process of relieving crystalline stresses in steel, allowing it to become harder, stronger, and more resilient. Glass is also tempered to minimize fracturing.

tempietto A small temple in the Italian manner.

*ter* The third use of the same number, as in 21, rue Blanche, 21 *bis* (21 again), and 21 *ter* (21 thrice).

terrace An Englishman's set of town houses, designed to be a single entity, à la John Nash, but meant for the masses as well as the classes.

tessera The unit of a mosaic.

TGV Train à Grande Vitesse. The fast trains of France that exceed 180 miles an hour.

*thermes* Baths (Latin: *thermae*).

torus A large half-round molding frequently seen at the base of an Ionic or Corinthian column, but used elsewhere on some facades.

*tourelle* Little tower, or turret, providing a view of the landscape, or perhaps the enemy.

transept The arms of a church in the Latin cross, the place for monks to worship.

transparente The concealed source of light in a Baroque church that illuminates a space or chapel melodramatically.

travertine Cousin of limestone, brother of marble, travertine is the mineral deposit at and near great springs. It is naturally pocked when sliced.

triglyphs The triad of incisions alternating with sculptured metopes in the frieze of a Classical Greek temple and its descendants.

truncated To replace an edge or point by a plane, as in a truncated pyramid, its top neatly lopped off, or the *pan coupé* of a Parisian *immeuble* where two streets join at an acute angle.

truss A network of structural parts that follow the stress lines for a great span, enclosing space for vast public assemblage, such as that truss (space-frame version) which covers the Palais Omnisports.

Tuscan The smooth and rounded Doric (no flutes) of later Roman architecture, popular in the 19th century.

tympanum The scuptured pediment in a Greek or Roman temple, or their revived successors (La Madeleine, for example), and the later arched, sculpted space over Romanesque and Gothic doors.

## V

vault A curved or warped surface of arches. Barrel vaults are linear continuous arches, both Roman and Romanesque; groin vaults are the crossed vaulting of the same eras that allow windows and light into the central space. Gothic ribs relieved vaulting of some of its burdens, relying on a cage of ribwork to carry loads, within which was an infilling of masonry panels.

vermiculated  Stone that has been tooled as if infiltrated by worms, popular in Renaissance and neo-Renaissance rusticated facades.

vernacular  The ordinary architecture of a society with—but mostly without—the benefit of architects: a vocabulary of life.

*verrière*  A stained-glass ceiling or skylight.

*villa*  A villa or country house; also used to describe a planned street, cul-de-sac, or grouping of buildings.

*ville*  City, town.

*volet*  An exterior shutter, mostly those of pre-Haussmannian Paris, later replaced by the folding and partially concealed *persiennes*.

volute  A spiral or scroll-like form, particularly that which crests an Ionic capital.

voussoir  A wedge-shaped stone, participating in forming an arch.

# W

wrought iron  Iron worked with heat and banging (the village blacksmith), which both hardens and tempers it, producing linear material for gates, grilles, railings, and horseshoes that is stronger than its source material.

# Z

ZAC  Zone d'Aménagement Concertée or "urban renewal district" in American parlance. Literally a zone planned in concert.

ziggurat  The mud-brick stepped pyramids of the Tigris and Euphrates valleys. Not tombs, like those of Egyptian pharaohs, but professional holy places.

# THE
# GUIDE
## TO THE
# ARCHITECTURE
## OF
# PARIS

# 1
# FIRST ARRONDISSEMENT

## SOUTH

### PLACE DE LA CONCORDE TO THE LOUVRE

Place de la Concorde, Les Palais de Gabriel: **Jacques-Ange Gabriel**
and **Jacques-Ignace Hittorf;** Jeu de Paume; rue Saint-Florentin; Aux
Trois Quartiers: **Louis Faure-Dujarric;** rue Saint-Honoré; Eglise
Polonaise: **Charles Errard;** place Vendôme: **Jules
Hardouin-Mansart;** Eglise Saint-Roch: **Jacques Lemercier;** Comédie
Française: **Victor Louis;** Bibliothèque Nationale: **Pierre Le Muet** and
**Henri Labrouste;** Eglise Notre-Dame-des-Victoires: **Pierre Le Muet;**
place des Victoires: **Jules Hardouin-Mansart;** Jardin du Palais-Royal:
**Victor Louis;** Galerie Véro-Dodat: **Constant Protain;** l'Oratoire du
Louvre: **Clément II Métezeau;** Eglise Saint-Germain-l'Auxerrois:
**Victor Baltard;** Louvre: **Pierre Lescot, Jacques Lemercier, Louis
Le Vau, Claude Perrault, Hector Lefuel, Percier et Fontaine,**
and **I. M. Pei;** Palais Royal: **Jacques Lemercier**

Métro: **Concorde**

[1s-63.] **Louvre, Cour Napoléon facade,** seen through the
pyramid/entry. **Hector Lefuel.** 1857. **I. M. Pei.** 1989.

1

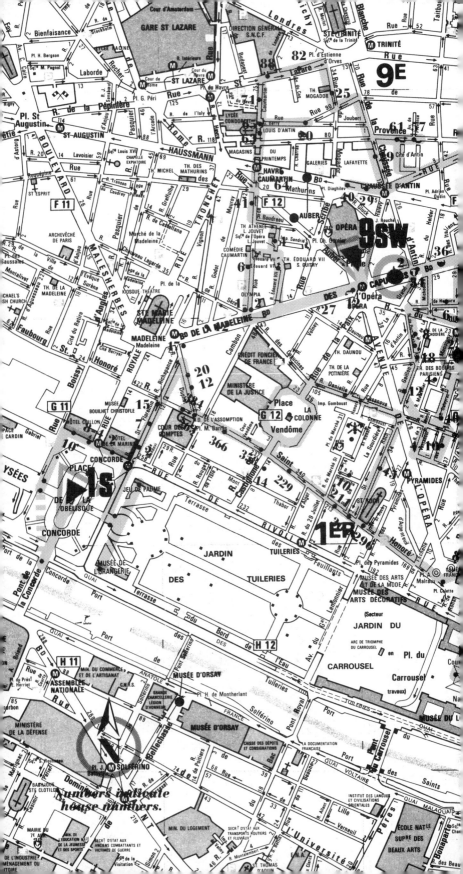

★★★★[1s-1.] **Place de la Concorde**/originally **place Louis XV,** joining avenue des Champs-Elysées, rue Royale, pont de la Concorde, and the Jardins des Tuileries. **Jacques-Ange Gabriel.** 1757–1772. Furnishings and fixtures, **Jacques-Ignace Hittorf.** 1836–1840.

The Italians wouldn't have approved, for here is a *place* that is relatively open on three sides and handsomely crowned on the fourth with the buildings of its designer, Jacques-Ange Gabriel. The later Hittorf additions include the obelisk, fountains, allegorical statues of the great cities of France—in effect, the urban furnishings. During the Revolution, place Louis XV was the scene of executions, and the name Concorde was later applied to it as symbolic balm.

Without Hittorf's paraphernalia, it must have been a sorry and amorphous place: modern traffic, using it as a *rond-point,* in fact articulates it more than the helter-skelter pre-Revolutionary activities of the late 18th century.

★★[1s-2.] **Obélisque de Louqsor,** centered in place de la Concorde. circa 1250 B.C. Reerected, **Apollinare Lebas.** 1836.

Certainly the oldest *thing* in Paris, this obelisk was one of several at the **temple of Ramses II** at Thebes (modern Luxor). It was a gift to Louis-Philippe from the Egyptian pasha Muhammad Ali in 1832. Hittorf used it smashingly to give a central axis to this grand space. Carved into its base are wonderful incisions recording its movement from Egypt and reerection here.

★★[1s-3.] **Aménagement, place de la Concorde,** including memorial columns, light standards, fountains. **Jacques-Ignace Hittorf.** 1836–1840.

The cast-iron columns, punctuating the sky in minor sympathy with the obelisk, are Corinthians, bearing urns and light standards. These are, according to the architect, "calculated so that the top of the capital corresponds to the height of the cornice of the lower floor of the buildings of the *garde-meuble* (now Ministère de la Marine)."

★[1s-4.] **Statues des Grandes Villes de France,** around periphery of place de la Concorde. 1830s. Lyons and Marseilles, **Petitot.** Bordeaux and Nantes, **Caillonette.** Rouen and Brest, **Cortot.** Lille and Strasbourg, **Pradier.**

★[1s-5.] **Chevaux de Marly,** flanking avenue des Champs-Elysées at the west end of place de la Concorde. Originals, now in the Louvre, **Guillaume Coustou.** 1745. Transferred here, 1795. Copies installed here, 1984.

Coustou's originals were sculpted for the **Abreuvoir de Marly,** so the move to the Louvre is their third siting.

★[1s-6.] **Pont de la Concorde,** on axis of Assemblée Nationale, place de la Concorde, rue Royale, and La Madeleine. **Jean-Rodolphe Perronet.** 1788–1791. Broadened, 1931.

The views along the axis and along the river are smashing. But on viewing the bridge itself, giant Tuscan piers conjoin with the arched spans—unassertive and handsome, triumphal arches for the river traveler.

★★★★[1s-7.] **Les Palais de Gabriel,** including the **Ministère de la Marine** at the northeast of place de la Concorde (entry, 2, rue Royale) and, at the northwest, **Hôtels de Coislin, Lambot de Fougères, de Pastoret,** and **d'Aumont** (entries at Nos. 4, 6, 8, and 10). No. 10 became the **Hôtel Crillon** in 1907. All by **Jacques-Ange Gabriel.** 1757–1770.

These symmetrical palaces have always had asymmetrical innards and functions, somewhat bizarre at first. The current Ministère de la Marine was built as the royal furniture warehouse, while its opposite twin was originally a series of *hôtels particuliers.*

The great colonnades took inspiration from **Claude Perrault's** eastern front to the Louvre, twelve freestanding Corinthian columns articulating the facades. At Logan Circle in Philadelphia is a baldly plagiarized twin pair (**Horace Trumbauer.** 1907). Inside the Crillon (**Pierre-Adrien Pâris,** interiors. Remodeling, **Destailleurs.** 1909) see the Salle des Aigles, the only Louis XVI interior still intact; gilded eagles mount the reentrant corner cornices.

★[1s-8.] **Statues équestres,** at entrance to Jardin des Tuileries, east side of place de la Concorde. **Antoine Coysevox.** Installed at Marly, 1702. Transferred here, 1719. Copies installed here (originals in the Louvre), 1986.

★[1s-9.] **Musée de l'Orangerie,** southwest corner, Jardin des Tuileries. 1853.

This now houses the Walter Guillaume collection, but more important, downstairs are *Les Nymphéas* of **Claude Monet.** Originally an *orangerie* for Napoléon III's Tuileries, it sheltered orange trees in tubs on wheels, which could be aired and viewed in good weather.

★[1s-10.] **Jeu de Paume**/onetime (1958–1986) **Musée de l'Impressionnisme**/now the **Musée du Jeu de Paume,** in the Jardin des Tuileries at the northeast corner of place de la Concorde. Original building, 1861. Conversion to museum of contemporary art, **Antoine Stinco.** 1991.

This former tennis court for Napoléon III's Tuileries has become a gallery of contemporary painting and sculpture. Stinco pulled back glass walls to leave what were flush arcades freestanding. The Impressionists have been moved to the attic of the **Musée d'Orsay.**

★[1s-11.] **Consulat des Etats-Unis**/originally **Hôtel de la Vrillière**/ also known as **Hôtel Talleyrand,** 2, rue Saint-Florentin, corner rue de Rivoli. Initial design, **Jacques-Ange Gabriel.** Execution, **Jean-François Chalgrin.** 1767.

A grand entrance court for this tight street, guarded by Marines.

★[1s-12.] **Hôtel Galitzine,** 7, rue Saint-Florentin, between rue de Rivoli and rue Saint-Honoré. **François Letellier.** 1761.

Ferdinand de Lesseps of Suez Canal fame lived here later. It is rusticated at the base, in the Italian Renaissance manner, with an arched entryway to its inner court.

★★[1s-13.] **Immeuble, 15, rue Saint-Florentin,** with another facade at 275, rue Saint-Honoré. **Sénet.** 1902.

This architect had a delicate hand, creating Art Nouveau window framing and glazing that would have made Mies tremble. But the man who ostensibly brought iron and glass to the 20th century must have passed through Paris, where such symbioses grew in lovely elegance before he was born. This was the avant-garde of the *Belle Epoque.*

★[1s-14.] **Aux Trois Quartiers (magasin), 17–25, boulevard de la Madeleine,** corner rue Duphot, facing place de la Madeleine. **Louis Faure-Dujarric.** 1932. Remodeled and extended, **Archi-Déco.** 1989.

Streamlined modernism that has cornered the *place* for sixty years. The redeveloper **Francis Bouygues** has unfortunately reduced the *magasin* to the *rez-de-chaussée*, as offices are more profitable at this point. The name comes from the conjunction of three arrondissements at this spot: 1st, 8th, and 9th.

**[1s-15.] Paribas Building,** 12, boulevard de la Madeleine, between rue Vignon and rue Godot-de-Mauroy. **Jean Pelée de Saint-Maurice.**

Lovely composite columns enrich this *retardataire* neo-Classicism.

★**[1s-16.] Aux Trois Quartiers (magasin), 20, rue Duphot,** between place de la Madeleine and rue Saint-Honoré. circa 1900.

An *earlier* Aux Trois Quartiers, with vigorous riveted steel and gently curved glass and sash—Art Nouveau elegance. The cornice of encurled strap-steel is a wonder.

★**[1s-17.] Immeuble, 10, 12, 14, rue Duphot,** between place de la Madeleine and rue Saint-Honoré. **L. Damesne.** 1806–1810.

The elevations of this ensemble are representative of the first great Parisian *immeubles à décor:* hard, carved, spare, spartan. The stone is travertine-like, with pilasters and arches classically abstracted. The vaulted entry leads into another world.

**[1s-18.] Magasin, 384, rue Saint-Honoré,** corner rue Duphot. circa 1900.

A *Belle Epoque* shop, Corinthian-pilastered and cartouche-cornered, enriches the street.

★★**[1s-19.] Eglise Notre-Dame-de-l'Assomption**/commonly called **Eglise Polonaise,** 263, rue Saint-Honoré, at rue Cambon. **Charles Errard.** 1670–1676.

Now the Polish presence in Paris, this cylindrical domed space is simple within, but in pilastered splendor. The outside provides more drama, as the volume of drum and dome, unlike the Panthéon or Val-de-Grâce, hovers right over you at the edge of the street.

★**[1s-20.] Hôtels particuliers, 366–368, rue Saint-Honoré,** between rue Cambon and rue de Castiglione. **Pierre Bullet.** 1705.

Light and sinuous iron, console-bracketed porte cochères, and grand doors are the serious enrichment of this wonderful ensemble. Don't overlook the courtyards behind.

★**[1s-21.] Hôtel particulier, 358, rue Saint-Honoré,** corner rue de Castiglione.

A place Vendôme participant as a guardian entrance portal. Its giant order and arched ground floor terminate the arcades of rue Castiglione.

**[1s-22.] Carré des Feuillants (restaurant),** 14, rue de Castiglione, corner rue Saint-Honoré.

The decor is 18th century.

★★★★**[1s-23.] Place Vendôme**/originally **place Louis-le-Grand,** on axis of rue Castiglione and rue de la Paix. **Jules Hardouin-Mansart.** 1687–1699.

A stage set for royal remembrances, this and **place des Victoires** are Louis XIV's great gifts to Paris. The uniform facades of this unequal octagon have since been modified. They were originally arcaded at the *rez-de-chaussée,* surmounted by two floors with engaged Corinthian pilasters, and crowned with a mansard roof with alternating dormer windows and *oeils-de-boeuf.*

The column (**Jacques Gondoin** and **Jean-Baptiste Lepère.** 1806–1810) commemorates Napoléon's victory at Austerlitz, in the manner of **Trajan's column** in Rome. Cast from over 1,000 Austrian cannons, it has spiral bas-reliefs (**Bergeret**) illustrating that campaign (1805). Napoléon himself bestrides it all (**Dumont.** Original, 1810. Copy, 1873). *Louis XIV* on horseback, by **Girardon,** was originally here, later dismounted and melted for artillery during the Revolution.

But why is it all so dry? Treeless with acres of asphalt and no place to sit, it *could* become a lush public garden—rather than a parking lot. The **Palais-Royal [1s-64.]** exiled the cars in favor of **Daniel Buren's Colonnes.** Vendôme might commission **Alexandre Chemetov** for some greensward dreams. (See **[19v-7.]**).

★★**[1s-24.] Rue Danielle-Casanova,** between rue de la Paix and avenue de l'Opéra. 18th century.

Console brackets faced with grim beauties, ironwork above of sinuous elegance. A series of handsome *hôtels* cluster along these blocks.

★★**[1s-24a.] Nouveau Marché Saint-Honoré,** place du Marché-Saint-Honoré, between rue des Petits-Champs and rue Saint-Augustin. **Ricardo Bofill.** 1991.

The horrendous bunker that occupies the site of the old Marché (1864–1959) will give way to a neo-Classical palazzo within a skin of glass by the king of columns, the Spaniard Ricardo Bofill, who has already tried columnar fantasies in Paris with **Les Colonnes et l'Amphithéâtre [14w-7.]** in the 14th arrondissement, near the Gare du Montparnasse.

**[1s-24b.] Grille Saint Honoré,** 15, place du Marché-Saint-Honoré.

A facade *classée.*

★**[1s-25.] Société des Cuisiniers de Paris,** 45, rue Saint-Roch, between avenue de l'Opéra and rue Saint-Honoré. **Bruno Pellissier.** 1917.

A flamboyant facade is held up by giant atlantes.

**[1s-26.] Hôtel des Tuileries,** 10, rue Saint-Hyacinthe. 18th century.

A handsome *hôtel particulier,* now a travelers' hotel.

★★★**[1s-27.] Eglise Saint-Roch,** 296, rue Saint-Honoré, corner rue Saint-Roch. **Jacques Lemercier.** 1653–1660. Chapel of the Virgin, **Jules Hardouin-Mansart.** Facade, **Robert de Cotte,** 1735 and later. Chapel of Calvary, **Etienne-Louis Boullée** (drastically modified).

Another bow to the *Jésuitique* source at **Il Gesù** in Rome, this time by de Cotte, who provides a front for this classy contemporary of **Val-de-Grâce,** which Lemercier designed simultaneously. The theatrical sequence of Baroque spaces within is appropriate as a social stage-set for the wealthy parishioners.

★**[1s-28.] Immeubles, 229–235, rue Saint-Honoré,** between rue Castiglione and rue d'Alger. **Jacques-Denis Antoine.** 1766.

Built for the Couvent des Feuillants, this is an asymmetrical ensemble, understated, cold, and proud.

★**[1s-29.] Hôtel Saint-James et d'Albany**/originally **Hôtel de Noailles,** 211, rue Saint-Honoré, between rue du 29 Juillet and rue Saint-Roch. 18th century.

The Tuscan portal is dour but powerful, the *Belle Epoque* storefronts wondrously ornate.

★**[1s-30.] Immeuble, 304–306, rue Saint-Honoré,** corner rue de la Sourdière. **A. J. Sellerier.** 1892.

Polychromy comes to this monochromatic street. Bay windows clad in sheet metal give these Parisians grand vistas up and down *la rue.*

**[1s-31.] Fontaine, place André-Malraux,** juncture rue Saint-Honoré, rue Richelieu, and avenue de l'Opéra. **Gabriel Davioud.** 1874.

A stiff work that needs water in motion to be alive.

★★**[1s-32.] Théâtre Français**/also known as **Comédie Française,** place André-Malraux, corner rue de Richelieu. **Victor Louis.** 1786–1790.

Snuggled against the Palais Royal are Tuscan columns in quantity, the detail hard-carved—but that is courtesy of restorers in 1900 and again in 1974. Feverish restoration can take away not only the natural patina of age but also its natural pockmarks.

★**[1s-33.] Immeuble, 8, rue de Richelieu,** corner place André-Malraux. **Constant Lemaire.** 1908.

Picturesque *lucarnes* punctuate a glorious arcade near the sky. Oh, to live on *that* fourth floor!

★**[1s-34.] Fontaine Molière,** 37, rue de Richelieu, corner rue Molière and rue Thérèse. **Ludovico Visconti.** 1844.

A Classical seat for this Classical playwright. Unlike its namesake, it is not much fun—just a lot of pomp, with the necessary paired columns, *fronton,* and entablatures.

**[1s-35.] Immeuble, 1, rue Thérèse,** corner rue Molière. 17th century.

Mostly interesting to see the 17th century's battering: walls thick at the base, becoming thinner as structural needs diminish.

_____

The present and past organs of the **Bibliothèque Nationale** occupy a superblock bounded by the rue des Petits-Champs, rue de Richelieu, rue Colbert, and rue Vivienne. All this will be supplemented by the Bibliothèque de France (*très grande bibliothèque,* or TGB), a grandiose center of towering stacks and study courtyards **[13se-51.]** over the Austerlitz rail yards in the 13th arrondissement (**Dominique Perrault.** 1995).

_____

★★**[1s-36.] Hôtel Tubeuf I,** 8, rue des Petits-Champs and 12–16, rue Vivienne. **Pierre Le Muet.** 1633.

The first of several elements of the Bibliothèque Nationale, this grand house belonged to Louis XIV's superintendent of finances, Jacques Tubeuf. The twin-columned portal is a potent entry symbol.

**[1s-37.] Hôtel de Nevers,** 12, rue Colbert, corner rue de Richelieu. **François Mansart.** circa 1645.

Here are the remains of the Hôtel de Nevers that housed, successively, the **Bibliothèque de Mazarin,** the salon of Mme. de Lambert, and **le Cabinet des Médailles du Roi.** There is some gutsy Mansart left up there.

★★★★**[1s-37a.] Main Reading Room/Salle de Travail, Bibliothèque Nationale,** 58, rue de Richelieu, facing square Louvois. **Henri Labrouste.** 1858–1868.

This grand and delicate essay in cast and wrought iron brings a host of hovering domes to form a glorious secular baldachino for the library's selected readers. Even a distinguished French intellectual has difficulty in getting a seat. But look in. It's worth it. Labrouste raised the art of iron to a level that transcends the elegance of engineering (in a strict mathematical sense) and creates a space of great beauty and joy. See his **Bibliothèque Sainte-Geneviève [5n-40.]** for a place of similar elegance, but differing form.

★**[1s-38.] Hôtel Tubeuf II**/later **Braquenie et Cie,** 16, rue Vivienne, opposite rue Colbert. **Pierre Le Muet.** circa 1650. Renovations, **Pierre Prunet** and **François Lerault.** 1991.

A nice relic, altered, surelevated on the street, that was converted from Tubeuf's elegant financial ministry to the work of ordinary mammon: now on the return road to its original splendor as an *hôtel particulier.*

★★★**[1s-39.] Galerie Vivienne**/originally **Galerie Marchoux,** 6, rue Vivienne and 4, rue des Petits-Champs. **François-Jacques Delannoy.** 1823.

Elegant, neo-Classical. The strong lateral structure offers a syncopated interruption to the skylights. The dome is of a quality that the former Galerie Colbert has lost. Its bas-reliefs are original, and the floor is inlaid with Italian tesserae (the work of the Italian artisan Faccina).

★**[1s-40.] Galerie Colbert,** 6, rue des Petits-Champs and 4, rue Vivienne. **J. Billaud.** 1826. Demolished and reconstructed, 1980s.

A sad story. The Bibliothèque Nationale demolished and reconstructed, for ostensibly practical needs, the whole works. Boutiques (à la Beaubourg, Louvre, or the lustful museums of New York) now line a rebuilt skylit gallery that has lost most of its elegance. Overdone, poorly detailed, and at times vulgar, it was a bad idea, a sorry contrast with the Galerie Vivienne next door.

**[1s-41.] Mairie (Second Arrondissement),** 8, rue de la Banque, between rue du 4 Septembre and rue des Petits-Champs. **Victor Baltard.** 1850.

Solid, arched, and pilastered, unfortunately without Haussmannian histrionics. Baltard's work was sober and somber, except for **Les Halles,** where he soared with engineering.

**[1s-42.] Hôtel du Timbre**/now **Direction Générale des Impôts,** 9-13, rue de la Banque, between rue du 4 Septembre and rue des Petits-Champs. **Victor Baltard** and **Lelong.** 1846–1849.

Official architecture, now officious. There is a strict neo-Roman portal to offend, if not affray, taxpayers.

★[1s-43.] **Immeuble, 12, rue Notre-Dame-des-Victoires,** between rue Réaumur and rue Paul-Lelong. **Jean-Alexandre-Edmond Navarre.** circa 1900.

The bay windows are boxed in by the 17th- and 18th-century structures adjacent. But the elegant curved glass reveals deserve a more gracious location.

★★[1s-44.] **Eglise Notre-Dame-des-Victoires,** place des Petits-Pères, between rue Notre-Dame-des-Victoires and rue de la Banque. Choir, **Pierre Le Muet.** 1629–1632. Transept and last bay of nave, **Libéral Bruant.** 1642–1666. Completed, **Sylvain Cartault.** 1740.

A cool *Jésuitique* facade faces an Italian-scaled piazza. It is a hard idea but in a picturesque position. Add to that Corinthian pilasters above, Composite pilasters below, and flanking obelisks.

[1s-45.] **Hôtel de Colbert,** 5, rue du Mail, between rue des Petits-Pères and rue Montmartre. **François Letellier.** 1650.

A maw lurks amid festoons.

[1s-46.] **Hôtel Gobert,** 7, rue du Mail, between rue des Petits-Pères and rue Montmartre. **Thomas Gobert.** 1669.

Great Corinthian pilasters rise for two floors above a rusticated and arcuated base.

[1s-47.] **Immeuble, 23, rue du Mail,** between rue des Petits-Pères and rue Montmartre. 1885.

A sturdy, stone-pilastered studio building, with glassy iron-framed infill. Precocious glass and iron and *retardataire* stone at the same time.

★[1s-48.] **Immeuble, 25 bis, rue du Mail,** between rue des Petits-Pères and rue Montmartre.

Much more elegance than at **No. 23** next door: delicately articulated iron (with rosettes), crowned, however, with a mansard *ordinaire.*

[1s-49.] **Ministère de la Culture,** 4, rue d'Aboukir, just off place des Victoires. circa 1815.

Rustications articulate great arches surmounted by Palladian windows.

★★★[1s-50.] **Place des Victoires,** originally served by rue Croix-des-Petits-Champs and rue d'Aboukir, later impaled by rue Etienne-Marcel. **Jules Hardouin-Mansart.** 1685.

The original standing statue of Louis XIV went the way of all bronze royalty during the Revolution—to the armaments foundry. The one now in place (**Bosio.** 1822) is a Restoration replacement, this time on a horse. Mansart's *place* is a bit too large for its buildings (four levels including the *comble*), which are more elegant close up than as a total entity. The car, of course, has come in to dominate, but perhaps some careful urbanism for pedestrians could improve this void. And maybe some trees?

★[1s-51.] **Hôtel Portalis,** 43, rue Croix-des-Petits-Champs, corner rue La Vrillière. circa 1685.

A *tourelle* with its bulging neo-Baroque balconies forms a swell swelling on two streets. The ironwork is lovely; rather than Baroquelike broken pediments, these are broken balustrades.

**★[1s-52.] Banque de France**/originally **Hôtel de Toulouse,** 39, rue Croix-des-Petits-Champs, off rue La Vrillière. **François Mansart.** 1643. Substantial alterations, **Robert de Cotte.** 1719. Totally rebuilt, 19th century.

Like Brigadoon, the Galerie Dorée is open only one day in September. The whole guts of the building were destroyed and rebuilt in the 19th century—gallery included. The latter was redone from drawings.

**★★★[1s-53.] Jardin du Palais-Royal,** between rue de Montpensier, rue de Beaujolais, and rue de Valois. **Victor Louis.** 1784.

A real estate venture of the duc d'Orléans, this grand and urbane garden is the by-product of its surrounding apartment buildings and shops. Annexed to the actual Palais Royal, it now seems an integral part of a symbiotic complex.
Around its melancholy arcades are elegant shops and some venerable, some merely good, restaurants. The central space, one of the most peaceful in Paris, is sparsely populated by nannies with their charges, relaxing office workers, and sometimes even a tourist. Enter.

**★[1s-54.] Le Grand Véfour (restaurant),** 17, rue de Beaujolais, between rue de Montpensier and rue de Valois, and 79–82, galerie de Beaujolais. Founded 1784.

The duc d'Orléans, later known as Philippe Egalité, can best be remembered in his architectural ventures for the apartments and Jardin du Palais-Royal and for the Rotonde de Chartres at the Parc Monceau. Here, at the edge of that garden, he installed what was at first known as the Café de Chartres, a hangout for royalty, nobility, and later a couple of presidents (Thiers and MacMahon). The interiors are painted in a neo-Pompeian manner, in a lavish display of intricate brushwork added 1820–1850. Expensive.

**[1s-55.] Théâtre du Palais-Royal,** 38, rue de Montpensier, corner of the Jardin du Palais-Royal. **Paul Sédille.** 1880. Restored, **Henri Bernouville.** 1905.

Pompous within, it bears fire escapes of iron elegance without. It replaces an earlier theater by **Victor Louis.**

**[1s-56.] Chez Armand (restaurant),** 6, rue de Beaujolais, between rue de Valois and rue de Montpensier. 16th century.

A converted carriage house, with lovely brick vaultings.

**★[1s-57.] Immeuble, 33, rue Radziwill,** just south of rue des Petits-Champs. 17th century.

Here is a double-timber spiral stair, an extraordinary blend of space and structure.

**★[1s-58.] Hôtel Mélusine,** 6–8, rue de Valois, between place de Valois and rue du Colonel-Driant. circa 1550. Balcony, 1636.

A handsome vernacular block opposite the **Palais Royal.** The consoles of lions are extravagant imbricated and gilded supports for the central balcony.

**[1s-59.] Place de Valois,** between rue de Valois and rue Croix-des-Petits-Champs. **Jean-Sylvain Cartaud.** 1750.

A space punctuating the progression from the rue Croix-des-Petits-Champs to **Daniel Buren**'s columns within the Palais Royal. Try it from the east.

**★★[1s-60.] Galerie Véro-Dodat,** 2, rue du Bouloi, between rue Croix-des-Petits-Champs and 19, rue Jean-Jacques-Rousseau. Perhaps **Constant Protain.** 1826.

Intact Classical storefronts enrich this very grandest of *galeries.*

**★★[1s-61.] Eglise Réformée de l'Oratoire du Louvre,** 147, rue Saint-Honoré, corner rue de l'Oratoire, through to rue de Rivoli. **Clément II Métezeau.** 1620s. Completed by **Jacques Lemercier** and **François Mansart.**

A Classical-Mannerist extravaganza, but the interior is rigorous and, appropriately, Protestant. The rue de Rivoli arcade and its monument to Admiral de Coligny by **Crauk** (1889) provide a rich and exciting counterpoint, unmatched by the works inside. Here is neo-Baroque outflanking the baroque reality.

---

**Rue de Rivoli**
Arcades were born here to challenge infinity. Happily, within, you'll have a more discrete idea of where you have been and where you are going, but the view from the **Tuileries**'s (gardens) north flank (who walks there?) is an "endless" vista, which in fact does end with a CRS (Compagnie Républicaine de Sécurité) submachine gun at the west end and the Oratoire at the east. The street was opened in 1800, between place de la Concorde and the Palais Royal (arcaded facades, **Percier et Fontaine**). This bold and plastic arcade, giving delight in shade and shadow, is in rich counterpoint to the gardens opposite and to the relatively bland north facade of the Louvre. Behind the arcade is a spectrum of shops, tourist traps, tearooms, hotels, and the English-language bookstore, **W. H. Smith.**
To the east, beyond place du Palais-Royal, is **Le Louvre des Antiquaires,** an assemblage of antique dealers in a later building that continues the arcade up to the rue du Louvre.

---

**★★[1s-62.] Eglise Saint-Germain-l'Auxerrois,** 2, place du Louvre, between rue de Rivoli and quai du Louvre. Tower, 12th century. Portal, choir, and chapel of the Virgin, 13th century. Reconstructions and porch, 15th century. "Restorations," **Jean-Baptiste Lassus** and **Victor Baltard.** 1838–1855.

A late Gothic eclecticism, its choir piers became fluted in the Classical manner. The white, translucent glass of the nave (1728) was a product of the Age of Reason in contrast to the rich red, blue, and purple glass and light of the choir. The 18th-century pendant chandeliers provide an elegance of brass, with sparkling highlights. This was the royal church. A *jubé* built by **Pierre Lescot** and decorated by **Jean Goujon** was created here (since removed) when they were working across the street on the west facade of the original small **Cour Carrée.**

**★★★★[1s-63.] Louvre,** between rue de Rivoli and the Seine, Jardin des Tuileries, and place du Louvre. **Plethora of architects.** 1546–1989.

The foundations of the Louvre of Philippe-Auguste, the first structure in the long ancestral line of the present complex, can be seen by entering the Pyramid and moving under the present **Cour Carrée.** Built as a bastion for his wall (1190–1210), it embraced a rectangular courtyard, 61 by 49 meters (200 by 161 feet). Charles V remodeled this fortification and prison into a sometime château (**Raymond de Temple.** 1360–1370), but it remained for François I to associate Paris, the capital, with the power of the Crown. French kings to this point had led a peripatetic life, moving the court from one château to another with no permanent centralized palace of authority. François wrote to the city counselors of Paris on March 15, 1528, "Very dear and good friends, it is our intention henceforth to make our home for the most part in our good city of Paris, more than in any other place in the kingdom, knowing that our château of the Louvre is both commodious and appropriate for us to lodge: to this end [we] have decided to repair this château and put it in order . . ."

In 1546 François commissioned Pierre Lescot to build a new west wing on the existing foundations, in what became the "modern" architecture of the Renaissance. Most subsequent architecture of the Louvre, through the 19th century, comprises variations on that theme by Lescot, including that of the sculpture by his collaborator, Jean Goujon. (West wing of Philippe-Auguste's Louvre. **Pierre Lescot,** architect. **Jean Goujon,** sculptor. 1546–1559, now visible in its original state on the courtyard, veneered by **Hector Lefuel** in the 1850s on the Cour Napoléon). Lescot and Goujon continued their work to complete the south wing, facing the river, between 1566 and 1600, also visible on the Cour Carrée, but veneered by **Claude Perrault** on the river side in the 1670s.

Henri IV entered Paris in 1594. His architectural impact was considerable **(place des Vosges, place Dauphine).** At the Louvre his grand decision was to quadruple the size of Philippe-Auguste's court and building, while continuing the connection of the Louvre to the new Tuileries palace: both that palace and the **Grande Galerie** had been started by Catherine de' Medici, and he extended both works. **Jacques Lemercier** was commissioned to continue Lescot's work, completing the west facade of the quadrupled courtyard and half of the north facade (1624–1654). It remained for **Louis Le Vau** and **François d'Orbay** to consummate the Cour Carrée under Louis XIV. (1650–1664). Finally, Colbert, superintendent of buildings, seeking a more grandiose eastern external facade facing the city, held a competition, to which **Gian-Lorenzo Bernini, François Mansart, Pierre Cottard, Jean Marot, Claude Perrault, Louis Le Vau,** and others were invited. Perrault (according to Boileau "a bad doctor who became a good architect") was the winner. The resulting colonnade (1667–1674) of twin Corinthian columns was at first almost invisible, pressed against the contiguous city; and a *place* to give it an appropriately monumental posture was not created for another eighty years, by **Jacques-Ange Gabriel** and **Jacques-Germain Soufflot** (1754 and later). The **Colonnade,** the most distinguished facade of the palace-museum, raises the somewhat bland skin presented elsewhere in the complex to a powerful statement, and the rediscovered "moat" now adds a posture of grandeur.

The Old Louvre, embracing the Cour Carrée, presents architecture of the 16th and 17th centuries facing the courtyard and on its three exterior elevations. The New Louvre, those grand arms embracing the Cour Napoléon (Napoléon III, that is), partially structured by the remnants of the Tuileries, is now invisible behind the 1850s veneering architecture of **Hector Lefuel.**

The Grand Axis, defined by the Louvre at its east and terminating at the 1989 Grande Arche of La Défense, seems to the traveler an almost eternal event. In fact, its marker, the **Arc de Triomphe,** was not completed until 1836, and the embracing arms of the Louvre in the 1860s and 1870s. The **Champs-Elysées,** originally a garden forest, was disciplined into an *allée perspective* by **André Le Nôtre** in 1664, but as a perspective for the Tuileries, and retained that role until the Tuileries was burned in the Commune of 1871. The small **Arc du Triomphe du Carrousel,** ultimately part of the eye's vista threading through the Arc de Triomphe to **La Défense,** was erected under Napoléon I **(Percier et Fontaine.** 1808) in what was originally a totally contained space. Its slight tilt from the present axis (7 degrees) is parroted in the similar tilt of the **Grande Arche** at La Défense.

The **pyramid** of **I. M. Pei** (1989) now serves as the principal entrance to the museum. As a crystalline island floating in the Cour Napoléon, it attempts to isolate itself from the stylistic embrace of Lefuel. The problem is that it is not crystalline enough: the trussed structure presents a heavy hand to the arriving traveler. As tall as the first cornice of the surrounding palace, it is not big enough, and the four surrounding satellite pyramids could well be eliminated. Once you are down and within the entrance space (on a stair more akin to Hollywood than to a world of neo-Classicism), the pyramid becomes a hole in a much vaster roof, an almost arbitrary incision. But from then on, the underworld is magnificent, offering services, restaurant, bookstore, parking, and distributing the visitor to both old and new sections of the museum with logic and grace. The Grand Louvre works.

The Louvre was only briefly used as the principal palace (1559–1666) of the kingdom, and its Grande Galerie was the habitat and ateliers of distinguished artists before it became a museum **(Boucher, Pigalle, Bouchardon, David, Hubert Robert).** The north wing was *never* a museum *or* a royal residence: most of it served as offices for the government, most recently for the **Ministry of Finance.** An eclectic building of eclectic usage, the Louvre is nevertheless a symbol of Paris and of its controlled urbanism. It is a grandiose icon that serves in concert with the Eiffel Tower, Sacré-Coeur, and the Arc de Triomphe as a touchstone for all travelers, whether or not they ever enter its portals or view its painting and sculpture. The Louvre is the symbolic palace of the world that was only briefly—and in small part—the royal residence.

★★★[1s-64.] **Palais Royal**/originally **Palais Cardinal**/now **Conseil d'Etat,** between rue Richelieu and rue de Valois along rue Saint-Honoré. **Jacques Lemercier.** 1629 and later.

Cardinal Richelieu's private *hôtel particulier* became, by his prudent gift to Louis XIII, the Palais Royal, to be inhabited by royalty and their relatives. The duc d'Orléans, later known as Philippe Egalité, constructed the vast annexed garden and its surrounding apartments, where revolutionary fervor excelled in the many cafés. The palace proper is bounded by place du Palais-Royal, the galerie d'Orléans, the Théâtre Français, and rue de Valois. Inside are the Conseil d'Etat and parts of the Ministère de la Culture.

In the courtyard, once a mere parking lot, are the **Colonnes de Buren** (★★) **(Daniel Buren.** 1986), a wonderful play of truncated neo-Classicism that concerns itself not only with the positive dimension but also with the negative. Voids below extend the rhythmic idea. Controversial, the columns providing a playground for children's bodies and adults' minds.

At the edge, the **galerie d'Orléans** offers a double colonnade **(Pierre Fontaine.** 1829) that triumphally joins Buren and the Jardin.

# 2
# FIRST AND FOURTH ARRONDISSEMENTS
## ISLANDS IN THE RIVER
### PONT DE SULLY TO SQUARE DU VERT GALANT

Hôtel Lambert: **Louis Le Vau;** Arcade de l'Hôtel Bretonvilliers: **Jean Androuet du Cerceau;** Hôtel Lauzun: **Louis Le Vau;** quai d'Anjou; Eglise Saint-Louis-en-l'Ile: **Louis Le Vau;** quai de Béthune; quai d'Orléans; quai de Bourbon; Hôtel Le Charron: **Sébastien Bruand;** les Déportées: **Georges-Henri Pingusson;** Cathédrale Notre-Dame de Paris: **Pierre de Montreuil,** then **Eugène Viollet-le-Duc;** pont d'Arcole: **Alphonse Oudry;** Sainte-Chapelle: **Pierre de Montreuil,** then **Eugène Viollet-le-Duc;** La Conciergerie; quai des Orfèvres: **Henri Sauvage;** place Dauphine; square du Vert Galant

Métro: **Sully-Morland**

**[Iles-19.] Mémorial des Martyrs de la Déportation. Georges-Henri Pingusson. 1962.**

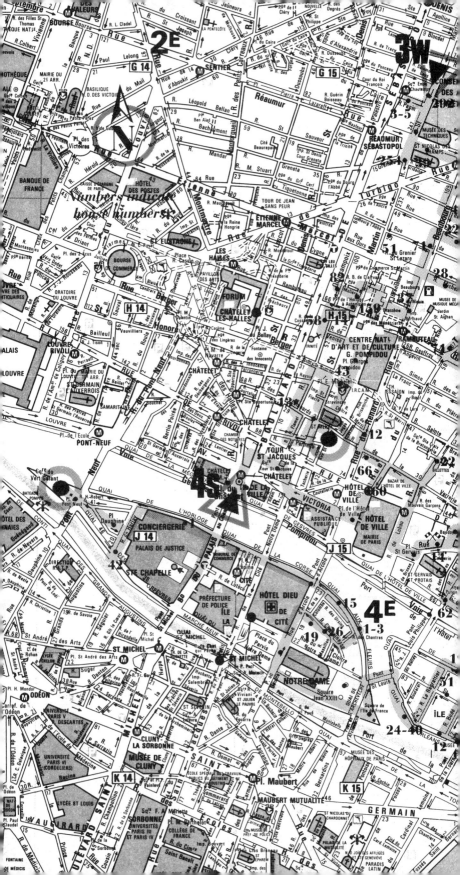

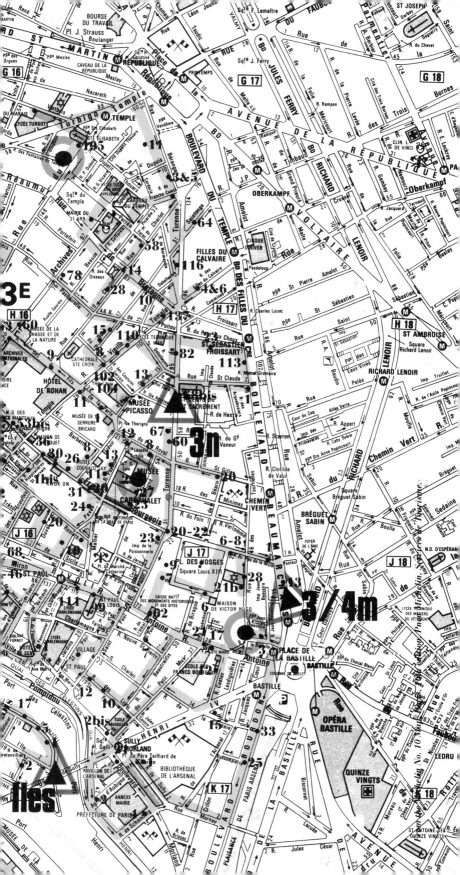

A nice way to slip onto these islands is over the pont de Sully (boulevard Henri IV). You'll find a pleasant park where you can gaze upstream before you move downstream.

★★★[Iles-1.] Hôtel Lambert, 1, quai d'Anjou and 2, rue Saint-Louis-en-l'Ile. **Louis Le Vau.** 1641.

The view from the bridge and *quai* shows the spectacular *galerie ovale* that pushes its busty form onto the very edge of the *quai.* Now a private house once again, it is visible only in random glimpses, including the grand portal on rue Saint-Louis-en-l'Ile.

★[Iles-2.] Arcade de l'Hôtel Bretonvilliers, 3, rue Bretonvilliers, between rue Saint-Louis-en-l'Ile and quai de Béthune. Apocryphal remnant. **Jean Androuet du Cerceau.** circa 1642.

The *hôtel* went into the drink with the construction of the Pont de Sully, but local apocrypha say that the building spanning the street is a vestige.

[Iles-3.] Petit Hôtel de Bretonvilliers, 2, rue Bretonvilliers, between rue Saint-Louis-en-l'Ile and quai de Béthune. circa 1639.

The doors are always open, but we monkeys must look through the locked and coded *grille* into the pleasant private inner court.

[Iles-4.] Petit Hôtel de Marigny, 5, quai d'Anjou, between pont de Sully and rue Poulletier. 1640.

Greatly altered and surelevated by later owners.

★[Iles-5.] Hôtel Jacques Brébart/now **Syndicat des Maîtres Boulangers de Paris,** 7, quai d'Anjou, between pont de Sully and rue Poulletier. 1642.

An iron merchant showed iron elegantly.

★★★ interiors [Iles-6.] Hôtel Lauzun, 17, quai d'Anjou, between pont de Sully and rue Poulletier. Probably **Louis Le Vau.** 1657.

What's wondrous here is mostly inside. The warm sandstone facade is made ornate by a gilded wrought-iron balcony. For more Le Vau, repair to **Vaux-le-Vicomte,** a heady place. Here, and only on the outside, you'll have to be content with the extraordinary downspouts.

★★★★ interiors [Iles-7.] Eglise Saint-Louis-en-l'Ile, 19 bis, rue Saint-Louis-en-l'Ile, corner rue Poulletier. **Louis Le Vau.** 1644 and later. **Gabriel Le Duc.** 1701 and later. **Jacques Doucet.** 1704–1725.

Parisian Baroque that continues the elegances of **Val-de-Grâce** and **Temple de la Visitation-Sainte-Marie.** The Jesuits counterattacked the Protestants here with vigorous vaults, light, and form—but inside; outside it is dour and almost unnoticeable.

★[Iles-8.] Immeuble, 29, rue Saint-Louis-en-l'Ile, between rue Poulletier and rue des Deux-Ponts. circa 1642. Reworked, 17th century.

Buzz in to a grand stair in wrought iron with steps that flower and cascade.

[Iles-9.] Maison Helena Rubinstein/once **Hôtel Hasselin,** 24, quai de Béthune, corner rue Poulletier. **Louis Le Vau.** 1642. Drastically altered, **Louis Süe.** 1935.

She may have had style, but this was a rape. The only remnant of Le Vau is the doors. The rest of the *hôtel* has vanished.

**[Iles-10.] Hôtel du Président Violle,** 36, quai de Béthune, between rue Poulletier and rue des Deux-Ponts. 1648.

A nice courtyard.

★**[Iles-11.] Immeuble, 33, rue des Deux-Ponts,** between rue Saint-Louis-en-l'Ile and quai d'Orléans. 17th century.

A magnificent stair in walnut, carved and sturdy.

★**[Iles-12.] Biblioteka Polska**/originally **Hôtel Antoine-Moreau,** 6, quai d'Orléans, between rue des Deux-Ponts and rue Budé. 1655.

Buzz in to Polish independence. The courtyard is in scale with this tiny island—compressed, but vigorous.

**[Iles-13.] Immeuble, 12, quai d'Orléans,** corner rue Budé. 17th century.

There is some elegant ironwork affixed to what is now a bland bulk.

★★**[Iles-14.] Hôtel de Chenizot,** 51, rue Saint-Louis-en-l'Ile, between rue Budé and rue Le Regrattier. Facade, **Pierre de Vigny.** 1726.

One extravagant hotel amid understated neighbors. Inside is a wonderful staircase.

★**[Iles-15.]** Originally **Demeure de Philippe de Champaigne,** 11, quai de Bourbon, between rue des Deux-Ponts and rue Le Regrattier. 1643.

Again a lovely courtyard, but if you pass through (enjoy the timber stair on the way), you will see the remains of a former *jeu de paume* (circa 1635) rising above the rooftops. It can be entered from 54, rue Saint-Louis-en-l'Ile, a residential hotel.

★**[Iles-16.] Hôtel Le Charron,** 15, quai de Bourbon, between rue des Deux-Ponts and rue Le Regrattier. **Sébastien Bruand.** circa 1650.

The main house is here on the streetfront, with a second mansarded block behind the majestic courtyard.

★**[Iles-17.] Hôtel de Jassaud,** 19, quai de Bourbon and 26, rue Le Regrattier. circa 1650. Reworked, 18th century.

The ironwork and entrance portal are lovely, ornate, and *classé;* the courtyard within is magnificent. See also **19 bis, quai de Bourbon** and **28, rue Le Regrattier** next door.

**[Iles-18.] Immeubles, 24–40, quai d'Orléans,** between pont Saint-Louis and rue Le Regrattier.

Standing at the ramp at the foot of rue Le Regrattier, the ensemble includes the elegant **Nos. 28–32,** with original ironwork. The architects here built cities rather than their own egos or those of their clients.

Cross the pont Saint-Louis to the east tip of the **Ile de la Cité.**

★★★**[Iles-19.] Mémorial des Martyrs de la Déportation,** square de l'Ile-de-France, at the eastern tip of the Ile de la Cité. **Georges-Henri Pingusson.** 1962.

Sunken below the adjacent park, constrained by narrow stairs and powerful masonry forms, you are shouldered through a memorial sequence. It would have been more effective without the stylish metal sculpture.

★[Iles-20.] **Square Jean XXIII,** between square-de-l'Ile-de-France and the chevet of Notre Dame. Fountain of the Virgin, **Vigoroux.** 1845.

A neo-Gothic presence in the spirit but without the venerability of **Notre Dame.** Like **Viollet-le-Duc,** it presents a Gothic-finialed perfection, exalted in the *flèche* seen rising from Notre-Dame's crossing. Henry Adams in *Mont Saint-Michel and Chartres* prefaced the whole book by its initial phrase: "The archangel loved heights." Here that same temptation to soar is expressed by the distant *flèche.*

★★★★[Iles-21.] **Cathédrale Notre-Dame de Paris,** place du Parvis Notre-Dame, pont au Double, and rue d'Arcole. Choir, 1162–1182. Three bays of nave, 1180–1200. Balance of nave and towers, 1220. Rose window, 1225. Elaborations and additions, **Pierre de Montreuil.** 1258–1265. **Jean de Chelles.** 1265 and later. **Pierre de Chelles.** 1300–1318. **Jean Ravy.** 1318–1344. "Restorations," **Eugène Viollet-le-Duc.** 1844–1879.

This ribcage of Paris, at the spot of pre-Christian pagan rites, became and remained the symbol of the ancient city. Around here the Romans camped, and here the city grew as a center of Gaul. Later symbols are more casual—and much, much later: the **Eiffel Tower** and **Sacré-Coeur,** both of the late 19th century, the **Arc de Triomphe,** not finished until 1836.

But symbol it is, elevated to neo-medievalism by Victor Hugo (*Notre Dame de Paris,* 1831), abetted by Charles Laughton by way of Hollywood. There are many quarrels about the almost dictatorial revisions of Viollet-le-Duc, who added the *flèche* and organized the facade into a rigid and "neatened" composition. But he gathered the failing building back into its extraordinary structural and visual integrity, as a somewhat arbitrary restorer, with what he hoped was a medieval soul.

★[Iles-22.] **Atelier de la RATP,** 19, rue Chanoinesse, opposite rue de la Colombe.

An electrical workshop for the city's subways and buses. The spiral strapwork forming iron console brackets are this steel building's graceful contribution to technological art.

★[Iles-23.] **Hôtel, 26, rue Chanoinesse,** between rue de la Colombe and rue des Chantres. 17th century.

A memory of the 17th century, stripped but enflowered.

★[Iles-24.] **Hôtel du Grand Chantre,** 1–3, rue des Ursins, corner rue des Chantres. 15th century.

Much fussed with: the frameless windows and the modern *garde-fous* are ludicrous. Where are you when we need you, Viollet-le-Duc? Only late ogives at the *rez-de-chaussée* keep a "foot" in their proper history.

★[Iles-25.] **Immeuble, 15, rue des Ursins,** between rue des Chantres and rue de la Colombe. 1899.

*Meulière* resplendent, with iron strapwork and glass and a *super* bay window. The real 19th century here displays vigor, while mostly neo stuff fills most of the rest of this island disconsolately.

★★[Iles-26.] **Pont d'Arcole,** connecting rue d'Arcole and place de l'Hôtel-de-Ville. **Alphonse Oudry,** engineer. 1855.

A clear span of 80 meters (262 feet) across this main branch of the Seine. The twelve iron arches, tapered in their soaring duties, make it the first wrought-iron bridge (as opposed to cast iron).

[Iles-27.] **Palais de Justice,** filling the Ile de la Cité between boulevard du Palais and place Dauphine. **Louis Lenormand.** circa 1874.

One of the great, if not grand, works under Haussmann, this vast ensemble embraces the remnants of medieval Paris, most strikingly that of the **Sainte-Chapelle** and the **Conciergerie.** The Palais is mostly banal (except for its preserved "organs") and presents a particularly pompous facade to the place Dauphine, which it sullied by removing the facing third side of that triangular space in order to allow Lenormand to display his vacuous self.

★★★★[Iles-28.] **Sainte-Chapelle,** within the embrace of the Palais de Justice, 4, boulevard du Palais. Probably **Pierre de Montreuil.** 1241–1248. Partially burned, 1630. Slow reconstructions in the 17th, 18th, and early 19th centuries. Restorations, **Félix-Jacques Duban** and **Jean-Baptiste-Antoine Lassus,** but particularly **Eugène Viollet-le-Duc.** *Flèche,* 1857.

Harbored in a courtyard that is not part of its own history, this glassy magnificence is a lithe crustacean structure, sheltering glass that dominates its incredible armature. Upstairs is the chapel of royalty; downstairs that of the lesser people. But all is bathed with a rich polychromatic light, the ultimate of Gothic virtuosity. At **Beauvais,** architects attempted almost impossible and melodramatic height. Here the skeleton was honed to a point that foresees the taut elegance of iron-and-glass French architecture of the 19th century (the roof of the **Grand Palais,** for example).

★★[Iles-29.] **La Conciergerie,** 1, quai de l'Horloge, between boulevard du Palais and place Dauphine. 14th–19th centuries, incorporated into the present Palais de Justice. "Reconstructions," **Louis-Joseph Duc** and **Pierre-Jérôme-Honoré Daumet.** 1868–1880.

This is a sometimes powerful and grisly place of justice, not only of the *ancien régime* but of the Revolution as well. Remnant spaces within are composed of some 14th-century Gothicisms, vastly recomposed by Duc and company in concert with the construction of the Haussmannian Palais de Justice. Particularly to be cited is the **Salle des Gens d'Armes,** a vast vaulted space now used for occasional concerts, 27 by almost 70 meters (88 by 229 feet) and 8.5 meters (28 feet) high. The present architecture, however, is largely that of Duc. Although the building burned in 1618, the restoration was not accomplished until the late 19th century; and, as with restorations of that era and ilk, it was intellectually passionate and cool.

★[Iles-30.] **Immeuble, 42, quai des Orfèvres,** corner rue de Harlay. **Henri Sauvage.** 1932.

Sauvage-*tardif,* a strange ending to his brilliant practice.

★[Iles-31.] **Place Dauphine,** filling the western end of the Ile de la Cité between the Palais de Justice and the pont Neuf. 1607, altered and disfigured in the 18th and 19th centuries. Eastern closure demolished, **Louis-Joseph Duc.** 1874.

A sad remembrance, though the trees try to create some ambience among its trashed houses. Its memory can best be savored in the **Turgot** engraving (1730). How can history be so strong in a place that has been denuded?

Across the street, facing onto what is the land portion, or *place*, of the **pont Neuf,** is the enhorsed **Henri IV,** patron of this *place* as well as that of **des Vosges.** Behind and below him is the **square du Vert Galant,** a restful oasis where one can enjoy the two arms of the Seine at this prow, and embark on a line of tourist boats.

# 3
# FIRST AND SECOND ARRONDISSEMENTS
## SOUTHEAST

### BOURSE DU COMMERCE, LES HALLES, AND ENVIRONS

Bourse du Commerce: **Nicolas Lecamus de Mézières** and **François-Joseph Bélanger**; Hôtel Thoinard de Vougy: **Germain Boffrand**; rue Jean-Jacques-Rousseau; passage du Grand Cerf; passage du Bourg-l'Abbé: **Lusson** and **Paul Blondel**; Tour de Jean sans Peur; Eglise Saint-Leu/Saint-Gilles: **Charles de Wailly** and **Victor Baltard**; Fontaine des Innocents: **Jean Goujon**; Café Costès: **Philippe Starck**; Forum des Halles: **Jean Willerval, Claude Vasconi,** and **Georges Pancreac'h**; Jardin des Halles: **Louis Arrètche**; Les Halles Souterraines: **Paul Chemetov**; Eglise Saint-Eustache: **Pierre Lemercier, Charles David, François Petit,** and **Mansart de Jouy**; La Samaritaine: **Frantz Jourdain** and **Henri Sauvage**

Métro: **Louvre**

**[1/2se-35.] La Samaritaine (grand magasin).** Interior ironwork. **Frantz Jourdain.** 1906.

23

★★[1/2se-1.] Bourse du Commerce/originally Halle aux Blés, 2, rue de Viarmes, off rue du Louvre. Original building, Nicolas Lecamus de Mézières. 1763–1767. Coupole No. 1, Roubo. 1781. Coupole No. 2, François-Joseph Bélanger. 1806–1811. Remodeled with glazed coupole, 1889.

The wheat exchange's original opaque dome, framed with wood members in 1781 to cover what was originally used as an open courtyard, burned in 1802. Bélanger's proposed replacement in iron was at first rejected in favor of stone (in the manner of Rome's Pantheon), but the perimeter structure would not bear the thrust. Nevertheless, it took nine years before agreement on the light and noncombustible substitute (and nine years of outdoor trading once more). The subsequent cast- and wrought-iron network was then covered with copper leaves (again à la Pantheon) until the 1889 remodeling. The then new Bourse de Commerce chose to remove the copper sheathing and replace it with glass—its present state.

The colonnaded street embracing the Bourse is named for the *prévôt de marchands* or mayor, in effect, under the *ancien régime,* who ordered it all. Behind, like a bustle confronting the garden of the **Forum des Halles,** is a column that served as observatory for the astrologer of Catherine de Médicis, a remnant of the **Hôtel de la Reine** that occupied this site.

[1/2se-2.] Immeuble, 15, rue du Louvre, between rue du Colonel-Driant and rue Coquillière.

The private place within, **Cour des Fermes,** is guarded by great twin atlantes flanking the double-vaulted entryway.

★[1/2se-3.] Caisse d'Epargne/originally Hôtel Thoinard de Vougy, 19, rue du Louvre, corner rue du Coq-Héron. Germain Boffrand. 1730.

A spectacular cornering of the juncture of rue du Coq-Héron, with a splendid 18th-century entrance portal.

[1/2se-4.] PTT (Hôtel des Téléphones), 55, rue Jean-Jacques-Rousseau, between rue Coquillière and rue Etienne-Marcel. 1930s.

There is a green cast to this glazed brick neo-Romanesque post office annex and a bulky modernism in both form and scale that is foreign to these parts.

[1/2se-5.] Hôtel Pierre Sageret, 62, rue Jean-Jacques-Rousseau, between rue Coquillière and rue Etienne-Marcel. 17th century.

This and its neighbor at **No. 64** were contextual elements into which the PTT charged.

[1/2se-6.] Hôtel de Mme. Dupin de Chenonceaux, 68, rue Jean-Jacques-Rousseau, between rue Coquillière and rue Etienne-Marcel. 17th century.

Rousseau's friend and adviser, Mme. Dupin, lived here, a short walk from his digs at (long gone) **No. 52.**

[1/2se-7.] Immeuble, 74, rue Jean-Jacques-Rousseau, between rue Coquillière and rue Etienne-Marcel. Julien-François Bayard. 1884.

Technology and brick join to open great windows.

★[1/2se-8.] Immeuble and passage, 48, rue Montmartre and 54, rue Tiquetonne, between rue Etienne-Marcel and rue Mandar. Remodeled, 1988.

What the best of old Paris can become—here a series of carefully detailed alleys, courts, and storefronts. The rue Montmartre streetfront is an unsuspecting mask to this interior world.

**[1/2se-9.] Immeuble, 15, rue Montmartre,** between rue Etienne-Marcel and rue du Jour. Restored.

**Le Cochon à l'Oreille** (circa 1890) has tile, mirrors, and a wonderful corniced zinc bar.

★**[1/2se-10.] L'Escargot d'Or (restaurant),** 38, rue Montorgueil, between rue Etienne-Marcel and rue Mauconseil. 1890s.

The golden snail is a welcoming and potent symbol guarding the canopy on this narrow street. A sumptuous *Belle Epoque* interior awaits. The snail and its patron have been in business since 1832, and over it all hovers a ceiling painted by **Clairin** for Sarah Bernhardt.

**[1/2se-11.] Immeuble, 51, rue Montorgueil,** opposite rue Marie-Stuart. 18th century.

An architect once dwelled here, his implements inscribed in stone over the entrance portal.

**[1/2se-12.] Immeubles, 15** and **22, rue Dussoubs,** between rue Saint-Sauveur and rue Greneta. 17th and 18th centuries.

Buzz in to No. 22—it's both grand and great. A stair of class and a handsome courtyard with a *classée* facade.

★★**[1/2se-13.] Passage du Grand-Cerf,** between 145, rue Saint-Denis and 8, rue Dussoubs. Covered, 1824. Restored, 1989.

**[1/2se-14.] Passage du Bourg-l'Abbé,** between 120, rue Saint-Denis and 3, rue de Palestro. **Lusson.** 1828. Rue de Palestro end reconstructed. **Paul Blondel.** 1863.

The two *passages* form a continuing glass-vaulted space. Note the caryatids at the rue de Palestro portal.

★**[1/2se-15.] Immeubles, 13** and **15, rue Tiquetonne,** between rue Saint-Denis and rue Dussoubs. 18th century.

At No. 13 the ironwork, cartouches, and cherubs enrich this narrow street with some special style. Buzz in to No. 15 to an 18th-century courtyard.

★★**[1/2se-16.] Tour de Jean sans Peur,** 20, rue Etienne-Marcel, between rue de Turbigo and rue Française, circa 1400.

Only extant part of the ancient **Hôtel de Bourgogne,** this medieval remnant is the only vestige of military feudalism in Paris. Now annexed to a public school, it stands today like an Englishman's folly, a venerable and picturesque artifact uninvolved with the modern city. The vaulted stairhall, with its central column spreading ribs in the manner of a great oak, will soon be reopened to the public. It is reputed that the tower was built for an insomniac assassin who later assassinated himself, a rather drastic solution for insomnia. But he did this deed elsewhere.

★**[1/2se-17.] Immeuble, 28, rue Pierre-Lescot,** between rue Etienne-Marcel and rue du Cygne. 1830s.

Sturdy Tuscans, two columns and two pilasters, bear a Greco-Roman entablature. It is a real event on the way to or from the **Forum des Halles.**

★★[1/2se-18.] **Eglise Saint-Leu/Saint-Gilles.** 92, rue Saint-Denis, between rue du Cygne and rue de la Grande Truanderie. Begun 1320. Choir, 1611. Side aisles, 1727. Crypt, **Charles de Wailly.** 1780. Other remodelings, **Victor Baltard.** 1857.

The 17th and 18th centuries attempted to impose a Renaissance discipline on a once-Gothic shell, but Haussmann and his architects preferred the Gothic, particularly on new and grand avenues such as **boulevard de Sébastopol.** Thus a sequential stylistic crossbreeding resulted: corbeled angel's heads support center ribs, with enough white glass above to assuage Jean-Jacques Rousseau. The nave is squat and wide without a triforium—how do they roof those aisle vaults? Go outside and see, and while you're there on rue Saint-Denis, deplore the facade, a spiky and typical French neo-Gothic (similar to neo-Gothicisms of the suburban United States and Canada). Too many architectural cooks were involved with this broth.

[1/2se-19.] **Pharamond (restaurant),** 24, rue de la Grande-Truanderie, between rue Pierre-Lescot and rue Mondétour. circa 1900.

Founded in 1832, the restaurant decorated its present interior in the best of the *Belle Epoque,* with ceramic tilework created for the 1900 Exposition. Outside is fake *colombage* but do not despair. Visual and gastronomic riches await within.

### Sex Shops and Peep Shows (rue Saint-Denis)

This more than venerable street vends more than venerable sex in multiple shops filled with sexual paraphernalia, books, and video booths. The incongruity of 17th-century architecture intermixed with sober restaurants and neon invitations to pubic entertainments is startling but, in retrospect, part of Parisian pragmatism. Limited to these blocks, all is legal, contained, and in view, while total exile to remoter enclaves (boulevard de Clichy) is impractical.

[1/2se-20.] **1992**/formerly **Ciné Sébastopol,** 41, boulevard de Sébastopol, corner rue de la Cossonnerie. Remodeled, 1989.

Chic salons replace X movies.

[1/2se-21.] **Immeuble, 44, rue Saint-Denis,** facing square des Innocents. 1890s.

A lone intruder amid the 17th- and 18th-century ensemble of rue Saint-Denis facades. Brick with cast-iron Ionics is tucked between overrestored and overstuccoed neighbors.

★★★[1/2se-22.] **Square** and **Fontaine des Innocents,** rue Berger and rue Saint-Denis. Original fountain, **Jean Goujon.** 1549. Moved to center of open market and fourth face added, **Pajou.** 1788.

Once three-sided at the corner of rue Berger and rue Saint-Denis, the fountain was modified by Pajou, who faithfully copied Goujon's style to create what seems to have always been this entity. This and adjacent open spaces were those of the **Cimetière des Saints-Innocents,** which, with its charnel houses, had received the bones of two million, the latter subsequently transferred (1780s) to abandoned quarries in the 14th arrondissement, the present **catacombs.**

The *tempietto* atop serves as a house of water delivering its secular cascades to the tourist hordes surrounding. But it is a place of sophistication in contrast to the noisy architecture of the **Forum des Halles** up rue **Pierre-Lescot.**

★**[1/2se-23.] Café Costès,** square des Innocents, at rue Berger and rue Saint-Denis. **Philippe Starck.** 1984.

The tense austerity of the self-conscious Starck—or is it stark? The stair doesn't go to paradise, but seems to.

**[1/2se-24.] Forum des Halles,** between rue Rambuteau, rue Pierre-Lescot, and rue Berger. Pierre Lescot building, **Jean Willerval.** 1979. Forum des Commerces, **Claude Vasconi** and **Georges Pancreac'h.** 1979.

Here lay the twelve pavilions of **Les Halles,** the great cast-iron-and-glass market buildings of **Victor Baltard** and **Félix Callet** (1857–1971). This belly of Paris, demolished in the name of efficiency, was replaced in function and on behalf of its resident produce wholesalers by suburban **Rungis,** near Orly airport, in 1971. The ensuing despair of concerned Parisians for this irreparable and unforgivable loss has focused attention on preservation, just as the destruction in 1963 of New York's Pennsylvania Station (**McKim, Mead & White.** 1910) was the catalyst for the creation of that city's Landmarks Preservation Commission.
The Forum underneath is a crossroads of commerce and transportation, serving the most complex transit interchange in Paris. That more than worthy program is topped, however, by vulgar and poorly detailed buildings. The poor old Comte de Rambuteau, prefect of Paris who hired Baltard originally, must be turning over in his grave. Mirrored windows and fanciful metalwork make a decorative shopping center that might better be at **La Défense,** where fellow spirits are abundant.

**[1/2se-25.] Jardin des Halles,** bounded by rue Coquillière, rue Rambuteau, the Forum des Halles, rue Berger, and the Bourse. **Louis Arrètche.** 1988.

A park that forms the lid of an underworld extension to the Forum. Here it seems more a gesture than a place of urban vitality; whatever is important is either below, aside, or elsewhere. The very word "important" is here suspect, starting with the Forum to the east. The gardens are a minimal bore, extravagant nonentities, with a sculpture (*Ecoute* by **Henri de Miller,** 1986) that confronts Saint-Eustache—a whimsy casually flaunted before serious architecture.

★★**[1/2se-26.] Forum des Halles/souterrain,** under the **Jardin des Halles,** bounded by rue Coquillière, rue Rambuteau, rue Berger, the Forum des Halles, and the Bourse. **Paul Chemetov.** 1988.

This underworld deserves more than mere casual mention. Officially it is an annex to the commercial center of the Forum, but architecturally it is a world apart. Chemetov, with this elegance of concrete, produces something as wondrous as his own writings about structural/architectural history (see *Architectures à Paris: 1848–1914* by Paul Chemetov and Bernard Marrey, and *Paris-Banlieue 1919–1939* by the same team with Marie-Jeanne Dumont). The gutsy beams, trusses, and columns produce a symphony that the resident commercialism can scarcely suppress. Chemetov's social housing is honorable, his **Ministère des Finances** an austere and somewhat totalitarian monument to the Mitterrand era, but here is an architectural lunch in the belly of Paris. *Formidable.*

★★★**[1/2se-27.] Eglise Saint-Eustache,** 2, rue du Jour, along the Jardins des Halles, rue Rambuteau, rue Montmartre, and rue de Turbigo. Aisle, **Pierre Lemercier.** 1532 and later. Nave, **Charles David** and **François Petit.** 1629–1637. New facade, **Mansart de Jouy.** 1754. **Moreau.** 1778.

Still Gothic in its organization, Saint-Eustache is detailed with Renaissance columns and capitals. It is magnificent and *retardataire*, an architectural historian's wonder, safely straddling 250 years of evolving taste. Nevertheless the Goths win, and the Renaissance supplies only the shoes, belts, ties, and other accessories, while 13th-century structuralism conquers.

Aside from its venerable past, it serves now to remind **Arrètche (Jardin des Halles** opposite) and others that history has retained its mark here from four hundred years before Baltard's **Les Halles.** Saint-Eustache soars within, as many Parisian churches do not, while remaining lofty and cool without.

**[1/2se-28.] Au Pied de Cochon (restaurant),** 6, rue Coquillière, between rue Jean-Jacques-Rousseau and rue du Jour. 1920s.

An Art Nouveau extravaganza within, normal commercial banality without. You can sup on oysters here twenty-four hours a day, twelve months a year! No *R*s in Au Pied de Cochon. Let's hope that they can also produce an occasional pig's foot.

**[1/2se-29.] Robert Vattier (restaurant),** 14, rue Coquillière, between rue Jean-Jacques-Rousseau and rue du Jour.

Shellfish, *choucroute*, et al.

**[1/2se-30.] Distrito (restaurant),** 49, rue Berger, just east of rue du Louvre. 1930s.

The bar and accompanying mosaics recall the vigorous 1930s.

**[1/2se-31.] Fontaine de la Croix-du-Trahoir,** corner rue Saint-Honoré and rue de l'Arbre-Sec. Reconstructed, **Jacques-Germain Soufflot,** architect. **Boizot,** sculptor. 1775.

A dripping, rusticated fountain-building.

**[1/2se-32.] Pharmacie**/originally **Pharmacie du Mont-Blanc,** 115, rue Saint-Honoré, between rue de l'Arbre-Sec and rue du Louvre.

Founded in 1715, it served Marie-Antoinette and her retinue. The venerable facade came later.

★**[1/2se-33.] Hôtel Trudon,** 52, rue de l'Arbre-Sec, opposite rue Bailleul. 1721.

Goats' heads are the console brackets that butt up an elegant balcony of 18th-century ironwork.

★**[1/2se-34.] Immeuble, 16, rue du Louvre,** between rue de Rivoli and rue Saint-Honoré. **Frantz Jourdain.** 1912.

A florid crossblend of the Beaux Arts and early modernism by the architect of the old Samaritaine department store. The latter (1905) was a more radical affair in steel, glass, and tile. Unfortunately, Jourdain became more orthodox as he grew older.

★★**[1/2se-35.] La Samaritaine (grand magasin),** between rue de Rivoli and the Seine, rue de l'Arbre-Sec, rue du pont-Neuf, and rue Boucher. **Frantz Jourdain.** 1906. **Frantz Jourdain and Henri Sauvage.** 1928 and 1930.

La Samaritaine (the good samaritan) was the name of the water-supply pump erected at the pont Neuf in 1605, one of the city's earliest public utilities. Ernest Cognacq borrowed the name in founding his shop at the corner of rue de la Monnaie and rue du Pont-Neuf in 1869.

Cognacq hired Jourdain in 1883, but site assembly and clearance delayed construction of the vastly expanded store across the street (between rue de l'Arbre-Sec and rue de la Monnaie) until 1900, then built only in increments, culminating in 1906. This was a loveliness in steel—hard, crisp, and ornamented with tile—which you still find on the side streets (rue de l'Arbre-Sec, rue Baillet, and rue de la Monnaie). Unfortunately, La Samaritaine was such a resounding success—commerce consummated by and within the architecture of Jourdain—that Cognacq sought bigger and bigger facilities. The result was the demolition and surelevation of the Seine end of Jourdain's greatest work; Henri Sauvage, younger at the time (1928), became his partner. The result is an architectural historian's special example of Art Deco—but a disaster for lovers of early steel and glass.

Elevate to the top floor served, then walk up to the roof terrace-restaurant-café that soars over the attics of Paris. One level yet higher provides free maps in each orientation to decipher the major monuments.

# 4
# SECOND ARRONDISSEMENT
## NORTH

### PORTE SAINT-DENIS TO PLACE DES VICTOIRES

Porte Saint-Denis: **Nicolas-François Blondel;** Eglise
Notre-Dame-de-Bonne-Nouvelle: **Hippolyte Godde;** passage du Caire;
Félix Potin: **Charles Le Maresquier;** 118, rue Réaumur: **Charles J.
Guiral de Montarnal;** 124, rue Réaumur: **Georges Chédanne;**
Théâtre des Variétés; passage des Panoramas; 8-10, rue Saint-Marc:
**Henri Sauvage;** Palais de la Bourse: **Alexandre-Théodore
Brongniart;** Le Vaudeville; rue des Colonnes; Crédit Lyonnais: **André
Narjoux;** Fontaine Gaillon: **Ludovico Visconti;** passage Choiseul

Métro: **Strasbourg Saint-Denis**

**[2n-5.] Passage du Caire.** 1799.

30

★★[2n-1.] **Porte Saint-Denis,** on the Grands Boulevards, the gate between rue Saint-Denis and rue du Faubourg-Saint-Denis. **Nicolas-François Blondel.** 1672. **François Girardon,** sculptor. Restored 1887.

Great ornamented obelisks flank the cheeks of this symbolic *porte* to Paris, a triumphal arch on the old royal way to the royal church of Saint-Denis. It sits just beyond the original *porte* that pierced the wall of Charles V on the site of these *Grands Boulevards.*

[2n-2.] **Prisunic, 15, boulevard Saint-Denis,** between boulevard de Sébastopol and rue Saint-Denis. 1930s.

The vegetative soffits and cubistic capitals make this latecoming Prisunic appear bedecked in attic finery.

[2n-3.] **Immeuble, 5 bis, rue de la Lune,** at boulevard de Bonne-Nouvelle. 1890s.

Bow windows with *grès de Bigot* and a lone maiden: iron and glass oversee the boulevard de Bonne-Nouvelle adjacent.

★[2n-4.] **Eglise Notre-Dame-de-Bonne-Nouvelle,** 25, rue de la Lune, corner rue Notre-Dame-de-Bonne-Nouvelle. **Hippolyte Godde.** 1830.

Tuscan columns before a bold, cool, neo-Classical barrel-vaulted interior. There is a coffered apse and dour, voluminous frescos dominated by more Tuscans, here arcaded.

★★[2n-5.] **Passage du Caire,** 2, place du Caire. Also entries at 16, 34, and 44, rue du Caire, 33, rue d'Alexandrie, and 237, rue Saint-Denis. 1799.

Once a center of printers and lithographers, le Caire is now filled with wholesale ready-to-wear. The facade on the *place* is neo-Egyptian, created during an era of concern with all ancient worlds (the Greek Revival was about to unfold more vividly), but especially with Napoléon's Egyptian campaign. Here the lotus and papyrus leaves ornament column capitals, and sphinx heads glower at those entering.

[2n-6.] **Imprimerie, 6, rue des Forges,** off rue du Caire and rue d'Aboukir. **A. Argouge.** 1929.

A concrete and steel piling of terraces in rampant, ugly, and wonderful technology. This whole area housed the printing industry.

★[2n-7.] **Félix Potin (magasin),** 51, rue Réaumur, corner boulevard Sébastopol. **Charles Le Maresquier.** 1910.

Gorge yourself with this luscious confection: a *poivrière* at the corner capped with a dome and finialed lantern, the place for an extravagant muezzin. The tile is laid in splendid exedra, and swags festoon commercial imperialism.

[2n-8.] **Immeuble, 61–63, rue Réaumur,** between rue Saint-Denis and rue Dussoubs. **G. Singary** and **Pierre Jouannin.** circa 1900.

An eclectic Romanesque-Byzantine-Gothic-Renaissance billboard (it is only two meters thick). Here is a facade that is almost all facade.

★[2n-9.] **Immeuble, 69, rue Réaumur,** between rue Saint-Denis and rue Dussoubs. **Louis-Ernest Pergod.** 1898.

A greenhouse crowns this place for garment fabrication: bright light for sewing, Surmounting ordinary *pierre de taille.* But a couple of cast-iron Corinthian columns give some substance at ground level.

**[2n-10.] Immeuble, 108–110, rue Réaumur,** corner rue des Petits-Carreaux. **Wattier.** 1898.

The stone-and-steel wars of modern architecture's gestation bring glass, elaborate stone ornament, and a *poivrière* to the streetcorner.

★★**[2n-11.] Immeuble, 97, rue Réaumur,** corner rue Cléry. **Philippe Jolivard** and **de Villard.** 1900.

Here is cast iron and glass, with minimal stone, supported by composite capitals of iron that attempt to compete with mineral enrichment. This is parallel to the work of **Ernest Flagg** in America.

★★**[2n-12.] Immeuble, 118, rue Réaumur,** between rue d'Aboukir and rue Cléry. **Charles J. Guiral de Montarnal.** 1900.

A winner in the *concours de façades,* this lush and glassy dowager offers riches at each level as the eye ascends. Metal, glass, and stone here marry happily. The *concours* was established at the time that this part of rue Réaumur was opened in 1895: the winning architects each received a gold medal, the building got one in bronze, and the owner the best prize of all: remission of half his real estate taxes. Money speaks, and some of the best facades in Paris came out of these competitions. Would you have given a prize to **Nos. 116 and 119?** The city did.

★★★**[2n-13.] Immeuble, 124, rue Réaumur,** between rue du Sentier and rue Montmartre. **Georges Chédanne.** 1905.

Mies was only nineteen when this blossomed on the street. No *prix de concours* here for this radical stoneless building, the steel-framed facade putting to shame most steel-structuralist and curtain wall buildings of the 1950s, 1960s, and 1970s everywhere. As to detail, one can even enjoy the rivets. It is a mystery building in the sense that Chédanne's other extant Parisian buildings include such extravagant turn-of-the-century exercises in stone and tile as the original **Galeries Lafayette** and the **Hôtel Mercédès** (off the Etoile), the latter with a touch of the Art Nouveau. The Mercédès was 1903, and No. 124 was begun only a year later. Talented assistant? Bolt of lighting? Tablets from the mountain?

★★**[2n-14.] Immeuble, 95, rue Montmartre,** between rue Lelong and rue Réaumur. **Sylvain Perissé.** 1898.

Superb: bay windows in green, yellow, and cream glazed tile, both radical and lovely. Compare Chédanne's guts at **No. 124** to Perissé's class.

**[2n-15.] Immeuble, 130, rue Réaumur,** corner rue Léon-Cladel. **Charles J. Guiral de Montarnal.** 1898.

With **Nos. 119** and **121** the bellied glass is an elegance elaborating the *Belle Epoque* limestone encrustations. Wonderful. Go in. The stair, elevator, and *entresol* are distinguished.

★**[2n-16.] Immeubles, 119** and **121, rue Réaumur,** corner (and off-corner) rue Notre-Dame-des-Victoires. No. 119, **S. Bousson.** 1903. No. 121, **Charles Ruzé.** 1900.

The corner *poivrière* with its bellied bow windows is *pâtisserie* with technical assistance. Here bow windows are bowed, not bayed.

**[2n-17.] Société Générale, 132–134, rue Réaumur,** corner rue Léon-Cladel and rue Notre-Dame-des-Victoires. **Jacques Hermant.** 1901.

A heavier hand was here than at **Nos. 119** and **121** across the street. But then again, poor thing, it's a bank.

**[2n-18.] La France/Le Soir,** 136, rue Montmartre, between rue du Croissant and rue Saint-Joseph. **Ferdinand Bal.** 1883.

Athletic caryatids support upper Corinthianism: the Beaux Arts before the *concours de façades.*

★**[2n-19.] Immeuble, 167, rue Montmartre,** between rue d'Uzès and boulevard Montmartre. 1890s.

There are bows in those bays: architecture is exploding out of its corset.

**[2n-20.] Immeuble, 13, rue d'Uzès,** between rue Saint-Fiacre and rue Montmartre. **Gustave Raulin.** 1886.

Go in: bold steel and glass over an ornate Beaux Arts atrium.

★**[2n-21.] Théâtre des Variétés,** 7, boulevard Montmartre, between rue Montmartre and passage des Panoramas. **Henri Celerier.** 1807.

Tuscan below, Ionic on top: this arresting neo-Classical facade is a traffic stopper on the boulevard. Its cadaverous porches with deep shadows give it a unique third dimension among flusher facades. Of its opening on June 24, 1807, Nicolas Brazier wrote: "From five o'clock in the evening, Parisians besieged the theater doors . . . they pushed, they crowded, they fought trying to enter; many were called but few were chosen. A charming and comfortable auditorium, a brilliant and select company, a sparkling play, actors drunk with mirth, a colossal success . . . bravos . . . encores, a work played almost twice that evening, such was the opening of this theater, which long enjoyed an unrivaled popularity."

★★**[2n-22.] Passage des Panoramas,** 11, boulevard Montmartre and 10, rue Saint-Marc. **Victor Grissart.** 1800. Modified, 1834.

The panoramas in question were those displayed by **Robert Fulton,** who introduced them to Paris in 1799. The developer of the first commercial American steamboat, Fulton was particularly welcome in the Paris of the Directoire, where American innovation was sought.
Neo-Classical columns and arches are a strong support and frame for luminous light. The stage door of the **Théâtre des Variétés** is on the *passage,* a fact that once called milling crowds to assemble on the evenings of popular performances. At **No. 47** the *graveur* **Stern** has done custom printing since 1840: letterheads, menus, calling cards, ex libris. Stop in. The interior is "late medieval–early Renaissance Revival" in magnificent carved wood (9:30 to 12:30 and 1:30 to 5:30, Monday through Friday). Napoléon III and the Emperor Maximilian of Mexico shopped here.

★**[2n-23.] Immeuble, 8–10, rue Saint-Marc,** between rue Vivienne and rue Montmartre. **Henri Sauvage.** 1929.

This is elder rather than vintage Sauvage, erected seventeen years after 26, rue Vavin **[6s-22.].** After this, nevertheless, he produced the fabulous **Magasins Decré** at Nantes (destroyed during World War II) and the bizarre *immeuble* on the Ile de la Cité at 42, quai des Orfèvres **[Iles-30.].**
The passage des Panoramas erupts into the rue Saint-Marc under this newcomer. Opposite, some concave *pans coupés* give an exedral signal to the presence of the *passage.*

**[2n-24.] Chambre de Commerce**/originally **Chambre des Ventes,** 2, place de la Bourse. **Félix Callet.** 1839. Reconstructed, 1857.

An Italian palazzo with an appropriately rusticated base and pedimented first floor.

**[2n-25.] Conseil des Bourses des Valeurs,** 6, place de la Bourse, between rue Vivienne and rue Notre-Dame-des-Victoires. **Gaston Bernier.** 1930.

A later, sadder, and hollower use of the Classics than at **No. 2** next door.

★**[2n-26.] PTT/La Poste, 8, place de la Bourse,** between rue Vivienne and rue Notre-Dame-des-Victoires. **Jacques Debat-Ponsan** and **Michel Roux-Spitz.** 1939–1950.

A smooth *retardataire* neo-Classicism. Both of these guys should have known better: compare Debat-Ponsan's post office at **La Villette (1931),** avenue Jean-Jaurès, or Roux-Spitz's old **Ford building (1929)** on the boulevard des Italiens. Like the early Dutch modernist **Oud,** they lost their pizzazz in their not-so-old age (Roux-Spitz was fifty-one in 1939). The construction was, of course, interrupted by the war.

★★**[2n-27.] Palais de la Bourse,** 4, place de la Bourse, where rue du 4 Septembre becomes rue Réaumur. **Alexandre-Théodore Brongniart.** 1808–1826. Expanded north and south. **Cavel.** 1903–1906.

Originally a Corinthian-columned neo-Classical Napoleonic temple (cf. **La Madeleine**), La Bourse was later expanded to a cruciform plan. Its center is a great glass-sheltered stock-trading hall.

★**[2n-28.] Le Vaudeville (restaurant),** 29, rue Vivienne, on place de la Bourse. 1920s.

High style still preserved: Art Deco in assorted marbles, mirrors, tubular lamps, and bronze figures.

★★★**[2n-29.] Rue des Colonnes**/originally **passage des Colonnes,** between rue du 4 Septembre and rue Feydeau. **Nicolas-Jacques-Antoine Vestier.** 1791.

Truncated by rue du 4 Septembre and interrupted by rue de la Bourse, this street bears witness to the neo-Classical mania that gripped Europe. Here are Doric columns in richly austere decorated arcades.

★**[2n-30.] Immeuble, 24, rue Feydeau,** between rue des Colonnes and rue Vivienne. **Fernand Colin.** 1929.

*Immeuble en accordéon* (a serrated facade) from the same year as **Jean Desbouis' Normandie Theatre [8w-36.].** *L'Architecture d'aujourd'hui* (December 1932) explained that the windows *en chevron* were intended "to obtain, in a street eight meters wide, bordered by seven-story buildings, natural light of the very highest order. . . . [The apartments and offices] take their light from the length of the street and enjoy a view of the sky provided by the nearby place de la Bourse." Perhaps Colin also just liked syncopated facades.

**[2n-31.] Immeuble, 18, rue Saint-Marc,** between rue Vivienne and rue de Richelieu. 1734.

An elegant entrance portal.

**★[2n-32.] Immeuble, 24, rue Saint-Marc,** between rue Vivienne and rue de Richelieu. **Louis Thalheimer.** 1894.

Iron and stone compete for honors in the Labroustian combination of taut technology and *pompier* stone. The central ironwork is gorgeous.

**[2n-33.] AGF/Assurances Générales de France,** 87, rue de Richelieu, between rue Saint-Marc and rue du 4 Septembre. **Joseph Belmont** and **Pierre-Paul Heckly.** 1979.

The architects invoke "the spirit of Haussmann," but that is a glib pretext for these banal modern buildings. One cannot excuse mediocrity by naming gods.
*Assurance* guarantees that something comfortable—nothing radical—will prevail.

**★[2n-34.] Crédit Lyonnais, 6, rue Ménars,** between rue de Richelieu and rue du 4 Septembre. **André Narjoux.**

Iron strappery, from which lovely console brackets are wrought. The balance of the body is a conservative shell. Narjoux completed the 4 Septembre end of the main offices of Crédit Lyonnais down the street, together with **Victor Laloux.**

**★[2n-35.] Immeuble, 8, rue de Port-Mahon,** between rue du 4 Septembre and rue Saint-Augustin. **L. Morel** and **Louis Filliol.** 1936.

"Propriété de la Société civile immobilière 'l'Avenir du Prolétariat!'" Some stacked "soldier" brick in a stylish bow-windowed, horizontally banded *immeuble* to ensure the future of the proletariat. Would that all workers could be so well housed.

**[2n-36.] Fontaine Gaillon,** place Gaillon, junction of rues de Port-Mahon, Saint-Augustin, de la Michodière, and Gaillon. **Ludovico Visconti.** 1828.

When fountains almost become buildings, here screening the restaurant Pierre à la Fontaine.

**[2n-37.] Restaurant Drouant,** 18, rue Gaillon, at place Gaillon. Staircase, **Jacques-Emile Ruhlmann.** 1926.

A stunning Art Deco setting, enhanced by Ruhlmann's stair (★★) and the **Cocteau** ceiling in the barroom (★ the original café). Expensive.

**★[2n-38.] Immeuble, 12, rue Gaillon,** between place Gaillon and avenue de l'Opéra. **Jacques Hermant.** 1913.

Layered metal and glass in a somber but striking British green. Reminiscent to Americans of the work of **Ernest Flagg.**

**★[2n-39.] Hôtels particuliers, 4–10, rue des Moulins,** between rue des Petits-Champs and rue Thérèse. 17th and 18th centuries.

A mostly 18th-century quartet, handsomely maintained No. 10 is 17th century.

**[2n-40.] Théâtre des Bouffes-Parisiens,** 4, rue Monsigny, between place du Marché-Saint-Honoré and rue Saint-Augustin. **Théodore Charpentier.** 1863. Bay window. **Auguste Bluysen.** 1913.

The theater was inaugurated by **Jacques Offenbach** and **Ludovic Halévy** in 1855, and then expanded in 1863, with interiors, it is said, by **Théodore Ballu.**

**[2n-41.] La Clé du Périgord (restaurant),** 38, rue des Petits-Champs, between rue Monsigny and rue Sainte-Anne.

Ceiling and furnishings of distinction.

★★**[2n-42.] Passage Choiseul,** 40, rue des Petits-Champs and 23, rue Saint-Augustin. Passage, **François Mazois** and **Antoine Tavernier.** 1825–1827. Hôtel/entry building rue Saint-Augustin, **Antoine Lepautre.** 1655.

Within there is architecture under the simple glass parasol: an Ionic-columned tribune. Here columns and arches discipline the shopfronts to a degree. The venerable Saint-Augustin entrance gives the stroller a sequence of "Back to the Future": from the present, through the 17th century, into a skylit 19th.

# 5
# THIRD ARRONDISSEMENT
## NORTH
### SAINT-DENIS-DU-SACREMENT
### TO SAINTE-ELISABETH

Eglise Saint-Denis-du-Sacrement: **Hippolyte Godde;** rue Vieille-du-Temple; rue de Saintonge; Hôtel de Tallard: **Pierre Bullet;** rue Charlot; 10, rue de Bretagne: **Hector Guimard;** rue des Filles-du-Calvaire; Fontaine Boucherat: **Jean Beausire;** Mairie; Marché du Carreau du Temple: **Jules de Mérindol;** Lycée Turgot; Eglise Sainte-Elisabeth

Métro: **Saint-Sébastien Froissart**

[3n-14.] Immeuble de bureaux, 14, rue de Bretagne. A. Sélonier and **Henri Dupussé.** 1926.

★★[3n-1.] **Eglise Saint-Denis-du-Sacrement,** 68 bis, rue de Turenne, corner rue Saint-Claude. **Hippolyte Godde.** 1826–1835.

A neo-Classical "temple" in concert with Godde's **Notre-Dame-de-Bonne-Nouvelle,** five years earlier. The crisp Classical colonnades within are parallel with similar English Regency efforts.

[3n-2.] **Immeuble, 13, rue de Thorigny,** opposite rue du Roi-Doré. **Jacques Vitry, Dominique Hertenberger, and Jacques Ivorra.** 1973.

Brick and concrete combine in Anglo-Saxon restraint. Underdone, like most of its 17th-century neighbors, it is bare and minor-scaled. Enter the court: a pleasantly modest building.

[3n-3.] **Hôtel de Cagliostro,** 1, rue Saint-Claude, corner boulevard Beaumarchais. 1719.

A secret garden.

[3n-4.] **Immeuble, 113, boulevard Beaumarchais,** corner rue du Pont-aux-Choux. 18th century.

An elegant serpentine Louis XVI facade corners the intersection.

★[3n-5.] **Ateliers, 23, rue du Pont-aux-Choux,** between boulevard Beaumarchais and rue de Turenne. 1888.

A bit of iron and glass interrupts an otherwise Beaux Arts essay. The colonnettes at the second floor and the eight-point starred stained-glass rondelles should be noted.

[3n-6.] **Immeuble, 82, rue de Turenne,** between rue du Pont-aux-Choux and rue Saint-Claude. circa 1705. Remodeled, 19th century.

A typical urban streetmaker of its time, long before Haussmann turned up.

★[3n-7.] **Hôtel d'Hozier,** 110, rue Vieille-du-Temple, between rue des Coutures-Saint-Gervais and rue Debelleyme. **Jean Thiriot.** 1623.

Newly cleansed, the rusticated window quoins and voussoirs sparkle, as do the light ironwork and an entrance portal with consoles of a delicate floral and vegetative elegance.

[3n-8.] **Hôtel Megret de Sérilly,** 106, rue Vieille-du-Temple, between rue des Coutures-Saint-Gervais and rue Debelleyme. Early 17th century.

Those deflecting entrance bollards are at the design apogee of street furniture.

[3n-9.] **Hôtel de Ferrary**/annex of **Lycée Victor-Hugo,** 102–104, rue Vieille-du-Temple, between rue des Coutures-Saint-Gervais and rue Debelleyme. Early 17th century.

[3n-10.] **Immeuble, 8, rue de Saintonge,** between rue de Poitou and rue du Perche. circa 1630.

There is a picturesque courtyard and a stair with a graceful railing.

★[3n-11.] **Boulangerie, 15, rue de Saintonge,** corner rue de Poitou. circa 1900.

Naïve paintings and good lettering make this shop *classé.*

★★[3n-12.] **Hôtel de Tallard**/also known as **Hôtel Amelot de Chaillou,** 78, rue des Archives, corner rue Pastourelle. **Pierre Bullet.** 1690.

A smoothly restored *hôtel.* Buzz in to the Belgian block—paved courtyard, with surprising trees. The carved wood tympanum at the street is naïve but lushly lovely. The stair within, by **Pierre Le Muet,** is now protected by the electronics of the restored tenants.

★[3n-13.] **Hôtel de Bérancourt,** 28, rue Charlot, between rue de Poitou and rue de Bretagne. 1680.

Within the courtyard is an exedral *hôtel* with a charming stair and railing.

★[3n-14.] **Immeuble de bureaux, 14, rue de Bretagne,** corner rue Charlot. 1920s. **A. Sélonier** and **Henri Depussé.** 1926.

Cubist caryatids greet the patrons of this glassy block of offices. This is halfhearted Sélonier; the modern open bays are there—but so are mansard roofs and caryatids.

★[3n-15.] **Hôtel de Chamillart,** 58, rue Charlot, opposite rue du Forez. 17th century.

A stripped and light-industrialized *hôtel,* but the portal still retains the mark of impoverished nobility. **No. 57,** opposite, has been slicked up for some yuppies **(Hôtel du Marquis de Boulainvilliers),** but counts not against Chamillart.

★[3n-16.] **Immeuble de bureaux, 10, rue de Bretagne,** corner rue de Saintonge. **Hector Guimard.** 1919.

Steel lintels and mullions, and some neo-Gothic buttresses, with assorted bay windows.

[3n-17.] **Immeuble, 137, rue Vieille-du-Temple,** corner rue de Bretagne.

A pre-Haussmannian survivor, with grand arches inside its buzz-in court.

★[3n-18.] **Immeubles, 4** and **6, rue des Filles-du-Calvaire,** between rue de Bretagne and boulevard des Filles-du-Calvaire. circa 1835.

Tuscan columns at No. 6 provide a taut architectural statement. At No. 4 there are Ionics at the first floor, with two columns and two pilasters.

[3n-19.] **Immeuble, 116, rue de Turenne,** between rue des Filles-du-Calvaire and rue de Saintonge. circa 1835.

Some non—load-bearing caryatids give life to this pre-Haussmannian place.

★[3n-20.] **PTT, 64, rue de Saintonge,** between rue de Turenne and boulevard du Temple. 1930s.

Stylish *moderne grillage* below, sawteeth on top—a statement that intercepts the old city and makes the latter more valid.

★[3n-21.] **Fontaine Boucherat,** corner rue de Turenne and rue Charlot. **Jean Beausire.** 1699.

A *pan coupé* corner fountain, rusticated and pedimented, that anchors this intersection.

★[3n-22.] **Mairie,** square du Temple, rue des Archives. circa 1870.

The stairwell within provides wonderful pomp, although it is not *pompier.* Outdoors the square is its best friend: here is a pseudo-château and its garden.

★★[3n-23.] **Marché du Carreau du Temple,** between rue Eugène-Spuller, rue Dupetit-Thouars, rue Perrée, and rue de Picardie. **Jules de Mérindol.** 1865.

Though this is only one-third of the original iron-and-glass market that extended three blocks to rue du Temple between rue Dupetit-Thouars and rue Perrée, it is nevertheless a happy remnant. Part of it is a discount clothing market, and part is a gymnasium. Mérindol was also responsible for the still extant **Grande Halle** at **La Villette [19v-9.]**

★[3n-24.] **Hôtel Bergeret de Frouville** (No. 3)/ and **Hôtel de la Haye** (No. 5 bis)/now **Collège Jean-Pierre-de-Béranger,** rue Béranger, corner rue de Franche-Comté. circa 1720.

Pierre Jean de Béranger (1780–1857) was a poet and polemicist who said that "tyranny could never settle in a country where one sings." His *chansons* were as popular as his politics.

[3n-25.] **Immeuble, 11, rue Béranger,** between rue de Dupuis and rue du Temple. 1980s.

What a dreadful thing to do to a street: *mural* turpitude. The setback balconies above are civilized; the glass-and-metal curtain-wall is not.

[3n-26.] **Lycée Turgot,** facade on rue du Vertbois, between rue de Turbigo and rue Volta. 1830s.

A side courtyard to this great *lycée* bears a marvelous Tuscan-columned atrium.

★★[3n-27.] **Eglise Sainte-Elisabeth,** 195, rue du Temple, with passage Sainte-Elisabeth passing through to rue de Turbigo. 1628–1646. Alterations, **Hippolyte Godde.** circa 1860s.

Godde made modifications on the behind necessitated by the piercing of the rue de Turbigo under Haussmann. The facade is *Jésuitique,* a bit stiff and pallid, with stones that were created either by a great mathematician or a machine. (Can something from the past look prefabricated? Or did man, early on, beat and better the machine, in the manner of an early Bauhaus?)
Within, it is neo-Classical (perhaps late remnants of Godde). His domical apse, with four Tuscan columns, presents a somber and lifeless mosaic.

# 6

# THIRD ARRONDISSEMENT

## WEST

### SAINT-MARTIN-DES-CHAMPS TO SAINT-MERRI

### VIA BEAUBOURG

Eglise Saint-Martin-des-Champs; Conservatoire Nationale des Arts et Métiers: **Léon Vaudoyer;** Réfectoire Saint-Martin-des-Champs: **Pierre de Montreuil;** Eglise Saint-Nicolas-des-Champs; rue Chapon; rue Michel-le-Comte; Hôtel d'Hallwyll: **Claude-Nicolas Ledoux;** quartier de l'Horloge; centre Georges-Pompidou: **Renzo Piano** and **Richard Rogers;** Café Beaubourg: **Christian de Portzamparc;** fontaine, place Igor Stravinsky: **Nikki de Saint-Phalle** and **Jean Tinguely;** IRCAM/Annexe: **Renzo Piano;** Eglise Saint-Merri

Métro: **Arts et Metiers**

[3w-6.] **Eglise Saint-Nicolas-des-Champs.** 12th–17th centuries. Columns made classical, 1745.

**★★[3w-1.] Eglise Saint-Martin-des-Champs,** within Conservatoire National des Arts et Métiers, corner rue Réaumur and rue Saint-Martin. Choir, 1140. Nave, circa 1290. Alterations into museum, 1798 and later.

There are bits and pieces of the Romanesque outside and a 19th-century entrance portal on the court. This distinguished abbey was coopted by the Revolution and was never returned to the faith. Its conversion in the 1790s to the Conservatoire National des Arts and Métiers was later supplemented by its extension and remodeling as the **Musée des Techniques** by **Léon Vaudoyer.** Most startling are the church contents: airplanes, steam engines and automobiles—technology within medievalism.

**★[3w-2.] Conservatoire Nationale des Arts et Métiers,** 292, rue Saint-Martin, bounded by rue du Vertbois, rue Vaucanson, and rue Réaumur. **Léon Vaudoyer.** 1845–1897.

Clocks, ships, industrial devices. Here is a museum of the history of the Industrial Revolution. Contents (★★★★).

**★★[3w-3.] Refectoire Saint-Martin-des-Champs,** across the courtyard from the church. **Pierre de Montreuil.** circa 1248 and later.

Now the library: a spectacular vaulted space.

**[3w-4.] La Planète Magique**/originally **Théâtre de la Gaité-Lyrique,** 3–5, rue Papin, on square Emile-Chautemps, opposite the Conservatoire. **Pierre-Alexis Kobakhozé.** 1990.

Unfortunately, a vertical Disneyland stands within this gutted 1862 landmark, the outside of which is *classé* and restored.

**★[3w-5.] Immeuble, 39, rue Réaumur,** between rue Saint-Martin and rue Vaucanson. **Germain Salard.** 1900.

A super *pompier* confection overlooking Eglise Saint-Martin-des-Champs across rue Réaumur. The Revolution secularized that abbey, but later lusties can savor its still vigorous remnants.

**★★★[3w-6.] Eglise Saint-Nicolas-des-Champs,** 254, rue Saint-Martin, between rue Réaumur and rue de Turbigo. 12th–17th centuries. Major expansions, circa 1615. Remodeling, circa 1745.

Mixed signals are received from sturdy "Gothic" ribbed vaults, becoming more and more supported by Classicism as you reach the altar: a march from Gothic piers to oval fluted Tuscan columns. These latter were the 18th century's architectural put-down of the Gothic. What were originally plain piers were channeled into quasi-Doric columns, and coiffed with some Ionic capitals.
The whole space is bathed with the clear light of reason as exemplified by Jean-Jacques Rousseau: a carapace of medievalism decorated and transformed by an architectural counterrevolution.

**[3w-6a.] Immeuble, 57, rue de Turbigo,** near rue Borda.

Here an *ange caryatide* bears witness to the proliferation of lady-bearers in 1860s Paris.

**[3w-7.] Immeuble, 7, rue Bailly,** between rue de Turbigo, rue Réaumur, and rue Beaubourg.

The smashing circular-spiral stair (★★) within is inscribed in the rosters of the *monuments historiques.*

**[3w-8.] Northwest corner, rue Volta and rue Réaumur.**

A cut-angle forms what was once the rue du Marché Saint-Martin (now rue Réaumur) and rue Frépillon (now rue Volta). The incised corner is elegant.

**[3w-9.] Immeuble, 3, rue Volta,** between rue au Maire and rue Réaumur. 17th century.

Once considered the oldest house in Paris, this handsome place is merely more mature than most. The *colombage* is picturesque and appropriately sagging.

**[3w-10.] Maison, 44, rue des Gravilliers,** between rue Beaubourg and rue du Temple. 17th century.

An elegant stair, behind glass.

**[3w-11.] Maison, 29, rue des Gravilliers,** between rue Beaubourg and rue du Temple. circa 1630.

A real innerworld of Louis XIII ironwork. Walk up to relish it.

**[3w-12.] Hôtel Jean-Bart,** 4, rue Chapon, between rue du Temple and rue Beaubourg. 17th century, with later modifications.

Here is a *fronton* Louis XVI.

★**[3w-13.] Immeuble, 13, rue Chapon,** between rue du Temple and rue Beaubourg. 18th century.

An elegant portal leads to a gracious courtyard and to the Galerie Philippe-Casini.

★**[3w-14.] Hôtel de Séré,** 22, rue Chapon, between rue du Temple and rue Beaubourg. 17th century.

Delicate sphinxes and an articulated and rusticated portal lead to a modest courtyard.

★**[3w-15.]** Originally **Dortoir Félix-Potin,** 71, rue Beaubourg, between rue Chapon and rue de Montmorency. **Paul Auscher.** 1910

The traditions of the *grands magasins* included housing their employees, originally in the stores themselves but here in a nearby annex. An austere bit of minor modern, it is more a historical artifact than a visual delight.

★**[3w-16.] Maison du Grand Pignon,** 51, rue de Montmorency, between rue Beaubourg and rue Saint-Martin. Possibly 1407. Restored, circa 1900.

Described as the house of **Nicolas Flamel,** this *might* be the oldest house in Paris.

★★★**[3w-17.] Hôtel d'Hallwyll,** 28, rue Michel-le-Comte, between rue Beaubourg and rue du Temple. Remodeled and expanded, **Claude-Nicolas Ledoux.** 1766. Restored, **Bernard Fonquernie.** 1989.

The portal is lusty, with fluted columns and a tympanum bearing winged ladies. Within the courtyard is a somber elegance, much "restored." There is little of Ledoux left in Paris, mostly in the *barrières* and *pavillons* of the wall of the Fermiers Généraux: at the Parc Monceau, place Denfert-Rochereau, place Stalingrad, and place de la Nation. All of them are more vigorous than Hallwyll, but they were done twenty years later.

**[3w-18.]** Once **Auberge de l'Ours et du Lion,** 16, rue Michel-le-Comte, between rue Beaubourg and rue du Temple. 15th–17th centuries.

Neutral on the street, with a charming cobbled courtyard that awaits within.

**[3w-19.] Logements, gymnase, archives, and parking, 2–14, rue Michel-le-Comte** and **89–99, rue du Temple. Agence d'architecture Ghiuliani.** 1989.

Some sophomoric histrionics in these understated streets. Tricky cantilevered concrete beams straddle an unnecessarily curved facade. Many contemporary architects seem to believe a curve is an ultimate solution.

**[3w-20.] Immeuble, 37, rue Beaubourg,** between rue du Grenier-Saint-Lazare and rue Rambuteau. **Charles Goujon.** 1903.

An island of sanity preserved in the *îlot* of the **quartier de l'Horloge.** Extravagant in the *pompier* style of the time. Its neighbors are described below.

**[3w-21.] Quartier de l'Horloge,** bounded by rue Beaubourg, rue Rambuteau, rue Saint-Martin, and rue du Grenier-Saint-Lazare. early 1980s.

A pretentious effort at contextualism. Smooth quasi-Haussmannian blocks are massaged with internal pedestrianways that give a maximum to commerce; the shopfront and the franc are in charge. The detailing is gross. To confront the experiment of Beaubourg with this banality is in bad taste, even though the latter, experimental and vigorous, may have its faults. Here is opportunism, rather than character.

**[3w-22.] Passage Molière,** between 159, rue Saint-Martin and 82, rue Quincampoix. 1791.

A *real* slice of Paris—in contrast to the quartier de l'Horloge across the street.

★ interior **[3w-23.] Immeuble, 147, rue Saint-Martin,** between rue aux Ours and rue Rambuteau. 17th century.

An elegant stair—buzz your way in.

★ interior **[3w-24.] Immeuble, 58, rue Quincampoix,** between rue Rambuteau and rue de Venise. circa 1630.

Louis XIII within, with a carved walnut stair that must lead to heaven.

★★★**[3w-25.] Centre Georges-Pompidou,** between rue Beaubourg, rue Rambuteau, rue Saint-Martin, and place Stravinsky. **Renzo Piano** and **Richard Rogers,** architects. **Gianfranco Franchini** and **John Young,** associates. **Ove Arup and partners,** engineers. 1977.

This extraordinary building was a result of President Pompidou's vision for Paris, which sought to blend modern technology, in the name of commerce and culture, into the fabric of the city. Other less happy results (of his) were the **Tour Montparnasse,** a solo skyscraper in that historic artists' enclave, and **La Défense,** the mini-Dallas just beyond the west edge of Paris proper (although a bit has been redeemed by Spreckelsen's **Grande Arche**). A competition awarded the Beaubourg commission to Piano and Rogers, a then young English-Italian partnership, at the nexus of the 1st, 3rd, and 4th arrondissements, halfway between the Louvre and place des Vosges.

The brash columns, trusses, and other braced steel form a fantastic filigree through which (on the rue Beaubourg side) is laced lusty tubular ductwork for air movement, inhaling and exhaling, conditioning the galleries and libraries—all in bright blue with red elevators and their balancing weights rising and falling in counterpoint. On the place Beaubourg facade the filigree harbors the long stepped escalators where people rise to the center's facilities but, more often, just rise to a point of view and survey the scene of Paris.

In fact, this vast structure, its bones exposed, its arteries resplendent, envelops a more traditional and serene world in the **Musée National d'Art Moderne** (remodeled in 1985, **Gae Aulenti**). The National Museum houses collections of the most significant modern French painters, the most important of whom include **Picasso, Matisse, Delaunay, Dufy, Lipchitz,** and the like.

The third floor houses a library of art, and the second the administrative offices of the Centre.

The *rez-de-chaussée* galleries present current works of contemporary artists but, more impressively, a sunken space for special shows of art and architecture.

Outside, on the plateau Beaubourg, street actors, acrobats, and con artists mingle in a kind of pseudo-neo-medieval gypsy world in a modern setting. The tourist crowds are thick; the action sometimes amusing, sometimes banal, and mostly not artful; and the threat of pickpockets is everywhere.

Beaubourg suffers from its own success. Visitors come in numbers vaster than any optimistic projections, and the building's high-tech tubes, struts, and sheet metal have acquired the kind of deterioration more familiar in a 1977 Ford than in a 1977 Pompidou.

★★**[3w-26.] Café Beaubourg,** 43, rue Saint-Merri, opposite Centre Georges-Pompidou. **Christian de Portzamparc.** 1980s.

A grand understated two-story space that brings a serene Portzamparc to Beaubourg. For distinguished Portzamparc housing, see **[13se-10.];** for flamboyant Portzamparc, see **[19v-17.].**

★★**[3w-27.] Fontaine, place Igor Stravinsky,** south of the Centre Beaubourg. **Nikki de Saint-Phalle** and **Jean Tinguely.** 1977.

Fun and games surmounting the underground world of IRCAM (Institut pour la Recherche et la Coordination Acoustique de la Musique). Tinguely's mechanical animations are supplemented by Saint-Phalle's ludicrous and colorful fantasies.

★**[3w-28.] IRCAM/Annexe,** south edge of plateau Beaubourg, corner of place Igor-Stravinsky. **Renzo Piano.** 1989.

The conning tower of Pierre Boulez's underground complex devoted to research into contemporary, electronically supported music. The submarine came along with Beaubourg; the conning tower is new and fits in admirably in scale and materials with the contiguous buildings: brick, in an articulated frame.

**[3w-29.] Immeuble, 13, rue Quincampoix,** between rue des Lombards and rue de La Reynie. circa 1598.

A wonderful courtyard; *entrez.*

★★**[3w-30.] Eglise Saint-Merri,** 78, rue Saint-Martin, at rue des Lombards. Nave, 1520. Choir, 1552. Tower, 1612. Assorted 18th- and 19th-century modifications.

Stylistically, the nave holds on to the Gothic, the choir to the 18th century. Here as usual, mixed centuries participate in the present-day reality. And with architects such as **Baltard** and **Viollet-le-Duc** around, nothing was safe from remodeling.

# 7
# THIRD AND FOURTH ARRONDISSEMENTS
## THE MARAIS
### A TRUE MEANDER FROM PLACE DE LA BASTILLE
### TO MUSEE CARNAVALET

Boulevard Beaumarchais; Hôtel Mansart de Sagonne: **Jules Hardouin-Mansart;** place des Vosges: **Louis Métezeau** and **Jacques II Androuet du Cerceau;** Hôtel de Sully: **Jean I Androuet du Cerceau;** Musée Picasso/Hôtel Salé: **Jean de Bourges;** Hôtel de Bruant: **Libéral Bruant;** Hôtel de Guénégaud: **François Mansart;** Hôtel de Soubise: **Pierre-Alexis Delamair;** Hôtel d'Albret: **François Mansart;** Hôtel des Juifs; Synagogue Pavée: **Hector Guimard;** Hôtel de Lamoignon: **Jean-Baptiste Androuet du Cerceau;** Musée Carnavalet: **Pierre Lescot** and **François Mansart;** Hôtel Le Pelletier de Saint-Fargeau: **Pierre Bullet**

Métro: **Bastille**

**[3/4m-48.] Tourelle, Hôtel de Lamoignon/now Bibliothèque Historique de la Ville de Paris (BHVP). Jean-Baptiste Androuet du Cerceau. 1584.**

Among the books and maps that explore the Marais in considerable detail are Pierre Kjellberg's *Le nouveau guide du Marais* and ARTGA's map, sold everywhere. Both offer detailed street-by-street histories and records that can supply the serious student with more information than provided here. Also a trip to the **Association pour la Sauvegarde et la Mise en Valeur du Paris Historique** would be in order. It's at 44, rue François-Miron, in the 4th arrondissement.

★**[3/4m-1.] Hôtel particulier, 13, boulevard Beaumarchais,** between place de la Bastille and rue du Pas-de-la-Mule. 17th century. Altered.

The building of the *Grands Boulevards,* beginning in 1680 on the emplacement of the old fortifications of Charles V, frayed the edges of the Marais. This complex reinforced the new edge.

**[3/4m-2.] Logements, 1, rue du Pas-de-la-Mule,** corner boulevard Beaumarchais. 1930s.

A brick-and-concrete block. But that perforated veil at the seventh-floor balcony, and the serrated teeth, are stylish.

★**[3/4m-3.] Logements, 6-8, rue du Pas-de-la-Mule,** between boulevard Beaumarchais and place des Vosges. 1930s.

This had a hard act to follow. Adjacent to the **place des Vosges** and a long block from the **Bastille,** here is 1930s modern fitting in with grace.

★★**[3/4m-4.] Hôtel Mansart de Sagonne,** 28, rue des Tournelles, between rue Saint-Antoine and rue du Pas-de-la-Mule. **Jules Hardouin-Mansart.** 1674–1685.

Hardouin-Mansart's own *hôtel particulier* that stretches through the block to boulevard Beaumarchais. The boulevard facade **(23, boulevard Beaumarchais)** through the entrance *grille* is elegant.

★**[3/4m-5.] Synagogue, 21 bis, rue des Tournelles,** between rue Saint-Antoine and rue du Pas-de-la-Mule. **Marcellin Varcollier.** 1861–1863. Burned, 1871. Metal frame, **entreprise Eiffel.** 1875

A dour and bland facade opens to neo-Romanesque space.

★★★★**[3/4m-6.] Place des Vosges** and **square Louis XIII**/originally **place Royale,** embraced by rue des Francs-Bourgeois, rue de Turenne, rue des Tournelles, and rue Saint-Antoine. **Louis Métezeau** and **Jacques II Androuet du Cerceau.** 1605–1612.

Here, the English, and **Inigo Jones**, in particular, found the prototype for Covent Garden, and the whole plethora of London (Bloomsbury) squares.
A great space, 140 meters (460 feet) square, is contained by thirty-six pavilions, separate segments of what was in effect a spectacular and wondrous real estate speculation. The brick facades, many of which were stucco painted to simulate brick and jointly crested with articulated high-pitched slate roofs, create an architectural ensemble rarely equaled in the western world, where the whole is far greater than the sum of the parts.

★★**[3/4m-7.] Musée Victor Hugo**/former **Hôtel de Rohan-Guéménée,** 6, place des Vosges.

Hugo lived here from 1832 to 1848 and is remembered here. Most unusual are his nonverbal remembrances: sketches of his 19th-century world, and the remarkable exotic oriental interiors that he designed. From his "Chinese" living room, you'll have a wonderful perspective of the place des Vosges. Can you feel the quality of life of an upper bourgeois of 17th-century Paris? The view is mostly the same. Only the people have changed.

★★[3/4m-8.] Originally **Hôtel de Chaulnes,** 9, place des Vosges, southwest corner.

The gallery of **Nikki Marquart** is housed behind all this grandeur in an industrial remnant of the pregentrified Marais. The great gallery space, reached through the frontal courtyard, is a special example of how Paris works. What seems to be the building is sometimes merely the portal to interior urbanism with another—older or newer—world of activity beyond.

★★★[3/4m-9.] **Hôtel de Sully**/now **Caisse Nationale des Monuments Historiques et des Sites,** 7, place des Vosges and 62, rue Saint-Antoine. **Jean I Androuet du Cerceau.** 1624. Restored, **Robert Vassas.** 1980.

Maximilien de Béthune, duc de Sully, gave his name to this wondrous *hôtel,* providing us with an extraordinary symbiosis and understanding of the relationship of the place des Vosges and the older city. Here Androuet du Cerceau tied the major artery of rue Saint-Antoine to the new urbanistic core of the **place Royale.** All around are similar but lesser enterprises. The urbane facade, with elegant gardens, officially confronts rue Saint-Antoine, but the innards of court-garden-viaduct to the place des Vosges are an urban designer's delight.

Behind, the *orangerie,* dubbed the **Petit Hôtel de Sully,** houses occasional exhibits and is a great foil and cooperating building for Androuet du Cerceau's.

[3/4m-10.] Originally **Hôtel Colbert de Villacerf,** 23, rue de Turenne, between rue Saint-Antoine and rue des Francs-Bourgeois. 1660. Drastically altered, 1931.

It is hard to separate the original body from surelevations and drastic defacements.

★[3/4m-11.] Immeuble, 20-22, rue de Turenne, corner rue des Francs-Bourgeois. **Joachim Richard** and **J. Roehrich.** 1929.

Ateliers on the first three levels, apartments above, from a time when the feverish Marais was laced with sweatshops. Here, however, a noble contract arose.

[3/4m-12.] **Immeuble, 20, rue Saint-Gilles,** between rue de Turenne and rue Villehardouin. 1980s.

The architecture is banal, but the garden court is worth savoring. Available to the eye, these private, midblock oases are hard to reach—visually or in person.

★[3/4m-13.] **Hôtel d'Equevilly**/known as **Hôtel du Grand Veneur,** 60, rue de Turenne, between rue Saint-Gilles and rue Saint-Claude. 1686. Remodeled, 1741.

A gracious court, screened by an entry wall, now regentrified.

[3/4m-14.] **Magasin, 67, rue de Turenne,** between rue du Parc-Royal and rue Sainte-Anastase. circa 1860.

Twin Doric columns support a simple mass above. To one side bulls act as modillions to support the hovering balcony.

**[3/4m-15.]** Société Saint-Raphaël/originally **Hôtel Duret-de-Chevry,** 8, rue du Parc-Royal, between rue de Sévigné and rue Payenne. 1620s. Converted to offices, 19th century.

A not so grand brick-and-limestone remnant serves as headquarters of this apéritif manufacturer. *A votre santé.*

★**[3/4m-16.]** Hôtel de Croisille/now **Bibliothèque du Service des Monuments Historiques,** 12, rue du Parc-Royal, opposite rue Payenne. 1619.

Over 98,000 photographs and 65,000 plans and documents are assembled here for archaeologists, architects, and historians. The **Hôtel de Vigny,** next door at **No. 10** (1628), houses the catalog of these and other inventories of France's historic monuments.

★★★**[3/4m-17.]** Hôtel Salé/now **Musée Picasso**/originally **Hôtel Aubert de Fontenay,** 5, rue de Thorigny, between rue de la Perle and rue des Coutures-Saint-Gervais. **Jean Bouillier,** known as **Jean de Bourges.** 1656. Conversion, **Roland Simounet.** 1985.

Picasso would have loved this environment of history in which his radical painting and sculpture are housed. It is perfectly consonant with his own personal and traditional environments, where he painted in places of 17th- and 19th-century architecture and furnishings.

The *hôtel* is magnificent. Savor particularly its entrance courtyard, the splendid entrance stair, and the elegant garden behind. Here is a prototypical 17th-century Parisian *hôtel particulier:* court, house, and garden. Simounet's detailing within presents a few cubistic tricks—niches, slots, and so forth—but, in general, is understated, happily.

★★**[3/4m-18.]** Hôtel de Bruant/now **Musée de la Serrurerie,** 1, rue de la Perle, corner rue Elzévir. **Libéral Bruant.** 1685.

This is the town house that Bruant, architect of the **Invalides** and the **Hôpital Salpêtrière,** built for himself—a perfect example, well restored, of the 17th century.

**[3/4m-19.]** Pavillon, **11, rue de la Perle,** between rue Vieille-du-Temple and rue Elzévir. 1683.

Those giant *clefs* (functioning as console brackets) are major strokes on the street.

★**[3/4m-20.]** Centre d'Accueil des Archives Nationales, 9, rue des Quatre-Fils, between rue des Archives and rue Vieille-du-Temple. **Stanislas Fiszer.** 1988.

This sleek and streamlined intrusion into the 17th century performs a noble function rather boringly. Perhaps that's appropriate for one that snuggles behind the **Hôtel de Soubise.**

★★★**[3/4m-21.]** Hôtel de Guénégaud/now **Musée de la Chasse et de la Nature,** 60, rue des Archives, corner rue des Quatre-Fils. Attributed to **François Mansart.** 1648–1651. Renovations, **André Sallez.** 1966.

Like many *hôtels particuliers* in the Marais, this was a near-ruin until it was bought by the City of Paris and renovated as the Hunting Museum by philanthropists M. et Mme. Sommer in 1966. The high floors and steep roof are typical of François Mansart, whose eponymous roofs crown houses in Great Britain and America.

★[3/4m-22.] **Fontaine des Haudriettes,** 53, rue des Archives, corner rue des Haudriettes. 1705. Remodeled, **Pierre-Philippe Mignot.** 1765.

A sensuous naiad is symbolic of this elegant watering place.

★[3/4m-23.] **Portail/Hôtel de Clisson,** 58, rue des Archives, between rue des Quatre-Fils and rue des Francs-Bourgeois. 1380.

A savored remnant attached to the Hôtel de Soubise. This is more venerable than the **Hôtel de Sens [4s-22.]** or the **Hôtel de Cluny [5n-26.]** which are *retardataire* Gothic of the late 15th century.

★[3/4m-24.] **Hôtel Lelièvre de la Grange,** 4-6, rue de Braque, between rue des Archives and rue du Temple. 1673.

Alive and not overrestored like most of its neighbors, Lelièvre presents within No. 4 a magnificent stair. Buzz in at No. 6.

★[3/4m-25.] **Hôtel de Montmor,** 79, rue du Temple, between rue de Braque and rue Michel-le-Comte. 1623. Remodeled, circa 1750.

An extravagant Baroque portal opens to a grand courtyard, another acquisition of the City of Paris.

★★[3/4m-26.] **Hôtel d'Avaux**/later **Hôtel de Saint-Aignan**/now **Archives de la Ville de Paris,** 71-75, rue du Temple, between rue Rambuteau and rue Michel-le-Comte. **Pierre Le Muet.** 1640s.

On the street, seemingly savage faces guard the sculpted entrance portals. The writer Piganiol de la Force called this "a great and magnificent house; the four facades of the building are decorated with great pilasters that rise from the ground floor to the roof." It is proposed that this become the **Musée d'Art Juif.**

[3/4m-27.] **Immeuble, 2-4, rue Rambuteau,** corner rue des Archives.

A late ornamentation of the rue Rambuteau, across from the Hôtel de Soubise. All those sculptured faces overlook the surrounding sea of tourism.

★★★[3/4m-28.] **Hôtel de Soubise**/now **Musée de l'Histoire de France,** part of the **Archives Nationales,** 60, rue des Francs-Bourgeois, corner rue des Archives. **Pierre-Alexis Delamair.** 1709. Interiors, **Germain Boffrand.** circa 1730. Alterations and additions, 19th century.

Here is grandeur for the present public, the great court embraced by a luscious Corinthian colonnade, and with a monumental entrance portal. The interiors are outrageously elaborate (we recommend the Salon de la Princesse de Soubise). Boffrand enlisted **Boucher, Vanloo,** and the **brothers Adam** in this venture. The *hôtel* is part of a vast complex that includes the **Hôtels de Fontenay, de Breteuil, d'Assy, de Jacourt,** and **de Rohan-Strasbourg.** This last (1718) is also by Delamair. The whole ensemble is the Archives Nationales, now entered from the **Centre d'Accueil** at 9, rue des Quatre-Fils.

★[3/4m-29.] **Tour/mur de Philippe-Auguste,** 57, rue des Francs-Bourgeois, opposite Hôtel de Soubise. circa 1190.

For those seeking a venerable remnant, there is this much restored annex of the modern **Crédit Municipal.** The stone foundations are the only original remnants.

★[3/4m-30.] **Eglise Notre-Dame-des-Blancs-Manteaux,** 12, rue des Blancs-Manteaux, between rue des Archives and rue Vieille-du-Temple.

**Dom Antoine de Machy.** 1685. Facade, 1701, moved 1863 by **Victor Baltard** from the Ile de la Cité (Eglise des Bernabites).

Baltard was almost equal to Viollet-le-Duc in "improving" historic archictecture, here by a masque of its time, relocated.

**[3/4m-31.] Le Domarais (restaurant),** 53 bis, rue des Francs-Bourgeois, between rue des Archives and rue Vieille-du-Temple.

Nouvelle cuisine in a converted 17th-century chapel.

★★**[3/4m-32.] Hôtel Amelot de Bisseuil**/commonly called **Hôtel des Ambassadeurs de Hollande**/now **Fondation Paul-Louis Weiler,** 47, rue Vieille-du-Temple, near rue des Rosiers. **Pierre Cottard and Jean-Baptiste Amelot de Bisseuil.** 1660.

A Baroque portal, enriched with cherub-caryatids but of the Italian putti order, leads to a grand but somewhat grimy courtyard beyond. Within are extant 17th-century rooms, such as the Galerie de Psyché and the *chambre à l'italienne.*

**[3/4m-33.] Mariage Frères (salon de thé),** 30-32, rue du Bourg-Tibourg, between rue du Roi-de-Sicilie and rue Sainte-Croix-de-la-Bretonnerie.

Under a great skylight are tastes from a menu of hundreds of teas. Supplement it all with pastries.

**[3/4m-34.] Boulangerie/Pâtisserie, 32, rue Vieille-du-Temple,** opposite rue Sainte-Croix-de-la-Bretonnerie.

A class act to enrich the streetscape. These small textural moments make the city whole.

★**[3/4m-35.] Hôtel de Vibraye,** 15, rue Vieille-du-Temple, corner rue du Roi-de-Sicile. 1650.

Buzz in to an elegant courtyard.

**[3/4m-36.] Laboratoire d'Hygiène de la Ville de Paris,** 1 bis, rue des Hospitalières-Saint-Gervais, between rue du Marché-des-Blancs-Manteaux and rue Vieille-du-Temple.

Polychromatic formalism, the side elevations worthy of **Viollet-le-Duc.**

**[3/4m-37.] Pharmacie Peladan,** 36, rue des Francs-Bourgeois, opposite rue des Hospitalières-Saint-Gervais.

A Classical storefront.

★★**[3/4m-38.] Hôtel de Fourcy**/also called **Hôtel d'Alméras,** 30, rue des Francs-Bourgeois, between rue Vieille-du-Temple and rue Elzévir. 1598.

Some Henri IV brick and limestone, an ornate baroque portal with pedimented gymnastics. Two dour goats guard it all.

★**[3/4m-39.] Hôtel de Sandreville,** 26, rue des Francs-Bourgeois, and 3, rue Barbette, between rue Elzévir and rue Payenne. Street facade, 18th century. Courtyard, 1630.

The courtyard is magnificent—if you can get in from either the Francs-Bourgeois or Barbette end.

★★[3/4m-40.] Hôtel de Guillaume Barbes/now **Maison de l'Europe,** 35, rue des Francs-Bourgeois, opposite rue Elzévir. 1634.

The Mairie de Paris, Direction des Affaires Culturelles, preserves another wondrous *hôtel particulier.*

★[3/4m-41.] Hôtel de Donon/now **Musée Cognacq-Jay,** 8, rue Elzévir, between rue des Francs-Bourgeois and rue du Parc-Royal. Perhaps **Philibert Delorme.** 1575.

**Fragonard, Boucher,** and **Chardin,** collected by the founder of the **Samaritaine [1/2se-35.],** have found a new home here to replace their lost building on boulevard des Capucines.

★★[3/4m-42.] Hôtel d'Albret/now **Bureau de la Direction des Affaires Culturelles de la Ville de Paris,** 31, rue des Francs-Bourgeois, opposite rue Elzévir. Court facades, **François Mansart.** 1640. Street facade, **Vautrain.** 1744. Exterior refurbishing, **Bernard Fonquernie.** Interior reconstruction, **Christian Germanaz.** 1989.

An 18th-century facade here is a match with London's then-contemporary Georgian. Within are some modern histrionics: a vast, curved, sleek, blue wall that would make Mansart shudder. A sad bit of stylish ego.

[3/4m-43.] Hôtel, 20, rue des Francs-Bourgeois, between rue Elzévir and rue Payenne.

Buzz yourself in to a lovely gardened inner world.

★[3/4m-43a.] Hôtel de Marle/also known as **Hôtel de Polastron-Polignac**/now **Centre Culturel Suédois,** 11, rue Payenne, between rue des Francs-Bourgeois and rue du Parc-Royal. circa 1600; 17th- and 18th-century alterations.

Behind a simple rusticated portal is the happily inevitable front courtyard.

★[3/4m-44.] Hôtel de Châtillon/also known as **Hôtel de Lude,** 13, rue Payenne, between rue des Francs-Bourgeois and rue du Parc-Royal. circa 1620.

A soul mate to **No. 11** next door.

[3/4m-45.] Hôtel des Juifs, 20, rue Ferdinand-Duval, between rue des Rosiers and rue du Roi-de-Sicile. circa 1600.

Buzz in to a pretty courtyard, with Corinthian pilasters and handsome dormers.

[3/4m-46.] Formerly **Boulangerie, corner rue des Rosiers and rue Malher.** circa 1900.

A dress shop occupies this lovely turn-of-the-century remnant. The painted graphics are distinguished.

★[3/4m-47.] Synagogue, 10, rue Pavée, between rue du Roi-de-Sicile and rue des Rosiers. **Hector Guimard.** 1913.

Not one of Guimard's star works, this was a transitional event between his early Art Nouveau wonders (**Castel Béranger** and the **Métro entries**) and the new modern style that ended with the 1920s Art Deco. Unfortunately it is set back, offering what he thought was a civilized gesture to a narrow street. But the result is broken urbanism.

**★★[3/4m-48.] Hôtel de Lamoignon**/once **Hôtel d'Angoulême**/now **Bibliothèque Historique de la Ville de Paris (BHVP)**, 24, rue Pavée, corner rue des Francs-Bourgeois. **Jean-Baptiste Androuet du Cerceau.** 1584. Expanded, 17th century. Portal, 1718. New building, 1966.

The giant Corinthian pilasters (to the left as you enter) are the grandest example of this 16th-century Italianate vocabulary in Paris. To the right is a modern insertion for efficient library purposes. And at the corner of rue des Francs-Bourgeois, a corbeled tower projects a powerful anchor to the intersecting streets.

**★★★[3/4m-49.] Musée Carnavalet**/originally **Hôtel Carnavalet**, 23, rue de Sévigné, corner rue des Francs-Bourgeois. **Pierre Lescot.** circa 1550. Remodeled, **François Mansart.** 1655–1661.

This grand ensemble presents a courtyard to both rue des Francs-Bourgeois and rue de Sévigné, centered with **Antoine Coysevox**'s statue of Louis XIV. Within there is a vast and rich collection of the history of Paris, but the facades without (and the courtyards within) are party to an architectural extravaganza.

"Un bel air, une belle cour, un beau jardin, un beau quartier," said the marquise de Sévigné, who once owned it.

**[3/4m-50.] Lycée Victor-Hugo,** 27, rue de Sévigné, between rue des Francs-Bourgeois and rue du Parc-Royal. **Anatole de Baudot.** 1896.

The first reinforced-concrete school in Paris. Nothing much to look at, but its guts were radical for its time.

**[3/4m-51.] Hôtel Le Pelletier de Saint-Fargeau**/now **annex to the Musée Carnavalet,** 29, rue de Sévigné, between rue des Francs-Bourgeois and rue du Parc-Royal. **Pierre Bullet.** 1686. Alterations, **Jean-Michel Wilmotte.** 1989.

This former home of the BHVP supplements the body of Carnavalet to make it the world's grandest museum of municipal history. In between, the **Lycée Victor-Hugo** interrupts the traffic, necessitating a connecting corridor built across its roof: an umbilical pedestrianway.

Here the grand staircase (★★) and its *rampe*, and a small *cabinet*, remain from Bullet. Transported from assorted Parisian buildings are a number of period rooms and shopfronts. Prominent among them are:

**★★★1. Boutique, bijoutier Fouquet. Mucha.** 1900.
A superb ensemble of Art Nouveau bronze, tilework, and stained glass—a bit like being in the entrails of a Jules Verne submarine.
**★2. Salon de bal de l'Hôtel de Wendel. José Maria Sert.** 1923.
A kitsch dreamworld, where in "muted dancing light, one would seem floating in space, detached from the orthogony of built reality that supports the dream."
**★3. Salon, Café de Paris. Henri Sauvage.** 1899.
Languid curves.

# 8
# FOURTH ARRONDISSEMENT
## SOUTH

### PLACE DU CHATELET TO PLACE DE LA BASTILLE

Théâtre Musical de Paris; Théâtre de la Ville de Paris: **Gabriel Davioud;** Tour Saint-Jacques; Hôtel de Ville: **Théodore Ballu;** Cloître des Billettes; Eglise Saint-Gervais-Saint-Protais: **Clément II Métezeau;** pont Louis-Philippe; Hôtel de Beauvais: **Antoine Lepautre;** Hôtel d'Aumont: **Louis Le Vau** and **François Mansart;** Hôtel de Sens; Eglise Saint-Paul-Saint-Louis: **Martellange** and **Père Durand;** Village Saint-Paul; Hôtel de Mayenne: **Jean II Androuet du Cerceau;** Chapelle de la Visitation-Sainte-Marie: **François Mansart;** Pavillon de l'Arsenal; Restaurant Bofinger

Métro: **Châtelet**

**[4s-36.] Pavillon de l'Arsenal. A. Clément.** 1879. Alterations, **Bernard Reichen** and **Philippe Robert.** 1988.

55

Along the Seine between the Châtelet and the Bastille is an island of rich architecture cut off by the rues de Rivoli and Saint-Antoine to the north, and by the river to the south.

★[4s-1.] Théâtre Musical de Paris, place du Châtelet, between the Seine and avenue Victoria. **Gabriel Davioud.** 1862. Alterations, **Claude Cuvelier** and **Jean-Louis Marin**/known as **Cabinet Synergos.** 1989.

A dour pavilion embracing the *place* with its opposite twin. Harder surfaces and added detail will hopefully improve the acoustics. Wall painting by **Adami.**

★[4s-2.] Théâtre de la Ville de Paris/once Théâtre Sarah-Bernhardt, place du Châtelet, between the Seine and avenue Victoria. **Gabriel Davioud.** 1862. Rear addition, rue Adolphe-Adam. circa 1898. Interior remodeled. 1968.

The bustle on this block is more fascinating than the building proper. On rue Adolphe-Adam iron and brick conjoin to make a special architectural gesture.

★★[4s-3.] Tour Saint-Jacques, centered in the square de la Tour-Saint-Jacques, between boulevard de Sébastopol, rue Saint-Martin, rue de Rivoli, and avenue Victoria. **Jean** and **Didier de Felin.** 1523.

The remnant tower of the **Eglise Saint-Jacques-la-Boucherie,** demolished in 1797 in the continuing fever of revolutionary anticlericalism. Now a meteorological station surmounts it all. This is late, or *retardataire*, Gothic, from a time when Michelangelo was drifting into mannerism in Italy.

★★[4s-4.] Hôtel de Ville, place de l'Hôtel-de-Ville, originally place de Grève. **Théodore Ballu** and **Edouard Deperthes.** 1882.

This careful reproduction replaces the original, burned by the Communards in May 1871, perhaps overelaborating the original architecture of the 16th-century Italian **Domenico da Cortona** (called **le Boccador**). This is neo-Renaissance at the moment that the Ecole des Beaux-Arts was at its peak power. The endless sculpture, and the supporting cast of Corinthian columns, Composite pilasters, roofs, chimneys, and *lucarnes*, creates a festival.
The revived plaza is bare of seats, a place for rallying rather than leisure. Its harsh fountains (**F. X. Lalanne.** 1980s.) seem to be more concerned with rigid aquatic engineering than joy.

★[4s-5.] Bazar de l'Hôtel-de-Ville: BHV, 60, rue de Rivoli, corner rue du Temple. **Auguste Roy.** 1913.

A second-echelon *grand magasin* that loads its power mostly at the corner cheeking the Hôtel de Ville. Sharp steel glazing, a half dozen sculpted putti, and a dome with oculi, and then oculi once more. In the basement is a vast do-it-yourself center of hardware and whatever.

[4s-6.] Immeuble, 66, rue de la Verrerie, between rue du Renard and rue du Temple.

Buzz in to an old Paris street, with a Louis XIII archway.

★[4s-7.] Syndicat de l'Epicerie Française, 12, rue du Renard, between rue de Rivoli and the Centre Beaubourg. **George-Raymond Barbaud** and **Edouard Bauhain.** 1901.

Spicy architecture.

★★★[4s-8.] Cloître des Billettes/now **Eglise Evangélique Lu-thérienne**/originally **Cloître de l'Ancien Couvent des Frères Hospitaliers de la Charité Notre-Dame,** 22, rue des Archives, between rue de la Verrerie and rue Sainte-Croix. Cloister, 1427. Church, **Frère Claude.** 1756.

This small and wonderful cloister sometimes houses visiting exhibitions under a vigorous ribbed-Gothic series of vaults.

★★[4s-9.] **Eglise Saint-Gervais-Saint-Protais,** place Saint-Gervais at rue François-Miron. Choir and transepts, 16th century. Nave, 1600–1620. Facade, **Clément II Métezeau.** 1621.

Doric, Ionic, and Corinthian stacked in a potent display of clustered columns. A Jesuit-Baroque facade, it screens late Gothicism within.

★[4s-10.] **Maisons de l'Orme**/sometime **Maisons du Pourtour Saint-Gervais,** 2-12, rue François-Miron, between place Saint-Gervais and rue des Barres. **Legrand.** 1732. Restored, **Albert Laprade.** 1957.

A lusty 18th-century block that is the architectural backup to Saint-Gervais-Saint-Protais. **No. 14,** adjacent, is by **Jacques-Ange Gabriel.** 1737.

[4s-11.] **Mairie,** place Baudoyer, between rue François-Miron and rue de Rivoli.

A bland entry in the 1860s Mairie sweepstakes, when those of the 10th to 20th arrondissements were almost simultaneously created. Check the 10th and 18th for winners.

★[4s-12.] **Immeubles, 11** and **13, rue François-Miron,** between rue du Pont-Louis-Philippe and rue Cloche-Perce. 15th century.

Here *colombage* supports and clads what may be the second-oldest buildings in Paris. **Le Grand Pignon [3w-16.]** may be the oldest.

★[4s-13.] **Hôtel Touchet,** behind 22 bis, rue du Pont-Louis-Philippe, between rue de l'Hôtel-de-Ville and rue François-Miron. 16th century.

If you brave the tempered-glass doors on the street, within is a lovely brick Renaissance facade that housed Marie Touchet, mistress of **Charles IX** in the 1560s.

[4s-14.] **Chez Julien (restaurant),** 62, rue de l'Hôtel-de-Ville, corner rue du Pont-Louis-Philippe. circa 1900.

A retired bakery, with its bucolic painted scenes both within and without. A venerable commercial relic.

★[4s-15.] **Pont Louis-Philippe,** between rue du Pont-Louis-Philippe and Ile Saint-Louis. 1862.

Three arches of 19th-century stonework trip across the Seine from the Ile to the Right Bank. Sober and more simplistic than the Pont Neuf, and three centuries later.

[4s-16.] **Cité Internationale des Arts,** rue de l'Hôtel-de-Ville, northeast corner rue Geoffroy-l'Asnier. **Paul Tournon** and **Olivier-Clément Cacoub.** 1965.

Barren modernism, with a disdain for Paris and for its site prominently edging the Seine. Tear it down.

**★★[4s-17.] Hôtel de Châlons-Luxembourg,** 26, rue Geoffroy-l'Asnier, between rue de l'Hôtel-de-Ville and rue François-Miron. circa 1608.

A monumental tympanum presents a lion, the cartouche supported by twin Ionic pilasters. Below are rare Henri IV carved wood entrance doors.

**★[4s-18.] Immeuble, 44-46, rue François-Miron/Association pour la Sauvegarde et la Mise en Valeur du Paris Historique,** corner rue Geoffroy-l'Asnier. circa 1550. Restored, 1990.

The window jambs are elegant, the *lucarnes* imposing. Underneath it all are grand late-Gothic (Abbaye d'Ourscamp) cellars. Ask to see them (★★★).

**★★★[4s-19.] Hôtel de Beauvais/now Association pour la Sauvegarde et la Mise en Valeur du Paris Historique,** 68, rue François-Miron, between rue de Jouy and rue de Fourcy. **Antoine Lepautre.** 1655.

The courtyard is dynamic, and the great stair a major Corinthian-columned architectural spectacle. It was from the balcony that the queen mother, Anne of Austria, together with Cardinal Mazarin, viewed the triumphant entry of Louis XIV into Paris in 1660 with his bride, Marie-Thérèse. Mozart played here, stopping for some time as a guest in 1763. Built on the site of a medieval abbey, the cellar comprises the original Gothic vaults of the latter.

**★★[4s-20.] Hôtel d'Aumont/now Tribunal Administratif,** 7, rue de Jouy, between rue des Nonnains-d'Hyères and rue François-Miron. Design of streetfront, **Louis Le Vau.** 1649. Execution, **Michel Villedo.** Garden facade, **François Mansart.** 1656. Remodelings, **Michel Roux-Spitz** and **Paul Tournon.** 1947.

For a good view of Mansart, walk up rue des Nonnains-d'Hyères and look back. Inside, the tribunal enjoys a *grand salon* painted by **Charles Le Brun.**
This was one of the most dilapidated *hôtels particuliers* of the Marais, "let go" by its owners in the mid-18th century. It subsequently served as *mairie* of the old 9th arrondissement and, later, as the **Pharmacie Centrale de France.** It is perhaps such marginal custody that has preserved what's left, avoiding the harsh and sometimes gut-and-rebuild gentrification of so many historic buildings.

**★★[4s-21.] Pont Marie,** from rue des Nonnains-d'Hyères to the Ile Saint-Louis. **Christophe Marie.** 1630. Partially reconstructed after collapse of two arches, 1658. Remaining buildings removed, 1758.

Marie, the speculator who developed the Ile Saint-Louis, largely in concert with architect **Louis Le Vau,** built this early bridge at his own expense. It is the umbilical cord connecting it to the fashionable Marais.

**★★★[4s-22.] Hôtel de Sens/now Bibliothèque d'Art et d'Industrie Forney,** 1, rue du Figuier, at rue de l'Hôtel-de-Ville and rue du Fauconnier. 1475–1519. Fanciful restoration, 20th century.

A late-Gothic town house for the bishop of Sens, under whose aegis the bishop of Paris was a mere suffragan, or assistant, bishop. It ranks with the **Hôtel de Cluny** on the Left Bank, and the house of **Jacques Coeur** in Bourges, as one of the three greatest laic medieval buildings remaining to France. The Gothic is embellished with some early Renaissance detail in the Flemish manner.

**[4s-23.] Hôtel de Vivre,** 111, rue Saint-Antoine, opposite rue Malher.

Within the courtyard are some lusty Ionics flanking the stair entrance.

**[4s-23a.] Lycée Charlemagne**/originally **Maison-mère de la Compagnie de Jésus,** 101, rue Saint-Antoine, opposite rue de Sévigné. **Père Turmel,** 1640+. Converted to school, 1795–1804.

Here was the Jesuitical home for pères Durand and Turmel.

★★★**[4s-24.] Eglise Saint-Paul-Saint-Louis,** 99, rue Saint-Antoine, opposite rue de Sévigné. **Ange Martel,** called **Martellange.** 1629. Facade and upper works, **Père Durand.** 1641. Interiors, **Père Turmel.** 1647.

Commonly called *Jésuitique* in French texts, this is full-blown Baroque, a term French historians have avoided in describing this and similar richnesses in Paris: **Sainte-Marie de la Visitation** and **Val de Grâce** included.
    The facade, as frequently perceived in Jesuit places, is a "false front" (compare the Church of the Gesù in Rome) but gutsy. Within, the decor is cool, perhaps cold, though those pendant lights are a dramatic scale-shifter, as at **Hagia Sophia** in Istanbul.
    In all, it is the grand patron of the whole Marais district, hovering over its wonderful *hôtels.*

★**[4s-25.] Village Saint-Paul,** between rue des Jardins-Saint-Paul, rue de l'Ave-Maria, rue Saint-Paul, and rue Charlemagne. Renovations, **Félix Gatier.** 1979.

A pleasant labyrinth of inner-block life, juxtaposing buildings of the 17th and 18th centuries with pleasant courtyards chockablock with stores of antiques and knickknacks. Behind, on rue des Jardins-Saint-Paul, to the west, are remnants of the 12th-century wall of Philippe-Auguste.

**[4s-26.] Immeuble, 7, rue Neuve-Saint-Pierre,** between rue de l'Hôtel-Saint-Paul and rue de Beautreillis. 1980s.

A Post Modern tour de force: grotesque sculptured hands play with the space of the street.

**[4s-27.] Hôtel d'Amelot,** 12, rue des Lions-Saint-Paul, between rue Saint-Paul and rue de Beautreillis. 1630s.

An eclectic (later modifications) neo-Classical remnant.

★**[4s-28.] Hôtel Fieubet,** in the court behind 10, rue des Lions-Saint-Paul, between rue Saint-Paul and rue de Beautreillis. **Pierre Le Muet.** 1647.

The stair and stairhall of the inner *corps de logis* share a magnificent massive oak balustrade and an Ionic-capped pier.

★★**[4s-29.] Hôtel de Mayenne**/now **Ecole des Francs-Bourgeois,** 21, rue Saint-Antoine, corner rue du Petit-Musc. **Jean II Androuet du Cerceau.** 1613–1617. Interior remodelings, **Germain Boffrand.** 1709. Restoration, **Bernard Fonquernie.** 1991.

The 1870s infill spliced the left and right wings together, a real estate speculator's wisdom that sullied the basic 17th-century form. Across the street at the **Hôtel de Sully,** one can see the restored airspace that Mayenne will also shortly reclaim.

Chimneys, *lucarnes,* and high-pitched slate roofs all serve the elegant 17th-century vocabulary.

★★★[4s-30.] **Chapelle de la Visitation-Sainte-Marie,** 17, rue Saint-Antoine, corner rue Castex. **François Mansart.** 1634.

Some Mansart Baroque, his first significant work, dedicated since 1802 to Protestants! Open only on Sundays (or weddings and funerals), its dynamic dome is surrounded by great pilasters, a miniature volume with a powerful scale. Nicolas Fouquet, Louis XIV's notorious finance minister (he built **Vaux-le-Vicomte),** is buried here, as is the marquise de Sévigné, sometime owner of the **Hôtel Carnavalet.**

[4s-31.] **PTT, 12, rue Castex,** between rue Saint-Antoine and boulevard Henri IV.

An exercise in 1930s grillework, tile, and raked brick. But craftsmen were still here.

★[4s-32.] **Hôtel Fieubet**/now **Ecole Masillon,** 2 bis, quai des Celestins, corner rue du Petit-Musc. **Jules Hardouin-Mansart.** 1671–1681. Vastly altered, 1858–1877.

Bare-breasted sphinxes guard the portal in a precocious preview of the neo-Classical use of such ancient symbols. The 19th century deflowered much detail and added an efflorescence of sculpture, presenting this contemporary wedding cake. Hardouin-Mansart's work is visible only on the rear facade.

[4s-33.] **Immeuble, 2, rue Agrippa-d'Aubigné,** corner quai Henri IV. circa 1900.

A lush apartment house at the edge of the Seine, just upstream from the Ile Saint-Louis. Haussmannian-*tardif.*

★[4s-34.] **Caserne de la Garde Républicaine,** 4, rue de Schomberg, corner boulevard Morland. **Joseph-Antoine Bouvard.** 1883.

Cast iron supports polychrome brick for the guardians. The column capitals and iron rivetwork are rich.

★★[4s-35.] **Ensemble de Bureaux et de Logements de la Caserne Schomberg,** quai Henri IV, between boulevard Morland and rue de Schomberg. **Yves Lion.** 1992.

Only the cast-iron polychromy of **Bouvard** will be preserved; the rest is gung-ho Lion.

★★[4s-36.] **Pavillon de l'Arsenal**/originally **Musée Populaire de Laurent-Louis Borniche,** 21, boulevard Morland, between boulevard Henri IV and rue Agrippe-d'Aubigné. **A. Clément.** 1879. Alterations for pavilion, **Bernard Reichen** and **Philippe Robert.** 1988.

A merchant of wood, Borniche here displayed his private collection of two thousand canvases, his popular (and populist) counterpoint to the official expositions. The Ville de Paris has restored this gracious cast- and wrought-iron building, which now displays a permanent collection of its good architectural works and frequently fascinating temporary expositions.

[4s-37.] **Bibliothèque de l'Arsenal,** 1, rue de Sully, off boulevard Henri IV. **Philibert Delorme.** circa 1563. Enlarged and remodeled, **Marceau Jacquet.** 1602. Again, 1637. Again, **Germain Boffrand.** 1715–1736.

Again, **Dauphin.** 1745. Most recently, **Théodore Labrouste.** 1856–1876.

Once a cannon-powder factory, it became a library at the beginning of the 19th century. Some rooms are still in their pristine state; the exterior is innocuous.

**[4s-38.] Direction de la Jeunesse et des Sports/Mairie de Paris,** 25, boulevard Bourdon, corner rue Bassompierre. 1989.

A stiff and heavy-handed hulk that is pretentious rather than civilized.

**[4s-39.] EDF/Station, 33, boulevard Bourdon,** corner rue de la Cerisaie.

Brick, glass, and steel conjoin in this neo-Romanesque electric utility.

★**[4s-40.] Hôtel particulier, 15, rue de la Cerisaie,** off boulevard Henri IV. 18th century.

A handsome remnant among 19th-century neighbors; buzz in and check the wrought-iron stair railings.

**[4s-41.] Bofinger (restaurant),** 3, rue de la Bastille, between rue des Tournelles and place de la Bastille. *Grande verrière,* **Neret et Royer.** 1900. Restaurant enlarged and redecorated, **Letay** and **Mitgen.** 1919. Remodeling of main salle, **Hansi.** 1930.

The oldest *brasserie* in Paris, this architectural and culinary symbiosis is rich with stained glass and tile detail. The women's room on the *rez-de-chausée* allegedly bears some of the richest tilework in France (the men's rooms aren't bad either).

# 9
# FIFTH ARRONDISSEMENT
## EAST

### PLACE VALHUBERT/GARE D'AUSTERLITZ

### TO ARENES DE LUTECE

Gare d'Austerlitz: **Louis Renaud;** Hôpital Salpêtrière-Pitié: **Libéral Bruant;** Hôtel Scipion-Sardini; Eglise Saint-Médard; rue Mouffetard; Jardin des Plantes; Galerie de Zoologie: **Jules André;** Les Serres Coloniales: **Charles Rohault de Fleury;** Les Serres Tropicales; Kiosque du Labyrinthe: **Edmé Verniquet;** Mosquée de Paris; Hôtel Le Brun: **Germain Boffrand;** Universités de Paris VII et VI; place Jussieu; Arènes de Lutèce
(The Gare and the Hôpital Salpêtrière-Pitié are in the 13th arrondissement)

Métro: **Gare d'Austerlitz**

**[5e-24.]** Les Serres Tropicales/Jardin des Plantes. René Berger.
1937.

**[5e-1.] Gare d'Austerlitz**/originally **Gare d'Orléans,** place Valhubert, between boulevard de l'Hôpital and quai d'Austerlitz. First station, **Félix Callet.** 1840–1862. Expanded, **Louis Renaud.** 1862–1870.

The Compagnie des Chemins de Fer d'Orléans later extended its service to the center of Paris, via a mostly underground route along the Left Bank of the Seine to the **Gare** (now **Musée**) **d'Orsay.** The Gare d'Austerlitz would make a major impact in a minor city other than Paris, where, in contrast to the gares du Nord, de l'Est, de Lyon, and Saint-Lazare, it is the *soeur mal-aimée.* Its facade is noted more for the academic sculpture by **Elias Robert** than for its architecture. To be substantially remodeled on the arrival of the new **pont Charles de Gaulle** that bisects its present body.

★**[5e-2.] Pont Charles de Gaulle,** on the alignment of rue Van-Gogh (12th arrondissement) and boulevard Saint-Marcel (13th arrondissement). **Louis Arrètche, Karasinki Bet: PX Consultants.** Engineer, **Beaulieu.** 1993.

Arrètche won the competition against Norman Foster, Jean Nourel, and others, who mostly offered a complex superstructure. Arrètche's low profile maintains views up and down the Seine.

★**[5e-3.] Hôpital Salpêtrière-Pitié,** 47, boulevard de l'Hôpital, between Gare d'Austerlitz and its access ways, rue Jenner and boulevard Vincent-Auriol. **Louis Le Vau, Pierre Le Muet,** and especially **Libéral Bruant.**

★★★**Chapelle Saint Louis-de-la-Salpêtrière,** on axis of the entrance. **Libéral Bruant.** 1657–1677.

On this site Louis XIII kept his grand arsenal for storing gunpowder, whence the name Salpêtrière, from saltpeter, a principal ingredient. In 1656, Louis XIV (then aged eighteen—do we hear his mother, Anne of Austria, talking?) decreed that it should become the municipal poorhouse and, in 1684, a pavilion for the compulsory detainment of women, including not only "bad girls" but also unwanted wives and daughters. After 1796 it became a mental asylum where many experiments in treating the insane with electricity were performed.
   The central chapel is at the scale of a grand cathedral, but with eight naves (in fact a Greek cross with four chapels between the arms). With the altar at the center, one could attend to eight unique congregations, the ensemble totaling four thousand souls.
   Walk through the interstitial gardens to enjoy a variety of green spaces and contrasting architecture.

★**[5e-4.] Logements, 1 bis, rue Nicolas Houël,** corner boulevard de l'Hôpital. Probably **Albert Chastignol.** circa 1931.

The bay windows of this limestone monolith are bracketed with spheres and ribbed in a neo-Classical manner, as if they were the flutings of engaged Greek columns.

**[5e-5.] Logements, 10, rue Poliveau,** between boulevard de l'Hôpital and rue Geoffroy-Saint-Hillaire. 1970s.

Modern but low-rise, with simple balcony railings—no smoked glass here, thank God! A street participant, it is a good citizen of its time.

★**[5e-6.] Logements sociaux, 20, rue Geoffroy-Saint-Hilaire,** between rue Poliveau and rue Buffon. **Jérome Delaage** and **Fernand Tsaropoulos.** 1981.

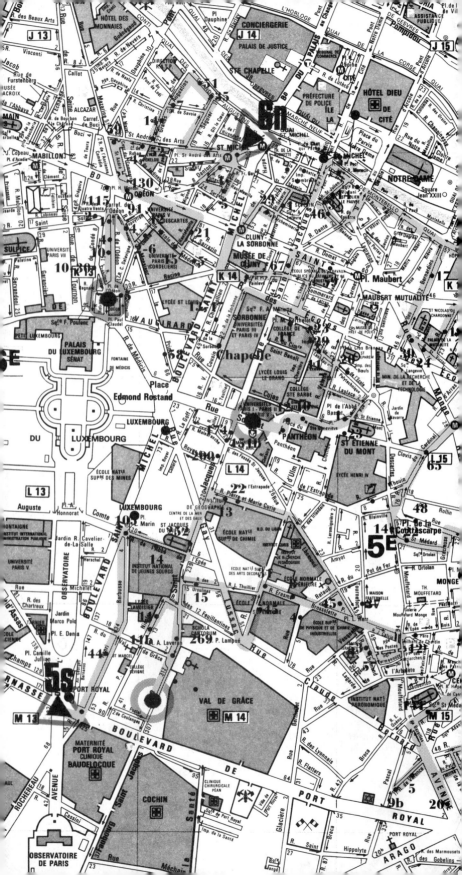

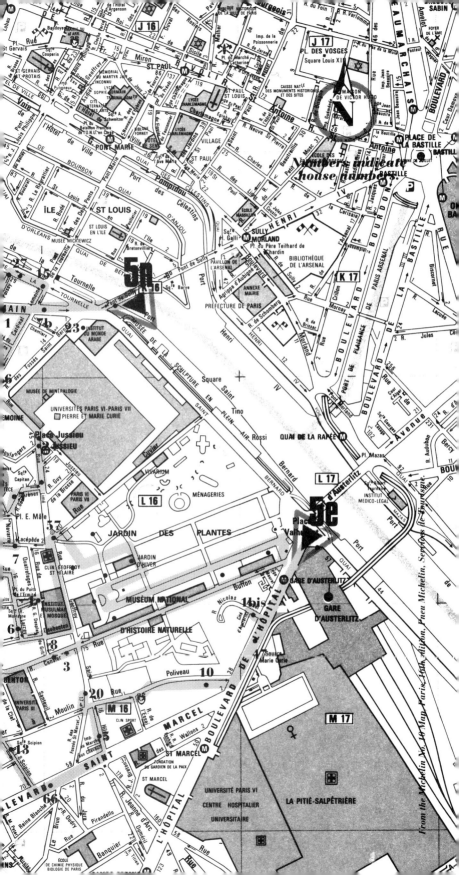

Numbers indicate house numbers.

Delaage intended to "preserve the structure of an old quarter and its dominant element, a small very Parisian square situated in front of the building."

Pretentious boxed pseudo-bay windows join a mirror-glass curtain wall behind. The streetfront scale is appropriate, but the costume flagrant.

★[5e-7.] Originally **Pavillon de Police du Marché aux Chevaux,** 5, rue Geoffroy-Saint-Hilaire, between boulevard Saint-Marcel and rue Poliveau. 1760s.

A stork and a rooster ornament this elegant "pavilion of surveillance" for inspectors at the outdoor horse market across boulevard Saint-Marcel. Dogs and pigs were allegedly sold there as well.

★★[5e-8.] **Collège d'Enseignement Technique,** 66, boulevard Saint-Michel, between rue des Fossés-Saint-Marcel and rue Scipion. **Michel Cuminal** and **Roger Lardat.** circa 1938.

Another study red brick facade of the prolific social architecture of the 1930s. The banded windows, like picture frames, join the *oeils-de-boeuf* as stylish statements of those times.

★★[5e-9.] **Hôtel Scipion-Sardini**/onetime **Boulangerie Centrale des Hôpitaux de Paris,** 13, rue Scipion, corner rue du Fer-à-Moulin. 1565. Conversion to *logements,* **Jean-Pierre Buffi** and **Italo Rota.** 1989.

Behind a tensely sculpted exedral entry lies a grand courtyard, in brick, limestone, and terra-cotta ornament. This Italianate *hôtel* anticipates those great brick buildings of Henri IV, the **place des Vosges** and the **Hôpital Saint-Louis.**

The new wing houses nineteen apartments for the research staff.

---

**L'Hôtel Scipion**

In *Coins de Paris* by Georges Cain: "Another handsome hotel, in rue Scipion, was built by Scipion Sardini under Henri III. This Scipion Sardini was a strange man, whose story deserves to be told. Of Tuscan origin, he came to France after the death of Henri II [1559], when Catherine de' Medici came to power. Amiable, witty, ingratiating, a great financial adventurer, clever in his endeavors, and unscrupulous, he quickly became an overpowering presence in this frivolous, dissolute, joyous court. He could mix business with pleasure: when an illustrious alliance seemed necessary to obliterate both the baseness of his origins and the rapidity of his fortune, he married 'la belle Limeuil,' one of the most ravishing beauties of the queen's ladies-in-waiting. . . . This lovable individual had been successively adored by the noblest lords of the court before conquering, in 1563, Condé, by whom she had a child. At Dijon, during a reception for the queen, the damsel of Limeuil felt indisposed and delivered a boy. . . . At that moment Scipion Sardini appeared on the scene; the richest financier of the time, he was banker to the king, the clergy, and the nobility. He got himself accepted, married her, and set her up in this handsome *hôtel* that we still admire and that was cited by Sauval as one of the finest in Paris, amid vineyards, orchards, and fields bordering the Bièvre. He lived there, surrounded by luxury, works of art, books, and flowers; he died around 1609."

---

★[5e-10.] **La Collégiale,** 33, rue du Fer-à-Moulin, between rue de la Collégiale and rue Scipion. **Jacques Kalisz.** 1986.

A somewhat-less-than monastic hotel for the recuperating aged. The street facade presents some modest form: balconies and their cornices; within is a handsome central all-weather atrium.

**[5e-11.] Brasserie Marty,** 20, avenue des Gobelins, between boulevard Arago and rue Claude-Bernard.

The classiest neighborhood stop for refreshment.

**★★[5e-12.] Logements, 5, rue de Valence,** between boulevard de Port-Royal and avenue des Gobelins. **Gérard Thurnauer.** 1981.

Shades of gray and white with brown-maroon sash play a mild Post Modern game. Simple, if not simplistic, the counterpoint of Nos. 3 and 5 presents the contrast of the rich gourmand and the nouvelle cuisine. Less is *more?* More of *what?*

**★[5e-13.] 9 bis, rue de Valence,** between boulevard de Port-Royal and avenue des Gobelins. **Georges Planche.** 1930.

Vanilla ice cream *moderne*, fluted, balconied, ribbed—and banal. And appropriate.

**★★[5e-14.] Eglise Saint-Médard,** 141, rue Mouffetard, at square Saint-Médard and rue Censier. Facade and nave, 15th century. Choir and chapels, 1560–1586, with work continuing into the 17th century. Chapel of the Virgin, and neo-Classical flutes added to the choir columns, **Louis-François Petit-Radel.** 1784. Surrounding houses cleared to create a freestanding church, 1868.

Gothic *retardataire* in a "country church" from a time when this actually was in the countryside outside the walls. Saint-Médard anchors the south end of the medieval rue Mouffetard, where the architecture has been updated to the 17th century and thereafter; that medieval street meanders up to the Lycée Henri IV, site of the vanished **Monastery of Sainte-Geneviève.**

**[5e-15.] Logements, 8, rue Censier,** between rue de Quatrefages and rue Geoffroy-Saint-Hilaire. 1930s.

Fluted Classical-modernism. Gray brick infills limestone clad with cream paint, a sorry covering for the quarrying of nature.

**[5e-16.] Restaurant Universitaire,** 3, rue Censier, and 30, rue Geoffroy-Saint-Hilaire. **Henry Pottier.** 1965.

A brooding black cube to the north (rue Censier side), a greenhouse to the south. The architect wanted "to close it [from the sun] to give the building the somber and powerful character of a grotto." However, on entering this would-be grotto, one is almost immediately flooded by sunshine from the south.

**★★★[5e-17.] Jardin des Plantes,** place Valhubert at the Pont d'Austerlitz, bounded by rue Buffon, rue Geoffroy-Saint-Hilaire, and rue Cuvier. Founded 1626.

Founded as the royal garden of medicinal plants by **Jean Hérouard** and **Guy de La Brosse,** physicians to the king, it assumed a greatly expanded role under the great naturalist **Buffon,** who was steward of the garden from 1739 to 1788. After this half-century of educational evolution, the Musée d'Histoire Naturelle was founded and expanded to include minerals, fossils, and animal skeletons. Here also a zoo was started after the Revolution with the surviving animals of Versailles: the Convention had renamed the garden Jardin des Plantes and brought the menagerie here in 1793.
The parterres are divided into ecological, alimentary, genetic, and ornamental sections.

**André Thouin,** chief gardener in the 1780s, wrote, "The garden of the king is situated so as to serve a quarter of the inhabitants of Paris. Situated in the east, at the edge of one of the *faubourgs*, its atmosphere is purified [in contrast to] the unwholesome vapors of the capital. . . . It offers different kinds of vegetation, places of repose, shelter against the north winds, shade during the summer, and lawns that are always green and on which one can always take all sorts of refreshment . . ."

The many buildings and structures of the Jardin are as follows:

**★★[5e-18.] Galerie de Paléontologie,** first on the left off place Valhubert. **Ferdinand Dutert.** 1894–1895.

An eclectic facade, with a great Romanesque Revival entrance arch surmounted by distyle in antis classicism, leads to grand galleries and a spectacular stair of cast iron and stone. The skeletons of animals (including the human animal) are densely clustered in the 19th-century manner: in a grand cultural attic.

**★[5e-19.] Robinier Faux-Acacia,** between Galerie de Paléontologie and Galerie de Botanique. Planted 1601.

This and its sister in square René-Viviani were planted by **Vespasien Robin** (hence Robinier), who maintained an experimental garden here before the garden of **de La Brosse.**

**[5e-20.] Galerie de Botanique.** 1833.

**[5e-21.] Galerie de Minéralogie et Géologie.** 1841.

**★★[5e-22.] Galerie de Zoologie,** on axis of the parterres and the entry, place Valhubert. **Jules André.** 1877–1889. Reconstruction, **Paul Chemetov** and **Borja Huidobro.** 1994.

The grandest gallery of them all, now closed for extensive renovation. Its two-storied skylit space, surrounded by a mezzanine, presents a Noah's Ark of large-scale animal life.

The poet Léon-Paul Fargue (1876–1947) in *Le Piéton de Paris:* "What a stockpile of patience, what mental presence, how many ghosts in this Parisian quadrangle of which the Jardin des Plantes constitutes some kind of capital. Physicians, scholars, and writers worked and meditated here: Fagon, Tournefort, Buffon, Bernardin de Saint-Pierre, the blind Lamarck, Cuvier, Geoffroy Saint-Hillaire, the Jussieus from Lyons, Daubenton, who as a good republican would not admit the 'king' of beasts, Claude Bernard, La Bruyère, Michelet, Balzac, the Goncourts, Bourget . . . Few places guard the memory of so many men. One has every right to prefer Berlin, Batumi, Hamburg, or Cádiz, to our own modest republican institution, which has been a bit spoiled by the powers that be, but how 'exciting for the mind,' as Barrès put it! One should not forget that the Jardin des Plantes of Paris has a gallery of ancestors like nobody else in the world, as well as souvenirs of knowledge, devotion, and passion that make it something more than a militarily organized square devoid of charm, like many foreign institutions."

**★★[5e-23.] Les Serres Coloniales,** next to the Galerie de Zoologie. **Charles Rohault de Fleury.** 1830. Restored, **Jules André.** 1874.

One for tropical, the other for plants of the desert—these two square pavilions were precocious greenhouses, based on avant-garde French technology in cast and wrought iron and, equally, on French leadership in glass manufacture. Panes 20 by 30 centimeters (8 by 12 inches) were the construction module, and an armature of slender wrought iron formed the clear-spanning skeleton.

In 1871 Prussian bombardment severely damaged both, and the architect who subsequently replaced the structures, Jules André, recreated them with much smaller panes and more metal, thereby not only reducing the sun's impact but also creating heavier buildings, with glazing that was almost neo-medieval.

★★[5e-24.] **Les Serres Tropicales,** adjacent to the Serres Coloniales, toward the Seine. **René Berger.** 1937.

More akin to the structure of the Galerie des Machines of 1889 or an aircraft hangar, this gutsy tropical greenhouse belies the delicate elegance of those of **Rohault de Fleury,** as reincarnated by André. But it has power and presence.

★★[5e-25.] **Le Labyrinthe,** northwest corner of the Jardin des Plantes. circa 1640.

The two small hills became a romantic garden, on the slopes of which is the great **cedar of Lebanon,** the first in France, planted by **Bernard de Jussieu** in 1734. Near the summit is the tomb of **Daubenton,** the second steward of the Jardin, after **Buffon.** At the crest is the **Kiosk of the Labyrinth (★★★)**, designed by **Edmé Verniquet** (1787). An iron structure, it was surmounted by a sphere that contained a globe (of the earth) and a mechanism intended to sound noon. A hammer struck "a dozen blows on a Chinese drum, cast in copper . . . which produced a sound heard over a great distance. The hammer was placed in movement precisely at noon by the rupture of a horsehair thread that had been burned by a magnifying glass placed on the . . . cornice."

[5e-26.] **Hôtel de Magny,** 57, rue Cuvier, corner rue Geoffroy-Saint-Hilaire. **Pierre Bullet.** 1690. Many later alterations.

The former porte cochère is the main access to the **Jardin des Plantes.**

★★[5e-27.] **Grand Amphithéâtre,** along the north flank of the Jardin des Plantes to the east of the 57, rue Cuvier entrance. **Edmé Verniquet.** 1788–1789. **Jacques-Guillaume Legrand** and **Jacques Molinos.** 1793–1794.

A neo-Classical gem with symmetrical exedra, now in the course of restoration.

★[5e-28.] **Mosquée de Paris** and **Institut Musulman,** 1, place du Puits de-l'Ermite, between rue Georges-Desplas, rue Daubenton, and rue Geoffroy-Saint-Hilaire. Tearoom entrance at the corner of rue Geoffroy-Saint-Hilaire. **Marcel Heubès, Robert-Alexandre Fournez,** and **Mantout.** 1922–1926.

The 1920s, expressed in green tile and stucco, seem more dominant than the spirit of North Africa in this Hispano-Moorish complex. The best of it is afforded by a peer into the courtyard off the entrance, and a cup of mint tea relished with sticky pastry.

★[5e-29.] **HBM, 6, rue Larrey,** between place du Puits-de-l'Ermite, rue Quatrefages, and rue Daubenton. **Georges Albenque** and **Eugène Gonnot.** 1926.

HBM heaven: a grand arch and vault, crowned with sinuousity, leads to gardens and populist housing. Extravagant detail abounds in brick, ceramic, and stone. This is an exuberant place to live.

**[5e-30.] Hôtel Le Pourfour-du-Petit,** 7, rue Lacépède, on axis of rue de Navarre. 1761.

The *hôtel* forms a porte cochère to 19th-century elegance, exotic in these simplistic surrounds.

**[5e-31.] Ecole maternelle, 22, rue Saint-Médard,** between rue Mouffetard and rue Gracieuse. **Philippe Canac.** 1973.

An obstreperous school, low-lying, with bits of Le Corbusier, a glass-clad stairway. It's rambling for Paris, but here in the zone Mouffetard *everything* rambles.

**[5e-32.] Au Nègre Joyeux (café),** 14, rue Mouffetard, between rue Blainville and rue du Pot-de-Fer.

A vintage signboard shows a black man delivering a plate of chocolates.

★**[5e-33.] Crèche, 48, rue Lacépède,** between rue Mouffetard and rue Monge. **Jacques Casanova.** 1985.

Quasi-historic end pavilions make a transition between a histrionic center and the neighboring buildings. The architect describes it as a "skinned" building that flaunts its intestines: "The skin is removed to reveal the organs—volumes that are resolutely modern." Is this revenge on rue Mouffetard?

★**[5e-34.]** Originally **Collège des Ecossais**/now **Ecole Sainte-Geneviève,** 65, rue du Cardinal-Lemoine, between rue Monge and rue Rollin. 1672.

The chapel, difficult to see without special permission from the Caisse Nationale des Monuments Historiques, contains the mausoleum of James II of England (his brain is in the gilded bronze urn), who died in exile at Saint-Germain-en-Laye in 1701.
James Drummond, duke of Perth, commissioned the tomb to **Louis Garnier,** a student of the sculptor **François Girardon.**

**[5e-35.] Fontaine du Pot-de-Fer,** at intersection of rue Descartes and rue de la Montagne. Perhaps **Michel Noblet.** Between 1671 and 1681.

Watered by the Aqueduc d'Arcueil from 1624, this is a reconstruction of the original.

★★**[5e-36.]** Originally **Hôtel Le Brun,** 49, rue du Cardinal-Lemoine, between rue des Boulangers and rue Jussieu. **Germain Boffrand.** 1700.

This Le Brun was a nephew of the painter **Charles Le Brun,** who decorated **Vaux-le-Vicomte** and **Versailles.** Seven "bays" wide, it projects three, surmounted by a pediment. Paradoxically, this elegant *hôtel* for an opulent client is now occupied (with modern extensions) by the national offices of HBM, the agency for social housing.

**[5e-37.] Universités de Paris VI** and **VII,** place Jussieu, bounded by rue Jussieu, rue des Fossés-Saint-Bernard, rue Cuvier, and quai Saint-Bernard (with the exception of the Institut du Monde Arabe). **Edouard Albert, Urbain Cassan, René-André Coulon,** and **Roger Seassal.** 1965.

A 1960s atrocity, this steel-and-glass warehouse of education is both an insult to the neighborhood and a cultural decline from its predecessor on this site, the **Halle aux Vins.** Intellects within are housed in a crass and rusting shell, worthy of a penitentiary. Why?

**[5e-38.] Logements, 24, rue Linné,** corner place Jussieu. **Adolphe-Paul Girard.** 1842.

An encrusted vulgarian.

**[5e-39.] Hôtel, 5, rue des Arènes,** between rue Linné and rue de Navarre. circa 1870s.

A sculptural neo-Gothic house overlooking the square Capitan and the Arènes de Lutèce. It makes an elegant corner.

★**[5e-40.] Arènes de Lutèce,** rue de Navarre, rue des Arènes. circa A.D. 200.

A pleasant park and arena for modern performances: this is where the Romans played, but there is no remnant architecture—only conjectural reconstructions of what might have been. Let your imagination supply what archaeologists could not.

# 10
# FIFTH ARRONDISSEMENT
## NORTH

### INSTITUT DU MONDE ARABE

### TO PLACE DU PANTHEON

Institut du Monde Arabe: **Jean Nouvel et al.** and **Architecture Studio;** boulevard Saint-Germain; Eglise Saint-Nicolas-du-Chardonnet: **Charles Le Brun** and **Victor Baltard;** Hôtel de Miramion: **Louis Le Vau;** Eglise Saint-Julien-le-Pauvre; Shakespeare and Company; Chapelle de la Communion-Saint-Severin: **Jules Hardouin-Mansart;** Hôtel and Thermes de Cluny; Chapelle de la Sorbonne: **Jacques Lemercier;** Saint-Etienne-du-Mont; Lycée Henri IV; Bibliothèque Sainte-Geneviève: **Henri Labrouste;** Le Panthéon: **Jacques-Germain Soufflot**

Métro: **Cardinal Lemoine**

**[5n-36.] Jubé, Eglise Saint-Etienne-du-Mont. Philibert Delorme,** architect of the *jubé.* circa 1550.

★★★[5n-1.] **Institut du Monde Arabe,** 23, quai Saint-Bernard, at pont de Sully. **Jean Nouvel, Gilbert Lézénès, Pierre Soria,** and **Architecture Studio.** 1987.

To honor nations known for their great hand-craftsmanship, wondrous architecture (also "handmade"), and avant-garde mathematics, here is a sleek elegance, mathematically complex, machine-crafted. The south plaza wall is screened by hundreds of diaphragms that mimic the opening and closing of an eye's iris, and hence the *moucharaby* of Islam.

Nouvel subdues his technical histrionics by containing them within the building's shell—stairs and railings of aluminum and steel, tensile cables, glazed elevators that glide within a central light well. All are high-tech, a style far in the future of the Arab world's own homelands because of the economics of arid lands with minimal resources.

Remember here the architectural technologists, from **Gustave Eiffel** to **Jean Prouvé,** from **Iskembard Brunel** to **Norman Foster,** from **John Roebling** to **Buckminster Fuller.**

The ninth-floor restaurant overlooking the Seine and **Notre Dame** is the eating site for modest budgets; it is equal to—if not better than—the **Tour d'Argent** for views of **Notre Dame**'s chevet.

[5n-2.] **Pont de Sully,** from the eastern end of boulevard Saint-Germain to the Ile Saint-Louis and boulevard Henri IV. 1876.

Here is a bridge not to look *at* but to look *from*—along the quais of the Ile Saint-Louis and to the east end of Notre Dame.

★[5n-3.] **Musée de la Sculpture en Plein Air,** quai Saint-Bernard between pont de Sully and pont d'Austerlitz. **Daniel Badani** and **Pierre Roux-Dorlut.** 1979.

A garden along the banks of the Seine that offers sculpture of the 20th century, from Brancusi to César (may I say good grief to the latter).

[5n-4.] **Logements, 7 bis, boulevard Saint-Germain,** between pont de Sully and rue du Cardinal-Lemoine.

A sliver building tucked between two Haussmanian dowagers.

[5n-5.] **Restaurant de la Tour d'Argent,** 15, quai de la Tournelle, corner rue du Cardinal-Lemoine.

An iron-and-glass marquise leads to (way upstairs) the most notorious restaurant in Paris, famed for its extravagant menu, extravagant prices, and extravagant view of the chevet and flying buttresses of Notre Dame. Here again the architecture is that of the view, not of the object.

On the *rez-de-chaussée* is the small **Musée de la Table,** opened by the management in 1958.

[5n-6.] **Logements, 27, quai de la Tournelle,** between rue du Cardinal-Lemoine and rue de Poissy. **Gabriel Leduc.** 17th century.

Giant console brackets flank the portal to a "buzz in" court. When in doubt, here or anywhere, buzz in during weekdays. In the evening and on weekends many, if not most, buildings are on "code," known only to residents and friends.

[5n-7.] **L'Ange Gourmand (restaurant),** 31, quai de la Tournelle, corner rue de Poissy. circa 1900.

A space from the turn of the century.

★[5n-8.] Logements, 21, boulevard Saint-Germain, between rue de Poissy and rue du Cardinal-Lemoine. **Jean-Marie Boussard.** 1882.

Busty and dis-armed caryatids lead to a classic Beaux Arts marble-and-limestone entrance hall. Here is pomp in advance of most *pompier.*

[5n-9.] **Paradis Latin (nightclub),** 26, rue du Cardinal-Lemoine, between boulevard Saint-Germain and rue des Ecoles. Main room, **Gustave Eiffel,** engineer-builder. 1890s.

Closed in 1907, it served as a pharmaceutical warehouse until 1977, when the Paradis Latin was reincarnated.

★★[5n-10.] **Caserne des Sapeurs-Pompiers**/originally **Réfectoire du Couvent des Bernardins,** 24, rue de Poissy, between rue des Ecoles and boulevard Saint-Germain. 13th century.

The firemen are on their way out of this remarkable refectory, which has three vaulted naves, each with seventeen bays. The space, 70 meters (230 feet) long, is constructed of rough limestone.

★[5n-11.] **Club Quartier Latin,** 19, rue de Pontoise, between boulevard Saint-Germain and rue Saint-Victor. **Lucien Pollet.** 1934.

A Frank Lloyd Wrightian brick symmetry, with a play of bas-relief brickwork, a hovering roof, and a square and squared steel entry—private athleticism for *les branchés.*

[5n-12.] **Maison de la Mutualité,** 24, rue Saint-Victor, between rue de Pontoise and rue des Bernardins. **V. Lesage** and **Charles Miltgen.** 1931.

★★[5n-13.] **Eglise Saint-Nicolas-du-Chardonnet,** 30, rue Saint-Victor, corner rue Monge and rue des Bernardins. Rue des Bernardins facade, **Charles Le Brun.** 1660s. Apse, **Victor Baltard.** 1862. Rue Monge facade, **Claude Halley.** 1934.

If we acknowledge some stonework remaining from a former church, dated 1625, construction spanned more than three hundred years. Baroque buttresses **(Le Brun?)** and some pyramids inspired by **Pope Sixtus V's** Rome festoon it all, but within rests a cool, Classical, emotionally limpid space.

[5n-14.] **Immeuble, 17, rue des Bernardins,** between boulevard Saint-Germain and quai de la Tournelle. **Jean-Marie Boussard.** 1890.

Amid all the 17th-century sobriety stands this ebullient wrought-iron-balconied *immeuble,* with a Tuscan column—arcuated crowning terrace. The terra-cotta soffits are a rich borrowing from the coffered polychromy of Baroque naves.

★[5n-15.] **Musée des Hôpitaux de Paris**/formerly **Hôtel de Miramion,** 47, quai de la Tournelle, between rue des Bernardins and rue de Pontoise. Entry facade and left courtyard facade, 16th century. Corps de logis, perhaps by **Louis Le Vau.** 1630–1633.

A partly 16th-century courtyard awaits within. According to *Le Grand Siècle au Quartier Latin,* catalog of a 1982 exposition, "The architecture of the Hôtel de Miramion has been compared with that of the Hôtel d'Aumont, built by Louis Le Vau, to the point where J.-P. Babelon has formulated a theory that it could be one of the first works of Le Vau, who was then eighteen years old but already associated with his father's work. Certain similarities are immediately apparent: features in common with the Hôtel d'Aumont. The facades behind the courts have much in concert: a width of five bays; dormer windows alternating with *oeils-de-boeuf*, as on the various courtyard facades of the Hôtel d'Aumont; the same approach to the design of the dormers; the same general silhouette; the same decoration of the windows with swags, clasps, and masks."

[5n-16.] 19, rue de la Bûcherie, corner rue de l'Hôtel-Colbert.

*Qu'est-ce que c'est?*

★[5n-17.] Square René-Viviani, between quai de Montebello, rue Lagrange, and rue Saint-Julien-le-Pauvre. Present garden limits, 1928.

What was originally the garden of **Eglise Saint-Julien-le-Pauvre** was extended to create this park, the major resident a *robinier* (locust) imported from Canada and planted in 1601.

★[5n-18.] Auberge aux Deux Signes, 46, rue Galande, between rue Dante and rue Saint-Julien-le-Pauvre. 13th, 14th, and 20th centuries.

Below (★★) are the vast rib-vaulted cellars of the refectory of the Chapelle Saint-Blaise (13th century). Also within are the great Gothic windows from the west gable of the same chapel.

★★[5n-19.] Eglise Saint-Julien-le-Pauvre, 3, rue Saint-Julien-le-Pauvre, between quai de Montebello and rue Galande. Some portions, 12th century. Nave vaults, 17th century.

A charming small parish church, now of the Eastern Orthodox rite, much restored, with a chancel vaulted with ribs, its walls supported by sturdy Romanesque columns. The altar is screened from the population by an iconostasis.

[5n-20.] Hôtel Isaac-de-Lafémas, 14, rue Saint-Julien-le-Pauvre, between quai de Montebello and rue Galande. Portal, 17th century.

Adapting the *hôtel* and its court to the random geometry of the Quartier Latin produces interesting space and form.

[5n-21.] Shakespeare & Company (bookstore), 37, rue de la Bûcherie, between rue du Petit-Pont and rue Saint-Julien-le-Pauvre.

A descendant of Sylvia Beach's Anglo-American center for intellectual encounters. The original was at **12, rue de l'Odéon.**

---

**Sylvia Beach,** daughter of a Presbyterian minister from Princeton, New Jersey, came to Paris in the summer of 1916. Julien Green wrote in *Jeunesse,* "Between these walls of multicolored books, I saw almost nothing at first, then found myself suddenly in front of a young woman with a pleasant face indeed, and well turned out in a short skirt, but whose expression froze me. It was not that she was hostile. To the contrary, a faint smile lifted the corners of her mouth, but what coldness . . . I don't know what I had expected . . . The smile was the one reserved for unknown customers and meant nothing."

The store became a magnet for expatriate American writers in Paris, led by **Hemingway** and **Fitzgerald.** Her most famous effort was in the original publication of **James Joyce**'s *Ulysses* in 1922.

---

★★[5n-22.] Eglise Saint-Séverin, 1, rue des Prêtres-Saint-Séverin, between rue Saint-Séverin and rue de la Parcheminerie. Basic building, 13th–15th centuries. Communion chapel, **Jules Hardouin-Mansart.** 1673.

Redecorated choir, 17th–18th centuries. Facade of Saint-Pierre-aux-Boeufs becomes facade of Saint-Séverin. 1837.

The flamboyant Gothic vaults within are elaborately ribbed, stoned, and bossed. At grade the promenade of columns and piers forms a historical walk to the altar: the first three columns with capitals, then four ribbed piers without, then a choir from the stilted 18th-century neo-Renaissance.
The stone is that of Saint-Leu *(calcaire Lutétien).*

★[5n-23.] rue Xavier-Privas, rue de la Huchette, rue de la Harpe.

Here is 17th- and 18th-century Paris (most of the buildings) on 13th-century streets, now filled with 20th-century Greek and Middle Eastern restaurants. The hucksters will, like the sirens of mythology (although these sirens are male), attempt to lure you into the world of tzatziki, moussaka, and retsina. Staunch tourists will see the rue du Chat-Qui-Pêche, but both cat and fish are long gone, and the street is a barren alley 2.5 meters (8 feet) wide. This is said to be the only street in Paris that banned not only one-way traffic but also one-way parking!

[5n-24.] Hôtel Dubuisson, 29, rue de la Parcheminerie, between rue des Prêtres-Saint-Séverin and rue de la Harpe. circa 1750.

Note the elegant balcony ironwork and the sculptured bas-relief of this exercise in stylish modesty.

★★[5n-25.] Thermes de Cluny, entry, 6, place Paul-Painlevé, between boulevard Saint-Michel and rue de Cluny. circa A.D. 200.

Viewed from the intersection of boulevard Saint-Michel and boulevard Saint-Germain, this is a striking ruin that ties the extant built history of Paris to this point almost 1,800 years ago. The *frigidarium* (cold bath) is the best-preserved segment (to the east), with the *tepidarium* (warm bath) nearer boulevard Saint-Michel. The *calidarium* (hot bath) has collapsed.

★★★★[5n-26.] Musée/Hôtel de Cluny, entry, 6, place Paul-Painlevé, between boulevard Saint-Michel and rue de Cluny. **Jacques d'Amboise.** 1485–1498. West arcaded gallery. 1500–1510.

The *hôtel,* transitional between Gothic and Renaissance, anticipates the urban arrangements of the great wave of Renaissance *hôtels* that followed in the 16th century. The *corps de logis* is opposite the entrance portal, with the arcaded service wing at its left, and "hanging" gardens were constructed in back of the main block, superimposed on the vaulted structure of the Thermes de Cluny's *frigidarium!*
Within, the only extant original architecture is that of the chapel, where a central column supports Flamboyant ribbed vaults, much in the manner of an English Perpendicular Gothic chapter house.
The *hôtel* became the Musée de Cluny in 1844, thanks to the interest (in the Middle Ages) and energy of Alexandre Du Sommerard and, later, his son, Edmond.

★[5n-27.] Maison, 67, rue Saint-Jacques, between rue des Ecoles and rue Du Sommerard. 18th century.

There is 18th-century class waiting on three of its five levels; but the fine scale is lost above. The balcony bears butterflies. Buzz yourself in to the rear court, where another handsome 18th-century structure resides.

★★[5n-28.] Ecole Spéciale des Travaux Publics du Bâtiment et de l'Industrie, 59, boulevard Saint-Germain, between rue Thénard and rue Jean-de-Beauvais. **Joannès Chollet** and **Jean-Baptiste Mathon.** 1936.

Brick, strip windows that corner roundly, and piers that crest in finials—all this is a bulky Art Moderne/Art Deco exercise, best savored in the grand detail at the street, where ironwork punctuates twin *oeils-de-boeuf.*

**[5n-29.] Immeubles, 13, 15, 17 rue Champollion,** between place de la Sorbonne and rue des Ecoles. **Jacques Curabelle.** 1670.

An investment property of the Sorbonne.

**★★★★[5n-30.] Chapelle de la Sorbonne,** place de la Sorbonne, off boulevard Saint-Michel. **Jacques Le Mercier.** 1635–1642.

The only extant monument of the Sorbonne created by Cardinal Richelieu, whose funerary monument (1675–1694) by **François Girardon** rests within. The remaining buildings are dour and lifeless 19th-century (**Henri-Paul Nénot.** 1881–1901) "barracks" built in the name of science—and to expunge the Sorbonne as a symbol of theology—under the aegis of **Jules Ferry,** who secularized the French educational system, from kindergarten to doctoral dissertations.

The chapel rests at the end of the *place,* an urban space worthy of Le Mercier's Italian Baroque inspiration. This rich domical ensemble shares special Baroque honors with those of the **Val-de-Grâce** and **Eglise Visitation-Sainte-Marie.**

Richelieu's tomb is a high point of 17th-century French sculpture.

**★[5n-31.] Collège de France,** 11, place Marcellin-Berthelot, between rue Saint-Jacques and rue Jean-de-Beauvais. Central portion, **Jean-François Chalgrin.** 1774. Additions, **Paul-Marie Letarouilly.** 1831–1842. **Albert & Jacques Guilbert** and **André Leconte.** 1928–1939.

Chalgrin is most often identified with the **Arc de Triomphe,** but he created more serious architecture at **Saint-Philippe-du-Roule,** the north tower of **Saint-Sulpice,** and the **Hôtel de Saint-Florentin/Talleyrand** (now the chancellery of the U.S. Embassy). Here his work was that of the catalyst in a great line of construction over 165 years.

The *collège* sits on a grand elevation over the *place.* The architecture is boring, the faculty exciting—**Pierre Boulez** and **Claude Lévi-Strauss,** among others.

**[5n-32.] Immeuble, 23, rue Jean-de-Beauvais,** between rue des Ecoles and rue de Lanneau. 1930s.

Elegant bay windows united with a modest brick polychromy.

**[5n-33.] Logements, 29, rue Jean-de-Beauvais,** corner rue de Lanneau. **Paul Herbé.** 1960.

Segmental arcs corner this awkward and gross modern ensemble.

**◢[5n-34.] Immeuble, 11, rue Lanneau,** corner rue Jean-de-Beauvais. 17th century.

A battered remnant at its most articulate; later dormered, it presents the tiniest *pan coupé* to those approaching the restaurant, **Le Coupe-Chou.**

**[5n-35.] HBM,** corner at **20, rue de l'Ecole-Polytechnique** and **21, rue des Carmes. Agence d'Architecture HBM.** 1934.

A grand Romanesque Revival arch constructed of rather repulsive yellow brick brings another scale to these ancient streets on the Montagne Sainte-Geneviève.

**[5n-35a.] Maison, 7, rue Valette,** between rue de l'Ecole-Polytechnique and rue Laplace. 1673.

An elegant and almost collapsed star, on the way to the Panthéon.

---

**Sébastien Mercier** wrote, on the eve of the Revolution: "This is the quarter where the poorest, the most transient and most undisciplined, of the Parisian population live. In these houses, removed from the central city, hide ruined men, recluses, alchemists, maniacs, pensioners of limited income, and also students seeking true solitude."

---

★★★**[5n-36.] Eglise Saint-Etienne-du-Mont,** 1, place Sainte-Geneviève between rue de la Montagne-Sainte-Geneviève and rue Clovis. Commenced, 1492. Choir, ambulatory, tower, and *jubé,* circa 1550. Nave and transept, 1585. Facade, 1610–1626. Restoration, **Victor Baltard.** 1868.

A Gothic body in Renaissance fancy dress (stone of **Saint-Leu**). Here the most famous element is the *jubé,* elevated at the same time as the choir, from designs by **Philibert Delorme.** Its twin spiral stairs are architectural icons that bring a dynamic Italian Renaissance intrusion into this equivocal Gothorenaissance space.

The organ's 17th-century *buffet* is the work of cabinetmaker **Jean Buron,** the pulpit that of his peer, **Germain Pilon,** with sculpture by **Claude Lestocard** after drawings by **Laurent de la Hyre.**

★★**[5n-37.] Lycée Henri IV,** 23, rue Clovis, between the Panthéon, rue Descartes, rue Thouin, and rue de l'Estrapade. 19th century. Within the first court, the **Tour de Clovis,** 12th–14th centuries.

The Romano-Gothic tower (★★★) (of the abbey church of Sainte-Geneviève, the abbey of which occupied this whole site and that of the Panthéon) is preserved within the first arcaded courtyard—Romanesque at the base, Gothic at its crest, its style changing with the times. Also within, by appointment through the custodian, you might see the kitchens (12th century), the refectory, now the school's chapel (13th century), and especially the galleries of the library, a cross in plan, with a dome over the crossing. The latter has extravagant Baroque-rococo details: capitals exploding with almost-solid beams of light, and putti floating among it all.

**[5n-38.] Logements** and **bureaux, 7, rue Thouin,** between rue Mouffetard and rue Tournefort. **Etienne Debré** and **Jean-Marie Hertig.** 1985.

An advertising agency on the first two levels, apartments above—all in big tiles and raw concrete, with a glassy, metallic-grill mansard crowning it all.

★★★**[5n-39.] Panthéon**/formerly **Eglise Sainte-Geneviève,** place du Panthéon, on axis of rue Soufflot. **Jacques-Germain Soufflot.** 1764–1780. **Maximilien Brébion** and **Jean-Baptiste Rondelet.** 1780–1791. Conversion to Panthéon, **Antoine Quatremère de Quincy.** 1791 and later. Inaugurated, 1822.

This cool and ungainly Classical pile oscillated between a house to worship God and a house to honor great men, until it finally chose the latter in 1885. Here are entombed **Voltaire, Le Pelletier de Saint-Fargeau, Rousseau, Victor Hugo,** the heart of **Gambetta,** the ashes of **Jean Jaurès,** and **Jean Moulin.**

For those who are gorged with the Baroque richness of **Val-de-Grâce** down the hill to the south, this is an austere and immense temple of reason.

## Who Was Saint Geneviève?

The patron saint of Paris, Geneviève was a rich Gallo-Roman landowner who lived from 420 to 500. Born in Nanterre (just west of today's **La Défense**), she was urged by **Bishop Saint-Germain d'Auxerre** to devote her virginity to Christ, after miraculously curing her mother's blindness with water from Nanterre's wells.

Most important for Parisians, she is credited with deflecting by prayer an invasion by **Attila the Hun** in 451, a feat for which she is remembered as a national and patriotic heroine.

★★★★**[5n-40.] Bibliothèque Sainte-Geneviève,** 10, place du Panthéon, corner rue Valette. **Henri Labrouste.** 1844–1850.

This was founded in 1624 as the monastic library of the Génovéfains; its contents were transferred here as the second cycle of change in the abbey's disappearance: the Panthéon occupies much of the abbatial grounds, and the **Lycée Henri IV** most of the balance. The latter, which still houses the abbey's library (physically, without books), exported the contents here into Labrouste's new shell.

The facade on the *place*, in an austere Florentine manner, shields the grand cast- and wrought-iron reading room that shares the honors with Labrouste's **Bibliothèque Nationale** as an important proto-Modern iron structure. Go in. The halls are crowded with waiting students, but at least you'll have a glimpse of the grand space.

★★★**[5n-41.] Faculté de Droit, Université de Paris I, II,** and **IV,** 12, place du Panthéon, between rue Cujas and rue Soufflot. **Jacques-Germain Soufflot.** 1763–1780.

Part of Soufflot's grand urban composition, this exedral half was later balanced by Hittorf's mairie with opposing symmetry (1846). The balance would have pleased Soufflot. Here are neo-Classical reinforcements for the Panthéon.

**[5n-42.] Logements, 174, rue Saint-Jacques,** between rue Soufflot and rue Malebranche. **Paul Tournon.** 1931.

Tournon is most noted for the **Eglise du Saint-Esprit [12s-33.]** of the same period (1928–1931). Here is a bourgeois transitional Art Moderne dwelling.

**[5n-43.] Hôtel, 151 bis, rue Saint-Jacques,** between rue Soufflot and rue Malebranche. **Lebas** and **Claude-Nicolas Dubuisson.** 1718.

A superb balustrade in wrought iron over the entrance portal, which in turn leads to a court where a second *hôtel* of the 18th century is resident.

**[5n-44.] Logements, 200, rue Saint-Jacques,** between rue Malebranche and rue Royer-Collard. **Remoissonnet Frères.** 1914.

Haussmannian-*tardif* in limestone. Those fourth-floor columns (don't count the *entresol*) are Romanesque Revival with entasis, porches for those wishing to be enframed.

# 11
# FIFTH ARRONDISSEMENT
## SOUTH

### PORT-ROYAL TO VAL-DE-GRACE

Station Port-Royal; Eglise Saint-Jacques-du-Haut-Pas: **Daniel Gittard**
and **Libéral Bruant;** Fondation Edmond de Rothschild: **Germain
Debré;** 53, rue Lhomond: **Paul Tournon;** passage des Postes, Ecole
Normale Supérieure, 31, rue d'Ulm: **Alexandre de Gisors;**
Val-de-Grâce: **François Mansart, Jacques Lemercier,** and **Pierre
Le Muet**

Métro: **Port-Royal**

**[5s-21.] Eglise Val-de-Grâce. François Mansart, Jacques Lemercier,
Pierre Le Muet. 1645–1667.**

★[5s-1.] **Station Port-Royal,** boulevard de Port-Royal at avenue de l'Observatoire. **Octave Rougier,** engineer. 1895.

The **Ligne de Sceaux** (railroad) passed through here on the way to the site of the **Cité Universitaire,** at a time when the national railroads were competing with the blossoming Métro. The marquise is lovely.

[5s-2.] **Ecole Française de Suggestopédie,** 44, rue Henri-Barbusse, between boulevard de Port-Royal and rue du Val-de-Grâce. **Jules Astruc.** 1899.

Astruc's most important work is the **Eglise Notre-Dame-du-Travail** near the Gare Montparnasse. Here is a vernacular effort in *meulière.*

[5s-3.] **Immeuble, 105, boulevard Saint-Michel,** corner rue de l'Abbé-de-l'Epée. circa 1900.

*Pompier-Classique* contrasting with *pompier-*Guimard down the block at 14, rue de l'Abbé-de-l'Epée.

★[5s-4.] **Immeuble, 14, rue de l'Abbé-de-l'Epée,** between boulevard Saint-Michel and rue Saint-Jacques. **Gaston-Georges Leroy.** 1909.

Post-Guimard *pompier,* with claw-footed lions supporting the bay windows.

★[5s-5.] **Eglise Saint-Jacques-du-Haut-Pas,** 252, rue Saint-Jacques, corner rue de l'Abbé-de-l'Epée. Cornerstone, 1630. Nave and facade, **Daniel Gittard.** 1675 and later. Chapel of the Virgin, **Libéral Bruant.** 1688.

Bland within, an altered and weathered hulk without. The Classical porch tries to tame the older bulk.

★★[5s-6.] **Fondation Edmond de Rothschild,** 13, rue Pierre-et-Marie-Curie, between rue Saint-Jacques and rue d'Ulm. **Germain Debré** and **Nicolas Kristy.** 1930.

Brick 1930s constructivism at the west end and a stucco conning tower at the entry. In between, there has recently been stuffed a volume of floor space with a particularly banal anodized-metal and glass curtain wall. The balance of the Ecole Supérieure de Chimie along this blockside is dour and bland 19th century, with some untalented modernisms tacked on above their original cornices.

[5s-7.] **Logements, 22, rue Pierre-et-Marie-Curie,** between rue Saint-Jacques and rue d'Ulm. **F. Saulnier.** circa 1900.

Three marquises and some modestly voluptuous stonework in flowing *pierre de taille.*

[5s-8.] **Maison, 45, rue Lhomond,** at place Lucien-Herr. 19th century.

The cast-iron *grille* in the court entrance door offers a view into this private space (go up the steps).

[5s-9.] **Logements, 37, rue Tournefort,** between place Lucien-Herr and rue du Pot-de-Fer. 1980s.

Limestone and granite. Post Modern.

★[5s-10.] **Immeuble, 53, rue Lhomond,** between place Lucien-Herr and rue de l'Arbalète. **Paul Tournon.** 1929.

Modern stucco, its rough walls constrasting with smooth columns. The crowning pediment and colonnaded porch give it special identity.

★[5s-11.] **Passage des Postes,** between 57, rue Lhomond and 104, rue Mouffetard. Buildings, 17th-18th centuries. *Passage* opened, 1830.

A cobbled *passage* open to the sky, except at its rue Mouffetard end, where it penetrates a building's mass.

[5s-12.] **Logements/surélévation, 12, rue de l'Epée-de-Bois,** between rue Mouffetard and rue des Patriarches. **Paul Chemetov.** 1967.

A truncated Haussmannian building, its construction stopped during World War I, was fulfilled here by the young Chemetov in his first commission in Paris. It obeys *all* the "laws" concerning materials and *gabarit* (envelope), and even sports a mansard roof. But it is a 1960s building, built when being thoroughly modern was more important than being right. For mature Chemetov, see the underground world at the **Forum/Les Halles.**

[5s-13.] **Ecole Normale Supérieure,** 4, rue Rataud, corner rue Erasme. 1930s.

The backside of the 45, rue d'Ulm complex. Here are oculi and mini bay windows.

★[5s-14.] **Ecole Normale Supérieure/Bâtiments de chimie et de sciences naturelles,** 8, rue Erasme, between rue d'Ulm and rue Rataud. **Albert Jacques Guilbert.** 1935.

A post-Perret ensemble: hard and hardhearted concrete symmetry produces an aura of centralized power.

★[5s-15.] **ENSAD (Ecole Nationale Supérieure des Arts Décoratifs),** 31, rue d'Ulm. **Robert Joly.** 1969.

Sleek and curvilinear ceramics clad an awkward addition to ENSAD. But such seems the fate of many distinguished schools of art and architecture.

[5s-16.] **Ecole Normale Supérieure, 31, rue d'Ulm,** between rue Erasme and rue Claude-Bernard. **Alexandre de Gisors.** 1841.

Penetrate the front court and building lobby into the garden court (★★ 1845), a peaceful treed and fountained space, surrounded by busts of the wise.

[5s-17.] **Logements, 15, rue des Ursulines,** corner rue Saint-Jacques. **Charles Labro.** 1900.

Guimardesque. The window heads at the second floor have singular sinuosity, with a tile frieze at the fourth.

★[5s-18.] **Logements, 11, rue Pierre-Nicole,** between rue des Feuillantines and rue du Val-de-Grâce. **André Contenay.** 1930.

The bourgeois 1930s in a crisp, no-nonsense *immeuble.* Its projecting bay offers oblique views of the neighborhood,

★[5s-19.] **Logements, 11 bis, rue Pierre-Nicole,** between rue des Feuillantines and rue du Val-de-Grâce. **E.D.** 1979.

Nonsense or fantasy? A busy "modern" facade is superposed above an eroded cave. The latter has the aura of the Viennese-American architectfantasist, **Frederick Kiesler,** as expressed in his visionary **Endless House** of the 1950s, a smooth egg shape on a pedestal.

**[5s-20.] Schola Cantorum**/originally **Couvent des Bénédictins Anglais,** 269, rue Saint-Jacques, between rue des Feuillantines and rue du Val-de-Grâce. 17th century.

Concerts of contemporary choral music take place here on Sunday mornings.

★★★★**[5s-21.] Eglise Val-de-Grâce,** 1, place Alphonse-Laveran, along rue Saint-Jacques. **François Mansart.** 1645–1646. **Jacques Lemercier.** 1647–1654. **Pierre Le Muet,** assisted by **Gabriel Leduc** and **Du Val.** 1654–1667.

The wife of an indifferent Louis XIII, Anne of Austria bought the old Hôtel Petit-Bourbon on this site in 1621, founding the monastery of Val-de-Grâce, where she would spend much of her energy and two days a week of her time. Her subsequent vow was to ''erect a magnificent temple to God if He would send her a son.'' That son became **Louis XIV** (born September 5, 1638. Five years later, after Louis XIII died, a five-year-old became king—and Anne became regent). Mansart, as architect of the Crown, was chosen to proceed. Louis XIV laid the first stone in April 1645.

The successor architects of Mansart were scrupulously faithful to his plans, although Le Muet apparently elaborated the external architecture of the dome. This is French Baroque, although the French have only recently accepted their own Baroque history. Mansart's first grand exercise in such a vocabulary was at the **Chapelle de la Visitation-Sainte-Marie [4s-30.]** in the Marais.

Certainly there is the influence of Michelangelo's St. Peter's in Rome on the dome, 19 meters (62 feet) in diameter, 41 meters (134 feet) tall. But some of Lemercier's design for the **Chapelle de la Sorbonne** is apparent, as well as Le Muet's urge for elaboration.

The spectacular space within is punctuated by a baldachino, based on **Bernini**'s in **St. Peter's,** perhaps designed by him (he had a contract with Anne of Austria in 1665) but probably created by Leduc based upon Bernini's inspiration.

The inner dome bears as its ''heaven'' the grand fresco of **Pierre Mignard,** the *Gloire des Bienheureux* (1663).

★★**[5s-22.] Monastère du Val-de-Grâce**/now **Hôpital Militaire,** surrounding the church, 1, place Alphonse-Laveran. **Pierre Le Muet.** 1655–1665.

The serene cloister harbors traces of the Hôtel Petit-Bourbon. Facing the open gardens to the east is a grand facade, punctuated at the monastery's northwest by the **Pavillon d'Anne d'Autriche,** where the regent, in her pious mode, maintained a modest two-room apartment.

# 12
# SIXTH
# ARRONDISSEMENT
## NORTH

### PLACE SAINT-MICHEL TO PLACE DE L'ODEON

Fontaine Saint-Michel: **Gabriel Davioud;** rue Saint-André-des-Arts;
Cour du Commerce-Saint-André; Librairie Magnard: **Roger Michaux;**
Confrérie des Barbiers-Chirurgiens: **Charles and Louis Joubert;**
Ancienne Faculté de Médecine: **Jacques Gondoin;** rue
Monsieur-le-Prince; rue de l'Odéon; l'Odéon: **Jean-François Chalgrin**

Métro: **Saint-Michel**

**[6n-4.] Maison des Trois Châpelets.** 1640. Rebuilt, 1748.

**★★[6n-1.] Fontaine Saint-Michel,** place Saint-Michel, between rue Danton and boulevard Saint-Michel. **Gabriel Davioud,** architect. **Francisque Duret,** sculptor. 1860.

Here is 19th-century neo-Baroque facademanship, glued to a *pan coupé.* Heroics are appropriate at this juncture of youth and an almost Roman road. This quarter's Latins abound—and did abound (see the **Thermes de Cluny** down the street **[5n-25.]).**

Davioud was, with Hittorf, a favorite architect of Haussmann, enriching the latter's avenues and boulevards with fountains **(Observatoire** and **place Félix Eboué),** *grilles* (Parc Monceau), urinals *(vespasiennes),* and buildings: the two theaters of the place du Châtelet plus the "Trocadéro," predecessor to the Palais de Chaillot.

This has been a rallying point for students of all ages, as well as the Commune of 1871 and the victorious tanks of General Leclerc in 1944.

**★[6n-2.] Logements,** 1, rue Danton, at place Saint-André-des-Arts. **François Hennebique** and **Edouard Arnaud.** 1900.

Behind all this bulky stonework is an early reinforced-concrete frame. But the carapace presents great arches and bay windows, as if it were supporting the space within, rather than being merely a screen wall.

**★★[6n-3.] Hôtel des Abbés de Fécamp,** 5, rue Hautefeuille, corner impasse Hautefeuille. 14th century.

Here is a glorious corbeled and decorated corner *tourelle* that allows its occupants to view three directions.

**★[6n-4.] Maison des Trois Châpelets,** 27, rue Saint-André-des-Arts, opposite rue Gît-le-Coeur. 1640. Rebuilt, **Dairler.** 1748.

Three great arcades, the central entrance surmounted by wrought iron of the 18th century.

**★[6n-5.]** Originally **Hôtel de Montholon**/now **Transports Fluviaux,** 35, quai des Grands-Augustins, corner rue Séguier. 1639.

Warm stone and cool iron for an *hôtel particulier* upgraded to national and international commerce.

**★[6n-6.] Restaurant Lapérouse,** 51, quai des Grands-Augustins, corner rue des Grands-Augustins. Building, 18th century.

A lush facade promises (and keeps it) a lush interior (à la Louis XIV) and a lush menu (★★). It has been here since 1768 (Louis XVI). After two hundred years a restaurant becomes an institution to be reckoned with.

**[6n-7.] Hôtel Savoie,** 7, rue des Grands-Augustins, between quai des Grands-Augustins and rue Saint-André-des-Arts. 1675 and later.

Tight and tall, it is the result of demolishing the hôtel d'Hercule in 1675 (the latter occupying the ground of both No. 5 and No. 7) and subsequently constructing two *hôtels* by dissident junior members of the Savoie family. Picasso's atelier was once here, and *Guernica* was painted here.

**[6n-8.]** Originally a portion of **Collège de Saint-Denis**/now **Jacques Cagna (restaurant),** 14, rue des Grands-Augustins, corner rue Christine. 16th century.

Inside are a stair and *salle* of note, but at these prices you should get more than just food. Expensive.

★★[6n-9.] Hôtel du Tillet de La Bussière, 52, rue Saint-André-des-Arts, corner rue des Grands-Augustins. 1750.

Ironwork supported by 18th-century goats. Behind it all is an 18th-century court. Buzz yourself in.

★[6n-10.] Hôtel de La Vieuville, 47, rue Saint-André-des-Arts, almost opposite rue des Grands-Augustins. Rebuilt, 1728.

The courtyard sports a bellied and domical corner pavilion of the 18th century. The stone is eroded but proud—no parvenu overkill here.

★★[6n-11.] Cour du Commerce-Saint-André, 59, rue Saint-André-des-Arts, and 130, boulevard Saint-Germain. 1776.

A *passage* covered, then uncovered, and re-covered. The buildings guarding its two streetfronts provide grand entrances to a bit of elder quaintness within. The rear of the **Procope** restaurant (opened on this site in 1689 by Signore Procopio, "Gentleman of Palermo") is a meandering urban cluster of 17th- and 18th-century structures (main restaurant entrance at 13, rue de l'Ancienne-Comédie). The Comédie Française, now at the Palais Royal, was at that time opposite at **No. 14;** thus this became the restaurant of artists, writers, and revolutionaries such as **Voltaire, Danton, Marat, Robespierre, George Sand, Verlaine,** and **Oscar Wilde.** More interesting to those with shallow pockets is the **Relais Odéon,** a brasserie (circa 1900) hidden in the corner (southwest) of the outlet of the cour to the rue de l'Ancienne-Comédie.

The cour de Rohan, to the east, offers a succession of small courtyards, in the second of which is the **Hôtel de Rohan** (1636). The court is surrounded by an exquisite ensemble of Henri IV houses.

The boulevard Saint-Germain facade is, of course, much later.

---

In 1672 an Armenian named Pascal opened the first Parisian café where one could consume that newly fashionable black beverage. The world of cafés then sprang forth from this fountainhead. Procope, which opened only fourteen years later (it was at a different site before its present location at rue de l'Ancienne-Comédie), became the most famous. Montesquieu in *Lettres Persanes* (1721) noted, "Coffee is very popular in Paris. There are a great number of public houses that carry it. In some of them they talk about the news, in others they play chess. In one of them coffee is taken in such a manner that it gives wit to those who drink it: at least, of everybody who leaves there, there is none who doesn't believe that he has four times as much wit as when he entered."

---

[6n-12.] Flash (magasin), 115, boulevard Saint-Germain, between carrefour de l'Odéon and rue Grégoire-de-Tours. 1900s.

The date is not of the shoes sold here but of the elegant woodwork storefront, in slender Classicism, where "frameless" glass is notched into the oak. The attenuated colonnettes are sleek.

★[6n-13.] Librairie Magnard, 91, boulevard Saint-Germain, between carrefour de l'Odéon and rue Dupuytren. **L. and Roger Michaux.** 1927.

The offices above enjoy a bay-windowed facade projecting from limestone, all lightly framed in steel. It is an elegant counterfoil to the Haussmannian street, maintaining the *gabarit* while punctuating its dour spirit with major facets of glass. Inside are medical and scientific books.

★[6n-14.] Hôtel particulier, 21, rue Hautefeuille, corner rue Pierre-Sarrazin. 16th–17th centuries.

An octagonal *tourelle* corners the *hôtel* at rue Pierre-Sarrazin, with an arched and rusticated entrance wall to the forecourt on rue Hautefeuille.

★★★[6n-15.] **Institut des Langues Modernes**/originally **Confrérie des Barbiers-Chirurgiens Saint-Cosme et Saint-Damien,** 5, rue de l'Ecole-de-Médecine, between rue Hautefeuille and boulevard Saint-Michel. Amphitheater, **Charles and Louis Joubert.** 1691–1695.

This squat dome owes much to Mansart and Lemercier: **Visitation-Sainte-Marie, Val-de-Grâce, Invalides.** Here, however, it has been brought down to a more human scale. At the extravagant portal, angel caryatids sound trumpets to the eye.
Other residents included an **Ecole Gratuite de Dessin** (1777–1875) and the **Ecole des Arts Décoratifs** (1875–1933). Hair, body, hand *(dessin)*, tongue.

★★[6n-16.] Originally **Réfectoire des Frères-Mineurs Franciscains (or Cordeliers),** 15, rue de l'Ecole-de-Médecine, opposite rue Hautefeuille. 1370–1510.

Rebuilt around 1500 by **Anne of Brittany,** the wife of two kings (Charles VIII and Louis XII), in Flamboyant Gothic, this is the only remnant of the Cordeliers. **Jean Paul Marat,** whom **Charlotte Corday** did in down the block (at what is now rue Antoine-Dubois), lay here, if not in state, before his burial.

★★[6n-17.] **Ancienne Faculté de Médecine,** 12, rue de l'Ecole-de-Médecine, between rue Hautefeuille and boulevard Saint-Germain. **Jacques Gondoin.** 1769–1774. **Léon Ginain.** 1878–1900.

The gallery along the street, its courtyard, and the hexastyle pedimented entrance beyond are Gondoin's, but further still the guts of modern medical education are those of Ginain. Ionic columns form a monumental screen to all this grand late 18th-century neo-Classicism.

[6n-18.] **Immeubles, 2, 4, 6, rue Antoine-Dubois,** between rue de l'Ecole-de-Médecine and rue Monsieur-le-Prince. 18th century.

The scale of the street has been sullied by the "new" university buildings on its east flank. Nos. 2, 4, and 6 bear handsome 18th-century ironwork with rusticated stone portals.

★[6n-19.] **Hôtel de Bacq,** 4, rue Monsieur-le-Prince, between carrefour de l'Odéon and rue Antoine-Dubois. 1750.

An extravagant portal on a simple 18th-century body. Next door at **No. 6** a neo-Gothic entrance supports neo-Classicism above.

An aside down rue Monsieur-le-Prince . . .

★[6n-20.] **Immeuble, 58, rue Monsieur-le-Prince,** between boulevard Saint-Michel and rue de Vaugirard. 18th century.

A classical remnant adorned with loving ironwork and console brackets. Saunter along this whole street to absorb its myriad low-key but wonderful details.

★[6n-21.] **Immeuble, 2, rue des Quatre-Vents,** at carrefour de l'Odéon. **Charles Gossart.** 1907.

Lots of glass, bay windows, and some Art Nouveau sinuousity to support them.

★[6n-22.] **Rue de Condé,** between carrefour de l'Odéon and rue de Vaugirard. Mostly 18th century.

*Hôtels* and *immeubles* on a neo-Classical pre-Haussmannian street. Note particularly **Nos. 10, 12, 14, 16,** and **30.**

[6n-23.] **1, rue de l'Odéon,** at carrefour de l'Odéon. **Brulé.** 1781. Surelevated, 19th century.

The cornice at the *pan coupé* is unique, masking two levels of mansarded space behind.

[6n-24.] **4, rue de l'Odéon,** between carrefour de l'Odéon and place de l'Odéon. **Jean Rougevin.** 1788.

A tight courtyard is screened by a wall with strong corniced entrance piers.

[6n-25.] **10-12, rue de l'Odéon,** between carrefour de l'Odéon and place de l'Odéon. Early 19th century.

Twin *Restauration immeubles,* well groomed but short on their original ironwork.

★★[6n-26.] **Place de l'Odéon. Thunot.**

The exedral space that receives the symmetry of the **Théâtre de l'Odéon.** An elegant crest to the street of the same name, the *place* is a rich topping to the gradually descending cascade of shops that ends in the more intellectual and plebian Carrefour.

To the east of the Théâtre is the **Librairie Moniteur,** the outlet of an architectural publishing house that has a broad range of books on architecture and urban design, including those of other publishers. (For other more eclectic selections try **La Hune** on boulevard Saint-Germain.)

★★[6n-27.] **Théâtre de l'Odéon**/also **Théâtre de l'Europe**/originally **Théâtre-Français,** place de l'Odéon. First building, **Marie-Joseph Peyre and Charles de Wailly.** 1782. Rebuilt after 1799 fire, **Jean-François Chalgrin.** 1807.

Neo-Classicism of the grandiose sort that Schinkel would pursue in Germany thirty years later. Peyre's work was influenced by **Ledoux,** and Chalgrin was at the center of such neo-Romanism—compare his **Arc de Triomphe** and **Eglise Saint-Philippe-du-Roule.**

---

To quote **Quatremère de Quincy:** "It [the Odéon] is the only theater in Paris that one can name as meriting the name *monument,* [because of] its access, the regularity of the *place* where it is situated, and of the streets connected to it. Moreover, its freestanding quality, rare in a city as compressed as Paris, commends its view. . . ."

# 13
# SIXTH
# ARRONDISSEMENT
## WEST

### PALAIS DU LUXEMBOURG
### TO CARREFOUR DE LA CROIX ROUGE

Palais du Luxembourg: **Salomon de Brosse;** Jardin du Luxembourg:
**Boyceau de la Barauderie** and **Jean-François Chalgrin;** Fontaine
Médicis: **Salomon de Brosse;** rue de Tournon; Institut Français
d'Architecture: **Pierre Bullet;** Marché Saint-Germain: **Jean-Baptiste
Blondel;** Eglise Saint-Sulpice: **Daniel Gittard** and **Jean-Baptiste
Servandoni;** Institut Catholique; Chapelle Saint-Joseph-des-Carmes; rue
du Regard; rue du Cherche-Midi; boulevard Raspail

Métro: **Luxembourg (RER)**

**[6w-36.] Immeuble, 67, boulevard Raspail. Léon Tissier,** architect.
**Henri Bouchard,** sculptor. 1916.

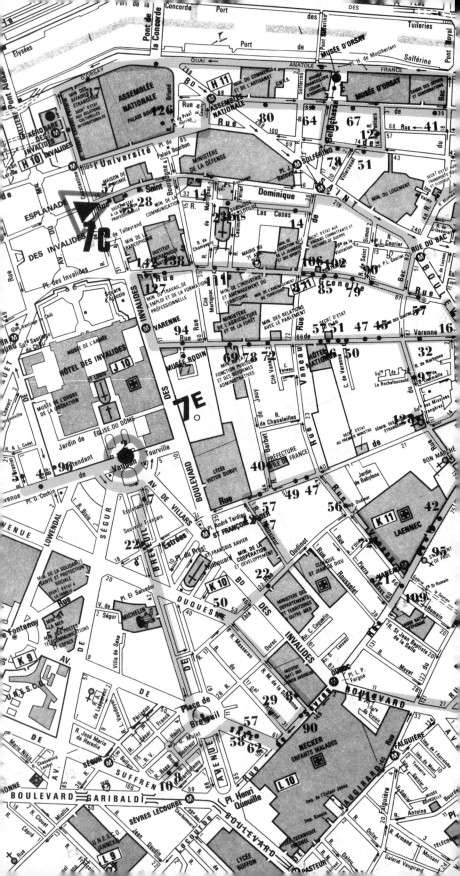

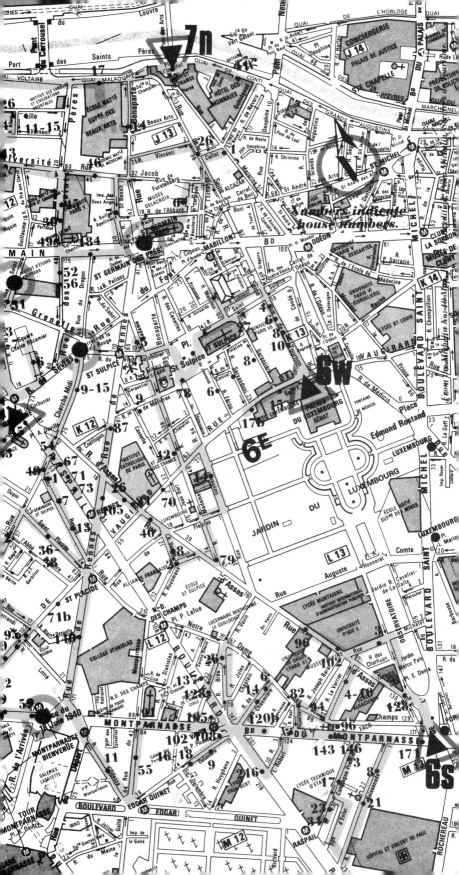

★★★[6w-1.] **Palais du Luxembourg**/now **Sénat de France,** 15, rue Vaugirard, on axis with rue de Tournon. **Salomon de Brosse.** 1615–1625. Vastly altered, **Jean-François Chalgrin.** 1802–1805. Enlarged and transformed, **Alexandre de Gisors.** 1836–1841 and again, 1852–1854.

This is the *grand* Luxembourg, as opposed to the *Petit* Luxembourg next door, the latter the original *hôtel,* bought by Marie de Médicis from the Gondi family.

From the rue de Tournon, the rusticated columns (stacked marshmallows?) give the central pavilion a powerful podium for what, in turn, seems to be a diminutive dome. In fact, from the garden the dome fades into oblivion. There is an obvious analogy with the **Palazzo Pitti** and the **Boboli Gardens,** a memory that Marie brought with her from her Florentine childhood.

Michael Dennis in *Court and Garden* wrote, "Like mini-châteaux, these buildings were manifestations of the independence and individuality characteristic of the period. Though forced by social pressure to be near the court, the nobility had reluctantly traded country houses for urban villas—but a pavilion in a controlled, private garden offered the best of both worlds. And one is compelled to believe that Salomon de Brosse's Luxembourg Palace (begun 1615), hovering as it did at the edge of the Fauborg St.-Germain, between the city and the gardens, also hovered in the imagination of the nobility, a grand ideal, attainable in miniature."

★[6w-2.] **Petit Luxembourg,** 17, rue de Vaugirard, just west of the Grand Luxembourg. Before 1612.

Now the residence of the president of the Senate.

★[6w-3.] Formerly **Couvent des Filles du Calvaire,** 17 bis, rue de Vaugirard, opposite rue Férou. 1622.

A proto-Baroque pediment crowns this elegant courtyard, all enriched in Italianate polychromy.

★★★[6w-4.] **Jardin du Luxembourg.** surrounded by rue de Vaugirard, rue Guynemer, rue d'Assas, rue Auguste-Comte, boulevard Saint-Michel, place Edmond-Rostand, and rue de Médicis. **Boyceau de la Barauderie.** 1613 and later. **Jean-François Chalgrin.** 1800 and later.

The grand gardens of the palace became the public gardens of Napoléon and Louis XVIII, an outdoor museum of mostly mediocre sculpture, with notable exceptions: included among the latter is the medallion of Stendhal by **Auguste Rodin,** just off place Edmond-Rostand. Sainte-Geneviève, Flaubert, Anne d'Autriche, Blanche de Castille, Marguerite de Valois, Baudelaire, Massenet, Verlaine, and even Phidias are present.

But the *pièce de résistance* is the **Medici Fountain:** see below.

Jean-Jacques Lévèque in *Guide des parcs et jardins de Paris* writes, "[The palace] frees itself from the ensemble [of the gardens], through the play of different levels, with gentle slopes leading from one to another, creating a kind of musicality that has a genuine and imposing beauty, without the ostentation of Versailles or the megalomania of a Tuileries extended by the Champs-Elysées. Everything here remains at human scale."

★★★[6w-5.] **Fontaine Médicis,** east of the Luxembourg Palace, near rue de Médicis. **Salomon de Brosse.** 1615.

In the spirit of Italian grottos, this is a magnificent testament to Marie de Médicis.

★[6w-6.] **Hôtel du Maréchal d'Ancre,** 10, rue de Tournon, between the Luxembourg Palace and rue Saint-Sulpice. 1607.

The last tenant, before its transformation into apartments, was the Garde Républicaine. Here the battle between Marie de Médicis, mother of Louis XIII, and Cardinal Richelieu seemingly ended with his brief exile (1630). Richelieu bounced back victorious; and Marie, in turn, was exiled to Cologne, where she died.

The distyle entrance is a later neo-Classical addition.

**[6w-7.] Immeuble, 8, rue de Tournon,** between the Luxembourg Palace and rue Saint-Sulpice. 1713.

Extravagant mini-caryatids.

★★**[6w-8.] Hôtel de Brancas**/now **Institut Français d'Architecture,** 6, rue de Tournon, between the Luxembourg Palace and rue Saint-Sulpice. Rebuilt, **Pierre Bullet.** 1719.

A grand court receives those interested, largely in the history of 19th- and 20th-century architecture. A separate entrance to the left leads to exhibition galleries. In the main building the Louis XIV staircase is impressive and worth a visit on its own. Continue through the entrance hall to the courtyard behind.

★**[6w-9.] Hôtel Jean de Palaiseau,** 4, rue de Tournon, between the Luxembourg Palace and rue Saint-Sulpice. 18th century.

Tuscan columns flank the door and thence the lovely cobbled courtyard. An elegant 18th-century railing is on view.

★**[6w-10.] Marché Saint-Germain,** rue Mabillon, off boulevard Saint-Germain. **Jean-Baptiste Blondel.** 1813–1818. Reconstruction, **Olivier-Clément Cacoub.** 1991.

This Blondel was unrelated to **Nicolas-François** of the **Porte Saint-Denis** but was perhaps the grandson of **Jacques-François,** who had built the **Aubette** at Strasbourg. Be chary of works attributed to Blondel, or **Jourdain,** or many others: there are, for example, at least four Blondels and three Jourdains in Parisian architectural history.

Threatened with total demolition and a replacement by the flamboyant Cacoub, the market was partially saved by the cry of an enraged citizenry. The architect has now been instructed to re-create the exact plans of Blondel, except for the central courtyard. That was uncovered in the original market and will now be covered. Cacoub, a favorite of Mayor Jacques Chirac, is the author of a new office complex in the **ZAC Citroën** at the Pont du Garigliano **[15w-26.]**; a more than flashy place.

**[6w-11.] Hôtel de Fougères,** 27, rue Saint-Sulpice, between rue de Tournon and Eglise Saint-Sulpice. 18th century.

An extravagant portal (★★) worthy of 17th-century Italy is in startling contrast to the now denuded facade surrounding.

At the rear of Saint-Sulpice is a door:

★★**[6w-12.] Eglise Saint-Sulpice,** place Saint-Sulpice, between rue Saint-Sulpice and rue Palatine. **Daniel Gittard.** 1646–1678. Then **Gilles-Marie Oppenordt.** Facade, **Jean-Baptiste Servandoni,** competition winner, 1732–1766. Completed by **Oudot de Maclaurin,** except for north tower, **Jean-François Chalgrin.** 1778–1780.

Greatly—if not grandly—inflated neo-Classicism, cool and excessive. The facade is reminiscent of the architecture of Roman theaters (as at **Orange**), creating a backdrop for actors *en scène*. The actors are the everyday citizens who pass to and fro, as well as those of the *foire* of secondhand furniture and furnishings that springs up here theatrically each June.

Here is quantity, and the square before it gives it room to hulk itself into these twisting streets.

Inside, there is a *buffet d'orgue* by Chalgrin (1781) and a pulpit by **Charles de Wailly** (1788). The **Chapelle de la Vierge** by de Wailly (★★★)(1774) is a French Baroque masterpiece, with the *Virgin and Child* by **Pigalle**. Murals by **Delacroix.**

★**[6w-13.] Fontaine des Quatre-Evêques,** centered on place Saint-Sulpice. **Ludovico Visconti.** 1844.

Visconti was inspired by the Renaissance **Fontaine des Innocents (Jean Goujon.** 1549) near the **Forum/Les Halles:** square in plan, arched on four sides.

★★**[6w-14.] Hôtel de Sourdéac,** 8, rue Garancìere, between rue Palatine and rue de Vaugirard. **Bobelini.** 1640.

A quasi-palazzo *alla fiorentina* with great ram's head pilasters. There is some lovely ironwork and a fine *culot.* It remains a stony stalwart in these streets. Built by René de Rieux, bishop of Léon, and left to his nephew, the marquis de Sourdéac, it became the office of the **Plon** publishing house in 1854.

**[6w-15.] Rue Servandoni,** between rue Palatine and rue de Vaugirard.

An undulating assembly, both in plan and elevation, provides the somewhat romantic tourist an appropriate route to Saint-Sulpice's south transept. It abounds in 17th- and 18th-century houses.

★**[6w-16.] Hôtel Luzy,** 6, rue Férou, between rue Palatine and rue de Vaugirard. 1750.

Stalwart sphinxes crest the pillared gates of this neo-Classical–Egyptoid *hôtel particulier.* Note the swagged festoons at the spandrels.

**[6w-17.] Mairie,** 78, rue Bonaparte, at place Saint-Sulpice. **Rolland** and **Vicomte.** 1849. Extended to rue Madame, 1889.

Cool, low of brow, and understated, it also shelters the **Bibliothèque des Arts Graphiques.**

★**[6w-18.] Lycée des Livres et des Arts Graphiques Maximilian Voss,** 5, rue Madame, between rue de Rennes and rue du Vieux-Colombier. **Jean-Henri Errard.** 1886.

Another sturdy brick, limestone, and tile monument to laic education, à la Jules Ferry, who exorcised the ghosts of clericalism from the French educational system.

★**[6w-19.] Logements, 9 bis, rue de Mézières,** between rue Madame and rue Cassette. **Paul Delaplanche.** 1933.

Solid cream, with ship's balcony railings. The bay windows even look up and down the street through polygonal portholes.

**[6w-20.] Ecole des Filles/Ecole Maternelle, 42, rue Madame,** corner rue Honoré-Chevalier. **Roger Bouvard.** 1923.

Here is a tapestry of brick and tile on a concrete skeleton, a pale work (à la **Perret**).

★[6w-21.] Immeuble, 14, rue Guynemer, between rue de Vaugirard and rue d'Assas. Michel Roux-Spitz. 1928.

Roux-Spitz's first Parisian *immeuble*, clad in limestone that conceals a reinforced-concrete skeleton.

★[6w-22.] Hôtel particulier, 79, rue Madame, corner rue d'Assas. Félix Werlé. 1892.

Glass, iron, and tile make a bay window of vigor on this *neo-Grec* town house.

★[6w-23.] Immeuble, 2, rue Huysmans, between rue d'Assas and boulevard Raspail. Raoul Brandon. 1919.

This is a decorative foil to 8, rue Duguay-Trouin opposite. The foliate Art Nouveau–*tardif* contrasts with Classical/Art Moderne.

★[6w-24.] Immeuble, 8, rue Duguay-Trouin, corner, rue Huysmans. F. Saulnier. circa 1930s.

Those stepped brackets supporting the bay windows would make good sets for a Fritz Lang film.

[6w-25.] Institut Arthur-Vernes, 40, rue d'Assas, between rue de Vaugirard and rue de Fleurus. Albert Ferran. 1926.

An exposed concrete frame surrounds pragmatic brick.

★★[6w-26.] Chapelle Saint-Joseph-des-Carmes, 70, rue de Vaugirard, between rue d'Assas and rue Cassette. 1613–1620.

One of the two earliest domes of Paris (the other is now part of the Ecole des Beaux-Arts [7n-3.]), here constructed of timber in imitation of Italian models.

[6w-27.] Institut Catholique, 21, rue d'Assas, between rue de Vaugirard and rue de Rennes. Reconstruction, 1930.

Neo-Renaissance brick and limestone, combining Art Deco spandrels with neo-Gothic bracketed dormer windows. An eclectic mélange.

[6w-28.] Maison, 26, rue d'Assas, between rue de Vaugirard and rue de Rennes. Hector Degeorge. 1894.

In its time this was a brave newness, informed by the revolutionary spirit of the 19th century's last years—a bit of Charles Voysey, a bit of Josef Hoffman, a bit of Louis Sullivan.

[6w-29.] Immeuble, 105, rue de Rennes, corner rue d'Assas. circa 1900.

Again caryatids, but industrialized.

★[6w-30.] Immeuble, 87, rue de Rennes, between rue d'Assas and rue du Vieux-Colombier. Jean-Marie Boussard. 1880.

A special island in the Haussmannian stream. Grand composite columns, winged goddesses, and vermiculated rustications. A face in the crowd.

[6w-31.] Hôtel particulier, 13, rue du Regard, between rue du Cherche-Midi and rue de Rennes. 18th century.

★[6w-32.] Hôtel de Beaune, 7, rue du Regard, between rue du Cherche-Midi and rue de Rennes. **Victor Bailly.** 1700 and later.

The 18th-century forebuildings signal entry to a forecourt, with the bulky *corps de logis* on the boulevard Raspail. The boulevard here was a Haussmannian incision that truncated and devoured the gardens of the *hôtels* on rue du Regard.

★[6w-33.] Hôtel de Dreux-Brézé, 1, rue du Regard, corner rue du Cherche-Midi. 18th century.

One of the inevitable ministries is housed here, its forecourt serving the ubiquitous cars of Parisian *fonctionnaires.*

[6w-34.] Sometime **Hôtel du Duc de Rochambeau,** 40, rue du Cherche-Midi, between boulevard Raspail and rue Saint-Placide. 18th century.

Arched and courtyarded in painted stucco, with delicate remnant ironwork. Rochambeau was party to the British defeat at Yorktown in 1781. At that famous surrender, abetted by the French navy, the British band played "The World Turned Upside-Down," while the troops stacked their arms.

★[6w-35.] Maison des Sciences de l'Homme, 54, boulevard Raspail, corner rue du Cherche-Midi. **Henri Beauclair, Paul Depondt,** and **Marcel Lods.** 1968.

An articulate steel structure with automatic *persiennes* that syncopate the facade in their variable states of folding and unfolding. Here is post-Mies (it moves), one of the less unfortunate intrusions of the 1960s. Even so, would that it were someplace else.

★[6w-36.] Immeuble, 67, boulevard Raspail, between rue du Cherche-Midi and rue de Rennes. **Léon Tissier,** architect. **Henri Bouchard,** sculptor. 1916.

The entrance sculpture and doors, together with the polychromy at the cornice, contribute a special grandeur. Look through the entry doors into a Secessionist stairhall, with stained glass and sinuous iron and bronze, the latter by **Bellery-Desfontaines.**

[6w-37.] Immeuble, 71, boulevard Raspail, between rue du Cherche-Midi and rue de Rennes. **Paul and Charles Wallon.** 1909.

A triad of arched tympani crowns the building in brilliant greens. Downstairs, don't bother.

[6w-38.] Maison, 73, boulevard Raspail, between rue du Cherche-Midi and rue de Rennes. circa 1895.

The *grand bourgeoisie* wished they were the *petite noblesse* of the Renaissance. Here, as in America and England, they created their stage set for others to admire.

★★[6w-39.] Hôtels, 9-15, rue du Cherche-Midi, between carrefour de la Croix-Rouge and rue d'Assas. 17th–18th centuries.

A tight and sinuous street, fulfilling its role as an elder pedestrian viaduct. The shutters, where extant, are flat *out*side, in contrast to the 19th-century *persiennes* folded into window reveals. Antiques and high fashion abound, from the minimal 500-franc bikini (minimal size, not price) to the maximal 150,000-franc armoire.

# 14
# SIXTH
# ARRONDISSEMENT
## SOUTH

### FROM CLOSERIE DES LILAS

### ALONG BOULEVARD DU MONTPARNASSE

Closerie des Lilas; Institut d'Art et d'Archéologie: **Paul Bigot;** rue d'Assas; rue Notre-Dame-des-Champs; Ateliers des Artistes: **Elkouken, Arfvidson, Astruc, Sauvage;** La Coupole; La Rotonde; Le Dôme; **Auscher; Davioud; Roux-Spitz;** rue du Cherche-Midi; rue de Vaugirard; Bistro de la Gare

Métro: **Port Royal (RER)**

[6s-30.] **Logements, 11, rue d'Odessa. Gabriel Blanche.** 1937.

★[6s-1.] Closerie des Lilas (café), 171, boulevard du Montparnasse, corner avenue de l'Observatoire. Building, **F. Gayaudon.** 1903. **Charles Julien,** sculptor. Altered, 1925.

One restaurant of the literati.

[6s-2.] Ecole Alsacienne, 128, rue d'Assas, between avenue de l'Observatoire and rue Le Verrier. 1980s.

PoMo brownstone—a jarring entry into this monochromatic street. The quantity of unrelieved brown is the problem.

★[6s-3.] Institut d'Art et d'Archéologie, Université de Paris, 3, rue Michelet, between avenue de l'Observatoire and rue d'Assas. **Paul Bigot.** 1927.

Brick, brick, brick . . . piered, arched, grilled, finialed . . . an exotic decorated box at the edge of avenue de l'Observatoire, with the "campus lawn" opposite. Flavors of Assyria, North Africa, and the Romanesque intermingle here. A belt of terra-cotta bas-reliefs offers remembrances of archaeological "stars."

★[6s-4.] Logements, 102, rue d'Assas, near rue Joseph-Bara. **Edouard Malot.** 1932.

Stucco modern, with some bay windows to enhance the view.

[6s-5.] Faculté de Droit et des Science Economiques, 96, rue d'Assas, between rue Joseph-Bara and rue Vavin. **Alain Lenormand.** 1962.

Poor Mies. See what your "children" have done with your God. He isn't in these details; and the graph paper–facade is relentless. The architect is excused, due to a bad case of *nineteensixtiesitis* (a dangerous but temporary disease).

★[6s-6.] Maisons, 4, 6, 8, and 10, rue Le Verrier, between rue d'Assas and rue Notre-Dame-des-Champs. 1887–1888.

Bourgeois houses on a Lilliputian scale in contrast to Brobdingnagian Haussmannism. Nos. 4, 6, and 10 are by **Henri Tassu;** No. 8 is the work of **Gustave Goy.**

★[6s-7.] Immeuble, 96, rue Notre-Dames-des-Champs, between avenue de l'Observatoire and rue Le Verrier. **Léon-Joseph Madeleine.** 1939.

Symmetrical Art Moderne in brick, glass, and glass block. The plan is Classical, the forms those of cubism—heavy, bold, and dour. Relish the concrete-shell vault over the lobby entrance, with its glass eyes (oculi).

★[6s-8.] Immeuble, 94, rue Notre-Dames-des-Champs, opposite rue Le Verrier. circa 1898.

An elegant set of bay windows in steel that has a greater freshness today than the aggressively "modern" **No. 96** next door.

★[6s-9.] Immeuble, 82, rue Notre-Dame-des-Champs, between rue de Chevreuse and rue Paul-Séjourné. **Constant Lemaire.** 1905.

Two busty caryatids and two voluptuous cupids guard the entrance to the Belle Epoque block.

**[6s-10.] Immeuble, 143, boulevard du Montparnasse,** between rue Paul-Séjourné and avenue de l'Observatoire. **Léon-Joseph Madeleine.** 1939.

The other side of 96, rue Notre-Dame-des-Champs. In those brick years of the HBMs and streamlined schools, this was a chunky bit of raked-brick cubism for those café frequenters who enjoyed their proximity to the **Dôme, Rotonde,** and **Coupole.**

★**[6s-11.] Logements, 146, boulevard du Montparnasse,** corner rue Campagne-Première. **Bruno Elkouken.** 1934.

A *pan rond,* those 1930s corners that sped through the mind as rockets might speed through space in the *Flash Gordon* (now *Star Trek*) era of static travel. Elkouken's limestone corner is a cool understatement, nevertheless.

**[6s-11a.] Ecole, 21, rue Boissonade,** between boulevard du Montparnasse and boulevard Raspail. circa 1930.

A flatiron fulfilled. Paris is filled with the *pan coupé,* but here is the stuff of which streamliners are made.

★★**[6s-12.] Ateliers, 31, rue Campagne-Première,** between passage d'Enfer and boulevard Raspail. **André Arfvidson.** 1912.

An ensemble of studios encrusted with a magnificence of tile, both flat and in bas-relief: roses, knobs, and angelic girls. Behind, on passage d'Enfer, is a house-scaled wing—the back door, in effect, where the *grès de Bigot* clads the bay window, its frame and soffit, with elegance.

**[6s-13.] Ateliers, 23, rue Campagne-Première,** corner passage d'Enfer. **Edmond Courty,** builder. 1931.

A rational studio building with clean lines.

★**[6s-14.] Impasse d'ateliers, 17, rue Campagne-Première,** between boulevard du Montparnasse and boulevard Raspail. 19th century.

Studios of assorted size, scale, and periods. At the first building on the right was the studio of the photographer **Eugène Atget.**

★**[6s-15.] Logements, 3, rue Campagne-Première** and **8, rue Boissonade,** between boulevard du Montparnasse and boulevard Raspail. **Gilles Bouchez, Didier Morax,** and **Francis Leroy.** 1975.

Ribbed concrete à la **Paul Rudolph,** smooth concrete, wood planting boxes, and greenery. An unabashed outsider of style slipping into an old Paris street.

★★★**[6s-16.] Logements, 216, boulevard Raspail,** between boulevard Edgar-Quinet and boulevard du Montparnasse. **Bruno Elkouken.** 1934.

Crisp limestone and glass with style that has held its own. Elkouken is more daring here than at 146, boulevard du Montparnasse. The Mondrianesque glazing pattern is a delight.
The anchor to this building was originally a cinema, the now private **Studio Raspail.** Buzz in, and through the court you will find a second, L-shaped, building embracing a helicoid stair.

**[6s-17.] Logements, 120 bis, boulevard du Montparnasse,** just east of boulevard Raspail. **Charles Lozouet.** 1913.

Gold, tan, and green tile inlays soffits and spandrels—enlivening an otherwise dour post-Haussmannian facade.

**[6s-18.] Académie de la Grande Chaumière,** 14, rue de la Grande-Chaumière, between boulevard Raspail and rue Notre-Dame-des-Champs. **Antoine Bourdelle,** sculptor. 1904.

Bourdelle was one of the *maîtres.* A neo–Henri IV facade of brick and limestone with bay windows and a mansard roof. Quite an eclectic mélange, both in the sense of the building outside and in the work of the ateliers within.

**[6s-19.] Ateliers, 6, rue de la Grande-Chaumière,** between boulevard Raspail and rue Notre-Dame-des-Champs. circa 1900.

An impressive atelier-studio; the metal and translucent glazing are largely original. The wood-paned doors are magnificent, although the transom is modern.

★★**[6s-20.] Ateliers, 9, rue Delambre,** between boulevard du Montparnasse and boulevard Edgar-Quinet. **Henry Astruc.** 1926.

Here are double-height ateliers, and here is pursued the game of squares within squares, which gives extraordinary presence to a modestly detailed building. At the time, Astruc was still a student at the **Ecole des Beaux-Arts,** and its American developer was host (or landlord) to many exotic talents, including **Isadora Duncan.**

**[6s-21.] Cinémas, logements,** and **passage, 16-18, rue Delambre,** between boulevard du Montparnasse and boulevard Edgar-Quinet. 1980s.

Modern with a vengeance, this aggressive, heavy-handed block applies the code (as in "dress code") material, travertine, to enter the *grand standing* sweepstakes. Not one, not two, but seven cinemas, lots of apartments, and a *passage,* Galerie les Parnassiens (wow!). It all adds up to architectural banality opposite Astruc's **No. 9** opposite.

★★★**[6s-22.] Maison à gradins sportive,** 26, rue Vavin, between boulevard Raspail and rue Notre-Dame-des-Champs. **Henri Sauvage.** 1912.

The title is Sauvage's, intended to attract a clientele of wealthy artists who also enjoyed sport—boxing was a cubist fad! This is where all that glazed whiteness began, with garden terraces receding for the sun. It would have been wiser to match the adjoining buildings (from an urban design viewpoint) and recede at the central pavilion, instead of vice versa. The cavetto cornices at floors one through five give it a lively aspect. Compare the larger **Immeuble à gradins [18ci-13.]** on the rue des Amiraux, where the *gradins* envelop a swimming pool.
Next door, at **137, boulevard Raspail,** Sauvage constructed an eclectic building thirteen years later.

**[6s-23.] Logements, 137, boulevard Raspail,** corner rue Vavin. **Henri Sauvage.** 1925.

The Parisian architect **Antoine Grumbach** wrote in *Henri Sauvage (1873–1932),* "A certain defect of vision seems to afflict historians of modern architecture and architects who visit the rue Vavin building. The defect is so pronounced that they literally do not see the adjacent building situated on the corner of boulevard Raspail, a building by the same Sauvage to whom they come to pay homage in visiting the ceramic setbacks. . . ."

**[6s-24.] Bureaux, 128, boulevard Raspail,** corner rue Vavin. **Michel Herbert.** 1980.

Herbert called it an "eye stopper" that "slips by." The form would be more satisfying if the detailing smacked more of crystal.

★[6s-25.] **La Rotonde (restaurant/café),** 105, boulevard du Montparnasse, corner boulevard Raspail. Founded 1898.

Once the hangout of such artists and writers as **Modigliani, Apollinaire, Zadkine,** and **Foujita,** the Rotonde has become a bourgeois restaurant where you can vicariously absorb the aura of writers and artists—who have, of course, long since left this neighborhood.

---

**La Rotonde,** according to **Jean Giraudoux** in *Siegfried et le Limousin* (1922): "At the corner of boulevard Raspail and boulevard du Montparnasse, on the terrace of a café in the middle of which, among the tables, the Métro emerged, I waited for Zelten. It was one of those fine March evenings, when the sun has not yet been propped up for another hour above the horizon by representatives of the workers, and as soon as it had crossed the city, it plopped like an egg over the Gare [Montparnasse] and the Eiffel Tower. At this intersection . . . were installed . . . all that Paris knows of Japanese expressionists, Swedish cubists, Icelandic engravers, Turkish medalists, Hungarians and Peruvians with complementary vocations, each one adorned with a mistress wearing distinctive makeup, none of whom used the same color for her eyes or lips; each one in a getup that would mark him for crazy in his hometown but that represented in this quarter, and for the concierge herself, the minimum outrage. Unescorted women would get up at times to get a light for their cigar from the pilot light at the counter. Across the boulevard was the rival café, in the shade when the Rotonde got the sun, in the sun as soon as the shade enveloped the Rotonde; but nobody ever crossed the street, except a Creole who moved along with the sun and a flushed pianist seeking fresh air. . . . I was certain before the war to meet Zelten in this Masonic triangle, at the very hour when drinking glasses flow at last with the colors of pharmacy bottles, when each table in turn is visited by dogs begging sugar and deaf-mutes two cents, of ladies bumming a light or one franc fifty for a taxi. . . . If you loved adventure, you had only to go answer the telephone, and strange voices would speak to you in an unknown language. It was onto this antheap that Damalli made plans to leap out of contempt and revenge, and he rented a room on the sixth floor, but, frightened by the subway entrance he turned to the career of parachutist that made him rich and famous. At the very table where I was sitting that evening, I had had for a neighbor for several weeks a diner wearing an overcoat who always ordered beef with a lot of salt or pepper. We since learned it was Trotsky, and nobody in the establishment was the least bit surprised, for nobody at the café—only at this café and perhaps only at this one place in the whole world—was so despairing of his most grubby, most indigent, or the most unrefined neighbor that he believed him incapable of one day becoming a king or tyrant."

---

[6s-26.] **Le Dôme (restaurant/café),** 108, boulevard du Montparnasse, corner boulevard Raspail. 1897. Altered, 1923.

The symbiotic mate of **La Rotonde,** across the boulevard.

★[6s-27.] **La Coupole (restaurant/café),** 102, boulevard du Montparnasse, between boulevard Raspail and rue du Montparnasse. **Le Bouc** and **Auffray.** 1927. Rebuilt 1989.

Surelevated by eight floors of commerce, this landmark of literati such as **Ernest Hemingway, Jean-Paul Sartre,** and **Gertrude Stein** retains its internal architecture and decor.
Opened on December 20, 1927, by two former managers of the **Dôme, E. Fraux** and **R. Lafon,** it was built on the foundations of an ancient

charcoal workshop. Belying the charcoal are the columns (but not in French, where they are *piliers:* French columns are only round), decorated by **Fernand Léger, Savant, Kisling, Zingg,** and **Grunewald.**

---

### La Coupole
**Françoise Planiol** in *La Coupole:* "La Coupole is an island right in the middle of the territorial waters of all those who paint, think, sculpt, and write about where they come from. That's how it was in 1927. Sixty years later, they are still there, the intellectuals and artists of the whole world, at more or less set times. It is meaningless to say that La Coupole is an institution. The Musée Grévin is also an institution. Here at La Coupole you don't cross paths with a single wax dummy; you meet sixty years of stylish figures. How strange it is that no one has ever written the history of La Coupole, the world's most famous brasserie, this mosque without prayer built by two Auvergnats, Fraux and Lafon, on the site of a charcoal shop. . . . The other Coupole, the one on quai Conti for at least a century, never witnessed such a parade of major talent. At the Académie Française, they are preparing a dictionary; at La Coupole, we are compiling a *Who's Who* of the geniuses who pass by. That's a big difference."

---

**[6s-28.] Eglise Notre-Dame-des-Champs,** 91, boulevard du Montparnasse, between rue du Montparnasse and rue Stanislas. **Girain.** 1876.

Within are groin vaults over neo-Renaissance arcades. The 19th century, when passive, reactionary, and antitechnological, could be cold. All the theoretical parts are in place in this Renaisso-Romanesque refrigerator.

★**[6s-29.] Residence des artistes, 55, rue du Montparnasse,** between boulevard du Montparnasse and boulevard Edgar-Quinet. **Jacques Bardet.** 1984.

To both hold and break the street at the same time in a grand gesture has been one of the better urban events of Paris, as in such *hôtels particuliers* of the Marais as **Soubise** and **Lamoignon.** Here the inevitable stucco, with tile trim, houses "artistes."

★★**[6s-30.] Logements, 11, rue d'Odessa,** between boulevard du Montparnasse and boulevard Edgar-Quinet. **Gabriel Blanche.** 1937.

A vigorous massing of creamy salient balconies against a ticktactoe of gray brick. This is creativity both disciplined and fulfilled, another observation of the continuous street. It is futurism with a future: not lovely but *wonderful.*

★★**[6s-31.] Magasin, logements,** and **bureaux, 140, rue de Rennes,** corner rue Blaise-Desgoffe. **Paul Auscher.** 1902.

Art Nouveau in concrete, producing whipped cream with reinforcing for a *magasin* that seems to crush the nakedness of the banal FNAC across the street.

**[6s-32.] Rue Saint-Placide,** between rue de Rennes and rue du Cherche-Midi. 19th century.

Napoléons I through III inclusive. **Nos. 36** and **38** are the work of **Gabriel Davioud.** The ground level enlivens some orderly boredom.

★**[6s-33.] Logements, 71 bis, rue de Vaugirard,** between rue de l'Abbé-Grégoire and rue Jean-Ferrandi. circa 1898.

A crisp bay window punctuates this placid street; the black steel is worthy of much of the later Mies van der Rohe. The shopfronts are venerable, avoiding the intrusion of artificial chic.

**[6s-34.] Logements, 72, rue du Cherche-Midi,** between rue de l'Abbé-Grégoire and rue Jean-Ferrandi.

Shuttered.

**[6s-35.] Logements, 86, rue du Cherche-Midi,** between rue de l'Abbé-Grégoire and rue Jean-Ferrandi. 18th century.

An arched vault leads to a court, past a bland but shuttered facade. Within is a fountain of Jupiter.

**★★[6s-36.] Petit Hôtel de Montmorency**/now **Musée Hébert,** 85, rue du Cherche-Midi, corner rue Jean-Ferrandi. 1743.

Be prepared for 18th-century grandeur in spades. Here the contiguous *hôtels* are made to seem bland, despite this understated elegance. Inside are the paintings of **Ernest Hébert,** a society painter, largely of the Italian countryside.

**★[6s-37.] Hôtel de Montmorency-Bours**/now **Ambassade de la République de Mali,** 89, rue du Cherche-Midi, between rue Jean-Ferrandi and boulevard du Montparnasse. 1756.

A heavier hand was here than at **No. 85;** surelevated, but with elegant windows and balconies.

**★[6s-38.] Hôtel particulier, 95, rue du Cherche-Midi,** between rue Jean-Ferrandi and boulevard du Montparnasse. 18th century.

An absolute anachronism: only two stories, a courtyarded *hôtel particulier.* Iron-balustraded, it sports an arch with Classical faces and anthemion ornaments—all with a skewed symmetry.

**[6s-39.] Groupe Scolaire Littré** and **logements, corner rue de Vaugirard and rue Littré.** 1980s.

Tile, stucco, painted *grilles,* and railings. An awkward but charmingly naïve attempt at a neighborhood school and minor housing.

**★★[6s-40.] Logements, 95, rue de Vaugirard,** between rue Littré and boulevard du Montparnasse. **G. Laize.** 1891.

A powerful place, in brick and limestone, with rough blocks of *meulière* below. The bay windows form an impressive verdigris copper column. Excellent, elegant, dour.

**[6s-41.] Cul-de-sac, 99, rue de Vaugirard,** between rue Littré and boulevard du Montparnasse.

A backwater in disguise: an alley of old Montparnasse secreted behind a mask. Open the wooden door and you'll see studios lining the cobbled cul-de-sac.

**[6s-42.] Logements, 122, rue de Vaugirard,** between rue Littré and boulevard du Montparnasse. 1970s.

Concrete in the hands of "talent" that shapes fenders and fins more often, presumably, than cities. It deserves its punishment of filthy spandrels. (Didn't the architect know about weather?)

★[6s-43.] **Logements, 11, boulevard du Montparnasse,** between rue de Sèvres and rue du Cherche-Midi. **Michel Roux-Spitz.** 1930.

A simple limestone bay-windowed facade, standing rather innocuously next to an adjacent *hôtel particulier.* The latter's garden space sings of luxury rather than the spartan Protestantism of No. 11. (Where would *you* have the party?)

★[6s-44.] **Le Paquebot (restaurant),** 39, boulevard du Montparnasse, between rue de Vaugirard and place du 18 Juin 1940. Building, **Louis Desfontaines.** 1912. Restaurant, 1980s.

An amiable excrescence in white-and-chrome Moderne, fronting a venerable Haussmannian facade that is the best on the block. Le Paquebot's style is that of the **Normandie,** one of the queens of French ocean liners.

★[6s-45.] **Bistro de la Gare,** 59, boulevard du Montparnasse, just west of place du 18 Juin 1940. circa 1900.

A wondrous iron-and-glass canopy shelters the iron storefront—metal painted to look like wood. There is a Belle Epoque interior of lights and mirrors—and *real* wood, too.

# 15
# SEVENTH ARRONDISSEMENT

## CENTER

### ESPLANADE DES INVALIDES

### TO MAISON DE VERRE

Esplanade des Invalides; rue Saint-Dominique; Eglise Sainte-Clotilde: **Chrétien Gau;** rue de Grenelle; Hôtel d'Estrées: **Robert de Cotte;** Eglise Reformée de Pentémont: **Constant d'Ivry;** Hôtel Biron/Musée Rodin annexe: **Henri Gaudin;** rue de Varenne; Hôtel Matignon: **Jean Courtonne;** 16, boulevard Raspail: **Henri Sauvage;** 26, boulevard Raspail: **Pol Abraham;** Maison de Verre: **Pierre Chareau**

Métro: **Invalides**

**[7c-30.]** Hôtel de Ségur/or Hôtel de Salm-Dyck. circa 1722.

One of the problems with strolling through these streets of fabulous *hôtels particuliers* is that much of their grandeur is concealed behind closed or guarded doors. We offer here only what the ordinary traveler can observe; spectacular interiors, private courtyards, and *corps de logis* that can't even be peeked at are ignored. Our reference is thus for the stroller's—rather than the privileged entrant's—eye. Other guides will provide the vicarious delights of what you *cannot* see.

★[7c-1.] Hôtel de William Williams Hope/now **Embassy of Poland,** 57, rue Saint-Dominique, between esplanade des Invalides and rue de Bourgogne. **Achille-Jacques Fédel.** 1838.

A tucked-in remnant: a Tuscan-porched, Greek Revival *hôtel* that replaced an earlier one (**Hôtel de Monaco. Alexandre-Théodore Brongniart.** 1777).

★[7c-2.] Hôtel de Gourgues/now **Ministère de la Culture,** 53, rue Saint-Dominique, between esplanade des Invalides and rue de Bourgogne. **Claude-Nicolas Ledoux.** circa 1770. Altered.

A lanterned court, mildly rusticated. The streetfront is a bore.

★[7c-3.] Hôtel de La Tour d'Auvergne/now **Maison de la Chimie,** 28 and 28 bis, rue Saint-Dominique, between esplanade des Invalides and rue de Bourgogne. **Lassurance.** circa 1710. Surelevated, **Lefranc.** 1935.

All in a warm sandstone, rusticated, with festooned first-floor lintels. A gracious bellied and understated 18th-century courtyard.

★★[7c-4.] Hôtel de Brienne/now **Ministère de la Défense,** 14, rue Saint-Dominique, between rue de Bourgogne and rue de Martignac. **Debias-Aubry.** 1728.

There is an elegant *corps de logis* behind armed guards and a two-story entrance-street-pavilion. You are advised not to run in.

★[7c-5.] Eglise Sainte-Clotilde, 23 bis, rue Las-Cases, between rue de Martignac and rue Casimir-Périer. **Chrétien Gau.** 1846–1853. **Théodore Ballu.** 1853–1856.

The first significant Gothic Revival church in Paris, a style embraced by Haussmann for ecclesiastical buildings in contrast to his "Classicist" boulevards. It has the symmetrical perfection achieved only in academic revivals—not during the Gothic period's long search for form that evolved such marvelous idiosyncrasies as **Chartres.**

[7c-6.] Hôtel particulier, 14, rue Las-Cases, between rue Casimir-Périer and rue de Bellechasse. circa 1890s.

A neo-Empire *hôtel,* now apartments. The bundled and gilt lances that fence the courtyard are elegant.

★★[7c-7.] Fontaine des Quatre-Saisons, 57, rue de Grenelle, between boulevard Raspail and rue du Bac. 1749.

An exedral facade that presents its giant scale to this narrow street. Here is grandeur in spirit with the aqueducts and fountains of Baroque Rome under Pope Sixtus V two centuries earlier.

[7c-8.] Immeuble, 90, rue de Grenelle, corner rue Saint-Simon. **Henri Deglane.** 1906.

The consoles stick out their tongues, plus brick and brackets.

★★[7c-9.] **Grand Hôtel d'Estrées,** 79, rue de Grenelle, just off rue Saint-Simon. **Robert de Cotte.** 1713.

Pale yellow and white, like Leningrad's **Winter Palace.** And before it is a Tuscan portal with diglyphed detail (Greek temples had triglyphed details as part of their cornice decoration).

Appropriately, this is the residence of the Soviet ambassador; before that it was the embassy of the tsars (from 1896).

★[7c-10.] **Hôtel de Maillebois,** 102, rue de Grenelle, between rue Saint-Simon and rue de Bellechasse. Transformed, **Jacques-Denis Antoine.** 1783.

Proto-Regency England or proto-Empire France? Urns mount the *corps de logis* in an outburst of neo-Classicism.

★[7c-11.] **Hôtel d'Avaray**/now **Residence de l'Ambassadeur de Hollande,** 85, rue de Grenelle, between rue Saint-Simon and rue de Bellechasse. **Leroux.** 1718–1723. Remodeled, 1920.

The family Bésiade d'Avaray lived here from its construction until 1920.

★[7c-12.] **Hôtel de Bauffremont,** 87, rue de Grenelle, between rue Saint-Simon and rue de Bellechasse. **Pierre Boscry.** 1721–1736.

Paired Composite columns flank a hooded neo-Baroque pediment.

★[7c-13.] **Eglise Reformée de Pentémont**/originally **Chapelle du Couvent des Bernardines de Pentémont,** 106, rue de Grenelle, between rue Saint-Simon and rue de Bellechasse. **Pierre Constant d'Ivry.** 1756.

A late dome and hard stone, sharp-edged, comes to this venerable street.

[7c-14.] **Cité Martignac,** 111, rue de Grenelle, between rue Casimir-Périer and rue Martignac.

A 19th-century barrel-vaulted entryway to an older world, with *hôtels particuliers* to the right and a 1930s PTT to the left.

★[7c-15.] **Hôtel de Normoutier,** 138, rue de Grenelle, between boulevard des Invalides and rue Martignac. **Jean Courtonne.** 1722.

Marshal Foch lived here.

★[7c-16.] **Hôtel du Châtelet**/now **Ministère du Travail,** 127, rue de Grenelle, between boulevard des Invalides and rue Martignac. **Cherpitel.** 1770.

The courtyard is spectacular, with colossal Corinthian columns.

★[7c-17.] **Hôtel de Chanac-Pompadour,** 142, rue de Grenelle, between boulevard des Invalides and rue Martignac. **Pierre-Alexis Delamair.** 1704.

Today this is the embassy of Switzerland.

★★★[7c-18.] **Hôtel Biron**/now **Musée Rodin,** 77, rue de Varenne, corner boulevard des Invalides. Design, **Jacques-Ange Gabriel.** Execution, **Jean Aubert.** 1728–1731. Annex, **Henri Gaudin.** 1993.

The delights are more in the gardens than in the understated house, where lovely rooms of the period contrast with the works of Rodin. Without, the *Burghers of Calais* is the most prominent single monumental sculpture. But most important for the history of Parisian *hôtels particuliers,* here is a rococo system of planning: a freestanding hotel in its gardens.

The annex should be exhilarating if it follows the wonderful work of Gaudin, such as the **Collège Tandou.**

★[7c-19.] **Immeuble, 94, rue de Varenne,** opposite the Musée Rodin, just east of boulevard des Invalides. **F. Leveque.** 1934.

A substantial Art Moderne building. Oh, to overlook the Musée Rodin and its gardens!

[7c-20.] **Ministère de l'Agriculture,** 78, rue de Varenne, between boulevard des Invalides and rue de Bellechasse. 1886.

A superinflated office building that attempts to match the scale of detail, if not building, of the true *hôtels particuliers* surrounding.

★[7c-21.] **Hôtel de Seissac/Clermont/**now **Premier Ministre/Service Juridique et Technique de l'Information,** 69, rue de Varenne, corner rue Barbet-de-Jouy. **Leblond.** 1708–1714. Altered, 1775.

Buried deep within these public precincts (and therefore private to bureaucracy) lies a companion *hôtel* to that of the **Hôtel Biron** up the street.

★[7c-22.] **Hôtel de Castries,** 72, rue de Varenne, opposite cité Varenne. circa 1700.

Inflated, rusticated, and vermiculated at its entry portal, the *corps de logis* bears some curvilinear proto–Art Nouveau curves.

★★★[7c-23.] **Hôtel Matignon,** 57, rue de Varenne, between rue de Bellechasse and rue du Bac. **Jean Courtonne.** 1721 and later.

This grand and lovely *hôtel,* perhaps the most wondrous of this precinct, is inaccessible to the public. It is accessible to the prime minister, however, as his official residence and workspace.

[7c-24.] **Hôtel de Gouffier de Thoix,** 56, rue de Varenne, between rue de Bellechasse and rue du Bac. **Baudouin,** entrepreneur. 1719–1727.

Another elegant annex for the prime minister in a *corps de logis* behind an 18th-century court.

★[7c-25.] **Cité de Varenne,** 51, rue de Varenne, between rue de Bellechasse and rue du Bac.

A cul-de-sac harbored behind a 19th-century streetfront, barrel-vaulted into a pre-Haussmannian world.

[7c-26.] **Ambassade d'Italie/**originally **Hôtel de Boisgelin,** 47, rue de Varenne, between rue de Varenne and rue du Bac. **Jean-Sylvain Cartaud.** 1732. Additions, 1787. 2nd story, **Henri Parent.** 1875. Reconstructed, **Félix Bruneau** and **Adolfo Leovi.** 1937.

Don't miss those long windows and turgid stone.

★★[7c-27.] **Hôtel de Gallifet/**now **Istituto Italiano di Cultura,** 50, rue de Varenne, between rue de Bellechasse and rue du Bac. **Jacques-Guillaume Legrand.** 1796.

There is a portal to Legrand's inner world, the *corps de logis* far within a meandering space. If you can penetrate through the conciergic maze, you'll be rewarded with a grand building and eight majestic Ionic columns.

★★[7c-28.] **Hôtel de Narbonne-Sérant,** 45, rue de Varenne, between rue de Bellechasse and rue du Bac. **Jacques-Denis Antoine.** 1785.

Four grand Ionic columns, two engaged, two freestanding, support a modest entablature. An elegant pavilion.

[7c-29.] **Immeuble, 32, rue de Varenne,** corner rue du Bac. **Gilbert-François Raguenet** and **Camille Maillard.** 1934.

Cream-crazy tile and loopy *garde-fous* support a serious 1930s curvilinear block.

★[7c-30.] **Hôtel de Ségur**/or **Hôtel de Salm-Dyck,** 97, rue du Bac, between rue de Varenne and rue de Babylone. circa 1722. Redecorated, **Antoine Vaudoyer.** 1811.

There is a *très beau* bow window (★★) on the court in rippling rhythm.

★[7c-31.] **Immeuble, 16, boulevard Raspail,** between rue de Varenne and rue de Grenelle. **Henri Sauvage.** 1924.

A muted Sauvage, less brave, reverting to a more academic-Classical Art Deco. The *gradins* have disappeared.

★★[7c-32.] **Immeuble, 26, boulevard Raspail,** between rue de Varenne and rue de Babylone. **Pol Abraham.** 1932.

Here is Abraham in the *grand standing* mode—and presenting it with vigor. The boulevard line is held, but he inhales part of the volume and articulates balconies and corner windows elegantly.

[7c-33.] **Sous-station Services/EDF**/now **Centre Cultural,** 6, rue Récamier, off rue de Sèvres.

Steel and glass; the plate girder at the stop with X-stiffeners becomes its decorative cornice. A greenhouse of culture.

[7c-34.] **Rue de la Chaise,** between boulevard Raspail and rue de Grenelle.

   ★ **Hôtel du Comte de Vertus,** 3, rue de la Chaise. 1640.
   ★ **Hôtel de Vaudreuil** or **Hôtel de Borghese,** 5–7, rue de la Chaise. 1763. "Modern apartments," **Jean-Jacques Fernier** and **André Biro.** 1973.

   Wow! When you open the door, bizarre serrated balconies confront the 18th-century surrounds. Around the corner, off the rue Récamier, you'll see an outbreak of this same eccentricity, which seems to smack of a misunderstanding of Frank Lloyd Wright—as well as of Paris.

   **Hôtel d'Ozembray,** 9, rue de la Chaise.

[7c-35.] **La Petite Chaise (restaurant),** 36, rue de Grenelle at the head of rue de la Chaise.

Reputedly the oldest restaurant (1680) in Paris, it is relatively inexpensive. But beware! There is a menu in Japanese that can turn the tide.

★★★★[7c-36.] **Maison de Verre,** 31, rue Saint-Guillaume, just north of rue de Grenelle. **Pierre Chareau.** 1931.

Better known as a "decorator" in the manner of **Mallet-Stevens,** Chareau produced a seminal work in the modern movement here. In concert with the developing works of Le Corbusier, and in contrast to the stripped classicism of **Roux-Spitz,** this was an experiment in steel and light. Though not open to the public, it can be viewed in its courtyard by buzzing in through the 18th-century streetfront.

# 16
# SEVENTH ARRONDISSEMENT
## NORTH

### INSTITUT DE FRANCE TO SAINT-GERMAIN

Institut de France: **Louis Le Vau;** Hôtel de la Monnaie:
**Jacques-Denis Antoine;** Ecole des Beaux Arts: **F. Debret** and
**Jacques-Félix Duban;** Gare/Musée d'Orsay: **Victor Laloux;** Palais
de la Légion d'Honneur: **Pierre Rousseau;** rue de Lille; Palais
Bourbon: **Lassurance, Jacques-Ange Gabriel, Alexandre de
Gisors, Frédéric Lecomte,** and **Bernard Poyet;** Eglise
Saint-Thomas-d'Aquin: **Pierre Bullet;** rue de l'Université; rue des
Saints-Pères; Saint-Vladimir-le-Grand: **Clavereau;** Eglise Saint-Germain;
Cafés de Flore and des Deux Magots

Métro: **Saint-Germain-des-Prés**

[7n-4.] Marquise, **Musée d'Orsay. Victor Laloux.** 1900.

111

★★★[7n-1.] Institut de France/formerly Collège des Quatre-Nations, place de l'Institut, between quai Malaquais and quai de Conti, on axis of Pont des Arts. 6th arrondissement. Louis Le Vau. Completed under the supervision of Théodore Lambert and François d'Orbay. 1663–1691.

The brainchild of Cardinal Mazarin (1602–1661), it was founded after his death as a college for the sons of gentlemen and the *haute bourgeoisie* from the four provinces annexed to France in 1659. Now it shelters the five prestigious French intellectual academies, of which the most prominent is the **Académie Française.**
The grand exedral facade, dominated by a pedimented portal and cupola, was carefully and consciously placed on visual axis of the **Cour Carrée** of the Louvre, but its umbilical cord, the **Pont des Arts,** didn't make the pedestrian connection until 1802. This is a typical and wonderful Parisian axial interplay realized over many centuries: Palais de Chaillot and Ecole Militaire; La Madeleine and Palais Bourbon, where architects of different centuries were visually conjoined.

★★[7n-2.] Hôtel de la Monnaie, 11, quai de Conti, between Pont des Arts and Pont Neuf. 6th arrondissement. Jacques-Denis Antoine. 1777.

*Monnaie* here refers to coinage and its mint. A rusticated and arcaded base supports a giant order of Ionic pilasters with a statement that almost seems English. Nevertheless, it is pompous, for this is a cash-on-the-line place.
But pass through into the courtyard, where a grand exedral *cour d'honneur* is marked by an elegant Tuscan-columned portal. On the first floor are some handsome 18th-century interiors, now used for expositions. Better inside than out.

★[7n-3.] Ecole Nationale Supérieure des Beaux-Arts, 14, rue Bonaparte and 17, quai Malaquais, 6th arrondissement. F. Debret. 1816–1832. Jacques-Felix Duban. 1858–1862.

From **Richard Morris Hunt** to **Louis Sullivan,** this is where the cream of late-19th-century American architects studied, for the Beaux-Arts was the first great architectural school. (The first in America was MIT in 1865. Hunt was here in 1846.)
But the architecture of the building that housed all this monumental teaching is an assembly of rather boring parts, except for the delightful cloister (**Cour du Murier:** enter the forecourt and penetrate the building). The chapel, now used for exhibitions, is a remnant of the **Couvent des Petits-Augustins** (1619). Here also is found the gabled entrance of the **Château d'Anet,** a major work of **Philibert Delorme.** Within the chapel, a second **Chapelle des Louanges** bears the oldest dome in Paris (1608). These inner spaces are accessible only when they house temporary exhibitions. Check, for they provide exotic experiences.

★★★★[7n-4.] Musée d'Orsay/originally Gare d'Orsay, 1, rue de Bellechasse, between quai Anatole-France and rue de Lille. Victor Laloux. 1898–1900. Remodeling, Pierre Colboc, Renaud Bardon, and Jean-Paul Philippon. 1985. Interiors for the museum, Gae Aulenti.

Built for the Exposition Universelle of 1900, this was linked to the Gare d'Austerlitz, enabling the Compagnie des Chemins de Fer d'Orléans to present its patrons with a grander station at the edge of the fair. All use of the building ended in 1973 with the closing of the hotel (the western facade).
Now reincarnated, it is a grand space, the internal architecture and arrangements of which are highly controversial. The exterior remains substantially its old bourgeois self, and the vast vaults within are still breathtaking. But the great steles that march down the nave are another matter, and have brought cries of Mesopotamian revival! and other sarcasms. They are

too much architecture for a museum that already has outrageously aggressive paintings. And some mountings of paintings within gallery arches are equally crass and overbearing.

The poor Impressionists are up at the top. While you're up there, enjoy a bizarre view of the Louvre through the glass clockface.

★★[7n-5.] Musée de la Légion d'Honneur/originally Hôtel de Salm-Kyrburg, 64, rue de Lille, between rue de Bellechasse and rue de Solférino. Pierre Rousseau. 1787.

A triumphal arch and a vast courtyard present startling grandeur to rue de Lille: very pompous and vast neo-Romanism. The Seine side, to the contrary, shows a more delicate semicircular pavilion. It has little of the urban grace of the best of the *hôtels particuliers* of the Faubourg Saint-Germain nearby. San Francisco copied it exactly. *Tant pis.*

★★[7n-6.] Palais Bourbon, 126, rue de l'Université, and along rue de Bourgogne and quai d'Orsay, comprising the original Palais Bourbon. Giardini, Lassurance, Jean Aubert, and Jacques-Ange Gabriel. 1722–1728. Hôtel de Lassay also incorporated to the west, Alexandre de Gisors and Frédéric Lecomte. Seine facade, on axis of Madeleine–rue Royale–Concorde, Bernard Poyet. 1807.

A makeshift complex, comprising an *hôtel particulier,* a palace, intermediate additions, and the vast Seine facade. Here sits the Assemblée Nationale, with its own twelve giant columns facing those of the Madeleine, twin mirrors of Roman pomp à la Napoléon I. On the rue de l'Université side (place du Palais-Bourbon) you can savor a very different flavor: that of an entrance courtyard to an urban national assembly. The river side is its public relations poster.

★[7n-7.] Ministère des Affaires Etrangères, 37, quai d'Orsay and 130, rue de l'Université. J. Lacornée. 1845–1853.

One of the few government buildings in this arrondissement that was built to order rather than being a revamping of an existing *hôtel.* Here 19th-century pomp flaunts itself in its inflated architecture. How did they lose the 18th-century panache? In the dusk or evening the great chandeliers make it seem like a stage set for an operetta.

[7n-8.] Aérogare des Invalides/originally Gare des Invalides, quai d'Orsay at Pont Alexandre III, facing esplanade des Invalides. Juste Lisch. 1900. Remodeled for Air France, Paul Bigot. 1945.

A minor event compared to that of the Gare d'Orsay down the quai, this also served to bring passengers to the 1900 Exposition Universelle. Giant Corinthian pilasters give it an outside grandeur. Buses for Orly leave from here.

[7n-9.] Hôtel de Seignelay/now Ministère du Commerce, 80, rue de Lille, between boulevard Saint-Germain and rue de Solférino. Germain Boffrand. 1714.

[7n-10.] Immeuble, 5, rue de Bellechasse, corner rue de Lille. 1930s.

Modern with an almost-*poivrière* (articulated at the top). The *garde-fous* are simple but expressive. And why not stucco?

★[7n-11.] Hôtel du Président Duret/now Caisse des Dépôts et Consignations, 67, rue de Lille, between rue de Bellechasse and rue de Poitiers. 1706. Reconstructed after fire, Marcou. circa 1798.

A somewhat vulgarized reconstruction that provides longer windows, a higher portal, and cruder detail. More is less!

★[7n-12.] Hôtel particulier, 78, rue de l'Université, between rue de Bellechasse and rue de Poitiers. 1687.

Recently restored, this is of an especial grandeur.

★★[7n-13.] Hôtel Pozzo di Borgo, 51, rue de l'Université, between rue de Bellechasse and rue de Poitiers. Lassurance. 1708.

A very grand Tuscan-columned portal stands high. If you are lucky, the great doors will stand open, and you can relish a double-deck order crowned with a pediment.

[7n-14.] Hôtel de Poulpry/now Maison des Polytechniciens, 12, rue de Poitiers, between rue de l'Université and rue de Lille. 1703.

A careful human scale is here extant, rather than pomp and a lusty presence—*except* at the imposing portal.

★[7n-15.] Maison des Dames des PTT, 41, rue de Lille, between rue de Poitiers and rue du Bac. E. Bliault. 1905.

A bit more Jugendstil than Art Nouveau. Angular brick and *pierre de taille* for some not-so-angular ladies. Within is a restaurant, La Télégraphe, where much of Bliault's interior remains. Try it.

[7n-16.] Immeuble, 26, rue de Lille, opposite rue Allent. 19th century.

A remarkable *verrière* floats over an interior courtyard.

[7n-17.] Immeuble, 15, rue de Lille, corner rue Allent. 17th century.

A battered facade, along with Nos. 11 and 13 next door, and lovely original 17th-century ironwork. Look for more.

★[7n-18.] Immeuble, 24, rue de Verneuil, corner rue Allent. 1930s.

Hard-cornered and corbeled bays with contrasting and lovely delicate *garde-fous.* The *pierre de taille* is a bit pocked, as is travertine.

★★[7n-19.] Eglise Saint-Thomas-d'Aquin, place Saint-Thomas-d'Aquin, off boulevard Saint-Germain, near rue du Bac. Pierre Bullet. 1688. Modified and extended, 1722–1769. Facade portal, François-Charles Butteaux. 1769.

A *Jésuitique* facade, as the Parisians would term it, based on Il Gesù in Rome in general but with a cool sense of detail. The old convent, adjacent to the east, is now an army barracks.

★★[7n-20.] Hôtel d'Aligre, 15, rue de l'Université, between rue des Saints-Pères and rue du Bac. 1681.

A wonderful concave-incised, pedimented, and rusticated portal. The streetfront building gives a barrel-vaulted entry into the courtyard.

★[7n-21.] Ecole Nationale d'Administration/formerly Hôtel de Venise, 13, rue de l'Université, between rue des Saints-Pères and rue du Bac. Gobert. 1713.

A dour beard in the key voussoir articulates the rusticated portal. Modern alterations behind have taken away much of the *corps de logis.*

★[7n-22.] **Hôtel de Sennecterre,** 24 rue de l'Université, between rue des Saints-Pères and rue du Bac. **Thomas Gobert.** 18th century.

A lovely ensemble.

[7n-23.] **Immeuble, 46, rue Jacob,** between rue des Saints-Pères and rue Bonaparte. 18th–19th centuries.

Niches house appropriate *neo-Grec* classicism with broken arms as if excavated at **Paestum.** And above, a hemispherical exedra with console-bracketed peering dames.

[7n-24.] **Université de Paris/Faculté de Médecine,** 45, rue des Saints-Pères, corner rue Jacob. **Léon-Joseph Madeleine** and **Jean Walter.** 1937–1953.

Another *retardataire* building suffering from World War II's timing. It has that authoritarian quality that came out of the 1937 exposition, translated into pompous offices in Washington as well as Paris. Unfortunately it is also ill-kempt, a factor that depreciates its image. For better Walter, see **[16h-40.];** and Madeleine scores particularly at **[15e-8.],** the **Villa Garnier.**

[7n-24a.] **Immeuble** and **courtyard, 30, rue des Saints-Pères,** between rue Jacob and boulevard Saint-Germain. 1830s.

**Louis-Philippe** plus a clutch of courtyard columns holding up the sky. Drop in.

★[7n-25.] **Eglise Saint-Vladimir-le-Grand** / originally **Chapelle Saint-Pierre,** 49, rue des Saints-Pères, corner boulevard Saint-Germain, 6th arrondissement. Facade, **Nicolas-Marie Clavereau.** 1790s.

A neo-Baroque portal presents paired Tuscan columns flanked by fasces and surmounted by a coffered vault.

★[7n-26.] **Hôtel de Cavoye,** 52, rue des Saints-Pères, between boulevard Saint-Germain and rue de Grenelle. **Daniel Gittard.** 1640.

The magnificent half-round portal creates a monumental compression of this narrow street.

★[7n-27.] **Fondation Nationale des Sciences Politiques**/originally **Hôtel de Cossé,** 56, rue des Saints-Pères, between boulevard Saint-Germain and rue de Grenelle. **Daniel Gittard.** circa 1660.

Composite columns and pilasters flank the portal to the courtyard.

[7n-28.] **Société de Géographie,** 184, boulevard Saint-Germain, between rue des Saints-Pères and rue de Rennes, 6th arrondissement. **Edouard Leudière,** architect. **Emile Soldi,** sculptor. 1877.

Here even *pompier* became dulled, fatigued with excess.

★[7n-29.] **Hôtel Latitudes Saint-Germain**/originally **Librairies-Imprimeries-reunies,** 7, rue Saint-Benôit, between boulevard Saint-Germain and rue Jacob, 6th arrondissement.

Articulated cast and wrought iron with two en-niched putti at the crest. Technology meets academic sculpture.

**[7n-30.] Immeuble, 26, rue de Seine,** at rue Visconti, 6th arrondissement. 17th century.

Savor the ironwork.

★**[7n-31.] Grande Masse des Beaux-Arts,** 1, rue Jacques-Callot, at rue Mazarine, 6th arrondissement. **Roger Expert.** 1932.

A rather tired modernism forewarning us of this idiom in New York and elsewhere twenty years later. These were originally ateliers for the faculty and students of the nearby **Ecole des Beaux-Arts.**

**[7n-32.] Atelier Delacroix,** 6, place Furstenberg, between rue Jacob and rue de l'Abbaye. **Eugène Delacroix,** designer. 1850s.

The museum occupies his apartment, but travel through to the studio (★★), a modest but entrancing cube with its own garden. Delacroix, although not known as an architect, designed the studio.

★★★**[7n-33.] Eglise Saint-Germain-des-Prés,** boulevard Saint-Germain at rue Bonaparte. Choir, 12th century. Nave vaulting, 17th century. Restorations, **Hippolyte Godde.** 1823. Further fooling around, **Victor Baltard.** 1842–1863.

This is an evolution and amalgam of styles both original and recycled. More a symbol than a great work, it ranks with the Eiffel Tower and Sacré-Coeur in the former status. Nevertheless it is a grand remnant of texture in this district, the very name of which is based on the Abbey of Saint-Germain-de-Prés. The abbey held vast lands and assorted buildings long before there was a boulevard Saint-Germain; the latter is another work of Haussmann and his minions (including Baltard). The tower is a stolid Romanesque symbol that outshines the body of the church.

Don't miss the dual cafés **de Flore** and **des Deux Magots** across the street. These are fancier versions of the original café life of the 1920s and 1930s (ghosts of painters and writers), but mostly filled with tourists from Minneapolis and Neuilly. Down the block at 170, boulevard Saint-Germain, is one of the best bookstores in Paris, **La Hune,** where art books vie with fiction in a wonderful interplay. Architecture, too, is well presented.

# 17
# SEVENTH ARRONDISSEMENT
## WEST

### TOUR EIFFEL TO QUAI D'ORSAY

Tour Eiffel: **Gustave Eiffel, Maurice Koechlin, et al.;** Champs de Mars; Ecole Militaire: **Jacques-Ange Gabriel;** 29, avenue Rapp: **Jules Lavirotte;** rue Saint-Dominique; 151, rue de Grenelle: **Jules Lavirotte;** Conservatoire Municipale VIIe: **Christian de Portzamparc;** Embassy of South Africa; American Church in Paris: **Ralph Adams Cram;** quai d'Orsay; passerelle Debilly: **Louis-Jean Résal**

Métro: **Bir-Hakeim** or **Champs-de-Mars** (RER)

[7w-1.] **Tour Eiffel** (within northwest leg). **Gustave Eiffel.** 1889.

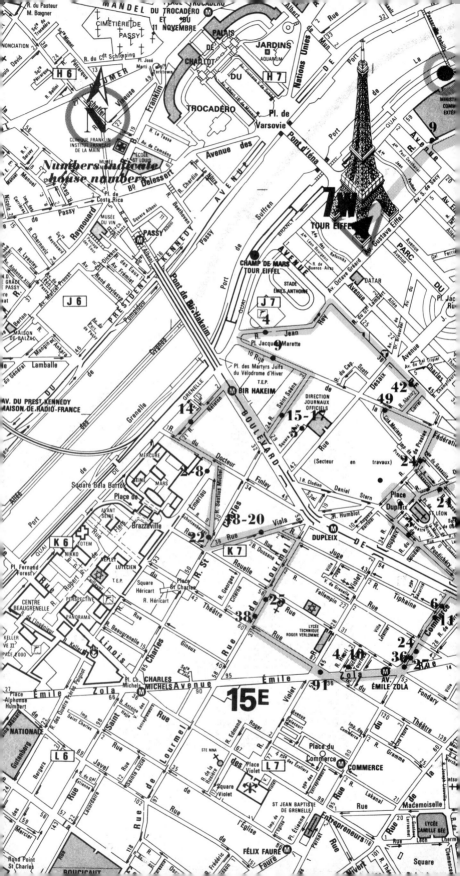

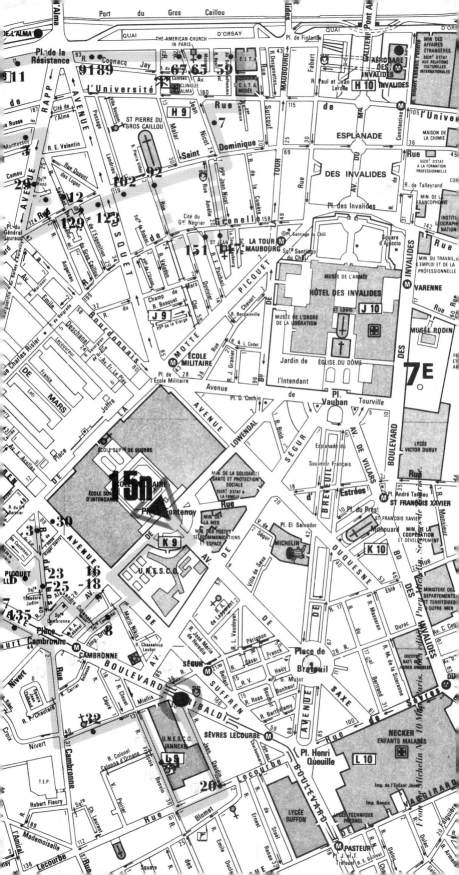

On the grounds of sequential expositions the Tour Eiffel, and the adjacent Champs de Mars, have seen vast competing experiements in architecture, particularly in 1878 and 1889. Strangely, this field of battle, contained at its east end by the **Ecole Militaire** of Jacques-Ange Gabriel, was counterpointed at its west, across the Seine, by the 1878 **Trocadéro** of Gabriel Davioud. The Tour in between did not arrive until 1889, and the Trocadéro was transformed (its skeleton remains within) for the 1937 Paris Exposition by Jacques Carlu and partners. All these essays in militarism, technology, international trade, and architectural experimentation are now one of the more dramatic episodes of the Paris scene.

★★★★**[7w-1.] Tour Eiffel,** on the Champs de Mars near quai Branly. **Gustave Eiffel,** entrepreneur. **Maurice Koechlin** and **Emile Nougier,** engineers. **Stephen Sauvestre,** architect. 1887–1889.

The articulation of roles as entrepreneur, engineer, and architect was still blurred in the 19th century, and that confusion sometimes persists in the 20th. Pier Luigi Nervi and Auguste Perret were principally entrepreneurs whose design talent (and that of their employees) made possible buildings that were both economically competitive and avant-garde.

Eiffel won a competition for the tower and gained a concession for ten years, during which his admission charges reimbursed and profited him, and he gave a percentage to the state. Wildly popular with the public (6 million entries in 1889 alone), it was passionately attacked by the art and architecture establishment, the fading architects of the years of Haussmann and Haussmannian-*tardif.* But as a symbol it rose above its initial self in concert with **Sacré-Coeur,** then under construction. It remains a great icon of French leadership in the development of iron, started at the Gare du Nord, cresting at Les Halles, and here brought to the ultimate fantasy, like a grand and giant Erector or Meccano set.

"An obnoxious column of bolted sheetmetal" was the comment of Contadin, supervising engineer of the exposition.

Sauvestre's role as nominal architect was mostly one of details and decoration. But he was no slouch—look in the index for some of his exotic works elsewhere.

★**[7w-2.] Immeuble, 9, avenue de la Bourdonnais,** corner rue de l'Université. **L. Pechard.** circa 1900.

*Pompier,* the local star in these posh yet severe precincts.

★**[7w-3.] Immeuble, 11, rue Franco-Russe,** between rue de l'Université and avenue Rapp. **E. Scheuret.** 1939.

A hoary stucco that gives a sense of some massive, inert, and dried paste, happily decorated with metal *grillages* in counterpoint.

★**[7w-4.] Immeuble, 3** and **3 bis, rue Franco-Russe,** between rue de l'Université and avenue Rapp. 1890s.

Romanesque Revival in brick, an H. H. Richardson kind of essay for Paris. The crowning studio with its balcony is a glorious place.

★★★**[7w-5.] Immeuble, 29, avenue Rapp,** between rue Edmond-Valentin and avenue de La Bourdonnais. **Jules Lavirotte.** 1901.

His dreams were fulfilled in polychromatic terra-cotta, wood, and sensuous iron doors, with bull's-heads bracketing the balcony and a green-columned arcade on high. Study it, scanning up and up. Lavirotte makes Guimard seem conservative in these years of Art Nouveau.

**[7w-6.] Salle Adyar/Société Théosophiqe de France,** 4, square Rapp, off avenue Rapp, just south of **No. 29.**

A Moorish fantasy that is mild compared to No. 29 around the corner. The dreamworld of theosophy could have made better use of the dreamworlds of Lavirotte.

★[7w-7.] **Liceo Italiano Leonardo Da Vinci/Collège Italien,** 12, rue Sédillot, between avenue Rapp and rue Saint-Dominique. **Jules Lavirotte.** 1899.

A milder and monochromatic Lavirotte, but all his wondrous sinuousity is there is both stone and iron.

★★[7w-8.] **Immeubles, 129-133, rue Saint-Dominique,** straddling rue de l'Exposition. Fountain, **J.-M. Bralle,** architect. **Beauvallet,** sculptor. 1809.

The complex not only straddles the street to form a small exedral *place* but also fills that place with Bralle's neo-Renaissance fountain. Surrounding are Tuscan-pilastered colonnades.

[7w-9.] **Ambassade de Roumanie**/formerly **Hôtel de Behague,** 123, rue Saint-Dominique, corner avenue Bosquet. 1770. Altered, 1866.

A 19th-century adaptation of an 18th-century grand *hôtel particulier.* Its tight streetfront urbanism conceals a gracious garden.

★[7w-10.] **Immeuble, 151, rue de Grenelle,** at cité du Général-Négrier. **Jules Lavirotte.** 1898.

An earlier and ordinary Lavirotte on the street—but buzz in to brick polychromy within. In his and others' early work, daring was exposed in the courtyard, while Haussmannian-*tardif* ensured streetfront propriety. Nevertheless, the entrance doors give something away.

[7w-11.] **Eglise Saint-Jean Evangélique Luthérienne** and **American University in Paris,** 147, rue de Grenelle, between avenue Bosquet and avenue de La Motte–Piquet. Church, **Buhler.** 1911

Neo-Gothic freestanding in an open space—an aspiring greensward without the grass. Behind, a fussy PoMo building is part of the university's stylish espansion.

[7w-12.] **Immeuble, 102, rue Saint-Dominique,** corner passage Landrieu. **Olivier Vaudou** and **R. Luthi.** 1974.

Cut-rate Corbu with sooty gray tilework over a cadaverous set of balconies. Downstairs the **Trésorie Principale** of the 7th arrondissement. How money subverts architecture!

★[7w-13.] **Eglise Saint-Pierre-du-Gros-Caillou,** 92, rue Saint-Dominique, between avenue Rapp and boulevard de La Tour–Maubourg. **Hippolyte Godde.** 1822 and later.

Stocky Tuscan columns and a low profile lead to a barrel-vaulted coffered nave with a gaggle of Tuscan arcades sheltering groin-vaulted aisles. Behind there is another modern nave. So-so.

★★★[7w-14.] **Conservatoire Municipal du Septième Arrondissement,** 7, rue Jean-Nicot, corner rue de l'Université. **Christian de Portzamparc.** 1984.

The precocious de Portzamparc brings to Paris what seems to be a bit of Tokyo, perhaps à la **Tange** or **Maki.** It is an aggressive building, but the incised cul-de-sac between itself and its dormitoried annex is inspired urbanism. But there is too much talent compressed into this tight set of lots.

**[7w-15.] Ambassade de l'Afrique du Sud,** 59, quai d'Orsay, at avenue Sully-Prudhomme. **Gérard Lambé, Jean Thierrat,** and **Jean-Marie Garret.** 1974.

Rapiers form a terrifying wall around this atrocious *kraal,* in an aggressive defense against the blackguards around. The building behind is nevertheless Hollywood modern—with or without its encirclements.

★**[7w-16.] American Church in Paris,** 65, quai d'Orsay, at rue Jean-Nicot. **Carroll Greenough,** with **Ralph Adams Cram** and **Frank W. Ferguson.** 1927–1931.

Neo-Cram—that is, a diluted example of the great neo-Gothic American architect's work unequal to **Princeton's chapel** or the **Cathedral of St. John the Divine.** But it is a quaint American anachronism in a Paris that was slipping concurrently from Roux-Spitz to Le Corbusier.

★**[7w-17.] Immeuble, 67, quai d'Orsay,** corner rue Jean-Nicot. **André Leconte.** 1935.

*Grand standing* with a great bellied corner in travertine and glass. Stylish—and what a fantastic view (from within)!

★**[7w-18.] Immeuble, 89, quai d'Orsay** and **22, rue Cognacq-Jay,** off place de la Résistance. **Michel Roux-Spitz.** 1929.

Sliced ice cream, bay-windowed: a leading participant in the Deco-Moderne rue Cognacq-Jay.

★**[7w-19.] Immeuble, 91, quai d'Orsay** and **26, rue Cognacq-Jay,** facing place de la Résistance. **Léon Azéma.** 1930.

Rustications borrowed from **Palazzo Diamanti,** with fanciful Art Deco balcony metalwork.

**[7w-20.]** Formerly **Ecuries, 11, quai Branly,** west of place de la Résistance. 1864.

Stables for Napoléon III present themselves as a minor palazzo with guarded gates leading to a handsome inner courtyard world. The arcades are powerful. All of it now houses apartments.

**[7w-21.] Centre des Conférences Internationales,** quai Branly, between avenue Rapp and avenue de la Bourdonnais. **Francis Soler.** 1995.

Crystalline boxes will shelter auditoriums, conference rooms, and support facilities in 450,000 square feet (41,600 square meters) of space. All are connected to the Palais de Tokio opposite by the passerelle Debilly.

★**[7w-22.] Passerelle Debilly,** quai Branly to avenue de New-York, between place de la Résistance and avenue de La Bourdonnais. **Louis-Jean Résal.** 1900.

Pedestrian access over the Seine was provided here for the Exposition of 1900 by the same architect who designed the great Pont Alexandre III for that same fair.

# 18
## SEVENTH ARRONDISSEMENT
### SOUTH

#### HOTEL LUTETIA TO LES INVALIDES

Hôtel Lutétia: **Louis-Hippolyte Boileau;** Eglise Saint-Ignace; Au Bon Marché: **Louis-Charles Boileau;** Fontaine Egyptienne; Station de Métro Vaneau; la Pagode: **Alexandre Marcel;** rue de Babylone; Maison Brongniart: **Alexandre Brongniart;** avenue de Saxe; avenue de Breteuil; Hôtel and Dôme des Invalides: **Libéral Bruant, Jules Hardouin-Mansart,** and **Ludovico Visconti**

Métro: **Sèvres-Babylone**

[7s-8.] **Métro Vaneau. Adolphe Dervaux. 1925.**

123

[7s-1.] **Hôtel Lutétia,** 45, boulevard Raspail, corner rue de Sèvres. **Louis-Hippolyte Boileau** and **Henri Tauzin.** 1912.

Art Nouveau detail undulates with bow windows; flowers, leaves, and fruit grow from a flat set of massive *pierre de taille*. But the overall volume is awkward.

★[7s-2.] **Eglise Saint-Ignace,** 33, rue de Sèvres, opposite square Boucicaut. 19th century.

A neo-Gothic surprise concealed behind a banal commercial building. Thus squeezed, its windows are mostly blocked by surrounding Mammon— but of its ilk, not bad! The problem is to find it. **Le Corbusier** had his atelier next door, at **No. 35.**

[7s-3.] **Au Bon Marché (grand magasin),** facing square Boucicaut between rue de Babylone and rue de Sèvres. **Alexandre Laplanche** and **Louis-Charles Boileau,** architects. Metal construction, **Gustave Eiffel** and **Armand Moisant.** 1869–1874. West building, rue du Bac. **Louis-Hippolyte Boileau.** 1920–1923.

Although much of its grandeur as the original *grand magasin* of Paris has vanished with alterations, this was where it all began, before **Magasins Réunis, Galeries Lafayette,** and **Au Printemps.** Thus Zola wrote *Au Bonheur des Dames* (1883) around this building and event. The collection of dozens of departments *(rayons),* with fixed and modest prices within a great architectural carapace, skylit and stylish, was a tremendous change from the myriad small shopkeepers who were the totality before.

★[7s-4.] **Chapelle du Séminaire des Missions Etrangères,** 128, rue du Bac, corner rue de Babylone. **Lebas** and **Claude-Nicolas Dubuisson.** 1691.

A modest facade of Ionic and Corinthian pilasters crowned by a spare and dour *fronton.*

[7s-5.] **Hôpital Laënnac,** 42, rue de Sèvres, between rue du Bac and rue Vaneau. 1878. Chapel, **Christophe Gamard.** 17th century.

The chapel (★) is a modest medieval remnant amid all this quite handsome neo–Henri IV brick and stonework.

[7s-6.] **Chapelle des Lazaristes**/also **Sacristie de Saint-Vincent de Paul,** 95, rue de Sèvres, between rue de l'Abbé-Grégoire and rue Vaneau. 1817.

Bland outside, it is a festival of granite, gilt, red, and blue within. A barrel "vault" hovers.

★[7s-7.] **Fontaine Egyptienne,** opposite 97, rue de Sèvres, between rue de l'Abbé-Grégoire and rue Vaneau. **J.-M. Bralle** and **Beauvallet.** 1810.

Napoléon's campaigns in Egypt unleashed a fury of interest in Egyptification, not the least of which is here. More can be savored at the place du Caire **[2n-5.].**

★[7s-8.] **Métro Vaneau,** opposite 97, rue de Sèvres, between rue de l'Abbé-Grégoire and rue Vaneau. **Adolphe Dervaux.** 1925.

An exotic Art Deco station in *béton armé,* tile, metalwork, and glass gives honor to its pseudo-Egyptian neighbor.

**[7s-9.] Immeuble, 109, rue de Sèvres,** corner rue Saint-Romain. circa 1900.

Lovely articulated bay windows with tiled spandrels.

**[7s-10.] Immeuble, 21** and **21 bis, rue Pierre-Leroux,** between rue de Sèvres and rue Oudinot. **Paul Lahire.** 1908. Tilework *(grès flammé)*, **Alexandre Bigot.**

Distinguished by its raincoat of gray tile, it is dour.

**[7s-11.] Immeuble, 72, rue Vaneau,** between rue de Sèvres and rue Oudinot. **Jules-Jacques Flegenheimer.** 1909.

There is a Tuscan porch at the fourth floor, but most of the surfaces are flat fields for growing vegetation.

**[7s-12.] Boulangerie Azrak,** 56, rue Vaneau, corner rue Oudinot.

Counters with marble neo-Classicism.

**[7s-13.] Immeuble** and **ateliers, 47, rue de Babylone,** between rue Vaneau and rue Barbet-de-Jouy. **Alexandre Fournier.** 1905.

The streetfront building attempts to emulate the *grande bourgeoisie,* and leads through its porte cochère to *colombage* in steel.

★**[7s-14.] Garde Républicaine,** 49, rue de Babylone, between rue Vaneau and rue Barbet-de-Jouy. 1934.

A *cité* of security and residence in elaborate brown-yellow brick, vestigial mansards, deep-revealed *persiennes,* and a series of buildings and courts that runs through to rue Oudinot.

**[7s-15.] Immeuble, 40, rue Barbet-de-Jouy,** just north of rue de Babylone. 19th century.

Pomp in neo-Renaissance dress.

★★**[7s-16.] Cinéma La Pagode,** 57 bis, rue de Babylone, corner rue Monsieur. **Alexandre Marcel.** 1895. Converted to cinéma, 1931.

Originally a reception pavilion for the Chinese embassy, next door at **No. 57,** it brought the traditional Chinese vernacular to Paris. Hardly a pagoda, it is of simple palace architecture, with supporting gardens along rue de Babylone. It is now a movie theater that serves aficionados not of China but of good cinema.

**[7s-17.] Hôtel Lefranc de Pompignan,** 7, rue Monsieur, between rue de Babylone and rue Oudinot. 18th century.

The *corps de logis* with its corbeled neo-Classical heads peers over a smooth entrance wall.

★**[7s-18.] Hôtel de Bourbon-Condé,** 12, rue Monsieur, between rue de Babylone and rue Oudinot. **Alexandre Brongniart.** 1786.

Its Ionic-pilastered body presents austere neo-Classicism. Within is a court of modest stance.

★★**[7s-19.] Maison de Brongniart,** 22, rue Oudinot and 49, boulevard des Invalides. **Alexandre Brongniart.** 1781–1785.

Here Brongniart dwelled, but the Tuscan sextet along boulevard des Invalides has been surelevated.

★[7s-20.] **Immeuble, 50, avenue Duquesne,** between rue Oudinot and avenue de Breteuil. 1930s.

Stolid *pierre de taille* with lovely ironwork and curved window heads of brown tile. The totality is a smooth plasticity.

★[7s-21.] **Ecole Sainte-Elisabeth,** 8, rue Maurice-de-la-Sizeranne and 90, rue de Sèvres. Hotel, 18th century. Additions, 1980s.

New brutalism on the garden side confronts the original château. The former has unfortunate, prissy strip windows and a specious flamboyant mural on the street, but the mass is powerful.

★★[7s-22.] **Studio Bertrand,** 29, rue de Général-Bertrand, between rue de Sèvres and rue Duquesne. 1930s.

Amber travertine with metalwork as sleek as the 1930s could provide. Study the entrance doors, the column, and the number *29.*

[7s-23.] **Immeuble, 62, avenue de Saxe,** between rue de Sèvres and place de Breteuil.

Cast iron and steel from two generations earlier than **No. 58.**

★[7s-24.] **Immeuble, 58, avenue de Saxe,** between rue de Sèvres and place de Breteuil. **Didier Maufras** and **Hervé Delatouche.** 1982.

*A la Corbu.* Of black and white, metal, glass, and tile, it is elegant yet understated. The red half-round balcony is a sassy punctuation. Turn across the street to **No. 57** to see, by contrast, a modern atrocity: PTT. Those grand patrons of the 1930s have become the yahoos of the 1980s.

★[7s-25.] **Immeuble, 8–10, rue Rosa-Bonheur,** corner rue Bouchut. No. 8, **Théodore Petit.** 1904. No. 10, **Noël-Martin et Cousin.** 1903.

Polychromatic brick and glorious multipaned leaded-glass bay windows. A terra-cotta frieze tops each tier of the latter.

[7s-26.] **Fountain/monument, intersection rue Valentin-Haüy and rue Bouchut.** After 1900.

Dedicated to Rosa Bonheur, Valentin Haüy, and others, this presents a mini neo-Baroque *rond-point.*

[7s-27.] **Immeuble** and **crèche, 22, avenue de Breteuil** and **14, rue d'Estrées.** 1980s.

A pretentious corner on the grand mall of the avenue de Breteuil, with clever detailing, mixed with a stylish intermingling of curtain wall and solids. Stop.

[7s-28.] **Maison, 7, avenue de Breteuil,** between rue d'Estrées and place Vauban. 1891.

An anachronistic brick building with iron lintels and cast-iron columns. An infill of floral tile at the cornice enlivens it all. The foundation is of dressed *meulière.*

[7s-29.] **Immeuble, 96, boulevard de La Tour–Maubourg,** north of avenue de Tourville. **E. Dutarque.** 1891.

This and its neighbor, **No. 94,** supply a rich texture to the streets around the Invalides.

**★[7s-30.] Immeuble, 4, avenue de Tourville,** corner boulevard de La Tour–Maubourg. 1890.

**Dutarque** may have struck here as well, with caryatids, bay windows, and wondrous articulations.

**★★[7s-31.] Immeuble, 5, rue Joseph-Granier,** corner avenue de Tourville. 1930s.

The rounded corner still echoes the more elderly *poivrières* but in the manner of the stylish 1930s. The strapwork *garde-fous* are elegant, and— look up! There is an incised Art Deco frieze at the top.

**Les Invalides** is a thirty-one-acre complex that includes the original hospital, or **Hôtel Royal des Invalides,** and two churches, one famous as the tomb of Napoléon, the **Dome;** and another behind it, the **Eglise Saint-Louis-des-Invalides.** Although the *hôtel* has been greatly diminished in hosteling soldiers invalided in the service of France, a small sector of the complex still serves that purpose. Most of the original *hôtel* is now the **Musée de l'Armée** and the **Musée des Plans-Reliefs.**

**★★★★[7s-32.] Dôme des Invalides,** facing avenue de Tourville and place Vauban. **Jules Hardouin-Mansart.** 1679–1706. Alterations for Napoléon's tomb, **Ludovico Visconti.** 1843.

Only **Val-de-Grâce** offers a dome of such Baroque grandeur. Newly regilded, it soars over this whole precinct with a stately and vigorous elegance that is more imposing in posture among its neighbors than either **St. Paul's** in London **(Christopher Wren)** or **St. Peter's** in Rome **(Michelangelo).**
Within it is vast but bland, partially because of its conversion from what might have become an equally ornate Baroque interior (cf. **Val-de-Grâce)** into the tomb of **Napoléon** and his coterie: **Joseph Bonaparte,** elder brother and onetime king of Naples; **Maréchal de Vauban,** marshal and military engineer. And, post-Napoléon, **Maréchal Foch,** hero of World War I.
The normal axis of the nave is interrupted by Visconti's incised sunken court for Napoléon's tomb. This gives the space a centrifugal quality, as you are continuously walking around a central point (Napoléon), from which everything radiates.

**★★[7s-33.] Eglise Saint-Louis-des-Invalides,** between the Dôme and the Cour d'Honneur des Invalides. Designs, **Libéral Bruant.** 1671–1676. Execution, **Jules Hardouin-Mansart.** 1677–1708.

A cold, calculated academic exercise, arched and Corinthian-pilastered within. The flags and pendant lamps attempt luxury, but in a stern and solemn place.
A couple of atlantes support, with the help of gilded cherubs, the silvered Baroque organ, an elegant moment amid blandness.

**★[7s-34.] Hôtel des Invalides,** facing esplanade des Invalides and surrounding the Cour d'Honneur. **Libéral Bruant.** 1671–1676.

Vast rather than fascinating, this was a grand social gesture of Louis XIV to the wounded and mutilated of his successful but bloody wars. Though majestic in scale and posture, it now serves principally as the **Musée de l'Armée** for those interested in the uniforms, armaments, and films of all of France's wars. Another museum, once minor, is now filling the attics of the whole ensemble: the **Musée des Plans-Reliefs** (★★★). Here are models of fortified French cities (more than four hundred existed) that were substantially started under Louis XIV and continued in a minor way to Napoléon III. At a scale of 1:600 (1 inch equals 50 feet), they are vast. The model of Strasbourg, for example, fills what might be a ballroom, and the detail is exquisite, showing every building.

# 19
# EIGHTH ARRONDISSEMENT
## EAST

### GARE SAINT-LAZARE TO LA MADELEINE

Gare Saint-Lazare: **Juste Lisch;** Brasserie Mollard: **Edouard Niermans;** Eglise Saint-Augustin: **Victor Baltard;** Magasins Majorelle: **Henri Sauvage** and **Charles Sarrazin;** Chapelle Expiatoire: **Pierre Fontaine;** Hôtel Suchet: **Etienne-Louis Boullée;** Parkings (sic) Garages de Paris: **Marcel and Robert Hennequet;** Restaurant Lucas-Carton: **Théodore Charpentier** and **Etienne de Gounevitch;** La Madeleine: **Barthélemy Vignon** and **Jean-Jacques Huvé;** Aux Trois Quartiers: **Louis Faure-Dujarric**

Métro: **Saint-Lazare**

[8e-25.] Galerie de la Madeleine. Théodore Charpentier. 1846.

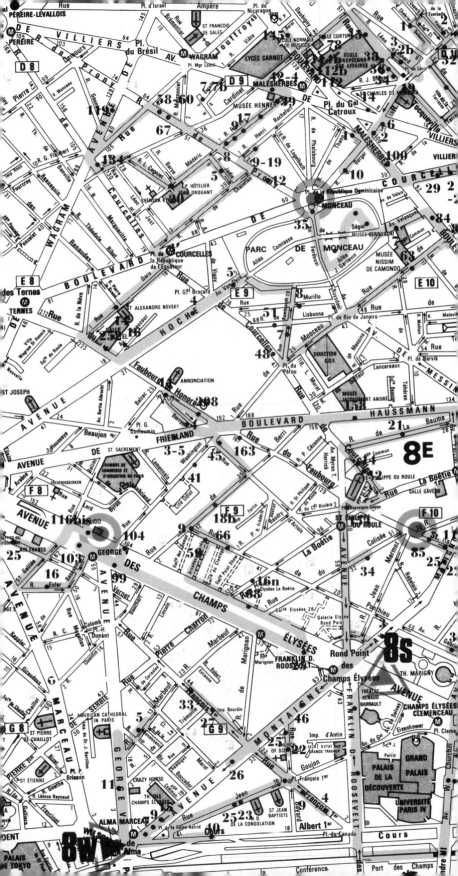

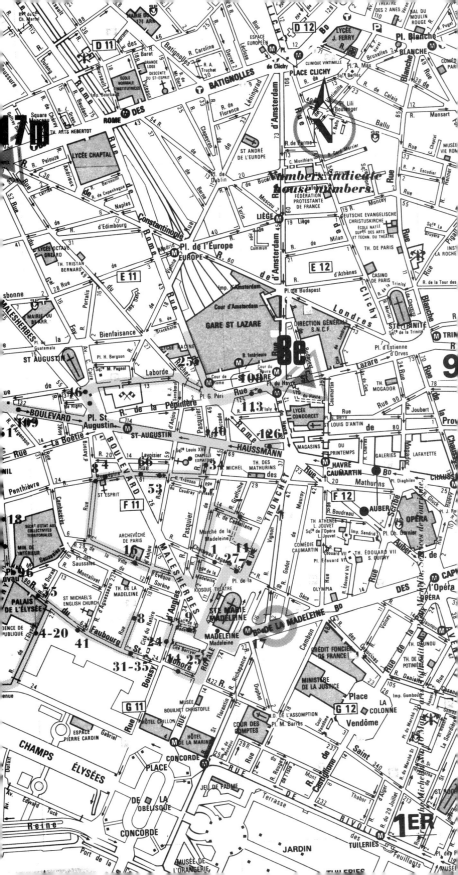

The railroad terminals of Paris are those of an ancient city, where the iron horse, astride its iron road *(chemin de fer),* could be tamed and stabled outside the walls—in this case (in 1832 first at the place de l'Europe) beyond the Grand Boulevards that traced the fortifications of Charles V and Louis XIII. The walls began coming down around 1670, but the lands beyond were still the little-developed *faubourgs* of the city. Cities, like the proverbial Topsy, always grew far faster and farther than any city or railroad planner first thought. The *gare* (and its five extant sibling stations) is surrounded by the 19th century and is now in effect "downtown."

★[8e-1.] **Gare Saint-Lazare,** 108, rue Saint-Lazare, between rue de Rome, rue de Londres, and rue d'Amsterdam. **Juste Lisch.** 1889. Minor renovations, 1930 and 1936.

This terminal does not lead one to any of the cities honored by surrounding streets; that is the function of the Gare du Nord. Never inspiring, the Gare assumed a romance when steam was still with us, and the diffuse impressionist paintings of **Monet** sanctified it in architectural memories, if not the architectural present. To see its best profile, walk up the rue de Rome past rue de Stockholm, look back, and there is the iron-and-glass that marks the soul of Parisian terminals, anchored by a corner stair tower that is much more exhilarating than the ponderous facade. In the plaza at each end, flanking the station hotel, the **Concorde Saint-Lazare,** are towers of the detritus of travelers, luggage to the west, clocks to the east, by the sculptor, **Arman.** Banal.

★[8e-2.] **Hôtel Concorde Saint-Lazare**/originally **Hôtel Terminus. Juste Lisch.** 1889.

The hotel and its terminus were completed for the Exposition of 1889, in consonance with the Eiffel Tower; but here the engineering wonders are restricted to the train shed behind all the terminal's pompous stone and to the elegant bridge that connects the hotel and terminal. The latter was apparently thought only utilitarian by Lisch and the Compagnie des Chemins de Fer de l'Ouest and lives on in sprightly and lithe elegance.

Inside the hotel lobby is a grandiose two-story space, with flamboyant Beaux Arts ornament: but technology lurks even here: at the right and left sides are cast-iron columns, worthy of Baltard's nave at Saint Augustin; and the walls are cast and glazed terra-cotta. Good grief, M. Lisch, there was a dangerous radical in your office.

[8e-3.] **Lycée Racine,** 25, rue de Rome and 20, rue du Rocher, between rue Saint-Lazare and rue de Stockholm. 1887.

A dour Jugendstil facade of a girls' high school that reaches through the block to the rue du Rocher. The stern facade is appropriate to this surrogate parent.

★★[8e-4.] **Brasserie Mollard,** 113, rue Saint-Lazare, between rue de Rome and rue du Havre. **Edouard Niermans,** architect. **Hubert et Martineau,** enamelists. 1895.

Mosaic, mirrors, and a compartmentalization of space give an endless quality to this small and vintage Belle Epoque restaurant.

★★[8e-5.] **Eglise Saint-Augustin,** 46, boulevard Malesherbes, between rue de Laborde and rue de la Bienfaisance. **Victor Baltard.** 1860–1871.

A splayed volume follows the spreading streets, and a framework of iron columns within (separate from the stone piers that they articulate) supports trussed iron arches, with filigreed metalwork infilling the dome's pendentives. Clever and rational, with precocious technology—and ugly. We need

Baltard's **Les Halles,** not this. The church at Farnborough, England, is a copy made for Napoléon III's family (in exile after 1871).

**[8e-6.] Cercle National des Armées de Terre, de Mer, et de l'Air,** place Saint-Augustin and rue de la Pépinière. **Charles Lemaresquier.** 1927.

Classical/Modern, officially Art Deco because of the date. It is ponderous and pompous, with a frieze of empty armor (vacated warriors) alternating with windows: the warriors are the triglyphs, the windows the metopes.

**[8e-7.] Papeterie, 109, boulevard Haussmann,** between rue d'Argenson and rue Roy.

Elegant. The graphics are party to the rich, carved architectural detail.

**[8e-8.] Logements, 51, rue Miromesnil,** between boulevard Haussmann and rue La Boétie. circa 1910.

Non–load-bearing caryatids voluptuously entertain the arriving visitor, a prolix ornamentation encrusting it all: the kind of vulgarity that one throws into an urban meal, the extra patisserie that nobody "needs" but can't resist. The diamond rustications recall Italy (see also the **Hôtel Fournier [17m-9.]**).

**[8e-9.] La Union et le Phénix Espagnol,** 40, rue Pasquier, corner boulevard Haussmann. 1931.

A flamboyant corner but no-nonsense on its side street. Atop is a bronze phoenix and a boy.

★★★**[8e-10.] Magasins Majorelle,** 126, rue de Provence, corner rue de Rome. **Henri Sauvage** and **Charles Sarrazin.** 1913.

Each level of this marvelously pristine and precocious *magasin* has a differing vocabulary. *Rez-de-chaussée:* storefront; 1st and 2nd: curtain walled; 3rd: balconies; 4th: bay windows; 5th: setback terrace; 6th: setback-some-more terrace. The only characteristic of Sauvage that relates to his distinguished housing is the setback of terraces at the top. But this is his most beautiful and sophisticated building.

★★**[8e-11.] Square Louis XVIe** and **Chapelle Expiatoire**/originally **Cimètiere de la Madeleine,** bounded by boulevard Haussmann, rue Pasquier, rue des Mathurins, and rue d'Anjou. **Pierre Fontaine.** 1826.

Here victims of the revolutionary guillotine were buried in quicklime, including **Louis XVI, Marie-Antoinette, Phillipe Egalité, Charlotte Corday, Madame du Barry, Danton,** and **Lavoisier.** Sold in 1797, the land came into the hands of a former royalist lawyer who later gave it to the restored Crown. And in 1815, the king and queen's remains were transferred to Saint-Denis. Louis XVIII then commissioned this chapel to expiate the tragedy of their fate.

In the neo-Palladian interior only symbolic biers remain. The coffered dome and exedra, and the statues (Louis XVI, **François Joseph Bosio;** Marie-Antoinette, **J. P. Cortot**) are rich neo-Romanism.

The complex is eerie, a floating island of symbolism in this ill-used park.

**[8e-12.] Bayerische Vereinsbank,** 34, rue Pasquier, corner rue des Mathurins. **Alexandre Fournier,** architect. **G. Saupique,** sculptor. 1929.

Neo-Classic, with a *comble* of three tiers overseeing the **Chapelle Expiatoire.** The bas-reliefs of exotic birds, animals, and fish (camel, elephant, alligator, shark, tiger, dolphin, eagle) are scattered ornaments intended to enrich bare architecture in this period when architecture and sculpture had taken separate paths.

★[8e-13.] Logements, 53, rue des Mathurins, corner rue d'Anjou. F. Farge. 1927.

Haussmannian-*tardif* is still viable two years after the Exposition of 1925 that heralded Art Deco. But *tardif* is a mild tag for this extravagance, complete with griffin atlantes and an icicle cascade. Le Corbusier's **Villa La Roche** and **Villa Jeanneret [16a-44.]** were already three years old; Mallet-Stevens completed his named street in the 16th arrondissement the same year.

★★[8e-14.] Maison de rapport, 32, boulevard Malesherbes and 66, rue des Mathurins. circa 1862.

With its cylindrical conservatories (sun rooms for some, plant rooms for others) for the lucky residents, this iron-and-glass assemblage makes a grand corner anchor. It precedes the rage for bay windows that came into play largely with a new law (1892) allowing "intrusions" into the volume of the street, making them "free" space for the developer. Here everything is within the property bounds.

[8e-15.] Logements, 4, rue Roquépine, between boulevard Malesherbes and rue d'Astorg. **Jacques Vitry.** 1982.

Variegated sandstone on this denuded block of flats. The play of scale (two stories versus one) is an asset, but the "mansard" is an affectation.

[8e-16.] Hôtel particulier, 8, rue Roquépine, corner rue d'Astorg. 1857.

An older generation's three-story-and-comble *hôtel*.

★★[8e-17.] Hôtel Alexandre or Hôtel Suchet, behind 16, rue de la Ville-l'Evèque, between rue d'Astorg and rue d'Anjou. **Etienne-Louis Boullée.** circa 1763.

Behind the gross building of the **Compagnie La Hénin** is secreted Boullée's only extant Paris work (the Chapelle du Calvaire de l'Eglise Saint-Roch was drastically altered in the 19th century). Here Boullée built a grandly columned hotel, neo-Classicism at its best. Pass though Hénin's lobby.

[8e-18.] Maison Henriette, 1, rue Chauveau-Lagarde, just west of place de la Madeleine. Founded, 1848.

The remains of an Empire storefront.

★★[8e-19.] Marché de la Madeleine, 7, rue de Castellane, through to 11, rue Tronchet. **Marcel and Robert Hennequet.** 1936.

The inner world of this market is a wonder of Art Deco, deep behind the posh rue Tronchet facade and equally tucked in back of the Restoration block on rue de Castellane. The lettering at Castellane's arched entry is one of the few "decorations" that architects "played with" in the denuded 1930s.

[8e-20.] Originally **Hôtel de Pourtalès,** 7, rue Tronchet, between place de la Madeleine and rue de Castellane. **Jacques-Félix Duban.** 1836.

The collector James-Alexandre Pourtalès-Gorgier commissioned this neo-Renaissance *hôtel particulier* for himself and his art collections (Etruscan works, glassware, paintings).

★[8e-21.] Parkings(sic) **Garages de Paris/Galerie Commerciale,** 27, place de la Madeleine, at rue Chauveau-Lagarde. **Marcel and Robert Hennequet.** 1932.

The paired columns and glazed cylinder shielding a spiral stair are jointly the knuckle, around which circulating cars and people reach the garage and shops behind. Together with **Aux Trois Quartiers** at the southeast corner of the *place*, this represents modernity at the Madeleine.

[8e-22.] **Epicerie Hédiard,** 21, place de la Madeleine, at rue de Sèze. circa 1850.

And don't miss the contents of **Fauchon** next door.

[8e-23.] **Confiserie Tanrade,** 18, rue Vignon, between place de la Madeleine and rue Tronchet.

★★[8e-24.] **Immeuble** and **Restaurant Lucas-Carton**/originally **Restaurant Scaliet,** 9, place de la Madeleine, southwest corner boulevard Malesherbes. *Immeuble,* **Théodore Charpentier.** 1846. Restaurant interiors, **Etienne de Gounevitch,** architect. 1903. Storefront, **Raymond Subès.** 1924.

Rich, sinuous Art Nouveau woodwork is a luscious counterfoil to the ornate and expensive food.
The craftsman **Planel** executed the sculpted woodwork "with his hand alone, imparting after forty months of unceasing work, [his] unique stamp, and a perfect homogeneity, to the ensemble of this masterly decor." Gounevitch's interior is sometimes ascribed to **Majorelle.** The facade, or storefront, is not the original but was added by Carton in 1924.

★★[8e-25.] **Galerie de la Madeleine,** 9, place de la Madeleine (see [8e-24.] above). **Théodore Charpentier.** 1846.

Classical arches span the bays of skylights. An upper-class *passage*, compared to those of the 10th arrondissement.

★★[8e-26.] **Eglise Sainte-Marie-Madeleine**/or **La Madeleine,** rue Royale, boulevard Malesherbes, rue Tronchet, and boulevard de la Madeleine. **Barthélemy Vignon.** (d. 1829). **Jean-Jacques Huvé.** consecrated, 1845.

Both Alexander the Great and Napoléon set out to conquer the world. In the former's case Greek culture, in the form of Hellenistic art and architecture, was left behind after later centuries of retreat. In the latter's case, the retreat came after only five years, but power was recorded by this originally-named **Temple de la Gloire,** which could almost be one of Alexander's discards (Ephesus, Sardis).
It all started as part of the ensemble remembering Louis XV (see place de la Concorde); but the first church, in the form of a Latin cross (**Pierre Constant d'Ivry.** plans, 1764), was succeeded by one Greek (**Guillaume Couture.** 1777–1789). The building at this time was considered as a new National Assembly, a Bourse, a National Library, and finally Napoléon's Temple of Glory, modified under the Restoration as a church.

★[8e-27.] **Cité Berryer,** 25, rue Royale and 24, rue Boissy-d'Anglas, just south of the place de la Madeleine.

Here is a passage, a sideline to the surrounding grandness, a bit of an older Paris.

★[8e-28.] **Immeuble, 14, rue du Faubourg-Saint-Honoré,** between rue Royale and rue Boissy-d'Anglas. 18th century.

Elegance on the street leads to a charming commercial courtyard. One of the truly venerable buildings along this stretch of strained (much refaced and redone) street.

★[8e-29.] **Aux Trois Quartiers (magasin), 17–25, boulevard de la Madeleine,** corner rue Duphot, off place de la Madeleine. **Louis Faure-Dujarric.** 1932. Drastic alterations, **Archi-Déco.** 1989.

A chic corner in black and white, it sought to be as up-to-date as its merchandise—who would seek the latest fashions under the dowdy cast iron and glass of **Printemps?** Everyone does now, but architectural style and the stylishness of *la mode* have diverged. The shop will be reduced to a minimum, the conversion and extensions rendered more profitable as very-high-rent offices.

# 20
# EIGHTH ARRONDISSEMENT
## WEST

### PLACE DE L'ALMA TO CHAMPS-ELYSEES

Pont et place de l'Alma; Théâtre des Champs-Elysées: **Henry van de Velde** and **Auguste Perret;** Eglise Notre-Dame-de-la-Consolation: **Daniel Guilbert;** 9, place François Ier: **Henri Labrouste;** Magasin Rochas: **Ricardo Bofill;** La Fermette Marbeuf; Eglise Saint-Philippe-du-Roule: **Jean-François Chalgrin;** boulevard Haussmann; Musée Jacquemart-André: **Henri Parent;** Bâtiment Shell: **Lucien Bechman;** Arcades du Lido: **Lefèvre, Julien & Duhayon;** Bâtiment Guerlain: **Charles Méwès,** Hôtel de la Païva: **Pierre Manguin,** Restaurant Fouquet, Théâtre Normandie: **Jean Desbouis**

Métro: **Alma-Marceau**

**[8w-3a.] La Fermette Marbeuf (restaurant). 1900.**

The **Pont de l'Alma** is a newcomer, the ancient one completed in 1855, the modern one in 1974.

**[8w-1.] Embassy of the People's Republic of China,** 11, avenue George V, between place de l'Alma, and avenue Pierre-Ier-de-Serbie.

A *grand hôtel particulier* that reeks of neo–Italian Renaissance trappings. China houses its proletarian puritanism in distinguished dress, analagous to those posh British buildings on Shanghai's Bund, bordering the Hwang Pu River. The proletariat from Russia, unfortunately, had less regal ideas and constructed their FBI-style headquarters in the 16th arrondissement.

**[8w-2.] Hôtels particuliers, 7,** and **9, avenue Montaigne,** between place de l'Alma and rue du Boccador. No. 9, **Ernest-Félix Trihle** and **Guinot.** 1883.

Here are 17th-century revivals for those in need of a past. No. 7 is more convincing in the scale of its dormer-attic-mansard and in its elegant bellied wrought-iron *garde-corps.* No. 9, however, is signed.

★★★**[8w-3.] Théâtre des Champs-Elysées,** 15, avenue Montaigne, between place de l'Alma and rue du Boccador. **Henry van de Velde,** design architect. **Auguste Perret,** follow-up architect. **Perret Frères,** builders. 1913. Restaurant surelevation, **Bertrand Bonnier.** 1990.

Somewhat modified (there were no windows at first), cleaned, and restored, this is marble-cased reinforced concrete, a wondrous principal auditorium within, the route to it served by lighting fixtures by **Lalique,** sculpture by **Bourdelle,** and a subtle neo-Classicism that invents elegant "moderne" capital and base junctures for the fluted structural columns. Perret, invited to be contractor, eased out van de Velde (the original director of the school that became the Bauhaus).
The Grand Théâtre seats 2,000. Two other halls share the volume: the Comédie (655 seats), over the main lobby, and the Studio (257 seats), above that. Their foyer is honored with paintings of **Vuillard.**
The *surélévation* is a banal box that looks like a cubistic goiter from afar. Hopefully it may be demolished, as the theater is a *classé* building.

---

In an interview published in *L'amour de l'art* in May 1925, Perret inveighed against the Art Deco exhibition, held that year: "Decorative art is to be suppressed. I would first like to know who joined these two words: art and decoration. It's monstrous. Where there is true art there is no need of decoration. What's necessary in art is nudity, beautiful ancient or medieval nudity. Under the pretext of making art decorative, they put ornaments everywhere and even go so far as sculpting columns, something that one has never seen done [in the past]. . . .
"I certainly allow in a handsome building a fresco intended to illustrate that edifice, to specify its purpose, but only in the reveals, in order to allow the framework to retain all its purity. That's why at the Théâtre des Champs-Elysées I allowed the bas-reliefs and frescos of Bourdelle, those of Roussel and of Marval."

---

★★**[8w-3a.] La Fermette Marbeuf (restaurant),** 5, rue Marbeuf, corner rue du Boccador. 1900.

An interior of extravagant stained glass and iron, blessed with a wondrous luminosity where gastronomy and architecture meet with vigor. The main room is original, the others simulated.

★[8w-4.] Logements, 40, cours Albert Ier, between place de l'Alma and rue Bayard. **Louis and Albert Feine,** architects. **Lalique,** glass-maker. 1903.

Lalique not only lived here and signed the facade but also created the translucent bas-reliefed glass-and-metal entrance doors. Floral bas-reliefs in stone further decorate the entry surrounds, and way above, architecture gives way to a François Ier silhouette, as modified by some eccentricities. Can one be an avant-garde eclectic?

[8w-5.] Offices, 25, rue Jean-Goujon, between place de l'Alma and place François Ier. **Pierre Parat** and **Michel Andrault.** 1964.

Zilch.

★[8w-6.] Eglise Notre-Dame-de-la-Consolation, of the Missione Cattolica Italiana, 23, rue Jean-Goujon, between place de l'Alma and place François Ier. **Daniel Guilbert.** 1901.

An Italian neo-Baroque attack on the Parisian streetfront presents a monumental staired exedra, next door to the "modern" offices at **No. 25.** Here the two fulfill the paired notion of the sublime and the ridiculous: **No. 23**'s talented flamboyance next to a block striving to be at least banal.

★[8w-7.] Place François Ier, collecting rue François Ier, rue Jean-Goujon, and rue Bayard. 1865.

A minor roundabout *(rond-point)* with a pallid fountain (**Gabriel Davioud.** 1865), confronted by six streets and six buildings seeking status. At **No. 14** rests the **Hôtel de Clermont-Tonnerre,** in neo–Louis XV trappings, the least boring of the surrounding ensemble.

[8w-8.] Hôtel de Vilgruy, 9, rue François Ier, at place François Ier. **Henri Labrouste.** 1865.

Only two years younger than his **Bibliothèque Nationale,** this was either bread-and-butter Labrouste or a product of an attitude, sometimes common: that dwellings shared the costumes of history, while places for thought and ceremony would be experimental environments.

[8w-9.] Logements, 4, rue François Ier, between cours Albert Ier and place François Ier. **Jean-Marie Boussard.** 1860s.

Neo-Renaissance.

★[8w-10.] Logements and **Magasin, 26, avenue Montaigne,** between rue François Ier and rue Clément-Marot. **Louis Duhayon.** 1938.

A swelling and undulating facade (disfigured at its base by the supposedly stylish pretensions of **Christian Dior**) gives life to the street within the same envelope as its original Haussmannian neighbors (but they have departed also).

[8w-11.] 27, rue François Ier, between avenue Montaigne and rue de La Trémoille.

★[8w-12.] Bâtiment Rochas, 33, rue François Ier, between rue de La Trémoille and rue Marbeuf. **AURA-3.** 1974. Reconstructed, **Ricardo Bofill.** 1989.

The AURA-3 facade was a pallid cross of off-white and gold, glass and some neo-neo-Classicism. This was a cheap shot for style. On the other hand,

Bofill proposed a "classic facade with a modern expression . . . treated in the manner of a jewel." Sorry, Ricardo, it is merely *banal:* the word as defined by **Robert Venturi.**

**[8w-13.] Offices, 25, rue Bayard,** at avenue Montaigne. **Roger Anger.** 1965.

Saw-toothed, for offices of grander-than-ever standing.

**[8w-14.] Radio-Télévision Luxembourg (offices),** 22, rue Bayard, between avenue Montaigne, and place François Ier. **Jacques Starkier** and **V. Vasarely,** graphicists. 1971.

An optic facade masks history, suggesting a disco world of more pretension than permanence. This is Times Square without Broadway.

★**[8w-15.] Logements, 46, avenue Montaigne,** between rue Bayard and avenue des Champs-Elysées. **R. and H. Bodecher.** 1930s.

A flowering of Art Moderne: balconies as petals punctuate this *grand standing.*

**[8w-16.] Logements** and **café, 3, avenue Matignon,** between avenue des Champs-Elysées and rue Ponthieu. **R. and H. Bodecher.** circa 1930.

The streetscape dominates this swath of cafés so much that one rarely bothers to look up at the parent buildings. Here is a lesser effort of Bodecher Frères, whose talent is better displayed at 46, avenue Montaigne, above.

★**[8w-16a.] Hôtel de la Païva**/now **Travellers' Club,** 25, avenue des Champs-Elysées, **Pierre Manguin.** 1860s.

Neo-Renaissance floridity, now somewhat debased by a *bureau de change* and its wall. Here is nouveau-riche affluence of the mid-nineteenth century, with bas-reliefs too low, too timid, and too much—all at one time. Look to the **Hôtel Massa** at the **Observatoire** for substantial qualities of the **Champs-Elysées** in its heyday.

**[8w-16b.] Le Boeuf sur le Toit (restaurant),** 34, rue du Colisée, between avenue Franklin-D.-Roosevelt and rue du Faubourg-Saint-Honoré.

A venerable restaurant.

★★**[8w-17.] Eglise Saint-Philippe-du-Roule,** 154, rue du Faubourg-Saint-Honoré, at avenue Franklin-D.-Roosevelt. **Jean François Chalgrin.** 1774–1784. Alterations, side aisles, **Hippolyte Godde.** 1845. Chapel of the Catechism, **Victor Baltard.** 1853.

Four neo-Classical Tuscan columns are pedimented toward the place Chassaigne-Goyon. Within is an exedral apse in Ionic splendor. This is a "temple," convincing in a way that **La Madeleine,** that remembrance of inflated Rome (or the dying Hellenism of Asia Minor), is not. Here, less is more; and modesty is appropriate.

★**[8w-18.] Maison, 12, rue de Courcelles,** between rue La Boétie and rue de La Baume. **Bernard Poyet.** 1812.

A modest Empire house, opposite the apse of Saint-Philippe. When the two were young, this whole neighborhood retained such a modest scale.

**[8w-19.] Passage commun, 14, rue de Courcelles,** between rue La Boétie and rue de La Baume.

An inner-stabled courtyard worth looking at for another glimpse of inside Paris urbanity. The maids and coachmen once lived in the *combles*, now as chic as the mews of London.

**[8w-20.] Maison, 21, rue de La Baume,** between rue de Courcelles and avenue Percier. **Auguste Bluysen.** 1903.

An austere outpost of Art Nouveau at the scale of a coach house.

★★**[8w-21.] Musée Jacquemart-André,** 158, boulevard Haussmann, between rue de Téhéran and rue de Courcelles. **Henri Parent.** 1860–1875.

Edouard André, a banker, married the portrait artist Nélie Jacquemart and brought her here six years after the hôtel's completion. Widowed in 1894, she was resident until her death in 1912, bequeathing building and contents to the Institute of France. The building and its interior are, jointly, a museum of painting and sculpture—as well as of the owners: a rich remembrance of grand *hôtels particuliers* of wealthy 19th-century philanthropists. The stairwell is an extraordinary neo-Baroque ensemble.

★**[8w-22.] Logements, 163, rue du Faubourg-Saint-Honoré,** at avenue de Friedland and boulevard Haussmann.

Glassy with steel and crystalline bay windows, upgraded by a new PoMo entrance gate. The side elevation, laced with an articulating grid and pierced with studio windows, owns the light and volume of this entry "garden" space.

★**[8w-23.] Hôpital Beaujon,** 208, rue du Faubourg-Saint-Honoré, between boulevard Haussmann and avenue Hoche. **Nicolas-Claude Girardin.** 1784.

Once the banker Nicolas Beaujon's philanthropic school for poor children, this has passed on to more bureaucratic things: Ecole Pratique des Gardiens de la Paix. The rusticated portal retains Girardin's touch.

★★**[8w-24.] Fondation Nationale des Arts Graphiques et Plastiques**/originally **Hôtel Salomon de Rothschild,** 11, rue Berryer, at rue du Faubourg-Saint-Honoré. **Léon Ohnet.** 1878. later, **Justin Ponsard.**

A grand *hôtel particulier* for this Anglo-French banking family. The gardens, later expanded, include the lands of Balzac's (demolished) house at 22, rue Balzac, and conserve (newly sited) the **Chapelle Saint-Nicolas** (architect: **Nicolas Beaujon**) (★★★) from Balzac's garden. Enter the garden proper at the corner of rues Balzac and Beaujon.

★**[8w-25.]** Originally **Bureaux de la Société Coty,** 4, rue Berryer, between avenue de Friedland and rue du Faubourg-Saint-Honoré. **Edmond Hugues.** 1930.

*Moderne* with Classical twinges, such as the railings and the gilt plaques facing the bay windows. However, a heavy hand was here.

★**[8w-26.] Offices, 3-5, avenue de Friedland,** between rue Washington and rue Lammenais. **Emile-Louis Viret.** 1928.

Doric forms merge into a bay-windowed facade above a bland, Tuscan-columned entry. Look up—the whole building is a mortuary temple of commerce to the coming crash of 1929.

**[8w-27.] Bâtiment Shell,** 45, rue d'Artois, corner rue Washington. **Lucien Bechmann.** 1932.

A Classical-Moderne pile with few redeeming graces save its internal plumbing: the pits of the period. This is an American import, from the period when Chicago wheat barons were sullying the memory of **Sullivan** (Louis Henry) with Classicized Modern.

**[8w-27a.] Immeuble, 41, rue Washington,** between avenue de Friedland and rue Lamennais. **Emile-Louis Viret.** 1928.

Tuscans at the base, a great Doric-moderne order above, on this rear facade of 3–5, avenue de Friedland.

**[8w-28.] Offices, 18 bis, rue de Berri,** between rue d'Artois and rue de Ponthieu. **Maurice Novarina.** 1978.

A flagrant intrusion onto the street: sleek, smooth, naïve, and egocentric.

**[8w-29.] Croix Rouge Française,** 9, rue de Berri, opposite rue de Ponthieu. **G. Acs** and **M. Natale.** 1969.

Precast brown mullions, with a speckled aggregate, corniced with blocky bays. Included to remind you how awful the 1960s were, worse than the 1970s.
    **No. 6** opposite is even less convincing and serves as entrance to another of the garish Champs-Elysées passages.

★**[8w-30.] Garage, 66, rue de Ponthieu,** between rue de Berri and rue Paul-Baudry. **Louis Dehayon** and **Julien.** 1935.

A graceful melding of garage and apartments above; the latter bay-windowed, bold, and still (if you gave it all a supercleaning) stylish. Perret's garage down the block, demolished in 1970, was *the* modern history-book event (51, rue de Ponthieu. **Auguste** and **Gustave Perret.** 1907), automated in the spirit of the new automobiles. Now, of course, garages are merely ramped warehouses. No. 66, however, is one of the best of its class.

★★**[8w-31.]** Arcades du Lido/originally **Arcades des Champs-Elysées,** 59, rue de Ponthieu, between rue de Berri and rue La Boétie. **Lefèvre, Julien, & Louis Duhayon.** 1925.

Ten years before the garage at **No. 66,** these architects composed the only wonderful passage/arcade left on the Champs-Elysées, with Classical-Composite columns and vaulted skylights. Though overcluttered with shops and light-standards, it retains, hovering over all that commerce, a carapace in neo-Renaissance cast iron and glass, in the manner of the Petit Palais.
    But how many other architects could also make the transition from Classical to Cubism in ten years?

★**[8w-32.] Bâtiment Guerlain,** 68, avenue des Champs-Elysées, between rue du Colisée and rue La Boétie. **Charles Méwès.** 1913.

Here the bay window in iron, black and articulate, enlivens the rich *pierre de taille.* The happy marriage of the Beaux Arts with French avant-garde technology is manifest in the exterior this time, the inverse of the Petit Palais's monumental exterior and glassy interior.
    In the words of Paul Chemetov: "It is the social, if not architectural, apotheosis of the bow window: originating in a petit bourgeois conception of space, it takes its place at last on the capital's chic avenue, and for the headquarters of a very 'Parisian' product: perfume. Better still, it is the

architect of banks, of great hotels (fittings of the Ritz in Paris, construction of the Carlton in London) and of transatlantic liners, who built it."

---

**IGN** (Institut Géographique National) is just around the corner at 107, rue La Boétie. Here you can find detailed maps of most of France and, better still, a variety of Paris maps: the classic **Turgot** (1730), a bird's-eye from the northwest; **Blondel's** latest bird's-eye from the southeast (either just central Paris or the whole works); a marvelous color photograph in plan of the whole city; various Michelin maps of Paris; and assorted ancient maps that illustrate, for example, the Ile de la Cité before the razing and rebuilding by Haussmann's minions.

---

**[8w-33.] Offices, 104, avenue des Champs-Elysées,** corner rue Washington. **Alexandre Durville.** 1895.

Perhaps this is what it all should have been: flamboyant and pompous, the architecture of power, whether business or governmental. A pompous avenue should have equally pompous architectural support. Look at Moscow and East Berlin: they learned of great avenues from Paris and lined them with bland, banal, bulky, and boring behemoths. The Champs-Elysées as a whole is almost as bad. At least you can look at the overpriced automobiles in endless show windows or immerse yourself in the movies.

**[8w-34.] Fouquet's (restaurant),** 99, avenue des Champs-Elysées, corner avenue Georges V.

An anchor for the Champs-Elysées, it has been a stylish presence stanching the crass commercialism surrounding. Some Kuwaitis bought it, but let's not despair; they may have more sense than dollars.

★**[8w-34a.] Crédit Commercial de France**/originally **Elysées-Palace Hotel,** 103, avenue des Champs-Elysées, between rue de Bassano and rue Galilée. **Georges Chédanne.** 1899.

Eight grand *lucarnes* face the avenue, each with twin Composite columns supporting a hollow neo-Baroque pediment. Floral relief sculptures, festoons, and putti play around the oculi at the street.

**[8w-35.] Logements, 16, rue Euler,** between avenue Marceau and rue de Bassano. 1930s.

Neo–Art Nouveau in its wrought-iron esses, the subsurface is Art Moderne. Here is style in a stylish sense, making it prominent on the street. Would Euler understand?

★**[8w-35a.] Hôtel Vernet,** 25, rue Vernet, between rue Galilée and place Charles-de-Gaulle. **A. Sélonier.** 1913.

A shell-formed iron-and-glass marquise displays handsome ironwork. Atop is a fourth-floor balcony with four vigorous Tuscan columns. In sum, a handsome Belle Epoque hotel.

★**[8w-36.]** Originally **Bureaux de la Poste**/then **Théâtre Normandie.** 116 bis, avenue des Champs-Elysées, between rue Washington and rue Balzac. **Jean Desbouis.** 1929.

This was a smashing addition to the avenue, its saw-toothed bay windows granting views to the inmates from the Arc de Triomphe to the Obelisk at place de la Concorde. And for the stroller, the lively facade brought some life to this too wide and too blandly homogeneous avenue. Many of the details have been "suppressed," such as the elegant ground-floor granite detailing and the chrome balcony railings. The bays of the first floor have also been extinguished by the urgent need of the cinéma within to flaunt its billboards. Otherwise, this is a major modern monument, mostly secreted from tourists and tourisms, for who looks up?

# 21
# EIGHTH
# ARRONDISSEMENT
## SOUTH

### ROND-POINT DES CHAMPS-ELYSEES

### TO AVENUE GABRIEL

Rond-Point des Champs-Elysées; Grand-Palais: **Henri Deglane** and **Charles Girault;** Petit Palais: **Charles Girault;** pont Aléxandre III: **Jean Résal;** United States Embassy/Hôtel de Pontalba: **Ludovico Visconti;** British Embassy Annex: **Grandhomme;** Palais Elysée: **Claude Mollet;** Hôtel de la Vaupalière: **Collignon**

Métro: **Franklin D. Roosevelt**

**[8s-16.] Résidence Marigny**/formerly **Hôtel de Rothschild.** 1885.

★[8s-1.] **Théâtre du Rond-Point,** avenue Franklin-D.-Roosevelt and avenue des Champs-Elysées.

The modest Greek Revival exterior hides the timber bones of the **Barrault-Renaud** theater, constructed for the interior vastness of the old Gare d'Orsay and transported here to infill this former ice skating rink. The architecture is within, infilling its carapace in the manner of a hermit crab.

★[8s-2.] **Palais de la Découverte,** avenue Franklin-D.-Roosevelt, between rond-point des Champs-Elysées and cours la Reine. 1937.

A western extension of the Grand Palais, here are thirty-two Composite-capitaled columns: sixteen pair, reminiscent in posture of the grand porch by **Perrault** that fronts the east end of the Louvre. The glazed terra-cotta frieze is a vulgar cartoon (or, alternately, perhaps not vulgar enough).

★[8s-3.] **Pont Alexandre III,** straddling the Seine between avenue Winston-Churchill and the axis of the Invalides. **Louis-Jean Résal,** architect. **d'Alby,** engineer. 1900.

Tsar Alexander III placed the first stone at a time of superb Franco-Russian relations, 1898, the year that brought us toward the edge of the twentieth century and its equivocation between perceived historical grandeur and technology; this great single span straddles the issue. For, unlike the glassy envelopes of the two **Palais,** concealed partially behind vast Beaux Arts facades, here are swags, lanterns, and structure in metal: an imperial bridgework connecting the exposition to the **Invalides.**

★★★[8s-4.] **Grand Palais,** avenue Winston-Churchill, between pont Alexandre III and avenue des Champs-Elysées. Facades, **Henri Deglane.** Iron and glasswork behind, **Charles Girault.** 1900.

Here is the ultimate crossbreeding of the Ecole des Beaux-Arts and technology. The facades are appropriately academic, grand, and a bit pompous. But within is iron and glass that sings a paean to wondrous developments in Paris from the **Gare du Nord** to **Beaubourg.**

★★[8s-5.] **Petit Palais,** avenue Winston-Churchill, between pont Alexandre III and avenue des Champs-Elysées. **Charles Girault.** 1900.

The technological extravagance of the Exposition of 1889, crowned by the Eiffel Tower, is veneered here, as with the neighboring Grand Palais, with extravagant pseudo-neo-Classicism, masked under the rubric: Ecole des Beaux-Arts.

★[8s-6.] **Théâtre Marigny,** avenue de Marigny, between avenue des Champs-Elysées and avenue Gabriel. **Charles Garnier.** 1883.

Although substantially remodeled, this remains one of Garnier's most modest and articulate works, a cool neo-Grec with a polygonal geometry that seems like an inflated **Tower of the Winds** (from Athens' Hellenistic times).

★[8s-7.] **Immeuble, 38, avenue Gabriel,** between avenue de Marigny and rue du Cirque.

The annex, to the right, bears four Ionic columns worthy of Jacques-Ange Gabriel himself.

[8s-8.] **Gardens, Palais de l'Elysée,** along avenue Gabriel, between avenue de Marigny and rue de l'Elysée. *Grille,* **du Coq.** 1900.

Grand gardens *à l'anglaise* serve the president's palace, with ironwork added at the turn of the century.

★[8s-9.] Maisons, 4–20, rue de l'Elysée, between avenue Gabriel and rue du Faubourg-Saint-Honoré. 19th century.

A handsome terrace in the English sense, complete with Classical porches and steps in cast iron. Here are some of Napoléon III's London memories.

[8s-10.] Ambassade des Etats-Unis/originally Hôtel de Pontalba/ later Hôtel de Rothschild, 41, rue du Faubourg-Saint-Honoré, between rue de l'Elysée and rue d'Aguesseau. Ludovico Visconti. 1842. Massive alterations, F. Langlois. late 19th century.

For the casual passerby, there is a monumental portal, twin-columned, flanking a central arch.

★[8s-11.] Annexe Ambassade de Grande Bretagne, 31–35, rue du Faubourg-Saint-Honoré, between rue d'Aguesseau and rue d'Anjou. Grandhomme. 18th-19th centuries.

At No. 31 there is a wonderful courtyard with a wrought-iron entrance canopy.

[8s-12.] Immeuble, 8 rue d'Anjou, between rue du Faubourg-Saint-Honoré and rue de Surène. Mazin. 1827.

Lafayette lived here in his dotage, which doesn't make for architectural grandeur, but there is a handsome courtyard. Buzz yourself in.

★★[8s-12a.] Palais de l'Elysée/originally Hôtel d'Evreux, 55–57 rue du Faubourg-Saint-Honoré. Armand-Claude Mollet. 1718. Expanded, J.-M. Alexandre Hardouin. 1740s. Later, Lassurance (1755), Boullée (1773), Paris (1787), Vignon (1805), Percier and Fontaine (1808+), Meunier (1848+), Lacroix (1857), Debressenne (1879 and 1896), et al., inside.

Residence of the president since 1873. Little can be seen, save the moments of arrival and departure of the president, his entourage, and his guests. Napoléon I, Tsar Alexander, the Duke of Wellington, Napoléon III, and numerous presidents have lived here.

★★[8s-13.] Hôtel Beauvau/now Ministère de l'Intérieur et de la Décentralisation, 96, rue du Faubourg-Saint-Honoré, on axis of avenue de Marigny. Nicolas Lecamus de Mézières. circa 1770.

A triumphal gate and Tuscan columns lead to magnificent 18th-century gardens behind the dour place Beauvau.

[8s-14.] Immeuble, 5, rue de Miromesnil, between rue du Faubourg-Saint-Honoré and rue de Penthièvre.

Doric pilasters and a fan-tympanum composing draped arrows remember the Revolution of 1789.

★[8s-15.] Immeuble, 18, rue de Miromesnil, between rue du Faubourg-Saint-Honoré and rue de Penthièvre. 18th century.

The cobbled court behind reeks of 18th-century *parfum.* And in front a simple Doric-pilastered entry bears dentiled lintels, friezes at both the first and second floors, and a handsome cornice at the third. All in all, it is understated elegance.

★[8s-16.] Hôtel de Rothschild/now **Résidence Marigny,** 23, avenue de Marigny, between avenue Gabriel and rue du Faubourg-Saint-Honoré. 1885.

This inflated *hôtel* now serves as a grand guesthouse for guests of the president, whose own house as guest of the French Republic is across the street, at the **Elysée.**

★[8s-17.] **Bureaux, 22, avenue Matignon,** between rue du Faubourg-Saint-Honoré and avenue Gabriel. **Vittorio Mazzucconi.** 1976.

This startling abstraction in metal, glass, and stone was intended to be an urban folly. But the only thing here meriting the idea of folly is the idea of doing it at all. This facade originally advertised its inhabitants: J. Walter Thompson (advertising), who, perhaps, have appropriate talents for the ephemera of TV, movie advertising, and the like, but shouldn't be permitted to commit instant ideas to the permanent street.

★★[8s-18.] **Hôtel de La Vaupalière,** 25, avenue Matignon, between rue du Faubourg-Saint-Honoré and avenue Gabriel. **Collignon.** 1761.

An *hôtel particulier* complete with part of its garden-street frontage. This is an exceptional remnant of a scale that one can see in group context only in the Marais or the Faubourg Saint-Germain.

[8s-19.] **Immeuble, 118, rue du Faubourg-Saint-Honoré,** corner avenue Matignon. 18th century.

Buzz in to the courtyard past the ironwork and a face-adorned voussoir keystone.

[8s-20.] **Immeuble, 85, rue du Faubourg-Saint-Honoré,** between avenue Matignon and rue Jean-Mermoz. **Poliakoff.** 1941.

A strange intermarriage of a Tuscan-Palladian shop with oculi and neo-Classic severity. It seems that 1941, for Poliakoff (see the index), was the year of Albert Speer.

# 22

# NINTH ARRONDISSEMENT

## WEST

### LA NOUVELLE ATHENES:

### LA TRINITE TO PLACE PIGALLE AND BACK

Eglise de la Trinité: **Théodore Ballu;** Casino de Paris; rue Ballu;
Hôtel Ballu: **Théodore Ballu;** 21, rue Blanche: **Charles Girault;** rue
de la Tour-des-Dames; Hôtel de Mlle. Mars: **Ludovico Visconti;** Hôtel
de Mlle. Duchesnois: **Auguste Constantin;** Musée Gustave Moreau;
square d'Orléans; place Saint-Georges; Hôtel Dosne-Thiers: **Alfred
Aldrophe;** Musée Renan-Scheffer; la Nouvelle-Athènes; avenue
Frochot; Cité Malesherbes; 68, rue Condorcet: **Eugène Viollet-le-Duc;**
Eglise Notre-Dame-de-Lorette: **Louis-Hippolyte Lebas;** La Grande
Synagogue: **Alfred Aldrophe**

Métro: **Trinité**

**[9w-13.] Ecole Nationale Supérieure des Arts et Techniques du
Théâtre. Charles Girault.** 1901.

149

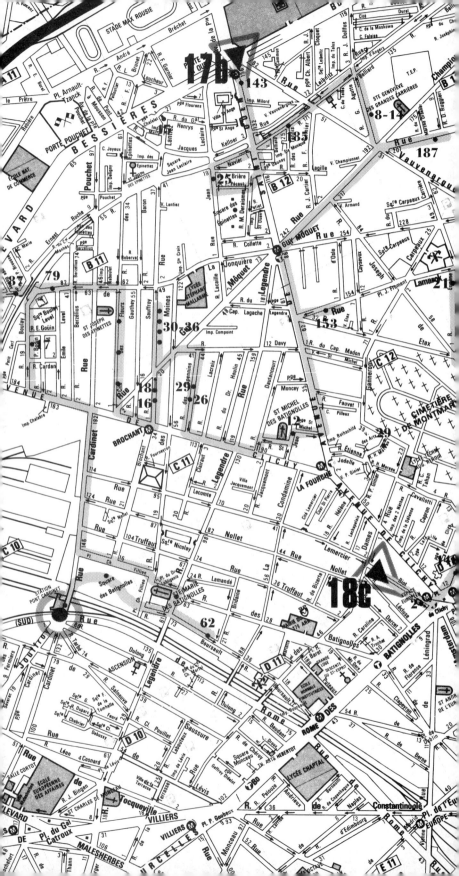

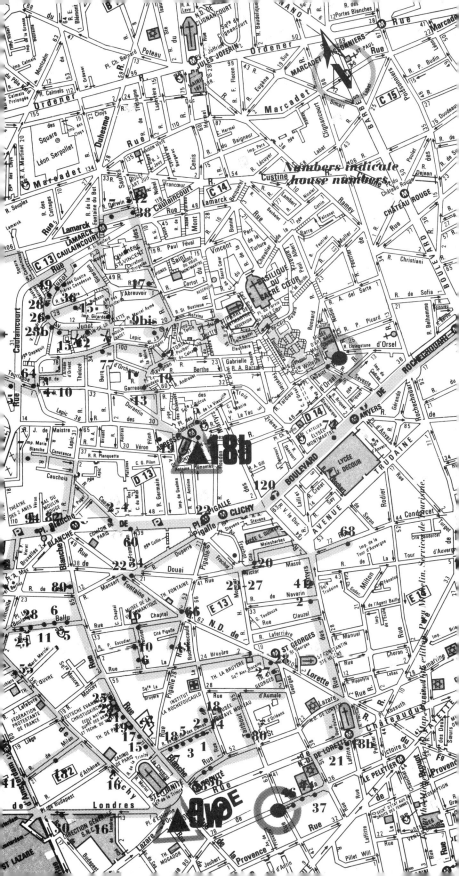

Numbers indicate house numbers

"There is a quarter that seems to have been built with a fairy's wand: Notre-Dame-de-Lorette. It's true that what's going on adds to the fantasy of it all. As if responding to Victor Hugo's challenge, the architects went to work and each found a developer who presented plans of houses: Italian, Spanish, Greek. It was as if the archives of Jean Goujon, Raphael, and Palladio had suddenly been discovered and reopened."

**Alexandre Dumas**

★★[9w-1.] **Eglise de la Trinité,** square de la Trinité, at junction of rue Blanche, rue de Clichy, rue Saint-Lazare, and rue de Châteaudun. **Théodore Ballu.** 1863–1867.

The pompous Gothic Revival of Ballu was instigated here by Haussmann, who wanted Gothic for the churches that punctuated his new Classical boulevards. Ballu's other major Parisian public work is the **Hôtel de Ville [4s-4.]**, recreated (1874–1882) as a replica of the 16th-century original.

★[9w-2.] **Mutuelle de Mans (bureaux),** 16, rue de Londres, between square de la Trinité and rue d'Amsterdam. 1881.

Some welcome commercial pomp on this boring street; columns, rustications, and other eclecticisms abound.

[9w-3.] **Immeuble Vals,** 30, rue de Londres, between rue de Clichy and rue d'Amsterdam. **H. Baranton.** circa 1920.

Pre-PoMo in tile, with a facade of stylized water. Vulgar and fascinating.

[9w-4.] **Androuet (restaurant),** 41, rue d'Amsterdam, almost opposite rue de Milan.

Handsome neo-Gothicisms harbor a marvelous local restaurant.

★[9w-5.] **Immeuble, 28, rue de Liège,** between rue d'Amsterdam and rue de Turin.

Elegant neo-Gothic hooded lintels in a field of carved and unpainted stone. The tendency to paint, rather than clean, is a sorry fate for good *pierre de taille.*

[9w-6.] **Immeuble, 18, rue de Milan,** between rue d'Amsterdam and rue de Clichy.

Post Modern flamboyance contrasts with an ancient balcony in a childish exercise that should have remained on the drawing board.

★[9w-7.] **Casino de Paris,** 16, rue de Clichy, between rue de la Trinité and rue Moncey. **Edouard Niermans.** 1890. Remodeled, 1922.

*Retardataire* Art Nouveau undulates around some elegant—and some banal—stained glass. The ground floor was subjected to a tawdry defacing. Josephine Baker was the greatest star in the vast space within.

★[9w-8.] **Théâtre de l'Oeuvre,** in cité Monthiers at 55, rue de Clichy between rue Jules-Lefebvre and rue de Parme. Cité, **J. Mesta.** 1905. Theater, 1892.

The *cité* was a later envelope for this once avant-garde theater, founded by Lugné-Poe: a high-relief remembers him. Works of Strindberg and Ibsen appeared here first for French audiences. Beyond the theater is a handsome block of ateliers. Follow your nose, and you will emerge on the rue d'Amsterdam—but return to rue de Clichy.

★★[9w-9.] **Rue Ballu,** between rue de Clichy and rue Blanche. A wild, wild street, a summation of the bad and the beautiful.

> ★**No. 28. Studio des Variétés. Sczermaux.** 1891. Bizarre Dutch Revival housing a school for singers.
> ★★**No. 23. Villa Ballu.** Here, at **Nos. 5** and **8,** are private hotels with treed gardens. The entry building harbors an Art Nouveau insert into its rez-de-chaussée.
> **No. 11 bis. Société des Auteurs et Compositeurs,** founded in 1777 by Beaumarchais.
> **No. 6. Immeuble. Jacques Bonnier.** 1932.
> **No. 5. Police Plus.** Symmetrical buildings flank a passage to a main building behind. **G. Brevet.** 1868.

But in between are some unmentionables.

[9w-10.] **Hôtel Ballu,** 78–80, rue Blanche, between rue de Douai and rue Mansart. **Théodore Ballu.** 1870s.

Neo-Renaissance. Like many of his 19th-century colleagues, Ballu speculated in real estate, here along the rue Blanche.

[9w-11.] **Deutsche Evangelische Kirche,** 25, rue Blanche, between rue La Bruyère and rue Pigalle. 1899.

Romanesque Revival with a heavy Germanic hand.

★[9w-12.] **Immeuble, 23, rue Blanche,** between rue La Bruyère and rue Pigalle. **Charles-Georges Raymond.** 1934.

The Art Moderne representative in this eclectic string of buildings, with bay windows glancing up and down the street.

★[9w-13.] **Ecole Nationale Supérieure des Arts et Techniques du Théâtre,** 21, rue Blanche, between rue La Bruyère and rue Pigalle. **Charles Girault.** 1901.

Beaux Arts bowed and bellied stone and glass. Note the Palladian window and a lovely *marquise.*

★[9w-14.] **Société des Ingénieurs Civils,** 19, rue Blanche, between rue La Bruyère and rue Pigalle. **Delmas.** 1896.

A blend of metal and glass and a Classical *pompier* frame that speaks of engineers beaten down by architects. When the two professions split at the beginning of the 19th century, those engineers who worked with architects were largely subjugated (as here), while those who worked alone built the great bridges, towers, and exposition halls of the time: **Eiffel, Paxton, Brunel,** and their peers.

[9w-15.] **Hôtel particulier, 17, rue Blanche,** between rue La Bruyère and rue Pigalle. 1830s.

A vestige of the Collège Chaptal.

[9w-16.] **Théâtre de Paris,** 15, rue Blanche, between rue La Bruyère and rue Pigalle. early 19th century.

The senior member present hereabouts.

★[9w-17.] Immeuble, 58, rue Saint-Lazare, between rue Blanche and rue de La Rochefoucauld. 1829.

A neo-Classical game in pink and gray, recently polychromatically restored. It seems to be an immigrant from Noto, that Sicilian city that forms a stage set for Greek Revival. The painter **Paul Delaroche** lived here.

[9w-18.] Immeuble, 56, rue Saint-Lazare.

A building that serves as portal to a handsome mews, with access to **Nos. 3, 5, 7,** and **9, rue de la Tour-des-Dames** at its end.

---

**La Nouvelle Athènes**

According to François Thiollet in *Choix de maisons . . . de Paris . . .* , "the quarter named the New Athens is made up of rue Saint-Lazare, rue de La Rochefoucauld, and rue de la Tour-des-Dames; it has for its developer Mr. de La Peyrière." His goal was "to create private houses according to the dictates of various financial situations, to arrange them so as to preserve forever a considerable volume of air that, by means of established rules, cannot be altered or diminished, to assemble, whenever possible, select people with a reputation acquired in letters, science, or the army; finally to publicize our young and talented architects by setting up some kind of competition that they could later take advantage of, thereby receiving an opportunity to show what they were capable of." De la Peyrière's master planner-architect was **Auguste Constantin** (1791–1842).

The war for Greek independence, which began in 1821, was certainly the emotional catalyst for creating this sea of Greek Revival architecture. "Nouvelle Athènes" was later applied to a larger area, extending from rue Blanche to rue des Martyrs, from rue Saint-Lazare to place Pigalle.

---

★★[9w-19.] Hôtel de Mademoiselle Mars/originally Hôtel Maréchal Gouvion Saint-Cyr, 1, rue de la Tour-des-Dames, corner rue de La Rochefoucauld. **Ludovico Visconti.** 1820.

The rue de la Tour-des-Dames facade has been drastically altered, from one of three arches flanked by windows, in the manner of **Brunelleschi,** to this Georgian pastiche. The only extant detail is the cornice and its dentils. On the garden, however, the arcade remains.

★[9w-20.] Hôtel de Lestapis, 2, rue de la Tour-des-Dames, between rue de La Rochefoucauld and rue Blanche. **Biet.** 1823.

A **Petit Trianon** in its miniature park, not part of the strictly New Athens development.

★★[9w-21.] Hôtel de Mademoiselle Duchesnois, 3, rue de la Tour-des-Dames, between rue de La Rochefoucauld and rue Blanche. **Auguste Constantin.** 1820.

The great exedral entry is reminiscent more of English Regency than anything Greek—original or revived. It is Classical Revival in spirit, where Greek geometry, rather than literal Greek architecture, is applied as the underlying ideal.
Decrepit.

[9w-22.] Maison de Horace Vernet, 5, rue de la Tour-des-Dames, between rue de La Rochefoucauld and rue Blanche. **Louis-Pierre Haudebourt.** 1822.

A lesser effort in this *lotissement.*

**[9w-23.] Maison de Paul Delaroche,** 7, rue de la Tour-des-Dames, between rue de La Rochefoucauld and rue Blanche. **Auguste Constantin.** 1835.

Vernet's son-in-law joined Vernet thirteen years later.

**[9w-24.] Compagnie Parisienne de la Distribution d'Electricité,** 18, rue de la Tour-des-Dames, between rue de La Rochefoucauld and rue Blanche. 1930s.

**Peter Behrens** remembered. Art Nouveau and *meulière* join in this ode to electrical technology. Was the EDF ever so classy?

★★**[9w-25.] Musée Gustave-Moreau,** 14, rue de La Rochefoucauld, between rue Saint-Lazare and rue d'Aumale. **Albert Lafon.** 1890s.

Rustications, Tuscan columns, and an empty niche are the detritus of this Italianate neo-Renaissance palazzo in which an affluent romantic painter lived and worked. The open staircase between the two gallery floors offers some stimulating vistas.

**[9w-26.] Immeuble, 18, rue de La Rochefoucauld,** between rue Saint-Lazare and rue d'Aumale. **M. Julien** and **Louis Duhayon.** 1930.

Limpid Classical-Moderne.

★★**[9w-27.] Square d'Orléans,** 80, rue Taitbout, between rue Saint-Lazare and rue d'Aumale. **Edward Cresy.** 1832–1842.

This speculation by the English architect and civil engineer Edward Cresy was built largely of that very English material, brick—only to be revived in Paris in the neo-Renaissance *hôtels* of the Plaine de Monceau fifty years later; but the latter arose more from an Henri IV revival.

The square, now entered off rue Taitbout, was originally entered from rue Saint-Lazare. The most notorious tenants were George Sand **(No. 5)** and Frédéric Chopin **(No. 9)**. Sand wrote in *Histoire de ma vie* that "the kindly Marliani had arranged for us to lead a family life. She occupied a handsome apartment between ours [i.e., **No. 7**]. We had only to cross a large courtyard, planted, sanded, and always neat, to get together, sometimes at her place, sometimes at mine, sometimes at Chopin's when he was disposed to play. We dined together at her house, sharing expenses. It was a very good arrangement, economical like all such partnerships, and it enabled me to see people at Mme. Marliani's, to receive my own friends more intimately at my place, and to return to my work when it was appropriate to withdraw."

★**[9w-27a.] Immeuble à loyer, 28, place Saint-Georges,** along rue Notre-Dame-de-Lorette. **Edouard Renaud,** architect. 1840. **Desboeufs** and **Garraud,** sculptors.

Thérèse Lachmann, the marquise de Païva, rented an apartment here in 1851–1852, prior to constructing her new mansion at 25, avenue des Champs-Elysées **[8w-16a]**. Neo-Renaissance and brocaded, the detail is hyperrich—too much of a good thing.

★**[9w-27b.] Hôtel Dosne-Thiers,** 27, place Saint-Georges, along rue Notre-Dame-de-Lorette. **Alfred Aldrophe.** 1873.

This is the second Hôtel Thiers; the first was demolished by the Commune in 1870. Now part of the Institut de France, this shelters the Bibliothèque Thiers and the **Fondation Dosne-Thiers.** Savor the garden behind.

**[9w-28.]** Hôtel particulier, 6, rue Henner, between rue La Bruyère and rue Chaptal. A. Feydeau. 1854.

A town house in tan sandstone.

**[9w-29.]** Immeuble, 10, rue Henner, between rue La Bruyère and rue Chaptal. circa 1930.

The bayed ensemble and its Art Deco supporting console brackets give *moderne* plasticity to these offices.

★★**[9w-30.]** Musée Renan-Scheffer, 16, rue Chaptal, between rue Blanche and rue Pigalle. 1820.

Enter into a private cobbled world with an ocher Italianate villa, twin studios (for the illustrator and "romantic" painter Ary Scheffer and his brother Henry), a conservatory, peace, and birds. Born in Holland, Ary Scheffer came to Paris at the age of sixteen (in 1811). His house is a vestige of another Paris, both in plan and scale.

**[9w-31.]** Hôtel, 5, cité Pigalle, 43, rue Pigalle, between rue Chaptal and rue La Bruyère.

A high rise Classical revival *hôtel* (above the first cornice) with two grand studios and a frieze from the **Parthenon.**

★**[9w-32.]** Hôtel particulier, 66, rue Pigalle, north of rue Notre-Dame-de-Lorette. Street building, 1854. *Hôtel* in court, **Rousseau.** 1788.

The building secreted within is a charming Palladian *hôtel*, columned and pedimented.

★**[9w-33.]** Immeuble, 22, rue de Douai/formerly **Hôtel particulier de Georges Bizet,** at intersection of rue Duperré and rue Fontaine. 19th century.

An extravagant Palladian/Beaux Arts block, shared by three streets. Great Corinthian pilasters embrace the first and second floors, over a *rez-de-chaussée* and *entresol.* Push the buzzer and enter.

★**[9w-34.]** La Poste (restaurant)/formerly part of **Hôtel particulier de Georges Bizet,** 34, rue Duperré, between rue Fontaine and place Pigalle.

Once demoted to a station of the PTT, this is now described as *le dernier-né des lieux hyper-mode de Pigalle,* featuring music (ranging from jazz to bel canto), drinking, eating, and billiards. Caryatids, great mirrors, and "oriental" paintings abound, but for four hundred francs there must be something more than food.

**[9w-35.]** Immeubles, 23, 25, 27, rue Victor-Massé, between rue Henri-Monnier and rue des Martyrs. **Davrange** and **Durup.** 1847.

The best is at **No. 27,** where neo-Renaissance virtuosity presents, for 19th-century Paris, a very glassy facade.

★**[9w-36.]** Avenue Frochot, between rue Victor-Massé and place Pigalle. 1830s.

A luxurious treed place of serenity abutting place Pigalle. Garishness, as on boulevard de Clichy, can sometimes be only skin-deep. But that is Paris: you can enter from a tawdry world into a lovely one in many places, where crass streetfronts conceal gardens and buildings of delight.

★★[9w-37.] Cité Malesherbes, 20, rue Victor-Massé, between rue Frochot and rue des Martyrs. 1900.

A luscious loop of *hôtels particuliers,* including:

No. 3. 1920s surelevation.
No. 11. Adolphe Jay, architect. Jollivet, sculptor. A psychedelic affair with a technological neo-Renaissance.

★[9w-38.] Cité des logements, 41–47, rue des Martyrs, between rue Victor-Massé and rue de Navarin. A. L. P. Blot. 1848.

A Louis-Philippe superblock embracing a treed lawn. Cool, cold, formal, distant, quiet. Check those corners, more recently borrowed by Ricardo Bofill.

[9w-39.] Immeuble, 2, rue de Navarin, corner rue des Martyrs. Joseph Charlet et Michel. 1903.

The local Haussmannian-*tardif.*

[9w-40.] Immeuble, 68, rue Condorcet, between rue des Martyrs and rue Rodier. Eugène Viollet-le-Duc. 1862.

Viollet-le-Duc (1814–1879) lived here from the building's birth until *his* death. The single caryatid (how do we know it's female?) is at once a structuralist and amusing stroke.

---

## Les Lorettes

Lorette was a euphemism for the young "kept" woman who permeated this quarter, bringing style—and stylish lovers—to the surrounds. Eugène Delacroix wrote to George Sand in 1844 (they were both longtime residents), "This new neighborhood has been created to daze a young man as hotblooded as I am. The first thing that struck my eyes on arriving was a magnificent Lorette of the finest kind, decked out in satin and black velvet, who, in descending from her carriage and as carefree as a goddess, let me see her leg up to the navel."

The Lorettes were instruments of real estate development and speculation by default. The fashionable bourgeois were reluctant to leave such favorite areas as the Faubourg Saint-Germain, and the lovely Lorettes filled this new precinct as lovers of those gentle- or not so gentlemen who would follow with their families. As Balzac noted in *Béatrix,* the Lorettes were the driving force in its development and construction: "Without the Aspasias of Notre-Dame-de-Lorette, there would not have been as many houses in Paris. Pioneers of new plasterwork, and conspicuous for their own speculation, they came to the hills of Montmartre, planting pegs for their tents, let it be said without a play on words, in the loneliness of the carved rubblestone that furnishes these streets . . . architectural steppes where the wind shakes countless signs that underscore the emptiness of it all with the words *Apartments to Rent!*"

---

★★[9w-41.] Eglise Notre-Dame-de-Lorette, 18 bis, rue de Châteaudun, between rue Notre-Dame-de-Lorette and rue Saint-Georges. Louis-Hippolyte Lebas. 1823–1836.

A Greek Revival hardness envelops a Roman portico; compare the Maison Carrée at Nîmes. Inside, thirty-four Ionic columns will remind you of an early Christian basilica and the ceiling supplies mock 17th-century Baroque coffering in gold and blue. When you've had enough of architectural pastry, but hunger persists, cross rue Bourdaloue to the left of the church, seeking No. 7, where the pâtissier Bourdaloue holds forth with sustaining *edible* pastry.

**[9w-42.] Bureaux, 21, rue de Châteaudun,** corner rue Laffitte. **Raymond Février.** 1933.

The rather pompous limestone-and-glass neo-Classicism borrowed from American examples of the era. For its peer, see the Shell building **[8w-27.]**

★**[9w-43.] Caisse Centrale de Réassurance,** 37, rue de la Victoire, corner rue Saint-Georges. **Jean Balladur** and **Benjamin Lebeigle.** 1958.

For its time, a valiant effort; in ours, it seems to represent the "bloated *paquebot* blues." "Modern" architecture in a dominant historical context has suffered most: its authors were not taught about context, and the stars, such as **Le Corbusier,** sought to destroy the streets of Paris. An *A* for effort—but we wish your building were not there.

★**[9w-43a.] Grande Synagogue,** 44, rue de la Victoire, also facing rue Saint-Georges. **Alfred Aldrophe.** 1865–1874.

A dour Romanesque Revival favored by 19th-century Jewry, whether in Paris, London, or New York (certainly not in Jerusalem). **Théodore Ballu** allegedly assisted in developing the plans, and **Gustave Eiffel** is said to have suggested the structure of the glass roof.

★**[9w-44.] Hôtel particulier**/now **Bains Chatereine,** 46, rue de la Victoire and 39, rue de Châteaudun. 1830.

Through the block by building . . . court . . . *corps de logis* . . . court . . . building . . . an essay in the multiple private internal worlds of Paris.

# 23
# NINTH
# ARRONDISSEMENT
## SOUTHWEST

### OPERA, GRANDS MAGASINS, GRANDES BANQUES,
### GRANDS BOULEVARDS

Palais Garnier: **Charles Garnier;** Café de la Paix: **Alfred Armand**
and **Charles Garnier;** boulevard des Capucines; place Edouard VIIe:
**Henri-Paul Nénot;** Printemps: **Paul Sédille, René Binet,** and
**Eugène Wybo;** Lycée Condorcet: **Eugène-Théodore Brongniart;**
Galeries Lafayette: **Georges Chédanne, Ferdinand Chanut,** and
**Pierre Patout;** Société Générale: **Jacques Hermant;** Eglise
Evangélique: **Crétien Gau;** Mairie: **Charles-Etienne Briseux;**
passages Verdeau/Jouffroy: **J. P. M. Deschamps** and
**François-Hippolyte Destailleur;** Musée Grévin: **Eugène-Alfred
Hénard;** passage des Princes; Maison Dorée: **Victor Lemaire** and
**Pierre Dufau;** Salle Favart: **Stanislas-Louis Bernier;** Crédit
Lyonnais: **William Bouwens van der Boijen, André Narjoux,**
**Victor Laloux,** and **Gustave Eiffel;** Cinéma Gaumont-Opéra: **Charles
Le Maresquier;** Cinéma Paramount-Opéra: **Auguste Magne**

Métro: **Opéra** or **Auber**

**[9sw-34.] Passage des Princes,** off boulevard des Italiens. 1860.

★★★★[9sw-1.] Palais Garnier/originally L'Opéra or Académie Nationale de Musique et de Danse, place de l'Opéra. Charles Garnier. Concours, 1861. Construction, 1862–1875. Sculpture, *La Danse,* by Jean-Baptiste Carpeaux.

Both fountainhead and symbol of the Napoléon III, or Second Empire, style, it inspired the encrustation with architectural and sculptural pomp of a dozen world capitals, in which were created the perfect settings (depending upon the program needed) for romantic operas, South American dictators, banks with or without capital, California lumber barons, amusement parks, and railroad stations.

Garnier won the competition in 1861 at the height of Napoléon III's power. When the emperor and empress were presented with the model, the latter was said to have questioned, "What is this style? It's not a style. It's not Greek, it's not Louis XVI." Garnier allegedly replied, "No, those styles have had their day. This style is Napoléon III, and you complain?" To which the emperor perhaps murmured, "Don't worry. She doesn't know anything about it."

Constructed by the *grand bourgeois* as a stage set for self-display, the vestibules, galleries, stairs, anterooms, and other areas are much vaster than the mere auditorium for the select 2,131 attending. Here one could stroll, step, sip, chat, ogle, and parade oneself in lengthy intermissions. This was the point of it all: the performance itself was an intermission between obligatory social strutting.

The British critic **Ian Nairn** summed it up as "a declamatory roulade of allegory that would pump a sense of occasion into the limpest libretto. The outside gives clear warning of what is about to happen, but it is only tuning up; overture, grand march, love duet, and final chorus are all inside, in the gorgeous sequence of double staircase leading to the auditorium on one side and a third floor foyer—what a name for it!—on the other, immediately behind the facade. This is more operatic than the opera, pulling the audience willy-nilly into grandeur. . . . Pay any price and go and see anything, however unsuitable: the experience will be worth it."

Garnier went on to do another extravaganza for the **Opera of Monte Carlo.** His son, Tony, was in the league of the Perret Frères in the development of reinforced concrete, creating his unbuilt **Cité Industrielle** and filling out his years as the city architect of Lyons.

Now one of a triad, the Palais Garnier will house only dance, the Salle Favart light opera, and the Opéra de la Bastille grand opera. The last is scarcely the place for grand personal display, but with a bigger auditorium (2,700) it will, hopefully, fulfill part of its programmed intentions: to bring opera to the people.

★★[9sw-2.] Café de la Paix, in the **Grand Hotel,** corner place de l'Opéra and 12, boulevard des Capucines. Building, **Alfred Armand.** Interiors, **Charles Garnier.** 1862.

This and the formal dining rooms above foresaw the magnificent aura of the **Opéra,** keeping one's eyes at a fever pitch before or after the concert, while feeding and watering the stomach with equal gastronomic extravagance. **Alphonse Daudet** said of the café, "It is principally during the evening that the terrace is invaded by strollers. Up to now I haven't seen those peripatetic boulevardiers for whom the windows of other cafés serve as 'ports of call'; decent women who gather at the tables of the Grand Hotel don't complain of the absence of those vulgar crinolines that the neighborhood makes so troublesome for them and so agreeable for their husbands or lovers."

The central ballroom of the hotel is covered with a great *verrière* sheltering stained glass and is surrounded by a Corinthian colonnade surmounted by two score of caryatids.

Such luxuries as elevators, central heating, a telegraph station, a staff of interpreters, and fifteen private bathrooms attracted many Americans to its seven hundred rooms.

Of the *salle à manger* Goncourt wrote, "Descending one of the last flights of the curved stair, I was struck by the handsome and grandiose appearance of this dining room, with its two-story height, skylight, and the pleasing arrangement of 310 places."

The colossal order of Corinthian pilasters that mark the facades was part of the requirements of an imperial decree for the whole place de l'Opéra.

★★[9sw-3.] Originally **La Samaritaine Deluxe/Annexe,** 27, boulevard des Capucines, between place de l'Opéra and rue Daunou. **Frantz Jourdain.** 1916.

Except for the entry, this is a magnificence of copper, Art Nouveau, *grès de Bigot,* and ironwork. The florid copper capitals would make **Lavirotte** jealous.

★[9sw-4.] **Hôtel Marin de la Haye** and **Hôtel d'Aumont,** 1 and 2, rue de Caumartin, corner boulevard de la Madeleine. **Jean André Aubert.** 18th century.

Corner-rounded neo-Classical twins that form a grand entry to this bland street. No. 2's great Ionic pilasters and ironwork are the more imposing. The roof once bore an Anglo-Chinese garden, comprising a kiosk, truncated columns, pyramids, false ruins, and a river (spanned by bridges) that supplied water to the bathrooms and dining rooms. It's enough to make Horace Walpole drool.

[9sw-5.] **Bar Romain (restaurant),** 6, rue de Caumartin, just off boulevard de la Madeleine. 1905.

A decor unchanged since 1905. Open until 2 A.M. with *steack tartare* and *tarte tatin* always waiting.

★[9sw-6.] **Rue** and **place Edouard VII,** between boulevard des Capucines and rue Boudreau. **Henri-Paul Nénot.** 1911. Sculpture, **Landowski.**

Here he sits superhorsed, a slenderer version of Victoria's son than in reality, amid late neo-Palladian pomp now devoted to the **Société Générale** except for the **Théâtre Edouard VII–Sacha Guitry.** This is a post-Haussmannian effort in combined architecture and urbanism, where both solid and void are under Nénot's control. For Nénot at the age of twenty-nine, see the Sorbonne. Here he was fifty-eight. He had improved.

[9sw-7.] **Théâtre de l'Athénée,** 4, square de l'Opéra-Louis-Jouvet, continuing the trace of rue Edouard VII. 1892.

Art Nouveau tracery ornaments this theatre in a quiet little square of antiquaires. Louis Jouvet directed the works of such as Giraudoux here from 1934 to his death in 1951. The statue is *The Poet Riding Pegasus* by **Alexandre Falguière** (1897). In 1897 myths became three-dimensional.

★[9sw-8.] **EDF Sous-Station Opéra,** 41, rue de Caumartin, between rue Joubert and rue Saint-Lazare. 1890s.

Crisp steel and glass lurks here near *The* Opera. Elegant and well-cared-for functionalism.

★★[9sw-9.] **Au Printemps,** 64, boulevard Haussmann, between rue du Havre and rue de Chartres. Founded 1865. First buildings, 1865, Destroyed by fire, 1881. New buildings, **Paul Sédille.** 1882–1889. Altered and surelevated. Nouveau Magasin and cupola, **René Binet.** 1907–1912. Destroyed by fire, 1921. Rebuilt. **Eugène Wybo.** 1924.

The cupola and grand skylight of the *Nouveau Magasin* were the *parapluies* of a great central hall, now infilled with selling spaces. But at the very top the pleated glory of stained glass still hovers over self-service "boutiques" for breakfast and lunch. You have a view of the heavens of Printemps up close, whereas in the full glory of six stories of space, it was the land of a distant god—a small recompense for spatial rape.

The rue du Havre facade is the purest Sédille, and the rue de Caumartin intersection (building-bridge-building) the most spectacular image.

A tearoom on another roof not only gives one aspect of the ornate details on this and neighboring aeries but also affords a sense of Paris in the air. Go up and out.

### Burning of Le Printemps, March 8, 1881

"It was at 5:30 in the morning when fire was discovered in the department of lace and embroidery on the ground floor near the boulevard Haussmann. One of the cleaning boys . . . lighted a gas jet for his work; the fire suddenly caught a muslin curtain, and in an instant the unhappy boy was surrounded with flames. Hearing his cries, the other cleaning boys ran, but the fire, finding in the lace, cardboard boxes and neighboring counters an easy fuel, propagated itself with such rapidity that the efforts of the assistants were in vain.

"Forewarned nearly as soon of the danger that menaced them, the employees lodged on the sixth floor were at least half-dressed, and had fled, some by the service stairs of 68, boulevard Haussmann, others reaching the roofs of neighboring houses. One can judge the disarray that reigned in that part of the building when one realized that more than two hundred young boys and girls were lodged in the main store as well as the annexes of the rue de Provence.

". . . Toward 5:50 the firemen arrived from stations on rues Blanche and de l'Opéra, but the manual pumps could have little affect against the power of the fire, and they had to content themselves with preventing the fire from extending to neighboring buildings. What's more, to fill these pumps, it was necessary to bring water in barrels from the rue de la Chaussée d'Antin."

**F. Evrard** in *La vie Parisienne à travers le XIXe . . .* 1901.

★★**[9sw-10.] Lycée Condorcet**/originally **Couvent des Capucines,** 65, rue de Caumartin between boulevard Haussmann and rue Saint-Lazare. **Aléxandre-Théodore Brongniart.** 1781–1783. Rue du Havre buildings, 1864.

Magnificent neo-Classical austerity on the rue de Caumartin facade, the Doric columns and pediment in stark contrast to bare, smooth stone. If you enter through the rue du Havre school entrance, you can reach the colonnaded court (former cloister), which reeks of late Greece and early Rome. Others who have enjoyed Brongniart's architecture include former students Dumas fils, Nadar, Ampère, Mallarmé, Süe (architect of rue Cassini), Proust, Haussmann, and Léon Blum.

★★**[9sw-11.] Eglise Saint-Louis-d'Antin**/formerly **Chapelle du Couvent Saint-Louis-des-Pères-Capucines,** 63, rue Caumartin between boulevard Haussmann and rue Saint-Lazare. **Aléxandre Brongniart.** 1782. Interior redecorated, 1904.

★★**[9sw-12.] Immeuble, 20, rue Joubert,** between rue de Caumartin and rue de la Chaussée-d'Antin. Rear courtyard, **François-Joseph Bélanger.** 1788. Surelevated, 1847.

A polygonal entry porte cochère gives way to an exedral courtyard open to the sky. The fluted Doric columns (in the original Greek manner) support elliptical arches. Elegant.

**[9sw-13.] Immeuble, 71, rue de Caumartin,** between boulevard Haussmann and rue Saint-Lazare. **Nicolas-Jacques-Antoine Vestier.** 1790s.

Some Hellenistic remnants among all the commercial visual cacophony of this street. It was a graceful neighbor of the **Lycée Condorcet** in the times of both Napoléons. But can detail conquer the Philistines?

★**[9sw-14.] Société Nationale des Chemins de Fer Français,** 88, rue Saint-Lazare, between rue de Caumartin and rue de Londres. 1870s.

Pomp in depth—the triumphal entry to SNCF headquarters behind.

★**[9sw-15.] Immeuble, 82, rue Saint-Lazare,** between rue de Caumartin and square de la Trinité. **Emile-Pierre Jarlat.** 1908.

Pomp without circumstance. There are blindfolded guardians at the fourth floor, bitted lions at the first.

**[9sw-16.] Théâtre de Mogador,** 25, rue de Mogador, between rue Saint-Lazare and rue de la Victoire. 1919.

Glazed terra-cotta classicism.

★**[9sw-17.] Galeries Lafayette/Annexe,** 29, rue de la Chaussée-d'Antin, between rue de Provence and boulevard Haussmann. **Pierre Patout.** 1932.

Glass with a bit of pomp, rather than pomp with a bit of glass. Patout here was a long way from his crisp white artists' ateliers.

★★**[9sw-18.] Galeries Lafayette/Main Store,** 40, boulevard Haussmann, between rue de la Chaussée-d'Antin and rue Charras. **George Chédanne.** 1906–1908. **Ferdinand Chanut.** 1910–1912. Extended 1932.

Though we bemoan the loss of the the great stair by **Majorelle,** the space is still here, unlike that of **Au Printemps** next door. The railings surrounding are probably also by Majorelle.

★★**[9sw-18a.] Société Générale,** 29, boulevard Haussmann, between place Diaghilev and rue Halévy. **Jacques-Ignace Hittorf** and **Charles Rohaut de Fleury.** 1867. Interiors, **Jacques Hermant.** 1906–1911.

In contrast to the popular music sung by the inner stained-glass cupola of **Au Printemps,** this multimuted alabaster/tortoise shell interior (★★★) is a symphony of glass. Walk in and around the glorious low counters *à l'anglaise* (no grilles), and imagine you had the money to be worth all of this.

**[9sw-19.] Cité d'Antin,** 57 and 61, rue de Provence, between rue de la Chaussée-d'Antin and rue Taitbout. 1830.

Two barrel-vaulted and Tuscan-columned triumphal arches lead to streets of bland commerce.

★**[9sw-20.] L'Européenne de Banque**/formerly **Banque Rothschild,** 21, rue Laffitte, between rue La Fayette and rue Pillet-Will. **Pierre Dufau** and **Max Abramovitz.** 1969.

An American-style invasion, largely by the hand of Abramovitz, one third of the team (**Harrison, Abramovitz & Harris**) that produced the later buildings of New York's **Rockefeller Center** (Exxon, McGraw-Hill, Celanese) and the **United Nations**. This "aerates a sad street" according to Dufau. In retrospect it intrudes foreign matter into an eyelid of Paris. The Banque Rothschild fled when the Socialists took power in 1981.

**[9sw-21.] Au Petit Riche (restaurant),** 25, rue Le Peletier, corner rue Rossini. Founded 1864.

Remodeled into the Belle Epoque.

**[9sw-22.] PTT, 23, rue Chauchat,** corner rue de Provence. circa 1925.

Classical modern, but the bas-relief is strong and gentle.

★★**[9sw-23.]** Originally **customs barrier**/now **Eglise Evangélique de la Rédemption,** 16, rue Chauchat, between rue de Provence and rue Rossini. **Lusson.** 1780s. Remodeled into church. **Chrétien Gau.** 1843.

A neo-Classical pediment, arch, and porch à la Ledoux. Powerful, rusticated, with Tuscan columns.

**[9sw-24.] Hôtel des Ventes Drouot,** 12, rue Chauchat between rue de Provence, rue Rossini, and rue Drouot. **Jean-Jacques Fernier** and **André Biro.** 1980.

The architects called it "a surrealistic reinterpretation of Haussmannian architecture." Were they taking hallucinatory mushrooms at the time? Its more sober facades are nothing but glass-and-metal curtain walls; the pan coupé is a pure Detroit "auto" of the 1960s.

**[9sw-25.] Mutuelle Electrique d'Assurances/Groupe PRIM,** 8, rue Chauchat, between rue Rossini and boulevard Haussmann. 1890s.

A Corinthian-columned, neo-neo-Classical *hôtel,* providing an aura of great assurance for the insured.

★★**[9sw-26.] Mairie**/originally **Hôtel d'Augny,** 6, rue Drouot, between rue Rossini and boulevard Montmartre. **Charles-Etienne Briseux.** 1748–1752. Entry portal, 1830. Wings and interior remodeled, 1870.

An *hôtel particulier* of the 18th century, now buried in a midblock of the 19th.

★**[9sw-27.] A la Mère de Famille (épicerie/confiserie),** 35, rue du Faubourg-Montmartre, corner rue de Provence. 19th century.

A superb shop with a decoration of paintings under glass and interior fixtures of the epoch.

★**[9sw-28.] Passage Verdeau,** 31 bis, rue du Faubourg-Montmartre and 6, rue de la Grange-Batelière. **J. P. M. Deschamps.** 1845.

Continues as the passage Jouffroy below.

★★**[9sw-28a.] Passage Jouffroy,** between 9, rue de la Grange-Batelière and 12, boulevard Montmartre. **François-Hippolyte Destailleur** and **Romain de Bourges.** 1846.

An ogival "vault" of glass hovers high over this shopping arcade with an entry to the two-star **Hôtel Chopin** and the **Musée Grévin.** If you want to study the *verrière* from on high, ask the room clerk for an overlooking room.

The passage des Panoramas continues the sequence across the boulevard.

★★[9sw-29.] **Restaurant Chartier,** 7, rue du Faubourg-Montmartre, between boulevard Montmartre and rue de la Grange-Batelière. 1896.

A 19th-century gastronomic and architectural heaven, serving good and inexpensive food in the original environment: stained glass, lamp standards in brass, and mahogany.

★★[9sw-30.] **Musée Grévin,** 10, boulevard Montmartre and off passage Jouffroy. Museum, **Esmault-Pelterie.** 1882. Théâtre Grévin, 1900. Palais des Mirages, **Eugène-Alfred Hénard.** 1906.

Madame Tussaud, move over. Here are a waxy Mitterrand and Reagan and the events of history frozen in time for the vicarious viewer. The *théâtre à l'italienne* within displays a curtain (carnival scene) by **Jules Chéret,** surmounted by an allegorical high-relief of **Bourdelle.**

But best of all, an ultimate architectural fantasy is presented in the **Palais des Mirages,** by means of stationary and rotating mirrors in a hexagonal space, built by Hénard for the exposition of 1900. Here you can "see" apparently endless space in the form of Hindu temples, Arabian palaces, and . . .

[9sw-31.] **Hôtel Mercy d'Argenteau,** 16, boulevard Montmartre, between rue du Faubourg-Montmartre and rue Drouot. 18th century.

A remnant from a different past of the Grands Boulevards. The courtyard is picturesque.

★[9sw-32.] **Les Maxévilles (cinéma),** 14, boulevard Montmartre, between rue du Faubourg-Montmartre and rue Drouot. **C. Lunel.** circa 1930.

Apartments perch over the cinema, with fins serrating the sky.

[9sw-33.] **Restaurant Drouot,** 103, rue de Richelieu, corner boulevard des Italiens. 1900s.

A lesser and upstairs **Chartier** (same owners), inexpensive and filled with character.

★★[9sw-34.] **Passage des Princes**/originally **passage Mirès,** 5 bis, boulevard des Italiens and 97, rue de Richelieu. 1860.

Not-so-delightfully seedy, but the original glass- and ironworks are still there, its ironwork wrought into curls. This is the last of the great covered *passages,* here built under Napoléon III.

★[9sw-35.] **BNP (Banque Nationale de Paris),** 16–18, boulevard des Italiens, between rue Le Peletier and rue Laffitte. **A. Marast** and **Charles Letrosne.** 1932.

The 1930s produced an austere autocratic architecture that we sometimes think of as fascist, although it appeared in New York and Oslo, as well as at the 1937 Paris Exposition. It has been said that Albert Speer was merely taking up the architecture of Queen Hatshepsut of ancient Egypt's New Kingdom, but it's doubtful that Marast and Letrosne spent much time on the Nile preparing for this scheme.

★★[9sw-35a.] **Maison Dorée (restaurant)**/now **BNP (Banque Nationale de Paris),** 20, boulevard des Italiens and 2, rue Taitbout. Maison

Dorée, **Victor Lemaire.** 1839. Alterations and rue Taitbout extension, **Pierre Dufau.** 1976.

A public outcry halted the planned demolition of the Maison Dorée and stimulated its adaptive reuse, with a sleek but bland addition. The Maison, a restaurant-café of the time of Louis-Philippe, was where Marcel Proust's Swann desperately sought Odette. The BNP and Dufau deserve credit for this rare Parisian combination of preservation and new construction, but why replace 19th-century window sash with fixed glazing? The scale of Lemaire's facade is destroyed by the elimination of such necessary detail.

★★**[9sw-36.] Salle Favart/Opéra-Comique,** place Boïeldieu off boulevard des Italiens, between rue Favart and rue de Marivaux. **Stanislas-Louis Bernier.** 1894–1898.

Two previous Opéra-Comiques on this site were destroyed by fire. This extravagant building for musical theater is junior to but endowed with the same spirit of exuberant internal architectural fantasy as the **Palais Garnier.**

**[9sw-37.] Immeuble, 28, rue de Gramont,** between boulevard des Italiens and rue du 4 Septembre. Jean-Claude Delorme. 1984.

Muted green, rose, and beige in a turgid and understated style: Post Modernism creeping up the flanks of the Grands Boulevards.

★★**[9sw-38.] Crédit Lyonnais,** 17-23, boulevard des Italiens, between rue de Choiseul and rue de Gramont. **William Bouwens van der Boijen.** 1878. **André Narjoux** and **Victor Laloux.** 1907–1913. Glass cupola over spiral stairs, **Gustave Eiffel.** 1882.

Laloux, architect of the **Gare** (now **Musée) d'Orsay,** finished what van der Boijen started, with a great glass-covered atrium on the rue du 4 Septembre side. Eiffel's earlier work can be seen off boulevard des Italiens, sheltering a double spiral stair (★★★) copied from Chambord. The heavy-handed stone carapace that envelops these elegances of glass and iron speaks strongly of banks and the safety of money. Ignore the message and go in.

**[9sw-39.] Immeuble, 6, rue du Hanovre,** between rue de La Michodière and rue de Choiseul. **Adolphe Bocage.** 1908. Tilework, **Alexandre Bigot.**

A green-ocher tiled Art Nouveau fantasy, with bay windows above and boxy dormers.

★**[9sw-40.] Banque Franco-Portugaise/**originally **Immeuble Ford,** 36, boulevard des Italiens, corner rue du Helder. **Michel Roux-Spitz.** 1929.

Now quite mute, this was originally an advertisement for Ford with flamboyant light streaking its facade, a brilliant showroom where the bank now rests, and a giant Ford logo illuminated atop it all. *Où sont les Modèles A d'antan?*

★**[9sw-41.] Palais Berlitz** and **Cinéma Gaumont-Opéra,** 31, boulevard des Italiens, between rue Louis-le-Grand and rue de La Michodière. **Charles Le Maresquier.** circa 1932.

Modern columns support the sky in a phalanx of fasces better than Mussolini's—and why not? This is the boulevard des Italiens, after all. The theater tries, in the terms of 1932, to emulate the power of the vintage **Paramount-Opéra** across the street.

★[9sw-42.] **Cinéma Paramount-Opéra**/originally **Théâtre du Vaudeville,** 2, boulevard des Capucines, corner rue de la Chaussée-d'Antin. **Auguste Magne.** 1869. Remodeled into cinema, 1925.

A *grand magasin* where caryatids are in the service of film rather than goods or money. Appropriately, in 1921 a bank considered converting the theater's shell to its own use, making a vaudeville of mammon. The cinema was a much better idea.

# 24
# NINTH AND TENTH ARRONDISSEMENTS
## POISSONNIERE
### CINEMA REX AND ENVIRONS OF
### RUE DU FAUBOURG POISSONNIERE

Cinéma Rex: **Auguste Bluysen** and **John Eberson;** Banque National
de Paris: **Edouard-Jules Corroyer;** Eglise Saint-Eugène-Sainte-Cécile:
**Louis-Auguste Boileau;** Folies Bergère: **Pico;** Hôtel de
Botterel-Quintin: **Pérard de Montreuil** and **Sébastien-Jean
Duboisterf;** Hôtels Titon and de Goix: **Jean-Charles Delafosse;**
Hôtel du Marquis de Thoix: **Munster**

Métro: **Bonne-Nouvelle**

**[9/10-1.] Cinéma Rex. Auguste Bluysen,** architect. **John Eberson,**
consulting architect. 1932.

★★★[9/10-1.] **Cinéma Rex,** 1, boulevard Poissonnière, corner rue Poissonnière. **Auguste Bluysen,** architect. **John Eberson,** consulting architect. **Maurice Dufrèsne,** interior architect. 1932.

The corner is a particularly Parisian architectural event. The *pan coupé* developed from Louis-Philippe to its apogee both in quantity and elaboration under Haussmann, and the *poivrière,* such as at **Félix Potin** on rue Réaumur, was the penultimate and enriched expression of a corner. Here Art Deco interprets the corner anew: crested with a modern version of a colonnaded ziggurat.

Bluysen and his American colleague, Eberson, created an auditorium with 3,500 seats, the first *cinéma à salle atmosphérique français* (Eberson had been party to over three hundred American movie theaters by then). With the **Gaumont-Opéra** and the **Paramount-Opéra,** it shares the memories of the vast movie theaters of the 1930s. The interior presents a wonderful cacophony of vision—all styles possible, with dancing fountains on occasion.

[9/10-1a.] **Théâtre du Gymnase,** 38, boulevard de Bonne-Nouvelle, between rue du Faubourg-Poissonnière and rue d'Hauteville. Original, 1820. Rebuilt, 1880.

[9/10-1b.] **Cinéma/Max Linder Panorama,** 24, boulevard Poissonnière, between rue du Faubourg-Poissonnière and rue Montmartre. Rebuilt, 1980s.

Frenchman Max Linder (1883–1925) has been called the greatest film comedian of the silent era. This may well be the finest spot in Paris to take in a movie.

[9/10-2.] **Immeuble, 10, rue du Faubourg-Poissonnière,** between boulevard de Bonne-Nouvelle and rue de l'Echiquier. **Auguste Perret.** 1900 and later.

Is this invisible, or merely skeletal, Perret?

★★[9/10-3.] **PTT, 2, rue Bergère** and **Centre Téléphonique, 17, rue du Faubourg-Poissonnière,** corner rue Bergère. **François Lecoeur.** No. 17, 1913. No. 2, 1921.

Exquisite ironwork and a glass-eyed oval dome at its unused Poissonnière monumental entry (enter rue Bergère). Add striped brick and a clock of filigree for a major effort that crosses the best of Art Nouveau ironwork with precocious modern experiments in concrete (the glass-eyed *marquise).*

★[9/10-4.] **BNP**/originally **Comptoir d'Escompte de Paris,** 14, rue Bergère, on axis rue Rougement. **Edouard Corroyer.** 1881.

Corroyer, who participated in the restoration of **Mont Saint-Michel,** created here what has been called a "magnificent palace of finance.... The handsome glazed ceiling that reigns over the great hall is so light that it seems to skim through the air. To see it at such a height, without perceptible supports, makes one believe it is made of light and pure air."

[9/10-4a.] **Théâtre du Conservatoire,** 2, rue du Conservatoire, between rue Bergère and rue Sainte-Cécile. **François-Jacques Delannoy.** 1811. Redecorated, 1866.

Inside, it is an austere Empire place, replete with neo-Roman frescoes and exuberant polychromatic, Composite, fluted columns. The exterior, however, is bland.

★[9/10-5.] **Eglise Saint-Eugène–Sainte-Cécile,** 6, rue Sainte-Cécile, corner rue du Conservatoire. **Louis-Auguste Boileau.** 1855.

The pasty Gothic Revival of the exterior offers no clue to the structural radicalism within: here is the first use of cast iron for a church. **Victor Baltard**'s later **Saint-Augustin [8e-5.]** (1860–1871) was certainly more spectacular and handled iron with more honor for its intrinsic value. Here was dissimulation, whereas at Saint-Augustin there was visual experimentation, a continuing process culminating in the steel filigree of **Notre-Dame-du-Travail [14w-8.].**

★★[9/10-6.] Originally **Hôtel Benoît de Saint-Paulle**/also known as **Hôtel Chéret,** 30, rue du Faubourg-Poissonnière. **Nicolas Lenoir.** 1776.

The streetfront has been much altered, a surelevation surrounding and muting the entry portal (columned, arched, and pedimented). But the *corps de logis* within is still present in neo-Classical elegance, with four Ionic columns announcing this great town house. Among the owners was François-Nicolas Lenormand, husband of Marie-Louis O'Murphy, notorious as the model for Boucher's canvas, *L'Odalisque Blonde,* and as mistress of Louis XV.

★★[9/10-7.] **Hôtel particulier, 26, rue d'Hauteville,** between rue Enghien and rue des Petites-Ecuries. circa 1810.

In the court the neo-Classical pavilion sports heads of men and lions in circular concave niches; to the Anglo-Saxon eye it seems like a bit of **John Soane.** A magnificent and powerful presence.

[9/10-8.] **Hôtel Mignon**/now **Fédération Nationale de la Presse Française,** 6 bis, rue Gabriel-Laumain, between rue d'Hauteville and rue du Faubourg-Poissonnière. circa 1840.

Off a tiny circular *place* sits an Italiante mini-palazzo, à la Brunelleschi at its entry porch, with engaged Corinthian pilasters above.

[9/10-9.] **Rue Gabriel-Laumain,** entry at 6, rue du Faubourg-Poissonnière, between rue Enghien and rue des Petites-Ecuries. 1820.

Two lost **Ledoux** hôtels **(d'Attilly** and **d'Espinchal)** once lived here. From rue du Faubourg-Poissonnière the view of mansarded regularity in perspective would have pleased a reincarnated **Palladio** (cf. **Teatro Olimpico** at Vicenza).

★[9/10-9a.] **Folies Bergère (cabaret),** 30, rue Richer, between rue du Faubourg-Poissonnière and rue Saulnier (west of rue de Trévise). Facade and new interiors, **Pico.** 1929.

A very stylish Art Deco facade displays an ebullient nude dancer amid her veils. The lettering itself is a sculptured alphabet of those years. The parent Folies, the bones underneath all this modernity, was built in 1869 (see *A Bar at the Folies Bergère* by Manet, 1882) and presented a Corinthian colonnade to the street:
"The illuminated facade of the establishment threw a great glow into the four streets that met in front of it. A line of carriages waited for customers to emerge. . . . He took the ticket that was presented to him, pushed the quilted leather door, and they were in the hall.
"A smell of tobacco veiled, like a very thin fog, distant parts, the stage, and the other side of the theater. And rising ceaselessly, in thin whitish streaks, from all the cigars and all the cigarettes that all the people smoked, this light mist rose, accumulated at the ceiling, and formed, under the large dome, around the chandelier, a smoky sky.

"In the vast entrance corridor, which led to the circular promenade where the costumed tribe of girls loitered, mixed in a somber crowd of men, a group of women awaited the arrivals before one of three counters, where were enthroned, made up and worn out, three merchants of drinks and of love. . . . On the stage, three young men in tights, one big, one medium, and one little, were, in their turn, exercising on a trapeze . . ." **Guy de Maupassant,** 1885.

**[9/10-9b.] Hôtel Bony,** 32, rue de Trévise and 11, rue Bleue. **Jules-Jean-Baptiste Bony.** 1826.

Neo-Classical with a *Restauration* interior, it is accessible through a long alley off rue Bleue, but better still through the garish street hotel on rue de Trévise. Here the free standing rococo is revived.

**[9/10-9c.] Maison Leclaire,** 25, rue Bleue, between rue de Trévise and rue Saulnier. **Bertrand.** 1911.

Neo-Classical contends with Art Nouveau, with glassy bay windows.

★★**[9/10-9d.] Cité de Trévise,** between 5, rue Bleue and 16, rue Richer. 1840s.

A private street and square.
"[Here are] elegant retreats that, while ensuring the calm necessary for work, are not, for professional men, far from downtown. . . . Situated near the boulevards, at the center of important business and banking, this new *cité,* where the hotels and houses surround a parterre emblazoned with flowers in the middle of which gushes a fountain, offers peace in the middle of the noise of business and pleasures." *L'Illustration.* Still very true.

★★**[9/10-10.] Hôtel de Botterel-Quintin**/now **Société Française des Ingénieurs-Conseils en Aménagements,** 44, rue des Petites-Ecuries, between rue d'Hauteville and rue du Faubourg-Poissonnière. **François-Victor Pérard de Montreuil** and **Sébastien-Jean Duboisterf.** 1780.

The restaurant **Le Lucas** is here. A Tuscan-columned portal marks the *corps de logis,* behind a well-manicured court.
The *salle à manger* is one of the most renowned extant 18th-century spaces (16 by 26 feet, with an oval glass cupola hovering 26 feet overhead). "The decor of this room is stupefying," remarks Laure Beaumont-Maillet in *Vie et histoire du Xe arrondissement.* "The floor is of white and blue (turquin) marble. All around the room stucco columns, painted to imitate the yellow marble of Sienna, support an opulent stucco frieze decorated with sphinxes, various animals, vases of flowers and fruit. Above this sculpted frieze runs, all around the ceiling, a great painted frieze representing mythological persons in the style of Prud'hon.
"Initially, the decor was richer still, when the four niches sheltered four groups of paired bacchantes. . . . They have been dispersed, but two of them have found refuge in the Musée des Arts decoratifs.
"For this dazzling room, Paul Marmottan has suggested three names: the architecture would be that of Bélanger, the painted decor that of his brother-in-law, Dugoure. As far as the bacchanale on the ceiling, it could be attributed to Prud'hon."

★★**[9/10-11.] Hôtel de Bourrienne** in the courtyard at 58, rue d'Hauteville, between rue de Paradis and rue des Petites-Ecuries. 1787-1793. Interiors, **François-Joseph Bélanger.** circa 1793. Garden facade, **Etienne-Chérubin Leconte.** Open on Saturdays and Sundays, 2–4 P.M. Entry building on the street. 1828.

The minor pieces left behind on the street in the great 19th-century reconstruction of Paris are sometimes shabby. Nevertheless, the scale of building and court remains proudly here. Within (★★★), the furnishings, paneling, and plasterwork are lovely and in an extraordinary state of preservation. The style of **le Consulat** relates much to the work of the British brothers **Adam.**

**[9/10-12.] Hôtel Cardon,** 50, rue du Faubourg-Poissonnière, between rue des Petites-Ecuries and rue de Paradis. **Goupy.** 1773.

The streetfront is 1820s *(Restauration),* but within the court the *corps de logis* exists, mildly altered. **No. 52,** also by Goupy, was built in 1774 for the painter **René-Hyacinthe Deleuze.**

★**[9/10-13.] Hôtel Sauvageot,** 56, rue du Faubourg-Poissonnière, between rue des Petites-Ecuries and rue de Paradis. **François-Joseph Nolau.** 1838.

A rusticated Italian Renaissance base supports shuttered Louis-Philippe architecture above. **Corot** maintained his atelier and died here in 1875.

---

*L'Illustration,* March 6, 1875: "It wasn't at all one of those ateliers encumbered with curios and knickknacks so dear to the heart of our fashionable painters; it was a sanctuary of art, nearly austere in its simplicity; the innumerable studies attached to all parts of the bare walls provided the only decoration. . . . Now some words about the apartment occupied by le maître (Corot) on the first floor of 56, rue du Faubourg-Poissonière: the simplest interior, furniture that, for the most part, came from his parents. The dinner had nearly finished, tobacco was lighted, and he played host by enlivening you with songs, or by witty sayings, and, to the extent that it interested you, his thoughts on the arts. Everyone then went into the salon to join the ladies for cards."

---

★**[9/10-14.] Hôtel Titon,** 58, rue du Faubourg-Poissonnière, between rue des Petite-Ecuries and rue de Paradis. **Jean-Charles Delafosse.** 1768. Surelevated on the court, 1820s; on the corps de logis, 1850s.

The unfortunate Jean-Baptiste-Maximilien Titon lost his head in the Revolution, but the architecture of his *hôtel* was well respected by later owners. The surelevation of the *corps de logis* copied the detail of its *rez-de-chaussée:* pediments, swags (or festoons), and window proportions.

**[9/10-15.] Hôtel de Goix,** 60, rue du Faubourg-Poissonnière, between rue des Petite-Ecuries and rue de Paradis. **Jean-Charles Delafosse.** 1768. Building on the street, **Alfred Aldrophe.** 1880s.

A smaller version of the style of **Delafosse,** whose *Nouvelle iconologie historique,* a handbook for artisans and craftsmen, appeared in the same year as his two extant buildings, **Nos. 58** and **60.** Andy Warhol said that everyone would be famous for fifteen minutes; Delafosse lasted a year.

**[9/10-16.] Immeuble, 51, rue du Faubourg-Poissonnière,** between rue Richer and rue de Paradis. **Charles Babet.** 1895.

Some shades of **Viollet-le-Duc** among the faithful Classical flock: polychromy, bay windows, steel lintels, and cast-iron colonnettes.

**[9/10-17.] Hôtel particulier, 65, rue du Faubourg-Poissonnière,** between rue Richer and rue de Paradis. 1820s within.

The court enjoys Greek pastry (edible, not architectural) and a Tuscancolumned portal: homey neo-Classical.

★[9/10-18.] Hôtel de Marmont/originally **Hôtel du Marquis de Thoix,** 51, rue de Paradis, between rue du Faubourg-Poissonnière and rue d'Hauteville. **Munster.** 1779. Surelevated, circa 1930.

In the tight courtyard, a bellied bay. There was no garden here; the marquis vicariously enjoyed views over that of the Hôtel Titon.

[9/10-19.] **Restaurant de la Grille**/formerly **Boutique de Marchand de Vin,** 80, rue du Faubourg-Poissonnière, between rue des Messageries and rue La Fayette.

Its *grille,* golden lances, pineapples, and all are worthy of **Hittorf.** This is a cozy, enfenced, traditional retreat.

# 25
# TENTH ARRONDISSEMENT
## EAST
### PLACE DE LA REPUBLIQUE
### TO LOUXOR AND BACK

Place de la République; Canal Saint-Martin; passerelle de la Douane; Groupe Scolaire: **Lionel and Daniel Brandon;** Gymnase Jenmapes: **Antoine Grumbach;** 100,000 Chemises: **Charles J. Guiral de Montarnal;** Gare de l'Est: **François-Alexandre Duquesney;** Gare du Nord: **Jacques-Ignace Hittorf;** Hôpital Lariboisière: **Gauthier;** Cinéma Louxor: **Ripey;** Eglise Saint-Vincent-de-Paul: **Jean-Baptiste Lepère** and **Jacques-Ignace Hittorf;** boulevard Magenta; Marché Saint-Quentin; Eglise Saint-Laurent: **Simon-Claude Constant-Dufeux;** Faïenceries de Choisy: **G. Jacobin** and **Ernest Brunnarius;** Mairie: **Jean-Eugène Rouyer;** Hôtel Goûthière: **Joseph Métivier;** Restaurant Chez Julien; Porte Saint-Denis: **Nicolas-François Blondel:** Porte Saint-Martin: **Pierre Bullet**

Métro: **République**

**[10e-37.] Julien (restaurant).** 1889. Remodeled.

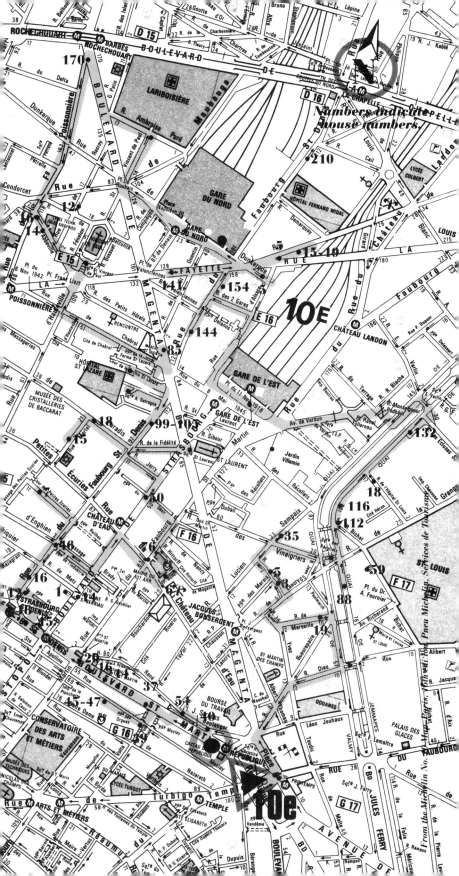

★[10e-1.] Place de la République (1883–)/formerly Place du Château-d'Eau (1811–1883)/and before that a mere carrefour on the Grands Boulevards.

A knuckle in the polygonality of the *Grands Boulevards*, it has been much rearranged in size, in the number and alignment of its radiating streets, and in the variety of centerpieces that have decorated it all since Louis XIV ordered the walls of Charles V to come tumbling down. First, it was an intersection, of the boulevards Saint-Martin and du Temple, but received its fountain *(château d'eau)* in 1811. Two fountains later (the latter was moved to place Félix-Eboué) the present monument, "La République," found its final resting place (statue, **Charles and Léopold Morice;** bas-reliefs, **Aimé-Jules Dalou**). Not particularly a place to tarry, save for a look at La République up close.

★★[10e-2.] Passerelle de la Douane, over Canal Saint-Martin, at rue Léon-Jouhaux. 1860.

This, the oldest extant metal pedestrian bridge over the canal, handles cast-iron voussoirs as if they were stone; but here, of course, each segmental piece is perforated with voids. Additionally, the three arches so composed are tied into a single unity by transverse tensile rods in wrought iron. If all this technological history is boring, just study its elegance, and walk on its light steps. The view is also graceful.

★[10e-3.] Groupe Scolaire, 19, rue de Marseille, at the quai de Valmy and the canal Saint-Martin. **Lionel and Daniel Brandon,** and then **Edouard Boegner.** probably 1933–1949. Addition, 1989.

Four periods of scholastic architecture appear in Paris: that of the church schools (everything until 1887); the first state public schools (1887–1914); the 1930s, under a social reform government; and postwar schools, although the last can be now further subdivided into, perhaps, "economy modern," "elegant modern," and both good and bad "post modern." Here is a good 1930s representative, with reinforced concrete bones, and that ubiquitous 1930s social clothing for housing and schools: red brick, joined by some stucco. The trellised terrace is elegant. The addition along rue Jean-Poulmarch is **Post Modern** at its best.

[10e-4.] HBM, 3-5, rue Legouvé, straddling passage des Marais. **Agence d'Architecture HBM.** 1935.

The extant lettering for the DOUCHES is a strong part of the architecture, when ornament was almost a sin. But a brave architect could, nevertheless, sneak in lettering of excellence (bootleg decor).

[10e-5.] Offices, 35, rue Lucien-Sampaix, between rue des Vinaigriers and rue des Récollets. **Léon Schneider.** 1934.

Oh, those neo-Classical flutes hold their sway still: here glass, curtain-walled with metal spandrels, shares space with the slowly vanishing Dorians. And the entrance tries a bit of Egyptian formalism. Seedy, unfortunately.

★[10e-6.] Passerelle Dieu, over the Canal Saint-Martin, at rue de la Grange-aux-Belles. 1891.

Another arch, where water traffic has been stilled. A mistake?—the absence of water traffic, that is, not the presence of the bridge. Lively barging would be both economic for bulky goods and a handsome and real activity for these sinuous waterways. And while we're at it, bring back the streetcars.

**★[10e-6a.] Immeuble, 88, quai de Jemmapes** and **59, rue Bichat,** between rue de la Grange-aux-Belles and avenue Richerand. 1980s.

A PoMo outpost closing in on the **Hôpital Saint-Louis.** *Pas mal,* and there is a garden court separating the two "wings."

**★[10e-7.] Immeuble, 112, quai de Jemmapes,** between rue Bichet and rue de l'Hôpital-Saint-Louis. **Georges Pradelle.** 1908.

The bay windows, here joined to concrete technology, ironwork, and tiling, sing. The infill brick is dour, a remembrance of a sadder past. But wow, those bays!

**★★[10e-8.] Gymnase Jemmapes/Centre d'Animation,** 116, quai de Jemmapes, between rue Bichet and rue de l'Hôpital-Saint-Louis. **Antoine Grumbach.** 1986.

Red brick and white tile join forces to solve an urban bend in continuous facades. A class act in these precincts, for here Post Modernism is upgraded to a state of urbanity. In effect there is a radical tile building "within" one of conservative brick.

**[10e-9.] Ecole Maternelle** and **Logements, 18, rue de l'Hôpital-Saint-Louis and quai de Jemmapes. Michel Duplay.** 1985.

Flamboyance in bay windows more regular and satisfying on the street than the quai. The urge for a corner architectural crescendo is a hangover from the time when all those cut and rounded corners honored the splay of Parisian boulevards. Here it is gratuitous.

**★[10e-10.]** Originally **Compagnie Parisienne d'Air Comprimé,** 132, quai de Jemmapes, between rue de l'Hôpital-Saint-Louis and rue des Ecluses-Saint-Martin. **Paul Friesé.** 1896.

An understated elegance in steel, infilled with glass and brick, surveys the canal. Even the rivets are joyful notes.

To the north is a worthwhile diversion, entailing a 400-meter (1300-foot) walk for aficionados of early metal-and-glass construction:

**★[10e-11.]** Originally **100,000 Chemises,** 26, rue Louis-Blanc, between quai de Valmy and rue du Faubourg-Saint-Martin. **Charles J. Guiral de Montarnal.** 1906.

A steel elegance again. Note the curved volutes at the crown of the *rez-de-chaussée.* Steel blossomed in Paris long before any of Mies van der Rohe's drawn dreams became reality: the latter's apartment building at 860 Lake Shore Drive in Chicago took form only forty six years later.

**★★[10e-12.] Gare de l'Est,** at the end of boulevard de Strasbourg, on place du 11 Novembre 1918. First half, **François-Alexandre Duquesney.** 1847–1850. Doubling and other expansions, 1924–1931.

Less grand than the Gare du Nord, the Gare de l'Est keeps its trains outside its great *parapluie.* Covered platforms here make arrival more ordinary. The half-rose windows illuminate the ticket and departure halls. Their cast-iron radiating ribs seem a pair of almost-rising suns.
In front stands, since 1988, a fountain by **Michele Blondel,** with rough blocks of blue crystal from Baccarat.

"For years I have dreamed of writing a 'Map of Paris' for very relaxed people, that is, for strollers who love Paris and have time to waste. And for years I've been promising myself to begin this tour by examining my own neighborhood, from the Gare du Nord and Gare de l'Est to La Chapelle, not only because we haven't parted company for some thirty-five years, but also because it has a special appearance and deserves to be known.

". . . We moved back to the 10th arrondissement for good. A kind of love brought us back to boulevard Magenta and then to Faubourg-Saint-Martin, and I would still be there if the Compagnie de l'Est [railroad] hadn't dispossessed us before sending us back up rue Château-Landon to La Chapelle, into that bustling and noisy circus where iron mingles with men, trains with taxis, cattle with soldiers: a country rather than an arrondissement, made up of canals, factories, the Buttes-Chaumont, the Port de la Villette, and beloved of old watercolorists.

"This kingdom, one of the richest in Paris in public baths where you wait as at the dentist's, is dominated by the elevated structure of the Métro, which crowns it like a tiara. . . .

"The noise of the Dauphine–Nation line, similar to the groan of a zeppelin, accompanies passengers all the way to precincts surrounded by factory chimneys, lakes of zinc from which the rue d'Aubervilliers flows like a river of varnish.

"For me, the tenth . . . is a neighborhood of poets and locomotives. The twelfth arrondissement has locomotives, too, but it has fewer poets. Let's get this word straight. There's no need to actually write a poem in order to have poetry in your pocket. First of all, there are those who write poems and who constitute a roving academy. Then there are those who know the secret reasons why sensitivity to the neighborhood makes for happiness. That is why I bestow the noble title of poet on carters, bicycle salesmen, grocers, truck farmers, florists, and locksmiths." Léon Paul Fargue in *Le piéton de Paris* (1932)

**★★[10e-12a.] UP 1 (Unité Pédagogique d'Architecture Villemin)/** originally **Couvent des Récollets/**later **Hôpital Villemin,** avenue de Verdun at rue du Faubourg-Saint-Martin. Convent, 1790. Hospice, then *hôpital,* 1802–1968. UP 1, 1970–. Alterations and new construction, **Francis Soler.** 1992.

Eight thousand square meters for eight hundred students in a new building of glass and steel, with articulated bridges and stairs, all abutting an old chapel that will serve as the exhibition hall. The split new building opens to a skylit central galleria.

**★[10e-13.] Offices, SNCF (Société Nationale des Chemins de Fer),** 144, rue du Faubourg-Saint-Denis, between rue du 8 Mai 1945 and rue des Deux-Gares. **Adrien Gouny.** 1887.

A Viollet-le-Duc handbook in three dimensions. Polychromatic brick à la Ruskin, terra-cotta spandrels, wrought-iron lintels and spandrel frames, cast-iron columns, and quite a lot of glass! Handsome, perfunctory, now a bit dowdy, this is a solid and wonderful citizen.

**[10e-14.] Immeuble, 154, rue du Faubourg-Saint-Denis,** between rue des Deux-Gares and rue La Fayette. **Paul Hubert.** 1900.

Some sinuous floral extravagances in the stonework, with *garde-fous* and balconies that belly out in the manner of Louis XIV furniture.

**★[10e-15.] Insurance Building, 5, rue de Dunkerque,** between rue La Fayette and rue d'Alsace. 1930s.

Neo-Classical (the workers' frieze), neo-Renaissance (the rusticated base), Art Deco (the corbeled and stepped central bay)—this is dichotomy elevated to trichotomy. A long glance reveals the disparate shreds of architecture that have *not* been integrated. But it is still a powerful presence.

**[10e-16.] Immeuble, 5, rue de l'Aqueduc,** between rue La Fayette and rue Demarquay. **A. Lefèvre.** 1878.

Precocious iron: the first steel-framed apartment house in Paris. It requires some careful study to see the almost flush steelwork, riveted and gusseted.

★**[10e-17.] Immeubles, 15, 17, 19, rue de l'Aqueduc,** between rue La Fayette and rue Demarquay. **Charles Thion.** 1895.

Bay windows modulate these Haussmannian-*tardif* buildings, and tilework enriches them. More fun to look at than the precocious **No. 5.**

**[10e-17a.] Immeuble, 210, rue du Faubourg-Saint-Danis,** between rue Demarquay and rue Cail. circa 1900.

Iron, glass, and tile bay-windows make a spritely interlude along Saint-Denis.

★**[10e-18.] Immeuble, 141, rue La Fayette,** between rue de Saint-Quentin and boulevard de Denain. **Auguste Berchon.** 1898.

This beautifully kept Belle Epoque confection is rich with sculptured detail (by this time done with machines). The consoles supporting the balcony at the second floor are Brobdingnagian, but the glazing bars (muntins) follow a sinuous Art Nouveau path.

★★**[10e-19.] Gare du Nord,** rue de Dunkerque at place Napoléon III. **Jacques Hittorf.** 1863.

Perhaps schizophrenic, this neo-Classical and pompous exterior shields a radical iron-and-glass interior: the architecture of the traditional boulevard joining the city, the architecture of the future (iron) joining the iron horses and their rails. Presenting a guard of honor, nine queens surmount the cornice, ten more mounting the first floor, while thirty Doric (this time not Tuscan) columns hold up the spirit of it all.
Within, the firm of builders, **Polonceau,** ironmakers, have made it *all* of iron, with some super columns that soar but nevertheless bear some neo-Grec traits. The space and light are the glory in this, one of Napoléon III's *parapluies* for Paris.
The architects of the Compagnie des Chemins de Fer du Nord contributed, perhaps more than has been credited to them in most accounts. **Laure Beaumont-Maillet** in *Vie et histoire du Xe arrondissment* (1988) attributes the basic plan and facade to **Léon Ohnet et Lejeune.** Does this solve the schizophrenia?

★**[10e-20.] Hôpital Lariboisière,** rue Ambroise-Paré, between boulevard de Magenta and rue de Maubeuge. **Gauthier.** 1854.

Here a legacy from the countess de Lariboisière constructed the original buildings, subsequently expanded. The chapel, however, is original, on axis at the end of the court. Its bold classicism is akin to the work of the early 18th-century English architect, **Nicholas Hawksmoor.** Within, there is a monument to Elisa Roy, the countess, by **Marochetti.** The whole complex has an informal civility so often missing from the "modern" hospital.

★★**[10e-21.] Cinéma Louxor**/originally **Magasins de Sacré-Coeur,** 170, boulevard de Magenta, corner boulevard de la Chapelle. Original store, 1900. Movie theater, **Ripey.** 1921.

Here the fantasies of Hollywood were clothed in trappings appropriate to Cecil B. DeMille's biblical movie epics: both Moses and Ptolemy might have played here. No Egyptian building ever looked anything like this, of course, but neither did Roman temples resemble the Madeleine, nor Renaissance palaces look like banks. The last screening took place years ago, but a savior has appeared in the form of a discotheque, La Dérobade, for those tuned to African and Caribbean rhythms.

For the architectural semanticist, note the cavetto cornice and the papyrus columns, enriched with a gold-green-blue-brown Art Deco tile frieze.

[10e-22.] **Renault Garage,** 12, rue de Rocroy, corner rue de Belzunce. 1956.

A modern tour de force, its asbestos and glass fiber mansard is a gesture to Baron Haussmann. The building's bulk below is a late 1930s-revival ensemble of concrete engineering; the spiraling ramps are sinuous.

★[10e-23.] **Immeuble, 16, rue d'Abbeville** and 114, rue du Faubourg-Poissonnière. **Georges Massa.** circa 1900. **Alexandre Chapuy,** sculptor.

Mostly Belle Epoque/Beaux Arts, it is a bejeweled and bedecked dowager on the way to a fancy dress ball. Four busty and voluptuous *jeunes filles* adorn (scarcely hold up) the bays.

★★[10e-24.] **Immeuble, 14, rue d'Abbeville,** between rue du Faubourg-Poissonnière and rue de Rocroy. **Edouard Autant.** 1901.

"Extravagant" is an understatement, for everything in the prolix vocabulary of the Beaux Arts is crossbred here with the fantasies of the Art Nouveau: **Lavirotte, Guimard, Plumet, Laloux,** and a crowd of others are combined.

★★[10e-25.] **Eglise Saint-Vincent-de-Paul,** place Franz-Liszt, rue La Fayette, and rue d'Abbeville. **Jean-Baptiste Lepère** and later **Jacques-Ignace Hittorf.** 1824–1844. Chapelle de la Vièrge, **Edouard Villain.** 1889.

A six-columned Ionic neo-Roman pediment crowns a cascade of stairs. The interior (early Christian revival) is reminiscent in arrangement, if not scale, of Sant' Agnese (Fuori le Mura) in Rome. Two tiers of "antique" columns, Ionic below, Corinthian above, support a gilded timber roof, the latter worthy of Monreale, or San Clemente, or Cefalù. But it is all good archaeology at work in the hands of Hittorf, whose more daring venture is the **Gare du Nord [10e-19.].**

Batteries of painters and sculptors worked here: pediment, **Charles Le Boeuf;** stained glass, **Charles-Edouard Maréchal** and **Bontemps** (gallery); painted frieze, **Hippolyte Flandrin.** 1848–1853.

★★[10e-26.] **Marché Saint-Quentin,** 85, boulevard de Magenta, between rue des Petits-Hôtels and rue de Chabrol. 1866. Renovations, **Rabourdin.** 1982.

An elegantly warped geometric plan: the rich canopy above is fulfilled by the juncture of tensile bars and filigreed wrought-iron trusses with foliated cast-iron capitals. At waist level the vendors are modern, with booths roofed with lighted canopies that detach one from the glories above.

★[10e-26a.] **Compagnie Parisienne de la Distribution d'Electricité,** Cour de la Ferme-Sainte-Lazare, between rue de Chabrol and boulevard de Magenta. 1930s.

Concrete, cavetto corniced, this is a rare sight at the end of a narrow alley. Art Nouveau and concrete à la **Perret** combine.

**[10e-27.] Amphithéâtre Saint-Vincent-de-Paul**/originally **Chapelle de la Prison Saint-Lazare,** square Alban-Satragne, rue du Faubourg-Saint-Denis, off boulevard de Magenta. **Louis-Pierre Baltard.** 1824.

Victor Baltard's father was obviously less radical than his son (cf. **Les Halles** and **Saint-Augustin**).

★**[10e-27a.] Immeubles de rapport de Saint-Lazare,** 99-105, rue du Faubourg-Saint-Denis, between boulevard de Magenta and rue de Paradis. 1720.

An investment property of the Lazaristes (priests of the Mission of Saint-Lazare). Sharply incised arches reveal a porte cochère and, within and on a recessed plane, an *entresol.* Cool, calm, and street-smart, they show slightly bellied *garde-fous* at the first two *étages,* flat ones at the third.

---

**99-105, rue du Faubourg-Saint-Denis**
"In 1719 and 1720, the priests of the Mission of Saint-Lazare built, on the main road to Saint Denis, a long succession of double houses of several floors, very solidly constructed, all of *pierre de taille,* in which many private families and various artisans could live most comfortably and which could produce quite a considerable rent.

"Since the priests are very zealous with regard to proper moral conduct, they suggested a situation that would be proper for large numbers of people who have a serious desire to work toward attaining salvation.

"In June 1724, they placed this notice on every streetcorner of Paris to inform the public:

" 'Honest and Christian retreat.

" 'If they can find several fine people, ecclesiastics or laymen, who wish to live apart from the crass world, the priests of the Mission of Saint-Lazare will be quite prepared to procure for them, at small cost, near their church, wholesome and commodious lodging, a large courtyard, a fine garden, a country house, and all the other things necessary for life, whether in sickness or in health.' " Germain Brice, *Nouvelle description de la ville de Paris et de tout ce qu'elle contient de plus remarquable,* 8th ed. (1725).

---

★★**[10e-28.] Eglise Saint-Laurent,** boulevard Strasbourg at boulevard de Magenta. Lateral chapels, 16th century. Most of nave, 17th century. Chapelle de la Vièrge, 1712. Two west bays of nave, and facade, **Simon-Claude Constant-Dufeux.** 1863–1867.

An originally neo-Classical facade was replaced with a Gothic one at the command of Baron Haussmann. Classical in his rulebook was for the profane world, whereas Gothic was an absolute for the sacred. His opportunity arose when his minions cut through the new boulevard de Magenta; the added bays and facade aligned Saint-Laurent more appropriately with the new urban configuration.

This neo-Gothicism is, however, still struggling with the Renaissance. Inside, the choir with its pedimented altar is a cool gray place; but the organ loft of 1682 is magnificent, and the pendant bosses centering the vaults are spectacular.

★★**[10e-28a.]** Formerly **Musée de l'Affiche et de la Publicité**/originally **Faïenceries de Choisy,** 18, rue de Paradis, between rue du Faubourg-Saint Denis and rue Martel. Facade, **G. Jacobin** and **Ernest Brunnarius.** 1889. Modernizations for museum, **Jean Prouvé et Fils.** 1978.

The facade, a self-advertisement for manufacturers of glazed tilework, shields an iron-and-glass exposition hall that displayed some of the museum's collection of fifty thousand posters. It is a grandiloquent entry to an austere place of display. The museum has moved to more glitzy quarters, but the extravagant tiled remnants remain.

**[10e-29.] Offices, 15, rue Martel,** between rue de Paradis and rue des Petites-Ecuries. **Charles Thomas** and **F. Dumarcher.** 1928.

A no-nonsense concrete frame once supported delicate steel-framed glass sash, now replaced with a gross aluminum ensemble. The *garde-fous* give a sense of an older elegance. To paraphrase Mies van der Rohe: Some of God is sometimes in some of the details.

**[10e-30.] Passage du Désir,** portion entered at 50, boulevard de Strasbourg, and east to rue du Faubourg-Saint-Martin, between boulevard de Magenta and rue du Château-d'Eau.

The portion west of the boulevard de Strasbourg is an alley of seedy repair shops; but east of the boulevard the image is grander: a stage set of neo–Henri IV brickwork and cut stone. The miniature urban perspective is reminiscent of Palladio's **Teatro Olimpico** at Vicenza.

★★**[10e-31.] Mairie,** 76, rue du Faubourg-Saint-Martin, between rue du Château-d'Eau and rue Hittorf. **Jean-Eugène Rouyer.** 1892–1896.

Hittorf the street remembers the architect but not the adjacent architecture. The *mairie* is appropriately ornate, with a Viollet-le-Duc–like *flèche* punctuating the sky (as does his *flèche* at Notre Dame).

★★**[10e-32.] Hôtel Gouthière**/now **Conservatoire Hector Berlioz,** behind the Mairie, at 6, rue Pierre-Bullet. **Joseph Métivier.** circa 1780.

A neo-Classic temple for a master "chaser of metals," this was merely a portion of his vast complex, which extended to rue du Faubourg-Saint-Martin (where the *mairie* now sits). "Inventor of a process of matte gilding which gave his works an incomparable brilliance, at once sumptuous and subtle, he was the appointed supplier to Louis XVI, Madame du Barry. . . . He had to consent to long periods of credit. . . . These clients (then) carried along in their own ruin the unpaid artisan . . . sober and hardworking . . . but he had the ambition of becoming a 'proprietor,' which was his undoing. In 1772, he became owner of swampy land on rue du Faubourg-Saint-Martin . . . where he built a vast corps de logis . . . [and], at the end of a court, the pavilion which still exists today. He couldn't pay his creditors. . . . He died in poverty in 1813." from *Vie et histoire du Xe arrondissement.*

**[10e-33.] Passage Brady,** connecting boulevard de Strasbourg with 46, rue du Faubourg-Saint-Denis, between rue de Metz and rue du Château-d'Eau. 1828.

This western arm of a two-block *passage* in glass and steel houses "Eastern" restaurants and groceries. Decrepit.

**[10e-34.] Théâtre Antoine,** 14, boulevard de Strasbourg, opposite rue de Metz. circa 1900.

A still active theater developed by André Antoine in the spirit of the "naturalism" of Emile Zola.

**[10e-35.] Immeuble, 1, rue de Metz,** corner boulevard de Strasbourg.

Concrete, tile, and both bow- and bay-windows.

**[10e-36.] Brasserie Flo,** 7, cour des Petites-Ecuries, between rue de Faubourg-Saint-Denis and passage des Petites-Ecuries. Founded 1909. Decorated, 1910–1913.

Brass and brown within, a venerable masculine bistro, in the English or pseudo-English tradition, like Boston's **Locke-Ober** or Brooklyn's **Gage & Tollner.**

★[10e-37.] **Julien (restaurant),** 16, rue du Faubourg-Saint-Denis, between porte Saint-Denis and rue de Metz. 1889. Remodeled.

Architectural gourmands and restaurant gourmets, assemble! Here is Art Nouveau in style and food to balance one's cultural perspectives: peacocks, mirrors, and a splendid stained-glass *verrière.*

★[10e-38.] **Passage du Prado,** 12, rue du Faubourg-Saint-Martin, between Porte Saint-Denis and rue de Metz: through to 18, boulevard Saint-Denis. 1830.

Better in black and white than in color, this garish *passage* is a dogleg between the street and avenue. The passage du Bois-de-Boulogne was formerly here (1785), so we are at a point of early life on the Grands Boulevards.

★★[10e-39.] **Porte Saint-Denis,** rue Saint-Denis, leading to rue du Faubourg-Saint-Denis, at the juncture of boulevard de Bonne-Nouvelle and boulevard Saint-Denis. **Nicolas-François Blondel.** 1672. **Michel Anguier,** sculptor.

Louis XIV commissioned Blondel to create a symbolic city gate on this royal road to the Cathedral of Saint Denis, sacred place of marriage and burial of French kings. Here, an actual door had penetrated the fortifications of Charles V, demolished at Louis' order, their footprints the space of what was to become the Grands Boulevards.
Blondel inscribed his arch in a 72-foot square, the arch occupying the central third. Either tall pyramids or fat obelisks mark the flanks, covered with Anguier's decor, all honoring the victories of Louis XIV in Holland.

[10e-40.] **Magasin, 15, boulevard Saint-Denis,** between porte Saint-Denis and boulevard de Sebastopol. 1930s.

Art Moderne. The vegetative soffits and cubistic capitals make Prisunic seem to have borrowed grandmother's attic finery.

[10e-41.] **Porte Saint-Martin,** rue Saint-Martin, leading to rue du Faubourg-Saint-Martin, at junction of boulevard Saint-Denis and boulevard Saint-Martin. **Pierre Bullet.** 1674.

The Latin inscription on its attic reads: "To Louis the Great [XIV], for having twice taken Besançon and the Franche-Comté, and conquered the German, Spanish, and Dutch armies: the provost of tradesmen and the aldermen of Paris. 1674."
Bullet was a student of Blondel. His arch, of vermiculated rustications, is three-fourths the size of Blondel's: 54 feet square. But size alone does not bring monumentality, which is a matter of design and placement. Both **Blondel** and Bullet succeed in those endeavors.

★[10e-42.] **Théâtre de la Renaissance,** 20, boulevard Saint-Martin, corner rue René-Boulanger. **Lalande.** 1872.

On the boulevard, the facade is subtly neo-Renaissance, albeit with voussoirs with grinning (or is it snarling?) masks. But there is exquisite cast ironwork, and the mermaids are svelte. The entry corner, however, facing Porte Saint-Martin, explodes with form—twin busty caryatids, paired Corinthian columns, and plump cherubs guarding oculi. This is Beaux Arts, but it is also *pompier.*
Sarah Bernhardt directed and played here from 1893 to 1899.

**★[10e-43.] Théâtre de la Porte Saint-Martin,** 16, boulevard Saint-Martin, between Porte Saint-Martin and place Johann-Strauss. Original building, **Sanson-Nicolas Lenoir.** 1791. Rebuilt after fire, 1873.

Its predecessor, built during the reign of Louis XVI, was another partial victim of the communards' incendiarism in 1871 (along with the Tuileries Palace and the Hôtel de Ville).
Sarah Bernhardt was director from 1883 to 1893, when she moved next door to the Renaissance.

**[10e-44.] Immeuble, 14, boulevard Saint-Martin,** between Porte Saint-Martin and place Johann-Strauss. 1930.

A cut-stone smoothy, bay-windowed and fresh in contrast to all that jazz around it. The counterpoint that makes the Renaissance at **No. 20** possible.

**[10e-44a.] Immeuble, 37, boulevard Saint-Martin,** between Porte Saint-Martin and place de la République. 1830s.

Cast iron and fine frieze carving. Is this where New Orleans (Nouvelle-Orléans) learned its rich ornament?
Pass through the passage Meslay to 32, rue Meslay.

**[10e-44b.] Hôtel particulier, 45-47, rue Meslay,** between rue Saint-Martin and place de la République (reached through passage des Orgues). 1830s.

Louis-Philippe ironwork and lovely female voussoirs (at No. 45). Their baggage includes apes, pianos, scrolls, and other aesthetic and intellectual impedimenta.

**★[10e-45.] Immeuble, 39, rue Meslay,** at passage du Pont-aux-Biches. 1830s. Renovation, **Michel Possompes.** 1989.

Understatement from the pre-Haussmannian days. Here is where buildings and streets cohabited to create a transcendental urbanism.

**★[10e-46.] Hôtel d'Aligre,** 54, rue René-Boulanger, facing place Johann-Strauss. 1770s.

This neo-Classical facade shelters industry behind in polychromatic brick. One of the oldest residents along the Grands Boulevards.

**[10e-47.] Offices, 40, rue René-Boulanger,** facing place Johann-Strauss. 1970s.

The French know how to do the best and sometimes have done the worst (perhaps that's over?). Here is porthole-eyebrow heaven for little green Martian movies.

# 26
# ELEVENTH
# ARRONDISSEMENT
## EAST

### PLACE AUGUSTE-METIVIER TO

### AVENUE PHILIPPE-AUGUSTE

Avenue de la République; 31, rue Saint-Ambroise: **Mario Heymann**
and **Roger Anger;** 25, rue Saint-Ambroise: **Louis Miquel** and
**Georges Maurios;** Direction de l'Eau: **Christian de Portzamparc;**
rue de la Roquette; rue de Charonne; avenue Philippe-Auguste

Métro: **Père Lachaise**

[11e-11.] Immeuble, 49, rue de la Folie-Régnault.

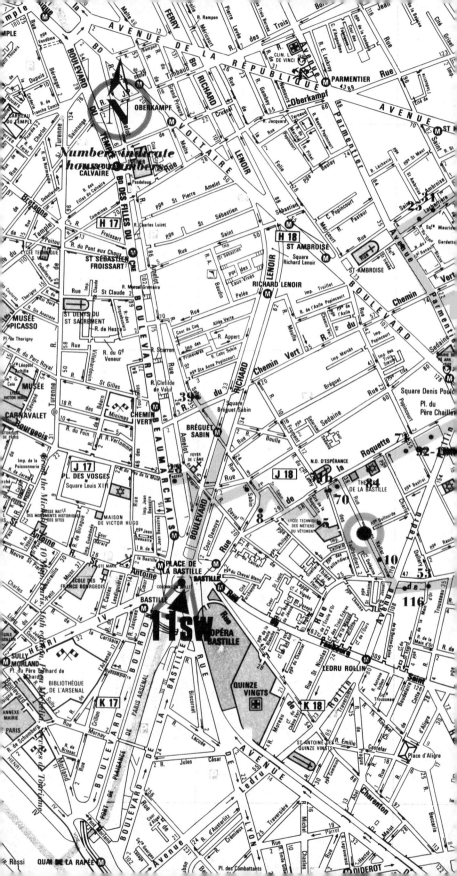

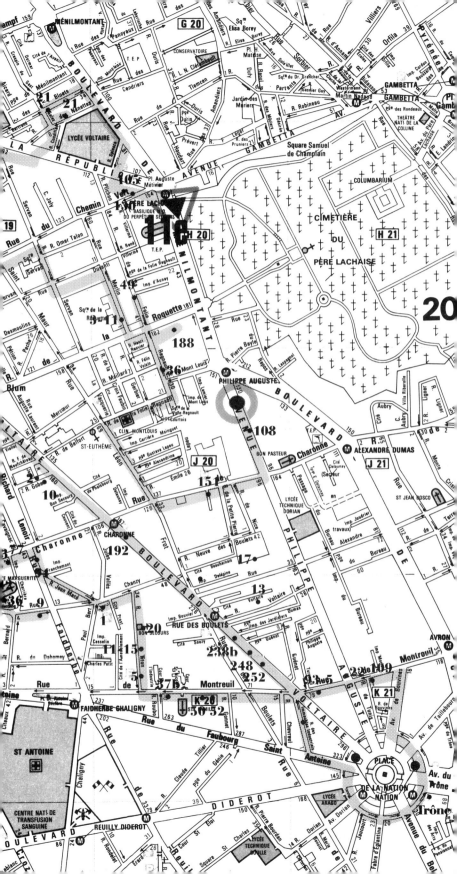

**[11e-1.] Immeuble, 105, avenue de la République,** near intersection with boulevard de Ménilmontant. **Henri Viet.** 1931.

Neo-Classic moderne with no shyness. Study it in relation to **No. 130** opposite.

**[11e-2.] Immeuble, 130, avenue de la République,** near intersection of boulevard de Ménilmontant. **Chrystophe and Dominique Dryjski.** 1981.

Sadly the materials are fragile, principally stucco, in this essay in recapturing some of the qualities of the 1930s. It succeeds at its crest with bold form but is banal at street level.

★**[11e-3.] Immeuble, 21, passage de Ménilmontant,** between boulevard de Ménilmontant and avenue de la République. **Michel Benoit** and **Thierry Verbiet.** 1985.

Some elaborate formal tricks, quite successful, but in blockwork. It is an exercise that is simultaneously crude and elegant.

**[11e-4.] Studios/Préfecture de Police,** 21, rue des Bluets, between boulevard de Ménilmontant and rue Victor-Gelez. **AUSIA.** 1987.

Cresting it all are three dunce caps, below which sit concrete-block and gray-stone lintels. A pretentious attempt.

**[11e-5.] Crèche, 56, rue Saint-Maur,** just south of rue Guillaume-Bertrand. **Christian Mauvette.** 1989.

★**[11e-6.] Immeuble, 31, rue Saint-Ambroise,** corner passage Saint-Ambroise. **Mario Heymann** and **Roger Anger.** 1969.

A bold statement in its time, perhaps particularly appropriate to the 11th arrondissement, which was then much in need of revitalization. It has the stylish constructivism one might associate with an early **Paul Rudolph.**

★**[11e-7.] Immeuble, 25, rue Saint-Ambroise,** corner passage Saint-Ambroise. **Louis Miquel,** assisted by **Georges Maurios.** 1965.

A slice of the Marseilles block, straight out of the **Le Corbusier** handbook, infilled with wood sash (in the manner of **Louis Kahn**). Only look up, because the streetscape collapses, with vulgar storefronts.

**[11e-8.] Eglise Saint-Ambroise,** boulevard Voltaire, at rue Saint-Ambroise. **Théodore Ballu.** 1863–1869.

A fussy twin-towered Romanesque Revival Haussmannian insert. Serenity was left behind by these nervous revivalists. How about some plain stone? Or go beserk à la Saint-Augustin (**Victor Baltard.** 1860–1871)?

★**[11e-9.] Direction de l'Eau et de la Propété, Ville de Paris,** 40, rue Pétion, between rue du Morvan and rue du Chemin-Vert. **Christian de Portzamparc.** 1987.

From here the managers of water and sanitation emerge, the agents of this white-tiled *salle de bain* of the streets. The curtain wall is here a foil: sorry you tried so hard.

**[11e-10.] Immeuble, 3-11, rue Merlin,** between rue de la Roquette and rue du Chemin-Vert.

Architecture and its maintenance are not the question here, but rather the park within—a bit of California where the arrangement is urbane, the materials and detailing tawdry.

★★[11e-11.] **Immeuble, 49, rue de la Folie-Régnault,** between rue de la Roquette and rue du Chemin-Vert.

Broken toys, bizarre slashes—the artist-architect James Wines (SITE) might be playing here. Orthodoxy cum mansard gives way to tile and stucco with a vestigial *paquebot* style—Darwinian evolution in a single blob.

★[11e-12.] **HBM, 188, rue de la Roquette,** between rue de la Folie-Régnault and boulevard de Ménilmontant.

Crisp concrete-framed public housing, submerged by the monsters next door. Very nice.

[11e-13.] **Ateliers/Housing, 36, rue de la Folie-Régnault,** between rue de la Roquette and rue de Mont-Louis.

Ateliers crowned by miniapartments: the workplace almost at home.

[11e-14.] **Immeuble, 151, rue de Charonne,** between rue Léon-Frot and avenue Philippe-Auguste. 1900.

A wonderful display of bay windows in this otherwise placid section of rue de Charonne.

★[11e-15.] **Immeuble, 108, avenue Philippe-Auguste,** between rue de Charonne and boulevard de Charonne. **Gilles Bouchez.** 1984.

Some architectural tricks are fun, like the double cross above. Such infill buildings are commendable, completing the urban fabric.

# 27

# ELEVENTH
# ARRONDISSEMENT

## NORTH

### PLACE DE LA REPUBLIQUE TO 61, BOULEVARD

### RICHARD-LENOIR AND BACK

Place de la République; passage Vendôme: **Jean-Baptiste Labadye,**
Magasins Printemps: **Gabriel Davioud** and **Marcel Oudin;** Eglise
Saint-Joseph; Palais de Commerce: **Ferdinand Bauquil;** Cirque
d'Hiver: **Jacques-Ignace Hittorf;** Le Bataclan; 61, boulevard
Richard-Lenoir: **Bernard Bourgade** and **Michel Londinsky**

Métro: **République**

[11n-11.] Immeuble, 82, rue du Faubourg-du-Temple, and 176, rue
Saint-Maur. Perhaps **Lucien Lambion.** circa 1929.

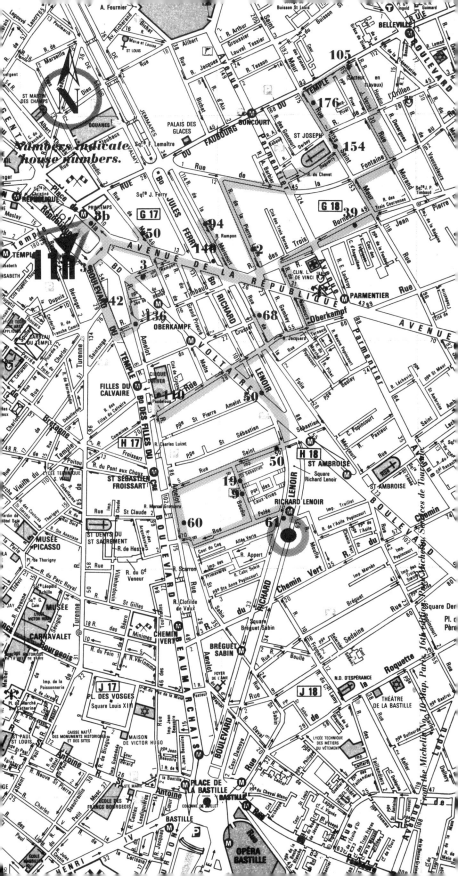

Numbers indicate house numbers.

★[11n-1.] **Place de la République**/originally **place du Château-d'Eau.** Monument, *La République.* **Léopold Morice** sculptor. **Charles Morice,** architect of pedestal.

The *place* was rearranged before 1865 by Haussmann's team, including **Gabriel Davioud,** whose fountain, which once graced it, was moved in 1883 to **place Félix-Eboué** to make way for *La République.* The name of the place and new avenue derive from the Morices' crowning statue.

★[11n-2.] **Passage Vendôme,** between 3, place de la République and 16, rue Béranger. **Jean-Baptiste Labadye.** 1828.

A radial void to place de la République: the ogive skylight is special. The rue Béranger facade is Louis XVIII, the *verrière* French rationalism.

[11n-3.] Formerly **Magasin Au Printemps**/originally **Magasins-Réunis,** 8 bis, place de la République, between rue du Faubourg-du-Temple and avenue de la République. **Gabriel Davoud.** 1865–1867. Altered, **Marcel Oudin.** 1894.

Haussmann hoped to "balance" the *place,* emulating the architecture of the Caserne du Prince-Eugène on the other side of rue du Faubourg-du-Temple. Davioud, always a good member of the team, complied in general, adding detail in the form of show windows, colossal pilasters, shells, garlands, and caryatids. The volume is now shared by the Holiday Inn.

[11n-4.] **Immeuble, 50, rue de Malte,** between rue du Faubourg-du-Temple and avenue de la République.

This Haussmannian presence shields the fantasies of URB (Utrecht Royale–Belge) with backbuildings sullied with glass and filigree that would shock downtown Brussels. Why did you do this to Paris?

★[11n-5.] **RATP, 3, rue Rampon,** between rue de Malte and boulevard Voltaire.

Steel and sash, those wrought-iron noodles create wondrous console brackets. A delicacy for aficionados of steel and glass.

[11n-5a.] **Immeuble, 42, boulevard du Temple,** between rue Jean-Pierre-Timbaud and place de la République. circa 1830s.

Not only did Gustave Flaubert live here from 1856 to 1869, but it is also a pre-Haussmannian class act with Corinthian pilasters at the entry and a wonderful first floor above the *rez-de-chaussée* and *entresol.* Savor the cast-iron railings.

★[11n-6.] **Immeuble, 136, rue Amelot,** northeast corner rue Jean-Pierre-Timbaud.

Half of an exedral place, this retains 18th-century details on its surelevated form: a wise and elegant urban participant.

[11n-7.] **Residence Folie-Méricourt,** 94, rue de la Folie-Méricourt, between rue du Faubourg-du-Temple and avenue de la République.

Neo-Grec from the 1930s, this presents another strong exedra to the street.

[11n-8.] **Immeuble, 140, boulevard Richard-Lenoir,** north of the avenue de la République. circa 1800.

This preceded both Haussmann and the covering of the Canal Saint-Martin. The self-conscious neo-Classicism of the sculptures and niches is more a 19th-century restored-exaggeration than a product of pure revolutionary fervor. The circular skylit stair within is wonderful.

[11n-9.] **Maison Pichenot**/successor **Jules Loebnitz**, 2, rue de la Pierre-Levée, between rue des Trois-Bornes and rue de la Fontaine-au-Roi. 1880.

A studied facade in the Beaux Arts manner but with Chicago Style infill.

[11n-10.] **Eglise Saint-Joseph**, 154, rue Saint-Maur, opposite rue de l'Orillon. **Théodore Ballu**. 1877.

Preordained or precut Romanesque Revival: a cold and sorry attempt at what, in the United States, was a rich and powerful vocabulary, led by H. H. Richardson. Why did the font of Parisian Romanesque Revival go dry?

★★[11n-11.] **Immeuble, 82, rue du Faubourg-du-Temple,** and **176, rue Saint-Maur.** Perhaps **Lucien Lambion.** circa 1929.

A wonderful *pan coupé*, bayed and burly, cream without ice. This is the first and only class act around here. The oriels at the summit are an extraordinary punctuation of a rich and lovely form.

★[11n-12.] **Palais de Commerce**, 105, rue du Faubourg-du-Temple, between rue Saint-Maur and boulevard de La Villette. **Ferdinand Bauquil.** 1924.

A gallery of ateliers centrally lit, all in *beton armé.* Now somewhat seedy, the space is exhilarating.

★★[11n-13.] **Groupe Scolaire, 39, rue des Trois-Bornes,** between rue Saint-Maur and avenue Parmentier. circa 1930s.

An elegant urbanism that sculpts an exedral garden within its embracing streetfronted wings. Stylish curved brick, it presents an oasis of supreme grace within otherwise bland blocks.

[11n-14.] **Immeuble, 68, rue de la Folie-Méricourt,** between rue Oberkampf and avenue de la République.

Industrial steel and brick. Dwellings crown their own ateliers; a vertical zoning stratification.

★★[11n-15.] **Cirque d'Hiver,** 110, rue Amelot, at intersection of boulevard des Filles-du-Calvaire and boulevard du Temple. **Jacques-Ignace Hittorf.** 1852.

Polychromatic, like the buildings of ancient Greece (the Parthenon was not nude stone), and polygonal in form, this was one of the 19th century's several circuses of the theater.

[11n-16.] **Le Bataclan,** 50, boulevard Voltaire, at intersection of boulevard Richard-Lenoir. **Duval.** 1864. Much altered.

Here a Napoléon III theater aped a Chinese pagoda fantasy. The exterior has been skinned, but within there are the original *pompiers* frescoes.

[11n-17.] **Immeuble, 50, rue Saint-Sébastien,** corner boulevard Richard-Lenoir.

Innocuous without, there is a pleasant courtyard with a lion and a lady in niches.

**[11n-18.] Ecole, 19, rue Alphonse-Baudin,** between rue Saint-Sébastien and rue Pelée. **Philippe Canac.** 1978.

The unfortunate 1970s inflicted modish hats on serviceable buildings.

**[11n-19.] Gymnase/Piscine Cour-des-Lions,** 9, rue Alphonse-Baudin, between rue Saint-Sébastien and rue Pelée. **Philippe Canac.** 1981.

Futuristic in form and scale, clad in yellow tile, the windows might be portholes for the swimmers within.

**[11n-20.] Immeuble, 2, boulevard des Filles-du-Calvaire,** corner rue Saint-Sébastien.

Rich Louis-Philippe cast ironwork: pilasters, *persiennes*, and a nougat-entry doorframe.

**[11n-21.] J. Alexandre/Régifilm,** 60, rue Amelot, between rue Saint-Sébastien and rue Pelée.

Wallace fountains, bicycles built for two, gendarme boxes, light standards, telephone booths, kiosks—the street furniture of Paris, old and current, rented by the movie and video industries.

**[11n-22.] Immeuble, 61, boulevard Richard-Lenoir,** between allée-Verte and rue Pelée. **Bernard Bourgade** and **Michel Londinsky.** 1984.

The central semicircular pediment is a 19th-century vestige, but the wings of lodgings seem inflated models, pasty and with too little shade and shadow. This one needs some metal railings *(garde-fous)* in contrasting color and/or values.

# 28
# ELEVENTH ARRONDISSEMENT
## SOUTHWEST

### PLACE DE LA BASTILLE TO PLACE LEON BLUM

### AND BACK

Place de la Bastille; Colonne de Juillet: **Jean-Antoine Alavoine;** rue de la Roquette; Eglise Notre-Dame-de-l'Espérance: **Julien Barbier;** Mairie: **Etienne-François Gancel;** place Léon Blum; boulevard Voltaire; Cité Beauharnais: **P. Colombier;** Habitations ouvrières: **Paul Héneux;** place de la Nation; Barrière du Trône: **Claude-Nicolas Ledoux;** Palais de la Femme: **Auguste Labussière;** rue de Charonne; Eglise Sainte-Marguerite: **Jacques-François de l'Espée** and **Victor Louis;** Café au Vrai Saumur: **Julien Galobin**

Métro: **Bastille**

[11sw-44.] Café au Vrai Saumur/originally **Carrefour Bouchez.** **Julien Galobin.** 1902.

195

**Place de la Bastille:** A void where there was once a solid, this is the site of the prison of the Bastille, originally a fort (14th century), a bastion on the fortifications of Charles V. Modified, reinforced, and girded with a dry moat, the fortified ensemble became **les Fossés Jaunes** under Louis XIII. Louis kept the alignment of Charles from here west to **Porte Saint-Denis,** beyond which the wall was extended to embrace the full **Louvre** and the **Tuileries'** gardens. One can saunter on the bed of the wall on the *Grands Boulevards,* starting with **Beaumarchais** and continuing with **Filles-du-Calvaire, Temple, Saint-Martin, Saint-Denis, Bonne-Nouvelle, Poissonnière, Montmartre, Italiens, Capucines, and Madeleine.** Here, only thirty-four years after Louis XIII's wall was completed, his son Louis XIV ordered its demolition, no longer necessary after his military victories and, at the same time, technologically outmoded. *Boulevard* is the word for the service road of fortifications, and, strictly speaking, the various boulevards of Paris are on the site of various, sequential fortifications. Some, like Voltaire, acquired the appellation *boulevard* in the 19th century, when eclecticism in architecture was matched by eclecticism in nomenclature.

The place de la Bastille is shared by the 4th, 11th, and 12th arrondissements, but when the fortress was demolished in 1789 it was part of the ensemble protecting Paris, and the 11th and 12th arrondissements were suburbs *(faubourgs)* outside.

★★**[11sw-1.] Colonne de Juillet,** center of the place de la Bastille. Base, **Jean-Antoine Alavoine.** 1825–1833. Column, **Joseph-Louis Duc.** 1840.

The July Revolution of 1830 put Louis-Philippe in power for eighteen years. Wishing to memorialize that revolutionary month, he preempted this growing monument, where Alavoine's original work was to have been merely a monument to the Ville de Paris. A giant Corinthian column (165 feet tall) is crowned with a bronze capital, all poured monolithically, an extraordinary feat of casting. The names of the fallen of July 1830 are inscribed on the column, and their remains were originally placed in a vault below, at a ceremony on the tenth anniversary of the uprising, to the sounds of a symphony for military band especially composed for the occasion by Hector Berlioz.

**[11sw-2.] Immeuble, 39, rue Saint-Sabin,** just north of rue du Chemin-Vert. **L. Depoix.** 1909.

Two demure ladies stretch a garland across the second floor . . . console brackets, *frontons,* and a slated mansard roof all conjoin in this island of Haussmannianism—admittedly *tardif*—among industrial neighbors.

**[11sw-3.] Boulangerie, 28, boulevard Beaumarchais,** corner rue Pasteur. 1900.

One of several wonderful shopfronts left from the *Belle Epoque.*

**[11sw-4.] Café de l'Industrie,** corner rue Sedaine and rue Saint-Sabin. 1900.

The stair within is special.

★**[11sw-5.] Médecins sans Frontière,** 8, rue Saint-Sabin, between rue Sedaine and rue de la Roquette. 1980s.

A more up-to-date *paquebot* than those of **Marcel Breuer**—and better. Their antenna on the roof must reach Sri Lanka. The Médecins are volunteer physicians serving the poor and oppressed in the world's sore spots: Nicaragua, Sri Lanka, Mozambique.

**★★[11sw-6.] Magasin Styles Dugasl,** 5, Cité de la Roquette, between rue de Lappe and rue des Taillandiers.

A romantic was here: timbers, bracketing, and finials in an extravagant remembrance of things not past. Gothic Revival.

**★[11sw-7.] Eglise Notre-Dame-de-l'Espérance,** 51 bis, rue de la Roquette, at rue du Commandant-Lamy. **Julien Barbier.** 1920.

A polygonal *clocher* surmounts an eclectic *moderne* facade. Behind, however, are concrete ribs and a concrete shell spanning the nave. A split personality.

**[11sw-8.] Fountain, 70, rue de la Roquette,** between rue des Taillandiers and rue Keller. 1846.

A neo-Renaissance grotto, decorated with shells, leaves, and the arms of the City of Paris. A public water supply was a product and symbol of dense urbanization; and here, as in other major European cities, its success was advertised at the point where ordinary people (without indoor plumbing) gathered it in buckets.

**[11sw-9.] Synagogue, 84, rue de la Roquette,** between rue Keller and passage Charles-Dallery. **A.-G. Heaume** and **Alexandre Persitz.** 1966.

A pleated/folded concrete roof within. Banal.

**[11sw-10.] Portal, 71, rue de la Roquette,** between passage Charles-Dallery and rue Basfroi. circa 1800.

Two Greek Revival ladies occupy the arched tympanum.

**[11sw-11.] Maisons, 92-100, rue de la Roquette,** between rue Basfroi and place Léon-Blum.

**[11sw-12.] Immeuble** and **café, 132, rue de la Roquette,** on place Léon-Blum. **Brouilhony.** 1860.

An eclectic facade is squeezed by Burger King and other pressing commerce. Look up. At the second floor (don't count the *entresol*) are busty caryatids with floral chastity belts.

**[11sw-13.] Mairie,** place Léon-Blum, between avenue Parmentier and boulevard Voltaire. **Etienne-François Gancel.** 1862–1865.

Bulky and boring, the latter as much a result of its squat volume as its posture at the end of a large urban space. Compare those of the 10th and 18th, the first with no square, and the latter with a small *place* and church. Both are dominant mini–*hôtels de ville.*

**★[11sw-14.] Compagnie Parisienne de la Distribution de l'Electricité,** 14, avenue Parmentier, between place Léon-Blum and rue du Chemin-Vert.

Iron arches below, colonnettes above, clear space inside. Another of the old electricity company's technically avant-garde works, now honored for their aesthetic value; see **[10e-26a.]** or **[9w-24.].**

**[11sw-15.] Hôtel particulier, 10, rue Gobert,** between boulevard Voltaire and rue Richard-Lenoir. **Gilet.** 1870.

The intricate iron balconies with medallions and garlands are extraordinary in this Napoléon III house.

★[11sw-16.] **Gymnase Japy**/formerly **Marché,** 2, rue Japy, near inter-section of boulevard Voltaire and rue Gobert. 1870. Converted to *gymnase,* 1884.

Cast and wrought iron and brick, skylit within. Here volleyball has replaced food: calories are worked off, rather than on. No-nonsense ele-gance.

[11sw-17.] **Immeuble, 192, boulevard Voltaire,** between rue de Cha-ronne and rue Chanzy.

Bay windows at a grand scale but crudely detailed, with oriel balconies for Rapunzel to let down her hair. A near miss.

[11sw-18.] **Cité Beauharnais,** off boulevard Voltaire between rue Alex-andre-Dumas and rue de Charonne. 1980s.

Sleek aluminum in a Post Modern play of forms creates a childish world of undergraduate architectural forms. Aging.

★[11sw-19.] **Jardin, 17, Cité Beauharnais,** off boulevard Voltaire be-tween rue Alexandre-Dumas and rue de Charonne. 1980s.

As you penetrate the *cité* to the lovely gardens behind, it all improves. The greensward and sculpture provide a delightful oasis.

[11sw-20.] **Immeuble, 13, Cité Voltaire,** between rue Alexandre-Dumas and rue de Montreuil.

Bay windows, iron, and glass with polychromatic brick.

[11sw-21.] **Immeuble, 238 bis, boulevard Voltaire,** between rue Alexander-Dumas and rue de Montreuil. circa 1930.

Bowed bays, oculi, and light stone vary this lengthy Haussmannian strip.

[11sw-22.] **Immeuble, 248, boulevard Voltaire,** between rue Alexan-dre-Dumas and rue de Montreuil. **A. Vaser.** 1863. Remodeled, **Henri-Anatole Moncel.** 1903. **Révillon,** sculptor.

Renaissance Revival with some Gothicisms thrown in. An eclectic strip of great richness.

[11sw-23.] **G. Caro (magasin),** 252, boulevard Voltaire, between rue Alexandre-Dumas and rue de Montreuil.

"BILLARDS, JEUX, JETONS
INSTALLATIONS COMPLÈTES DE CERCLES ET DE CASINOS.
INSTALLATIONS COMPLÈTES D'ACADÉMIES ET DE SALLES DE BILLARDS"
Building, shopfront, and business—the last since 1789—give a cultural solidity to this newer neighborhood. A stylish iron storefront with Beaux Arts above.

★[11sw-24.] **Habitations ouvrières, 93-95, rue de Montreuil,** be-tween boulevard Voltaire and avenue Philippe-Auguste. **Paul Héneux.** Streetfront, 1892. Housing behind, before 1908.

Bourgeois in front, proletarian behind in low barracks. The entry arch conceals the glazed colored tile of the porte cochère ceiling, resting on exposed iron T bars.

**[11sw-25.] Immeuble, 22, avenue Philippe-Auguste,** corner rue de Montreuil. **L. I. Jourdain.** 1904.

Some mild late *pompier.*

**[11sw-26.] Garage, 109, rue de Montreuil,** between avenue Philippe-Auguste and avenue de Bouvines. 1920s.

Sinuous pencil lines for sash, with tile and translucent glass. Naive cubist.

★**[11sw-27.] Place de la Nation.**

The hub of ten radial ways, five of which (two boulevards, one avenue, one rue, and the cours) go somewhere, and five of which have brave beginnings but soon falter. The nation did not receive its crown, Dalou's central "Triomphe de la République," until 1899, in fulfillment of Haussmann a generation after he lost power. What has been important, however, for three hundred years is the eastern portion, where the avenue du Trône enters, the point of ceremonial entry for the kings of France since the 17th century. It is there also that we find the pavilions of Ledoux.

The *place,* 800 feet in diameter, is so vast that the periphery buildings do not visually contain it. The *boule* players on various islands might just as well be in the country.

★★★**[11sw-28.] Barrière du Trône**/sometimes called **Barrière de Vincennes,** avenue du Trône, between boulevard de Charonne and boulevard de Picpus. **Claude-Nicolas Ledoux.** 1788. Sculptures atop by **Etex** and **Dumont.** 1830s.

La Ferme Générale was an organization of forty *fermiers généraux,* subcontractors, in effect, who collected indirect taxes for the king—of course taking, in turn, their own cut. These worthies erected the wall of the Fermiers Généraux in the mid-1780s, its fifty-two points of entry serving as tollgates for collecting taxes on food and other necessities entering Paris. All of the pavilions were designed by Ledoux, but only four survive. Two of them actually were collection points (this and that at Denfert-Rochereau), one was administrative (the Rotonde at La Villette), and one was an "extra" viewing platform for the duc d'Orléans at Parc Monceau.

The Barrière du Trône includes two collecting buildings and two guardhouses, the latter surmounted by monumental columns. This is neo-Classical architecture of the first rank, one set of the fifty-two chessmen briefly in place. These so exacerbated the discontent of Parisians that they were contributory to the Revolution and were sacked by mobs to vent their wrath.

★**[11sw-29.] Rue des Immeubles-Industrielles,** between rue du Faubourg-Saint-Antoine and boulevard Voltaire. **Emile Leménil.** 1873.

Three levels of housing over ateliers below . . . with a uniformity that makes the rue de Rivoli look lush. The orderliness is still extant, in a spirit that might be termed *Hollandaise.*

A vast steam-engine in the cellar powered machinery on the first three levels *(rez-de-chaussée, entresol,* and *premier étage),* above which were three floors of apartments.

---

**Rue des Immeubles-Industrielles**
"It's a completely new street, pretty, which will create an elegant small town in this immense faubourg. The street, which the Company will deliver to the city of Paris completed, with its sidewalks and roadway, bears the name of 'rue de l'Industrie-Saint-Antoine' and connects the two great arteries of rue

Saint-Antoine and boulevard Voltaire. The concept that inspired the creation of these new buildings has for its ultimate purpose the availability to the worker of a single complete complex for his family and his workplace."
*L'Illustration,* July 12, 1873.

---

**[11sw-30.] Immeuble, 52, rue de Montreuil,** between rue des Boulets and rue Titon. **Romeur** and **Varenault.** 1830s.

En-niched, with six neo-Classical figures in search of the True, the Good, and the Beautiful (proper ancient Greek values). Two vacant niches await residents.

**[11sw-31.] Immeuble, 50, rue de Montreuil,** between rue des Boulets and rue Titon. **Honoré-Lucien Pers.** 1885.

Iron brought to a high level of strapwork.

**[11sw-32.] L'Aiguière (restaurant),** 37 bis, rue Montreuil, near rue Titon. 17th century.

A Louis XIII *auberge,* where—would you believe it?—the real Porthos, Athos, Aramis, and d'Artagnan hung out. The surrounding buildings are ateliers served by great wood-timbered skylights, reached through sequential courts.

**[11sw-33.] Immeuble, 5, rue Titon,** between rue de Montreuil and rue Chanzy. **P. Robuchon.** 1932.

A 1930s *Moderne* presence in this bland, variegated street.

**[11sw-34.] Ateliers** and **logements, 11, 13, 15, rue Titon,** between rue de Montreuil and rue Chanzy. 1900.

Here orthodox streetfronted housing leads to ateliers for the same population behind, a widespread practice at one time in Paris. Some are still in timber.

★**[11sw-35.] Eglise Notre-Dame-de-Bon-Secours**/also **Eglise Protestante–Luthérienne,** 20, rue Titon between rue de Montreuil and rue Chanzy. **Jean-Emile Rey.** 1896.

Some silly romanticisms outside. Within (★★), great handsome hammer beams support a stained-glass skylight—heaven on earth—and stubby Composite capitals keep it all together below. The dark wood remembers a northern European culture.

**[11sw-36.] Immeuble** and **Restaurant Chardenoux,** 1, rue Jules-Vallès, corner rue Chanzy. **Emile Laurent.** 1908.

The iron-and-glass marquise is a distinguished entry to the period restaurant within: stucco, patterned glass, and a marble-and-zinc bar. The outside is every bit as rich in detail.

★**[11sw-37.] Palais de la Femme/Armée du Salut,** 94, rue de Charonne, corner rue Faidherbe. **Auguste Labussière** and **C. Longerey,** architects. **Camille Garnier,** sculptor. 1910.

*Meulière,* brick, *pierre de taille,* terra-cotta, and wood-bracketed eaves. There are skylights over the court within, and an inexpensive restaurant for the patient; 750 single rooms.

**[11sw-38.] Immeuble** and **ateliers, 77, rue de Charonne,** between rue Godefroy-Cavaignac and rue Basfroi. Street building, **Emile Bonnet.** 1886. Ateliers behind, circa 1917.

This many-tiered assembly of iron and glass, balconied for access, is an intense workplace that is masked by the Haussmannian streetfront.

**[11sw-39.] Immeuble, 73-75, rue de Charonne,** between rue Godefroy-Cavaignac and rue Basfroi. 1980s.

A bellied apartment block.

★**[11sw-40.] Immeuble** and **court, 42, rue Saint-Bernard,** between rue de Charonne and rue Charles-Delescluze.

A delightful flowered and vined interior court remembers the scale and *faubourgs* of years past. Walk in.

★**[11sw-41.] Eglise Sainte-Marguerite,** 36, rue Saint-Bernard, between rue de Charonne and rue Charles-Delescluze. 1637–1734. Chapel of the Virgin, 1734. New choir, **Jacques-François de l'Espée.** 1737. Chapel of the Souls of Purgatory, **Victor Louis.** 1760, with trompe l'oeil by **Brunetti** and **Briard.**

With its Square Nording, it forms an ensemble in the manner of a country church (compare Saint-Médard). The chapel is a space of illusion by Brunetti, its false perspective of Composite colonnades and grand coffered barrel vault leading to broken entablatures that frame Briard's painting *The Passage of Souls from Purgatory to Heaven.*

**[11sw-42.] Maison, 9, rue Chanzy,** between rue Saint-Bernard and rue Faidherbe. **Achille Champy.** 1902

Even here a heavier Art Nouveau intervenes (and next door at **No. 7** is a "modern" atrocity).

★**[11sw-43.] Hôtel de Mortagne,** 53, rue de Charonne, corner of passage Charles-Dallery. **Delisle-Mansart.** 1652–1670.

Now concealed behind a banal modern block, this 17th-century *manoir* still houses a central octagonal rotunda, with ornamental plasterwork and parquetry restored.

★★**[11sw-44.] Café au Vrai Saumur**/originally **Carrefour Bouchez.** 116, avenue Ledru-Rollin, corner rue de Charonne. Building, **Julien Galobin.** 1902.

A sinuous wood Art Nouveau storefront sheltered by a monumental glass-and-iron marquise. Inside are bacchanalian putti consorting across the ceiling, and some ceramic panels à la Mucha.

**[11sw-45.] Groupe scolaire, 10, rue Keller,** between rue de Charonne and rue de la Roquette. **Louis-Hippolyte Boileau** and **E. Olombel.** 1932.

A rigid frame of concrete with cream and ochre tile infill. Precocious and difficult to see behind its encircling walls.

And return to **place de la Bastille.**

# 29
# ELEVENTH AND TWELFTH ARRONDISSMENTS
## SAINT-ANTOINE
### PLACE DE LA BASTILLE TO
### MAISON EUGENIE-NAPOLEON

Place de la Bastille; Opéra de la Bastille: **Carlos Ott;** rue du Faubourg-Saint-Antoine; Magasins le Bihan: **Charles de Montalto;** Eglise Saint-Antoine-des-Quinze-Vingts; Marché Beauvau: **Nicolas Lenoir;** square Trousseau; Cuisine de l'Hôpital Saint-Antoine: **Henri Ciriani;** Centre Hospitalier Universitaire/Hôpital Saint-Antoine: **André Wogensky;** passage du Génie; Maison Eugénie-Napoléon: **Jacques-Ignace Hittorf**

Métro: **Bastille**

[11/12-15.] Marché Beauvau/or Marché Lenoir. Nicolas Lenoir. 1843.

The **place de la Bastille** is where, symbolically, the French Revolution "began." Although the mob attacking that medieval bastion, later prison, released only seven detainees, the event is remembered every July 14 as the special focus of a multifaceted revolution that had many striking events. What is remembered here is as arbitrary as selecting the remains for the tomb of the unknown soldier but no less moving.

The **Colonne de Juillet** remembers another revolution (1830) [11sw-1.]. But looming over this, like a beached leviathan, is the new **Opéra de la Bastille.**

★★★[11/12-1.] **Opéra de la Bastille,** place de la Bastille, between rue de Lyon and rue de Charenton. **Carlos Ott.** 1989.

The new opera more than fills the site of the former **Gare de Vincennes,** a redundant railroad station in its last years, due to the development of the RER (super Métro). And perhaps equally important, this opera for the people, as it was programmed, sits at the edge of a revolutionary *place*, among the eastern zones of Paris, traditional quarter of workers and revolutionaries.

The building is the design product of an international architectural competition won by Ott, a young Canadian born in Uruguay. Its 2,700-seat auditorium seems a great visual and acoustic success; its bulky posture on the place de la Bastille is another matter. The sheer volume, charging toward the **Colonne de Juillet,** is overwhelming, the result of a program given to competitors that forced onto the site much too much to allow any building to assume a friendly posture vis-à-vis its contextual neighbors. The **Palais Garnier** is a striking contrast: there the building and its context were designed as an integrated architectural and urbanistic ensemble.

The cladding, or not-so-fancy dress of this behemoth, doesn't help. The glass-and-metal panels, and the broken forms that work with them, seem already dated, part of an overanxious attempt to be new, to be the latest. A little understated serenity, with classic but not Classical form, would have been more appropriate.

★★[11/12-2.] **Magasins le Bihan**/originally **Magasins Wimphen,** 25, rue du Faubourg-Saint-Antoine, between place de la Bastille and rue de Charonne. **Charles de Montalto.** 1894.

Cast iron with extravagant capitals. The added bracing at the fourth floor displays a delightful structural rescue. This is the best facade on the whole rue du Faubourg-Saint-Antoine.

★[11/12-3.] **Cour du Bel-Air,** 56, rue du Faubourg-Saint-Antoine, between place de la Bastille and rue de Charonne. circa 1830.

*It never ceases to amaze me* is an apt expression for Paris open spaces intra-*îlot*, such as this: a handsome, verdant, private square.

[11/12-4.] **Fontaine Trogneux,** 61, rue du Faubourg-Saint-Antoine, corner rue de Charonne. 1719.

More neo-Renaissance than neo-Classical, this served also as a "milestone" *(borne)* marking the beginning of the rue de Charonne.

"He showed him the opening of the rue de Charonne, with its old windows, its mansards, its ornamented walls; the piece of wall at the fountain that made one dream of a château or of a park." **Jules Romain.**

[11/12-5.] **Ateliers, 74, rue du Faubourg-Saint-Antoine,** opposite rue de Charonne. circa 1885.

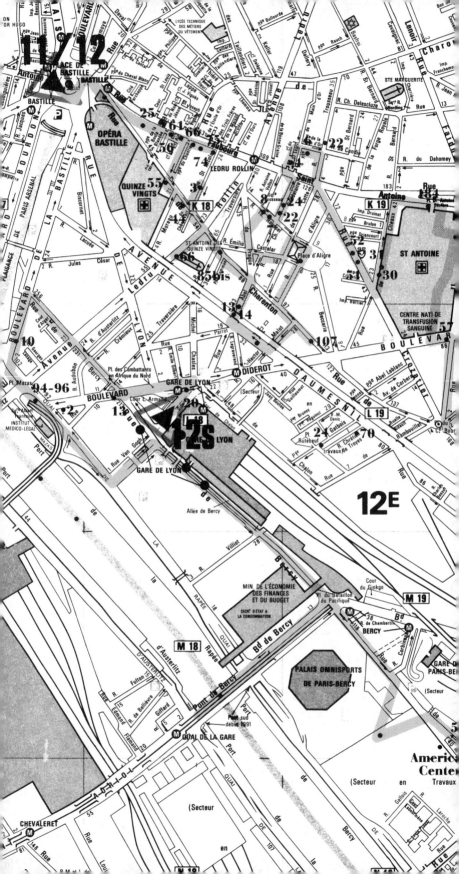

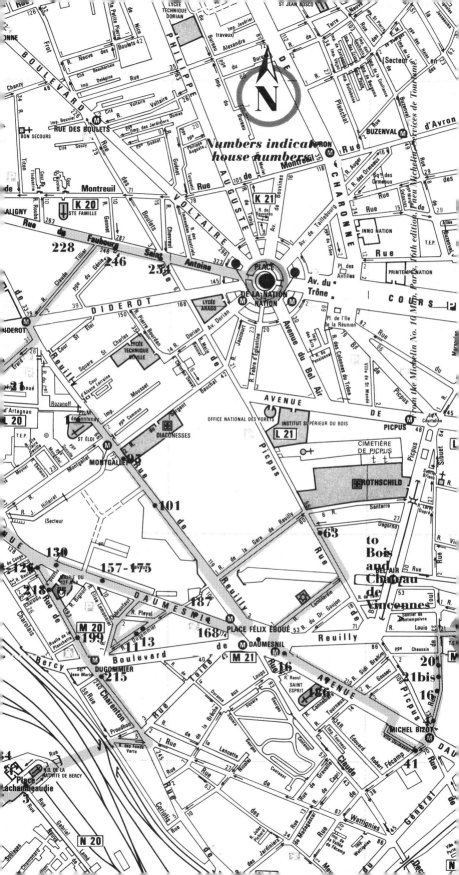

The glass roof that shelters loading and unloading is an appropriate skylight at this furniture factory, where light was welcome before electricity, and wood finishes were fragile in wet weather. Handsome.

**[11/12-6.] Courtyard, 75, rue du Faubourg-Saint-Antoine,** between rue de Charonne and avenue Ledru-Rollin. **M. de Chabot.** 1883.

**[11/12-7.] Passage du Chantier,** between 66, rue du Faubourg-Saint-Antoine and 55, rue de Charenton. 1842.

A welcome shortcut to rue de Charenton, past work sites of the furniture trade.

★**[11/12-8.] Immeuble, 44, rue de Charenton,** between passage du Chantier and avenue Ledru-Rollin. 1890s.

Bay windows and glazed brick join in this modestly polychromatic building. Savor the wrought-iron frames supporting the bays: curlicued.

**[11/12-9.] Immeuble, 3, rue Saint-Nicolas,** between rue de Charenton and rue du Faubourg-Saint-Antoine. **Alexandre Ghiulamila.** 1988.

Streamlines and columns enliven this old street of furniture and fabric vendors.

**[11/12-10.] Eglise Saint-Antoine-des-Quinze-Vingts,** 66, avenue Ledru-Rollin, between rue de Charenton and avenue Daumesnil. 1909.

Awkward without, the neo-Romanesque interior sports a glass-eyed dome over the crossing. A delightful detail.

**[11/12-11.] Boulangerie/Patisserie, 85 bis, rue de Charenton,** corner rue Emilio-Castelar.

An exterior *classé*. Hungry?

★**[11/12-12.] HBM, 13 and 14, rue Abel,** between avenue Daumesnil and rue de Charenton. **Emile Bois. 1921.**

Some original massing in brick and limestone, with stepped gables fronting the street in the Dutch manner. Bois won the competition in 1913, but World War I intervened between concept and completion. A barrel vault at No. 14 bears the municipal cartouche.

★**[11/12-13.] Viaduct, Chemin de Fer de Vincennes, avenue Daumesnil,** between place de la Bastille and intersection with rue de Charenton.

The **Gare de Vincennes** was demolished to make way for the **Opéra de la Bastille,** but the viaduct that led to it, happily elevated to leave foot and horse traffic free, remains. The most fertile imaginations foresaw on its vacant route a rebirth of the hanging gardens of Bercy, if not Babylon. Some efforts have been made for pedestrian-ways to the east between rue Picpus and boulevard Soult, but most of its length is waiting. Here, near rue Abel, the arches shelter appropriate shops and give a handsome rhythm to the street.
At rue de Charenton and rue de Rambouillet, competition winner **Wladimir Mitrofanoff** has been commissioned to build apartments.

**[11/12-14.] Logements, 107, rue de Charenton,** between rue d'Aligre and boulevard Diderot. **P. Malluin** and **J. P. Mauduit.** 1984.

Big square cream tile in a foil to tiles that are tiny and black. Stylish, and of course it will shortly be dated, as is its next-door neighbor. But it's better.

**★★[11/12-15.] Marché Beauvau**/sometimes called **Marché Lenoir,** place d'Aligre, between rue de Cotte and rue d'Aligre. **Nicolas Lenoir.** 1843.

Timber at this market, in contrast to the more sophisticated iron and glass at the *marchés* **Saint-Quentin** or **Secrétan.** The structure has the guts of rural France, with trussed members that create powerful interplay overhead. Unfortunately bird screens and fluorescent lights diminish the glory of it all.

**[11/12-16.] Logements/Fondation Rothschild,** 7, rue Théophile-Roussel, between rue de Prague and rue Charles-Baudelaire. **Henri-Paul Nénot.** 1909.

*"Pour l'amélioration des conditions de l'existence matérielle des travailleurs"* . . . the barons Alphonse, Edmard, James, Gustave, Edouard, and Robert de Rothschild.

The great greeting Romanesque Revival arches are the most impressive element.

**★[11/12-17.] Le Square Trousseau (restaurant),** 8, rue Théophile-Rousseau, corner rue Antoine-Vollon.

Lush plaster- and woodwork, a potted palm, flowers, and mirrors make this a wonderful middle-class *Belle Epoque* place. With the arrival of the Opéra, it should be swamped.

**★[11/12-18.] Square Trousseau,** between rues du Faubourg-Saint-Antoine, Théophile-Rousseau, Charles-Baudelaire, and Antoine-Vollon. 1906.

A late-blooming square, it replaces the bulk of the **Hôpital Trousseau.**

**22, rue Charles-Baudelaire. Joseph Charlet & F. Perrin.** 1908. Beaux Arts.

**24, rue Charles-Baudelaire. Joseph Charlet & F. Perrin.** 1908. Winner, *concours de facades.* 1910.

Architects **Charlet & Perrin; Veber & Michau; Merlaud;** and **Achille Champy** and **L. Plousey** accomplished the whole east and west facades of the square immediately after it opened in 1905; their buildings were completed between 1906 and 1908.

**★[11/12-19.] Ateliers, 4, passage de la Main-d'Or,** between rue du Faubourg-Saint-Antoine and rue de la Main-d'Or. circa 1880s.

Go into the court. There is wild *colombage,* not as refined (some would say elegant) as iron but with more pizzazz.

**[11/12-20.] Maison, 6, rue de la Main-d'Or,** between passage de la Main-d'Or and rue Trousseau. **J. Lombard.** 1894.

Eclectic but with a handsome Gothic-Renaissance portal.

**[11/12-21.] Immeuble, 22, rue Trousseau,** corner rue de Candie. 1904.

Not so *nouille* but a sinuous presence in these hard-lined streets, a modest spiritual import from the 16th arrondissement.

**[11/12-22.] Immeuble, 52, rue Crozatier,** between rue du Faubourg-Saint-Antoine and rue de Cîteaux. **J. Neel.** 1959.

Some dated but nice neo-1930s balconies—Seaside Style or perhaps vintage Miami Beach (that's a compliment) but downstairs at pedestrian level is 1950s doldrums.

**[11/12-23.] Maison, 51, rue Crozatier,** between rue du Faubourg-Saint-Antoine and rue de Cîteaux. 19th century.

Composite pilasters with entwined cherubs.

**[11/12-24.] Immeuble, 31, rue de Cîteaux,** between rue Crozatier and rue du Faubourg-Saint-Antoine. circa 1900.

Here the Germanic influence creeps in, for this is Jugendstil, the more Nordic and harder version of Art Nouveau.

★★**[11/12-25.] Cuisine de l'Hôpital Saint-Antoine,** 30, rue de Cîteaux, between rue Crozatier and rue du Faubourg-Saint-Antoine. **Henri Ciriani.** 1985.

A minor modern monument tucked into this side street, linking two medium ancient buildings. At the left, the kitchen structure matches the building height adjacent; at the right, the two buildings interlock. But, more important, the building proper has a play of free form behind bands of stone that hold the street's line. This is neo–Le Corbusier.

**[11/12-26.] Fontaine de Montreuil,** place du Docteur-Antoine-Béclère, at junction of rue du Faubourg-Saint-Antoine and rue de Montreuil. 18th century.

The only visible remnant from the site of the old royal abbey of Saint-Antoine-des-Champs, later Hôpital Saint-Antoine, probably built around 1770, when **Lenoir** remodeled the old conventual buildings.

★**[11/12-27.] Centre Hospitalier Universitaire**/appended to **Hôpital Saint-Antoine,** place du Docteur-Antoine-Béclère, 184, rue du Faubourg-Saint-Antoine. **André Wogensky** with **Maître.** 1965.

Enter and turn left, and you will instantly see this 1960s slab in the spirit of international hospitals everywhere, but one expects more from Wogensky, sometime protégé of **Le Corbusier.** In that light, it's an economy model, perhaps the **Salvation Army,** without the *brise-soleil* (although there are some north-south eyelids here). But what *does* one do with the western sun? Once upon a time this sort of International Style minimalism could draw a passionate flock of architectural students, but in the 1970s they gave up looking because it cut into their time for talking. Now only some form of bold Post Modern license can raise their very slow pulse.

**[11/12-28.] Caserne des Sapeurs-Pompiers,** corner 57-63, boulevard Diderot, corner rue Chaligny.

The guardhouses in front are like mini-Ledoux *pavilions d'octroi,* protecting a mansarded Beaux Arts ensemble behind.

★**[11/12-29.] Logements, 11-21, rue Erard,** between rue de Reuilly and rue Crozatier. **Mario Heymann, Roger Anger,** and **Pierre Puccinelli.** 1969.

Although architects and planners ignored the urban fabric of Paris in the 1960s, they occasionally created a *cité* so striking that it impresses as architecture, even though we deplore its overwhelming posture. These blocks are analogous to English New Brutalism, inspired by the rough concrete and bolder forms that **Le Corbusier** used in his later work, and intellectually honored by the writings of London architects **Alison and Peter Smithson.**

**[11/12-30.] Immeuble, 228, rue du Faubourg-Saint-Antoine,** between rue de Reuilly and rue de Picpus. **Bernard Oge** and **Jean-Jacques Faysse.** 1977.

A setback suburban building in the city. Why not that wondrous Parisian quality of savoring urban open space inside the site, rather than wasting it on a noisy, unfashionable, unattractive street?

**[11/12-31.] Passage du Génie,** 246, rue du Faubourg-Saint-Antoine, between rue de Reuilly and rue de Picpus.

A skewed void in a Haussmannian facade allows the older city behind access to the rue du Faubourg-Saint-Antoine: the worker's world veneered.

**[11/12-32.] Maison Eugénie-Napoléon,** 254, rue du Faubourg-Saint-Antoine, corner rue de Picpus. **Jacques-Ignace Hittorf.** 1856.

Built as an orphan asylum, this is a neo-rococo *hôtel particulier* in form but not in function. The *grilles* are vintage Hittorf.

# 30
# TWELFTH ARRONDISSEMENT
## SOUTH

### GARE DE LYON TO CHATEAU DE VINCENNES

Gare de Lyon: **Marius Toudoire;** Le Train Bleu: **Marius Toudoire;**
Hôtel Le Massilia: **Marcel Oudin;** Préfecture de Paris: **Ayméric
Zublena;** Viaduc d'Austerlitz: **Jean-Camille Formigé;** pont Charles
de Gaulle: **Louis Arrètche;** Ministère des Finances: **Paul Chemetov**
and **Borja Huidobro;** pont de Bercy; Palais Omnisports: **Michel
Andrault, Pierre Parat,** and **Jean Prouvé;** Parc de Bercy: **Bernard
Huet et al.;** American Center: **Frank Gehry;** Eglise
Notre-Dame-de-la-Nativité: **André-Marie Châtillon;** Mairie:
**Antoine-Julien Hénard;** La Poste Daumesnil: **Moineau;** place
Félix-Eboué: **Gabriel Davioud;** rue de Reuilly; Institut
Sainte-Clothilde: **Roland Schweitzer;** Eglise du Saint-Esprit: **Paul
Tournon;** Musée des Arts Africains et Océaniens: **Albert Laprade**
and **Léon Jaussely;** Bois de Vincennes: **Adolphe Alphand, Gabriel
Davioud,** and **Pierre Barrillet-Deschamps;** Château de
Vincennes/Pavillons du roi et de la reine: **Louis Le Vau**

Métro: **Gare de Lyon**

**[12s-8.]** Ministère de l'Economie, des Finances, et du Budget. Paul
Chemetov and Borja Huidobro. 1989.

★[12s-1.] **Gare de Lyon,** 20, boulevard Diderot at the end of rue de Lyon. **Marius Toudoire.** 1899–1900. Expanded, 1927.

Toudoire made the necessary use of a *grande verrière* for mere trains. For people approaching he created a splendid Beaux Arts facade, punctuated by a tower sometimes termed *beffroi,* sometimes *campanile,* that closes the axis of the rue de Lyon. And if you stand at the foot of that tower, your countervista is that of the **Colonne de Juillet.**

The glory of the Gare de Lyon is the restaurant, **Le Train Bleu (★★★),** of extraordinary architectural opulence, both in its lofty sequential spaces and in its lush decor of sculptured and gilded plaster and paintings: forty-five paintings dedicated to the cities served by the *chemin de fer* PLM (Paris–Lyon–Mediterranée). This is a traveler's *pompier de luxe* in preparation for a luxurious tour to the Côte d'Azur and beyond, perhaps aboard the Train Bleu itself, perhaps while reading Agatha Christie's *The Mystery of the Blue Train.* You are welcome to come merely for lunch or dinner, but you may not have time to look at the food with all this grandeur abounding.

★[12s-2.] **Hôtel Le Massilia,** 13, boulevard Diderot, corner rue de Bercy. **Marcel Oudin.** 1911.

A block unto itself, this small hotel is an early structural and visual experiment in *béton armé,* infilled with brick. Some mannerisms remain in the neo-medieval false fronts and finials at the skyline, with fake *colombage* between, but Oudin was a pioneer. See his **Printemps** store at the juncture of avenues des Ternes and Niel **[17t-5.]** for equal but different creativity.

★[12s-3.] **Immeuble, 10, boulevard de la Bastille,** between rue de Bercy and quai de la Rapée. **U. Gaillot.** 1930.

The 1930s left their strong and ubiquitous mark in Paris, here again at a modest architectural essay. The balcony serves as a vestigial capital for the continuing equivocation: classical/*moderne.*

---

**Port de Plaisance: Paris/Arsenal**
A marina fills this wide basin, which gives access to the Canal Saint-Martin, Bassin de la Villette, and canals de l'Ourcq and Saint-Denis. From here the waterway is concealed beneath the boulevard Richard-Lenoir until it emerges again north of the rue du Faubourg-du-Temple. The port occupies the *fossé* (dry moat) of the fortifications of Charles V: the wall from place de la Bastille to the Seine was along boulevard Bourdon on the other side. On this bank a pleasant park has been manicured, and one can pass across to the opposite side via the 1895 steel bridge.

---

★[12s-4.] Formerly **Pumping Station/Ancienne Usine élévatrice des Eaux de Bercy,** 4, avenue Ledru-Rollin, corner quai de la Rapée. **Pierre Chabat.** 1888.

Steel, brick, and glazed terra cotta that got its deserved washing and rehabilitation only when displaced by the police, whose new precinct station **(Ayméric Zublena)** stands here. The factory, demounted, is being reassembled on the **Canal Saint-Denis.**

★★[12s-4a.] **Préfecture de Paris,** 94–96, quai de la Rapée, between avenue Ledru-Rollin and boulevard Diderot. **Ayméric Zublena.** 1991.

The state's presence in aluminum and glass. More than a bit stylish, it intrudes into the city's context aggressively, perhaps given license by its proximity to the towers of Bercy along the Seine east of the Gare de Lyon.

**★★[12s-5.] Viaduc d'Austerlitz/Métro Aérien**, spanning the Seine between quai de la Rapée and quai d'Austerlitz. **Jean-Camille Formigé,** architect. **Louis Biette,** engineer. 1904.

The Métro spans the Seine with engineering brilliance enriched with cast iron and carved stone decorations. The abutting pylons at each end give lip service to the Beaux Arts, but the sleek three-hinged arches with pendant trainway are precocious works in steel. Formigé was architect for all the **Métro Aérien,** whereas **Hector Guimard** ruled the entries to the **Métro Souterrain.**

**★[12s-6.] Immeuble, 2, boulevard Diderot**, corner quai de la Rapée. 1930s.

This may be extinct, as a permit to demolish has been posted. It is one of the best of its genre: strip-windowed with oculi, a handsome curved corner overlooking the Seine.

**★★[12s-7.] Pont Charles de Gaulle**, on axis of the rue Van-Gogh, from the quai de la Rapée to the quai d'Austerlitz. **Louis Arrètche.** 1992.

The last bridge for Paris will participate in the activation of the 13th arrondissement opposite: product of a 1988 *concours* in which such as **Richard Rogers** and **Paul Chemetov** participated. This, the winner, avoided all superstructures to keep the sight lines along the Seine clear, a tactic that may have influenced the jury. Other than the elevated Métro at the viaduc d'Austerlitz and ponts de Bercy and de Bir-Hakeim, the thirty-two bridges of Paris are without substantial superstructure.

**[12s-7a.] Immeuble, 24, rue Crétien**, along passage Gatbois, between Gare de Lyon and avenue Daumesnil. 1990.

A display of elaborate *grillage* floats around dour red masonry: a stark melodrama in these industrial streets.

**★[12s-7b.] Ecole maternelle, 70, avenue Daumesnil,** corner passage Gatbois. 1989.

A serene and classy school that is serious modernism, thoughtfully detailed.

**★★★[12s-8.] Ministère de l'Economie, des Finances, et du Budget,** boulevard de Bercy, rue de Bercy, and quai de la Rapée. **Paul Chemetov** and **Borja Huidobro.** 1989.

This Brobdingnagian megaslab, its two feet wading boldly in the Seine, forms a wall, with portals, to Paris on the approximate line of the wall of the Fermiers Généraux of the 1780s—a metaphor for the Ministère des Finances? The architecture, however, is hardly that of Ledoux. The bulk of the great slab is a center for computerized analysis of the comings and goings of the franc into and out of the national coffers. At the river's edge, some drama appears with the salient suite of the Ministre him- or herself. And behind it all, along the rue de Bercy, is a series of lower, courtyarded blocks to fulfill the enormous terrain of the program.

Like many talented architects, Chemetov is erratic in that he tries many ideas, and all ideas are not intrinsically successful; the *logements sociaux* at Pantin comprise a serious effort, but the bulk overwhelmed him. To see Chemetov at his best, descend into the netherworld of the Jardin des Halles, where sophisticated guts (of concrete beams and columns) discipline a chaotic underworld.

There are 113,000 square meters (1,200,000 square feet) of construction, 40 meters (130 feet) high and 365 meters (1186 feet) long. It has a sort of Moscow bureaucratic visage on the exterior of this main bar, but inside, if the bureaucracy will allow you, are some breathtaking spaces.

**[12s-9.] Pont de Bercy,** 1832, with later remodelings. Métro viaduct, 1904.

A rusticated Métro viaduct rides atop a neo-Renaissance series of arches. The pedestrian arcade that results is a grand walkway from the Left Bank to **Chemetov** and **Omnisports.**

★★**[12s-10.] Palais Omnisports de Paris-Bercy,** boulevard de Bercy, quai de Bercy, rue de Bercy. **Michel Andrault** and **Pierre Parat.** Consulting engineer for the space frame, **Jean Prouvé.** 1984.

A 17,000-seat arena for the lions of sport, rock, opera, and politics is within, banked with berms of green sod, forming for the approaching viewer a verdant truncated pyramid, surmounted by high-tech decorative space frames. These advertise a real structure behind. Without the exterior decorative trusses, the palais would be a superb success. It almost assumes the dual role of park and center of events, a happy conscious duality best expressed at the multilevel Oakland, California, museum of **Kevin Roche** and **John Dinkeloo,** where a park surmounts the stepped forms as public terraces.

A surrealistic event occurs when these green planes are mowed with machines, leashed from a girt around the mounds, from which they march up and down the slopes under the direction of two gardeners. Are there wildflowers in the spring?

★**[12s-11.] Canyoneaustrate/"Petit Grand Canyon" (sculpture),** on the *parvis* east of Omnisports, between quai de Bercy and rue de Bercy. **Gérard Singer,** sculptor. 1988.

Deep concrete incisions into the *parvis,* fed by water, give the illusion of a Lilliputian version of the canyons of the Little Colorado river. It is a fine fate for 1,500 cubic meters of *béton un petit peu armé.*

★★**[12s-12.] Parc de Bercy/les Jardins de la Mémoire/site of Entrepôts Bercy,** between parvis d'Omnisports and the boulevard Périphérique, along the Seine. **Bernard Huet, Marylene Ferrand, Jean-Pierre Feugas, Bernard Leroy,** architects. **I. Le Caisne,** landscape architect, 1990.

The *entrepôts* went, save for a few artifacts and sites for wine tasting and dining that evoke memories of what was once here. With a 2,500-space car park planned, many tourists are expected. The park will enjoy the multiplicity of existing trees—plane, linden, and ash—that have shaded this little city for warehousing wine barrels. Lawns, parterres, and romantic gardens intermingle, remembering the orderly network of André Le Nôtre's Château de Bercy gardens.

★★**[12s-13.] American Center,** rue de Bercy at rue de Pommard. **Frank Gehry.** 1992.

Gehry, an American pop high-tech master, will construct lodgings for passing faculty and artists, an auditorium, a library, and research facilities for art, technology, and applied arts. His work, a deconstructivist fantasy, appropriately satirizes the hectic vulgarity of America without, of course, telling of its sometimes graceful urbanism. Here is an antiurban ego at work.

**[12s-13a.] Immeuble, 36–48, rue de Bercy,** between rue de Macon and rue Léopold. **Roland Schweitzer.** 1989.

A strong street-fronted architectural statement.

**[12s-13b.] Immeubles, 20–34, rue de Bercy,** between rue de Chablis and rue Léopold.

The inner courtyard is a delight, with subtle interplay of forms surrounding a place of human scale.

**★[12s-13c.] Ecole Maternelle, rue Neuve-de-la-Garonne and place Lachambeaudie. Pierre-Louis Faloci.** 1990.

A gray marble and metal construction pierced by an internal street that forms a structural spine, from which hovering roofs are cantilevered.

**[12s-14.] Eglise Notre-Dame-de-la-Nativité,** place Lachambeaudie, at the end of rue de Dijon. **André-Marie Châtillon.** 1823–1826. Reconstructed after burning by the Commune, **Antoine-Julien Hénard.** 1873.

Four Tuscan columns for this neo-Classical church at the center of the former wine *entrepôts* de Bercy. Here is God confronting Bacchus.

**[12s-15.] Immeuble, 215, rue de Charenton,** corner boulevard de Reuilly. 1890s.

A luxurious vision in this backwater of Paris: a *grande poivrière* corners the streets with the manners of the rue Réaumur, for a discount department store **(Monoprix)** and dwellings above.

**★[12s-16.] Immeuble, 199, rue de Charenton,** between boulevard de Reuilly and rue Bignon. **Raoul Brandon,** architect. **Alexandre Morlon,** sculptor. 1911.

Four worker atlantes support the bays: a miner, reaper, mechanic, and sailor-fisherman. One of the winners of the Paris *concours de façades* of 1913.

**★[12s-17.] Immeuble, 218, rue de Charonne,** between ruelle de la Planchette and rue Baulant. **Wladimir Mitrofanoff.** 1983.

An urbane through-block private passage and court with whimsical entrance arches and iron gates makes this simple place simply grand.

**[12s-18.] Mairie,** 130, avenue Daumesnil, at rue de Charenton. **Antoine-Julien Hénard.** 1877.

Mansarded limestone and patterned brick; the porch has an almost-minaret crowning it.

**[12s-19.] Immeuble d'habitation, on the former Viaduc de Vincennes,** at avenue Dausmesnil, rue Montgallet and rue de Charenton. **Wladimir Mitrofanoff.** 1991.

**[12s-20.] Logements sociaux/Fondation de Mme. Jules Lebaudy,** 124–126, avenue Daumesnil, corner rue de Charenton. **Auguste Labussière,** architect. **Camille Garnier,** sculptor. 1907.

Early low-rent housing for workers financed by a private foundation. The arch is triumphant, as at many HBMs and their social equals.

**[12s-21.] Immeuble, 157–175, avenue Daumesnil,** between rue de Charenton and rue de Reuilly. **D. Honegger.** 1960.

A concrete *grillage* that crosses the technology of Perret with the relentless geometry of Mies. The result is an overwhelming and oppressive wall that screens the old railroad yards of Reuilly from view but is spalling, pitted, and maintenance-abandoned.

**[12s-22.] Immeuble, 11, rue Dugommier**, between avenue Daumesnil and boulevard de Reuilly. **Marcel Marchand.** 1932.

Flaking and externally dingy, this is one of those forgotten landmarks. Those wonderful colonnettes articulate the corner bay windows with tile capitals (flush but rich). With some cosmetics this could be a great spectacle; it waits for rent control to die.

**[12s-23.] Immeuble et garage, 13, rue Dugommier**, between avenue Daumesnil and boulevard de Reuilly. **Georges Ardouin** and **Lemaistre.** 1931.

Though the flutes give the bays a vestigial neo-Classical quality, this is a vigorous modern concrete building at heart.

★★**[12s-24.] La Poste, 168, avenue Daumesnil**, between rue Dugommier and place Félix-Eboué. **Moineau.** 1937.

Post Modernists in America are enthralled by these articulated-attached single and paired columns. The stylish lettering above is a wonderful world of its own, the incisions originally colored Pompeian red, now faded. The lettering at the street, 168 bis, is one thoughtful detail now almost always missed in current works.

★**[12s-25.]** Originally **Central Téléphonique Daumesnil,** 187, avenue Daumesnil, at place Félix-Eboué. **Paul Guadet.** 1926.

Brick and terra-cotta within a rich grid of concrete, festooned. This is a wondrous building, a substantial place where spandrels titillate with multicolored tile.

★**[12s-26.] Place Félix-Eboué,** gathering boulevard and rue de Reuilly and avenue Daumesnil. Fountain, **Gabriel Davioud,** sculptor. 1874 (first sited on place de la République). Sited here, 1883.

Sprawling, the peripheral architecture vainly tries to hold it together. The central fountain is too weak and the edges too distant to control the space, in the way that an obelisk à la place de la Concorde would. Davioud moved the fountain here to give way to *La République* at the *place* of the same name, a more important sculpture at a larger scale. But Davioud's work *up close* is delightful, those thirst-quenching lions spouting relentlessly.

★**[12s-27.] Institut et Collège Sainte-Clothilde,** 101, rue de Reuilly, between place Félix-Eboué and rue du Sergent-Bauchat. **Roland Schweitzer.** 1976.

Arrhythmic louvers in the syncopated manner of **José Luis Sert** at Harvard University's **Hopkinson Center,** with a pleasant front rock garden and pool.

★**[12s-28.] Ecole des Infirmières,** 95, rue de Reuilly, corner rue du Sergent-Bauchat. **Roland Schweitzer.** 1971.

A competent brick-and-concrete modern block for training nurses. Understated and with style, without being stylish.

★**[12s-29.] Eglise Saint-Eloi,** 1, place Maurice-de-Fontenay, opposite 77, rue de Reuilly, between rue Montgallet and rue Erard. **Marc Leboucheur.** 1967.

Structural steel sheathed with corrugated steel for this industrialized church, lit with translucent louvers. It has a fresh panache for the fading churchviewer and -goer.

**[12s-30.] Foyer des Jeunes Travailleurs,** 68, rue de Reuilly, between rue Montgallet and rue Erard. **Beatrice Dollé** and **Christian Labbé.** 1990.

★**[12s-31.] Immeuble, 63, rue de Picpus,** corner rue Dagorno, north of boulevard de Reuilly. **Marc Solotareff.** 1931.

Stuccoed *pan coupé* and the *garde-fous* are nice, all making a sober outpost of architecture among the superarchitectural trivia.

★**[12s-32.] Immeuble, 16, place Félix Eboué,** corner rue de la Brèche-aux-Loups. **Weber** and **Michaud.** 1905.

*Belle Epoque* exuberance in a Haussmannian-*tardif* apartment house presents a minor *poivrière* corner. As often, in this radial-avenue world of Paris, the corner is the opportunity for the grandest statement, sometimes flamboyant.

★★**[12s-33.] Eglise du Saint-Esprit,** 186, avenue Daumesnil, at rue Cannebière, between place Félix-Eboué and avenue du Général-Michel-Bizot. **Paul Tournon.** 1928–1931, with later additions and alterations.

Hagia Sophia lent the dome, but the modern concrete technology of France (à la Perret, Hennebique, Tony Garnier) provided the structure. Inside this Byzantine form there is mostly raw concrete: its very nudity gives it power. Outside, the immense *clocher* (85 meters/275 feet) is perhaps inspired by Perret's more modest one at Le Raincy (there in concrete, here in brick).

This church was built to coincide with the Exposition Coloniale of 1931, as a memorial church dedicated to the missionaries but not without apprehensiveness about the reaction of the neighborhood's inhabitants, who were "noted for their communist ideas." The Revolution of 1789 was as much anticlerical as antiroyal, and so, in turn, was the Commune of 1871. The 12th, 19th, and 20th arrondissements were the center and fountainhead of revolutionary fervor. No wonder Bishop Eugène Jacques despaired.

More than thirty artists were assembled to paint the history of world evangelization by honored missionaries on the surrounding walls of the upper church.

★**[12s-34.] HBM, 41, rue de Fécamp,** bordered by avenue Daumesnil, rue Tourneux, and rue Edouard-Robert. **Alexandre Maistrasse** and **Léon Besnard.** 1924.

An early and regimented HBM that shows powerful corner entries supported by articulated concrete columns.

**[12s-35.] Immeubles, rue de Toul,** between avenue Daumesnil and rue Louis-Braille.

★**4 SCAU,** architects. 1988.
A modest curved reentry articulates this simple but well proportioned facade.
**16** Whereas No. 20 is quietly powerful, No. 16 is full of tricks and fussy: textured block spandrels, frames for gardes-fous that exceed any need, and a generally excessive, if not careful, detailing.
★**20** Carefully articulated boxed-cantilevered balconies in white against a tan body (here the glass balustrades are forgiven). Understated good scale and handsome.

**[12s-36.] Garage, 21 bis, rue de Toul,** between avenue Daumesnil and rue Louis-Braille.

An added structure of *grand standing* atop a 1930s garage. Such layer-caking had been started even under the Restoration, when any building corniced below 17.54 meters (the exact limit before the setback *comble*, about 57 feet) was ripe for real estate profits by *surélévation*.

**[12s-37.] Immeuble, 20, rue de la Véga,** corner rue Rottembourg. circa 1930.

A modest infill that brings novelty if not imagination to this quarter of mixed functions and tired styles.

**[12s-38.] Immeuble, 10, rue de la Véga,** between rue Rottembourg and avenue Daumesnil. **G. Delanoe.** 1972.

The bold simplicity of **Skidmore, Owings & Merrill** on this deeply sculpted facade.

★**[12s-39.] HBM, square Van-Vollenhoven,** corner boulevard Ponia-towski and avenue Daumesnil.

A park embraced by an HBM, where spiral staircases within enliven the park's facades. Gracious housing for modest means.

★**[12s-40.] Lycée Technique Elisa Lemonnier,** 22, avenue Armand-Rousseau, corner rue Montesquieu-Fezemsac, off boulevard Soult, **S. Menil.** 1972.

Concrete ululations veneer this huge complex, with styling akin to the fins on now perversely beloved Cadillacs. Aging vulgarity attracts aficionados.

★★**[12s-41.] Musée des Arts Africains et Océaniens,** 293, avenue Daumesnil, at Porte Dorée. **Albert Laprade** and **Léon Jaussely.** 1931. Salon Paul Reynaud, **Jacques-Emile Ruhlmann.**

Laprade had been active in Morocco before creating this monument to the French Empire, which is perhaps the nadir of the conflicting movements of modernism and neo-Classicism. The colonnade, tall and attenuated, belies Classical proportions without offering any new vigor; it is matchbox-and-matchsticks, as forty years later **Edward Durell Stone** outdid even this matchstick competition at the **Kennedy Center** in Washington, D.C. It is an appropriate, if bizarre, relic of that great display of colonial cultural eclecticism in 1931.

Ruhlmann's interior (★★★), however, is a classy memory of those early 1930s.

And, as a tour offshoot and addendum, one may visit:

**[12s-42.] Immeuble, 81, boulevard Soult**, between rue du Sahel and avenue de Saint-Mandé. **Wladimir Mitrofanoff.** 1986.

Pink and gray with blue window-sash, this is a somewhat outrageous PoMo intrusion in contrast to the sober HBM at No. 64 across the boulevard.

★**[12s-43.] Collège Vincent d'Indy,** 8, avenue Vincent-d'Indy, between avenue Courteline and rue Jules-Lemaître.

A virtuoso statement in *béton armé* that seems more appropriate to downtown Tokyo.

★[12s-44.] **Bois de Vincennes,** beyond Porte Dorée, and bounded by boulevard Poniatowski, avenue Daumesnil and avenue de Grevelle. **Adolphe Alphand,** chief engineer. **Gabriel Davioud,** architect. **Pierre Barillet-Deschamps,** landscape architect. 1858–1860.

To balance the Bois de Boulogne to the west, Napoléon III's team rebuilt this old bois, the center of former military maneuvers. The Lac des Minimes was excavated, and other pilings and diggings remolded the topography as much as they had done at Montsouris and Batignolles; but they could never match the drama of Buttes-Chaumont. Later, for the 1931 exposition, the new zoo offered an artificial concrete mountain for goats to climb and for people to look on in wonder (even at **Buttes-Chaumont,** around the central island and particularly at the restored feeding-waterfall, the "rocks" are simulated of concrete).

Other curiosities include the **Buddhist Temple,** a remnant from 1931 that is still party to an active Buddhist congregation and compound (ring the bell), and the **Chalet de la Porte Jaune,** on an island in the **Lac des Minimes.**

★★★[12s-45.] **Château de Vincennes,** east of the Porte Saint-Mandé on the edge of the Bois de Vincennes. Dungeon, 1370. Chapel, 1552. Royal pavilions, **Louis Le Vau.** 1658.

A medieval hunting park of the king, this evolved into a sometime royal residence that competed with Saint-Germain in the *banlieue* and, later with Versailles. Although he left many urban remnants such as the **place Vendôme,** Louis XIV was not enamored of Paris, preferring to decorate its edges (as here) and observe its elegance from a slight distance.

# 31
# THIRTEENTH ARRONDISSEMENT
## NORTHWEST
### PLACE D'ITALIE TO PORT-ROYAL

Place d'Italie; Mairie; 163, boulevard de l'Hôpital: **Henri Sauvage**; Théâtre des Gobelins sculpture: **Auguste Rodin**; Manufacture Nationale des Gobelins: **Jean-Camille Formigé**; Mobilier National: **Auguste Perret**; Locaux Universitaires Saint-Hippolyte: **Jacques Ripeault** and **D. Duhart**; Cité Fleurie: **Montmorin Jentel**; Cité Verte; Maison d'arrêt de la Santé: **Joseph Vaudremer**; Hôtel de Massa: **Leboursier**; rue Cassini: **Louis Süe, Paul Huillard, Jules Saulnier,** and **Charles Abella**; Cloître de Baudelocque: **Antoine Lepautre**; Station Port-Royal: **Octave Rougier**

Métro: **Place d'Italie**

[13nw-16.] Cité Verte. 1920s.

219

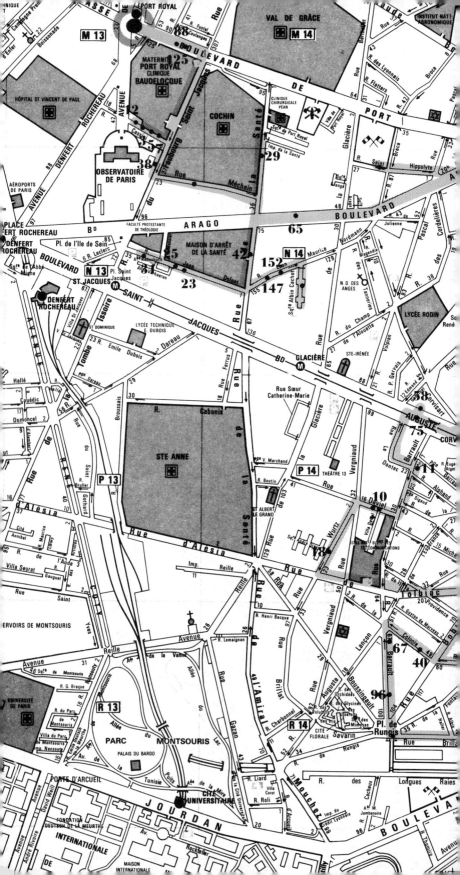

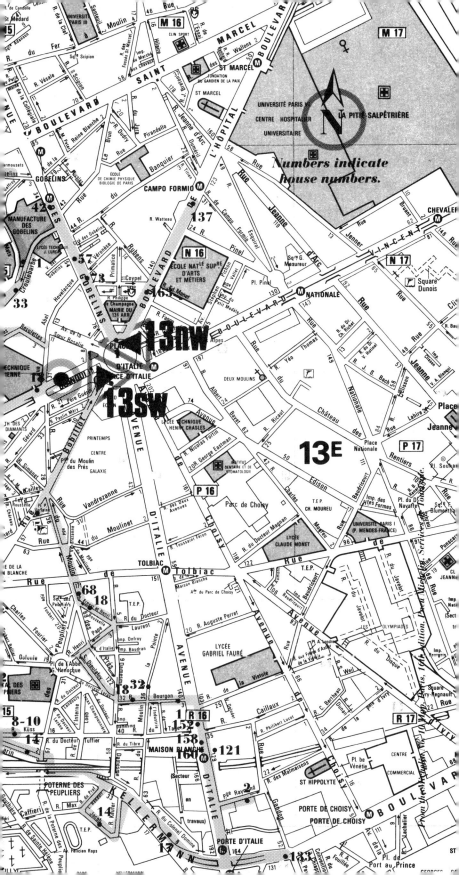

**[13nw-1.] Place d'Italie.**

See **[13se-1.]** and **[13sw-1.]**.

**[13nw-2.] Mairie,** 1, place d'Italie, between boulevard de l'Hôpital and boulevard des Gobelins. **Bommet.** 1873–1877.

Bland, but a little *tourelle* attempts some class. Here, on the place d'Italie, is a toy house overwhelmed by urbanization, the not so distant towers, and the powerful forms of Kenzo Tange.

Inside seek the **Salle des Fêtes,** recently restored by architect **Chocas.** You'll find a vaulted (false) ceiling of gilded plaster and a handsome parquet floor under pendant chandeliers.

★★**[13nw-3.] Logements, 163, boulevard de l'Hôpital,** between rue Fagon and rue Edouard-Manet. **Henri Sauvage.** 1908.

Hygienic low-cost housing crowned with a triad of colonnaded lookouts. This is an essay in stucco, with elegant *garde-fous* (look up) and some memorable chamfered forms.

**[13nw-4.] HBM, 137, boulevard de l'Hôpital,** between rue Pinel and rue de Campo-Formio. **Joseph Charlet** and **F. Perrin.** 1926.

Brick, polychromatic tile, and picturesque mansard roofs with attached balconettes. The playing detail on these bulky facades make them good understated urban neighbors.

★**[13nw-5.] Salle Fauvette (cinema)**/originally **Théâtre des Gobelins,** 73, avenue des Gobelins, between rue Coypel and rue Véronèse. **Alphonse-Adolphe Cusin.** 1860.

A youthful Rodin was employed here (1864–1865) carving the bas-relief of the facade. A Palladian arch gives this small entry pavilion (to the theater behind) great monumentality, creating a tiny but powerful statement on the street.

★**[13nw-6.] Logements, 57, avenue des Gobelins,** between rue du Banquier and rue Véronèse. **Henrick Lassen/Camus-Sandjian.** 1989.

A modest but large (110 apartments) streetfronted building, self-effacing but with handsome details. Crisp, precast concrete balconies and trellised terraces.

**[13nw-7.] Manufacture Nationale des Gobelins,** 42, avenue des Gobelins, between rue des Gobelins and rue de Croulebarbe. **Jean-Camille Formigé.** 1914.

A Beaux Arts facade is the formal entry to this complex of tapestry and carpet making near the site where Jean Gobelin started his dye works in 1443. **Henri IV** added tapestry makers in 1601, and it all was nationalized by **Colbert** in 1662. **Charles Le Brun** (interior "decorator" for Vaux-le-Vicomte, then Versailles) was onetime director, and painters from **Boucher** to **Chagall** contributed designs.

**[13nw-8.] Logements, 33, rue de Croulebarbe,** between rue des Reculettes and rue Berbier-du-Mets. **Edouard Albert, Roger Boileau,** and **Labourdette.** 1960.

A tarnished tower with busy details, timidly structural in its wind bracing, usurps the sky, the view, and the middle of the block. The only safety is to be inside, where you can't see it. Technically, it was the first skyscraper in Paris, but, at twenty-one stories, it is, at least, less intrusive than the Tour Montparnasse [14w-1.] (1973).

★★[13nw-9.] Crèche, 25, rue des Reculettes, between rue de Croule-barbe and rue Abel-Hovelacque. 1980s.

A Post Modern neo-1930s *crèche* forms a knuckle or pivot on this doglegged street, leading to the backyard of the **Lycée Estienne.** It is stylish with its "portholes" and great multipaned glass bay.

★★[13nw-10.] Garde-meuble du Mobilier National, 1, rue Berbier-du-Mets, between rue de Croulebarbe and rue Emile-Deslandres. **Auguste Perret.** 1934.

A somber neo-Classicism here in the traditional form of an *hôtel particulier,* with its gated forecourt flanked by service wings (the concierge's residence is at the right) and the *corps de logis,* here the museum, at the back. As a national warehouse, it harbors furniture for the government elite.
Articulated concrete panels in concert with the window spacing retain the Perret updating of a basically Classical rhythm.

---

**Rue Berbier-du-Mets and la Bièvre**
**Jean-Jacques Lévèque** in *Vie et histoire XIIIe arrondissement:* "The rue Berbier-du-Mets was the little street of the Gobelins, and it owes its curvilinear aspect to the fact that it was established on the bed of la Bièvre, still visible at the beginning of the century, offering, if one is to believe numerous witnesses, the most astonishing and picturesque views imaginable on what remained of an exhausted river, colored by all the products of industry, watered by all the oils dumped there. Simultaneously superb and infected, like a sick body that will soon be enveloped by the earth."

---

★[13nw-11.] Folie Gobelins, 19, rue des Gobelins, between rue Berbier-du-Mets and avenue des Gobelins. 1490–1510, with later modifications.

In the 1530s Rabelais speaks of this in his great novels *Gargantua* and *Pantagruel.* Buzz yourself in to a tight stone courtyard and a spiral stone stair. On the facade are traces of early Renaissance windows; savor the pediment over the spiral stair's entrance doorway.

[13nw-12.] Hôtel particulier, 14, boulevard Arago, between boulevard de Port-Royal and rue Pascal. **Eugène Becquet.** 1901.

Beaux Arts toying with the edges of Art Nouveau, with cast-iron columns at the *rez-de-chaussée* supporting a tesseraed frieze.

★★[13nw-13.] Locaux Universitaires Saint-Hippolyte, rue Saint-Hippolyte, corner rue Broca. **Jacques Ripeault** and **D. Duhart.** 1990?

A double-decked amphitheater leaves a naturally lit void between two volumes.

★★[13nw-14.] Cité Fleurie, 65, boulevard Arago, between rue de la Santé and rue de la Glacière. **Montmorin Jentel.** circa 1880.

Here is a romance of cottage and *colombage,* an island of *anti-*Haussmannianism for the ateliers of twenty-seven painters (Picasso and Modigliani passed here, and Rodin even shared a foundry with Maillol). Quaint and arty, it has lush vegetation that makes it more rural than a suburban villa.

**[13nw-15.] Square Albin-Cachot**, off rue Léon-Maurice-Nordmann, between rue de la Glacière and rue de la Santé. 1930s.

A cul-de-sac embraced by 1930s concrete.

★★**[13nw-16.] Cité Verte**, 147, rue Léon-Maurice-Nordmann, between rue de la Glacière and rue de la Santé. 1920s.

A somber villa of ateliers, with glass and steel envined and a less bourgeois quality than No. 152 below. The *allée* is long, eerie, sunstroked—and wonderful.

**[13nw-17.] Cité des Vignes**, 152, rue Léon-Maurice-Nordmann, between rue de la Glacière and rue de la Santé. circa 1920s.

A mini cul-de-sac—and yes, it is envined. What could be more inexorably possible for the middle-middle-artist class?

**[13nw-18.] Maison d'arrêt de la Santé (prison)**, 42, rue de la Santé, between boulevard Arago and rue Jean-Dolent. **Joseph Vaudremer**. 1861–1867.

Speaking of *meulière,* it is here aggrandized, piled, debased, and honored in the monumental walls of this sinister slammer.

**[13nw-19.] Maison de campagne** (once upon a time)/sometime residence of **Maréchal Masséna**, 23, rue Jean-Dolent, between rue de la Santé and rue du Faubourg-Saint-Jacques. 1870s.

★★**[13nw-20.] Allée Verhaeren** and **Allée Rodenbach**, 25, rue Jean-Dolent, between rue de la Santé and rue du Faubourg-Saint-Jacques.

Secreted behind the facades of rue Jean-Dolent are brick, mansarded Georgian *blocks* in a lovely cul-de-sac of gardens, trees, and understatement.

★**[13nw-21.] Logements, 31, rue Jean-Dolent**, between rue de la Santé and rue du Faubourg-Saint-Jacques. **Pierre Mouret**. 1931.

Wonderfully equivocal brickwork—corbeled, stepped, and with bas-relief for the neo-Classicists—and ironwork of semi-*grand standing*. A lost lover.

★★**[13nw-22.] Maison mère des Dames Augustines du Sacré Coeur de Marie**, 29, rue de la Santé, between boulevard Arago and boulevard de Port-Royal. **Chalut**. 1840.

This is the Greek Revival of Anglo-Saxon lands, which produced the great plantations of Dixie and myriad churches, museums, banks, and what-have-you in England and America.
Here is a handsome Ionic-columned courtyard, with a great breath of fresh space behind some dour walls, in stark contrast to the Santé prison opposite.

**[13nw-23.] Hôpital Cochin/Annex**, rue Méchain, between rue de la Santé and rue du Faubourg-Saint-Jacques. **J. P. Bellon, B. Paczowski, and P. Sobota**. 1989.

Stylish concrete.

★**[13nw-24.]** Originally **Hôtel de Massa**/ now **Société des Gens de Lettres**, 38, rue du Faubourg-Saint-Jacques, between rue Méchain and rue

Cassini. **Leboursier**. 1774. Moved to its present site from 52–60, avenue des Champs-Elysées, 1928.

An 18th-century *hôtel particulier* becomes involuntarily a *maison de campagne*, perched on the escarpment of the **Observatoire.**

**[13nw-25.] Rue Cassini between avenue de l'Observatoire and rue du Faubourg-Saint-Jacques/various hôtels particuliers:**

> **No. 7. ★Louis Süe** and **Paul Huillard**. 1903.
>> Built for the painter Czernikowski, this assymetric attack on Classicism has giant console brackets at the timid pediment.
>
> **No. 5. ★Louis Süe** and **Paul Huillard**. 1905.
>> The "respected" academic painter, Jean-Paul Laurens, sought medievalism. Süe responded with this smooth incised plane of brick, crowned with a glassy studio supported on an arched corbel-table, more neo-Roman than Romanesque Revival (too smooth for H. H. Richardson).
>
> **No. 3 bis. ★★Louis Süe** and **Paul Huillard**. 1906.
>> House for M. et Mme. Lucien Simon, both painters, each with an atelier. In the instant progression of styles, Süe assembled Classical, medieval, and early modern symbols contiguously and sequentially on this same street. No. 3 bis owes much to **25 bis, rue Franklin** of 1904 (**[16c-22.]**). This idiom (concrete frame infilled with brick) is often repeated by others, as at **4–10, rue Victor-Duruy [15c-26.].**
>
> **No. 3. Jules Saulnier.**
>> A late Beaux Arts foothold on this radical street.

---

After a trip to Vienna in 1909 with the couturier Paul Poiret, **Louis Süe** wrote, "I attended, in Vienna and Berlin, all the exhibitions of decorative art. I made the acquaintance of the heads of all the schools, such as Hoffmann, creator and director of the Wiener Werkstätte, Karl Witzmann, M. Muthesius, Bruno Paul, and Gustav Klimt. . . . I met in Berlin a group of architects who sought the new and who found it sometimes. I spent whole days visiting modern interiors, planned and constructed with so many new ideas; I have never seen anything like it at home. Villas in the environs of Berlin, sited in pine forests, at the edge of lakes, surrounded with gardens filled with the unforeseen and the surprising, seemed to me delicious. I returned to create in France a new fashion in furnishing and decoration.

"I went out of curiosity to Brussels, expressly to see the home of M. Stocklet, constructed by the architect Hoffmann of Vienna, who had designed not only the house and its outbuildings but also the garden, the carpets, the furniture, the chandeliers, the chairs, the silver . . ."

---

**★★[13nw-26.] Logements** and **ateliers, 12, rue Cassini**, between avenue de l'Observatoire and rue du Faubourg-Saint-Jacques. **Charles Abella.** 1930.

A transitional building presents pebble-textured cubistic form, tempered with a neo-Classical/Moderne sculpture in high relief at the side entrance court (**Xavier Haas**, sculptor).

**★[13nw-27.]** Originally **Abbaye de Port-Royal de Paris**/ now **Maternité Port-Royal and Clinique Baudelocque**, 121–125, boulevard de Port-Royal between avenue de l'Observatoire and rue du Faubourg-Saint-Jacques. Chapel and cloister, **Antoine Lepautre**. 1648.

The cloister is an oasis of repose. Go in.

**[13nw-28.] Bibliothèque, 88 ter, boulevard de Port-Royal,** corner rue Pierre-Nicole. **Jean Willerval and Pierre Rignols**. 1975.

A sleek grid—perhaps *too* sleek.

**[13nw-29.] Immeuble, 88, boulevard de Port-Royal,** between rue Pierre-Nicole and rue Saint-Jacques. **P. L. Alinot**. 1884.

The bay windows (bow windows in French) are early (the law of 1892 allowed greater projections into the "public space"). Go around the corner to the rue Fustel-de-Coulanges to see the rear facade—iron and brick.

★**[13nw-30.] Station Port-Royal,** boulevard de Port-Royal and avenue de l'Observatoire. **Octave Rougier**, engineer. 1895.

Now a stop on Line B of the RER, this was originally the conning tower of the Ligne de Sceaux, which led to the present **Cité Universitaire** and suburbs. Iron and glass provide magnificence in the marquise of entry.

# 32

# THIRTEENTH ARRONDISSEMENT

## SOUTHEAST

### PLACE D'ITALIE TO

### LA BIBLIOTHEQUE DE FRANCE

Place d'Italie; square de Choisy; Clara Clara: **Richard Serra;** Faculté des Lettres/Tolbiac: **Pierre Parat** and **Michel Andrault;** Logements, rue des Hautes-Formes: **Christian de Portzamparc;** 106, rue du Château-des-Rentiers: **Architecture Studio;** École Maternelle: **Edouard Crevel;** Cabinet d'Architecture: **Paul Chemetov** and **Borja Huidobro;** Maison Planeix: **Le Corbusier;** SUDAC: **Joseph Leclaire;** Hôtel Industriel Masséna: **Dominique Perrault;** Armée du Salut: **Le Corbusier;** Eglise Notre-Dame-de-la-Gare: **Claude Naissant;** place Jeanne-d'Arc; 112–118, rue du Chevaleret: **Edith Girard;** allée des Arts; Bibliothèque de France: **Dominique Perrault**

Métro: **Place d'Italie**

[13se-10.] Logements sociaux, rue des Hautes-Formes. Christian de Portzamparc. 1979.

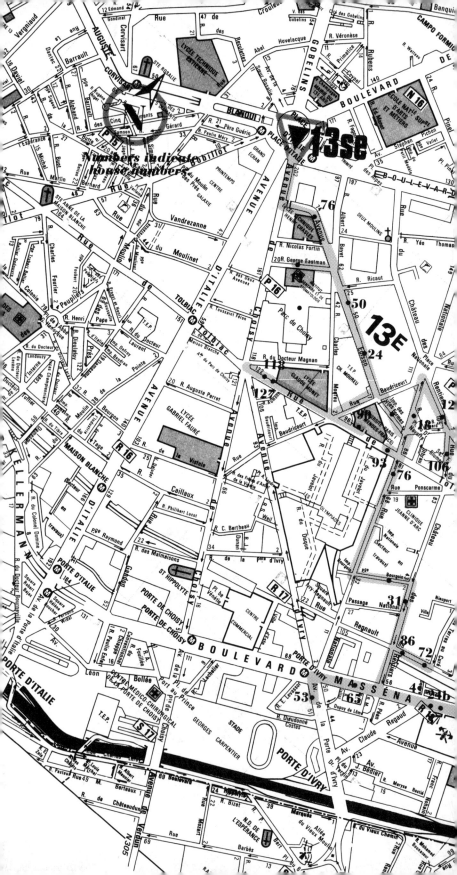

**[13se-1.] Place d'Italie**

Foreign countries, cities, and heroes are honored in the street and place names of Paris—unrelated, however to ethnic migrations. Here the *Italie* of *place* and *avenue* shelters Asians of all latitudes: Chinese, Vietnamese, Cambodians, Laotians.

**[13se-2.] Centre de Santé Mentale**, 76, avenue Edison, between avenue de Choisy and rue Albert-Bayet. **N. Sonolet. 1980.**

Literally child's play: building blocks frivolously rotated for the sake of some desperately sought character. Here is form without either space or the discipline of an urban participant. It is boorish, whereas the overbearing towers nearby are merely bland, boring, and banal.

★**[13se-3.] Donation George Eastman/Institut Dentaire et de Stomatologie**, 11, rue George-Eastman, between avenue de Choisy and avenue Edison. **Edouard Crevel. 1937.**

In concert with the brick social architecture of Paris in the 1930s, this blossomed coincidentally with the 1937 *Art Moderne* exposition. The latter's off-white monumentalism of power (German and Russian pavilions—and even the Palais de Chaillot) offered its elite presence to the common citizen. Eastman's gift offered succor to the mouths of the same common citizen, but in red brick.

★★**[13se-4.] Clara Clara (sculpture)**, square de Choisy, between avenue de Choisy and rue Charles-Moureu. **Richard Serra. 1980.**

These tense Cor-Ten walls form an axial passage centered on the Donation Eastman. Their spatial compression-expansion is an exhilarating urban element in a sea of grass.

**[13se-5.] HBM, 50, rue Edison**, corner rue Ricaut.

A little *style* goes a long way: the 1930s stenciled frieze, together with the simple but elegant entrance gates and ironwork, make it a good citizen in Sunday best accessories—cuff links, necklace, tie, or bonnet.

**[13se-6.] HLM, 24, avenue Edison**, between rue Ricaut and rue Baudricourt. **Maurice Cammas. 1967.**

*Retardataire* **Perret.** The entrance portal, distyle in antis, is a reprise of Classicism, now newly flowering in PoMo architecture.

★**[13se-7.] Faculté des Lettres et des Sciences, Centre Pierre Mendès-France**, 90, rue de Tolbiac, between rue Baudricourt and rue Nationale. **Pierre Parat** and **Michel Andrault. 1973.**

If this were New York, this sleek bronze tower would be honored for its elegant detailing and stately (would-be) freestanding presence. But next to Portzamparc's Hautes-Formes (see below) it seems like a philistine.

The elevator traffic is a nightmare. No office building holds classes at hourly intervals, when all present must shift to another floor almost simultaneously.

**[13se-8.] HBM, 118, rue de Tolbiac**, between avenue de Choisy and rue Charles-Moureu. **Lucien Prudon** and **Toussaint-Pascal Contresti.** 1931.

A solid citizen that anchors the neighborhood to a brief but lusty past.

**[13se-9.] Archives d'Architecture de l'IFA (Institut Français d'Architecture),** 127, rue de Tolbiac, between avenue de Choisy and rue Charles-Moureu. Rehabilitation and new quarters, **Bernard Reichen and Philippe Robert.** 1989.

Documents of architecture are analyzed, classified, restored, and evaluated here for eventual deposit in French national or regional archives. Visiting professionals may inspect or assist.

The new entranceway presents overkill akin on its own tiny scale to the twelve columns that form the shallow billboard/facade of the Palais Bourbon. There, the National Assembly is the important place—within. Here, the archives in transit are what's important. Architects rarely know when to stop.

★★★**[13se-10.] Logements sociaux, rue des Hautes-Formes,** between rue Baudricourt et rue Nationale. **Christian de Portzamparc. Georgia Benamo,** associate. 1979.

Here the thirty-five-year-old Portzamparc introduced another form of high-density urbanity to Paris, far from the banal towers of Croulebarbe **[13nw-8.]**, the Front de Seine, and the pervasive *grands ensembles* surrounding the city proper. A rich quality of public space serves in counterpoint to the eight carefully modeled blocks that contain it—an urbane symbiosis. But one can quarrel with the detailing (why must Portzamparc have curtain-wall segments inlaid into his once-pristine stucco blocks?). By the way, stucco (all over) painted, as at the Villas Laroche/Jeanneret **[16a-44.]**, or stucco (all over) plain, as at the Ecole des Garçons **[13sw-21.]**, is a bonnie material. Perhaps we lost our technical touch in the 1980s.

★**[13se-11.] Logements, 18, rue Sthrau,** on the place du Docteur-Navarre, at rue Nationale. **Michel Benoit and Thierry Verbiet.** 1985.

A refreshing monolith of brick ornamented with ironwork. The polygons in metal are elegant, but those in brick are not. Here again a powerful building is encumbered with too many ideas. The simplicity of Hautes-Formes could have been borrowed to fulfill the rue Sthrau.

★**[13se-12.] Foyer pour les personnes âgées, 120, rue du Château-des-Rentiers,** between place Nationale and rue Baptiste-Renard. **Christian de Portzamparc.** 1984.

The revolution of 1968 produced coins with two sides: the refreshing new look at architecture and the city and, conversely, a splash of egoism in the young. Creativity is not complexity and exaggeration. Even the *pompiers* architects of 1900, although extravagant in their ornamentation of facades, worked within the discipline of the then post-Haussmannian streets. Here, though the street gap is plugged to form continuity, it is plugged with a *conch*. Would that **Emile Aillaud** had never foisted the undulating building on France!

★**[13se-13.] Logements, 106, rue du Château-des-Rentiers,** at rue Jean-Colly. **Architecture Studio.** 1980s.

The Métro map facing rue Jean-Colly is a tour-de-force. The building sans map is even better—a structural-geometric game with a play of grid and *grillage*. This is the apotheosis of the *pan coupé*, on elegant stilts.

★★**[13se-14.] Médiathèque/Bibliothèque, 93, rue de Tolbiac,** corner rue Nationale. **CANAL (Daniel and Patrick Rubin).** 1990.

A sleek, curving glass envelope for electronic access to documents that included a vast body of work devoted to feminism.

**[13se-15.] Logements** and **bureaux, 76, rue Nationale**, between rue de Tolbiac and rue Ponscarme. **Francis Fixot** and **Laurent Toussaint.** 1987.

Socially if not architecturally redeeming: stucco, blue bay windows, a bit of mansard, a bit of brick. Urban propriety, architectural pseudodecoration.

★**[13se-16.] Passage Bourgoin**, between rue Nationale, rue du Château-des-Rentiers, rue Ponscarme, and passage National.

When in doubt (while in the 13th arrondissement) that you are in the Paris of storybooks and their reality, pass among small houses, real flowers, and a domestic and pedestrian loveliness.

**[13se-17.] Ecole Maternelle Elémentaire, 31–37, rue du Château-des-Rentiers,** between passage Bourgoin and rue Regnault. **Maurice-Achille Bernier.** 1983.

Blues, broken forms, and polyglotish windows—do these make a children's world? And are children an island populace, severed from the scale of the real city surrounding?

**[13se-18.] Bureaux, 86, rue Regnault,** corner rue du Château-des-Rentiers. **Jacques de Brauer.** 1976.

Serrated (saw-toothed) glass and a tiny plaza bring an American-style import to this bleak neighborhood.

**[13se-19.] Bureaux, 72, rue Regnault,** corner rue des Terres-au-Curé. **Jacques de Brauer.** 1971.

More appropriate to Los Angeles, it is a sort of aspiring yuppie's heaven: modern*istic* if not modern, styl*ish* if not of a style. The sloping windows and spandrels are redolent of automobile fins and fenders.

★★**[13se-20.] Ecole Maternelle, 53, avenue de la Porte-d'Ivry,** corner boulevard Masséna. **Edouard Crevel.** 1933.

A skylit canopy is enriched with lights of glass shards, at the entrance portal of an early modern cubism in stucco.

**[13se-21.] Hôtel industriel, 65, boulevard Masséna,** between avenue de la Porte-d'Ivry and avenue Claude-Regaud. **Jean-Marie Charpentier** and **Ros Borath.** 1989.

Structural bones are rather crudely displayed in front of a crass curtain wall: schoolkid stuff.

★★**[13se-22.] Cabinet d'Architecture, 4, square Masséna,** off boulevard Masséna, opposite avenue Claude-Regaud. **Paul Chemetov** and **Borja Huidobro.** 1986.

An elegant cube of glass, both in sheets and block, is umbilically attached to some 19th-century *meulière* that sports a period canopy of iron and glass. The cube's frame is of galvanized steel at its most sophisticated. Architects work here.

★**[13se-23.] Caserne des Pompiers, 37, boulevard Masséna,** between avenue Claude-Regaud and rue Darmesteter. **Jean Willerval.** 1971.

A first-rate superblock worthy of Skidmore, Owings & Merrill, the American Internationalists who have both blessed (Lever House, New York) and sullied (Tour Fiat, Paris) America and Europe. It is the best of the unhappy 1970s.

★★★[13se-24.] Maison Planeix, 24 bis, boulevard Masséna, between square Masséna and the viaduct to the Pont National. Le Corbusier and Pierre Jeanneret. 1927.

An artful cube of stucco, glass, and steel, now an artifact in its seventh decade, demeaned by a barrier wall at the ground floor. Originally this served the sculptor Antonin Planeix for his atelier and those of two painters. The facade is an exquisite example of Corbu's trigonometric composition, based on the proportions of the human body as elaborated in his *Modulor* (cf. Leonardo Da Vinci's inscribed man).

[13se-25.] Bureaux, 27, rue du Dessous-des-Berges, between rue de Patay and rue Regnault. André Biro and Jean-Jacques Fernier. 1975.

In the space of a prior *immeuble,* Biro and Fernier have inserted this trio of self-conscious sawteeth.

[13se-26.] Logements and Ecole, 14–24, rue de Patay, between rue Regnault and rue Eugène-Oudiné. Jacques Kalisz. 1985.

Neo-Godzilla, as in a Japanese hallucination, leads to a nursery school. Such histrionics make most of the 13th arrondissement's modernism seem cut and dried, and the best of the Post Modern (PoMo: cf. 44, rue de Ménilmontant by Henri Gaudin [20m-48a]) seem serenely magnificent.

★★[13se-27.] SUDAC (Société Urbaine d'Air Comprimé), 13, quai de la Gare, between the Pont National and rue Watt. Engineer, Joseph Leclaire. 1891.

A rich construction of steel, infilled with brick and glass, where the very structure is a complex ornament. This was a successful marriage of steel technology and "art," present in neo-Classical cast-iron buildings but denuded in the works of Mies and his peers.

★★[13se-28.] Hôtel industriel, boulevard Masséna between Porte de Vitry and the Pont National. Dominique Perrault. 1990.

"The networks for fluids are presented along the facades, ready to be distributed according to each tenant's needs. Ventilation and heating ducts, electric and communication cables, pipes for water and compressed air will remain visible, underscoring the building's ever-transient state. They will thus delineate on the exterior the vital fluids of the industrial organism." —Jean-Paul Robert in "L'architecture d'aujourd'hui," October 1987.
Remember the Beaubourg? Remember the Trusteeship Council of the United Nations? In 1976 and 1951 tubes and ducts were flaunted. Here is not an innovation but, rather, a crutch. Louis Kahn created such flexibility at the Salk Institute, but invisibly, concealed in alternate service "floors" and elsewhere.
The box is a sleek, crystalline container, nevertheless.

★★★★[13se-29.] Refuge de l'Armée du Salut, 12, rue Cantagrel and 47, rue du Chevaleret. Le Corbusier and Pierre Jeanneret. 1931–1933.

*Brise-soleils* were added in the 1940s to mute the sun's radiation in this hermetically sealed "air-conditioned" dormitory for the unfortunate, intended as "a factory for human good, where one overhauls those parts of the human machine which are worn out by life." This, Corbu's second multiunit complex—and a dormitory like his first, the Pavillon Suisse at the Cité Universitaire—is the fruit of a patron's will, that of a Singer sewing machine heiress, the American-born Princesse de Polignac. The Salvation Army had other, more orthodox, architects in mind, but money talked in the language of the avant-garde. The play of cubistic form, cylinder and cube-proper, still presents a dynamic interplay to the arriving pedestrian.

"This is where it all began. It is here that Le Corbusier had placed his most cancerous cell (the building for the Salvation Army, rue Cantagrel), cell that the epigones of the pseudo-genius of Châteaux-de-Fonds are later employed to proliferate, to believe, and embellish like their queen. The sickness has reached the avenues d'Italie, and de Choisy, the boulevard Masséna, the quartier de la Gare, etc., and some other arrondissements, certainly, but the 13th seems to be the most stricken. Giant pustules of glass and concrete have been erected, one of them insolently called 'Galaxie,' to better tell us that we are entering another world."—Léo Malet (see p. 73, *Vie et histoire du VIIIe* arrondissement)

The philistines here counterattack.

**[13se-30.] Logements, 105, rue du Dessous-des-Berges,** between rue de Domrémy and rue de Tolbiac. **André Biro** and **Jean-Jacques Fernier.** 1971.

Shocking blue jazz, fireworks for this unsuspecting quarter. The architects "rediscovered" color without any sense of sensitivity or grace in its use.

★**[13se-31.] Logements, 16, rue de Domrémy,** between rue Dunois and rue du Chevaleret. **Architecture Studio.** 1984.

A layered grid is simultaneously both subtle and fussy, the tilted plane above too arrogant. A clever work, it tests ideas without a built sense of completion. Walk between the screened street wall and the building proper to sense the architects' message.

★**[13se-32.] Logements, 18, rue Dunois,** corner rue Charcot. **Gilles Bouchez.** 1981.

Two gables and a windowed parapet in a block so understated that it is consciously invisible. Although a torus and minor rustications at the base fail to make us take notice, it is an appropriate modern vernacular.

**[13se-33.] Logements, 10, passage Chanvin,** between rue Pierre-Gourdault and rue Duchefdelaville. 1988.

Moderately sober multihued brick leads through a PoMo portal to the *passage* proper. Behind are bow balconies and de rigueur glass block. On rue Duchefdelaville next door are beflowered ateliers, a narrow remembrance of this arrondissement's simpler past.

**[13se-34.] Eglise Notre-Dame-de-la-Gare,** place Jeanne-d'Arc, on axis of rue Jeanne-d'Arc. **Claude Naissant.** 1855–1864.

Dutiful Romanesque Revival serves this district as an urban anchor, providing a pivot around which markets spring each week and some secondhand history for the history-impoverished 13th.

★**[13se-35.] Ateliers des artistes, 2, rue Lahire,** corner place Jeanne-d'Arc. **Jacques Bardet.** 1984.

An exercise in grids à la Mondrian, with tiled columns and articulated capitals. Cubistic and straightforward.

★[13se-36.] PTT, 36, place Jeanne-d'Arc, corner rue Jeanne-d'Arc. 1930s.

Style here stands out of the ordinary crowd surrounding. Sober brown-gray brick with crisp white window sash is accentuated by handsome, understated steel detailing.

[13se-37.] Logements, 34–38, rue Clisson, corner rue Dunois. 1980s.

Banal.

[13se-38.] Ecole élémentaire, 64–70, rue Dunois, between rue Clisson and boulevard Vincent-Auriol. **Jérome Delaage and Fernand Tsaropoulos.** 1975.

Fins, slopes, mirror glass—the worst sets from "Star Trek." The orange brick school behind is relatively sober in this heteroclitic ensemble, but the adjacent towers: "Look on my works, ye Mighty, and despair."

[13se-39.] Bureaux, 2, rue Clisson, corner rue du Chevaleret. **Maurice Novarina.** 1973.

Dirty brown tile, ranged in tone and value. The pits.

[13se-40.] Logements, 23–29, rue Louise-Weiss, off rue du Chevaleret. 1989.

White tile, green sash, and a triumphal and vulgar arch. This is an improvement only in a relative way.

★★[13se-41.] 112–118, rue du Chevaleret, corner of rue Clisson. **Edith Girard.** 1990.

A happy reentrance onto the urban scene of Girard, whose lovely apartments in the 19th arrondissement [19r-8.] make that district a better environment. The main block, a symbolic *corps de logis*, raises elegant undulations above its courtyard.

[13se-42.] Bureaux 55–65, boulevard Vincent-Auriol, between rue du Chevaleret and the railroad yards. **Henry Ciriani** and **Adrien Fainsilber.** 1990.

Twin office buildings flank a new commercial street.

★[13se-43.] Logements, Hôpital Salpêtrière. 36–42, boulevard Vincent-Auriol, between rue Bruant and the railroad yards. **Gilles Bouchez.** 1989.

An outpost of housing on this eclectic stretch of boulevard, but it hugs the street, and delivers form to define it.

★★[13se-44.] Pavillon, Pathologies de la Tête, Salpêtrière/Pitié, boulevard Vincent-Auriol. **Pierre Riboulet.** 1992

A *concours* won. Riboulet, the architect of the marvelous **Hôpital Robert-Debré [19b-3.]**, here brings his talents combining distinguished hospital planning and distinguished architecture to the **Salpêtrière/Pitié** complex.

[13se-45.] Hôtel industriel/Ministère des Finances, 41–43, boulevard Vincent-Auriol, between rue du Chevaleret and the railroad yards. Remodeling, **Robert Grosjean** and **Jean-Philippe Pargade.** 1980s.

The conversion of SNCF offices into shops for the maintenance services of the Ministry of Finance.

**[13se-46.] PTT, 26, boulevard Vincent-Auriol,** corner rue Edmond-Flamant. **Joseph Bukiet.** 1956.

Wow! Here is very *retardataire* Perret, with exposed concrete, stained and neglected. Clean windows, high-pressure water cleaning, and awnings (to solve the obvious sun problems) might recoup its spirit.

**[13se-47.] Foyer pour les personnes âgeés, 10, boulevard Vincent-Auriol,** corner rue Giffard. **Marie-Christine Gangneaux.** 1985.

Intellectual stucco clads neo-Fascist architecture (Mussolini's Third Rome of 1939–1940).

**[13se-48.] Foyer de travailleurs, 6, rue Giffard,** between boulevard Vincent-Auriol and quai d'Austerlitz. **Jean Caillat.** 1980.

African workers temporarily in Paris come home to this dour ensemble in ocher tilework. From rue Giffard you can see the sleek back of 5, rue de Bellièvre:

★★★**[13se-49.] Logements, 5, rue de Bellièvre,** between quai d'Austerlitz and rue Edmond-Flamand. **Fabrice Dusapin** and **François Leclerq.** 1987.

Winner of the Grand Prix d'Architecture *(Moniteur)* / Prix de la Première Oeuvre. The modest facade on rue de Bellièvre belies the rich plasticity of its rear, with a spiral ribbon (stair) soaring to its crest. If you sneak into the court of 6, rue Giffard, you can savor that soar.

★**[13se-50.] Allée des Arts,** 26, rue Edmond-Flamand, north of rue Fulton. **Bernard Le Roy, Marylene Ferrand, Jean-Pierre Feugas,** and **Bernard Huet.** 1983.

Formerly a barrel warehouse, this now shelters studios and living quarters on each side of its central nave; a timber frame holds up the sky. Parisian artists are sometimes honored and frequently coddled in their culture-oriented society. Splendid! And such urban recycling is a necessity in an always growing, changing city.

★★★**[13se-51.] Bibliothèque de France,** quai de la Gare, over the tracks of the Gare d'Austerlitz. **Dominique Perrault.** 1995.

Already popularly known as the **TGB** (très grande bibliothèque), an acronym after the **TGV** (train à grande vitesse), this is a futuristic technological symbol of the high-tech symbiosis of the 300 km/hour train and the electronic library. Here diskettes, microfiches, tapes, CDs, and deep, hard memory banks will supplement books.

Four thirty-story towers, warehouses of books and information for the TGB's readers, viewers, and listeners, will surround a grand sunken court. Not only is it inappropriate to put books in glass towers subject to the harsh rays of the sun, it is also totally inappropriate urbanistically to have such towers at the edge of the city of Paris. This is 1960s-*retardataire* planning.

# 33
# THIRTEENTH ARRONDISSEMENT

## SOUTHWEST

### PLACE D'ITALIE TO STADE CHARLETY AND BACK

Place d'Italie; Grand Ecran: **Kenzo Tange**; Piscine de la
Butte-aux-Cailles: **Louis Bonnier**; place Verlaine; avenue d'Italie; 152,
avenue d'Italie: **Vittorio Mazzucconi**; Les Palmes d'Italie: **Michel
Bourdeau**; tour Super-Italie: **Maurice Novarina**; boulevards des
Maréchaux; Stade Sébastien-Charléty: **Henri Gaudin**; rue Kuss/Groupe
Scolaire: **Roger-Henri Expert**; Cité Florale; Eglise
Sainte-Anne-de-la-Maison-Blanche: **Prosper Bobin**; Petite Alsace: **Jean
Walter**; Lycée Estienne: **Mansot** and **Dammartin**; Le Métro Aérien:
**Jean-Camille Formigé**

Métro: **Place d'Italie**

[13sw-7.] Logements, 32, rue du Moulin-de-la-Pointe, and 18, rue
Bourgon. Damir and Maya Perinic. 1988.

237

**[13sw-1.] Place d'Italie**

To quote the Association du Quartier pour de Développement et l'Aménagement du XIIIe Arrondissement, "Neither round nor square, neither mineral nor vegetable, neither flat, nor concave, nor convex. It marks a frontier of Paris and the beginning of a symbolic descent toward Turin and Perpignan; it suggests not a gate, but merely the summit of the last slope before leaving Paris."

★★**[13sw-2.] Grand Ecran**/also known as **Ensemble d'Equipement** and **Campanile**, place d'Italie, between avenue d'Italie and rue Bobillot. **Kenzo Tange**. 1990.

A hotel, two cinemas, and offices for film and video. This segmental reinforcement of the place d'Italie supports the cry of ADA XIII (see **[13sw-1.]** above), but for only one of the eight enclosing blocks. If place d'Italie is to become an urban gate or an urban *place*, a vastly more monumental response is needed.

The building proper is Tange's first European commission, part of the one-upmanship between Mayor and sometime Prime Minister Jacques Chirac and President François Mitterrand over who might be the greatest patron (the former, for example, with Omnisport and La Villette, the latter with the Grand Louvre and the Grande Arche). Mitterrand is winning hands down, but Chirac's counterattack with Tange is impressive.

★★**[13sw-3.] Piscine de la Butte-aux-Cailles**, 5, place Paul-Verlaine, between rue Bobillot and rue du Moulin-des-Prés. **Louis Bonnier**, architect, assisted by **Emile Bois**. Engineer, **Girard**. 1924.

A Romanesque Revival crustacean envelops a sleek reinforced-concrete structure—vaulted, with seven light arches. Might this be an analogous urban hermit crab, with a wandering structure slipped into the Romanesque shell? Underneath it all is its "fountain of youth," an artesian (self-flowing) well providing mineral water at 28°C (82.4°F.)—therapeutic rather than refreshing.

★**[13sw-4.] Square des Peupliers**, 68, rue du Moulin-des-Prés, between rue de Tolbiac and passage Foubert. 1920s.

No poplars here but, rather, a grand urban enclave for people in a paved and quiet cul-de-sac.

**[13sw-5.] HBM/Cité Ernest et Henri-Rousselle**, 18, rue Ernest-et-Henri-Rousselle, corner rue du Moulin-des-Prés. **Georges Albenque** and **Eugène Gonnot**. 1922.

Sometimes it seems that it would be just grand to be "poor" in Paris, but this is only an external architectural assessment. Toilets in HBMs were originally shared by four families, and a one-bedroom apartment (the bedroom splittable into two small ones) comprised only 28 square meters (300 square feet). The most simplistic HBMs were termed *taudis officiels* (official slums) by some. In retrospect they were far more savory than the shantytowns that had filled the space outside the 1845 walls—not totally demolished until 1919.

★**[13sw-6.] Rue Dieulafoy**, between rue Henri-Pape and rue du Docteur-Leray. 1920.

A "terrace" of false gables, ivy-covered and precious. The simple street, ironwork, and no-nonsense scale are a delight.

**[13sw-7.] Logements, 32, rue du Moulin-de-la-Pointe,** and **18, rue Bourgon,** between avenue d'Italie and rue Damesme. **Damir** and **Maya Perinic.** 1988.

Tiled jazz, its yellow beating the eyes, the detailing (windows, sills) gross. If this won a competition, where were the jurors? The interior courtyard is somewhat more serene.

**[13sw-8.] Immeuble, 1, rue Bourgon**, between avenue d'Italie and rue du Moulin-de-la-Pointe. 1930s.

The ironwork at No. 1 is distinguished, as is the interplay of brick and concrete (painted and stuccoed inevitably).

★**[13sw-9.] Logements, 152, avenue d'Italie,** corner rue du Tage. **Vittorio Mazzucconi.** 1984.

Mazzucconi speaks of this as a "fortress besieged by all the catastrophes that menace our epoch . . . [by] the worst excesses of postwar architecture, which have presided over the reconstruction of this quarter." One wonders whether architects should speak about their own works.

Here is a crossblend of Italian postwar romance and the constructivism of the 1920s in the USSR: flamboyant, egocentric, with complication and "originality" for its own sake. It does, however, respect the old scale of Paris.

★**[13sw-10.] Les Palmes d'Italie (logements)**, 158, avenue d'Italie, between rue du Tage and the railroad. **Michel Bourdeau.** 1980s.

This strange work is doubtlessly "Learning from [the] Las Vegas" of Robert Venturi, chief guru of the banal (his word) for others (his own work is usually subdued). Described as an architectural prodigy (Bourdeau was barely thirty at the birth of this block), he shares the blame and honors with his mentor at UP 1 (Unité Pédagogique = school of architecture), **Henri Ciriani**, and his client, the City of Paris.

Another analogy might make him the Arquitectonica of Paris, full of semitropical plasticity and colors. This is a building to be excerpted in magazines in color, not inflicted on the city.

**[13sw-11.] Immeuble, 160, avenue d'Italie,** between rue du Tage and the railroad. **J. Duflos** and **F. Arnoux.** 1934.

Bourdeau next door should have paid more attention to this modest, moderate, middle-class neighbor.

★**[13sw-12.] Tour Super-Italie,** 121, avenue d'Italie, between rue Caillaux and the railroad. **Maurice Novarina.** 1976.

Unfortunately if there must be a tower (a terrible Parisian urban-design idea of the 1960s and 1970s) here is an elegant one that defies the city. As a detached point-block and a solo event, this might be tolerated in a way that the low-rise theatrics of **Nos. 152** and **121** across the street cannot.

★★**[13sw-13.] Lycée Gaston-Bachelard,** 2, passage Raymond, between avenue d'Italie and rue Gandon. **J. Creulot et E. Denis.** 1947.

A high point in the history of this arrondissement's modern architecture. The date makes it officially *retardataire* 1930s, excused because the war removed six years from French architectural history. Struck red brick, it wears an Art Moderne entrance and offers housing in the same complex along the side streets.

★★[13sw-14.] Logements/ZAC Gandon-Masséna, facing the internal garden of the ZAC (corner avenue des Maréchaux et avenue d'Italie). **Jean Dubus.** 1990.

Homage to Le Corbusier, in a reprise of his never-built *immeuble*-villa.

[13sw-15.] HBM, 133, boulevard Masséna, between avenue de la Porte-d'Italie and rue Paulin-Enfert. **Joseph Bassompierre, Paul Sirvin, and Paul de Rutté.** 1931.

Vast neo-Classical columns give this social housing a powerful architectural presence.

[13sw-16.] HBM, 17, boulevard Kellerman, between rue du Docteur-Bourneville and rue Keufer.

[13sw-17.] Crèche, 14, rue Max-Jacob, between rue Keufer and rue du Professeur-Louis-Renault. **Philippe Dubois.** 1973.

★★[13sw-18.] Stade Sébastien-Charléty, 83, boulevard Kellerman, between rue Thomire and avenue de la Porte-de-Gentilly. **Henri Gaudin.** 1991.

A new complex (20,000 seats) on the site of the former Charléty stadium, where Michel Jazy broke the world's 2,000-meter record in 1960. The $90 million project will include facilities for international sporting events, the PUC, a *maison de sport,* and a complex to finance part of the works ($40 million). Intended to form an urbane transition to contiguous Paris, housing has unfortunately been stricken from the program, to be replaced by trees. Trees, of course, don't vote, and the housing's occupants would have voted against the present political hegemony of the City of Paris.

★[13sw-19.] Logements, 14, rue Brillat-Savarin, between rue des Peupliers and rue Kuss. **A. S. Agopian.** 1932.

Bellied bay windows in a stylish *immeuble* of the 1930s.

★[13sw-20.] HBM, 18, rue Brillat-Savarin, between rue Kuss and rue Albin-Haller. **André Arfvidson, Joseph Bassompierre,** and **Paul de Rutté.** 1913–1924.

The great crowning two-story loggias are richly decorated in stenciled Art Deco—rich and glorious detail for these delightful HBMs. The war intervened, as with all of the HBMs commissioned in the *concours* of 1913.

★★★[13sw-21.] Groupe Scolaire, 8-10, rue Kuss, between rue Brillat-Savarin and rue des Peupliers. **Roger-Henri Expert.** 1934.

A cascade of half-round terraces spills down the side of a garden sheathed in stone-textured stucco. Expert designed the interiors of the *Normandie,* as well as the fountains at the Trocadéro (Palais de Chaillot). His stylish palette spanned the manmade world. These schools are a substantial landmark in the history of modern—as opposed to Art Deco and Art Moderne—Parisian architecture. Le Corbusier would have been pleased.

[13sw-22.] Logements, place de Rungis, between rue Brillat-Savarin and rue de la Fontaine-à-Mulard. 1930s.

Fluted pilasters, spandrels with fasces, and a studied skyline. This 1930s stalwart is both ordinary and marvelous.

★[13sw-23.] **Cité Florale**, comprising several streets surrounded by rue Brillat-Savarin, rue Auguste-Lançon, and rue Boussingault. 1928.

Botany baptised the rue des Orchidées, rue des Glycines, square des Mimosas, rue des Iris, and rue des Volubilis. Tiny but urbane row houses *(villas mitoyennes)*, sometimes luxuriant with foliage but certainly not luxurious. An island of human scale in the 13th arrondissement.

[13sw-24.] **Ecole particulière du Ministère de l'Education,** 96, rue Barrault, between place de Rungis and rue de la Colonie. **Roger Dhuit.** 1962.

If the date is correct, this is *neo*-1930s, a blend of the International Style and the Paris exposition of 1937.

★[13sw-25.] **Logements, 67, rue Barrault**, corner rue de la Colonie. **Roger Anger** and **Pierre Puccinelli**. 1958.

Constructivist boxed balconies provide a pleasant childscape to reinforce this strong corner.

★[13sw-26.] **HBM, 40, rue de la Colonie,** between rue Barrault and rue Bobillot. 1930s.

Red raked brick, many-balconied, with rampant oculi. (Or are they *oeils-de-boeuf?*) This is distinguished social architecture from a maligned decade.

★★[13sw-27.] **HBM, 72, rue de la Colonie,** corner rue de la Fontaine-à-Mulard. **George Vaudoyer**. 1911.

A grand and lovely Romanesque Revival arch leads to a garden oasis.

[13sw-28.] **Eglise Sainte-Anne-de-la-Maison-Blanche,** 186, rue de Tolbiac, corner rue Bobillot. **Prosper Bobin**. 1891–1912.

A free and easy Romanesque/Byzantine Revival, domes great and small. It has the aura of an exposition never held, say that of 1914.

[13sw-29.] **HBM, Square André-Dreyer, 18, rue Wurtz,** between rue de Tolbiac and rue Daviel. **Louis Heckly**. 1934.

Another 1930s HBM with a powerful arched entrance and bold balconies.

★★[13sw-30.] **Petite Alsace,** 10, rue Daviel, between rue Vergniaud and rue Barrault. **Jean Walter**. 1912.

Here a gated facade leads to an Arts and Crafts courtyard or what might be called, alternately, a woodsy mini–New Town, as at Letchworth (England) or Forest Hills (New York City),

[13sw-31.] **Villa Daviel,** 7, rue Daviel, between rue Vergniaud and rue Barrault. 1912.

There are, miraculously, myriad of these wonderful pedestrianways. Variously termed *villas, passages,* or *squares,* they are all family-scaled retreats of the true middle class—particularly in the 13th, 19th, and 20th arrondissements. In the 16th and 17th the similarly meandering streets serve the freestanding houses of the *haute bourgeoisie.*

★★[13sw-32.] **Logements, 11, rue Barrault,** between passage Barrault and rue Alphand. 1930s.

One Brave New World in stucco, with oculi and ship's railings for the *garde-fous.* Opposite is the civilization of more HBMs flanking the rue Le Dantec.

**★[13sw-33.] HBM, 75, boulevard Auguste-Blanqui,** between rue Barrault and rue Vergniaud. **Agence d'Architecture HBM.** 1935.

Rue Le Dantec forms the spine of this delightful complex.

**[13sw-34.] Maison, 58, boulevard Auguste-Blanqui,** between rue Edmond-Gondinet and rue Corvisart. 1880s.

Neo-Gothic structuralism in a modest villa, with its two neighboring peers, here at a hot center of "urban renewal." Some streetfronted *immeubles* are near, but most new construction is still in the manner of a freestanding suburbia. This is flavor from the 13th arrondissement's distant past.

**[13sw-35.] Lycée Supérieure Estienne des Arts et Industries Graphiques,** 18, boulevard Auguste-Blanqui, corner rue Abel-Hovelacque. **Mansot** and **Dammartin**. 1896.

A pallid neo–Henri IV limestone-and-brickwork school. The sign over the boulevard portal is unworthy of graphics and even more unworthy of art. The 1896 wrought-iron fence and gate put such vulgarity to shame.

---

### Le Métro Aérien

**Jean-Jacques Lévèque** in *Vie et histoire du XIIIe Arrondissement:* "It erupts from its underworld at the Saint-Jacques station and triumphantly enters the XIIIe arrondissement. In its voyage leading to the Seine, interrupted only by its return to the underworld at the place d'Italie, the Métro aérien offers an ideal view over the boulevard Auguste-Blanqui and the boulevard Vincent Auriol, the former boulevard de la Gare, of which it follows the trace.

"Banal at ground level, in the flood of traffic, the route, thanks to the Métro aérien, acquires a poetic allure. This trip through the living texture of the city allows one to read it as if it were a rich and fruitful book."

**Roland Barthes** noted that "he who moves in the city, that is to say the user of the city, is a sort of reader who, according to his obligations and his movements, foresees the articulated parts as a secret reality."

The 20th-century poet **Léon-Paul Fargue,** who said "we leaf through the boulevards like an album," did not hide his love for the Métro, if one believes his friend and biographer, **André Beucler.**

The Métro aérien traverses the quarters of Paris in depth, "an X-ray of daily life." If it offers a fragmented view, made dynamic by speed, it also has its underside, the life that takes place under the high columns which support it.

Construction of the line Sud (Passy–place d'Italie) began in 1902 (**Jean-Camille Formigé**, architect), and on May 11, 1905, the company took possession of it. The extension of the line up to the Viaduc de Bercy, a kilometer and a half (.93 miles), started in 1904 and was placed in service in 1907.

With the opening of a competition for its construction, the section between the quai de la Rapée and the quai d'Austerlitz, which required the construction of a viaduct, fell to the Société de Construction de Levallois in 1903. At 143 meters (470 feet), the Viaduc d'Austerlitz holds the record for the longest span in Paris.

---

# 34
# FOURTEENTH ARRONDISSEMENT
## EAST

### PLACE DENFERT-ROCHEREAU TO

### SAINT-PIERRE-DE-MONTROUGE AND BACK

Place Denfert-Rochereau; Barrière d'Enfer: **Claude-Nicolas Ledoux**;
Les Catacombes; Lion de Belfort: **Frédéric-Auguste Bartholdi**;
Observatoire de Paris: **Claude Perrault**; Ecole Spécial d'Architecture:
**Cuno Brullman** and **Arno Fougeras-Lavergnolle**; 11, rue
Schoelcher: **Gauthier et Gauthier**; Cimetière Montparnasse;
Logements, 3, rue Lalande: **Thierry Gruber**; 7, rue Danville: **Henri
Sauvage**; Annexe/Mairie: **Georges Sébille**; Eglise
Saint-Pierre-de-Montrouge: **Joseph Vaudremer**; Villa Adrienne; La
Rouchefoucauld: **Jacques-Denis Antoine**

Métro: **Denfert-Rochereau**

[**14e-1.**] Barrière d'Enfer. **Claude-Nicolas Ledoux.** 1785–1787.

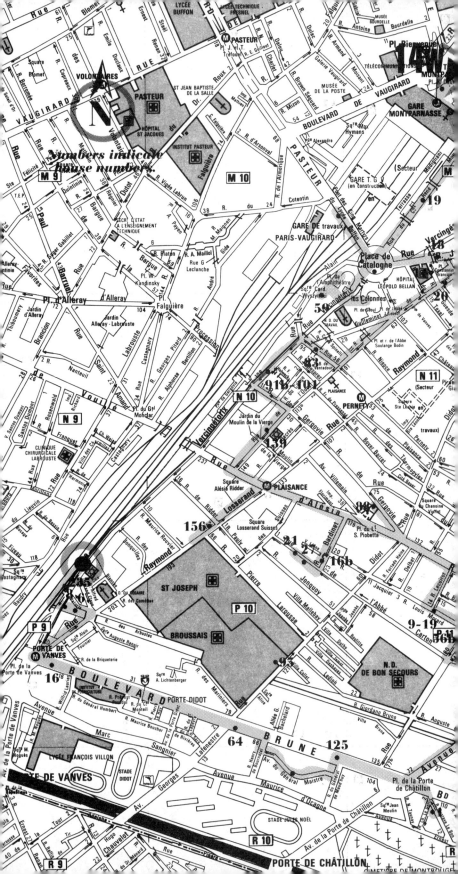

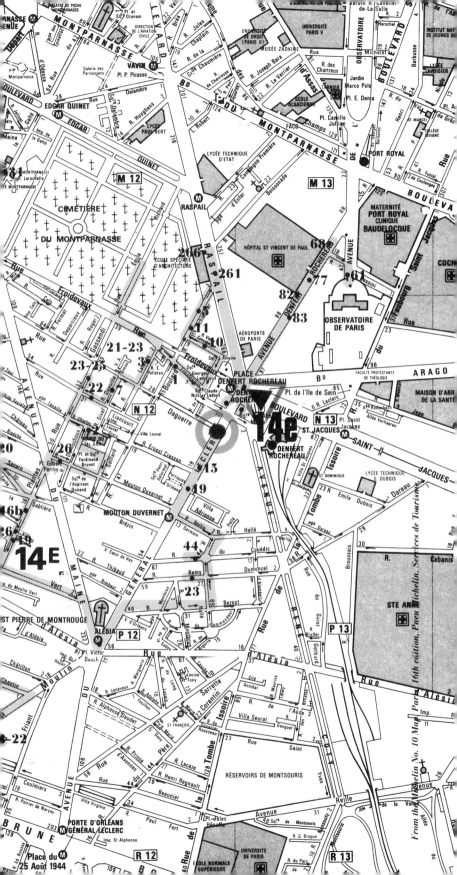

**★★★[14e-1.] Barrière d'Enfer**, avenue du Général-Leclerc, south side place Denfert-Rochereau. **Claude-Nicholas Ledoux**. 1785–1787.

Four vestiges from the tax-gathering wall of the Fermiers Généraux remain: this tollgate, that of the **Trône** at place de la Nation; the administrative **Rotonde de la Villette** at place de Stalingrad; and the **Rotonde de Chartres** at the Parc Monceau, a viewing *folie* for the duc d'Orléans. Only here and at place de la Nation did money actually change hands, as customs fees on farmers' produce entering Paris.

These twin pavilions are rusticated to a mannerist's delight. They still serve the public realm as offices of the Inspection Générale des Carrières de Paris and (the easterly one) as entry to the Catacombs, which occupy part of the quarries being inspected. The third act of *La Bohème* takes place here.

**★[14e-2.] Les Catacombes/Ossuaire Général de Paris**, under the street system south of place Denfert-Rochereau, between avenue René-Coty and Avenue du Général-Leclerc and, particularly, under rue Hallé, rue Rémy-Dumoncel, and rue d'Alembert. Entrance, 1, place Denfert-Rochereau. Exit, 36, rue Rémy-Dumoncel.

The bones of six million Parisians rest in these vast caverns created by the quarrying of limestone for building Paris, and these catacombs are only 7 percent of the total area of quarries once in use. The trip here is more to see these mines for the architecture of Paris than to see bones—but there is a bit of the ghoul in us all. The original installation came from the reclamation of Parisian land, relocating the fruit of cemeteries into these more efficient halls.

---

### Manhunt in the Catacombs

"This hunt in the Catacombs was one of the most dramatic episodes in the great tragedy of the capture of Paris (1871) by the army of Versailles. . . . The battle in the streets of the city ended. The insurgents [communards] were tracked down to all their positions. Those who weren't killed fighting, captured, or shot sought safety in flight.

"Some sought refuge in the sewers, others in the *carrières d'Amerique* [plaster of paris quarries], still others and in greater numbers, in the Catacombs. . . .

"In the first days of June 1871 the manhunt began in the Catacombs. Some troops entered through the gate in the Barrière d'Enfer, while others secured the other gate, opening on the plaine de Montsouris. Then, armed with torches, the soldiers cautiously descended into the immense boneyard.

"What happened then is not hard to guess. . . . It must have been horrible—this final battle fought as the red glow of torchlight bizarrely illuminated the tense faces of the combatants. Violent tramplings, shouts of rage, screams of pain, agonized death rattles, the clanking of bayonets, the clatter of explosions—what a spectacle! And all of it happening in the long corridors of these crypts carpeted with bones, under the very eye of the dead, disturbed in the rest that had been promised them." (*Vie et histoire du XIVe arrondissement*, p. 62)

---

**[14e-3.] Lion de Belfort**, place Denfert-Rochereau. **Frédéric-Auguste Bartholdi**. 1880.

This is a reduced copy of the Lion created by Bartholdi at Belfort honoring the city's successful defense from the Prussians in 1871 by a force led by Colonel Denfert-Rochereau. Another work of Bartholdi is the **Statue of Liberty**. Neither the Lion nor Liberty is great sculpture although Liberty, like **Sacré-Coeur,** has become a symbol that transcends its value as a work of art. For super-Bartholdi see the fountain of horses at Lyons, where they snort vapor.

**J.-H. Rosny Aîné,** in *Dans les rues de Paris,* 1913: "That afternoon Maurice found himself at that knot of avenues and boulevards where the Lion muses on his defeat: boulevard Raspail, boulevard Arago, boulevard Saint-Jacques, avenue d'Orléans (now avenue du Général-Leclerc), avenue Montsouris (René-Coty), rue du Champ-d'Asile (Froidevaux), rue Denfert-Rochereau. Only the Etoile produces a more ample urban image, but the Lion's landscape is more variable, more profound, and more tragic, with its little city of hospitals, hospices, the Great Observatory bathed in the eternity of the stars and, on a green hill . . . the other observatory, which sets a trap for the wind, measures rainfall, and captures fugitive electricity [the meteorological observatory of the City of Paris]. The Luxembourg is nearby with all its legends, the Montparnasse cemetery with all its corpses; three railway stations (Montparnasse, Sceaux, and Petite Ceinture) hurl their iron mammoths far and wide, the Métropolitain disgorges its human rats; and each path serves a different humanity."

**[14e-4.] Chapelle de la Sainte-Trinité et de l'Enfant-Jésus-Christ,** 68, avenue Denfert-Rochereau, between place Denfert-Rochereau and avenue de l'Observatoire. **Daniel Gittard.** 1655–1657.

**★[14e-5.] Pharmacie, Hôpital Saint-Vincent-de-Paul,** 82, avenue Denfert-Rochereau, between place Denfert-Rochereau and avenue de l'Observatoire. **J. A. Fourquier** and **Jean Filhol.** 1986.

A beautifully detailed bit of PoMo intermingles with history.

**[14e-6.] Cité des petits hôtels,** 83, avenue Denfert-Rochereau, between place Denfert-Rochereau and avenue de l'Observatoire. early 1900s.

In this small oasis of urbanism, small *hôtels* and ateliers flank a cul-de-sac leading to the **Hôtel Fontaine (François Le Coeur.** 1913) in brick and reinforced concrete.

**[14e-7.] Cité d'artistes/**originally **Ecuries de la Barrière d'Enfer,** 77, avenue Denfert-Rochereau, between place Denfert-Rochereau and avenue de l'Observatoire. 1780s.

These fourteen ateliers were once the stables attached to the **Barrière d'Enfer.**

**★★[14e-8.] Observatoire de Paris,** 61, avenue de l'Observatoire, between boulevard Arago and boulevard du Montparnasse. **Claude Perrault.** 1668–1682. (Opened for work, 1672.) Wings and cupolas, 1834.

Claude Perrault, architect of the east colonnade of the Louvre (where he had beat out both Le Vau and Bernini), was "a bad doctor who became a good architect," according to Boileau. On a grand axis with the Luxembourg Palace and Gardens, it was described by the astronomer Grillot as having a particularly well chosen site: in the countryside, where "the horizon was perfectly free on all sides and the spot propitious for observations."

**[14e-9.]** Formerly **American Center,** 261, boulevard Raspail, between place Denfert-Rochereau and rue Boissonade. 1920–1988.

When redevelopment is completed, these grounds will at least be visually open to the passing public as a great garden harboring a Cedar of Lebanon planted by Châteaubriand (ca. 1800). The center sold its land (profitably) and moved to Bercy, where its new building by **Frank Gehry [12s-13.]** stands at the edge of the new Parc de Bercy, site of the old Halles aux Vins.

★★[14e-10.] Ecole Spéciale d'Architecture, Ecole Camondo, and Ecole Supérieure de Communication Visuelle, 266, boulevard Raspail, between rue Schoelcher and boulevard Edgar-Quinet. Cuno Brullman and Arno Fougeras-Lavergnolle. 1989.

They tried for a mini-Beaubourg and got an incomplete erector set in the form of a rather ordinary commercial glass box festooned with an awkward would-be constructivist open stair. To inflict such opportunistic architecture on students is foolishness. (The cobbler's children either have no shoes or ones with holes in them.) Such was the fate of many new School of Architecture buildings, such as that at Yale, which functions badly and remains a bit like last year's hat, safely preserved in the closet of the mind as a memory of ephemeral style.

The Ecole Spéciale d'Architecture was founded in 1865 under the direction of Emile Trélat in reaction to the Ecole des Beaux-Arts, to be the instrument of an "art appropriate to our modern times" and to train men "possessing the science of the engineer and the art of the architect." At No. 266 the architect of this imaginary team is off-base, playing the effete engineer.

★[14e-11.] Maison, 5, rue Schoelcher, between boulevard Raspail and rue Froidevaux. Paul Follot. 1911.

Curved and extravagant ironwork, baked ornamentation, geometric tile, and a soaring *comble* create an extraordinary and wild former private house.

★★[14e-12.] Ateliers d'artistes, 11, rue Schoelcher and 12, rue Victor-Considérant. Gauthier and Gauthier. 1927.

Father and son created ateliers that overlook the Cimetière du Montparnasse. Blue sash set in white stucco provides real and imaginary studios to real and imaginary painters. (Did you think all those ateliers were reserved for actual artists?) In the same manner that Greenwich Village and SoHo were coopted by the yuppies of their time, many Parisian ateliers became fashionable for the bourgeoisie.

[14e-13.] RATP (Métro de Paris), 10, rue Victor-Considérant, east of rue Schoelcher. circa 1915.

A power station for the Métro, unfortunately modernized with a false mansard.

★[14e-14.] Logements, 1, rue Boulard, corner rue Froidevaux. 1900.

Concave and convex, a sinuous play of stone, metal, and glass. Tile banding enlivens the facade, which has depth and vigorous shadow.

★★[14e-15.] Cimetière du Montparnasse/also called Cimetière du Sud, principal entry, 3, boulevard Edgar-Quinet, and surrounded by boulevard Raspail, rue Schoelcher, and rue Froidevaux. First burials, 1654. City cemetery, 1824.

Here you will find the memory of Jean-Paul Sartre and Simone de Beauvoir, Chaim Soutine, Charles Baudelaire, Antoine Bourdelle, Jean Seberg, Camille Saint-Saëns, Constantin Brancusi, Frédéric-Auguste Bartholdi, Colonel Dreyfus, François Rude, Tristan Tzara, Pierre Larousse, César Franck, Guy de Maupassant, André Citroën, Henri Pétain, and Antoine-Chrysostome Quatremère de Quincy, the archaeologist responsible in 1791 for converting the Eglise Sainte-Genevieve of Soufflot, still under construction, to a Panthéon "to receive the great men of the epoch of French liberty."

★[14e-16.] **Logements, 21–23 rue Froidevaux**, between rue Lalande and rue Gassendi. **Georges Grimbert**. 1929.

Art Deco polychromatic-geometric floral work on a Haussmannian brick body. Two-story glazed paired windows overlooking the cemetery illuminate the "atelier" spaces. Somber, naive, but searching for the new truth.

★★[14e-17.] **Logements, 3, rue Lalande,** between rue Froidevaux and rue Daguerre. **Thierry Gruber**. 1987.

What a joy to turn onto this street and see truly distinguished modern architecture—not just the slick of instant PoMo. Here is a building that is thoughtful and rich, with a skin of white precast stone far superior to the acres of white tile seen elsewhere. The massing of the balconies, details of columns, and roof silhouette border on the magnificent.

[14e-18.] **Logements, 7, rue Danville,** between rue Daguerre and rue Liancourt. **Henri Sauvage**. 1905.

Ironwork on the small balconies allows flowers galore and a step outside. This is early Sauvage, seven years before the **Maison à gradins sportive [6s-22.]**, and intended for the financially modest rather than the jet set.

[14e-19.] **Immeuble/Bureaux, 22, rue Liancourt,** between rue Gassendi and rue Boulard. 1980s.

Figured tile on an asymmetrical building that would have considerable style in a better material and with better detailing.

★[14e-20.] **Logements, 23–25, rue Gassendi**, between rue Daguerre and rue Liancourt. **Albert and Jacques Guilbert** and **Michel Luyckx**. 1931.

Bay windows for the poor in dour brick and concrete. Just think what steam cleaning and some painted chromatics would do for the counterpoint of *garde-fous*, railings, and window sash.

[14e-21.] **Mairie, 2, place Ferdinand-Brunot. Claude Naissant.** 1852–1855. East and west wings and central tower, **Alexandre-Emile Auburtin**. 1889.

Second Empire stuff again, boring except for the central tower that reeks of extenuated Mansart. The square is a pleasant park of trees, playgrounds, bushes, and gravel. Remember these oases from dogs.

★[14e-22.] **Mairie/Annexe, 26, rue Mouton-Duvernet,** west side of place Ferdinand-Brunot. **Georges Sébille**. 1933.

Brick from those short interbellum years from 1919 to 1939, which witnessed a renaissance of Parisian architecture weighted toward social action. Here is a transition from the architecture of the 1925 Exposition to that of the Exposition of 1937.

★[14e-23.] **Logements, 20, rue Sévero,** between rue des Plantes and rue Hippolyte-Maindron. **Henri Sauvage**. 1905.

A simply stated HBM, now renovated and "promoted" to HLM status. Steel lintels, prow windows, and corniced with some picturesque eaves. This is before Sauvage really got going with form—producing the stepped terraces that gave a "Magic Mountain" aspect to his later work.

[14e-24.] **Logements, 16 bis, rue des Plantes,** between rue Sévero and rue de la Sablière. circa 1930.

The ironwork of and around the small curved balconies is simple but stylish, and at the sky two-story vestigial Classical columns provide a stance for a muezzin (IMA **[5n-1.]** take note) or just a bit of sixth-floor ego.

**[14e-25.] Ateliers d'artistes,** 26, rue des Plantes, between rue Bénard and rue Léonidas. **S. Dessauer.** 1930.

The salient ribs seem structural—are they pseudo or real? Here is Art Deco in white stone between beige stucco, an austere place except for those Cadillac fins.

**[14e-26.] Villa Garnier,** 19, rue des Plantes, between rue Bénard and rue Léonidas. **DLM.** 1985.

A simple form clad with stone slabs projects a subtle bay window over the entrance to its garden courtyard. But the south corner lets loose with an extravagant circular bay crowned with a pergola-gazebo. The Italians were here.

★**[14e-27.] Eglise Saint-Pierre-de-Montrouge,** place Victor-Basch, between avenue du Maine and avenue du Général-Leclerc. **Joseph Vaudremer.** 1870.

A somewhat cold and very inflated neo-Romanesque. Compared to the virtuosity of Victor Baltard at Saint-Augustin, built at the same time, this is barely an also-ran.
The columns of the nave are of granite (de Vire), appropriate to the everlasting technical hardiness (or is it hardness?) of the 19th century. Over the altar floats a ciborium, a more ancient version of the baldachino still found in the early Christian churches of Rome (San Clemente).

★★**[14e-28.] Quartier de la rue Neuve-d'Orléans** (now rue du Couédic), generally between avenue du Général-Leclerc, rue d'Alésia, rue de la Tombe-Issoire, avenue René-Coty, and rue Hallé and rue Sophie-Germain. 1830s.

Mostly from the time of Louis-Philippe, these are modest houses. Of particular interest is the one at 23, rue Rémy-Dumoncel, at the corner of rue Hallé, which gives the scale of an earlier Paris; **44, rue du Couédic,** at the corner of rue Hallé, presents an exedra to the intersection. The surrounding streets give a vignette of Parisian history, an excerpt from time—even though this did not become part of Paris proper until 1860. Small buildings are endemic to this precinct, the roof of the catacombs.

★★**[14e-29.] Villa Adrienne,** 19, avenue du Général-Leclerc, between rue Sophie-Germain and place Denfert-Rochereau. 1895.

An "English" square with buildings à la Viollet-le-Duc on three sides, a neo-Georgian on the fourth—all off the good general's garish avenue, along which he entered in 1944.

★**[14e-30.] Hospice de La Rochefoucald,** 15, avenue du Général-Leclerc, near place Denfert-Rochereau. **Jacques-Denis Antoine.** 1781. Extended, **Nicolas-Marie Clavereau.** 1802.

Antoine's better-known work is the **Hôtel de la Monnaie [7n-2.]** on the quai de Conti. This surprising pre-Revolutionary survivor, standing amid great lawns and gardens, was built as a private hospital for impoverished churchmen, magistrates, and military officers. Its ultimate construction was due to the supplementary francs of the duchesse de La Rochefoucauld–Doudeauville.

# 35
# FOURTEENTH ARRONDISSEMENT
## WEST

### GARE MONTPARNASSE TO PORTE DE VANVES

Tour Montparnasse: **Eugène Baudouin et al.**; place de Catalogne; Les
Colonnes et l'Amphithéâtre: **Ricardo Bofill;** Eglise
Notre-Dame-du-Travail: **Jules Astruc**; rue de l'Ouest: **Antoine
Grumbach et al**; HBM, 156, rue Raymond-Losserand: **Maurice
Peyret-Dortail**; Villa Léone; 9-19, rue Louis-Morard: **Henri Robert**;
avenue du Général-Maistre

Métro: **Montparnasse-Bienvenue**

**[14w-7.] Les Colonnes/logements sociaux. Ricardo Bofill.**
1985–1988.

**[14w-1.] Tour Montparnasse,** place Raoul-Dautry, between boulevard de Vaugirard and rue du Départ. **Eugène Beaudouin, Urbain Cassan, Louis Hoym de Marien,** and **Jean Saubot.** Consulting architect, **A. Epstein.** 1973.

The first true *gratte-ciel* within the traditional walls of Paris, this remains an insolent intrusion (fifty-seven stories, 210 meters [682.5 feet]) into the cityscape—33, rue de Croulebarbe **[13nw-8.],** built in 1960, has a mere twenty-one floors. Here, within a city of elegant scale both in street and building, looms a commercial enterprise worthy of Dallas, not Montparnasse. To partially excuse those concerned, there was a consulting architect from Chicago—a two-edged sword, for Chicago is a center of both banal and magnificent skyscrapers. But there is no remembrance of Louis Sullivan or Mies van der Rohe here. André Malraux, was it really you who issued the permit?

**★[14w-1a.] Porte Océane de la Gare Montparnasse/TGV-Atlantique,** place Raoul-Dautry, between boulevard de Vaugirard and rue du Départ. **Jean Duthilleul.** 1990.

A triumphal and glassy entrance portal to the vastly restructured (in the interior) Gare Montparnasse, the latter capped above by a slab and park. **TGV** trains newly directed to the Atlantic coast are within. One day they will take you to Bordeaux in two hours and a half.

**[14w-2.] Ensemble Montparnasse,** bounded by place Raoul-Dautry, boulevard de Vaugirard, rue du Commandant-René-Mouchotte, and Pont des Cinq-Martyrs. **Eugène Baudouin, Raymond Lopez, Louis Hoym de Marien, Louis Arrètche,** and **Jean Dubuisson.** 1964.

These are Chinese walls that, seen from across Paris, sever the skyline. Such vast slabs have permeated the banlieues of several countries (in St. Louis they blew them up) and have no redeeming qualities except for their developers' profits. To fill the huge void between them (over the Gare Montparnasse), a concrete deck and its surmounted park are now in place: **Jardin des Hespérides.**

**★[14w-3.] Théâtre Montparnasse,** 31, rue de la Gaîté, at rue Larochelle. **Charles Peigniet** and **Louis Marnez.** 1886.

The third theater on this site, this was where the plays of André Gide and Oscar Wilde bloomed. Now surrounded by pornography, it boasts two dis-armed caryatids modestly supporting its cornice. A lone place of quality.

**[14w-4.] Hôtel Montparnasse-Parc,** 19, rue du Commandant-René-Mouchotte, between avenue du Maine and place de Catalogne. **Pierre Dufau.** 1974.

Built for the Sheraton hotel chain, this brings the dregs of the 1960s' lesser efforts to Paris. A sky*reacher,* if not a sky*scraper,* it is good only insofar as it intruded here, next to the Tour Montparnasse, rather than elsewhere.

**★[14w-5.] Operation Pasteur-Montparnasse,** embracing Pont des Cinq-Martyrs between the slabs of the Ensemble Montparnasse. **Jean Willerval.** 1990.

An exedral pair make a simulated *rond-point* on the Pont des Cinq-Martyrs for a bulky set of offices. A park behind has been created on the slab covering the new **TGV/Porte Océane** station. Ponderous.

**★★[14w-6.] Place de Catalogne,** collecting rue Jean-Zay, rue du Commandant René Mouchotte, Pont des Cinq-Martyrs, rue Alain, rue Vercingétorix, and rue du Château. **Shamaï Haber.** 1988.

A serene sloping circular plane of granite slides water quietly to one side. Here is a water-place that silently and handsomely reinforces the crescent space. And at night the lighting is eerily magnificent.

★★[14w-7.] **Les Colonnes et l'Amphithéâtre,** place de Catalogne, between rue Vercingétorix and the railroad. **Ricardo Bofill.** 1985–1988.

Palaces for the people in the architect's words, here employed in a facile and virtuoso manner. The ultimate drollity is in the mirror-glass columns that house apartment bay windows.

Bofill is an urbanist happily in sync with the needs of urbane Paris, providing a sense of place rather than monster freestanding blocks. But his architecture misses the mark: poorly detailed and lacking the vigor of an **Henri Gaudin** or **Charles Moore.**

★★★[14w-8.] **Eglise Notre-Dame-du-Travail,** 59, rue Vercingétorix, entrance at 36, rue Guilleminot, behind Les Colonnes. **Jules Astruc.** 1892–1902.

Steel—lithe and filigreed, trussed and bolted—created a basilica for the workers. Iron, in the evolution of great Parisian churches, markets, and railroad stations, long antedates this crisp place. But the steel here unleashed provides a supple and crisp elegance that the iron (cast and wrought) couldn't match.

[14w-9.] **Ecole primaire, 18, rue Jean-Zay,** corner rue Vercingétorix. **Jean-Claude Bernard.** 1984.

A concrete frame interplaying with trussed steel, providing a gateway to the vast ZAC beyond.

★★[14w-10.] **Immeuble, 20, rue de l'Ouest,** at place Constantin-Brancusi. **Antoine Grumbach.** 1985.

This mannered play of forms is modest compared to the histrionics afoot at the plaza's east end: **16, rue de l'Ouest.** But the building is in scale with Paris, presents itself to a minor plaza, and hence becomes a good citizen.

★[14w-11.] **Crèche municipale, 14, rue Jules-Guesde,** between rue Jean-Zay and rue de l'Ouest. circa 1900.

Polychromatic architecture for this place of surrogate motherhood brings an elegance that the surrounding PoMos envy.

★[14w-12.] **Immeuble, 9–11, rue Lebouis,** between rue de l'Ouest and rue Raymond-Losserand. 1988.

Glass block, stucco, and tile—strong yet modest until it acquires a warship's bridge at its summit. But bravo!

★[14w-13.] **Immeuble, 7, rue Lebouis,** between rue de l'Ouest and rue Raymond-Losserand. **Emile Molinié.** 1913.

Stucco and tile grace this venerable studio building in the style of **Bonnier** and **Guimard.**

★★[14w-14.] **Immeuble, 83, rue Pernety,** between rue Vercingétorix and rue de l'Ouest. **P. Malluin** and **J. P. Maduit.** 1986.

Embracing its own cul-de-sac, this presents some vigorous architectural ideas at its crest but is a bit confused and heavy-handed at the bottom. Its streetscape is urbane and enhanced by the incised "square."

**[14w-15.] Immeuble, 91 bis–101, rue Vercingétorix,** spanning rue Fernand-Holweck. **N. Soulier.** 1985.

Stratified in materials between the *rez-de-chaussée*, first, and second floors, it shows tile at the third and stucco at the fourth, fifth, sixth, and seventh. A play of forms above, with assorted solids, voids, and cutouts, is fun; but there is a banality, if not brutality, at the street level.

But a building harboring a street always has a special charm and exoticism.

**[14w-16.] Immeuble, 139, rue de l'Ouest,** at rue du Moulin-de-la-Vierge and rue Decrès.

Aggressively vulgar, this makes everything else of ordinary Parisian modern look good. This is an architectural prostitute as drawn by a modern Daumier—even Los Angeles would have trouble matching it.

★★**[14w-17.] HBM, 156, rue Raymond-Losserand,** opposite rue Pierre-Larousse. **Maurice Payret-Dortail.** 1929.

Corbeled brick and rounded corners. Pass behind the balconied facade into a series of courtyards where the main blocks are carefully oriented to the southern sun.

★**[14w-18.] Foyer pour les personnes âgées, 88, rue de Gergovie,** between rue d'Alésia and rue Raymond-Losserand. **Eva Paszkowski.** 1977.

A serrated facade of single rooms in fine gray tile. A garden graces the interior of this triangular site.

★★**[14w-19.] Villa Léone,** 16 bis, rue Bardinet, between rue d'Alésia and rue de l'Abbé-Carton.

An urban oasis for the urbane middle class. Outside on rue Bardinet are Haussmannian remnants and some bad modern blocks; here is a bit of semirural heaven.

**[14w-20.] Immeuble, 21, rue de l'Abbé-Carton,** between rue Bardinet and rue des Suisses. 1980s.

A fantasy of trellises decorates a tile facade. Rather childish—look at its better modern neighbor at **No. 27.**

★**[14w-21.] Immeuble, 27, rue de l'Abbé-Carton,** between rue Bardinet and rue des Suisses. 1930s.

Moderne but seedy, it has magnificent guts. The semicircular iron balconies are particularly worthy.

a short way to one side:

**[14w-22.] Entrance Portal/Hôpital Broussais–La Charité, 95,** rue Didot, opposite Villa Collet. 1930s.

An excursion for the specialist, this portal is a glorious blend of stripped Doric architecture with a concrete-and-glass dome that hovers over the entrance portal. Verlaine stayed here and wrote a dozen poems.

★**[14w-23.] Immeubles, 9–19, rue Louis-Morard,** between rue Didot and rue des Plantes. **Henri Robert.** 1905.

An eccentric and personal collection by a maverick architect. Strange and wonderful bay windows decorate the first floor of these polychromatic brick-and-tile facades.

★[14w-24.] Bussières Arts Graphiques/originally Usine de Photogravure Ruckert, 56 bis, rue des Plantes. Louis Périn. 1901.

Polychromatic brick in a lusty industrial style. The glazed tile flowers and artichokes are a personal elegance of note. The whole thing is a tender set.

★[14w-25.] HBM, 36, rue Antoine-Chantin, corner rue des Plantes. Emmanuel Pontremoli, Joseph Bassompierre, Paul Sirvin, and Paul de Rutté. 1929.

Sponsored by the Weill Foundation, this was built for the petit bourgeois employees of commerce, rather than for the "poor" envisaged by earlier philanthropists such as the Rothschilds. Here is brick corbeled, stepped and patterned, in a tour de force that presents wondrous detail to conquer boredom.

★[14w-26.] Immeuble, 19, rue Antoine-Chantin, between rue des Plantes and avenue Jean-Moulin. Bernard Bourgade and Michel Londinsky. 1982.

Lodgings and an *école maternelle.* Where No. 7 (below) is a strong personality, No. 19 is a noisy but well-bred child, grasping for attention on this child-filled street (there is a school opposite).

★★[14w-27.] Ateliers, 7, rue Antoine-Chantin, between rue des Plantes and avenue Jean-Moulin. Eugène Gonnot. 1927.

Studios in vestigial Art Nouveau crossed with Art Deco; sinuous forms with geometric decor. The glass-roofed negative bays at the street (original glazing to the right) are elegant. Here is a strong personality. Bravo!

[14w-28.] Immeuble, 35–37, avenue Jean-Moulin, corner square de Châtillon. Jean Boucher and André Gendrel. 1930.

Syncopation of bowed spandrels in a triad with a corner bow and *garde-fous.* Here is 1930s Art Moderne styling at a subtle level.

[14w-29.] Maisons, 8–22, square de Châtillon, off avenue Jean-Moulin.

A small cul-de-sac surrounded by 1930s town houses. Bayed and stuccoed, they are party to a quiet place.

[14w-30.] Centre de Tri-Postal, 125, boulevard Brune, just west of avenue Jean-Moulin. Georges Tourry. 1961.

A rather shoddy tour de force: the encylindered bays are all that's left of an idea. It emerged from the age of histrionics, when one held up one's shoes with one's suspenders.

★[14w-31.] HBM, 1, rue Gustave-Le-Bon, corner boulevard Brune. Agence d'Architecture HBM. 1935.

Another winner among the very good standards of the HBM, and this one is better than most. Detailing, not bulk, makes the difference in balconies, bay windows, and other facial features. Everyone has admired a beautiful nose, a wondrous smile, a handsome ear. Here are their inanimate counterparts.

**★★[14w-32.]** HBM, avenue du Général-Maistre, between rue du Général-de-Maud'huy and rue Henry-de-Bournazel. **Agence d'Architecture HBM.** 1935.

Wonderfully articulated brickwork, occasionally punctuated by Art Moderne entranceways with fading neo-Classical allusions, mostly *within* this vast complex. It is banal at the external streets.

**★★★[14w-33.]** HBM, 64, boulevard Brune, corner avenue Georges-Lafenestre. **Agence d'Architecture HBM.** 1934.

Superb: polygonal, bayed, and balconied around the garden court. This is one of the very best *îlots* of 1930s social housing.

**★[14w-34.]** HBM, 16, boulevard Brune, at the Porte de Vanves. 1930s.

They didn't quit—quality is *everywhere* on this string of old fortification sites served by the boulevards des Maréchaux.

**★[14w-35.]** Immeubles, 6 and 8, rue Paturle, between rue Vercingétorix and rue Raymond-Losserand. No. 6, 1980s. No. 8, 1890s.

A valiant attempt at integrated urbanism, and No. 6 almost makes the grade. The columns are more apparently structural and less self-conscious than those around the corner at **No. 235**. The steel *"colombage"* at No. 8 is fascinating. Don't turn around, or you'll wish you hadn't.

**[14w-36.]** Immeuble, 235, rue Vercingétorix, at rue Paturle. **D. Drummond.** 1986.

The *fronton* above and the columns below are an unnecessary PoMo affectation on this 1930s revival overlooking the new **TGV-Atlantique.**

# 36
# FOURTEENTH ARRONDISSEMENT
## SOUTH

### CITE UNIVERSITAIRE, PARC DE MONTSOURIS,

### AND THEIR SURROUNDS

**Le Corbusier, Lucio Costa, Willem Dudok, Louis-Hippolyte Boileau, Marc Solotareff, André Lurçat, Raymond Fischer, Auguste Perret, Jacques Bonnier, Jean Delechette, Paul Huillard, Louis Süe, Lenin**

Metro: **Cité Universitaire (RER)**

[14s-21.] **Edicule Pavilion, Réservoir de Montsouris.** circa 1900.

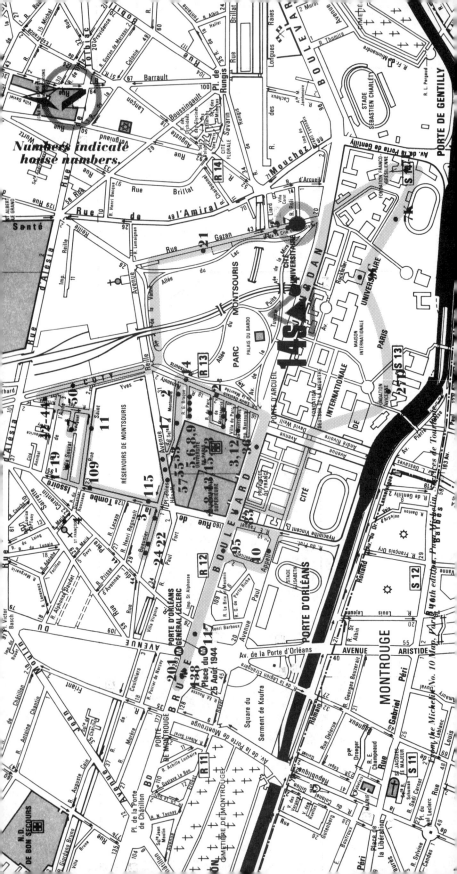

Numbers indicate
house numbers.

★[14s-1.] Cité Universitaire Station/RER, 24, boulevard Jourdan, at the edge of the Parc de Montsouris, opposite Cité Universitaire. **Louis-Loÿs Brachet.** 1932.

Nestled into the edge of the Parc de Montsouris, an eclectic *moderne* building, its cornice borrowed from Egypt (the *cavetto* cornice), serves as the house of em- and debarkation for the six thousand students commuting to their Quartier Latin studies.

Cross boulevard Jourdan, and walk east on its south flank to an entrance of the Cité that veers to the southeast. You are heading toward the **Maison Franco-Brésilienne** as your first stop on the campus. There is a posted *plan* for your guidance.

---

**The Cité Universitaire Internationale de Paris** is a vast residential community for students at the University of Paris. Here, on forty hectares of campus are set both buildings as common ground for all resident students, philanthropically financed, and thirty-six national pavilions. The latter shelter an average each of 60 percent of their own citizens, with a mixture of other cultures filling the balance—six thousand residents. The grounds were set aside from a sector of the old Thiers fortifications, built in 1845 and demolished around 1930, although the **Fondation Emile-Deutsch de la Meurthe** was built in 1921 in anticipation of further clearance. John D. Rockefeller contributed the **Maison Internationale** (library, restaurants, salons, theatres) in 1935, but the individual national pavilions blossomed from 1927 to 1960.

Here you will find a spectrum of architecture, ranging from the English Collegiate Gothic of the **Deutsch Foundation** through DeStijl of the Dutch Pavilion, to both early and late works of Le Corbusier. Aside from these staccato moments of surprise amid a lot of green, wander around the campus to savor its casual parklike ambience.

---

★★[14s-2.] Maison Franco-Brésilienne, 7L, boulevard Jourdan, at the edge of avenue de la Porte-de-Gentilly (pedestrian gate from the avenue). **Le Corbusier** and **Lucio Costa.** 1959.

Here is another page from Corbu's Cité Radieuse, first inscribed at Marseilles in 1952. The exposed and painted reinforced concrete came to be known in English as brutalism (a complimentary, not pejorative, word), a vast change, and to be expected, from the sleek smoothness of his 1932 Swiss Pavilion. Corbu was later enamored of sunshades *(brise-soleils)*, even where there was no sun. Certainly the progenitor of them in his vocabulary was the Ministry of Education in Rio di Janeiro (with **Costa and Oscar Niemayer** as associates), where the north (or sun) facade was composed of *brise-soleils* and the south of pure glass (the latter in the manner of the Pavillon Suisse).

This is a marvelous sculptural object, enriched by the painted balcony reveals (said to be the colors of the Brazilian flag). But one can quarrel with his rationality, for Corbu, who seemed to be the patron saint of light and air in such schemes for rebuilding Paris as the Cité Radieuse and Ville Verte, here orients the sunshades east—and, to boot, faces them on a noisy boulevard. Perhaps he realized that Brazilians were a noisy people.

★★★★[14s-3.] Pavillon Suisse, 7K, boulevard Jourdan. **Le Corbusier.** 1932.

One of the greatest moments of the Modern movement, this petite ensemble moved mountains and trembled the grounds of academia. Built at a time when Parisian boulevard architecture was struggling mostly with ways to cut stone in an Art Deco, Moderne, or simplified neo-Classical manner, this dormitory relieved itself of the street and displayed a sheet of glazed rooms to the southern sun (see Brazil above for later news)—not to mention a roof garden with terrace that allowed the cool Swiss youth to sun themselves among the treetops. The most telling innovation, uniquely presented here, was the support system: pilotis, or pilings, brought right out of the ground as visual piers, freeing the ground space to float under. Here the building in the park was fulfilled: streetless, sun-filled, suspended over greensward, enterraced. This is the first built realization of Corbu's composite high-density ideas for high-density habitation—scarcely urban but perhaps urbane. Corbu is now more fondly remembered for this as architecture rather than as a block in a city-building system.

★★[14s-4.] Pavillon du Mexique, 9C, boulevard Jourdan, along the walkway passing by the Pavillon Suisse, and then further west. Medellin and Urbain Cassan. 1953.

Post–World War II Modern architecture flourished vigorously in Latin America before the United States or Europe; and by the time of this pavilion, Mexico's own national university was a showplace of its national architecture.

[14s-5.] Fondation Avicenne/formerly Pavillon d'Iran, 27D, boulevard Jourdan. Claude Parent, Mossem Foroughi, and Hedar Ghiai. 1968.

A pavilion for the *périphérique*, the skyscraper of the Cité, unfortunately debased with an advertising billboard on top (how can the cité permit such trash?). It is a structural tour de force, with some virtuoso spiral stairs to provide "architectural" enrichment. This is a sorry bit of ego that provides illustrations for architectural magazines but is an intruder in the green-swarded environment.

★★★[14s-6.] Pavillon Néderlandais, 83, boulevard Jourdan, corner rue Emile-Faguet. Willem Dudok. 1927.

Dudok's interlocking cubistic architecture is less notorious than that of Le Corbusier, Mies, Gropius, and others of the 1920s and 1930s, but it is powerful stuff (his school and town hall in Hilversum, Holland, are of the same vocabulary but in Dutch brick). Here white pristine stucco so dear to the 1920s is arranged with a tower, cantilevered balconies, strip windows, and a rounded stair form, to compose a less pure but more dynamic set of forms than those of Le Corbusier. Much underrated in the textbooks, it needs some exterior housekeeping.

★[14s-7.] Immeubles, 10, avenue Paul-Appell and 55, boulevard Jourdan, between rue de la Tombe-Issoire and 95, boulevard Jourdan. Louis-Hippolyte Boileau and Marc Solotareff. 1934.

Pink-brown stucco on avenue Paul-Appel and muted sand tones on boulevard Jourdan—classy, streamlined, and crisp. The entrance on avenue Paul-Appel is a striking statement (Boileau), and the views from rue Emile-Faguet give striking contrasts between the two segments. Boileau's half wins, but it is a wonderful interchange.

★★[14s-8.] HBM, 95, boulevard Jourdan, between rue de la Tombe-Issoire and avenue du Général-Leclerc.

Stepped and corbeled brick in the central block . . . supporting rhythmic bays in red-brown, interrupting the yellow brick (brown-spandreled) facade. And this is for the modest poor.

[14s-9.] HBMs, 138, boulevard Brune and 117, boulevard Jourdan, at the Porte d'Orléans. Albert Pouthier. 1926.

The concrete caged stairs are strong and lovely additions to the court-yards—a triumphal entry to Paris anticipating that of General Leclerc's reentry on August 25, 1944.

**[14s-10.] Immeuble, 201, boulevard Brune,** just west of avenue du Général-Leclerc. **Louis Périn.** 1903.

Gargantuan foliage wraps around the bay windows, with a blue and dirty cream frieze above. It is an amateur Art Nouveau attempt in the time of the more elegant **Charles Plumet.**

★**[14s-11.] Maison, 36, boulevard Jourdan,** at the end of impasse Nansouty. **F. Medvès,** decorator. 1920s.

An unheralded bit of the avant-garde best viewed from the boulevard, even though its primary access is the impasse. A curved bay-window form, stucco, and glass block suggest that Dudok—or a friend—was here.

**[14s-12.] Maison, 12, villa du Parc-de-Montsouris,** off rue Emile-Deutsch-de-la-Meurthe, between boulevard Jourdan and avenue Reille. 1920s.

In contrast to the austere modern villa-ateliers of artists that abound in these small streets, here is the Tyrol in Paris, its half-timbering giving an exotic rural quality on this cul-de-sac. The modern neighbors are crass, but this is an oasis of quiet and planting.

**[14s-13.] Ateliers, 3, villa du Parc-de-Montsouris,** off rue Emile-Deutsch-de-la-Meurthe, between boulevard Jourdan and avenue Reille. circa 1915.

Stucco and tile; its ateliers of industrial glazing bring a conservative air of artistry to the cul-de-sac.

**[14s-14.] Rue du Parc-de-Montsouris,** off rue Nansouty, between boule-vard Jourdan and avenue Reille.

> **No. 4** An Art Deco hotel in two-toned stucco, with tiny balconies that give the "French" windows a special purpose. 1920s.
> **No. 8** A polychromatic Italianate villa, enriched with a polygonal corner tower and a verdant garden. circa 1890.
> **No. 13** Stone and timber villa with a red tile roof—the "bourgeois" rustic style.
> **No. 15** Post Modern white tile sheathes this oversized banality. One should protect not only buildings in this district as significant architecture but also the scale of the ministreets. **Patrick Rufener.** 1974.
> **No. 23** Another *meulière* romantic villa.

↟**[14s-15.] Immeuble, 2, rue Emile-Deutsch-de-la-Meurthe,** corner rue du Parc-de-Montsouris. 1880s.

A polygonal bay window (or winter garden) overlooks the Parc Montsou-ris greensward. A spectacular but noissome vantage place.

★★★**[14s-16.] Villa Guggenbuhl,** 14, rue Nansouty, corner rue Georges-Braque. **André Lurçat.** 1927.

This is what the best of the International Style is all about: sun, view, all crisply within a cubist form. The soaring cantilever must have inspired **Edward Durell Stone** and **Philip Goodwin** at the Museum of Modern Art in New York, opened twelve years later. Lurçat is right up there with

**Mallet-Stevens** and **Le Corbusier**—but had a less-skilled publicity campaign.

---

**Lurçat** wrote in 1965, reflecting on the flood of "modern" buildings in the postwar years (such as those at **La Défense**): "Between 1925 and 1939 commissions were rare and the architects promoting the functionalist movement had time to reflect, to study, to analyze, and to slowly build a doctrine . . . 1945 suddenly brought a reality of a totally different character.

". . . The time for reflection had passed. It was now necessary to produce (architecture) under particularly difficult conditions . . . the poorly controlled principles of functionalism.

"Meanwhile, applied for the most part mechanically, they were the source of multiple errors . . . poorly assimilated, they led to simplistic solutions.

"It was apparently a complete victory of the ideas of functionalism, but in reality, what was retained the most often were certain rudimentary aspects where creative imagination was replaced by systematic and uncontrolled application . . ."

---

★★as a totality **[14s-17.] rue Georges-Braque,** off rue Nansouty between boulevard Jourdan and avenue Reille.

**No. 5** Timid stucco internationalism: modern style without modern form. **Raymond Fischer.** 1929.

**No. 6** Georges Braque's studio snuggled into the top floor of this stodgy neo-Classicism in concrete. The vines and foliage seem to be conquering it. **Auguste Perret.** 1927.

**No. 8** Brick with load-bearing ivy. Zilch. **Zielinsky.** 1932.

**No. 9 Villa Kroyer Kielberg.** Same comment as at **No. 5,** except this one is bigger. **Raymond Fischer.** 1929.

★★★**[14s-18.] Square de Montsouris,** between rue Nansouty and avenue Reille. **Jacques Bonnier.** 1922–1923.

A romantic housing development that leads from the promiscuous modernism of the rue Georges-Braque to the classic modernism of the Maison Ozenfant. At **No. 2** is an incursion of modernism, the Maison Gaut (**Auguste Perret.** 1923.); at No. 17, another (**Zielinsky.** circa 1930.) But all in all, it is another romantic suburban ensemble, intent more on timbers, bracketing, bay windows, and tile than on purity of purpose.

★★★★**[14s-19.] Maison** and **atelier Ozenfant,** 53, avenue Reille, corner of the square de Montsouris. **Le Corbusier** and **Pierre Jeanneret.** 1923.

Amédée Ozenfant was Le Corbusier's first, and one of his foremost, French clients, but his house is now sullied by its truncation. The flat terrace atop replaced a saw-toothed set of skylights that illuminated Ozenfant's studio. Ozenfant painted jointly with Corbu, and together they founded the review *L'esprit nouveau* in 1920.

Here are elegant steel industrial sash and crisp forms. In comparison with Lurçat's Guggenbuhl villa four years later, this seems like a bland exercise, but what if Guggenbuhl had lost its soaring perforated roof?

Modernists (and, even more so, some Post Modernists) are sometimes concerned more with the idea of a construction than with its reality or even aesthetic *quality.* They can become infatuated with ideas for the "betterment" of the environment—even though you'd rather live in a tacky villa down the block on the square de Montsouris. Nevertheless here are ideas that once resonated as a concerto and have lost a whole movement.

★**[14s-20.] Maisons, 55** and **57, avenue Reille,** between square de Montsouris and rue de la Tombe-Issoire. **Jean Delechette.** 1925.

These neighbors to **Ozenfant** acquire stature by proximity; simple and spartan, they lack any of O's vigor. We would hope that they were commissioned by those merely riding the bandwagon of modernity rather than governed by the taste of superior patrons. But, no: No. 55 was constructed for **Georges Braque,** who later moved to rue Auguste-Perret. Like many painters, he was less a connoisseur of avant-garde architectural environment than of painting.

★★**[14s-21.] Réservoir de Montsouris,** 115, rue de la Tombe-Issoire, bounded by avenue Reille and the L-shaped rue Saint-Yves. **Eugène Belgrand,** supervising engineer. 1858–1874. Edicule pavilions. circa 1900.

The reservoir proper contains two vast superposed tanks, the lower with a capacity of 125,000 cubic meters (4.4 million cubic feet) the upper with 77,000 (2.7 million cubic feet), drawing water from the Vanne (1874), Loing (1900), Lunain (1900), and Voulzie (1925) rivers. To oversee the operation there are viewing points, called *bâches,* to check the water at its influx. Here, to protect the water from pollution, edicule pavilions have been built that are the conning towers of this complex, architectural symbols that punctuate the great bermed-shape's simplicity.

These are some of Paris's more extravagant cast-iron structures. Tiered bases of rubblestone *(meulière)* edged with cut limestone *(calcaire)* are surmounted with pavilions of cast iron and translucent glass, with intricate glazed tile spandrels.

The reservoir was built here, at what was then considered the *edge* of probable development. As history has demonstrated everywhere, development passed by (land was cheap beyond), creating inexpensive opportunity for the villa-ateliers cited above.

★**[14s-22.] Immeuble, 3, rue Beaunier,** between rue de la Tombe-Issoire and rue du Père-Corentin. **Paul Huillard** and **Louis Süe.** 1907. Surelevated, 1910–1912.

Elegantly bracketed bay windows in articulated concrete, on a lesser brother to 40, rue Boileau.

**[14s-23.] Immeubles. 22, rue Beaunier,** between rue de la Tombe-Issoire and rue du Père-Corentin. 1890s.

Post Modern bay windows in a stylish but heavy-handed envelope. Neighboring No. 24 gives the architectural flavor of the old neighborhood, which was a more vigorous bourgeois place. Lenin lived here from December 1908 to July 1909. Finding the rent too high, he decamped.

★**[14s-24.] BMW Garage,** 109, rue de la Tombe-Issoire, corner rue Saint-Yves. 1930s.

A crisp, white place, but it's doubtful that BMW's always went there for their health. The corner tower, glass-blocked, is vigorous and lovely.

**[14s-25.] Immeuble, 4, rue Marie-Rose,** between rue du Père-Corentin and rue Sarrette.

When he left rue Beaunier (above), Lenin stayed here until June 1912. It must have been a lively street of revolutionary comings and goings.

★★★**[14s-26.] Villa Seurat,** off rue de la Tombe-Issoire, between rue Saint-Yves and rue de l'Aude. 1920s.

Largely the work of **André Lurçat,** this cul-de-sac has housed, in addition to those who commissioned the ateliers, writers such as **Anaïs Nin** and **Henry Miller,** as well as the painters **Chaïm Soutine** and **Salvador Dali.**

| No. 1 | **Maison Townshend.** | **André Lurçat** | 1926 |
|---|---|---|---|
| | Something of a ruin. | | |
| No. 3 | **Atelier Goerg** and **Gromaire** | **André Lurçat** | 1925 |
| | The bow front modulates | | |
| No. 3b | **Atelier R. Couturier** | **Jean-Charles Moreux** | 1938 |
| No. 4 | **Atelier Jean Lurçat** | **André Lurçat** | 1924 |
| | Ivy has conquered. | | |
| No. 5 | **Atelier Paul Bertrand** | **André Lurçat** | 1925 |
| | Bland. | | |
| No. 7 | **Maison Chana Orloff** | **Z. Rechter** | 1931 |
| | Out of context. | | |
| No. 7b | **Atelier Chana Orloff** | **Auguste Perret** | 1926 |
| No. 8 | **Maison Quiller** | **André Lurçat** | 1926 |
| No. 9 | **Maison Bertrand** | **André Lurçat** | 1925 |
| No. 11 | **Atelier Huggler** | **André Lurçat** | 1926 |
| No. 18 | Bowed balconies. | | |
| No. 19 | The local romantic. | | |

"If this ensemble of villas lacks the luxurious elegance of the rue Mallet-Stevens, it nevertheless possesses a certain charm that, despite the modesty of the means employed, expresses a new manner of creating space. The villa Seurat was a true artists' enclave in its time, for it accommodated Soutine, Gromaire, Goerg, and Henry Miller, who occupied No. 18 and wrote his *Tropics* there." **Jean-Claude Delorme** in *Les villas d'artistes à Paris.*

★[14s-27.] **Cité du Souvenir,** 11, rue Saint-Yves, between rue de la Tombe-Issoire and rue des Artistes. **Léon Besnard** and **Boulanger.** 1926–1930.

A strongly modeled, multiuse ensemble surrounding a central court and overlooking the "lawn" surmounting the Réservoir de Montsouris. Outside, ateliers complementing the tenancy line the street at ground level. Inside, the founder, **Abbé Keller,** has provided the Chapel of Memories.

With a bit of paint this could be fascinating. The drying laundry on the terraces is part of the whole architectural ensemble, as with the multicolored curtains on Mies van der Rohe's Esplanade apartments 860 Lake Shore Drive (annex) in Chicago.

★[14s-28.] **3, 5, 7, rue Gauguet,** off rue des Artistes, between rue Saint-Yves and rue de l'Aude. **Zielinsky.** 1929–1931.

White ice cream for greater artists' studios, with black "pencil-lined" sash. Unfortunately, at No. 3, renovators have fattened the metalwork, muting the original elegance.

We come upon the next entry from above, at the level of its penthouse and conning tower entry. Although we are at the end of the rue de l'Aude, the address is on the street below:

★★[14s-29.] **Maison/Atelier, 50, avenue René-Coty,** between avenue Reille and rue d'Alésia (also 1, rue de l'Aude). **Jean-Julien Lemordant** and **Jean Launay.** 1929.

This bizarre bulwark flanks the old quarries of Montsouris, many of which were recycled in the 19th century to form the ghoulish catacombs [14e-2.]. Here cheap land was available, narrow at the avenue René-Coty level and splaying upward as the quarry walls sloped away.

Lemordant, a popular painter before World War I, was wounded therein and lost his sight, but regained it partially after several operations. Modeling his vision in wood, he created this construction with the aid of the Belgian architect, **Jean Launay.** Shipshape.

**Léandre Vaillant** in *L'Illustration* wrote: "Major Tristani . . . had been a prisoner of war with Pierre Fervacque and the painter Lemordant at the camp at Ingolstadt in Bavaria. . . . He spoke to me of Lemordant, whose blindness was progressive in the sense that his sight narrowed little by little toward the center in such a manner that at the end he saw only a luminous point directly in front of him. His suffering was intolerable. The astonishing strength of his spirit was necessary to master the pain. In his youth he had studied architecture. Blind, and wishing to construct a house, he explained where one should place the doors, the windows, the solids, the voids. To translate his intentions, pieces of wood were placed on a plank: in this manner he 'read' the plans as if they were 'braille' . . . he corrected thereby the proportions. . . . In his house he took charge like a clairvoyant, leading the visitor to a painting, explaining the values, the colors. . . ."

**[14s-30.] Ateliers, 42-44, avenue René-Coty,** between avenue Reille and rue d'Alésia. **Emmanuel Ladmiral**. 1914–1920.

A stacking of styles. Duplex *(maisonette)* studios are entered from the street. First there are Classical cornices, then a bit of Arts and Crafts. **No. 46,** next door, is a baldly stated place of ateliers without pretensions.

Walk down (south) on avenue René-Coty to the corner entrance of the park at avenue Reille. Take the path to the left, along the park's northern edge, exiting at the northeast corner, at the rue Gazan.

**★★[14s-31.] Parc de Montsouris,** bounded by avenue Reille, rue Gazan, rue de la Cité-Universitaire, boulevard Jourdan, rue Emile-Deutsch-de-la-Meurthe, and rue Nansouty. **Adolphe Alphand**, supervising engineer. 1867–1878.

In counterpoise to the Parc des Buttes-Chaumont in the northeast, Napoléon III ordered Montsouris to the south. Now used by its later neighbors, the students of the **Cité Universitaire,** the residents of the streets of ateliers along its flanks, it was in splendid isolation at the time of construction, waiting for the city to arrive (not unlike Central Park in New York). The **Pavillon Montsouris,** a pricey restaurant, remains open after the park closes, nestling in a verdant semiprivate evening setting.
"At the summit of the Parc de Montsouris stands the **Bardo [★★★,** BURNED TO THE GROUND, January, 1991], former pavilion of Tunisia at the Universal Exposition of 1867; having occupied the corner of the Champ de Mars formed by the quai and the avenue de Suffren, it was moved to this site the following year. Dilapidated but undergoing restoration, this astonishing specimen of neo-Moorish architecture, needing to rediscover its past splendor, deserves attention.
"Built at the bey's expense by Alfred Chapon (1834–1893), architect of the Compagnie de Suez and of all the exposition's "eastern" structures, the Bardo is a reduced copy of the palace of the same name at Tunis, formerly the summer residence of the beys." **François Macé de Lépinay** in the catalog of the exhibition "De Montparnasse à Montsouris," Musée Carnavalet, 1986.

**[14s-32.] Immeuble d'ateliers, 21, rue Gazan,** between avenue Reille and rue Liard. **J. Pelée de Saint-Maurice.** circa 1930.

Stark studios with a splendid view over the park. No. 21 is an austere early outpost, but the neighboring post–World War II buildings are ghastly.

**★[14s-33.] Immeuble d'ateliers, 3, rue de la Cité-Universitaire,** between rue Liard and rue Roli. **Michel Roux-Spitz.** 1930.

Roux-Spitz's work, sometimes ponderous, shows a lighter hand here. The small balconies provide stance for an airy look over the park but those great glazed studios must suffer terribly from the brilliance of the afternoon sun all year—ovens in summer! We need Corbu's *brise-soleils* from the Brazilian pavilion at the Cité to shield the sun (see discussion at [14s-2.]).

[14s-34.] **Immeuble, 7, rue de la Cité-Universitaire,** between rue Liard and rue Roli. **Albert Pouthier.** 1930.

Art Moderne on the same block with Roux-Spitz. Look up at the sinuous bronze railings along the terraces on high. They can sparkle in the afternoon sun.

# 37
# FIFTEENTH ARRONDISSEMENT
## CENTER

### PLACE HENRI QUEUILLE

### TO PLACE DU COMMERCE

Boulevard Garibaldi; rue Ernest-Renan; Square Blomet: **Joan Miro**; 81-83, rue Mademoiselle: **Klaus Schulze;** 11, place Adolphe-Chérioux: **Marcel and Robert Hennequet;** 166, rue de la Convention: **Emile Bois**; square Saint-Lambert: **Georges Sébille;** 138, rue du Théâtre: **Bruno Elkouken;** Beaugrenelle: **Léonard Violet;** place du Commerce

Métro: **Sèvres-Lecourbe**

**[15c-21.] Immeuble, 11, place Adolphe-Chérioux. Marcel and Robert Hennequet. 1933.**

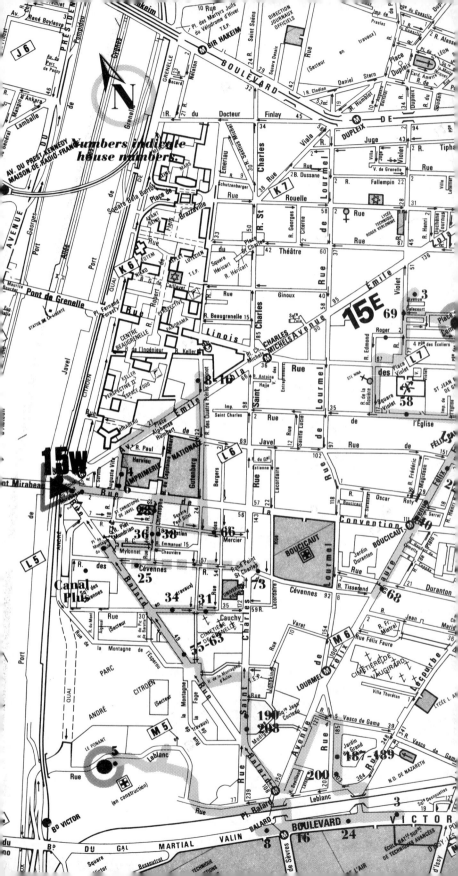

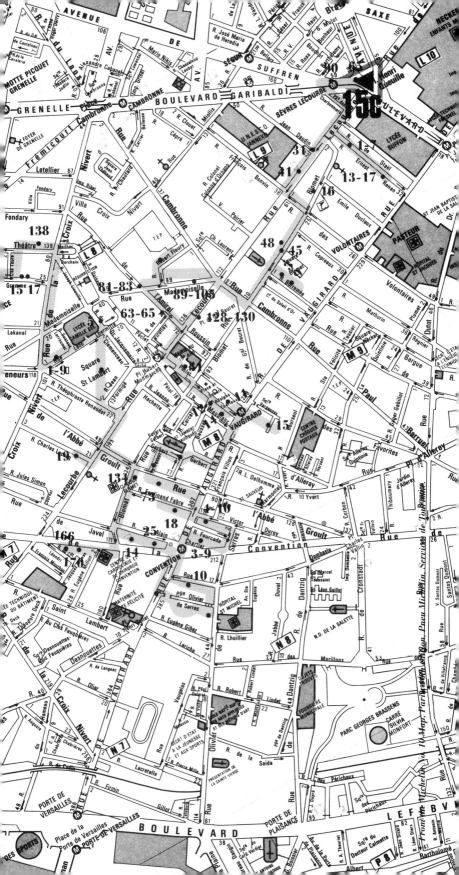

**[15c-1.] 90, boulevard Garibaldi**, between place Henri-Queuille and passage des Charbonniers. **Charles Peigniet** and **Louis Marnez.** 1890.

Iron-and-glass ateliers above some compromising masonry. A schizophrenic building, for those conservatives who never look up—and those radicals who do.

**[15c-2.] Immeuble, 65, boulevard Garibaldi**, between avenue de Breteuil and avenue de Suffren. **Jean Bouchard** and **Pierre Soulard.** 1929.

Angular, as in Art Deco/neo-Classicism.

★**[15c-3.] Immeubles, 1, 3, 5, 7, rue Ernest-Renan,** between rue Lecourbe and rue de Vaugirard. circa 1900.

For aficionados of bay windows, here are twenty-four: six square, eighteen polygonal. with leaded lights they are worthy of London's Arts and Crafts, that late 19th century revival of things Medieval, here expressed with these small panes.

★**[15c-4.] Immeubles, 13, 15, 17, rue Ernest-Renan,** between rue Lecourbe and rue de Vaugirard. circa 1900.

No. 13, with bay windows in multihued stained glass, leaded, has elegant ironwork to contain and enrich it all; one of the best of this genre in town. No. 15 is lesser, a bit *retardataire*, with neo-Classical bays; No. 17 is the most spartan, in this grouping a weak follower.

**[15c-5.] Immeuble, 31, rue Lecourbe**, between rue Blomet and rue des Volontaires. **M. Gouverneur.** 1930.

The balconies are fluted with reminiscences of Classical ribbings, although convex, rather than the concave of Doric and Ionic. The frieze in bas-relief is noteworthy.

★**[15c-6.] Ateliers/immeuble, 41, rue Lecourbe**, between rue Blomet and rue des Volontaires. **Jean Pelée de Saint-Maurice.** 1927–1929.

Monumental steel and glass bay windows are framed with attenuated mullions and muntins.

★**[15c-7.] Immeuble, 16, rue Blomet**, between rue Lecourbe and rue des Volontaires. **Jean Pelée de Saint-Maurice.** 1926–1927.

The earlier construction, to which 41, rue Lecourbe was added. Here are elegant polygonal bay windows.

**[15c-8.] Maison, 48, rue Blomet,** between rue Copreaux and rue Borromée. 18th century.

A bit of old Vaugirard, now mostly obliterated by 19th-century construction.

**[15c-9.] Square Blomet,** 45, rue Blomet, between rue Copreaux and rue Borromée.

Here were once the ateliers of **Joan Miró** and **André Masson.** In memory of those years Miró donated the bronze sculpture centered within the square.

**[15c-10.] Habitation ouvrière, 3, rue Borromée,** between rue Blomet and rue de Vaugirard. **Torlet.** 1897.

Somber but stolid brick over *meulière;* the end bay windows work, but the central pair are bland. Nevertheless, it won a silver medal in the first competition held by the Committee of "Habitation à bon marché." (HBM) de la Seine in 1901.

★[15c-11.] **Etablissement National des Invalides de la Marine,** 9, rue Borromée, between rue Blomet and rue de Vaugirard. 1980s.

The blue metal-and glass-facade waves like a ship's sail against this Post Modern white facade of large tiles.

[15c-12.] **Immeuble, 89-105, rue Mademoiselle** between rue Robert-Fleury, rue Cambronne, and rue Lecourbe. 1980s.

Polygonal jazz tiled in muted grays. At least it's low and streetfronted, and harbors a garden.

[15c-13.] **Rue Robert-Fleury,** between rue Cambronne and rue Mademoiselle. **A. Huset** and **J. Chartieau.** 1890s.

A whole streetscape created by two architects in sync and symbiosis: one story lower than the boulevards, here are *rez-de-chaussées, entresols,* and four *étages.* The crook in the street, caused by the two arms being perpendicular to rue Cambronne and rue Mademoiselle, gives it a sense of place.

★★[15c-14.] **Crèche, 81-83, rue Mademoiselle,** corner rue de l'Amiral-Roussin. **Klaus Schulze.** 1980s.

An aspiring **Gaudí** bricked and tiled these undulating and plastic anthropomorphic forms. Behind is a more sober (in a relative sense) house-scaled tiering of pastel stucco and wood wonders.

★★[15c-15.] **Groupe des Maisons Ouvrières,** 63-65, rue de l'Amiral-Roussin, opposite rue de Viroflay. **Auguste Labussière.** 1907.

A minor triumphal arch creates a neo-Baroque entry to a grand courtyard. Brick, *pierre de taille,* and iron with bay windows, mansards, and gables. Another project by the Fondation Lebaudy.

[15c-16.] **Immeuble, 128–130, rue Lecourbe,** between rue de l'Amiral-Roussin and rue Cambronne. **Léon Chesnay.** 1907.

Transitional Haussmannian-*tardif* with a touch of Art Nouveau à la **Charles Plumet.** There are lovely balconettes at the fifth floor (there is no *entresol).*

[15c-17.] **Mairie, 31, rue Péclet,** between rue Lecourbe and rue Blomet. **Devrez.** 1876.

Another in the indefatigable dectet of post-1860 *mairies* for those new arrondissements of the *couronne d'or* added to the first ten by Napoléon III and his prefect Haussmann in 1860.

★[15c-18.] **Place** and **square Adolphe-Chérioux**, between rue Blomet and rue de Vaugirard. **Jean-Camille Formigé.** 1896.

Paired rows of plane trees (fourteen on each side) flank a central flower garden and playground. A stylistic potpourri surrounding is nevertheless at a sympathetic scale to create a handsome urban ensemble. Formigé was architect for all the elevated sections of the **Métro,** as well as the **Jardin Fleuriste [16s-1.].**

[15c-19.] **Immeuble, 14, place Adolphe-Chérioux,** between rue de Vaugirard and rue Blomet. **Henri Regache.** 1902.

*Pierre de taille* with florid neo-Classical parts intermingle with a modest Art Nouveau sinuosity. Guess who built it? **Adolphe Chérioux,** contractor!

★[15c-20.] **Immeuble, 12, place Adolphe-Chérioux,** between rue de Vaugirard and rue Blomet.

A giant order (Ionic) embraces three floors of generous multipaned French doors. Paired with **No. 14,** it makes a lush contrast in forms.

★★[15c-21.] **Immeuble, 11, place Adolphe-Chérioux,** between rue de Vaugirard and rue Blomet. **Marcel and Robert Hennequet.** 1933.

Crisp off-white International style with triangulated bay windows as twin prows to the street; a modest understatement.

★★[15c-22.] Originally **Maison Barillet**/now **Ecole, 15, square Vergennes,** between rue d'Alleray and rue des Favorites. **Robert Mallet-Stevens.** 1932.

The school provided an awful 1960s curtain wall, but this was once a class act in the International style: crisp, white, rounded, and roof-terraced. The square's continuation displays a charming set of studios and small houses.

[15c-23.] **Eglise Saint-Lambert-de-Vaugirard,** place Gerbert, between rue Blomet and rue de Vaugirard. **Claude Naissant.** 1853.

Neo-Romanesque with two tiers of differing stone: body and base set in the arms of the two rues Gerbert and place Gerbert. A bit too slender for true Romanesque, it is neither gutsy nor stolid enough.

[15c-24.] **Ecole, rue Fenoux,** behind 6, rue Gerbert. **Philippe Gazeau.** 1985.

A small facade on this side street flags intense activities behind. It makes a strong presence for a modest volume.

[15c-25.] **Immeuble, 73, rue de l'Abbé-Groult,** between rue Blomet and rue de Vaugirard. **Edouard Jacquemot.** 1931.

Simple and austere, with playful balconies at the top.

★★[15c-26.] **Immeubles, 3, 5, 7, 9, rue Fourcade** and **4, 6, 8, 10, rue Victor-Duruy** between rue de Vaugirard and rue Olivier de Serres. **Léon Chesnay.** 1909.

Articulated iron-framed bay windows and multihued brick, with glazed and unglazed tile, in a lively, lovely set of *logements sociaux*. The metal console brackets, perforated elegantly, are fun.

[15c-27.] **Passage Olivier-de-Serres,** between 30, rue Olivier-de-Serres and 363, rue de Vaugirard.

The *place* is more important than the buildings proper in this a complex of architecture that is a joy to pass through.

[15c-28.] **Immeuble, 10, rue Dombasle,** between rue de Vaugirard and rue Olivier-de-Serres. 1930s.

Stucco plasticity and columns articulate this 1930s facade more than most of its chronological peers. The patina of the stucco is a pleasant contrast to painted *pierre de taille* in many pretentious Haussmannian buildings.

**[15c-29.] Immeuble, 18, rue Ferdinand-Fabre,** between rue de Vaugirard and rue Blomet. **Gaston Ernest.** circa 1910.

A lesser spectacle than **Nos. 4-10, rue Victor-Duruy,** but the bay windows make charming apartments within and handsome modulations without.

**[15c-30.] Ateliers/hotel, 25, rue Alain-Chartier,** between rue de Vaugirard and rue Blomet. 1930s.

The bay windows start as neo-Classical-moderne and end as bold polygonal concrete. A frieze with squirrels amid a vegetative bas-relief is another dating style.

**[15c-31.] Ville de Paris/Direction d'Architecture**/originally **Pavillon du service des eaux**, 14, rue Alain-Chartier, between rue de Vaugirard and rue Blomet. 1895.

A light industrial building, lightly handled and happily reincarnated for the City of Paris's working architects.

★**[15c-32.] Immeuble, 170, rue de la Convention,** between rue Eugène-Millon and rue Lecourbe. **Paul Legriel.** 1900.

A tooled and rusticated base in the Italian Renaissance manner: smooth above to a stolid solidity. **No. 168**, next door, has a similar character but its richness is upstairs, not down.

**[15c-33.] Immeuble, 166, rue de la Convention,** between rue Eugène-Million and rue Lecourbe. **Emile Bois.** 1912.

A modest but heavy-handed effort by Bois, who did better elsewhere.

**[15c-34.] Clinique Blomet**/originally **Maison de Santé des Soeurs de Sainte-Marie-de-la-Famille,** 134, rue Blomet, between rue Alain-Chartier and rue de l'Abbé-Groult. 1842.

A neo–17th-century portal leads to a neo-Gothic chapel (★★) tucked in next to the clinic proper at **No. 136**. The latter is blessed with some peaceful gardens.

**[15c-35.] Crèche Lecocq** and **Postes Télécommunications,** 19, rue Charles-Lecocq, between rue Lecourbe and rue de la Croix-Nivert. 1980s.

A stepped stucco Post Modern ensemble, more understated than many and not a bad neighbor. The blue sash is elegant.

★**[15c-36.] Square Saint-Lambert,** flanked by rue Jean-Formigé, rue Théophraste-Renaudot, rue Léon-Lhermitte, and rue du Docteur-Jacquemaire-Clemenceau. **Georges Sébille.** 1933.

Terraced changes in level make this 1930s park a formal Classical ensemble symmetrically disposed. The great circular pool sits in the abandoned vat of an earlier gas plant!

**[15c-37.] Maison des Dames des PTT, 5,** rue du Docteur-Jacquemaire-Clemenceau, corner rue Léon-Lhermitte. **Henri Ploquin.** 1930s.

Neo-Classical-moderne in stone and tile; a sharp-edged residence of modest pretensions.

★[15c-38.] Immeubles, 1-9, rue Léon-Lhermitte, between rue de la Croix-Nivert and rue Gustave-Larroumet. **Louis C. Heckly.** 1934.

A vigorous block of concrete and brick overlooking the pleasant verdure of the square Saint-Lambert. Vitality without any special posturing makes it a parallel to the best of Haussmann and Haussmannian-*tardif.*
Heckly also did the whole west side of the square on rue Théophraste-Renaudot, the same year, a sorry and lesser work.

★[15c-39.] Immeuble, 138, rue du Théâtre, between rue de la Croix-Nivert and rue du Commerce. **Bruno Elkouken.** 1930.

Stucco and bay windows, with crisp stucco and crisper sliding sash. This is a place for light.

[15c-40.] Immeuble, 15, rue Gramme, between rue de la Croix-Nivert and rue du Commerce. **G. Dejouy.** 1928.

As if the reincarnated Empire had built an *immeuble* with great angled console brackets. The cité Thuré adjacent is charming.

★★[15c-41.] Immeuble, 17-21, rue Gramme, between rue de la Croix-Nivert and rue du Commerce. 1930s.

Smooth and pebbled stucco, streamlined and creamy, presents an unaffected early modern block with a touch of neo-Classicism. With horizontal bandings, the surfaces here are matte, whereas the tiled Post Moderns sometimes create an excessive sleekness.

---

**Beaugrenelle** was a town just outside the walls of Charles X's Paris in 1824, when it was developed by **Léonard Violet,** who was city councilman of Vaugirard. It occupied the area (about 105 acres) bounded by boulevard de Grenelle, rue de la Croix-Nivert, rue des Entrepreneurs, and rue de Lourmel.
On June 27, 1824, speaking at inaugural ceremonies to celebrate the project, the mayor of Vaugirard said: "Gentlemen, it is a richness with good luck, and forever to be remembered, that this day presents to us fortune associated with charity, and which offers simultaneously for our admiration a city being born, misfortune aided, virtue recompensed.
"Yes, gentlemen, on this shore we will see erected the retreat of the peaceful citizen, the workshop of the manufacturer, the shops of commerce, and this great result is the work of a single man."

---

[15c-42.] Immeuble, 87, rue du Commerce, corner rue Lakanal. 1830s.

Faces from the time of Louis-Philippe peer from the curved pediments at the first floor. A remnant of Violet's original development of the town of Beaugrenelle.

[15c-43.] Eglise Saint-Jean-Baptiste-de-Grenelle, place Etienne-Pernet, between rue des Entrepreneurs and rue de l'Eglise. **Bontat.** 1828–1831. **Eugène Viollet-de-Duc.** 1865.

An eclectic mélange that could have blossomed in Regency England. It is awkward in proportions: the steeple seems Lilliputian in this context.

★[15c-44.] Immeuble, 24, place Etienne-Pernet, between rue des Entrepreneurs and rue de l'Eglise. **Alfred Wagon.** 1905.

Thick "spaghetti" *(nouilles)* festoons the *pierre de taille.* Léonard Violet and Saint-Jean-Baptiste would both be startled.

★**[15c-45.] Immeuble, 2, place Etienne-Pernet** corner, rue de l'Eglise. **S. Wagon**. 1935.

A sharp-edged foil to the limpness across the street. **Wagon**, son of **Wagon**, did the honors.

**[15c-46.] Immeuble, 13, avenue Félix-Faure,** between rue de l'Eglise and rue de Javel. **S. Dauger-Cornil**. 1907.

Hard polychromy rather than soft Art Nouveau, with *meulière* supporting it all: a hard-hearted and -faced eclecticism.

**[15c-47.] Immeuble, 22, avenue Félix-Faure,** southwest corner rue de Javel. circa 1900.

Multipaned bay windows spandreled with mixed white and gray-cream brick.

★**[15c-48.] Immeuble, 31, avenue Félix-Faure,** between rue de Javel and rue Serret. **Clément Feugueur**. 1912.

Late Haussmannian-*tardif* influenced lightly by Art Nouveau. A flat wall gives way to floral relief and simplified console brackets.

**[15c-49.] Immeuble, 40, avenue Félix-Faure,** between rue Oscar-Roty and rue de la Convention. **H. Audiger** and **Joachim Richard**. 1907.

Sinuous bas-reliefs become plastic over the entrance portal, set in a flat and smoothly undulating facade.

★**[15c-50.] Immeuble, 68, avenue Félix-Faure,** corner rue Tisserand. **Clément Feugueur**. 1913.

The manners in this *pierre de taille* high-rise are 18th-century; the height is more than the 18th century could even imagine. *Superior eclecticism.*

Walk back along avenue Félix-Faure to the rue de l'Eglise.

**[15c-51.] Immeuble, 58, rue de l'Eglise,** between place Etienne-Pernet and rue de la Rosière. 1989.

So-so PoMo by someone without talent.

**[15c-52.] Square Violet,** between rue de l'Eglise and place Violet. 1824 and later. City park, 1875.

Here were the gardens of Léonard Violet's château, where the inauguration of the subdivision was celebrated. It is now a charming public park.

★★**[15c-53.] Château Violet**/now **Caserne des Sapeurs/Pompiers,** place Violet off rue des Entrepreneurs, on axis of rue Violet. 1824 and later. Restored and remodeled as caserne, 1860.

Palladian–Greek Revival with Ionic pilasters stacked upon Doric ones. This is an elegant *hôtel particulier* that assumes the posture of a chateau, on axis of developers Violet and Letellier's main street.

**[15c-54.] Ilot, UAP d'Immeubles Bourgeois**, rue des Entrepreneurs, rue Violet, and rue Edmond-Roger. 1927.

Some cadaverous balconies over salmon-colored and yellow brickwork, a brick frieze, and floral-basketed ironwork. The monotony of the bulk is relieved by intervening courtyards and the dogleg of rue Edmond-Roger.

★[15c-55.] **Union des Institutions Sociales du XVe Arrondissement**/formerly **Mairie de Grenelle**/originally **hôtel particulier**, 69, rue Violet, at place du Commerce. 1820s. Mairie, 1842–1860.

A modest *hôtel* shuttered with *volets*, pilastered with Ionics atop Tuscans. It could be a modest Greek Revival building in England or America.

[15c-56.] **Maison, 3, avenue Delécourt,** between place Violet and avenue Emile-Zola. 1890s.

A pleasant cul-de-sac presents at No. 3 an ivy-covered villa with convoluted ironwork.

★★[15c-57.] **Place du Commerce,** between rue Violet and rue du Commerce.

Twin rows of horse-chestnut trees flank a cast-iron kiosk-bandstand. Long and thin, the park is particularly graceful as the front garden of the surrounding buildings—another Anglophiliac urban oasis.

# 38
# FIFTEENTH ARRONDISSEMENT
## EAST

### TOUR MONTPARNASSE TO

### SAINT-ANTOINE-DE-PADOUE

Tour Montparnasse: **Eugène Baudouin et al.**; TELECOM: **Jacques Debat-Ponsan**; Le Monde; Musée Bourdelle expansion: **Christian de Portzamparc**; Villa Garnier: **Léon-Joseph Madeleine**; Faculté de Médecine/Necker: **André Wogensky**; Necker Morgue: **Paul Chemetov**; Institut Pasteur: **E. Bréhant**; 106, rue Falguière: **E. D.**; 10, rue Aristide-Maillol: **AURA-3**; Maison Chirurgicale: **René Patouillard-Demoriane**; Centre des Chèques Postaux: **Michel Roux-Spitz**; Eglise Notre-Dame-de-la-Salette: **Henri Colboc**; Villa Santos-Dumont; Collège Modigliani: **Pierre Sardou**; Marché du livre ancien et d'occasion de Paris: **Ernest Moreau; La Ruche: Gustave Eiffel**; Parc Georges-Brassens; Eglise Saint-Antoine-de-Padoue: **Léon Azéma**

Métro: **Montparnasse-Bienvenue**

[15e-45.] **La Ruche**/originally **Pavillon des Vins. Gustave Eiffel,** entrepreneur. 1900. Relocated, 1902. **Duvelle,** caryatid sculptor.

**[15e-1.]** **Tour Montparnasse**, place Raoul-Dautry, off boulevard Montparnasse, between rue de l'Arrivée and rue du Départ. **Eugène Beaudouin, Urbain Cassan, Louis Hoym de Marien**, and **Jean Saubot**. Consulting architect, **A. Epstein and Sons**. 1973.

An American intrusion by an American developer, Wylie Tuttle, and his Chicago-based consulting architect. It is also certainly a fall from grace for Beaudouin, whose wondrous school at Suresnes (with partner Marcel Lods) is a landmark of the serious modern movement.

Here is a banal point-block in glass and metal that attempts a break from the rectangle with sinuous form, not dissimilar to an equal disaster, New York's Pan Am building, where, similarly, Walter Gropius and Pietro Belluschi were consulting architects for a similar travesty (there, more architectural than urbanistic). Why does the French team want to claim this building? Let the American secret partner be the fall guy. But, in sum, it is a symbol of the rape of Montparnasse, that artists' enclave of small and human scale which is not so slowly succumbing to lesser but equally intrusive change in the name of modernism.

**★★[15e-2]** **TELECOM/Direction Regionale d'Ile de France**, 18, boulevard de Vaugirard, between avenue du Maine and rue Armand-Moisant. **Jacques Debat-Ponsan**. 1935.

First-class 1930s limestone that atones, in advance, for the bad pastry of the Musée de la Poste at **No. 34** on the next block. Here strength, function, and style brings Firmness, Commodity, and halfhearted Delight.

**[15e-3.]** **Musée de la Poste**, 34, boulevard de Vaugirard, between rue Armand-Moisant and boulevard Pasteur.

Brutalism weakened by its vulgar and amateurish ribbing and bas-reliefs. Would that the architecture of the PTT in the 1970s and 1980s were equal to the quality of its stamps—or to the architecture of the PTT in the 1920s and 1930s.

**[15e-4.]** **Le Monde (newspaper)**, 15, rue Falguière, between rue Antoine-Bourdelle and rue de Vaugirard. **Dominique Lyon** and **Pierre Besset**. 1990.

A pregnant curtain wall, or perhaps its pregnant shift, lunges into the streetscape on both Falguière and Bourdelle. Shame on you, Monde, not for your fabric, but for your form. It seems more appropriate for a Robert Maxwell publication.

**★[15e-5.]** **Musée Bourdelle**, 16, rue Antoine-Bourdelle, between avenue du Maine and rue Falguière. Studio, before 1884. Salle des Monuments, **Henri Gautruche**. 1961. Further extended, 1968. New wing connecting to Villa Garnier, **Christian de Portzamparc**. 1991.

Brick of those years between the wars conceals a studio in *colombage*, a no-nonsense place of early technology, and gardens within gardens—all with the seemingly endless histrionic sculpture of Antoine Bourdelle. To the left, in the Salle des Monuments, is the sculptured detritus of 1930s Art Moderne, where fascism, communism, and liberal democracies all embraced such a clean neo-Classical pomposity.

**★[15e-6.]** **Garage, 7** and **7 bis, rue Antoine-Bourdelle**, between avenue du Maine and rue Falguière. 1930s.

A surelevation has modified this bold Art Moderne garage. No-nonsense, with a powerful scale of rounded columns, steel, and glass. Paint, love, and graphics could make this extraordinary once more.

★[15e-7.] Immeuble, 6, rue Antoine-Bourdelle, between avenue du Maine and rue Falguière. 1930s.

Ice cream (but only vanilla) on this crisp and austere street-facade that leaves all Classicism behind and speaks only of its whitewash.

★★[15e-8.] Villa Garnier, 131, rue de Vaugirard, corner rue Falguière. Léon-Joseph Madeleine. 1936.

Random tiles *(grès cérame cassés)* wrap around this sleek Art Moderne block, which harbors a triumphal arch to the PoMo architecture beyond. This happy surprise, secreted from the street, blossoms as you explore the villa's entrails.

★[15e-9.] Service Assistance Médicale d'Extrême Urgence de Paris, 144, rue de Vaugirard, opposite rue Dulac. ACAUR. 1986.

SAMU Ambulances housed in PoMo style. Here tile at least has a psychological function, and lithe curves with freestanding columns are proportioned with grace.

★[15e-10.] Citroën Garage, 165, rue de Vaugirard, between rue Dulac and rue Dalou. A. Galey. 1928.

Another in the avant-garde automobile architecture that enlivened the 1920s and 1930s in Paris. Opposite is its more vigorous but ruined ancestor—or perhaps an elder and poorer brother.

★[15e-11.] Faculté de Médecine/Necker-Enfants Malades, 156, rue de Vaugirard, opposite rue Dalou. André Wogensky. 1968.

Excellent academic modernism within; the small street-entry building is less successful, although a gesture to urban Paris. If such a mock portal could not at least come to the street line and match the height of its neighbors, why bother?
The sleek block within is in the same vocabulary as Wogensky's addition to the Hôpital Saint-Antoine in the 12th arrondissement [11/12-27.].

★★[15e-12.] Morgue et Laboratoires/Hôpital Necker, off impasse de l'Enfant-Jésus, next to 144, rue de Vaugirard. Paul Chemetov. 1984.

A serious essay in morbid programming, where both elegance and proportion abound. The vermilion scuppers are a bit off-putting, considering the functions within; but Chemetov provides a far more impressive depth of architecture and detailing than most of the glib current Post Modern architects.
The *crèche* for the hospital staff opposite (Georges Maurios. 1983) gives a note of new life, in contrast.

[15e-13.] Siège du Crédit-Agricole, 90, boulevard Pasteur, corner rue du Cotentin. Renée Genin and Jean-Louis Bertrand. 1975.

For farmers? Here is crystalline high style, high-tech glitz in the spirit of suburban Dallas. Nevertheless, it is lovely in comparison with the Maine-Montparnasse complex.

[15e-14.] Hôtel Arcade, passage Alexandre and boulevard de Vaugirard, just off boulevard Pasteur.

Instant PoMo that may age ungraciously in only a few more instants. Can all that casual glass, steel, and stucco weather the fickle Paris weather?

**[15e-15.] Eglise Saint-Jean-Baptiste-de-la-Salle**, 9, rue du Docteur-Roux, just south of boulevard Pasteur. **Jacquemin**. 1910.

A neo-Baroque stair is an awkward entrance to this sorry, gloomy church, where somber brick and dirty stone reign.

★**[15e-16.] Institut Pasteur**, 24, 25, rue du Docteur-Roux, between boulevard Pasteur and rue des Volontaires. No. 24, **E. Bréhant**. 1900. No. 25, 1888.

Part of a campus on *both* sides of the rue du Docteur-Roux that extends to the rue de Vaugirard. At No. 24 is a broken neo-Baroque pediment (enclocked), with brick and limestone, quoins, and pilasters.

★★**[15e-17.] Serres/Hôpital Pasteur**, 213, rue de Vaugirard, between boulevard Pasteur and rue des Volontaires. 1880s.

Little greenhouses give some flavor from the time of Louis Pasteur himself. Plants, rather than microbes, abound under steel and glass. It's a short walk in off the street entrance.

★**[15e-18.] Ateliers, 32, rue Mathurin-Régnier,** between rue de Vaugirard and rue Dutot.

A bizarre relic of the 1920s, with vast-scaled bay windows, unhappily in a dirty and turgid condition. Precocious.

**[15e-19.] Square Necker,** between rue de la Procession and rue Bargue.

A calm island, with the ever-present cast- and wrought-iron bandstand.

**[15e-20.] Immeuble, 16, rue de la Procession,** corner rue Sainte-Félicité. **Théodore Lambert**. 1913.

Undulating bays enliven the facade, supported by imbricated tile spandrels.

★★**[15e-21.] Immeuble, 106, rue Falguière,** corner rue Vigée-Lebrun. **E. D.** 1985.

The void between the wings is a powerful slot that belies the mannerisms at the sky. At least the tile is gray, and stucco is exiled to the penthouses. This is distinguished urbanism—Next time the *architecture* might match it.

**[15e-22.] Société Anonyme de Logements Economiques pour Familles Nombreuses/Immeuble No. 3,** 36-38, rue du Cotentin, corner rue Falguière.

★**[15e-23.] Immeuble, 10, rue Aristide-Maillol**, off rue Falguière. **AURA-3.** 1985.

Another place of pleasant urbanism, with the architecture to the south (No. 10) far more elegantly detailed than that to the north. Seats and playplaces make this a civilized pause, and a Périgordian restaurant, La Dordogne, brings the countryside to Paris.

**[15e-24.] Ecole Maternelle, 15, rue Aristide-Maillol,** off rue Falguière. **Alexandre Ghiulamila**. 1986.

A somewhat awkward exedra (tiled in white) joins the apartments next door. It is *too much:* too much ego, too much form for a program that should be modest and understated.

**[15e-25.] Logements, 127, rue Falguière,** opposite rue Bargue. **Alexandre Ghiulamila**. 1985.

Less graceful than its **10, rue Aristide-Maillol** neighbor around the corner; the articulated columns and struts are awkward and out of scale. And why throw in that soupçon of curtain wall?

★**[15e-26.] Logements, 129, rue Falguière,** opposite rue Bargue.

An elegant neighbor to **No. 127**, whose composition shows a careful expression of differing functions.

**[15e-27.] Immeuble, 27, rue André-Gide**, at rue de la Procession.

A building as a triumphal arch? Good idea, lousy architecture. All those curves would sell well on the Côte d'Azur.

**[15e-28.] Ecole, 66, rue de la Procession,** corner rue d'Alleray. **Joseph Belmont, A. Pelletier**, and **J.P. Gautron**. 1979.

The color of mud (but tiled), this has vestiges of the 1937 exposition (the corner columns), 1960s curtain walling, and flying beams. A silly place.

★**[15e-29.] Maison Chirurgicale,** place d'Alleray, between rue d'Alleray and rue Brancion. **René Patouillard-Demoriane**. 1935.

A glassy bracketed bay sits atop this concentric brick pile. The side entrance on rue Brancion and its attached stair are much more interesting.

**[15e-30.] Immeuble, 66, rue d'Alleray,** just west of place d'Alleray. **Anthony Bechu**. 1980.

*Grand Standing* and a lush park. Ribbed concrete balconies (crowned with that continuous smoked glass that has festered in the 16th arrondissment and in Boulogne) in a broken form: the neo-Niemeyer *pilotis* are both obscene and structural gimmickry. Some of them don't even reach the ground!

**[15e-31.] Maison, 41, rue d'Alleray,** opposite rue Corbon. circa 1900.

Tailored *meulière*, brick, and glazed terra-cotta, with vines embracing it all.

**[15e-32.] Ecole, 3, rue Corbon,** corner rue d'Alleray. 1896.

*Pierre de taille* laced with brick and supported by a *meulière* base. Somber late 19th-century, but stolid and serious.

**[15e-33.] Centre de Chèques Postaux,** 16, rue des Favorites, corner rue Bourseul. **Michel Roux-Spitz**. 1933.

When the stylish Roux-Spitz turned from *logements de grand standing* to public architecture, he became pompous. Here neo-Classicism is reduced to an insipid flat cornice and columns of concrete. There's no joy for you when the *chèques postaux* are cashed, except in the francs brought home.

**[15e-34.] Logements** and **Ville de Paris/Section des Egouts,** 52, rue Dombasle, east of rue de Dantzig. **Jacques Branchereau**. 1983.

The architects have "tried to regain the continuity of the street by making a transition between a small old building and a recent structure twice as high and set back." The product is jazzy, unlike the understated connection that should have been achieved.

★★[15e-35.] **Square Léon-Guillot**, between rue Dombasle and rue des Morillons. 1934.

Banded-metal balconies, bay windows, octagonal oculi, and a fluted frieze. This is a *cité* of first-class elegance.

★[15e-36.] **Eglise Notre-Dame-de-la-Salette**, midblock between rue de Dantzig and rue de Cronstadt. **Henri Colboc**. 1967.

Buried in the middle of a block, this modern concrete truncated cone is illuminated with stained glass. Better within than without.

★[15e-37.] **Villa Santos-Dumont**, off rue Santos-Dumont, between rue des Morillons and rue de Vouillé. 1926.

Belgian block, Virginia creeper, and ateliers in a cul-de-sac of charm. See especially **No. 15's** brick and tilework; **No. 13,** protomodern; **No. 9's** elegant *garde-fous*—everything minor in an urban space that is major.

★★[15e-38.] **Maison, 8, rue Charles-Weiss**, between rue Castagnary and rue Labrouste. circa 1930.

A venerable modern à la Mallet-Stevens that needs a bath and paint but is artistically glorious.

★[15e-39.] **Immeuble, 25, rue Rosenwald**, corner rue des Morillons. 1980s.

*Mirabile dictu:* an import from Miami with class. Those pregnant balconies are stylish.

[15e-40.] **Maison, 14, rue de Cherbourg**, between rue des Morillons and rue Fizeau.

A bit of precocious concrete brutalism in these mixed precints.

★★[15e-41.] **Groupe Scolaire/Collège Modigliani**, 66, rue des Morillons, between rue de Cherbourg, rue Fizeau, and rue de Lieuvin. **Pierre Sardou**. 1934.

Brick: "stacked," ribbed, bellied, curved, and honored. It ripples around the block, its mild bays surveying the street.

[15e-42.] **Immeuble, 5, rue du Bessin**, corner rue Castagnary.

Sleek white tile spoiled by some pretentious dirty-brown brick wandering around its base. This student exercise shouldn't have left the drafting board.

★★[15e-43.] **Marché du livre ancien et d'occasion de Paris**/originally **Marché aux Chevaux**, 106, rue Brancion, between rue Castagnary and rue des Morillons. **Ernest Moreau**. 1904–1907.

Buildings in *meulière*, but the pavilions are exquisite in cast iron and steel, trussed and tiled. Where horses were once slaughtered for the dinner table, old and rare books are now sold on Saturdays and Sundays.

[15e-44.] **Immeuble, 31, rue Robert-Lindet**, off rue de Dantzig. 1930s.

Brick and stucco 1930s; the bellied balconies are in counterpoint to the central bay windows. **No. 33,** next door, offers a "cleaner" modernism, with its white stucco.

★★★[15e-45.] La Ruche/originally **Pavillon des Vins, Exposition Universelle, 1900,** 246, passage de Dantzig, between rue de Dantzig and rue de la Saida. **Gustave Eiffel**, entrepreneur. 1900. Relocated, **Alfred and Albert Boucher,** sculptors. 1902. Caryatids, **Duvelle.**

Here was a phalanstery of artists established by Boucher that, unlike the avant-garde enclave of the Bateau-Lavoir, provided an eclectic mantle. Here briefly worked Leger, Archipenko, Chagall, Zadkine, Modigliani, Soutine, and Lipchitz. The central pavilion is bordered by other ateliers that were added at the time of the relocation of the Pavillon des Vins. The whole ensemble is a delightful and verdant enclave.

"In 1895, Alfred Boucher, a relatively celebrated academic painter and sculptor of his time, acquired land comprising 54,000 square feet in this place, removed from Vaugirard. He had the idea of creating there a cité d'artistes and a cultural center. At the close of the Exposition of 1900, he bought and rebuilt the wine pavilion. Created by Eiffel and his team, this building, with a polygonal plan, constructed with iron beams and red brick, is composed of three floors covered with a roof pagoda-like. Two caryatids decorate the entry." . . . *Vie et histoire, XVe arrondissement.*

★★[15e-46.] **Groupe de Maisons Ouvrières, 15, rue de la Saida,** between passage de Dantzig and rue Olivier-de-Serres. **Auguste Labussière.** 1912. Additions on rue Olivier-de-Serres, **Albert Guilbert.** 1927.

Early concrete exposed frame infilled flush with brick, with a modest tile and polychromatic frieze—an airy place for the modest worker. "All apartments comprising a common room and three bedrooms, with a water closet, should be rented at 5 to 6 francs a week. Each apartment will include a fireplace, a source of water in the common room, and a fireplace in one bedroom. We ask that you do not construct a chimney for the two small bedrooms." Superb.

[15e-47.] **Parc Georges-Brassens**, between rue de Dantzig, rue des Morillons, rue Brancion, and rue Castagnary. **Alexandre Ghiulamila** and **Jean-Michel Milliex,** architects. **Daniel Collin,** landscape architect. 1977–1985.

Vestigial horse sheds became a *crèche,* and the symbolic tower now lords it over a small jet d'eau and pond. Peaceful, dull, and overlooked by giant residential slabs that are attacking from the south. The Théâtre Sylvia-Monfort by architect **Claude Parent**, now underway, will provide 450 seats in these *sub-*urban precincts.

[15e-48.] **HBM, 82, boulevard Lefebvre,** between avenue de la Porte-Brancion and rue Jean-Sicard. **Louis C. Heckly.** 1933.

A solid brick-and-limestone triad of blocks: the corbeled bays are of a knuckled neo-Classicism.

[15e-49.] **Eglise Saint-Antoine-de-Padoue,** 52, boulevard Lefebvre, between rue de Dantzig and rue Olivier-de-Serres, **Léon Azéma**. 1934–1936.

A harsh essay in concrete and red brick that punctuates the boulevard with its campanile.

# 39
# FIFTEENTH
# ARRONDISSEMENT
## NORTH
### ECOLE MILITAIRE TO UNESCO ANNEX

Ecole Militaire: **Jacques-Ange Gabriel**; UNESCO: **Marcel Breuer, Bernard Zehrfuss,** and **Pier Luigi Nervi**; 23–25, rue de Laos: **Charles Thomas**; Eglise Saint-Léon: **Brunet;** place Dupleix; Australian Embassy: **Harry Seidler**; Groupe Scolaire/Grenelle: **Louis Bonnier;** rue de Lourmel; 36, rue du Commerce: **Théodore Judlin** and **P. Gravereaux;** UNESCO Annex: **Bernard Zehrfuss**; Métro Aérien: **Jean-Camille Formigé**

Métro: **Ecole Militaire**

[15n-35.] **Métro Aérien,** boulevard de Grenelle. **Jean-Camille Formigé.** 1904.

★★★[15n-1.] Ecole Militaire, place de Fontenoy, between avenue Duquesne and avenue Suffren. **Jacques-Ange Gabriel**. 1751–1773. Expanded, 19th century.

The facade on the **Champ de Mars** is the most familiar but is understated to the point where the roving families in the Champ proper scarcely notice it. But on place de Fontenoy, it is another matter, not only embracing its **Coeur d'Honneur** but also working symbiotically with neo-Classical ministeries *and* the **UNESCO** building of Marcel Breuer.
Corinthian columns and pilasters abound.

★★[15n-2.] UNESCO, place de Fontenoy, between avenue de Lowendal, avenue de Saxe, avenue de Ségur, and avenue de Suffren. **Marcel Breuer**, architect. **Bernard Zehrfuss**, associate architect. **Pier Luigi Nervi**, engineer. 1958.

Le Corbusier blessed it as "a respectful salute to the past, while opening itself to the future"—but he *would.* Breuer attempted to give an urban completion to the exedral space of place de Fontenoy, while simultaneously articulating his three-armed body of a building, The umbilically corded great hall is spanned with some of Nervi's wonderful engineering, folded concrete that makes a great accordion. Later additions are buried in the sunken garden.
Here are the code marks of modernism of the 1950s: *brise-soleils*, exposed concrete, *pilotis,* and a less than convincing concern for the city's fabric.

[15n-3.] European Space Agency, 8, rue Mario-Nikis, between square Lowendal and avenue de Ségur. **Jean Perrotet** and **Valentin Fabré.** 1977.

A clunky land ship, with thick window frames and sash that don't even make its neo-1930s corner. Without grace, it imposes a vacuum on this street.

[15n-4.] Immeuble, 16–18, avenue de Lowendal, corner avenue de Suffren. **Jean Boucher** and **Paul Delaplanche.** 1932.

The ironwork of the 1930s was still derived from Art Deco; but surrounding, neo-Classicism still reigned.

★[15n-5.] Immeuble, 23–25, rue de Laos, between avenue de Suffren and place Cambronne. **Charles Thomas.** 1930.

An almost industrial-styled *grand standing* clad in a smooth stone that successfully simulates concrete. The stepped-back forms are a link with the *immeubles à gradins* of Sauvage.

[15n-6.] Hôtel particulier, 3, rue de Laos and 90, avenue de Suffren, just off corner. 19th century.

Tucked behind a corner apartment block (1914, that used to be part of its greenery), this town house gives a taste of what it was once like hereabouts.

[15n-6a.] Immeuble, 2, avenue Emile-Acollas, corner rue Jean-Carries. 1930s.

Some creatively splayed console brackets enliven this bay-windowed Moderne facade.

★[15n-6b.] Immeuble, 41, avenue Charles-Floquet, between rue Jean-Carriès and avenue du Général Petrie. 1930s.

Smooth and pregnant bay windows, *oeuils-de-boeuf,* and a small, but monumental columned entry bring some architectural guts to this bland and arriviste neighborhood.

★**[15n-7.] Garage Citroën, 6, rue de la Cavalerie,** off avenue de La Motte–Picquet. **R. Faradèche.** 1929.

Plain stucco, mildly bayed, gives way to pergolas borne by tiled columns against the sky. **No. 7,** opposite (**P. Sonrel** and **F. Davin.** 1935), is a barren cousin, where—not to diminish the words of Mies van der Rohe— less is less. No. 6 combines seven levels of parking with a rooftop sports complex.

**[15n-8.] Bureau, 3, rue de Pondichéry,** between rue Dupleix and rue du Soudan. 1980s.

A client with interests neither urban nor urbane, an architect who believes that a curtain wall is one that curtains history. *Atrocious.* But look—and wonder when it will all end.

★**[15n-9.] Eglise Saint-Léon,** place Dupleix and place du Cardinal-Amette. **Brunet.** 1934.

Concrete, brick, and tesserae, with a beehive neo–Sacré-Coeur spire, facing a pleasant "English" square.

**[15n-10.] Caserne Dupleix,** facing place Dupleix through to rue Desaix.

This vast ex-army barracks will give way to 1,200 apartments (225 moderate-income, 750 deluxe, and 225 for the army).

★**[15n-11.] Groupe Scolaire, 21, rue Dupleix** at place du Cardinal-Amette. **Edouard Boegner.** circa 1935.

From that rash of red brick designed to have the populace think modern by chromatic shock.

**[15n-12.] Immeuble, 5–7, rue Alasseur,** between rue Dupleix and avenue de Champaubert. **Joannès Chollet** and **Jean-Baptiste Mathon.** 1930.

A complex plan and section within provides five levels visible on the street and eight on the interior court. Brick and stucco produce a bland architecture at the sidewalk (those arches infilled with unrelated windows) but staccato form crests at the sky.

★**[15n-13.] Immeuble, 24, rue de Presles,** opposite rue du Guesclin. **Franck Hammoutène.** 1980s.

A PoMo annex to a giant slab, this seems like the creative gesture to relieve a major boredom.

★**[15n-14.] Immeuble, 49, rue de la Fédération,** between rue Desaix and rue Alexis-Carrel. **Jean-Pierre Buffi.** 1984.

Green stone and some style distinguish this from the sea of modern banalities in this neighborhood.

**[15n-15.] Immeuble, 42, avenue de Suffren,** between rue Alexis-Carrel and rue Desaix. **Pierre Koemptgen.** 1936.

Simple, austere, Art Moderne/Art Deco in *un-*polished travertine. A good neighbor.

★★[15n-16.] Ambassade d' Australie, quai Branly, 4, rue Jean-Rey, and 9, rue de la Fédération. **Harry Seidler** and **Peter Hirst**, architects. **Marcel Breuer**, consulting architect. **Pier Luigi Nervi**, consulting engineer. 1978.

A class act that owes nothing to Paris, yet still stands boldly alone with style. Seidler, an Austrian by birth, worked with Breuer on UNESCO and later emigrated to Australia. His work owes much to his experience with Breuer.

★[15n-17.] Immeuble, 15–17, rue Saint-Saens and 5–9, square Desaix, between rue de la Fédération and boulevard de Grenelle. 1930s.

No-nonsense stone at the *rez-de-chaussée,* stucco above, with bay windows for lookers-out.

★[15n-18.] Immeuble, 14, rue Nélaton, between rue Nocard and rue du Docteur-Finlay. **L. Veber** and **Michau**. 1907.

The whole block is V & M, with oculi, bellying *pierre de taille,* rustications, and iron, and at No. 14 a proto-PoMo colonnade. Who could ask for anything more? But look at what they have to look *at:* flunking freshmen who became developers.

[15n-19.] Fondation Michel Darty, 2–8, rue Emeriau, corner rue du Docteur-Finlay. **Phillipe François**. 1983.

A grossly detailed ensemble of white tile and bay windows. The fat aluminum structure of the latter belies Parisian elegance in 19th-century iron. Why become heavy-handed in the wake of graceful ancestors?

We will avoid the Front de Seine, which is totally devoid of any redeeming qualities; the ensemble is a hideous affront to Paris in particular and to modern architecture in general. To pick through the morass of it all would yield only oddities like the Tour Totem (**Michel Andrault** and **Pierre Parat**. 1978), an affront to the Native Americans who created the totem poles. These and other banalities are marked not only by their Dallas-like posturing but also by horrendous detailing.

★★[15n-20.] Groupe Scolaire/Grenelle, 22, rue Saint-Charles, between rue Rouelle, rue Emeriau, and rue Schutzenberger. **Louis Bonnier**. 1912.

A grand tiled entrance arch meets rue Saint-Charles, but along rue Rouelle is a veritable side aisle of brick—corbeled, stepped, and glorious.

[15n-21.] Caisse d'Allocations Familiales, 18–20, rue Viala, opposite rue Béatrix-Dussane. **Raymond Lopez** and **Reby**. 1959.

The siting is unbelievable, ignoring sun, city, and architectural neighbors. *And* the architecture is banal. This, happily, is a symbol of the past. For a breath of fresh architecture, go to the 19th arrondissement, where quality flowers.

★[15n-22.] Immeuble, 25, rue de Lourmel, corner rue Fondary. 1930s.

Smooth concrete bay windows, like ribbed ice cream, with an infilling of yellow brick. *Very nice.*

[15n-23.] Immeuble, 38, rue de Lourmel, corner rue du Théâtre. **Clément Feugueur**. 1913.

Eclectic brick and *pierre de taille.* The grand console brackets at the *premier étage* support the brick world above.

★**[15n-24.] Immeuble, 4–10, rue Henri-Duchêsne**, 133–135, avenue Emile-Zola, and 91, rue du Théâtre. **Ernest Mallet**. 1930.

*Retardataire* Haussmannian-*tardif* for those who missed the last boat. The whole ensemble is a Parisian stage set, with monotony tempered by rich detail.

★**[15n-25.] Immeuble, 36, rue du Commerce**, corner rue Fondary. **Théodore Judlin** and **P. Gravereaux**. 1907.

Transitional in that it maintains a bit of *pompier* with a touch of Art Nouveau. There are vermiculated rustications and some elegant ironwork.

**[15n-26.] Immeuble, 27, rue du Commerce,** corner rue Letellier. circa 1824.

This stems from the original subdivision of Beaugrenelle by Violet in 1824. There are remnants of a painted facade: LA GRANDE CREMERIE DE GRENELLE.

**[15n-27.] Boulangerie, 24, rue du Commerce,** corner rue Letellier. 1920.

A painted ceiling with an elegant curvilinear glass front. Not nostalgia, this is the real thing.

**[15n-28.] Immeuble, 11, rue du Commerce,** between rue Letellier and boulevard de Grenelle. 1930s.

Modern/neo-Classical pilasters with a floral frieze; the spandrels are equally vegetative. It matches the old scale of Beaugrenelle.

★**[15n-29.] Immeuble, 6, rue du Commerce,** corner rue Tiphaine. **Paul Alegre**. 1931.

Sturdy nude columns support tiered balconies, with the usual and pleasant frieze atop. This has understated strength, an architecture without tricks.

**[15n-30.] EDF/GDF, 127, boulevard de Grenelle,** between avenue de La Motte–Picquet and avenue de Lowendal. 1980s.

A precocious event for this dour avenue—or Attack of the Killer PoMos.

★**[15n-31.] RATP/Métro de Paris, 135, boulevard de Grenelle,** between avenue de La Motte–Picquet and avenue de Lowendal. circa 1900.

Iron and glass in a class act.

**[15n-32.] Immeuble, 32, rue Miollis,** between rue Cambronne and boulevard Garibaldi.

More Côte d'Azur, the plastic surgeon's Parisian mistake—for that's who must live here in another of the latest, most expensive grand trivialities. (Would that it were a folly.) Swerving balconies make this another of the various Parisian neo-Watergates (cf., **Remondet** at the Passy Kennedy **[16p-16.]**).

★**[15n-33.] UNESCO Annex, 31, rue François-Bonvin, between rue Mi-ollis and rue Lecourbe. **Bernard Zehrfuss**. 1978.

Orthodox modernism again avoids the street structure of Paris, giving an elegantly detailed but foreign intrusion into the body of this precinct. Zehrfuss was party to the basic UNESCO building (with **Marcel Breuer**) and was also present at La Défense with the CNIT (Centre National des Industries et Techniques) building. But he is an unreconstructed modernist, still hypnotized by the antiurban visions of Le Corbusier; as is the later work of his contemporary, **André Wogensky**.

★**[15n-34.] Immeuble, 20, rue Jean-Daudin,** between rue Miollis and rue Lecourbe. **Proudin d'Hartwic**. 1924.

Stripped neo-Classical columns and colonnettes with accompanying vestigial frieze and console brackets. But wow for those dentils!

★★**[15n-35.] Métro Aérien,** along boulevard Garibaldi and boulevard de Grenelle. **Jean-Camille Formigé**. 1904.

A marvelous mixture of structural virtuosity, practical construction, and Classical remembrances. Here trusses march down the boulevards supported on Doric columns (of cast iron) that bear neo-Assyrian supercapitals. In between, shallow brick arches jump between minor steel beams to form an undulating ceiling to what is now largely parking space. It's fun to be under—and even more fun to ride on top and view the crest of Paris at a modest speed.

# 40
# FIFTEENTH
# ARRONDISSEMENT
## WEST

### ROND-POINT DE PONT MIRABEAU

### TO PARC CITROEN

Rond-Point de Pont Mirabeau; Pont Mirabeau: **Louis-Jean Résal**;
Station Javel: **Juste Lisch**; Eglise Saint-Christophe-de-Javel: **Charles
Besnard**; Immeuble/Sébastien-Mercier/Léontine: **Pol Abraham**; 25,
rue Cévennes: **Gérard Thurnauer**; rond-point Saint-Charles: **Charles
and Henri Delacroix**; Canal Plus: **Richard Meier**; rue Cauchy;
boulevard Victor; "Paquebot"-Immeuble: **Pierre Patout**; Ministère de
la Marine: **Auguste Perret**; Parc André-Citroën:
**Patrick Berger et al.**

Métro: **Javel**

[15w-7.] Eglise Saint-Christophe-de-Javel. Charles H. Besnard. 1934.

**★★[15w-1.] Pont Mirabeau**, across the Seine from place de Barcelone to rond-point du Pont-Mirabeau. **Louis-Jean Résal**. 1896.

Résal was designer of both the Pont Alexandre III and passerelle Debilly. Here is Beaux Arts happily incarnate with most of its venal sins intact.

**★[15w-2.] Station Javel**, rond-point du Pont-Mirabeau, adjacent to the Pont Mirabeau. **Juste Lisch**. 1889.

Originally at place d'Alma for the Exposition Universelle of 1889, it was disassembled and moved here, and now serves the RER. A Lilliputian *hôtel* in iron, brick, and tile. Lisch is better known for the Gare Saint-Lazare, memorialized magnificently in the paintings of Monet.

**★★[15w-3.] Immeuble, 7, rond-point du Pont-Mirabeau**, between rue Balard and rue de la Convention. **Joseph Bassompierre, Paul de Rutté, and Paul Sirvin**. 1936.

An undulating double *pan coupé* flanked by articulated, projecting, square and round balconies. The ground is in orange *crazy tile* popular at the time, the balconies in fine pebbled stucco. The entrance ironwork on the *rond-point* is magnificent.

**[15w-4.] Maisons, 4** and **6, rue Auguste-Vitu**, between avenue Emile-Zola and rue de la Convention.

"Dutch" Art Nouveau in stucco, a creative and exciting duet. The entrance doorways are rich essays.

**[15w-5.] HBM, 8–16, rue des Quatre-Frères-Peignot**, corner avenue Emile-Zola. **Alexandre Maistrasse**. 1926.

Some stolid relief from the omnipresent Front de Seine around the corner. A handsome porch articulates the *pan arrondi* at the corner.

**★★[15w-6.] Bureaus, 66, rue Sébastien-Mercier**, between rue Gutenberg and rue des Bergers. **Franck Hammoutène**. 1985.

A sleek post-Miesian wall fits into the streetfront—and at the scale of its old Parisian (Javel) surrounds.

**★★for its insides[15w-7.] Eglise Saint-Christophe-de-Javel**, 28, rue de la Convention, corner rue Saint-Christophe. **Charles H. Besnard**. 1934.

*Béton armé* that forms wonderful filigrees within at the clerestory windows. This is an eclectic modern church with elegant details—the whole is less than the sum of the parts. The exterior is ungainly brick.

**★[15w-8.] Immeuble, 36, rue Sébastien-Mercier**, corner rue Léontine. **Pol Abraham**. 1930s.

A bold bellying bay holds the corner of this intersection.

**[15w-9.] Immeuble, 38, rue Sébastien-Mercier**, corner rue Léontine. **Charles Devillard**. 1903.

Crisp bay windows and iron shielded with brick spandrels—a bit of history to anchor this corner.

**★[15w-10.] Immeuble, rue Balard**, on axis of rue Clément-Myionnet. **Ayméric Zublena**. 1986.

A great exedra of white, blue, and gray tile cornered by columned *tourelles.* If only the joints were not so prominent, a sense of a monolith might prevail.

★[15w-11.] **Immeuble, 25, rue Cévennes,** between rue Balard and rue Léontine. **Gérard Thurnauer**. 1985.

Even these simple forms are fussed with: some pink tile, some blue tile, and three colors of stucco. But the curved balconies, with their blue rails, are right on.

a short walk away:

★★[15w-12.] **Immeuble, 73, rue des Cévennes,** corner rue Saint-Charles. **Charles and Henri Delacroix**. 1935.

Responding to the rond-point of rue Saint-Charles, this is a vigorous modern experiment, a symbolic red brick building articulated—unusually for Paris—with white balconies and black metalwork. The petits bourgeois here have better trappings than most of the 16th arrondissement's *grand standing.*

★★★[15w-13.] **Canal Plus (television station and studios**), quai André-Citroën, between rue Cauchy and rue des Cévennes. **Richard Meier**. 1992.

An architectural competition held by this private television station resulted in some powerful form and elegant detailing. Meier has grown from being a disciple of Le Corbusier to his present distinquished architectural vocabulary, best expressed elsewhere in his museums in Atlanta and Frankfurt.

★[15w-14.] **Immeuble, 34–38 rue Cauchy,** southeast corner, rue Balard. **Georges Maurios**. 1986.

A rather bald cornering of the intersection, this aggressive Post Modern building is very interested in presenting its own ego. There is scrambled tile (not glazed) and some histrionic shapes at the corner entry: an airplane-wing canopy that continues the tradition of styling buildings like women's hats.

★[15w-15.] **Maison** and **atelier, 31, rue Cauchy,** between rue Gutenberg and rue Saint-Charles. 1980s.

An individualistic three-level complex with a glass-roofed studio *(verrière)* atop, overlooking the cemetery of Grenelle. An elegant neighbor in perfect sync with Grenelle's 19th-century scale.

[15w-16.] **Immeuble, 55–63, rue Balard,** corner rue Gutenberg. 1980s.

A low-key, understated, modern dwelling, at the edges of Post Modernism.

[15w-17.] **Immeuble, 190, rue Saint-Charles**, opposite rue Jongkind. **Alexandre Ghiulamila**, 1986.

When you have 1930s revival with rounded corners and dark sash, why spoil it all with aluminum bay windows with opaque glass spandrels?

★★★[15w-18.] **Collège l'Artense**. 208, rue Saint-Charles, corner rue Balard. **Olivier Brenac** and **Xavier Gonzale**. 1989.

An elegant cornering of this triangularization; the detailing is superb at all levels. A masterful entrance to these twin streets.

★[15w-19.] **Immeuble, 200, rue Lourmel,** between rue Vasco-de-Gama and boulevard Victor. **Daniel Badani** and **Pierre Roux-Dorlut.** 1980.

An eccentric but refreshing entry among the sleek smoked-glass and great sweeping curves. It might be by a minor student of Frank Lloyd Wright transported to Paris, but it belongs in the suburbs. It is distinguished, in contrast, to the terrifying **No. 187** opposite.

[15w-20.] **Immeuble, 187–189, rue de Lourmel,** between rue Vasco-de-Gama and boulevard Victor. 1980s.

Giganticism, megalomaniacalism, egoism, egotism—an anathema to Paris. Those within are protected from seeing it.

★[15w-21.] **Cité de l'Air,** 24, boulevard Victor, between rue de la Porte-d'Issy and rue de la Porte-de-Sèvres. **L. Tissier.** circa 1932.

An ensemble of gutsy early modernism, clad in bits of neo-Classicism.

★[15w-22.] **HBM, 16, boulevard Victor,** between rue Desnouettes and rue Lecourbe. **Agence de l'Office Public d'HBM.** 1935.

A wondrously textured brick ensemble.

★★★[15w-23.] **Immeuble, 3, boulevard Victor,** between rue Lecourbe and avenue Félix-Faure. **Pierre Patout.** 1934.

Certainly the *ne plus ultra* of the *style paquebot,* this slender building was squeezed in between the railroad and the original boulevard. **Patout** exploited the site and the style to produce a building of great power and elegance. He did, in concert, design the interiors of transatlantic liners, but his talent is remembered here in more solid terms.

[15w-24.] **Ministère de la Marine,** 8, boulevard Victor, corner avenue de la Porte-de-Sèvres. **Auguste Perret.** 1932.

Almost three decades after his great triumph at **25 bis, rue Franklin,** Perret slid into a self-academic style. It is huge and boring.

The **ZAC** (Zone d'Aménagement Concertée) **Citroën-Cévennes** is in a state of advanced flux, with many buildings under construction, and the grand park awaiting completion.

★★[15w-25.] **Parc André-Citroën,** quai André-Citroën, between boulevard du Général-Martial-Valin and rue Cauchy. **Patrick Berger, Jean-Paul Viguier,** and **Jean-François Jodry,** architects. **Gilles Clément** and **Alain Provost,** landscape architects. 1993.

An urbane park is expected on the grounds of the old Citroën works, surrounded by architecture of both social purpose and mixed use. The quality of the surrounds has expressed itself from modest to terrible, the latter in advance of the park at its southwest corner, a building that would make Detroit shudder.

Here, however, 12 hectares of greenery will extend to the very cheek of the Seine, the roadway suppressed, and the RER elevated. Theme gardens will surround the central lawn, the Jardin Blanc to rue Saint-Charles, the Jardin Noir to rue Balard, and the gardens of gold, silver, copper, aluminum, mercury, and iron.

**[15w-26.] Le Ponant (bureaux)**, 5, rue Leblanc, corner quai André-Citroën. **Olivier-Clément Cacoub**. 1989.

This is a silver carbuncle on the revitalization of these precincts. Up rue Balard are some elegant and intelligent buildings, but this gross importation lacks any redeeming social significance. That Paris could allow this in the 1980s is a retrogradation, while in other arrondissements—especially the 19th—distinguished architecture blossoms.

# 41
# SIXTEENTH ARRONDISSEMENT
## AUTEUIL
### PLACE D'AUTEUIL TO RUE MALLET-STEVENS

Eglise Notre-Dame-d'Auteuil: **Josseph Vaudremer**; Chapelle
Saint-Bernadette: **Paul Hulot** and **Busse**; Square Henri-Paté: **Pierre
Patout**; Logements: **Joachim Richard, Jean Ginsberg, François
Heep, Berthold Lubetkin, Hector Guimard, Bernard Reichen,
Philippe Robert, Henri Sauvage, Pol Abraham, Le Corbusier,**
and **Robert Mallet-Stevens**

Métro: **Eglise d'Auteuil**

**[16a-3.] Chapelle Sainte-Bernadette. Paul Hulot and Busse.**
1936–1953.

**Haussmannianism versus the Villas: A Reverie;** or, a bourgeois Battle of the Styles, being the *Account,* never *bloody* or *melodramatic,* of how those indomitable Stalwarts from the Backwoods conquered Society by commissioning the latest *ARCHITECT* to do the LATEST THING, and how *ARCHITECTS* used this useful Vehicle to invent the Word "MODERN"; and how modern *ARCHITECTURE* is, therefore, *in fact,* and for evermore, a whimsical Device to advertise COMMERCIAL SUCCESS; and, where foisted upon the Poor, it was so *foisted* that the View of the Bourgeoisie would not be *sullied,* and, therefore, it was *spread about* a bit, ruralized, in effect, so that one could see where the B\*\*\*\*\*\*s were in case they became *uppity* (this latter came to be known as *URBANISM*).

**[16a-1.] Eglise Notre-Dame-d'Auteuil**, 2, place d'Auteuil, at avenue Théophile-Gautier, opposite rue d'Auteuil. **Joseph Vaudremer**. 1877–1892.

A bit of Sacré-Coeur crowns this neo-Romanesque cut-stone pile. It is a solid middle-class corner, with a picturesque profile for this charming square. This was the heart of the village of Auteuil.

★**[16a-2.] Logements, 2, rue Verderet**, at the edge of place d'Auteuil. **Joseph Bassompierre, Paul de Rutté**, and **Paul Sirvin. 1936.**

Crazy random mosaic tile clads this streamlined corner overlooking the pleasant plaza and Notre Dame d'Auteuil. The balcony metalwork at the fifth and sixth floors is bizarre, if not beautiful.

★**[16a-3.] Chapelle Sainte-Bernadette**, 4, rue d'Auteuil, at place d'Auteuil. **Paul Hulot** and **Busse.** 1936–1953.

Straddling the Second World War, this building's evolution shows again the ambivalence of architects between Classical and Modern ideology. A strange giant ruddy-brick portal screens a sunken chapel. You would hope for more joy for Saint-Bernadette. It has a similar ambience to the work (1943) of Eliel Saarinen at the Cranbrook Academy of Art in Bloomfield Hills, Michigan.

★**[16a-4.] Hôtel Véron** or **Pérignon**, 16, rue d'Auteuil, between place d'Auteuil and rue des Perchamps. 17th century. Remodeled, 1806.

The garden facade *(classée)* can be viewed from the intersection of rue des Perchamps and rue Leconte-de-Lisle.

★**[16a-5.] Immeuble, 85, rue La Fontaine**, between rue d'Auteuil and rue Pierre-Guérin. **Ernest Herscher.** 1914.

Skip the facade. The avant-garde world of its time is within the courtyard and lobby.

**[16a-6.] Hôtels particuliers, 8–10, rue Leconte-de-Lisle,** between rue des Perchamps and avenue Théophile-Gautier. **Pol Abraham** and **Paul Sinoir.** 1924.

Low Countries' brick and bay windows at a modest scale. A far cry from the radicalism of **Abraham:** cf. **[16a-40.].**

★**[16a-7.] Hôtel Antier** or **des Demoiselles de Verrières**, 43–47, rue d'Auteuil, between rue Boileau and rue Michel-Ange. 1715.

★★**[16a-8.] Square Henry-Paté**, between rue François-Gérard and rue Félicien-David. **Pierre Patout** and **C. Daman.** 1930.

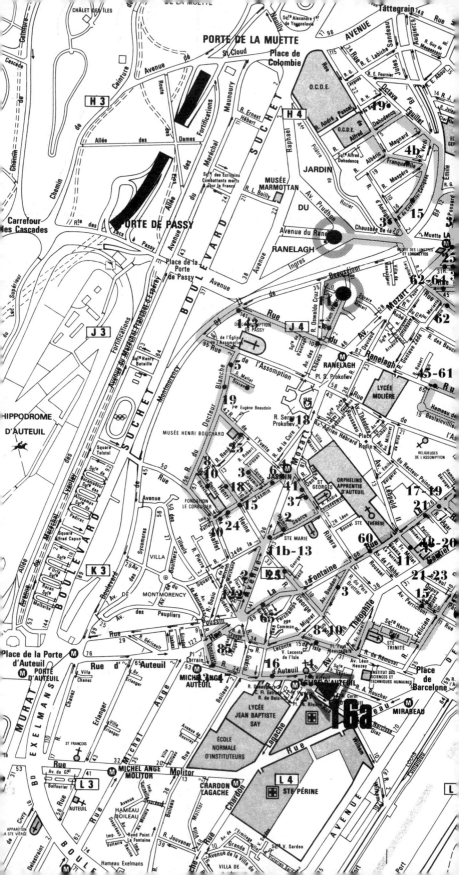

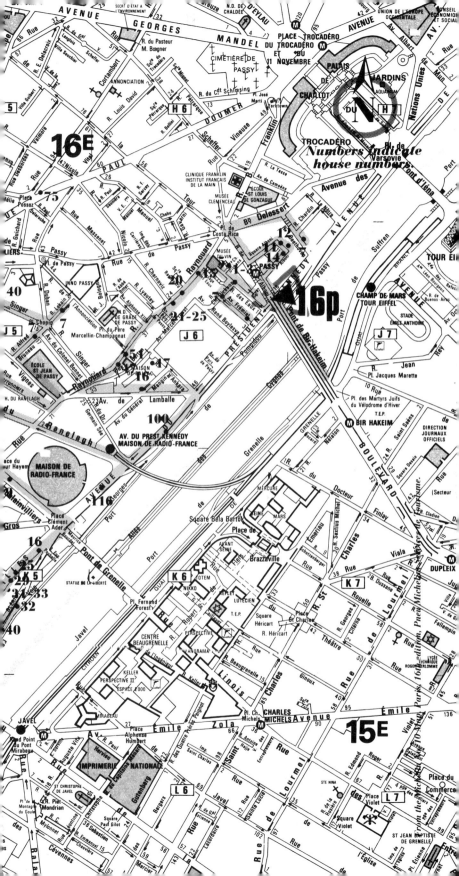

Numbers indicate
house numbers.

**16ᴱ**

**16p**

**15ᴱ**

Here is a square in the English sense, unfortunately incomplete on one side, with a looming monster *immeuble* replacing the south flank. This quiet place surmounts a garage that allows grand trees within its embrace. A lonely oasis for Paris that is still urbane.

★[16a-9.] **Logements, 15, avenue Perrichont,** between avenue Théophile-Gautier and rue Félicien-David. **Joachim Richard.** 1907.

Here is *grès de Bigot,* with yellow bricks accented in blue forming a lovely polychromy. Spandrels and lintels display Art Nouveau organic growth and the *garde-fous* have playfully floral but sinuous ironwork.

★[16a-10.] **Logements, 6, rue des Pâtures**, between rue Félicien-David and avenue de Versailles. **Jean Ginsberg** and **François Heep.** 1937.

A small toothy *immeuble* in an appropriate scale: seven levels and a pleasant cubistic play of form. Modern architecture should have been more like this, displaying character and an elegance of detail in the wood window frames, railings, and light wrought-iron balustrades.

★★[16a-11.] **Logements, 42, avenue de Versailles**, corner rue des Pâtures. **Jean Ginsberg, François Heep**, and **Maurice Breton.** 1933.

Another way to turn a corner *(Haussmannian pans coupés),* dating from the passionate 1930s. **No. 25** down the block is a simpler but more elegantly considered building. This is a bit of a splash—too didactic and self-conscious, perhaps, but an important remnant from those hardy years.

[16a-12.] **Logements, 3, rue Degas,** corner avenue de Versailles. **Gilbert.** 1935.

This owes more to its rich orange-ocher tile than to any strong architectural form or detail. An understatement of form; an overstatement of surface.

[16a-13.] **Logements, 32, quai Louis-Blériot**, between rue Degas and place Clément-Ader. **G. Lesou.** 1932.

Nothing remarkable, but one of a row of developing styles along the quai. There are several to savor, including **Nos. 10** and **12–16,** No. 32, **No. 36 (Compoint** and **Beaulieu.** 1931) and **No. 44** (circa 1932).

★[16a-14.] **Logements, 40, quai Louis-Blériot,** between rue Degas and place Clément-Ader. **Marteroy** and **Bonnel.** 1932.

Tile again (see 3, rue Degas), but more subtle and complex, flecked with gold as it rises, darkening and ending in an Art Deco frieze of blues, browns, and gold. Otherwise, its mannerisms include that 1930s symbol, rampant oculi.

★[16a-15.] **Logements, 31–33, avenue de Versailles,** opposite rue Florence-Blumenthal.

Glassy flat and bay windows enliven these brick, stone, and—yes, *wrought-iron*—facades. 1890s.

★[16a-16.] **Logements, 29, avenue de Versailles,** between rue Pierre-Louÿs and rue Florence-Blumenthal. **B. Boessé.** 1929.

Gracious ateliers in an architecture by no means in the same class as **No. 25.** If someone could wash the windows, matters would be clearer.

★★[16a-17.] 25, avenue de Versailles, between rue Pierre-Louÿs and place Clément-Ader. **Jean Ginsberg** and **Berthold Lubetkin**. 1931.

An elegant modern *immeuble,* worth of the **CIAM** (Congrès International d'Architecture Moderne) and the *International Style*'s accolades. It is still fresh and crisp; note the wonderful curved glass at the terraces. It makes you wonder where "modern" architecture, including Ginsberg's, went astray. Lubetkin was a strong presence here, as in his famous Penguin Pool (1933) at the London Zoo.

[16a-18.] Logements, 16, avenue de Versailles, between rue Pierre-Louÿs and place Clément-Ader. **P. Branche**. 1954.

The ghost of the late **Frères Perret** hovers over this taut concrete grillage, a no-nonsense building with the vertical window proportions traditional to Paris, however (also encore Perret). Branche was certainly *not branché.*

[16a-19.] Logements, 9, rue de Boulainvilliers, between rue Gros and rue La Fontaine. **Roger Taillibert**. 1987.

A visually noisy island for the common man amid the sea of the affluent. Unfortunately, it's not in the same class architecturally as much of the housing for its residents' confrères in the 19th and 20th arrondissements.

★[16a-20.] Ecole, 16, rue Gros, between place Clément-Ader and rue La Fontaine. **Roger Taillibert**. 1985.

Red steel sash and tan tile—it seems appropriate for children, one of those intrusions that many find a necessary cut into the urban form. Why do children need a "house" scale and no stairs in a city where apartments and stairs are the norm?

★★★★[16a-21.] Castel Béranger, 14, rue La Fontaine, between rue de l'Assomption and avenue du Recteur-Poincaré. **Hector Guimard.** 1898.

Certainly his *chef-d'oeuvre,* this is a complex *immeuble* of polychromatic brick (some glazed), stone (both *pierre de taille calcaire* and *meulière*), and the wonderful, inevitable wrought iron. The entrance gate, a worldwide symbol of Art Nouveau, opened the same year that Samuel Bing named this namesake's shop, L'Art Nouveau. Stroll down Hameau Béranger adjacent and savor the interior court from afar. Then buzz yourself in to that same court for a tactile view.

★[16a-22.] Conservatoire Municipal de Musique du XVIe Arrondissment, rue La Fontaine, corner rue Gros. **Roger Taillibert**. 1988.

At first it seemed that the "arcane" symbolism of cut-stone windows on rue La Fontaine had an iconographic Levantine significance. These "exclamation points" do well to classify this intrusive white stone presence as a gaudy monochrome that does some insult to the serene polychromy of Guimard *en face.*

★[16a-23a.] Café/Bar Guimard, 17, rue La Fontaine. **Hector Guimard.** 1911.

Guimard delivers elegance at the commercial level.

★★[16a-24.] Logements, 19 and 21, rue La Fontaine, flanking rue Agar and 8 and 10, rue Agar. **Hector Guimard.** 1911.

Little of the lush detail celebrated on Castel Béranger subsists here, but the ironwork twists with elegance and the stone flows under the carvers' hands. This is an economy model, a Rolls-Royce without the Flying Lady, burled walnut dash, and leather upholstery. But the basic lines are still there.

★[16a-25.] Immeuble Tremois, 11, rue François-Millet, between rue La Fontaine and rue Théophile-Gautier. **Hector Guimard.** 1910.

Another popularized Guimard, the bread and butter after the passion and complexity of Castel Béranger.

[16a-26.] Logements, 18–20 rue Théophile-Gautier, corner rue François-Millet. **Charles Blanche.** 1899.

Those elegant *saillies* that were permitted as bay windows under the 1892 law.

[16a-27.] Logements, 21 and 23, rue Théophile-Gautier, between rue Gros and avenue Perrichont. **Deneu de Montbrun,** architect. **P. de Folleville,** sculptor. 1907.

★★[16a-28.] Hôtel Mezzara, 60, rue La Fontaine, between avenue Léopold II and rue Ribéra. **Hector Guimard.** 1911.

Guimard's Art Nouveau sinuousity is a matter of stone as well as iron. The plastic flow attempts to enliven and extend a static space between what is now a Haussmanian model to the south and a 1960s modernist to the north.

★★★[16a-29.] Logements, 3, avenue Boudon, between rue La Fontaine and rue George-Sand. **Bernard Reichen** and **Philippe Robert.** 1979.

*Grand standing* redeemed by architects who fit within the Haussmannian envelope despite the absence of Haussmanian buildings here. The bay windows and *garde-fous* all have elegant detailing; the metal, glass, and *pierre de taille* are neatly tailored. And those drooping plants! They knew about Mies, Wright, Perret, and Prouvé but did their own thing anyway. *Lovely.*

[16a-30.] Logements, 25, rue George-Sand, between rue La Fontaine and avenue Mozart. **Gabriel Brun.** 1914–1922.

★[16a-31.] "Studio Building," 65, 65 bis, and 65 ter, rue La Fontaine, 2–4, rue du Général-Largeau, and 21, rue des Perchamps. **Henri Sauvage.** 1926. **Alphonse Gentil** and **François Bourdet,** ceramists.

A pre-PoMo, or whence comes the contrasting tile, before its 1980s rediscovery? A fat, bulky box relieved by its polychromatic bay windows and by the jump of scale from studios to flats. Sauvage's greatness was often errant; this is a studied and somewhat vulgar building.

★★[16a-32.] Hotel Guimard, 122, avenue Mozart, between rue du Capitaine-Olschanski and rue de la Source. **Hector Guimard.** 1909.

Guimard lived and worked here, while his wife, Adeline Oppenheim Guimard, painted. He moved here from Castel Béranger after his marriage, for his wife's fortune permitted him to build this sinuous and somber house exactly to their wishes. Note the elegant *garde-fous* at the second floor and the dormer windows that seem to scoop the light of the sky.

**[16a-33.] Maison, 2, villa Flore**, off avenue Mozart. **Hector Guimard**. 1926.

Late Guimard.

**★[16a-34.] Garage Citroën**, 11 bis and 13, rue de la Source, corner avenue Mozart. **Pol Abraham**. circa 1930.

The concrete frame and serrated glass facade punctuate these Haussmannian blocks for the auto. The infill, off-white and black, nevertheless respects the *gabarit.*

**★[16a-35.] Logements, 2, rue Chamfort**, corner rue de la Source. 1890s.

Metal and glass bay windows articulated in off-white armatures, and brown, roll-down, accordion shutters—like your old desk. Elegant foils on a plain brick body.

**[16a-36.] Logements, 37, rue Ribéra**, between rue de la Source and avenue Mozart. **José Imbert**. circa 1975.

Imbert, obsessed with Classical detritus, again brings his concrete training to the 16th arrondissement (see rue de Franqueville **[16p-34.]**). But here the image is hardly unique. Next door both caryatids and Composite columns abound around terrace spaces.

**★[16a-37.] Logements, 41, rue Ribéra**, between rue de la Source and avenue Mozart. **Jean-Marie Boussard**. 1894.

Three discrete caryatids at the third floor support the fourth, and Composite columns below allow balconies and ironwork. It makes Imbert's banal "modern" next door seem like a gelded pastiche.

**[16a-38.] Logements, 4, rue Jasmin**, corner **rue de l'Yvette. Jean-Marie Boussard**. 1909.

Atlantes and bosomy maidens enrich this grandiloquence, providing something to react against for those down the street on rue Jasmin and, around the corner, on square du Docteur-Blanche and rue Mallet-Stevens.

**[16a-39.] Immeuble, 6, rue Jasmin**, at square Jasmin. **Jean-Marie Boussard**. 1914–1916.

More Boussard.

**★[16a-39a.] Maison, 3, square Jasmin**, off rue Jasmin. **Hector Guimard**. 1922.

Concerned more with the technology of construction than with aesthetic presence, this is late Guimard. This is *precast concrete*, which Guimard hoped would provide housing in the aftermath of the First World War's great loss of life—and, therefore, unhappily—manpower for construction.

**★[16a-40.]** Originally **Collège Montmorency**, 15, rue Henri-Heine, corner rue Jasmin. **Pol Abraham**. 1930.

A single complex of classrooms, library, offices, and eighteen rooms for American graduate students. It is an event to write home about, not one to *look at.* **Abraham** was a theorist whose built work here smacked of self-flagellating penitence.

★[16a-41.] **Logements, 18 bis-18, rue Henri-Heine,** between rue Jasmin and rue du Docteur-Blanche. **Hector Guimard.** 1926.

*"C'est un immeuble bourgeois de bonne tenue, qui n'exhibe pas son rang avec l'ostentation d'un parvenue 'haussmannien,' mais dont le dessin est conçu avec finesse pour dégager le regard du niveau de la rue et le conduire progressivement, par émerveillements successifs, jusqu'a la pyramide qui couronne le salon du dernier étage."* **Paul Chemetov, et al.** *Architecture à Paris 1919–1939.*

★[16a-42.] **Maison, 24, rue Jasmin,** between rue Henri-Heine and rue Raffet. circa 1925.

Bay windows prow the street, with vestigial Doric fluted half-columns rising between. And the ironwork tries hard.

★[16a-43.] **Logements, 40, rue Jasmin,** corner rue Raffet. **Antoine Morosoli.** 1929.

Brown precast concrete curved and balconied. An early streamliner at rest in this jet-set-section-to-be.

★★★★[16a-44.] **Villas La Roche** and **Jeanneret,** 8-10, square du Docteur-Blanche, off rue du Docteur-Blanche. **Le Corbusier** (Charles-Edouard Jeanneret). 1924.

Some buildings are worth writing home about; a few are worth leaving home for. This pair is in the latter category. Few will have the opportunity both to see and experience internally and externally the remarkable talent of this great architect, one of the five who changed the course of 20th-century architecture, with Frank Lloyd Wright, Mies van de Rohe, Louis Kahn, and Aalvar Aalto. Unfortunately, his ideas on urbanism have obscured for some his immense talent for working within a small scale and controlled parameters. In the latter category, are included buildings ranging from the **Monastery of La Tourette** and the pilgrimage church at **Ronchamp,** to the **Villa Savoye** at Poissy (western suburb of Paris) and the **Villa Stein** at Garches. But here a cul-de-sac scale of urbanism was conceived, although only two of the whole enclave were finally constructed, one for his friend, the banker **Raoul La Roche,** the other for his brother, **Albert Jeanneret,** the musician.

The La Roche house is now the museum of both itself, its space, and exhibits of Corbusian history; Villa Jeanneret houses the **Fondation Le Corbusier.** Within La Roche a great ramp sails up by the sleek exedral windows.

[16a-45a.] **Musée Henri-Bouchard,** 25, rue de l'Yvette, between rue du Docteur-Blanche and rue Jasmin. 1924.

★★[16a-46.] **Logements, 19, rue du Docteur-Blanche**, rue de l'Yvette and rue Mallet-Stevens. **Massé, Jean Ginsberg,** and **Alinsky.** 1953.

In 1954 this was postwar Paris's most thoughtful modern architecture and, atop it all, a duplex apartment with swimming pool–terrace for one of the architects.

Who wouldn't then dream of the rosy architectural future? With care, a renewed facade would sparkle. Bring it back. The long, flanking, low wings are a good transition to the streetfront; under the *pilotis* you can see the garden behind.

★★★★[16a-47.] **Rue Mallet-Stevens,** off rue du Docteur-Blanche, between rue de l'Yvette and rue de l'Assomption. **Robert Mallet-Stevens.** 1927.

A brilliant and stylish designer, Mallet-Stevens worked at once on stage designs, movie sets, and apartment and shop interiors. His approach to architecture was as a cubistic modeler, and the ensemble of his cul-de-sac (named for him while he was still living) is a test of the theater of the street—more successful, on reflection, in its parts than in its whole. Glasswork, *grilles*, doors, and ironwork were the careful studies of variegated talent, including work by **Pierre Chareau** (Maison de Verre, [**7c-36.**]). But these were in fact *hôtels particuliers* for the rich, not multiple dwellings for the bourgeois or less.

His close collaboration with **Marcel L'Herbier** produced the sets of a dozen films, including *L'Inhumaine* (1923), *Le Diable au coeur* (1924), *Le Vertige* (1928), and *L'Argent* (1928).

★[16a-48.] Logements, 5, rue du Docteur-Blanche, between rue Mallet-Stevens and rue de L'Assomption. **Pierre Patout**. 1928.

Studios again in an equivocal moderne; the ironwork seeks ingenuity, but it is a confused whole. The later setback of **No. 7** is a shame, taking away the smooth street front participation of No. 5.

[16a-49.] Immeuble, 143, rue du Ranelagh, corner boulevard de Beauséjour. **Emile Bainier**. 1901.

*Retardataire* Flemish neo-Renaissance—but with panache.

[16a-50.] Avenue des Chalets, entry at 101 bis, rue du Ranelagh, opposite avenue Vion-Whitcomb.

Stone, timber, and picturesque profiles for the identity of those in search of such: a pleasant private world, of the sort that repeats itself in the middle of many Auteuil blocks. Try **3 bis, square du Ranelagh** next door.

★★[16a-51.] Logements, 5, avenue Vion-Whitcomb, off rue du Ranelagh. **Jean Ginsberg** and **François Heep**. 1935.

*Grand standing* when new was grander than old. There is a definite relationship between this precocious travertine building and that of Le Corbusier at 24, rue Nungesser-et-Coli, three years earlier. But, as they say, if you copy someone, copy someone good.

The detailing is excellent—sometimes even elegant, except at the ground floor.

[16a-52.] Logements, 11, avenue Vion-Whitcomb, off rue du Ranelagh. **Christian and Herve de Galera**. 1985.

Fifty, count them, fifty, years after **No. 5,** this gross vulgarian intrudes (and withdraws) to banalize (more travertine) this private street. Perhaps *clients* should be awarded aesthetic licenses, to protect the public from their selection of specious architecture.

Return to the rue du Ranelagh and avenue Mozart, for Métro Ranelagh.

# 42
# SIXTEENTH ARRONDISSEMENT
## CHAILLOT

### PALAIS DE CHAILLOT TO CIMETIERE DE PASSY

Palais de Chaillot: **Jacques Carlu, Léon Azéma,** and
**Louis-Hippolyte Boileau;** Musée Guimet; Palais Galliera: **Louis
Ginain;** Église Saint-Pierre-de-Chaillot: **Emile Bois;** Musée d' Art
Moderne de la Ville de Paris/Palais de Tokio: **Alfred Aubert et al.;**
Conseil Economique et Social: **Auguste Perret;** 25 bis, rue Franklin:
**Auguste and Gustave Perret;** 17, rue Franklin: **Marcel and
Robert Hennequet;** 39, rue Scheffer: **Ernest Herscher;** Cimetière de
Passy entrance: **René Berger**

Métro: **Trocadéro**

**[16c-13.] Eglise Saint-Pierre-de-Chaillot. Emile Bois,** architect. **Jean
Bouchard,** sculptor. 1933–1937.

Before the Revolution, little attention was paid to the small village of **Chaillot,** resting on the north slopes of its hill (crowned by the modern **Trocadéro**), roughly between the modern avenue Marceau, avenue Kléber, and the Seine. The waters of Passy and Auteuil, and their location on the royal route to Versailles, were two stimulating attractions for modest development of those villages. But Chaillot did not gain any focused attention until the First Empire and, in particular, as a site selected by Napoléon for the palace of his son, the future king of Rome. "I wish," he said, "to create, in a word, a Kremlin a hundred times more beautiful than that of Moscow. It will be my imperial city, the Napoleonic city." Ironically, Cossacks, part of the victorious allied armies that defeated Napoléon, camped on this site in 1815.

Foundations were actually laid in 1811 **(Percier and Fontaine)** before the fall of the Empire and, of course, were later abandoned. Nevertheless, these first works led to the initial topping of the hill, work that continued with the development of its crest: well articulated by the old Cimetière de Passy, a remnant of the ancient topography, that now sits behind vast retaining walls on a prominence overlooking the *place.*

The name Trocadéro commemorates the victory in 1823 of the duc d'Angoulême, who captured the fort of this name near Cádiz, in a war to restore Ferdinand VII to absolute power on the Spanish throne. To glorify that victory, a monument was proposed for Chaillot; one proposal took the form of a Classical temple, another called for an obelisk with fountains. A mock fort was actually built so that troops could "storm" it on the anniversary of the victory of Trocadéro.

For the better part of the 19th century the surrounding land was the property of the Delessert family but it was not developed until the late 1840s. Modest subdivision was then undertaken, and the exposition of 1867 gave rise to the hill's first use for substantial public building. In 1878 a memorable structure arrived, the Palais du Trocadéro **(Gabriel Davioud)**. Built on the axis of the Champ de Mars and Ecole Militaire (no Eiffel Tower yet), it had a footprint that became the skeleton within the 1937 Palais de Chaillot. That Palace now forms a symbiosis with the Eiffel Tower and the Champ de Mars, one of the city's major axial events, second only to the Louvre–Arc de Triomphe–Grande Arche ensemble.

★★★[16c-1.] **Palais de Chaillot,** place du Trocadéro, restrained by rue Franklin and avenue du Président-Wilson. **Jacques Carlu, Léon Azéma,** and **Louis-Hippolyte Boileau,** 1937.

This building, much despised by modern architects in the postwar years as a flaccid, pseudomodern, neo-Classic pastiche, is again beloved: by some (including a gaggle of Post Modern architects) for its surviving Classicism, and by others for its brilliant role in urban design. Carlu's stroke of genius was in removing the central pavilion from the 1878 Davioud building (he used the inner structure of the curved wings, adding to them), to open an axial vista to the Eiffel Tower. *Le Figaro* quipped at the time, "The architect removed the building's belly but left its wings." This void is a much more powerful statement than any volume. The stepped gardens below **(Roger-Henri Expert, P. Thiers,** and **A. Maître,** 1937), cascading to the Seine, make a splendid visual forecourt for the Tour Eiffel, particularly at night. The lighted fountains work in counterpoint to the tower's intraskeletal lighting, enlisting every bone in the service of its rightful filigree.

The spectrum of museums and activities within ranges from the Musée de la Marine to the Cinémathèque. But for architecture buffs the great events are those at the **Musée des Monuments Français** (every day but Tuesday). The brainchild of **Viollet-le-Duc,** Frank Lloyd Wright's favorite Frenchman, the museum opened in 1882 in the Palais du Trocadéro (the ghost within). Although nominally a museum of sculpture, it is by default a museum of architectural details (full-scale copies, cast in plaster) of buildings from Merovingian times to the 18th century, and includes models of whole buildings and complexes. Have you ever wondered what the Crusad-

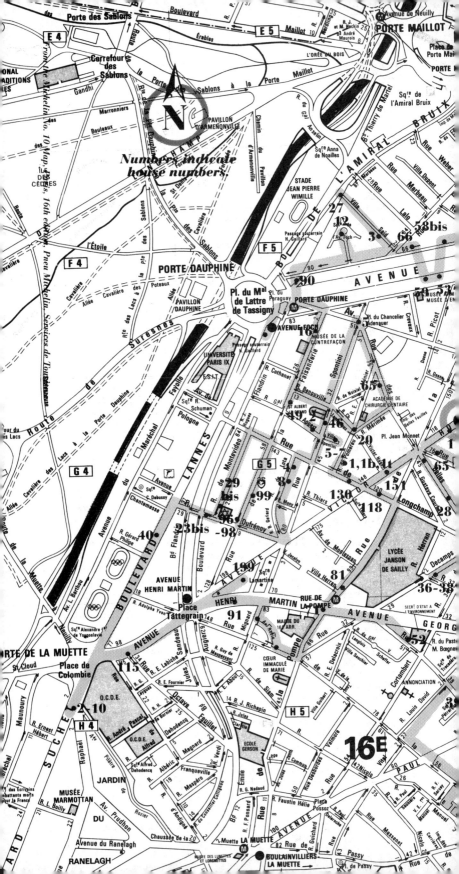

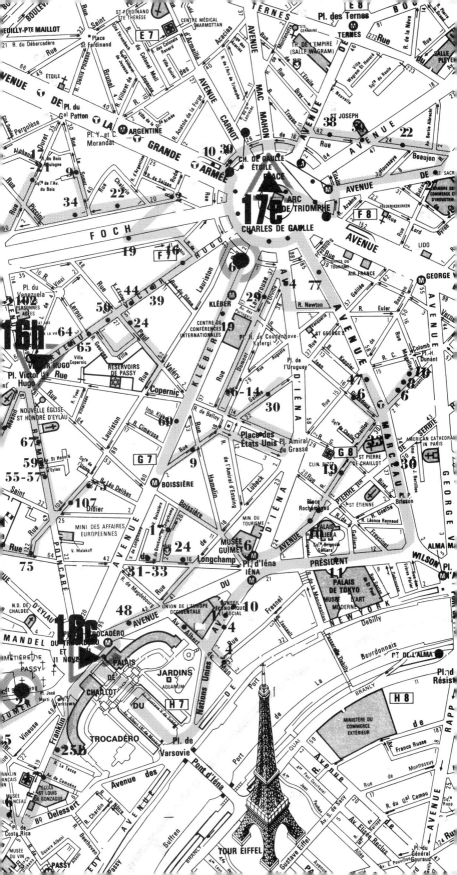

ers' castle in Syria looked like? Or the Romanesque abbey and church of Cluny?

One excellent possibility is that of comparing the detail of medieval facades standing in the same room.

**[16c-2.] Immeuble, 48, avenue du President-Wilson**, between place du Trocadéro and rue de Magdebourg. **Charles Adda**. 1908.

A breakaway attempt by someone who feared the Art Nouveau. The colonnade at the fourth floor and the balconies everywhere give it a lush plasticity.

**★[16c-3.] Immeuble, 24, rue de Longchamp**, between rue de Lubeck and rue du Bouquet-de-Longchamp. **H. Dubouillon**. 1930s.

Cubistic console brackets and vestigial dentils support the central bay. The ironwork well represents the 1930s.

**[16c-4.] Immeuble, 31-33, rue de Longchamp**, between rue du Bouquet-de-Longchamp and avenue Kléber. **Charles Lefèbvre**. 1899.

Three-story Composite pilasters, with their mates, the usual monster console brackets. *Vigoureux!*

**[16c-5.] Immeuble, 17, rue du Bouquet-de-Longchamp**, between rue de Longchamp and rue Boissière. **François Bertaux**. 1908.

Bay windows with supporting strap-iron bracketwork in a field of polychromatic brick. A crisp presence.

**★[16c-6.] Musée Guimet/Collection Nationale d'Art Asiatique**, 6, place d'Iéna, between avenue d'Iéna and rue Hamelin. 1885.

Look up! *Helicarnassus*: a pierced, freestanding colonnade supports this Asiatic dome, from a time when Greece, Ionic division, was Asia Minor.

A very dry exterior otherwise. Within is the original collection of oriental art donated by Emile Guimet, supplemented both in situ and by the collections of the Louvre.

**★★[16c-7.] Palais Galliera/Musée de la Mode et du Costume**, 10, avenue Pierre Ier-de-Serbie, off place Rochambeau. **Louis Ginain**. 1892.

An extravagant Beaux Arts *hôtel particulier*, built as a museum. The rear garden (it seems like the front), facing the Palais de Tokyo, is unusual: the space in front of such an *hôtel* was usually walled and paved. Here the scale of a château is sought.

The building was originally intended as a repository for 17th-century Italian Baroque art, but that collection went elsewhere, and the husk was left to the City of Paris.

**[16c-8.] Place Rochambeau**, at the crossing of avenue Pierre Ier-de-Serbie, rue de Chaillot, and rue Freycinet.

A pleasant triangle in front of the Musée Galliera, this honors the comte de Rochambeau, commander of the French army at the battle of Yorktown (1781).

**[16c-9.] Maison de l'Architecture**, 7, rue de Chaillot, at place Rochambeau.

The contents (★★), not the building, are what matters here: temporary expositions, particularly of the young architects of France.

**[16c-10.] Logements, 19, rue de Chaillot**, between rue Freycinet and rue Georges-Bizet. **André Biro** and **Jean-Jacques Fernier**. 1981.

*Grand standing*—and, of course, one veneers it with (what else?) travertine, crested with glassed balconies. Here is more architecture for the Hollywood set in Paris.

**[16c-11.] Bureaux, 6, rue Jean-Giraudoux**, between avenue Marceau and rue de Bassano. **Pierre Figarol**. 1929.

The avant-garde in this retardataire quarter, but in a pasty stuccoed concrete. The new windows have dispelled Figarol's spirit, for in the architecture of the 1920s details were scant, and hence detailing was of paramount importance. Many buildings of the era have been similarly trashed.

**[16c-12.] Logements, 6, 8,** and **10 rue Quentin-Bauchart**, between avenue Marceau and avenue George V. No. 8, **Ernest Bertrand**. 1927. No. 10, **H. Dupusse**. 1927.

The Classical-Modern wars here are illustrated in their life-throes: No. 6, the anonymous best of the triad, is bold and trendy, with high bay windows crisply breasting the street; No. 8 has a recessed torso and wings achieving the form of giant columns; No. 10 tries floral bas-reliefs to update its Classicism.

**★[16c-13.] Eglise Saint-Pierre-de-Chaillot**, 33, avenue Marceau, between rue de Chaillot and avenue Pierre-Ier-de-Serbie. **Emile Bois**, architect. **Jean Bouchard**, sculptor. 1933–1937.

There is a gesture to the Romanesque in its arched and sculpted triple portal. This chunky, prismatic stone church stops 'em dead on the bland avenue Marceau.

**[16c-14.] Teinturerie Huguet**/originally **Grande Teinturerie de Chaillot**, 47, avenue Marceau, between rue Jean-Giraudoux and rue de Bassano. 19th century.

Neo–18th-century, built in the middle of the 19th, and still around for the 21st. If you can afford the prices, the interiors are a handsome fringe benefit.

**★[16c-15.] Logements, 30, avenue Marceau,** between avenue Pierre Ier-de-Serbie and avenue du Président-Wilson. **André Granet**. 1916.

A stone vineyard friezes the cornice, and a hovering hood marks the pedimented grand balcony for the chief vintner. An en-snaked radical marquise speaks of modern *fer et verre*, as do the *garde-fous*.

**★★★[16c-16.] Musée d'Art Moderne de la Ville de Paris/Palais de Tokio**, 11, avenue du Président-Wilson, between rue Gaston-de-Saint-Paul and rue de la Manutention. **Alfred Aubert, D. Dastugue, J. C. Dondel,** and **Paul Viard**. 1937. Reconstruction, museums of photography, cinema. **Franck Hammoutène**. 1990.

Through this and its 1937 neighbors, the hill of Chaillot became a haven of 1930s neo-Classical monuments: Palais de Chaillot, Musée des Travaux Publics, Eglise Saint-Pierre-de-Chaillot, in the manner that geographical development leaves a sea of style in any developing quarter (the 16th, 17th, and 18th centuries in the Marais, the late 20th century spreading over the whole east of Paris).
It is neo-Classical in that architecturally merged world of the late 1930s. Speer admired it, but so did the bureaucrats of Washington and Moscow.

The columned void between the Modern (to the north) and the Tokio (to the south), the square piers on the avenue that become round columns on three sides of the court, the concavely curved west facade—all these were popular mannerisms of French architecture of the time.

★★[16c-17.] Conseil Economique et Social/originally Musée des Travaux Publics, 1, avenue d'Iéna, at avenue du Président-Wilson and avenue d'Iéna. Auguste Perret. 1937.

Concrete concrete. Tapered and fluted columns, with a soupçon of entasis and a floating stair that honors the idea of *béton armé* (for tension): a tense ribbed ribbon. Perret and his brothers were general contractors, but Auguste in particular adapted the new technology of concrete to a largely neo-Classical aesthetic here and at the Mobilier National (1934). Earlier, he had been more daring (down the street at 25 bis, rue Franklin), but that may have been a matter of youthful abandon, before he saw the light of Classicism. At rue Franklin, he was twenty-nine at the moment of design; here he was sixty-three.

[16c-18.] Centre Français du Commerce Extérieur/originally Hôtel du Prince Roland Bonaparte, 10, avenue d'Iéna, off place d'Iéna. Janty. 1899. Remodeled, Michel Roux-Spitz. 1929.

John Soane Regency at the top (or is it simple protocubism?) with lush Beaux Arts supported by atlantes below.

[16c-19.] Ambassade d'Iran/formerly Hôtel du Comte de Combacéres. 4, avenue d'Iéna, between avenue Albert-de-Mun and place d'Iéna. Xavier Schoellkopf. 1898. Boussard. 1909.

A 19th-century *hôtel particulier*, in white limestone and gendarmes, that wants to be 18th-century. A strange environment for representatives of the late ayatollah from Qum.

★[16c-20.] Immeuble, 4, avenue Albert-de-Mun, corner rue Fresnel. Jean Fidler. 1934.

Elegant white-painted ships' railings and a cubist's play of curves and rectangles overlook the park of the Palais de Chaillot.

[16c-21.] Direction des Phares, avenue Albert-de-Mun, between avenue d'Iéna and avenue du Président-Wilson.

A 19th-century brick-and-limestone "lighthouse" with an almost-Hawksmoor power. Here are great console brackets and a wonderful broken pediment.

★★★[16c-22.] Logements, 25 bis, rue Franklin, between place du Trocadéro and rue Scheffer. Auguste and Gustave Perret. 1904.

Vintage Perret. Concrete is glorified in this early skeleton of apartments. But all is veneered with *grès de Bigot*, flat, floral, and geometric. These cool clear lines are the best of Perret, who could later be quite heavy-handed.
    Would that his colleagues and students—Imbert, among them—had inherited his spirit rather than his manners.
    In 1952, Perret, in remembrance of this early work, wrote: "The structure orders the appearance of this building, and those who conceal any portion of the frame deprive themselves of the single legitimate and finest ornament of architecture."

**Le Corbusier** wrote of his experiences: "I knew Auguste Perret at the beginning of 1908. Arriving in Paris with no relations and no money, I felt horribly alone for several days. A decision: I knocked at the door of Eugène Grasset and explained myself: 'Here is my problem: I can't enter the Ecole des Beaux Arts. Where is modern architecture, who are the creative architects?'

"He answered: 'why did you come to Paris, for there aren't any, there is nobody. Reactionary (architecture) is everything: The 19th century's era of iron has served for nothing. . . . Nevertheless, go see the Perret brothers. . . . They build with reinforced concrete.'

"The Perrets served at that time in a new function: the Builder. They were not only engineers, not only architects, but both. Good fortune allowed them to play the role, including temperament, a family business tradition, and the capital that they needed, plus the presence of a third brother, Claude, who did everything that the pencil couldn't do.

"They had already to their credit, since 1905 or 1906, the rental building, 25 bis, rue Franklin: a trailblazer of the modern period."

★[16c-23.] **Logements, 17, rue Franklin,** corner rue Scheffer. **Marcel and Robert Hennequet.** 1928.

Precocious in style, this multifaceted collection of bay windows has a new and temporary look, as if it were folded cardboard for the world's largest model. But it brought a glassy openness, in contrast to the heavy masonry windows of its neighbors. Perret, on the next block, has more style in the "forever" sense rather than Hennequet's stylishness.

★[16c-24.] **Hôtel Regina de Passy,** 6, rue de la Tour, between place de Costa-Rica and avenue Paul-Doumer. **Gabriel Brun.** 1930.

Those four stacks of bay windows are the heart of this hotel; the rest is awkward, all clad in tiny geometric and/or random tiles. A street with bays like that could give a bit of juice to Haussmannianism, while respecting his urban discipline.

★★[16c-25.] **Logements, 9, rue Claude-Chahu,** corner rue Eugène-Manuel. **Charles Klein,** architect. **Emile Muller,** ceramist. 1903.

Muller's terra-cotta takes over in polychromatic but muted greens, ochers, and spots of red. The entrance doors show a bit of *nouille*, but it is mostly a dreamy pastiche of Art Nouveau on a Classical body. Extravagant.

an aside:

[16c-26.] **Immeuble, 77, avenue Paul-Doumer**, corner rue Paul-Delaroche. **Armand and Pierre Sibien**, architects. **Pierre Seguin**, sculptor. 1901.

Look up at those tiered balconies, which give this cornered block a strongly cadaverous quallty.

★[16c-27.] **Logements, 39, rue Scheffer,** corner rue Louis-David. **Ernest Herscher,** architect. **Pierre Seguin,** sculptor. 1911.

*Lucarnes en parasol* float above an intricate cornice. This exuberant departure from Classicism touches on the Art Nouveau, becoming increasingly clumsy as it descends to the street.

[16c-28.] **Logements, 25, avenue Paul-Doumer**, corner rue Scheffer. **Roger Anger, Mario Heymann, Pierre Puccinelli**, and **L. Veber**. 1965.

Apartments in a sleek block that offers a sexy corner, instead of a *pan coupé*, on a body that could well be in downtown Athens. Marble can be a filthy material in an air-polluted city.

★★[16c-29.] **Cimetière de Passy**, 2, avenue Paul-Doumer, at place du Trocadéro. First interments, 1874. New gates and entrance pavilions (★★), **René Berger**. 1937. Bas-reliefs, **Janthial**.

Here repose **Manet, Cognacq-Jay** (founder of La Samaritaine), **Gabriel Fauré, Fernandel, Debussy, Giraudoux, Lefuel** (Napoléon III's architect for the Louvre), the decorator **Jacques-Emile Ruhlmann,** whose tomb is by the architect Pierre Patout—all at the former crest of the hill of Chaillot. The view is magnificent. All of the place du Trocadéro was once at this level.

The entrance gates and lodge are a spirited work by René Berger, architect of the tropical greenhouses in the **Jardin des Plantes [5e-24.].**

# 43
# SIXTEENTH ARRONDISSEEMENT
## VICTOR HUGO

### PLACE VICTOR-HUGO THROUGH PASSY

### AND BACK

Place Victor Hugo; 50, avenue Victor-Hugo: **Charles Plumet;** Restaurant Prunier Traktir: **Louis-Hippolyte Boileau;** 58 bis, avenue Foch: **Alfred Fasquelle;** 53, avenue Foch: **Charles Abella;** Musée d'Ennery; 27, villa Saïd: **Auguste Perret;** Métro Dauphine: **Hector Guimard;** St. James Club: **Alfred Aldrophe;** Institut Supérieur de Gestion: **William Bouwens van der Boijen;** Logements: **Michel Roux-Spitz, Jean Walter,** and **Charles Thomas;** Mairie: **Godeboeuf;** Cinéma Victor-Hugo: **Jean Charaval** and **Marcel Mélendes;** Hôtel Pauilhac: **Charles Letrosne;** Caserne des Sapeurs/Pompiers: **Robert Mallet-Stevens;** Cité Commercial d'Argentine: **Henri Sauvage**

Métro: **Victor Hugo**

**[16h-57.] Hôtel Pauilhac. Charles Letrosne,** architect. **Camille Garnier,** sculptor. 1911.

**★★[16h-1.] Place Victor Hugo.**

A decimal *rond-point*, its radiating spokes gather a precinct into a discipline that includes avenue Victor-Hugo, avenue Foch, the Quartier Dauphine, and the surrounds of the place de Mexico. The grand fountain here will cool your eyes, while you cool your throat at a surrounding café. Victor himself was once mounted on the pedestal at the center, but was a casualty of World War II. Guimard was also here, as designer of the Métro entrance.

**★[16h-2.] Garage Citroën,** 64, avenue Victor-Hugo, between place Victor-Hugo and rue Leroux. 1930s.

An almost no-nonsense white concrete structure, with some vestigial Classical framework and two added stories of bland commercial "modern" on top. Interrupting many Haussmannian boulevards, these showplaces of the mass-produced automobile asserted the technocratic wonder of the automobile through similar architectural attitudes. A serious event.

**★[16h-3.] Logements, 65, avenue Victor-Hugo**, at rue Georges-Ville. **A. Sélonier.** 1902.

The bow window gives a graceful swelling and a maximum of glass to this Belle Epoque doyenne. Up rue Georges-Ville the whole street is by Sélonier (1904–1911).

**★[16h-4.] Logements, 50, avenue Victor-Hugo,** between rue Leroux and rue Paul-Valéry. **Charles Plumet.** 1902.

"Adroitly, and with a remarkable versatility, the architect has been able to avoid startling those who worship the 18th century, and, surreptitiously, he has slipped modern elements into a Louis XVI interior décor that makes an elegant marriage of reason." **Frantz Jourdain** in *Art et Decoration,* May 1903.
Behind is the **Fondation Dapper** in a bourgeois house of 1910.

**[16h-5.] Immeuble, 24, rue Paul-Valéry**, between avenue Victor-Hugo and rue Lauriston.

Fancy brickwork with Art Nouveau iron; atop is a pergola and gabled, decorated dormers.

**[16h-6.] Réservoir de Passy,** between rue Paul-Valéry, rue Lauriston, and rue Copernic.

Like a giant Egyptian mastaba, here are battered walls (touch that volcanic texture of *meulière*) and limestone quoins. Within, the clear waters water Passy.

**★[16h-7.] Logements, 39, avenue Victor-Hugo,** between rue Paul-Valéry and rue du Dôme. **Charles Plumet.** 1913.

Oak leaves enrich this portal and the soffit of the first-floor bay windows, and serpentine iron wends its way in the *garde-fous* and *petits balcons.* An arcade at the fourth floor bears more soffited leaves and incised decor, with hooded "eyebrows" leering from the *comble.*

**[16h-8.] Villa d'Eylau,** 44, avenue Victor-Hugo, between rue Paul-Valéry and rue de Traktir.

A gated cul-de-sac with three- and four-level mansarded miniatures of the boulevard from which they branch. The modern "behinds" at the left are in glossy contrast to the sober brick-and-sandstone facades that they reflect.

**★★[16h-9.] Restaurant Prunier Traktir,** 16, avenue Victor-Hugo, at rue de Traktir. **Louis-Hippolyte Boileau** and **Léon Carrière**. circa 1925.

Art Deco expressed in black marble, molten glass, and onyx. A designated *monument historique.*

**[16h-10.]** Originally **Hôtel Rothschild**, 19, avenue Foch, between rue de Traktir and rue Paul-Valéry. 1850s.

A vast private garden for the Rothschilds supplements this early Napoléon III *hôtel particulier.*

**[16h-11.] Ambassade d'Irlande**/originally **Hôtel du Marquis de Breteuil**, 2, rue Rude, corner avenue Foch.

Here putti surmount the balustrades of a grand *hôtel particulier.*

**[16h-12.] Immeuble, 22, avenue Foch**, between rue Chalgrin and rue Lesueur. **Alexandre Durville**. 1893.

Corinthian pilasters make this an appropriate place for the better-than-middle-class.

**★[16h-13.] Immeuble, 9, rue Lesueur**, between avenue Foch and avenue de la Grande-Armée. **Roger Kohn**. 1926.

Cool and stripped "moderne" Classicism.

**[16h-14.] Hôtel particulier, 34, avenue Foch,** corner rue Lesueur.

Grand Corinthian pilasters hover over an arcaded garden porch with a couple of guarding sphinxes.

**★[16h-15.] Immeuble, 17–21, rue Duret,** between avenue Foch and avenue de la Grande-Armée. 1930s.

Streamlined corners, but note the flat limestone arches. Some brick appears in counterpoint, and there is elegant Art Deco ironwork at the entry.

**[16h-16.] Ambassade des Emirats Arabes Unis**, 56, avenue Foch, between avenue de Malakoff and rue Laurent-Pichat. **Henri-Paul Nénot**.

Boring Nénot, the architect of the rebuilt Sorbonne.

**★[16h-17.] Immeuble, 58 bis, avenue Foch**, between rue Laurent-Pichet and rue Pergolèse. **Alfred Fasquelle**. 1893.

Four grand half-round Corinthian columns attached, then two flat pilasters, and cadaverous twin-columned porches. Add festooned console brackets. Yuppies of the 1890s lived here.

**★[16h-18.] Logements de grand standing, 53, avenue Foch,** between rue Picot and rue Crevaux. **Charles Abella**. 1939.

Smooth, antirusticated, a decoration of windows in size and shape—assorted circles and rectangles. A pair of maidens not so demurely prance atop. Here curtains (a Parisian specialty) are part of the facade. **No. 55,** next door, is of a more lusty ancestry.

**[16h-19.] Musée d'Ennery**, 59, avenue Foch, between rue Picot and rue Crevaux.

A potpourri of orientalism is scattered within, the amateur collection of the 19th-century playwright Adolphe d'Ennery, assembled before such objects made it to the Louvre.

★**[16h-20a.] Hôtel particulier, 66, avenue Foch,** near rue Pergolèse. 1890s.

Twin paired giant Corinthian columns support a broken neo-Baroque pediment, the composition reinforced by oculi and oeils. This is avenue Foch at its most appropriate state of Haussmannian-*tardif* grandeur.

★**[16h-21.] Maison, 3, villa Saïd.** off rue Pergolèse. 1930.

Smooth stone and ribbon glass for some *avant-gardiste*. This street is one of the medium bourgeois, a bit of Neuilly almost downtown.

★**[16h-22.] Maison, 27, villa Saïd,** off rue Pergolèse. **Auguste Perret.** 1928.

A simple repeat of the *béton armé* bays of Perret's neo-Classicism. A background building, it lacks the vitality of **No. 3**—Perret, except perhaps at 25 bis, rue Franklin (where *grès de Bigot* jazzed it up), was a bit of a bore. The Théâtre des Champs-Elysées was in fact largely designed by Van de Velde, and the history book adulation of **No. 25 bis** is based largely on its precocious engineering, baldly presented to the street.

**[16h-23.] Square Foch,** off avenue Foch, between rue Pergolèse and boulevard de l'Admiral-Bruix.

An awkward private square, with varied and undistinguished buildings. However, **No. 12,** a mock Bavarian chalet, is the embassy of Singapore **(Stephen Sauvestre. 1885).**

★★★**[16h-24.] Métro Porte Dauphine**, at approximately 90, avenue Foch, edge of place du Maréchal-de-Lattre-de-Tassigny. **Hector Guimard.** 1905.

Super Guimard. Here the whole shelter is a concerto of iron and glass. Sinuous, cast organic members embrace serrations of scalloped glass, with a marquise in front. The wrought finials of the cast frame comb the air elegantly. The only other extant Guimard Métro shelter is at Abbesses.

**[16h-25.] RER/SNCF,** avenue Foch, boulevard Flandrin, and place du Maréchal-de-Lattre-de-Tassigny. 1900.

A small palazzo, balustraded, curved, and arched with a Napoléon III rounded *comble*. A little vulgar, a little proud . . . perhaps a peasant in fancy dress, in contrast to sleek Guimard across avenue Foch.

**[16h-26.] Musée de la Contrefaçon,** 16, rue de la Faisanderie, between avenue Foch and rue Cothenet. 19th century.

Imitations of everything are exhibited in this 19th-century imitation of the 18th century.

★**[16h-27.] Services commercially de l'ambassade de l'URSS**/originally **Hôtel Hériot,** 49, rue de la Faisanderie, corner rue Benouville. **Tersling.** 1905.

The profits of the Magasins du Louvre were partially spent by the Hériots, but now, at least in spirit, it supplies shades of the tsars. The entrance portal is mighty, and a powerful engaged Ionic colonnade faces rue Benouville.

★[16h-28.] St. James Club/formerly Fondation Dosne-Thiers, 5, place du Chancelier-Adenauer, between avenue Bugeaud and rue des Belles-Feuilles. Alfred Aldrophe. 1890.

A lone but not lonely *maison particulière* in this posh section: Second Empire-*tardif*, mansarded, and lucarned, with a front garden that gives opportunity to a miniature *rond-point*. It is a happy preservation of an anachronistic nouveau-riche palace.

[16h-29.] Ambassade de la République de Tchad, 65, rue des Belles-Feuilles, between avenue Bugeaud and avenue Victor-Hugo. Louis Sorel. 1906.

Eastlakian brick and limestone with leaping arches, supporting split lintels at the top. A show-off.

★[16h-30.] Maison, 20, rue Emile-Menier, at rue Mérimée. 1900s.

Ice cream Art Nouveau. Melting.

★[16h-31.] Villa Spontini, off rue Spontini, opposite rue du Général-Appert. 1900.

A very human-scaled cul-de-sac, with leaded bay windows at No. 5 and multicolored brick and tile at No. 7.

[16h-32.] Immeuble, 46, rue Spontini, corner rue du Général-Appert.

A polygonal *poivrière* holds the corner over a venerable bakery.

★[16h-33.] Immeuble, 4, rue de Lota, between rue de Longchamp and avenue Victor-Hugo. Fernand Delmas. 1894.

Griffins, serpents, and chimera hold bracketed bays of composite colonnettes with a stepped gable against the sky. Terrific!

[16h-34.] Institute Supérieur de Gestion, 8, rue de Lota, between rue de Longchamp and avenue Victor-Hugo. William Bouwens van der Boijen. 1900.

Smooth glazed green, white, and cream-gray tile, with a crowning colonnaded dour brow. Thoughtful but somber—an intellectual rather than visual exercise.

★[16h-35.] Logements, 96-98, rue de la Faisanderie, corner rue Dufrénoy. 1930s.

Stepped terraces, à la Sauvage, tubular railing à la Breuer: here sun and air become compelling, if not an obsession (but a laudable one). Stylish.

[16h-36.] Logements, 99, rue de la Faisanderie, between rue de Longchamp and rue Dufrénoy. 1980s.

A bit of Skidmore, Owings & Merrill gridlock imported to this eclectic street. Bold, brutal, well-detailed and cared for. But, nevertheless, it is boring *grand standing*.

★[16h-37.] **Logements, 29 bis, rue de Montevideo**, between rue Dufrénoy and rue de Longchamp. **Michel Roux-Spitz**. 1928.

Roux-Spitz had an ego: incised into the facade is his name (as usual) followed by PREMIER GRAND PRIX DE ROME. The building can stand on its own merits, without such self-promotion, from its general stripped Classicism to its stepped-corbeled bow windows.

The synagogue next door at **No. 31** is less daring.

[16h-38a.] **Maison, 23 bis, rue Dufrénoy,** between rue de Montevideo and boulevard Flandrin. **Laurent Farge.** 1890.

A Stick Style urban chalet with brick, stone, and timber—urban archaeology.

[16h-39.] **Ambassade de l'URSS,** 40, boulevard Lannes, between square Claude-Debussy and rue Gérard-Philip. **Pokrowski.** 1977.

This monumental intrusion has the same bulky, aggressive posture as the FBI headquarters in Washington, D.C. The bully on the block, it is unrelated to the city, the street, or the Bois and might just as well be on the plains of Turkestan. (But why wish it on those hardy shepherds?)

★[16h-40.] **Logements de grand standing, 2-10 boulevard Suchet,** at place de Colombie. **Jean Walter.** 1931.

A "fortified" enclave for the rich—if not the talented—with stone piled in a form that Perret had long since converted to concrete. And within the floors are travertine. A billionaire from Moroccan lead and zinc mines, Walter was also a philanthropist and art collector of note.

★[16h-41.] **Logements, 115, avenue Henri-Martin,** between rue de Franqueville and rue Octave-Feuillet. **Michel Roux-Spitz**. 1931.

A blocky *îlot* of ice cream, barely articulated, it has the vision of vanilla without the wondrous flavor of those beans. It is a period piece from a period when some, Roux-Spitz included, rejected ornament while simultaneously rejecting the avant-garde in a "strip the temples" attitude.

[16h-41a.] **Immeuble, 90, avenue Henri-Martin**, between boulevard Lannes and boulevard Flandrin. **Charles Labro.** 1927.

Neo-Classical/Moderne sculpture shows magnificent craftsmanship with somewhat insipid content.

[16h-41b.] **Immeuble, 199, avenue Victor-Hugo,** between avenue Henri-Martin and square Lamartine. circa 1900.

A glorious marquise that announces your entry, more than sheltering anything or anyone.

[16h-41c.] **Immeuble, 91, avenue Henri-Martin,** between boulevard Emile-Augier and rue Mignard. circa 1900.

More of **199, avenue Victor-Hugo,** above.

★[16h-42.] **Logements, avenue Rodin,** between rue Mignard and rue de la Tour. **Charles Thomas.** 1930.

Even in Paris an artist's name is veneered onto a developer's greedy fantasies. Here precocious Art Moderne gives a bland, curvy, and multiwindowed private street to the mildly grand bourgeois. Boring. Send the maid out to shop in the real world.

**[16h-43.] Mairie,** 71, avenue Henri-Martin, at rue de la Pompe. **Eugène Godebeuf.** 1875–1877.

A pompous bourgeois palace on a pompous post-Haussmanian street. Avenues Henri-Martin and avenue Georges-Mandel lead to the Trocadéro, along an avenue attempting to be a junior avenue Foch.

**[16h-44.] Logements, 52, rue Scheffer,** at avenue Georges-Mandel. **Thibeault.** 1893.

Crisp Parisian bay windows illuminate an otherwise dour facade. The law of 1892 allowed projections beyond the regular building line, and hence giant ornament and bow windows could appear. At the time such bays were often termed *moucharaby,* in honor of their polychromatic tile spandrels and soffits.

**[16h-45.] Villa Herran,** 81, rue de la Pompe, between avenue Georges-Mandel and rue de Longchamp.

More villas here, with the intrusion of Gargantua from the left—but eyes right! one can discipline the charm.

**[16h-46.] Hôtel particulier, 118, rue de Longchamp,** corner avenue Victor-Hugo. 1890s. Alteration and extension adjacent, **Charles Kimmoun.** 1988.

A descendant of the 19th century's leaner years (creatively), it has grown an appendage worthy of the most lustful bourgeoisie from Lille, or Detroit, or Newcastle. Extravagant materials cannot atone for taste developed in *Playboy.*

**[16h-47.] Crèche** and **ecole, 130, rue de Longchamp,** between avenue Victor-Hugo and rue de Pomereu. **A. Cazes** and **Armin Einschenk.** 1980.

A jazzy facade plays with the idea of function matching opening: some flush, some inset, some punched, some stepped groups of curtain-walling. *Pierre de taille* is a sheet of surface here, a bland but oddly foreign presence on the street.

**[16h-48.] 1, 1 bis, 1 ter, rue de Pomereu,** between rue de Longchamp and rue Charles-Lamoureux.

Three stories of *pierre de taille,* mansarded and complete with both freestanding and bracket gas lamps.

★★**[16h-49.]** Originally **Cinéma Victor-Hugo,** 65, rue Saint-Didier, at avenue Victor-Hugo and place Jean-Monnet. **Jean Charaval** and **Marcel Mélendes.** circa 1928.

Balconies for Rapunzel, bow-windowed studios (two floors high), smooth, streamlined, and rippling. This is a theatrical Art Moderne wonder, crowning a cinema that has now been demoted to a mere bank. Theater of the street.

★**[16h-50.] Logements, 28, rue des Belles-Feuilles,** between avenue Victor-Hugo and place de Mexico. **P. Schroeder.** 1912.

The carving (by **Camille Garnier**) is elegant, but the smooth ripple of pregnant stone is more elegant still. Smooth and ornate in high contrast bring a special savoir-faire to this Haussmann-*stijl.*

★**[16h-51.] Place de Mexico.**

Septet, where the sands meet the leaves *(sablons et feuilles).* But avenue d'Eylau is a dramatic western approach to the Tour Eiffel, seen through the twin wings of the Palais de Chaillot. Named for the city, not the country, this remembers the Aztecs of Tenochtitlán.

★★**[16h-52.] Logements, 36** and **38, rue Greuze,** corner rue Descamps. **Hector Guimard. No. 36, 1925. No. 38, 1928.**

Late Guimard, who mixes a brew of Art Deco with his Art Nouveau; here brickwork and stone, cut into roundels, play with other, both sinuous and stepped, corbeled shapes. Look carefully—the *garde-fous* have a serpentine Art Nouveau elegance.

**[16h-53.] Ateliers** and **garage, 11, rue des Sablons,** between place de Mexico and rue Saint-Didier. 1909.

Timber, in modern terms, makes a structural wall in articulated *colombage.* Here is Mies before Mies, with a purity that he could not beat (fireproofing did him in). Would that a savvy entrepreneur would construct a bottom worthy of the top.

**[16h-54.] Logements, 75, rue de Longchamp,** opposite rue Lauriston. **R. Thomas.** 1928.

A knuckle on the street that manages a slight shift of the urban plane, while creating an inhalation with more windows on the street, where a court is not available.

**[16h-55.] Logements, 107 rue Lauriston,** between rue Saint-Didier and rue Léo-Delibes. **Maurice Bonnemaison.** 1930.

Smoo-ooth stone gives this a *béton armé* look. Two-story studios and negligible detail combine to break the street scale, while remaining within the Parisian envelope.
The small triangular bay windows on the second and fourth floors are intimate counterpoints at the balcony bedrooms.

**[16h-56.] Hôtel Park Avenue–Central Park,** 55-57, avenue Raymond-Poincaré, between rue Saint-Didier and place Victor-Hugo. **Paul Robine.** 1912.

Check the interior court, self-consciously restored as a stage set for the pleasure of hotel and restaurant guests.

★**[16h-57] Hôtel Pauilhac,** 59, avenue Raymond-Poincaré, between rue Saint-Didier and place Victor-Hugo. **Charles Letrosne,** architect. **Camille Garnier,** sculptor. 1911.

Hats dominate here—the dunce cap of "school." Garnier's pine cones *(pommes de pin)* festoon the *grès* in relief, with wrought ironwork everywhere. Craftsmen abound, wondrously overpowering the basic building.

**[16h-58.] Logements, 67, avenue Raymond-Poincaré,** between rue Saint-Didier and place Victor-Hugo. **Charles Plumet.** 1894.

**[16h-59.] Ambassade de la République de la Côte d'Ivoire,** 102, avenue Raymond-Poincaré, between place de Mexico and avenue Foch.

A superbourgeois *hôtel particulier* for the cocoa suppliers and pineapple growers to Paris. Breaking the streetfront, it presents an ironmongered forecourt with appropriate wings cheeking the street facades adjacent.

★★★[16h-60.] **Caserne des sapeurs/pompiers,** 8, rue Mesnil, between place Victor-Hugo and rue Saint-Didier. **Robert Mallet-Stevens.** 1936.

This is a modern monument gelded by pseudomodern neighbors; set back, they create an imbalance rather than the support that this vigorous fire station had once given to a traditional street.

Mallet-Stevens originally allowed cubism here to intermingle gracefully with Haussmannism. His greatest work is the complex of private houses off the rue du Docteur-Blanche, on the short street named for himself [**16a-47.**]

★[16h-61.] **Marché Saint-Didier,** 50, rue Saint-Didier, at rue Mesnil. 1867.

Cast iron, now infilled with brick.

★★[16h-62.] **Cité Commerciale d'Argentine,** 111, avenue Victor-Hugo, between rue des Belles-Feuilles and place Victor-Hugo. **Henri Sauvage.** 1903.

*Colombage* in steel and brick with some *nouille* brackets for the bay windows. The skylit *impasse* within now offers seedy shops. *Why?* This is a daring, thinking, commercially clever building in the midst of a rich neighborhood, counterpoint to the Haussmannian street adjacent.

The most appealing shopfront within is that of **Les Livres Anciens.**

# 44
# SIXTEENTH ARRONDISSEMENT
## CENTRAL PASSY
### SQUARE ALBONI TO LA MUETTE

Square Alboni: **Pol Abraham**; rue Beethoven: **Georges Thirion**; pont de Bir-Hakeim: **Jean-Camille Formigé**; Ambassade de Turquie; Maison de Balzac; 51, rue Raynouard: **Auguste Perret**; Maison de la Radio: **Henri Bernard**; Hameau Boulainvilliers; Station Boulainvilliers: **A. Barret**; Logements: **André Remondet, Charles Blanche, Maurice du Bois d'Auberville**, and **José Imbert**; Fleuriste Orève: **Lecourtois**; La Muette

Métro: **Passy**

**[16p-2.]** Logements, 12, square Alboni. Pol Abraham. 1930s.

**Passy, a commune in 1790, annexed to Paris in 1860:** A country village, at one time merely a dependency of Auteuil, Passy was on the route to Versailles, but, more important, its waters were seemingly endowed with almost magical curative powers. A spa, owned by the ubiquitous Delessert family (see Chaillot), was centered where the modern avenue Marcel-Proust, rue d'Ankara, and avenue du Président-Kennedy border the Ministry of Urbanism (before its move to the **Tête de La Défense**).

**[16p-1.] Square Alboni,** off rue de l'Alboni, at Métro Passy.

A doglegged street remains from an "English" square, bifurcated by the Métro; the other side of the tracks is now square Charles-Dickens and the Musée du Vin. The green space is now privately appended to **No. 11** but remains within view as you escalate from the Métro to the high ground above.

★**[16p-2.] Logements, 9–11, 11 bis, 12,** and **14, square Alboni,** off rue de l'Alboni. No. 12, **Pol Abraham.** 1930s. No. 14, **Charles Wenner.** 1929.

The 1930s in triad, bayed with bold balconies—polygonal, curved, and straight. A prismatic world in this peaceful cul-de-sac.

★**[16p-3.] Ateliers, 7, rue Beethoven,** between boulevard Delessert and avenue du Président-Kennedy. **Georges Thirion.** 1913.

A bit more decorated (at the sky) than his Saint-Senoch buildings **[17t-49.],** these glassy studios fill a concrete frame veneered with stone and infilled with brick. The interior spaces must be glorious.

**[16p-4.] Square Charles-Dickens,** at 4, rue des Eaux. 1936.

A tail of the street here climbs up a steep, stepped cul-de-sac; quiet, secluded, and charming, it is all guarded by a Greek Revival temple (Algerians within) at its portal.
The **Musée du Vin,** at **No. 5,** occupies old 15th-century quarries that had previously been wine cellars of the Abbaye de Passy.

**[16p-5.] Logements, 1–3, rue Charles-Dickens,** between rue des Eaux and avenue Frémiet. **Adolphe Bocage.** 1911.

**[16p-6.] Logements, 7, rue Charles-Dickens,** between rue des Eaux and avenue Frémiet. **Albert Vèque.** 1909.

**[16p-7.] Logements, avenue Frémiet** (both sides), between rue Charles-Dickens and avenue du Président-Kennedy. **Albert Vèque.** 1913.

A private street, resulting from a speculative ensemble.

At the end of the rue Frémiet, look back to the Pont de Bir-Hakeim.

★★**[16p-8.] Pont de Bir-Hakeim**/originally **Viaduc de Passy,** across the Seine between rue de l'Alboni/Métro Passy and boulevard de Grenelle/Métro Bir-Hakeim. **Louis Biette,** engineer. **Jean-Camille Formigé,** architect. **Gustave Michel,** sculptor. 1905.

Elegant columns with entwining wrought-iron foliage once supported the Métro, in consonance with pendant lamps. The columns have given way to more simplistic ones—to paraphrase Chemetov, "Progress doesn't always progress." The supporting bridge beneath is a swan song to academic enrichment so popular at the Exposition of 1900, which had produced the Grand and Petit Palais and the Pont Alexandre III.

**[16p-9.] Batiment UAP, 15, rue Raynouard,** between place de Costa-Rica and rue Chernoviz. **M. Julien** and **Louis Duhayon**. 1931.

Gold and white mosaics and a garden.

**[16p-10.] Logements, 20, rue Raynouard**, between place de Costa-Rica and rue Chernoviz. **Albert Vèque**, architect. **Mourques**, sculptor. 1910.

★**[16p-11.] Logements de grand standing, 21, 23, 25, rue Raynouard,** opposite rue Chernoviz. **L. Nafilyan**. 1933.

This mammoth block drops off 15 meters to avenue Marcel-Proust behind, where it becomes a thirteen-story monster. The rue Raynouard facade is a mild set of prismatic stones, notched and articulated.
Visit the garden (★★) through the entry at No. 23, with its high terraced view over Paris.

**[16p-12.] Ambassade de Turquie/** originally **Hôtel de Lamballe**, 17, rue d'Ankara, between rue Berton and avenue du Président-Kennedy. 18th century.

An *hôtel* inaccessible to the stroller in its present function.

★**[16p-13.] Maison de Balzac,** entry at 47, rue Raynouard, between rue de l'Annonciation and rue Singer.

This country house, that Honoré de Balzac inhabited from 1841 to 1847, moving here from les Jardies at Ville-d'Avray to avoid his creditors, is the sole remembrance of rural Passy. It is an 18th-century pavilion on the grounds of an *hôtel particulier* that has since disappeared.
**Gérard de Nerval** wrote: "This house was the exact antipode of the former. At les Jardies, it was always necessary to go up; at Passy it is always necessary to descend. The first lacked any stairs, the second had three floors of them. One (now) arrived at a little door on the street that skirted the heights of Passy, heights that opened a distant view over the plain of Grenelle, the île des Cygnes, and the Champs-de-Mars. Not a house in front of him. A wall, a green door, and a bell. The concierge would open it, and one found oneself on the landing of the first level in the open air. At the last level, one was in a court. Two terra cotta busts indicated, at the end, the house of the novelist. Once the door opened, a delicious smell floated from this man of taste. It was an office, where, on shelves carefully arranged, one could admire all the varieties of pears from Saint Germain that it was possible to find."

★★**[16p-14.] Logements, 51-55, rue Raynouard,** between rue de l'Annonciation and rue Singer. **August Perret**. 1932.

The Frères Perret maintained their contracting business here, with Auguste living in the penthouse. An exposed concrete frame is here matter-of-factly infilled with precast concrete slabs, rather than with the great enrichment of *grès de Bigot* as at 25 bis, rue Franklin. It is old hat Perret—tired, gray, seedy, and something of a bore, except to the scholar.

---

The **Frères Perret** inherited a contracting enterprise from their father, and were first builders before both **Auguste** (1874-1954) and **Gustave** (1876-1952) completed training as architects. No registration laws limited the use of the professional title in 1902, when 25 bis, rue Franklin was begun. The drawings were signed **A.-G. Perret,** and brother **Claude** (1880–1960) remained firmly on the entrepreneurial side. But Auguste and Gustave both studied with Guadet, and, in later years, Auguste taught, maintaining an atelier at the Ecoles des Beaux Arts, his original nemesis. He continued, however, a strong French tradition in his work, expressed succinctly by his onetime employee, Le Corbusier: "Perret isn't a revolutionary, but one carrying forward the great, noble and elegant truths of French architecture."

★[16p-15.] **Chancellerie de l'Ambassade de Turquie,** 16, avenue de Lamballe, between rue Raynouard and avenue du Président-Kennedy. **Henri Beauclair.** 1976.

Give this architect an exotic client, and he will release fantasies if not solid creativity. This glassy undulation ululates, visually violating a district already ravaged by nouveau-riche excess. Look down the hill to the right, to "Passy Kennedy," where the felony is compounded.

★[16p-16.] **Passy Kennedy/Logements de grand standing**, 100, avenue du Président-Kennedy. **André Remondet.** 1982. Office additions, 1988.

The Watergate of Paris: forms intended to be sexy in marble, granite, and glass are reminiscent of Luigi Morelli's complicated stylishness in Washington's Foggy Bottom. This complex is sadly appropriate to the banal Front de Seine and the gross Maison de Radio-France adjacent. One of the penalties of its tenants' great financial success can be (for others) bad taste, based on the quick glitz of the fast franc.

[16p-17.] **ORTF/Maison de la Radio,** 116, avenue du Président-Kennedy, between rue du Ranelagh and rue de Boulainvilliers. **Henri Bernard** and **Lhuiller**, **Niermans** and **Sibelle**. 1955–1963.

The pits, although pits are usually negative space, and this is a monster in positive scale that dominates a whole sector. What is good happens within, where **Radio-Musique** and **Radio-Culture** broadcast intelligence and fine music. From the outside it is a boorish warehouse more in concert with the lesser buildings of **La Défense** than with this architecturally vibrant sector of the 1920s and 1930s.

[16p-18.] **Hameau de Boulainvilliers,** 45-61, rue du Ranelagh, between rue de Boulainvilliers and rue Gustave-Zédé. 1838.

A subdivision of villas on land that was once part of the park of the Château du Boulainvilliers.

★[16p-19.] **Maison, 40, rue du Ranelagh,** corner rue de Boulainvilliers. 19th century.

Carpenter Gothic for the Hansel and Gretel crowd, beautifully detailed, elegant, and lovely—and completely out of its later Passy context.

[16p-20.] **Immeuble, 28, rue des Marronniers,** corner rue de Boulainvilliers. 1925 and later.

Vestigial column flutes and a wonderful bas-relief frieze at the fifth floor.

[16p-21.] **Immeuble, 7, rue Alfred-Bruneau,** between rue des Vignes and rue Singer, opposite avenue du Colonel-Bonnet. 1930s.

A hard set of forms veneered with tile and stone.

★[16p-22.] **Immeuble, 7, rue Lekain,** between rue Singer and rue de l'Annonciation.

Colonnettes symbolically flank the first floor with strapwork supporting bay windows—all intercolored with red and gray brickwork.

★★[16p-23.] **PTT, 40, rue Singer,** corner rue Talma. **Paul Bessine.** 1931.

A wonderful surprise in reinforced concrete infilled with tile, and the ironwork is elegant. The public architecture of the 1930s is recalled here and should be revered.

★[16p-24.] **Station Boulainvilliers,** rue de Boulainvilliers at 52, rue des Vignes. **A. Barret.** 1900.

This shuttle station connected the line of the Petite Ceinture with the Champ de Mars, for the Exposition of 1900. A bit of extravagant eclecticism à la Frank Furness (Philadelphia), it assembles brick, cut stone, and a slate roof in a freestanding statement to the glories of Passy, when these were more suburban parts.

★[16p-25.] **Immeuble, 62, rue des Vignes** and **43, rue Singer,** between avenue Mozart and rue de Boulainvilliers. **Charles Blanche.** 1907.

Bay windows and brick, with modest ironwork, that signals an architecture transitional between Haussmannian and technocratic.

[16p-26.] **Maisons, 62-64, rue Singer,** between rue de Boulainvilliers and rue des Vignes. circa 1900.

Vestigial villas that speak of early Passy's entry into Paris as the 16th arrondissement, front-gardened, with an elegance of wrought iron, and styled to the newly eclectic taste of the turn-of-the-century bourgeoisie.

★[16p-27.] **Logements, 26, rue Bois-le-Vent,** between rue de Boulainvilliers and rue Talma. circa 1925.

A Classical-moderne studio building (forget the two floors of surelevation). Simple cylindrical columns support concrete trellises at the fourth and fifth *étages.*
This is a well-kept period piece.

[16p-28.] **Logements, 25, rue Bois-le-Vent,** between rue de Boulainvilliers and rue Talma. **Lecourtois.** 1902.

[16p-29.] **Logements, 34–36, rue Bois-le-Vent,** between rue de Boulainvilliers and avenue Mozart. **Maurice Du Bois d'Auberville.** 1909.

Fancy brickwork a bit more sincere than that of **No. 25** opposite. If the building doesn't have enough class, the architect's name makes up for it.

[16p-30.] **Logements, 1, 3, 5, avenue Mozart,** corner rue de Boulainvilliers. **Maurice Du Bois d'Auberville,** architect. **P. Seguin,** sculptor. 1906.

More **M.D.B. d'A.** Who could resist employing such an elegant name?

[16p-31.] **Logements, 3, rue François-Ponsard,** between chaussée de la Muette and rue Gustave-Nadaud. **José Imbert.** 1970s.

This is the *père* of Saudi Arabia's mission **[16p-34.]**, almost identical. It could be a Greek motel in a bad dream, not worthy of a nightmare.

★**[16p-32.] Orève (restaurant)**/originally **Fleuriste Orève,** 25, rue de la Pompe, between rue Gustave-Nadaud, and rue Jean-Richepin. **Lecourtois.** 1910. Decor, **Maurice Marty.**

A floral shop that has become a restaurant, its Art Deco interior wanders around back courtyards under glassy greenhouses.

---

The French drama critic **Jules Janin** lived in a rustic chalet on the site of what is now 11, rue de la Pompe, in the 1850s. "A certain courage was necessary to install myself in this desert," he wrote. "On a path hardly traced, and during three winters, we remained alone, frightened by this solitude and great silence."

---

**[16p-33.] Logements, 19, rue Octave-Feuillet,** between rue Alfred-Dehodencq et rue Henri-de-Bornier. **Maurice Du Bois d'Auberville,** architect. **S. Seguin,** sculptor. **Alphonse Gentil** and **François Bourdet,** ceramists. 1909.

**[16p-34.] Saudi Arabian Military Mission,** 4 bis, rue de Franqueville, between rue Verdi and rue Albéric-Magnard. **José Imbert.** 1976.

Unbelievable *neo-Grec* Perretian galleries allow perambulations to nowhere. It is bizarre but at least holds the line of the street.

**[16p-35.] Hôtel particulier,** 3, rue d'Andigné, at rue Conseiller-Collignon.

Neo-Renaissance, engardened.

**[16p-36.] Logements, 15, rue du Conseiller-Collignon,** between rue d'Andigné and rue Octave-Feuillet. **C. H. Blanche.** 1939–1948.

Some jazzy ironwork gives this Art Moderne block a bit of style, and two-story atelier–living rooms make a special counterpoint. The construction period embraced the whole Second World War, and thence this is *retardataire* Art Moderne.

---

The Château de la Muette (demolished in 1926) lay on the approximate site of the rue d'Andigné, and its park extended over the blocks now bordered by avenue Henri-Martin, the Jardin du Ranelagh, and boulevard Emile-Augier. Originally a hunting pavilion, it was a place of assignation for Louis XV: three sequential daughters of the comtesse de Mailly-Nesle, not to mention Madame de Pompadour. The château was entirely reconstructed for the latter by **Jacques-Ange Gabriel** (it had been drastically altered in the 1560s for Charles IX by **Philibert Delorme**). But its role in history was very different than that of its vanished 18th-century architecture:
In 1783 the **Montgolfier brothers,** Etienne-Jacques and Michel-Joseph, papermakers from Annonay, south of Lyons, created the first hot-air balloon, made of a special paper stretched over a willow framework. Here, on the lawns of la Muette, the first manned ascension took place, by the chemist Jean-François Pilatre de Rozier (remembered by an *allée* in his name in the Jardin du Ranelagh) and the marquis d'Arlandes. That first voyage took place in the presence of the Dauphin, in a globe 70 feet tall and 46 feet in diameter. The intrepid travelers left on November 21, 1783,

at one hour and 54 minutes after noon, rising to an altitude of 950 meters (3,100 feet). They landed in good shape on the Butte aux Cailles (13th arrondissement) between the Moulin de Merveilles and the Moulin Vieux, having traveled eight kilometers (five miles) in about twenty minutes without the slightest inconvenience.

---

Métro: **La Muette**

# 45
# SIXTEENTH ARRONDISSEMENT
## PASSY/SOUTH AND BOULOGNE
### JARDIN FLEURISTE TO HAMEAU BOILEAU

Jardin Fleuriste: **Jean-Camille Formigé**; Piscine Molitor; Atelier Lipchitz-Miestchaninoff: **Le Corbusier**; Logements/allée des Pins: **Georges-Henri Pingusson**; Villa Collinet: **Robert Mallet-Stevens**; Villa Cook: **Le Corbusier**; Villa Zed: **Raymond Fischer**; Maison Lombard: **Pierre Patout**; Atelier Huré; **Auguste Perret**; Atelier Gordin: **Auguste Perret**; Villa Dury: **Raymond Fischer**; Villa Froriep: **André Lurçat**; rue Nungesser-et-Coli: **Le Corbusier, Jean Fidler, Poliakoff**, and **Michel Roux-Spitz**; Parc des Princes: **Roger Taillibert**; 95, boulevard Murat: **Paul Guadet**; Ecole du Sacré-Coeur: **Hector Guimard**; Atelier Carpeaux: **Hector Guimard**; Immeuble Jassedé, Hôtel Deron-Levent, Hôtel Jassedé, and Villa Rosze: **Hector Guimard**; Ambassade d'Algérie: **Joachim Richard** and **H. Audiger**; Hameau Boileau

Metro: **Porte d'Auteuil**

[16s-33.] Hôtel Jassédé. Hector Guimard. 1893.

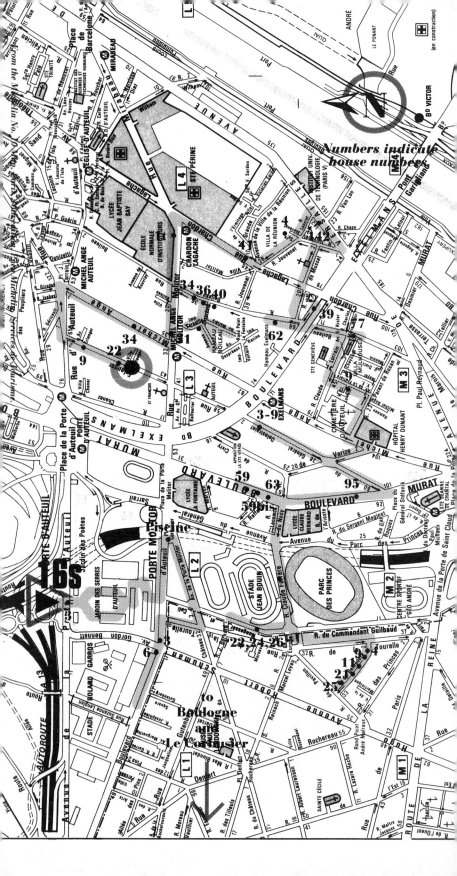

Numbers indicate
house numbers

From place de la Porte-d'Auteuil, walk west along avenue de la Porte-d'Auteuil, crossing over the Périphérique. Don't despair, it's a good distance to **No. 3.**

★★★**[16s-1.] Jardin Fleuriste Municipal,** 3, avenue de la Porte-d'Auteuil, **Jean-Camille Formigé,** architect. **Schwarz** and **Meurer,** engineers of the central greenhouse. 1898–1901.

Here, on the site of the botanical gardens of Louis XV, Formigé and friends planned an enclave of formal gardens and greenhouses, as nurseries for flowers, shrubbery, and trees that ornament the Mairie of Paris and those of its twenty arrondissements. A lovely park, it is quiet and little-utilized by Parisians, let alone travelers.

The house of palms, the central pavilion of a symmetrical complex embracing a grand lawn, is 100 meters (325 feet) long, with a central dome reaching almost 16 meters (52 feet)—and the palms yearn further. Walk through this and the side greenhouses and then to the back of the palm house, to see the handsome brick service buildings along a parallel courtyard.

★**[16s-2.] Piscine Molitor,** place Le Corbusier, corner boulevard d'Auteuil and avenue de la Porte-Molitor. 1929.

The last of the Art Deco swimming pool complexes, with both indoor and outdoor *piscines,* where summer sunbathers can find topless heaven.

**[16s-3.] Maisons des Gardiens, Jardin Fleuriste**, 3 and 6, avenue Gordon-Bennett. **Jean-Camille Formigé.** 1900.

A bit of Napoléon III's London memories: imported England at the edge of the Jardin Fleuriste.

★★★**[16s-4.] Atelier Jacques Lipchitz–Oscar Miestchaninoff,** 9, allée des Pins, corner rue des Arts (Boulogne). **Le Corbusier.** 1924.

Interlocking spaces served the ateliers of two sculptors, who had their living quarters above. Ivy has almost conquered the pristine white stucco prisms, the revenge of a well-caring but philistine bourgeoisie.

★★**[16s-5.] Logements, 15, allée des Pins** corner (5), rue Denfert-Rochereau (Boulogne). **Georges-Henri Pingusson.** 1936.

Apartments in the *paquebot* style (see particularly Pierre Patout's work), complete with a streamlined and glassy prow, and portholes at the entrance stairs. It would have been more powerful without the icebreaker beak at the *rez-de-chaussée.*

★**[16s-6.] Villa Collinet,** 8, rue Denfert-Rochereau, between allée des Pins and boulevard d'Auteuil (Boulogne). **Robert Mallet-Stevens.** 1926.

An awkward preface to the rue Mallet-Stevens but noted for its role with its party-wall neighbors at **No. 6** and **No. 4,** by Le Corbusier and Raymond Fischer, respectively. The current owner has restored some later grossness to its pristine state (particularly the front door and balcony).

★★★**[16s-7.] Villa Cook,** 6, rue Denfert-Rochereau, between allée des Pins and boulevard d'Auteuil (Boulogne). **Le Corbusier.** 1927.

Built simultaneously with the **Villa Planeix [13se-24.]** and the **Villa Stein** at Garches, this was commissioned by an American journalist friend of Gertrude Stein (whose brother Leo was client for the Villa Stein).

"Here are applied very clearly the characteristics [I have] acquired up to now, the pilotis, the roof garden, the open plan, the free facade, the horizontal ribbon window. The controlling rule is . . . furnished by simple elements at human scale, such as the height of the floors, the dimensions of the windows, doors, and balustrades. Classic organization is overthrown: Underneath the house, it's open. The living room is at the summit of the house, opening on the roof-garden, from which one overlooks the vastness of the Bois de Boulogne. One is no longer in Paris; it is like being in the country." *Les Villas d'Artistes à Paris.*

Jeanneret did thus romance himself a bit.

★[16s-8.] **Villa Zed,** 4, rue Denfert-Rochereau, between allée des Pins and boulevard d'Auteuil, (Boulogne). **Raymond Fischer.** 1928.

This completes the triptych with Mallet-Stevens and Le Corbusier. The three jointly express what was, for the **Ecole des Beaux-Arts,** "barbarism, the anti-architecture that for some years had created a furor in northern and eastern Europe, a veritable offense against sanity and good taste."

Fischer had been fascinated with, and studied firsthand, the work of Adolph Loos in Vienna—Loos built the Tristan Tzar house [18b-21.] in 1926—and was equally fascinated by Gropius and the Bauhaus. His interest and passion, however, were not matched by talent, for his Parisian houses are boring.

★[16s-9.] **Maison Lombard,** 1, avenue Jean-Baptiste-Clement and 2–4 rue Gambetta (Boulogne). **Pierre Patout.**

Patout's name is identified with the *paquebot* style, although here in Boulogne Pingusson's paquebot seems more in the spirit of the great transatlantic ships. But Patout, of course, did the interiors of the **Normandie** (with his partner, Jacques-Emile Ruhlmann. 1935).

The painter Alfred Lombard maintained his studio at the crest of the blunt *pan coupé.* All in all, a disorderly place in both the Classical and cubistic senses, and another landmark to remain more in the written than in the visual history of Parisian architecture.

In *Les Villas d'Artistes à Paris,* Jean-Claude Delorme writes, "Patout's architectural vocabulary has the same elegance as that of Mallet-Stevens, the same expressive massing as that of Dujarric, and the dynamics of form of a Pingusson. . . . Patout was never properly part of the 'heroic avant-garde'; he was a great architect in love with his art, who brought to this last work a degree of mastery rarely equaled." An opposing view.

★[16s-10.] **Villas, 3, 5, 7, 9, rue Gambetta,** between carrefour des Anciens-Combattants and rue Claude-Monet (Boulogne). No. 3, **Jean Niermans.** 1935. No. 5, **Emilio Terry.** 1930.

This quartet shows well the struggling ambivalence of lesser French architects in the late 1920s and early 1930s. Niermans produced a correct International Style document at No. 3, but Terry at No. 5 is lost, with a pediment and rustications applied to a plain box behind. No. 7 is better than either Fischer's or Mallet-Stevens' around the corner—but by whom?

[16s-11.] **Maison, 2, rue des Pins,** corner rue Denfert-Rochereau (Boulogne). circa 1920.

The work of an anonymous mason, this is the vernacular that glues Boulogne together: the common bourgeois house, mansarded, in *meulière.*

One field of 1920s architectural experimentation centered around Boulogne's rue Denfert-Rochereau, the other on rue du Belvédère. Here we find Fischer once more, as well as Perret and André Lurçat.

[16s-12.] **Atelier Marguerite-Huré,** 25, rue du Belvédère, between rue du Pavillon and rue de la Tourelle (Boulogne). **Auguste Perret.** 1928.

Perret's articulated concrete frames studio windows, the center divided into the famous nine squares (see Tschumi's pavilions at the Parc de La Villette [19v-6.]). A not-so-special place on a street of eclectic houses.

[16s-13.] Atelier Dora-Gordin, 21, rue du Belvédère, between rue du Pavillon and rue de la Tourelle (Boulogne). Auguste Perret. 1929.

A rational distillation of the facade produces a thoughtful, if not wonderful, studio/house.

★[16s-14.] "Maison Carrée"/Villa Dury, 11, rue du Belvédère, between rue du Pavillon and rue de la Tourelle (Boulogne). Raymond Fischer. 1928.

Stripped, this is the closest of the 1920s villas to the work of Adolph Loos: no compromise with its austere white form. Nevertheless, its fame was such that the painters Soutine and Chagall, and the architect-decorators, Chareau and Mallet-Stevens, were present at its "inauguration."

★★[16s-15.] Villa Froriep de Salis, 9, rue du Belvédère, between rue du Pavillon and rue de la Tourelle (Boulogne). André Lurçat. 1926.

Lurçat's contribution to rue du Belvédère is the boldest. Froriep's sculpture atelier is on the first floor facing the street, and the living spaces behind faced the southern garden. It is, however, simplistic, with none of the exuberant creativity of his Villa Guggenbuhl. [14s-16.]

★[16s-16.] Villa Godefroy, 4, rue du Belvédère, between rue du Pavillon and rue de la Tourelle (Boulogne). Raymond Fischer. 1928.

Here, for once, a "modern" architect bows to the geometry of the street—and wins some points. This great bellied house gains, therefore, some geometry that is fortunately in concert with the nature of cubism. The window sash and doors were originally painted green, enlivening today's bland monochromy.

★[16s-17.] Logements, 22, rue Nungesser-et-Coli, between rue Claude-Farrère, and avenue de la Porte-Molitor. Michel Roux-Spitz. 1931.

It is fascinating to see this in contrast with Le Corbusier's No. 24 next door, built one year later. Roux-Spitz was in the same atelier as Fischer at the Ecole des Beaux-Arts. Winner of the Prix de Rome, he went on to a brilliant career of public works, the due (so it seems) of such lauréats. Poor Corbu went on to lose the League of Nations competition (disqualified for improper drafting materials) and had to content himself with becoming, to many, the greatest architect of the 20th century.

★★★[16s-18.] Logements, 24, rue Nungesser-et-Coli, between rue Claude-Farrère and avenue de la Porte-Molitor. Le Corbusier. 1932.

You see, Corbu could fit into the Haussmannian envelope, even when his spirit was with the Ville Verte, imagining the total destruction of central Paris to create "towers in a park" (he would save the great "monuments"). Glass, steel, and glass block are here assembled in a rich interplay of facade elements, bayed, balconied, terraced. It does make Michel look pretty silly.

★[16s-19.] Logements, 26, rue Nungesser-et-Coli, between rue Claude-Farrère, and avenue de la Porte-Molitor. Jean Fidler and Poliakoff. 1933.

Another of Corbu's neighbors in contrast.

**[16s-20.] Stadium du Parc des Princes,** avenue du Parc-des-Princes. **Roger Taillibert.** 1972.

You can't miss it, and where else would Michael Jackson want to sing? Here 50,000 spectators more often enjoy sporting events, as the traffic of the Périphérique speeds beneath them. The great concrete fin-buttresses give it a futuristic air, styled for *Star Trek*, perhaps. Stadia have a difficult program to conquer, the bulk of their form inevitably out of scale with a proximate city. At Expo 70 in Osaka, the American architects Davis, Brody & Associates presented one potential solution, an earth berm sheltered with a low tensile roof, producing minimal built volume in profile.

**[16s-21.] Logements, 59, boulevard Murat,** between place de la Porte-Molitor and rue de Varize. circa 1930.

A *moderne immeuble* of studios.

★**[16s-22.] Logements, 59 bis, boulevard Murat,** between place de la Porte-Molitor and rue de Varize. **Jean Fidler and Poliakoff.** 1929.

Neo-Classical and Art Deco fight it out once more, with more nonsense—and more fun—than the relatively spare studio building next door.

★**[16s-23.] Logements, 63, boulevard Murat,** corner rue de Varize. circa 1930.

Another stylish attempt to break the academic pattern, this time with a corner opportunity that complements curves with oculi—those 1930s windows that seemed to architects appropriate for the modern view.

★**[16s-24.] Maison Guadet,** 95, boulevard Murat, between rue de Varize and rue du Général-Delestraint. **Paul Guadet.** 1912.

A concrete tour de force, now out of scale but perhaps once in happy juxtapositions. Never handsome, it is an intellectual exercise that fortunately was never repeated.

**[16s-25.] Logements, 3, 5, 7, 9, rue du Général-Delestraint,** between rue de Varize and boulevard Exelmans. **Joachim Richard,** architect. **Gentil and Bourdet,** ceramists. 1912.

Richard was at a wilder stage when he designed **40, rue Boileau** (**[16s-36.]**).

★★**[16s-26.] Ecole du Sacré-Coeur,** 9, avenue de La Frillière, between rue Claude-Lorrain and rue Parent-de-Rosan. **Hector Guimard.** 1895.

Designed in Guimard's heyday (he was 28) with the help of an illustration from Viollet-le-Duc's *Entretiens.* What remains is a facade without Guimard's 'organs' behind, a sorry fate for organic architecture.

**[16s-27.] Logements, 77, rue Boileau,** between rue Charles-Marie-Widor and boulevard Exelmans. **Devinant and Poigin.** Ironwork, **Hector Guimard.** 1902.

It was remarkable that Guimard produced ironwork for other architects. Perhaps this allowed him a sufficient income to support himself before his marriage to the wealthy Mademoiselle Oppenheim.

★**[16s-28.] Atelier Carpeaux,** 39, boulevard Exelmans, between rue Boileau and rue Chardon-Lagache. **Hector Guimard.** 1895.

This was the site of the sculptor **Jean-Baptiste Carpeaux's** studio, but his widow commissioned Guimard to design this memorial replacement twenty years after his death. An early Guimard design, it seems that two coy Carpeaux children are niched and corbeled on the facade. The brick second floor seems reminiscent of Louis Sullivan.

**[16s-29.] Ambassade de la République Socialiste du Vietnam**, 62, rue Boileau, between boulevard Exelmans and rue Molitor. **Vo Thanh Nghia**. 1977.

Some traditional Vietnamese forms are encrusted with white tile, that ubiquitous French material that throws down the gauntlet: I am modern—or, better still, Post Modern. It would have been nice to see, in this semi-suburban area next to hameau Boileau, traditional Vietnamese forms in traditional Vietnamese materials. This one seems to have been designed for a World's Fair, the rest of which never was built.

★★**[16s-30.] Immeuble Jassedé**, 142, avenue de Versailles, corner (1) rue Lancret. **Hector Guimard**. 1905.

Lintels, *garde-fous,* balcony rails, stonework, dormers—all give territory for Guimard's sinuous imagination. At the *entresol,* the *garde-fous* are cast; the first-floor-balcony infilling is both cast and wrought; lintels rolled, cast and wrought.
Unfortunately, the details are much more interesting than the whole. But don't miss the stair.

**[16s-31.] Logements, 4, square Jouvenet,** off rue Jouvenet at rue Lancret. **M. Quent**. circa 1930.

A determined Classicist was here, with fluted balconies acting as surreal column capitals, and a frieze in imbricated stucco. Moderne, translucent glass lights the stair, and all is set back in the name of light and air.

**[16s-32.] Hôtel Deron-Levent,** 8, grande avenue de la Villa-de-la-Réunion, between avenue de Versailles and rue Chardon-Lagache. **Hector Guimard**. 1908.

Guimard, forty-one.

★★**[16s-33.] Hôtel Jassédé,** 41, rue Chardon-Lagache, between grande avenue de la Villa-de-la-Réunion and rue Molitor. **Hector Guimard**. 1893.

Guimard, twenty-six.

**[16s-34.] Hôtel Delfaut,** 1 ter, rue Molitor, off rue Chardon-Lagache. **Hector Guimard**. 1895.

Guimard, twenty-eight.

★**[16s-35.] Villa Rosze,** 34, rue Boileau, between rue Molitor and rue Jouvenet. **Hector Guimard**. 1891.

Guimard, twenty-four. An Italianate villa, with a floral terra-cotta frieze (*grès de Bigot,* but in plaques). Brick, tile, stone, and encrusted pebbles all meld here in Guimard's youthful and eclectic fantasy.

★**[16s-36.] Ambassade d'Algérie**/originally **hôtel particulier,** 40, rue Boileau, at entrance to hameau Boileau. **Joachim Richard** and **H. Audiger,** architects. **Alphonse Gentil and François Bourdet**, ceramists. 1907.

The Algerians got ready-made neo-Arabic architecture, covered with ceramic blues. Here *béton armé* is made to look like sinuous steel—(but, of course, sinuous steel rods are inside those serpentine shapes).

★**[16s-37.] Hameau Boileau,** 36, rue Boileau, between rue Molitor and rue Jouvenet. circa 1838.

The developer, a lithographer named **Rose-Joseph Lemercier,** established rigid rules of cooperative ownership: "It will forever be the requirement of (the owner of) each lot and building . . . never to sell or rent all or part of these lands or buildings to factories, industrial establishments, to people in the business of selling wine or liquor, to restauraunts, delicatessens, butchers, food stores, or other individuals holding dances, public balls, or creating noisy conditions, or giving out disagreeable and unhealthy odors, or to women of ill repute, and finally to anybody carrying out any business in a shop of such sort that said houses could never be occupied by their owners, artists, office workers, clerks, assistants, stockholders, or other tranquil people."

Here is 19th-century semirural romanticism unleashed à l'anglaise, with an individualism in sharp contrast to the Louis-Philippe or Haussmannian flat. Edith Wharton's heroes would be at home here, (although Mrs. Manson Mingott, of *The Age of Innocence*, would not).

Savor the gothic manor directly ahead of the entry gates (**Danjoy.** circa 1845). Danjoy was steeped in Gothicism as a restorer of medieval churches.

Office buildings in both 1926 and 1955 were erected despite the deed restrictions. Both were demolished in the 1960s on court orders. *Succès fou.*

Métro: **Michel-Ange Molitor**

Other nearby buildings might be added to this tour:

**[16s-38.] Logements, 31, rue Molitor,** between rue Boileau and rue Michel-Ange. **Charles Lemaire.** 1906.

**[16s-39.] Logements, 34, rue Michel-Ange,** between rue Molitor and rue d'Auteuil. 1979.

Michelangelo would faint. This is *grand standing,* the best graces of which are in the absence of smoky glass balconies. A rather sleek and pompous set of bay windows punctuates the inevitable nouveau-riche wallpaper: travertine.

★**[16s-40.] Ecole, 9, rue Erlanger,** between rue d'Auteuil and rue Molitor. **Francois-Louis Girollet.** 1910.

The spirit of Frank Lloyd Wright (Chesney House?) passed by here. The bracketed cornice is in the Italian Villa style, and the frieze is in *grès*. Here was an independent architecture, adjacent to Haussmannianism on the left, and grand blah 1960s *grand standing* to the right.

★★**[16s-41.] Logements, 22, rue Erlanger,** between rue d'Auteuil and rue Molitor. **Bernard Oge** and **Jean-Jacques Faysse.** 1976.

Despite the ubiquitous travertine of *grand standing,* this articulate block brings life and lively presence to the street. Pictorially reminiscent of the Richards Medical Research Laboratories at the University of Pennsylvania by Louis Kahn, with some mannered projecting planting boxes, it is nevertheless a superior modern work.

# 46
# SEVENTEENTH ARRONDISSEMENT
## BATIGNOLLES

### PORTE DE SAINT-OUEN TO PONT CARDINET

Porte de Saint-Ouen; square des Epinettes; Montmartre aux Artistes: **Adolphe Thiers** and **Henri Résal**; Eglise Saint-Michel-des-Batignolles: **Bernard Haubold**; Cité des Fleurs: **L'Henry et Becqueville**; 17, passage Petit-Cerf: **Bernard Bourgade** and **Michel Londinsky**; square des Batignolles: **Adolphe Alphand, Pierre Barrillet-Deschamps**, and **Gabriel Davioud**; Eglise Sainte-Marie-des-Batignolles: **Jacques Molinos** and **Pierre-Eugène Lequeux**; 62, rue Boursault, **René Simonet** and **Alexandre Bigot**; RER/pont Cardinet: **Julien Polti**

Métro: **Porte de Saint-Ouen**

[17b-17.] Logements, 17, passage Petit-Cerf. Bernard Bourgade and Michel Londinsky. 1988.

★[17b-1.] **Logements/HLM, 143, avenue de Saint-Ouen,** rue Jean-Leclaire, and boulevard Bessières. 1988.

A gray set of volumes accented with articulated blue columns. Don't look too closely—this sort of public housing is not strong on detail but is handsome in the handling of its interior open spaces: a plaza, allowing pedestrian thoroughfare from block to block.

[17b-2.] **Logements, 15, rue du Général-Henrys,** at boulevard Bessières.

A building as a bridge makes this a not-so-triumphal arch to the neighborhood behind, interesting more as a stroke of urbanism than as architecture to contemplate.

★★[17b-3.] **Logements, 25, rue Jean-Leclaire,** corner rue Navier. 1938.

Crazy tile (as if a surface were subsequently crazed) veneers Art Moderne, with bay windows to modulate the facade. A first-class outpost of style in this neighborhood of Les Epinettes.

[17b-4.] **Square des Epinettes,** bounded by rue Jean-Leclaire, rue Collette, rue Félix-Pécaut, and rue Maria-Deraismes. 1893.

Such small Parisian parks are vestiges of earlier villages, with an earlier geometry than that of Haussmann. Les Epinettes is a northern sector of what was, before 1860, Les Batignolles. Cropped, clipped, and graveled, this is a wondrous escape from the frantic markets that line the avenue de Saint-Ouen between rue Guy-Môquet and the boulevards des Maréchaux. Unlike the English as in Bloomsbury, planned building did not create the square: the French found opportunities for a variety of surrounding buildings.

★[17b-5.] **Logements, 185, rue Belliard,** corner rue des Tennis. **Henri Deneux.** 1913.

Constructed by the chief architect of Monuments Historiques for himself, this is an amalgam of the style of Perret Frères and bizarre tile, a superencrustation equal to those towers of Simon Rodilla at Watts in Los Angeles. The flat roof is a "modern" architectural affectation, intended more to cry "style!" than to serve any functional purpose.

★[17b-6.] **Logements** and **crèche, 8-14, rue Georgette-Agutte,** between rue Belliard and rue Championnet. **Alexandre Ghiulamila** and **Jean-Michel Milliex.** 1983.

The metal and glass bay windows are an unhappy use of 1960s detailing to surround an elegant idea: that of bay windows per se. On the entrance side to the south, and the *crèche* to the north, such *retardataire* stuff gives way to PoMo games, more successful and logical at the *crèche*.

★★[17b-7.] **Montmartre aux Artistes (ateliers),** 187, rue Ordener, between rue Championnet and rue Damrémont. **Adolphe Thiers** and **Henri Résal.** 1932.

Neo-Romanesque arches support artists' studios in a more spartan style. Pass through into the first courtyard, where off-white stucco, steel sash, and glass give an appropriate neutral "industrial" setting for the "artists." No competition with their work is brooked. It's interesting to note, nevertheless, that many of the greatest modern painters preferred to live in 19th-century surroundings (e.g., **Picasso**).

★[17b-8.] Logements, 153, rue Lamarck, at avenue de Saint-Ouen and rue Etex. L. Dupont. circa 1910.

Bay windows and bay balconies infilled partly with floral tilework. The great verdanda and roof at its crest give a rakish hat to this *pan coupé*.

★★[17b-8a.] Bureaux, 29, rue Ganneron, corner rue Hégésippe-Moreau. 1989.

Some powerful articulations display columns embraced within a thoughtful curtain wall. Logic and elegance make a distinguished building.

★[17b-9.] Eglise Saint-Michel-des-Batignolles, 12 bis, rue Saint-Jean and passage Saint-Michel, off avenue de Saint-Ouen. Bernard Haubold. 1913–1924.

Neo-Romanesque in reinforced concrete clad with brick. The tower soars over the passage St. Michel. A heavy and spacious gloom gives a pleasant mystery to the interior.

★★[17b-10.] Logements, 26 and 29, rue des Apennins, between avenue de Clichy and rue Davy. André Bertin and Abro Kandjian. circa 1930.

Small *immeubles* in the International style, early modern in the spirit of such as Mallet-Stevens. This lovely pair, opposite each other, allows residents to savor their own "reflected" image.

★[17b-11.] Logements, 16, rue Sauffroy, between rue Guy-Môquet and avenue de Clichy. circa 1900.

Industrialization: first brick, then steel, lintels, wrought-iron balconies with suspended brick soffits. Virtuoso technology.

★[17b-12.] Logements, 18, rue Sauffroy, between rue Guy-Môquet and avenue de Clichy. Lamoreux. 1902.

A bit of art for art's sake: Art Nouveau, carved (the machines were now doing the carving), but the apparent product was not "industrial."

[17b-13.] Logements, 30, 32, 34, 36, rue Sauffroy, between rue Guy-Môquet and rue de La Jonquière. 1860.

Old hands that preceded Haussmann (the outer arrondissements were not annexed until 1860)—the scale here is more that of the July Monarchy (1830–1848). The decoration at No. 36 includes extravagant panels honoring music, architecture, painting, and sculpture, with some heady voussoirs to watch over us.

★★[17b-14.] Cité des Fleurs, between 59, rue de La Jonquière and 154, avenue de Clichy. 1847 with later additions.

There are 350 meters (more than 1,000 feet) of continuous villas, now mostly multiple apartment buildings, in a variety of styles, mostly "Classical" à la Louis-Philippe and Haussmann, but also with Moderne, neo-Renaissance, and some medieval revival entries.
  The original deed restrictions required each front garden to be planted with three fruit trees—such was the wont of Messrs. L'Henry and Bacqueville, the original developers.

[17b-15.] Piscine Bernard Lafay, 79, rue de La Jonquière, between rue Emile-Level and rue Boulay. J. A. Fourquier and Jean Filhol. 1982.

Low-rise brick and metal roofing gives this the character of a suburban place—but with 1970s styling at its best. The square Boulay-Level beyond is an appropriate foil.

★[17b-16.] Logements, 87, rue de La Jonquière, corner rue Fragonard. Bernard Bourgade and Michel Londinsky. 1985.

Neo-1930s with a curved rather than cut corner, oculus windows, pipe railings à la Breuer, a rich ocher-brown stucco, and tile. Overdone (take away the tile and the polygonal corner window wall), but these guys can detail, even if it's a bit berserk at times. See 17, passage Petit-Cerf. WOW!

★★[17b-17.] Logements, 17, passage Petit-Cerf, between rue de La Jonquière and avenue de Clichy. Bernard Bourgade and Michel Londinsky. 1988.

A Mediterranean extravaganza in tan pastel stucco, but the caryatid and her symbiotic tree are fertility rampant. What will cold winter evenings bring to the new inhabitants?
The *passage*, as usual, is more interesting than the buildings.

★★[17b-18.] Square des Batignolles, between rue Cardinet, place Charles-Fillion, and rue des Moines. Adolphe Alphand, supervising engineer. Barillet-Deschamps, horticulturist. Gabriel Davioud, urban furnishings. 1862.

A surprising, full-grown, and treed "English" garden (one of twenty-four by Alphand under Haussmann) in the sense of Kew or New York's Central Park—but much milder in drama than the folly of Buttes-Chaumont. Here are a copper beech and many horse chestnuts flanking an artificial romance, a stream with reeds and other supporting flora. Lovely.

★★[17b-19.] Eglise Sainte-Marie-des-Batignolles, place du Docteur-Félix-Lobligeois, on axis of rue des Batignolles. Jacques Molinos. 1829. Enlargements, including transepts and side aisles, Eugène Lequeux. 1839–1851.

Greek Revival without, its charm within is largely in the *transparente*, with Mary ascending through plastic clouds to the heaven above the altar—a neo-Baroque delight.
The *place* is of a charming scale and semicircular form, with low-rise but innocuous buildings serving to form a positive urbanism.

★[17b-20.] Logements, 62, rue Boursault, between rue Legendre and rue Bridaine. René Simonet, architect. Alexandre Bigot, ceramist. 1901.

Schizophrenic—or the work of the unlinked right and left halves of the brain. The articulate and sinuous steel supports bay windows in what seems avant-garde Art Nouveau to the right—with ordinary balconies to the left. For similar sinuousity (structural division), see 19–21, and 25, rue Boyer [20m-49]; and 40, rue Boileau [16s-36.]; and 124, rue Reaumur [2n-13.].

[17b-21.] RER Station, Pont Cardinet, 147, rue Cardinet at rue de Rome. Julien Polti. circa 1924.

You can ride from here to the Musée d'Orsay or the Gare d'Austerlitz, and so forth. Here are vaulted ogival shells that bring back a hint of Viollet-le-Duc—massacred, however, by SNCF alterations.

# 47
# SEVENTEENTH ARRONDISSEMENT
## ETOILE, WITH ADJACENT ARRONDISSEMENTS
### PLACE CHARLES-DE-GAULLE/ETOILE

Arc de Triomphe: **Jean-François Chalgrin;** Hôtels des Maréchaux: **Jacques-Ignace Hittorf** and **Charles Rohault de Fleury;** Hôtel Potocki: **Louis Renaud;** 22, rue Beaujon: **Henri Sauvage;** place des Etats-Unis; 60, avenue Kléber: **Charles Letrosne;** Hôtel Mercédes: **Georges Chédanne**

Métro: **Charles de Gaulle/Etoile**

**[17e-3.]** Hôtel Potocki/now **Chambre de Commerce de Paris. Louis Renaud.** 1857. Expanded.

The twelve-pointed star of the Etoile is the *rond-point* of the world. No other network of streets is gathered into such grandeur, tracing a spider web of Brobdingnagian proportions. Crowning it is that inevitable symbol of Paris, the Arc de Triomphe: superior corn. But so are its sibling symbols, the Tour Eiffel and Sacré-Coeur, the former more because its image has become jaded, the latter because it is the largest effort in banality that France has ever undertaken.

Once upon a time, before Catherine de Médicis asked for the Elysian Fields to be planted before her Palais des Tuileries, and long before there were any streets—let alone houses—in these parts, the site of the future *place* was a greater hill. Cut down to a gentler swell in 1768–1774 to make a circular place of promenade, it was then bypassed by the wall of the Fermiers-Généraux and its *barrières de l'octroi*, twin buildings in this case, that flanked the axis of what was then boulevard de Neuilly. The *barrières* coexisted with the Arc until 1860, when they were demolished, along with the wall.

★★★[17e-1.] **Arc de Triomphe,** centered on place du Général-de-Gaulle, until recently called place de l'Etoile, and its twelve radiating avenues. **Jean-François Chalgrin,** architect for Napoléon. 1806. **Jean-Nicolas Huyot,** architect for Louis XVIII. 1823. **Blouet,** architect for Louis-Philippe. 1830–1836.

Almost 50 meters (164 feet) tall, the Arc could fit the arches of Constantine and Titus and Septimius Severus within its volume, with space to spare. This is colossal, as Napoléon would have it, and mightily in the scale of the avenues of the Elysian Fields and Grand Army, which serve as the vista between the Louvre and the Grande Arche, threaded through this gargantuan eyelet.

The architecture of the Arc is simple, but Chalgrin's second, interpenetrating arch and vault on the Wagram-Kléber cross-axis was his stroke of genius. Visually ventilated, it now forms the nave and transepts of the **Unknown Soldier,** and on national days the great flag of France floats majestically within this eloquent space.

On its flanks, sculpture commemorates the feats of the armies and generals of France: **François Rude**'s *Le départ des Volontaires* is not only the best work in place but was also popularly called *Le Marseillaise*, inspiring the national anthem of the same name. Take the elevator to the roof terrace. From here the view is magnificent, at a height where human scale is still perceptible, and the work of Haussmann can be apprehended with leisure. Walk down to the museum of the history of the Arc and the Etoile, with the drawings of Chalgrin and Blouet and some *son et lumière* (cinema style) telling of things past: the funeral of Victor Hugo, the liberation of Paris—you guess which was more important.

★★[17e-2.] **Hôtels des Maréchaux,** rue de Tilsitt and rue de Presbourg, two halves of a concentric ring around the Etoile. **Jacques-Ignace Hittorf** and **Charles Rouhault de Fleury**. 1860–1868.

These knuckles of the twelve avenues radiating from the Etoile comprise eight small and four large exercises in neo-Renaissance architecture, with grand pilasters, at the colossal scale, in the manner of **Michelozzi**. But they are not buildings to contemplate; they are meant to participate in the grand ensemble of the *place*.

★[17e-3.] **Hôtel Potocki**/now **Chambre de Commerce de Paris,** 27, avenue de Friedland, corner rue Balzac. **Louis Renaud.** 1857. Expanded, **Jules Reboul.** 1881. Expanded for the Chambre, **Paul Viard** and **D. Dastugue**. 1927. *Salle de fêtes*, **Jacques-Emile Ruhlmann.**

The monumental marble stair is a wondrous essay in pomp—including neo-everything. Potocki's daughter-in-law termed it the *Crédit Polonais*. You figure that one out.

★[17e-4.] Logements, 22, rue Beaujon, between rue Arsène-Houssaye, and avenue Hoche. Henri Sauvage. 1925.

A kind of banal neo-Classicism erupts in the tasteless 1920s. The flutes of the balconied bays seem more like fasces bundled than Doric invested. Sauvage probably needed the money.

[17e-5.] Bureaux, 50, avenue Hoche, corner rue Beaujon. 1970s?

Semi-*pilotis* (at the right but not the left) participate in a virtuoso performance of tensile suspension of the projecting facade. Nervi, who didn't believe in suspenders, would have cantilevered.

[17e-6.] Logements, 38, rue Beaujon, between avenue Hoche and avenue de Wagram. Jean Ginsberg. 1969.

Travertine is now de rigueur among the affluent near the Etoile. Here cubism is sullied by its *pierre de taille*—cut and jointed slabs. Did you ever see articulated ice cream?

★[17e-7.] Bureaux/sometime piscine, disco, and restaurant, 30, rue Tilsitt and 10, avenue de la Grande-Armée. 1934.

A crisp entry in the series of facades that blandly (and, at Porte Maillot, vulgarly) march down this extension of the axis beyond the Etoile, on its way to La Défense. Next door on rue Tilsitt is an extravagance in the form an *hôtel particulier*, now commercialized: flamboyant neo-Renaissance of the very late 19th century.
Downstairs at No. 30 you may float in the former swimming pool (now filled with air) while dining.

[17e-8.] Ambassade de Danemark, 77, avenue Marceau, between rue de Presbourg and rue Newton. Preben Hansen and Bernard Zehrfuss. 1966.

The 1960s rash of multiple picture frames in a frenzy of decorative excess: semi-kitsch. In the United States architects such as Yamasaki and Edward Durell Stone fostered a similar frosty confectionery. One thought the Danes were above that sort of thing.

[17e-9.] Logements, 4, avenue d'Iéna, between rue de Presbourg and rue Newton. Léopold George and Xavier Schoellkopf. 1897.

[17e-10.] Compagnie Bancaire, (bureaux) 29, rue La Pérouse, between rue de Presbourg and avenue des Portugais. Michel Herbert. 1978.

A vain attempt to match the quality of the 19th-century street. Yes, Virginia, there *is* stone, but the harsh curtain wall and absence of secondary and tertiary levels of detail make this an elephant of the 1970s.

[17e-11.] Fédération Nationale du Bâtiment, 6–14 rue La Pérouse, between avenue des Portugais and rue de Belloy. Roger Saubot and Francois Jullien. 1972.

Glassy, but the deep structure at least gives some weight to the street commensurate with its more ancient (1890s–1940s) neighbors. The earlier building opposite (Gravereau and Lopez. 1951) is typical of that period of bland, modernity (frequently an excuse for cheap buildings).

★[17e-12.] Immeuble, 30, rue Galilée, between place des Etats-Unis and avenue d'Iéna. Paul Sédille, architect. André Allar, sculptor. 1895.

Twin busty caryatids (★), their pedestals making them mermaids, in an otherwise mixed-up, eclectic facade.

★★[17e-13.] **Place des Etats-Unis,** between avenue d'Iéna, rue Copernic, and rue Dumont-d'Urville. 1881.

A handsome garden surrounded by horse chestnuts. To the west the small square envelopes *Lafayette et Washington, Hommage à France,* sculpture by **Bartholdi** (1895).

[17e-14.] **Immeuble, 9, rue Galilée,** corner rue Hamelin. 1890s.

Brick and limestone, eclectic François I–Henri IV, adapted to an *immeuble de rapport.* François I's heraldic salamander stands atop his convoluted attached colonnettes. Galileo in glazed tile watches over it all.

★★[17e-15.] **Bureaux, 60, avenue Kléber,** between rue Cimarosa and rue Copernic. **Charles Letrosne,** architect. **Camille Garnier,** sculptor. 1912.

Brick and stone share this facade of sinuous balconies and floral carvings. Question: How do you get in? Answer: From the neo-Renaissance **No. 58** next door, of which this is an extension.

[17e-16.] **Centre de Conférence Internationale/** originally **Hôtel Majestic,** 19, avenue Kléber and 5, avenue des Portugais. **Armand Sibien.** 1908.

A mediocre block, more famous for its infamous use as German army headquarters during World War II.

★[17e-17.] **Hôtel Mercédes/**originally **Palace-Hôtel,** 9, rue de Presbourg and 6, avenue Kléber. **Georges Chédanne,** architect. **Gasq, Sicard, Boutry,** sculptors. 1902.

Hovering hats (or umbrellas) give this a skyscape. Why don't architects enrich, to this plastic degree, the level of the pedestrian? Why not fancy bottoms and naked tops?
"Even from afar, one is informed, won over, and charmed by its picturesque roof, which dominate the gloomy piles of the rond-point de l'Etoile. . . . The sport of the automobile, of particular prestige in this luxurious neighborhood, has informed the sculptors' inspiration." Roger Marx, in *Art et Décoration,* November 1904.

# 48
# SEVENTEENTH ARRONDISSEMENT
## MONCEAU

### PLACE GOUBAUX AND PLACE DU GENERAL
### CATROUX TO ROTONDE DE CHARTRES

Place Goubaux; 29, rue de Courcelles: **Xavier Schoellkopf;** Hôtel
Gaillard: **Victor-Jules Février;** Hôtel Fournier: **Duttenhofer;** rue de
Lévis; 27, rue Legendre: **Henri Sauvage;** 2 bis, rue Cosnard: **Charles
Plumet;** Les Procédés: **Frédéric Bertrand;** Salle Cortot: **Auguste
Perret;** Lycée Carnot: **Gustave Eiffel;** rue Fortuny; 134, rue de
Courcelles: **Théodore Petit;** Eglise Saint-Alexandre-Nevsky:
**Kouzmine;** Salle Pleyel: **Marcel Auburtin, et al.;** Hôtel Menier:
**Henri Parent;** Galerie C. T. Loo; Musée Nissim de Camondo: **René
Sergent;** Musée Cernuschi; Parc Monceau: **Carmontelle, Adolphe
Alphand,** and **Pierre Barrillet-Deschamps;** Rotonde de Chartres:
**Claude-Nicolas Ledoux**

Métro: **Villiers**

**[17m-49.] Pyramide de Carmontelle/Parc Monceau. Carmontelle.**
1773.

## La Plaine Monceau

"In former times a house, inhabited by a single family, constituted a luxury available only to those with titles, or millionaires. For some time now, thanks to some considerations too lengthy to discuss here, each can have his own *hôtel* . . . and the *hôtels* (whether) important, middle class, or minuscule, sprout up, thick and stylish.

"To satisfy this appetite for construction, it was necessary to seek out, beyond the former limits of the capital, vacant land. There was, precisely beyond the exterior boulevards (line of the Fermiers Généraux wall)—hardly twenty minutes from the Madeleine—an immense plain, called the Plaine Monceau, absolutely bare of habitations.

"In the times of which I speak (1850), this quasi-suburban territory was composed of wheat fields, 'enameled' with poppies and *bleuets,* furrowed by paths where the Juliets of Batignolles got lost in the arms of Romeos from Ternes.

"The Plaine Monceau presented, at that time, a spectacle unknown up to the present, even at the height of Haussmannian fevers. In two years, an immense town was created. Certain parts, still incomplete in the part neighboring the fortifications (those of Thiers/1845), are still the prey of a myriad of workers of all kinds, and nothing is so curious—when the meal hour sounds—as watching the debacle of masons, stone cutters, painters, carpenters, and locksmiths. . . . It is a true bouquet of flowers. These workers spread out through the quarter in the search of a restaurant with wine; for the wine-shop is still rare. Everybody is then seated outside or inside temporary eating places at plank-tables. . . . I must say that one of these taverns serves giblets for which one licks one's fingers up to the shoulders.

"Before going back to work, the workers smoke a pipe or read a newspaper (which is not generally the Revue des Deux Mondes) in the shade of the plane trees of the surrounding streets." **Adrien Marx** in *Les petits mémoires de Paris* (1888)

---

**[17m-1.] Centre d'Etudes Sociales Familiales,** 9, boulevard de Courcelles, at rue du Rocher. **Architecture Studio.** 1984.

Light and form at this place, not for *boulevardiers* but for serious studies. The excised form of man stands on one hand, a fractured Post Modern exercise in stone, tile, metal, and glass.

★**[17m-2.] Garage Renault,** 21–23, boulevard de Courcelles, between rue Miromesnil and boulevard Malesherbes. 1920s.

Lusty concrete and glass in slender steel framing, here for Renault. The garages of Paris are one whole chapter in avant-garde experimentation. As a modern appliance, the automobile could inhabit a modern building without questions of historical style—a Louis XIV garage?

★**[17m-3.] Logements, 29, rue de Courcelles,** between rue de Miromesnil and boulevard Malesherbes. **Xavier Schoellkopf,** architect. **Marcel-Alexandre Rouilière,** sculptor. 1902.

A paradoxical place of heavy and massive Art Nouveau. The floral sculpture becomes more sinuous and aggressive toward the top, where walls, balconies, and columns participate in a static raging sea.

The rusticated and vermiculated base is ponderous, a sturdy bottom to the typhoon above.

**[17m-4.] Logements, 6, place du Général-Catroux,** corner avenue de Villiers. **Georges Hennequin.** 1907.

*Pompier* style, even to the crossed torches entwined in the balcony railings. Ornate carving makes an ornate foil to the wrought-iron-and-glass entrance canopy (★).

**[17m-5.] Hôtel particulier, 2, place du Général-Catroux,** corner boulevard Malesherbes. **André Fiquet.** 1899.

The Belle Epoque bourgeois conjured up such neo-Renaissance brick and limestone remembrances of François I. A fantasy for those snobs who seek a "royal" past.

**★★[17m-6.] Banque de France**/originally **Hôtel Gaillard, 1,** place du Général-Catroux, between rue Georges-Berger and rue de Thann. **Victor-Jules Février.** 1884.

Février built this urban château to the order of Emile Gaillard, regent of the Banque de France, loosely inspired by the Louis XII wing of Blois. Fortuitously escaping demolition, it was purchased by the same Banque de France in 1919 and has remained their offices until this day. Its inauguration as Gaillard's house (furnishing took a year) was attended by 2,000 invited dancers.

"Two superb lancebearers, the fleur de lys of France emblazoned on their chests, struck the ground at the entry of the guests. The buffet was laid out in the dining room, with a superb peacock as its centerpiece. Monsieur Gaillard wore the costume of Henry II, in violet satin. . . . " from a newspaper account at the time. "At 11 o'clock a gentleman arrived on horseback. Proudly mounted, he wore with grace a charming Henri III costume . . . on his shoulder a short silk cape embroidered with gold; at his side, a long rapier, its guard gilded and carved.

This gentleman was none other than the painter **Jacquet** who, wishing to perpetuate the memory of the party, had painted, in his atelier of the rue de Prony, his own portrait showing him entering on his great roan horse, in the court of the chateau of la place Malesherbes (Catroux)."

**[17m-7.] Hôtel Saint-Marceaux,** 100, boulevard Malesherbes, corner rue de la Terrasse, **Victor-Jules Février.** 1875.

**[17m-8.] Hôtel, 10, rue Georges-Berger,** between boulevard Malesherbes and boulevard de Courcelles. **Jacques Hermant.** 1907.

An exedral trio of buildings off Georges-Berger includes this eclectic palazzo.

**★[17m-9.] Hôtel Fournier, 14,** place du Général-Catroux, between rue Legendre and rue Jacques-Bingen. **Hippolyte Duttenhofer.** 1878.

Duttenhofer not only was architect of this Viennese pastry but also modeled all the sculpture himself. A neo–Italian Renaissance *hôtel particulier,* with a touch of the multiplied pyramids of the Palazzo dei Diamanti in Verona (1582). Look up and down the north side of the square for variations on rising capitalists' dreams.

**★[17m-10.] Rue** and **square de Lévis,** between rue Legendre and boulevard de Courcelles.

A teeming street market serves the 19th-century grandeur of the Plaine Monceau. Your *pique-nique* can be bought here.

**[17m-11.] Immeuble, 27, rue Legendre,** between square Gabriel-Fauré and rue Salneuve. **Henri Sauvage.** 1928.

A modest and dulled Sauvage passed by here.

**[17m-12.] Chez Léon (restaurant),** 32, rue Legendre, between square Gabriel-Fauré and square Claude-Debussy.

A restaurant for the stroller, this has been described as "a true Parisian bistrot," where Georges Simenon may have sent his Inspector Maigret to dine.

★**[17m-13.] Ateliers, 1, square Emmanuel-Chabrier,** a cul-de-sac at the left end of square Claude-Debussy. 1920s.

Studios in an exposed concrete frame and with delicious, geometrically divided glass, like parquetry—all enhanced with *paquebot*-style balcony railings.

**[17m-14.] Maison, 19, rue Legendre,** corner rue Léon-Cosnard. 1880s.

A neo-Renaissance miniature with a great bay window guarding the street.

★**[17m-15.] Immeuble, 2 bis, rue Léon-Cosnard,** between rue Legendre and rue de Tocqueville. **Charles Plumet.** 1893.

A Plumet eclecticism. The bay windows are grand, the brick above provides novelty.

**[17m-16.] Immeuble, 3, rue Léon-Cosnard,** between rue Legendre and rue de Tocqueville.

Steel-framed glass studios interrupt brickwork and iron balconies.

**[17m-17.] Immeuble, 34, rue de Tocqueville,** between rue Legendre and rue Cardinet. **Léon Benouville.**

Iron strapwork of note.

**[17m-18.] Immeuble, 36, rue de Tocqueville,** between rue Legendre and rue Cardinet.

Polychromatic arcades against the sky.

**[17m-19.] Immeuble, 38, rue de Tocqueville,** between rue Legendre and rue Cardinet. 1930s.

Art Deco.

★**[17m-20.] Les Procédés/**originally **Enterprise Dorel (ateliers et domicile),** 45, rue de Tocqueville, between rue Legendre and rue Cardinet. **Frédéric Bertrand.** 1923.

Art Nouveau and tile, tile, tile. Polychromatic glass tile over a *béton armé* frame.

★**[17m-21.] Salle Cortot/Ecole Normale de Musique,** 78, rue Cardinet, between boulevard Malesherbes and rue de Tocqueville. **Auguste Perret.** 1929.

The frieze ventilates the auditorium, turning ornament into a functional asset. And the auditorium, squeezed into a building that is 9 by 29 meters (30 by 95 feet), sounded, according to Alfred Cortot, "like a Stradivarius." Wood acoustical panels floating in front of the walls and below the ceiling provide an appropriate resonance.

**[17m-22.] Ecole Normale de Musique de Paris,** 114 bis, boulevard Malesherbes, corner rue Cardinet. **Léopold Cochet.** 1881.

A retired mansion by the architect of **No. 112.** Look into the entry hall, where a grand stair is a stage set of inspiration, a neo-Baroque space ornamented with assorted marbles and painted *trompe l'oeil.*

★**[17m-23.] Hôtel particulier, 112 bis, boulevard Malesherbes,** between place du Général-Catroux and rue Cardinet. **Léopold Cochet.** 1881.

Chemetov calls it "an exercise in the rational style" by an architect whose work at 22, place du Général-Catroux, is concealed behind "an order that one would tend to term 'bourgeois.' " But for that matter, what *isn't* bourgeois around here?

Look into the quiet treed courtyard, accessible through the gate of No. 112 adjacent, through a building behind *(porte cochère),* and out again into a backwater.

**No. 22** is reminiscent in scalelessness of the inflated palace of the kings of the Two Sicilies at Caserta north of Naples. Here we have twenty-one windows in width, as if one were creating a *super-Haussmannianism* without party walls.

---

**Rosa Bonheur** (painter and sculptor, 1822–1899) speaks: "We lived in the faubourg Roule, at which time my father gave lessons (sketching) while I worked 'after nature' outdoors. . . . You would have no idea of what it was like, this quarter so elegant, so luxurious today, with the boulevard de Courcelles, the avenue de Villiers, the place Malesherbes (i.e., Général Catroux). . . . It was the country, the real country, where one saw market gardens, dairies, farms, cow-barns, country taverns . . . where one went to eat an omelet under flowering acacias. The cows, the goats, the sheep filled the fields . . . we studied moss. There exists a painting by Chabat (displayed in 1900) that one would believe painted in the "Morvan." I painted there some animals, and there were plenty of models. . . . I remember a student of Drolling who played the French horn between his lessons. . . . When the weather was bad, I worked in the abattoirs at Roule . . . it was necessary to truly adore art to work in the middle of such horrors: I took my place in the *bouveries* next to the point of slaughter. I heard jokes there. . . . Providence sent me a protector; seeing me lunch on a little *pain d'un sou,* he led me to his house, situated very near the atelier of our friend Detaille, where his brave wife had prepared a comforting meal. . . ." (*Vie et Histoire XVIIe,* p. 63.)

---

**[17m-24.] Lycée Carnot**/originally **Ecole Monge,** 145, boulevard Malesherbes, between rue Cardinet, avenue de Villiers, and rue Viète. **Hector Degeorge,** architect. Gymnasium, **Gustave Eiffel,** engineer. 1874.

In 1894 the Lycée Carnot inherited the building of the monumental Ecole Monge, a modern construction erected on plans of Hector Degeorge and Gustave Eiffel with exceptional qualities of comfort and hygiene.

"It was in 1869, and with a group of former students of the Ecole Polytechnique, that the Ecole Monge was founded; it was given for a start as a program, and has not failed since in it: alleviating the difficulties of teaching, and developing, at the same time as the intelligence of children, their bodies, which make men strong and valiant." **Alexis Martin,** *Promenade dans le 17e arrondissement.* 1892.

**[17m-25.] Hôtel particulier, 42–44, avenue de Villiers,** opposite rue Fortuny. **Lucien Magne.** circa 1890.

Entry arches à la Bramante in brick and limestone. A so-so hotel—but big.

**★[17m-26.] Aux Delices (café)**/once **Atelier Barrias,** 39, avenue de Villiers, corner rue Fortuny. circa 1900.

A delicious interior, both visually and gastronomically. Before conversion to a *pâtisserie* in 1900, it was the atelier of Louis **Barrias,** sculptor and friend of **Gustave Eiffel.** Stop in.

**★★[17m-27.] Rue Fortuny (even side),** between avenue de Villiers and rue de Prony. Circa 1878–1888.

> **No. 46. Charles-Eugène Flamant.** Neo-Renaissance brick and limestone.
> **No. 44. Hôtel** denuded.
> **No. 42. Hôtel Ponsin. Antoine Boland.** 1879. *Pompier* with attached caryatids over a raped *rez-de-chaussée* that once harbored a great stained glass window by Joseph-Albert Ponsin, originally displayed at the exposition of 1878.
> **No. 40. Charles Gudel.** 1958. A terrifying "modern" annex to **No. 42.**
> **No. 38.** Comfortable neo-Georgian.
> **No. 36.** Wandering eclectic.
> **No. 34.** Neo-Gothic (look at that leading).
> **No. 32.** More of **No. 38.**
> **No. 30.** Spartan neo-Gothic.
> **No. 28.** No-nonsense *pierre de taille* with bay window.
> **No. 26.** No-nonsense *pierre de taille* without bay window.
> **No. 22.** More of the neo-Goths.
> **No. 8. Lycée Mariano Fortuny. Antoine Boland** and **Latapy.**

**★★[17m-28.] Rue Fortuny (odd side),** between avenue de Villiers and rue de Prony. circa 1878–1888.

> **No. 17. Hôtel particulier. Weyland.** 1883.
> > "Our climate is most often gray; rain falls during two thirds of the 365 days of the year. Also isn't it important as a first principal, for our health as well as for the gaiety of our dwellings, to let enter there a flood of light, and sometimes warmth. Instead of large walls between windows, here are as large glazing as is necessary, and the more the window assumes importance, the more also it will be fitting to decorate it and embellish it. . . ." **César Daly,** an architect acting as critic. 1883. (*Ternes aux Batignolles,* p. 170)
> **★★★ No. 9. Ministère de l'Education Nationale. Ferdinand Gouny.** 1892. Glazed tile by **Loebnitz.**
> > A polychromatic phantom in multicolored brick, cut stone, and *grès de Bigot.* The frieze, cornice, bay window, and *lucarne* in silhouette are all strongly picturesque elements—a photographer's holiday.

**[17m-28a.] Immeuble, 7** and **7 bis, rue Edouard-Detaille,** between avenue de Villiers and rue Cardinet.

A grand two-story bay window presents iron strapwork and tiled pilasters (composite-capital capped) to the entry courtyard.

**[17m-29.]** Formerly **Hôtel particulier, 58–60, rue de Prony,** between rue Meissonnier and rue Jouffroy. 19th century. Surelevated, 1980s.

Modern architecture here vanquishes Haussmann-*tardif.* An elegant vestige of the plaine Monceau maltreated by commercial glass.

**[17m-30.] Hôtel particulier, 67, rue de Prony,** between rue Cardinet and rue Jouffroy. 1890s.

Ateliers housed in a neo-Renaissance town house.

★★**[17m-31.] Immeuble, 134, rue de Courcelles,** corner avenue Wagram. **Théodore Petit,** architect. 1907. **L. Binet,** sculptor of the frieze. **Henri Bouchard,** sculptor of the consoles.

The sinuous concrete-framed corner towers must be points of spectacle in this Classical/Art Nouveau mélange. As with many transitional—that is, going on from "Classical"—Parisian buildings, the interest is greatest at the top and in silhouette against the sky, where columns, colonnades, domes, dormers, mansards, chimneys, studios, and what-have-you, proliferate.

**[17m-32.] Immeuble, 119, avenue de Wagram,** between rue Gounod and rue de Prony. **Perret Frères.**

★**[17m-33.] Lycée Technique Jean Drouant/**originally **Ecole de l'Hôtellerie et de la Restauration,** 20, rue Médéric, between rue Jadin and rue Léon-Jost. **Raymond Gravereaux.** 1936.

Burnt red brick, raked to accentuate its horizontality, clads this Art Moderne school, styled in the spirit of the social architecture of the 1930s.

★**[17m-34.] Ateliers, 5 bis, rue Jadin,** between rue Médéric and rue de Chazelles. 1890s.

Polychromatic brick and glass veneering vast studios make this an oriental rug of a facade. Note the steel lintels, exposed and vigorous. Wouldn't *you* like to live here?

**[17m-35.] Hôtel particulier, 12, rue de Prony,** between boulevard de Courcelles and rue Henri-Rochefort. **Jean-Louis Pascal.** 1883.

The lands of the Pereire brothers included this street, opened in 1863 and lined with *hôtels* of this character. Pascal was a leading member of the architectural establishment: prominent in the administration of the Ecole des Beaux-Arts, secretary of the Société des Artistes Français, and inspector for Lefuel on the continuing construction of both the Louvre and the Tuileries—the latter, obviously, in his earlier years.

★**[17m-36.] Rue Henri-Rochefort,** between rue de Prony and place due Général-Catroux. Nos. 9–19. **Charles-Eugène Flamant.**

By creating, neo-Renaissance, neo-Gothic, and Dutch-eclectic houses, Flamant expressed individuality for those *arriviste* clients.

★**[17m-37.] Eglise Russe Saint-Alexandre-Nevsky,** 14, rue Daru, on axis of rue Pierre-le-Grand. **Kouzmine.** 1859–1861.

Six golden onion domes punctuate the sky in this stone Orthodox neo-Romanesque extravaganza. The unique forms make the front garden a necessary and pleasant buffer to Haussmannian urbanism.

★**[17m-38.] Salle Pleyel,** 252, rue du Faubourg-Saint-Honoré, between rue Daru and avenue Hoche. **Marcel Auburtin, André Granet,** and **Jean-Baptiste Mathon.** 1927.

Stripped Classical forms, with octagonal oculi, at that confused time when many potentially talented architects were producing their most bland work in the name of the "functional" idea. The doors on rue Daru (★) are exceptional.

**[17m-39.] Logements, 16, avenue Beaucour,** at avenue Hoche and rue du Faubourg-Saint-Honoré. 1930s.

There is some lovely ironwork, and the recessed entry provides a neo-Classical and functional touch.

**[17m-40.] Logements, 4, avenue Hoche,** between rue du Faubourg-Saint-Honoré and rue de Courcelles. **E. Ricard** and **Lefoll.** 1892.

Here great *Atlantides* crowned with Composite capitals flank the entrance and support the second-floor balconies. The vermiculated and rusticated stonework is an Italian touch. The patron was the chocolatier, Emile Menier, who built here for his relatives. He dwelt at 5, avenue Van Dyck, a block away, as if the Parc Monceau were his private garden.

**★★[17m-41.] Hôtel Menier,** 5, avenue Van Dyck, at the west entrance of Parc Monceau. **Henri Parent.** Interiors, **Aimé-Jules Dalou.** 1868–1872.

An *hôtel particulier* with a grand front courtyard, open to the street, that advertises the chocolate-dipped wealth of a once-great industrialist in an elaboration of stone, ironwork, *combles,* and *lucarnes.* Here a *grand bourgeois* was truly grand.
Next door, on the park side, his brother Henri built in an ornate neo-Renaissance style: pilasters, coquilles Saint Jacques, and anthemia ornament this white (for Paris) stone (cf. Sacré-Coeur). At **8, rue Alfred-de-Vigny** is the entrance, with a bit of neo–15th-century fantasy in the courtyard. Look!

**[17m-42.] Logements, 8, rue Murillo,** corner rue Rembrandt. **Tronquois.** 1899.

A building of splendiferous *grand standing* in the form of an inflated *hôtel particulier.* Brick, with stone quoins and rustications, embraces a small courtyard. Visible technology bows here with light, steel-framed bay windows.

**[17m-43.] Logements, 7, avenue Rembrandt,** between rue de Lisbonne and place du Pérou. 1890s.

Cast- and wrought-iron bay windows vastly enrich the facade.

**[17m-44.] Logements, 51, rue de Lisbonne,** corner rue Rembrandt. **Gustave Rives.** 1896.

A corner bay's half-cylinder brings technology to the merely affluent.

**★★[17m-45.] Galerie** and **Hôtel Ching Tsai Loo,** 48, rue de Courcelles, at place du Pérou. **Fernand Bloch.** 1928.

A bourgeois fantasy in muted and matte reds. The tiled eaves are more convincing for the entrance than those that hang from the floors above.

**★★[17m-46.] Musée Nissim de Camondo**/originally **Hôtel Moïse de Camondo,** 63, rue de Monceau, between avenue Ruysdaël and boulevard Malesherbes. Reconstructed as museum, **René Sergent.** 1910–1914.

The house within the courtyard is based on the Petit Trianon at Versailles. The last descendents died at Auschwitz.

**[17m-47.] Immeuble, 84–88, boulevard Malesherbes,** between rue de Monceau and boulevard de Courcelles. **J. M. Lesoufaché.** 1862.

★**[17m-48.] Musée Cernuschi**/originally **Hôtel Cernuschi,** 7, avenue Velasquez, between boulevard Malesherbes and Parc Monceau. Reconstructed as museum, **Bouvins.** 1898.

A personal collection of oriental art, housed in the former *hôtel particulier* of the politician and economist Henri Cernuschi.

★★★**[17m-49.] Parc Monceau,** between boulevard de Courcelles, boulevard Malesherbes, rue de Monceau, rue Murillo, and rue Alfred-de-Vigny. **Adolphe Alphand,** supervising engineer. **Pierre Barillet-Deschamps,** horticulturist. 1862.

Originally a romance or "stage set" of the playwright **Carmontelle** for the duc de Chartres (1773, only his pyramid survives), this was replanned in a more limited area by Haussmann's landscape team, who produced a very English garden with appropriate *folies,* including the apocryphal colonnade (speciously attributed to a chapel at Saint-Denis demolished in 1719), an arcade torn from the old Hôtel de Ville in 1871 by the communards, and Carmontelle's pyramid. Lush green grass, cropped and clean (where only small children intrude), a lake, and many Sunday morning joggers at the perimeter. The balance (half) of the original park became a subdivided property of the Pereire brothers.

Before the Revolution, this was the domain of the duc de Chartres, who opposed the wall of the Fermiers Généraux that would form a barrier to his view. Ledoux, architect of the wall's pavilions, or *barrières,* was enough of a politician to negotiate with the duke, proposing a moat, instead of a wall, along the gardens, and a vantage point atop what was to become the **Rotonde de Chartres.**

★★★★**[17m-50.] Rotonde de Chartres,** 35, boulevard de Courcelles, at entrance to Parc Monceau. **Claude-Nicolas Ledoux.** 1784–1791. Dome, 1861.

The sixteen archaic Doric columns, which form a tempietto at the edge of the park, are "archaic" in the sense that their capitals emulate those flatter, less taut ones of the 7th century B.C., as at Paestum, rather than those of the **Parthenon.**

Louis-Phillipe d'Orléans, duc de Chartres (later known under the Revolution as Philippe-Egalité), received a salon atop this pavilion in return for withdrawing his opposition to the newly built wall of the Fermiers Généraux. From it, he could survey his lands (the present Parc Monceau) and the open territory to the north. This was apparently an extra structure, not a tollgate like the other *barrières* but solely a vantage point for the duke. Located inside the walls, therefore, it was saved at the time of the wall's demolition. Ledoux is remembered by architectural historians mostly as a dreamer of ideal cities (cf. the City of Salt); but with the Rotonde and the fifty-odd *barrières* he extrapolated a whole Classical vocabulary. Perhaps Variations on a Theme by Palladio would be a fair classification.

# 49
# SEVENTEENTH ARRONDISSEMENT
## TERNES

### PLACE DES TERNES TO PORTE MAILLOT/
### PORTE DE CHAMPERRET AND BACK

Place des Ternes; Métro Entrance: **Hector Guimard;** 7–9, place des
Ternes; Ceramic Hôtel: **Jules Lavirotte** and **Paul Bigot;** Au
Printemps: **Marcel Oudin;** avenue Carnot; place Saint-Ferdinand;
square Gaston-Bertandeau: **Léon Gaudibert** and **P. Jumelle;** villa des
Ternes; 48, boulevard Gouvion-Saint-Cyr: **André Arfvidson;** Palais des
Congrès: **Alain Gillet;** rue de Dardanelles; rue Dobropol: **Raymond
Perruch;** Eglise Sainte-Odile: **Jacques Barge;** Logements/rue Jacques
Ibert: **Wladimir Mitrofanoff;** 174, boulevard Berthier: **Auguste
Perret;** HBM Berthier: **Joseph Bassompierre, et al.;** 14, 16–18, rue
Eugène-Flachat: **Stephen Sauvestre** and **Charles Girault;** rue
Ampère; Hôtel Mercédès: **Pierre Patout;** ateliers/rue Saint-Senoch:
**Georges Thirion;** Château des Ternes

Métro: **Ternes**

[17t-49.] Ateliers/logements, 10, rue de Saint-Senoch. **Georges
Thirion.** 1910–1912.

**[17t-1.] Place des Ternes,** at junction of avenue des Ternes, avenue de Wagram, boulevard de Courcelles, and rue du Faubourg-Saint-Honoré. 1860 and later.

Here was the Barrière du Roule on the old road to Neuilly. Ternes is a tardy place-name, from the Château des Ternes, now straddling rue Bayen, along rue Pierre-Demours. The *barrière,* one of Ledoux's grandest, was a two-story complex at the scale of a minor castle.

The modern *place* is no great shakes, but is host to a wonderful building at **Nos. 7–9(★),** the central courtyard of which forms a great Classical cylinder of space, articulated with grandiose pilasters. Buzz yourself in.

Here also is a crisp **Hector Guimard** entrance to the Métro, complete with light standards peering with the eyes of Martians at those entering and exiting. Look. You'll agree.

★★**[17t-2.] Ceramic Hôtel,** 34, avenue de Wagram, between place des Ternes and rue Beaujon. **Jules Lavirotte,** architect. **Paul Bigot,** ceramist. 1904.

A great essay in Art Nouveau, this excerpt from a Haussmannian avenue bears an exuberant encrustation of tiles *(grès de Bigot).* **Lavirotte's** play of forms is precocious pre-modernism of a sort that arranges a rich drapery of stone and tile rather than the slim glass and metal curtains (walls), of "modern." Post Modern is back with such masses and volumes, but in a less revolutionary and more childlike (sometimes childish) sense.

**[17t-3.] Logements, 17, avenue MacMahon,** corner of rue du Général-Lanrezac. 1930s.

The corner, towered with a polygon, gives a *paquebot* prow to this radical—for the street and arrondissement—*immeuble de rapport.*

**[17t-4.] Boulangerie/patisserie, 19, rue de l'Etoile,** corner rue de Montenotte. 1890s.

Classy and *classée.*

★★**[17t-5.]** Formerly **Magasins du Printemps**/originally **Magasins Réunis,** 28–30, avenue des Ternes and 24, avenue Niel. **Marcel Oudin.** 1912. Altered.

Oudin created one of the great sinuous Art Nouveau buildings, here in *béton armé,* but much of its detail was erased by a one-story surelevation and by simplification of the dome. Churches and department stores (God and mammon) were the two great experimental grounds for the technology of iron and concrete, where their aesthetic merits could evolve.

The bourgeois store implanted amid its clientele gave its only salute to Haussmann in its slate slopes. Inside, the great central light well and staircase have been replaced by decorators' blandness.

Alas, Printemps has withdrawn, and we await a new tenant. Because it is not a *monument classé,* the building could be demolished in favor of an *immeuble de grand standing* with horrendous smoked-glass balcony railings.

**[17t-6.] Logements, 45 ter, rue des Acacias,** between avenue MacMahon and avenue Carnot. **F. Carrer.** 1930s.

Smooth and textured stone contrast on this equivocal Moderne/neo-Classical lodging. At **No. 45,** next door, in the first step in the process of "stripping," only the balcony columns still seek to be Classical vestiges.

**[17t-7.] Bureaux, 46, rue des Acacias,** between avenue MacMahon and avenue Carnot. **Jean-Emile Rey.** 1973.

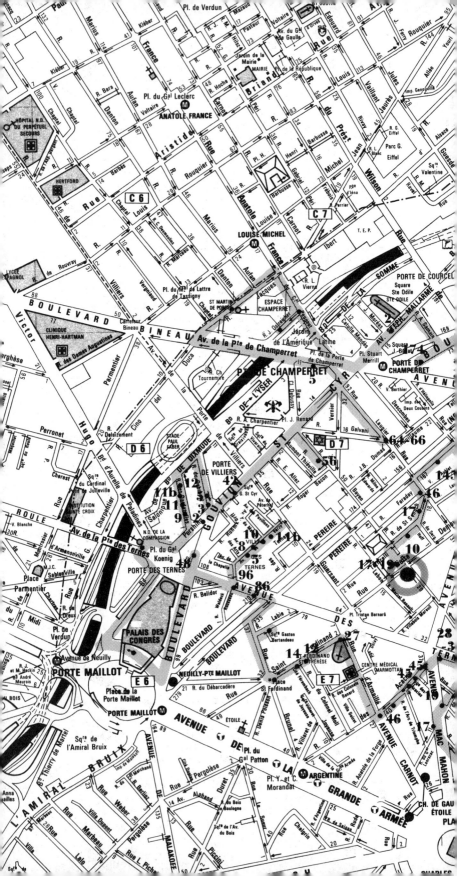

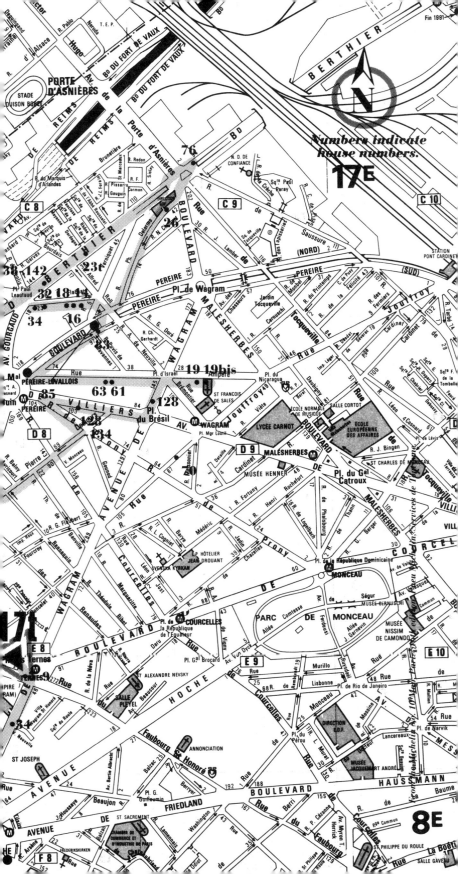

The glass, pinned to a gasketed facade, will remind you of nautical architecture, where the opening is excised from a sheet of steel, and stresses can comfortably round a corner.

★★[17t-8.] **Avenue Carnot,** between place du Général-de-Gaulle and rue des Acacias. 1857.

One of the five avenues that Haussmann added, this is a ray in the 12-pointed *Etoile.* And here are two blocks of pure, early Haussmannian architecture.
The shortest of the five, it ends not with a bang but a whimper at the little rue d'Armaillé.

[17t-9.] **Eglise Saint-Ferdinand-des-Ternes,** 27, rue d'Armaillé, corner of rue Saint-Ferdinand, off avenue des Ternes. **Théodon, F. Bertrand** and **P. Durand.** 1937.

A rather pompous "modern."

★[17t-10.] **Rue Saint-Ferdinand,** between avenue des Ternes and place Saint-Ferdinand.

One of the arrondissement's older streets; note particularly **No. 12 (P. Convert.** 1847) and **No. 14 (D'Aurange.** 1853). For the neighborhood of Ternes, these are early lodgings.

★★[17t-11.] **Place Saint-Ferdinand,** at the intersection of rue Saint-Ferdinand and rue Brunel.

A strongly contrasting group of architecture from the Belle Epoque to the 1960s. It nevertheless holds the cylindrical space, at the center of which is a romantic stone memorial to Léon Serpollet (1858–1907), inventor of a steam-powered auto, here remembered in "molten," naturalistic stone.

★[17t-12.] **Square Gaston-Bertandeau,** between rue Brunel and avenue des Ternes. **Léon Gaudibert** and **P. Jumelle.** 1927.

More dedicated *moderne-*ism, where Classical remembrances are subdued by smooth detail.

[17t-13.] **Ecole, 86, avenue des Ternes,** between boulevard Pereire and avenue de Verzy. 18th century.

Tucked into a courtyard behind the avenue's facades is an 18th-century country house from another era of architecture and street configuration.

★★[17t-14.] **Villa des Ternes,** between 96, avenue des Ternes and 39, rue Guersant. Late 19th century.

A semisuburban enclave on a quiet, private street tucked behind the surrounding streetfronts. Here is again a panorama of architecture from Art Nouveau to the terrible 1970s.

> **No. 5.** Ceramics and a cavetto cornice.
> **No. 8.** Art Nouveau wrought iron.
> **No. 10.** Art Nouveau with neo-Egyptian.
> **No. 11 bis.** A bit of *Star Trek* among conservative villas and apartments. (**Michel Londinsky** and **Bernard Bourgade.** 1980).

★★[17t-15.] **Logements, 48, boulevard Gouvion Saint-Cyr,** between boulevard Pershing, and 10, place du Général-Koenig. **André Arfvidson.** 1932.

Art Deco tesserae crown the silhouette in gold—but muted tesserae are everywhere. Details and craftsmanship of this order would redeem much Post Modern architecture. Could they be revived to this level of quality?

**[17t-16.] Palais des Congrès** and **Hôtel Concorde Lafayette,** place de la Porte-Maillot. **Alain Gillet.** 1974.

Only a preview of coming attractions. This exile from Detroit stands at the gates of Paris, at the end of the avenue de la Grande-Armée, the penultimate blow to the rapid degradation of that avenue between the Etoile and the boulevard périphérique.

The Palais serves as a center for professional meetings. In America they would be conventions, and supposedly staid citizens would shed their somber demeanor, drink, dance, and wear funny hats. The French seem to seek the same sort of bizarre behavior here through architectural empathy—the building is a funny hat.

Inside, the *grande salle* seats 4,000; overhead there are 1,000 rooms.

---

**Olivier-Clément Cacoub** wants to join those architects participating in the grand Louvre/Champs-Elysées/Arc de Triomphe/La Défense axis: **Percier & Fontaine** (Arc de Triomphe du Carrousel), **Chalgrin** (Arc de Triomphe de l'Etoile), **Pei** (Pyramide du Louvre), and **Spreckelsen** (La Grande Arche). His first proposal was for a pair of half-arched buildings, borrowed from *Star Wars.* Happily, this was discarded after a universal reaction approaching violence. A second proposal, floated in the spring of 1988, modified the first. Whatever is finally built at this great traffic circle, it will not be a precinct of the pedestrian. What is already in place honors the automobile, and to attain the *place* proper (the park in the center of the *rond-point*), you must pass over inconvenient bridges or brave the herds of autos en route to the Périphérique.

---

**[17t-17.] Chapelle Notre-Dame-de-la-Compassion,** porte des Ternes, between avenue de la Porte-des-Ternes and boulevard d'Aurelles-de-Paladines. **Lefranc,** architect. **Jean-Auguste-Dominique Ingres,** stained glass. 1842.

This memorial to the duc d'Orléans, son and heir apparent of Louis-Philippe, once marked the site of the grocery store where he died in 1842 after falling from his runaway carriage. It was moved here for the construction of the boulevard Périphérique. It is an awkward complex at a miniature scale.

★**[17t-18.] Rue des Dardanelles,** between boulevard Pershing and boulevard de Dixmude. 1930s.

A neo-Classical versus Moderne struggle in stucco and stone. **No. 5** attempts some precocious boxy balconies, and **No. 7** unleashes a whole retine of tricks.

> **No. 9. Charles Venner.** 1932.
> **No. 11. Jack Gerodias.** 1930.
> **No. 11 bis. J. Bellat.** 1930.
> **No. 12. A. Coudray.** 1931.

**[17t-19.] Immeuble, 2, boulevard Pershing,** corner rue du Dobropol. **J. Bellat.** 1930.

Note the leafy bas-reliefs.

★★**[17t-20.] Logements, 3** and **5, rue Dobropol,** between boulevard Gouvion-Saint-Cyr and boulevard de Dixmude. **Raymond Perruch.** 1931.

Jazz Art Deco forms at No. 3, with *retardataire* metalwork, redeemed at No. 5 in tubular shipboard-style iron bands. Perruch is one of the unsung modernists of Paris.

★[17t-21.] **Logements, 42, boulevard Gouvion-Saint-Cyr,** between rue Dobropol and avenue de la Porte-de-Villiers. **Raymond Perruch.** circa 1930.

More Perruch, here in heavy Art Deco, unfortunately very poorly cared for. The balcony railings are sinuous tree silhouettes. Here modernity confronts the Haussmannian scale.

★[17t-22.] **Ecole, 56, rue Bayen,** between boulevard Gouvion-Saint-Cyr and rue Roger-Bacon. **Jean Dubuisson.** 1987.

A graceful Post Modern school, both strongly and modestly stated. Color is essential in such a simple scheme, and the strong greens, with counterpoints of yellow, red, and blue, are just right. Bay windows add some plasticity to the street.

★[17t-23.] Originally **Archives de la Banque de France,** 64–66, rue Laugier, between boulevard Gouvion-Saint-Cyr and rue Guillaume-Tell. **J. Flegenheimer, Henri Bard,** and **F. Garella.** 1931. Remodeled, **Bernard Reichen & Philippe Robert.** 1987.

The intermingling of the 1930s and 1980s leaves a classic-smooth *moderne* mix. This offbeat orphan is hard to place but very appropriate to the 17th arrondissement.

[17t-24.] **HBM, 5, place de la Porte-de- Champerret,** between boulevard Gouvion-Saint-Cyr and rue Claude-Debussy. **Bali.** 1934.

*Meulière,* red brick, cast stone, and rock-face granite. One essential in these 1930s public housing complexes was the inclusion of shops along the streetfronts, activating them.

★[17t-25.] **Logements, rue Jacques-Ibert,** between avenue de la Porte-de-Champerret and rue du Caporal-Peugeot. **Wladimir Mitrofanoff.** 1988.

Almost as willful as a sophomore, Mitrofanoff gives us five tiers of casual histrionics: a black truss supports the sky, with a vermilion pediment floating above it all. Do people really live here, or is this merely an occasion to look at all that unleashed genius? Underneath the jazz is poor detailing.
The court within furthers an architecture of children, innocence, willfulness, impetuousness. No serenity, calm, or vernacular is allowed here.

[17t-26.] **Espace Champerret,** underground, between boulevard Périphérique, avenue de la Porte-de-Champerret, and rue du Caporal-Peugeot. **Michel Andrault** and **Pierre Parat.** 1988.

A jazzy netherworld.

★[17t-27.] **Jardins d'Amérique Latine,** over and around Espace Champerret. **Landowski.** 1988.

Pyramid fever has struck again, here with a remembrance of the Aztecs and the Mayans: Mexico at the gates of Paris.

★[17t-28.] **Ecole, rue du Caporal-Peugeot,** adjacent to boulevard Périphérique. **Alain Gillet** and **Jean Daveau.** 1988.

Those little white tiles clad a snuggled-down clutch of pavilions, the amusing fenestration of which plays a nice game within its walls. Little children, little windows—and close to the floor. Most buildings around this *non aedificandi* zone of the old fortifications of Thiers (1845–1920s) are more worthy of the Côte d'Azur than of Paris. This is an exception.

★★[17t-29.] **Eglise Sainte-Odile,** 2, avenue Stéphane-Mallarmé, between rue Jean-Moréas and rue de Courcelles. **Jacques Barge,** architect. 1936–1942. Stained glass, **Decorchement.**

Three pseudo-Byzantine domes, more akin in their external expression to gears of a machine than to the domes of Anthemius of Tralles (Hagia Sophia). But all this is forgiven 1,400 years later. After all, the Moslems copied Hagia Sophia to create the Blue Mosque 500 years after Anthemius.
Outside are brick, the domes, and a finned and lanceted tower.

[17t-30.] **Logements, 174, boulevard Berthier,** between avenue de Villiers and rue Albert-Samain. **Auguste Perret.** 1953.

Very *retardataire* Perret, as are his buildings at Le Havre and Marseilles. An articulated concrete frame is infilled here with sandstone panels. The balcony railings and *garde-fous* are naïve in comparison to rich versions both old and new (for the latter compare the ironwork at 58, rue Bayen). Even those Art Deco tubes have more guts.
Perhaps gracious within, it is an intellectualized and entrepreneurial version of Paris.

★★[17t-31.] **HBM, 138–142, boulevard Berthier,** between rue de Senlis and rue Jules-Bourdais. **Joseph Bassompierre, Paul de Rutté,** and **Paul Sirvin.** 1933.

An exceptionally crisp *îlot* of these HBMs, encircling to form a "red belt" around Paris—"red" in both senses of the word.

★[17t-32.] **Hôtel, 23 ter, boulevard Berthier,** between rue Verniquet and rue Alfred-Roll. **A. Sélonier.** 1900.

A special star on the two blocks between rue Eugène-Flachat and rue Verniquet. Selonier's eclecticism crosses late Gothic with early Renaissance, including the salamanders of François I. It was built for an opera singer known as Alvarez.

★★[17t-33.] **Groupe Scolaire, 76, boulevard Berthier,** corner avenue de la Porte-d'Asnières. **Alexis Dresse** and **Léon Oudin.** 1938.

The ship in full sail (arms of the city) is an intricate bas-relief of complex brickwork, as if carved into this Art Moderne block. *Moderne* but not modern, it is full of memories, like the rings of a brick tree.

[17t-34.] **Immeuble, 26, rue Philibert-Delorme,** between boulevard Malesherbes and boulevard Pereire. **Alexandre and Pierre Fournier,** 1930.

Limp *moderne,* with stalactites that conjure a watery character.

[17t-35.] **Maison, 32, rue Eugène-Flachat** and **51, boulevard Berthier** between boulevard Berthier and rue Verniquet. **Paul Sédille.** 1890s.

Hallucinating "Arabic" neo-Renaissance vulgarity. Wow!

[17t-36.] **Maison, 34, rue Eugène-Flachat,** corner boulevard Berthier. **J. Brisson.** 1891.

★[17t-37.] Maisons, 16 and 18, rue Eugène-Flachat, between boulevard Berthier and rue Alfred Roll. Stephen Sauvestre. 1890s.

More hallucinations in a battle between **John Ruskin** (for England) and **Viollet-le-Duc** (for France). The result might be termed a Stick Style extravaganza. Sauvestre collaborated with **Eiffel** on the "decoration" of his tower.

[17t-38.] Maison, 14, rue Eugène-Flachat, between boulevard Berthier and rue Alfred-Roll. Charles Girault. 1890s.

The architect of the **Grand Palais** made this "modest" house a few years before his 1900 extravaganza.

[17t-39.] Hôtel particulier, 83, boulevard Pereire, between rue Alphonse-de-Neuville and rue Puvis-de-Chavannes. J. Brisson. 1883.

Ateliers top this *hôtel* in brick and limestone.

★★[17t-40.] Ateliers, 85, rue Ampère, between boulevard Pereire and rue Puvis-de-Chavannes. Circa 1890.

Three grand studio floors face north in delicate steel and glass. Slender Corinthian columns support decorated steel lintels.

[17t-41.] Hôtel/ateliers, 61 and 63, rue Ampère, between boulevard Pereire and rue Puvis-de-Chavannes. Stephen Sauvestre. No. 61, 1881. No. 63, 1890.

Eiffel didn't influence him much here—or at least not as much as the wood translations from steel on rue Eugène-Flachat.

[17t-42.] Chapelle de l'Eglise Saint-François-de-Sales, 15, rue Ampère, between avenue de Wagram and boulevard Malesherbes. E. Ewald. 1913. Adjoining housing, Van Lysbeth. 1930.

Neo-Romanesque crowned with those Lombardian arched corbel tables from the north of Italy.

★[17t-43.] Logments, 19, rue Ampère, between avenue de Wagram and boulevard Malesherbes. 1898.

The curved glass, in an elegant crystalline bellying, is surrounded by Beaux Arts pomp.

★[17t-44.] Hôtel Mercédès/originally immeuble à usage de pension de famille de luxe, 128, avenue de Wagram, corner rue Brémontier. Pierre Patout. 1929.

Another stationary Patout *paquebot*, modern in its smooth, rounded nudity—but certainly not in fenestration or plan.

★[17t-45.] Hôtels particuliers, 128, 130, 132, 134, avenue de Villiers, between place du Maréchal-Juin and avenue de Wagram. Stephen Sauvestre. 1883.

The canopy at No. 134 is a supreme vulgarism, but this quartet nevertheless presents a northern European stylistic mélange. No. 134 affects a stepped Dutch gable, patterned brickwork, and inset decoration of enameled tile. The other three, in brick and *pierre de taille*, are in vigorous neo–17th-century styles—*lucarnes*, broken pediments, and all.

**[17t-46.] Logements** and **bureaux, 70, rue Jouffroy,** between avenue de Villiers and boulevard Malesherbes. **Paul Vimond.** 1983.

Sandstone + brick spandrels = overcomplicated—sandstone alone would have been super. Vimond is already sufficiently enriching his forms with a play of splayed openings.

**[17t-47.] Ateliers/logements, 145, boulevard Pereire,** between rue Rennequin ad rue Laugier. **G. A. Dreyfus and V. Metté.** 1931.

A heavy-handed attempt at artists' *ateliers* in an otherwise very bourgeois district.

**[17t-48.] Villa Aublet.** 46, rue Laugier, between boulevard Pereire and avenue Niel. 1900–1980.

A mingle of styles, most delightful at the Stick-Style timberwork entry of **No. 17.**

**[17t-48a.] Wallace fountain,** on an island at the intersection of avenue Niel, rue Laugier, and rue Pierre-Demours. **Charles Lebourg,** sculptor. 1871.

Sir Richard Wallace gave Paris sixty-six fountains, each with four caryatids carrying an imbricated dome. Here was public potable water in a city then with an imperfectly sanitary water supply.

★★**[17t-49.] Ateliers/logements, 10** and **17, rue de Saint-Senoch,** between rue Laugier and rue du Sergent-Hoff. **Georges Thirion.** 1910–1912.

Ateliers that may not have been for artists but, rather, for bourgeois lovers of light and space. The long vertical panes in industrial steel sash are elegant, and brick infill spandrel panels complete the industrial aesthetic. Only traces of Classicism remain, in the *rez-de-chaussée* rustication and a cartouche or two.

★**[17t-50.] Château des Ternes,** 17–19 rue Pierre-Demours, straddling rue Bayen. Circa 1740, with terrifying alterations and denuding.

The remains of the château span rue Bayen, symbolizing what was later a split use: separate families living in each half. The scale of the 18th century is the most of what remains, with a freestanding courtyard portal.

# 50

# EIGHTEENTH ARRONDISSEMENT

## BUTTE

### SAINT-JEAN-DE-MONTMARTRE TO SACRE-COEUR

Métro/Abbesses: **Hector Guimard;** Théâtre/Conservatoire Nationale:
**Charles Vandenhove;** Eglise Saint-Jean-de-Montmartre: **Anatole de
Baudot;** Le Bateau Lavoir; Moulin de Radet; Moulin de la Galette;
26–36, avenue Junot: **Adolphe Thiers;** Maison Tristan Tzara: **Adolf
Loos;** Maison Casadesus; Cimetière Saint-Vincent; Eglise
Saint-Pierre-de-Montmartre; Basilique du Sacré-Coeur: **Paul Abadie;**
Halle Saint-Pierre

Métro: **Abbesses**

**[18b-1.] Métropolitain Abbesses. Hector Guimard. 1898–1901.**

Montmartre is a magic word in tourist circles. Like Camelot, it is romantic fiction; but at first hand it can also be delightful or tawdry fact. Images of artists in their garrets, dancing in the streets, evenings at the **Moulin Rouge,** and that castle on the hill, **Sacré-Coeur,** intertwine in a worldwide daydream. And so the Americans, Japanese, and many others, puff up those hundreds of steps of the **Butte,** jostle one another to have their images sketched in the place du Tertre, flock into the vastness of Sacré-Coeur, buy awful paintings, drink wine (and eat hamburgers) in cafés, and go home assured that they have reached Mecca, soared to Valhalla, brought home the Holy Grail.

Meanwhile, all around them was a richness of wondrous architecture— ancient (**Saint-Pierre**), 18th-century (**Château des Brouillards**), Art Nouveau (**Métro Abbesses**), early modern (**Maison Tzara**)—that belies the schlock that they were led to believe was the soul of this venerable place. To start, we will emerge from the Métro under one of **Guimard**'s last remaining covered structures at

★★[**18b-1.**] **Métropolitain Abbesses,** place des Abbesses. **Hector Guimard.** 1898–1901.

One of Guimard's two remaining volumetric exercises for the Métro (the other is at **Porte Dauphine,** see [**16h–24.**]. Many of his railings, light standards, and map-display panels remain, but here is a glorious Art Nouveau crustacean that shelters the body until it emerges from the underworld, level with the *place.*

[**18b-2.**] **Théâtre/Conservatoire National,** place des Abbesses. **Charles Vandenhove.** 1992.

The reincarnation of the 18th and 19th centuries both in tandem and surelevated. An Ionic temple lurks behind logements, entered through a *porte cochère.* Atop it all, lead-coated steel roofs house Post Modern *combles.*

[**18b-3.**] **Crèche, logements,** and **parking,** 14–16, place des Abbesses, along rue de La Vieuville and embracing Parc Jehan-Rictus. **Charles Vandenhove.** 1991.

An adopted site for the children of [**18b-2**]. Will neo-Classical architecture create neo-classic infants?

★★★[**18b-4.**] **Eglise Saint Jean-l'Evangeliste**/commonly called **Saint-Jean-de-Montmartre,** 19, rue des Abbesses, 2, place des Abbesses. **Anatole de Baudot,** architect. **Paul Cottancin** and (later) **Degaine,** engineers. **Alexandre Bigot,** ceramist. 1894–1904.

The reinforced concrete ribs and shell recall Gothic, without being literal: the material here was promoted for a poor parish seeking to save money. The result is a memorable tour de force by Baudot, the first architect interested in concrete as an architectural material rather than merely as an invisible structure. For this, he is at the fountainhead.

In Baudot's own words, the vaults were "formed of two membranes of 7 centimeters of reinforced cement: the inner one was covered with a skin of plaster to receive paint; the other constituted a proper roof. Between these two, in a space of .04 centimeters, slag was placed, forming an excellent means of isolation against changes in temperature."

Precocious engineering, precocious architecture. Baudot was a star student of **Labrouste,** a student and assistant of **Viollet-le-Duc,** and the teacher of many followers.

★[**18b-5.**] **Le Bateau-Lavoir,** 13, place Emile-Goudeau, at rue Ravignan, gallery entrance, rue Garreau. 1978.

A concrete incarnation in general function, if not true spirit, of the true Bateau-Lavoir, where Picasso painted the "Demoiselles d'Avignon." That ramshackle wooden structure succumbed to the flames of an "urban renewal fire" in May 1970. Its peer survives around the corner at **1, rue Orchampt.**

Among those who might be seen (with benefit of a séance) are Max Jacob, Harry Baur, Georges Braque, Henri Matisse, Juan Gris, and Guillaume Apollinaire. The photographer Andreas Feininger termed the old rotting place "The Acropolis of Cubism." Behind the new building, on the rue Garreau, you can enter a quiet courtyard and study the studio building's full volume; through a passage, you can enter a gallery open to the public.

**★[18b-6.] Atelier, 1, rue Orchampt,** off rue Ravignan.

A glass house to catch northeast light; the volume of the whole is a whole glazed studio. See **Le Bateau-Lavoir** above.

**[18b-7.] Hôtel particulier,** 19, rue Ravignan, at place Jean-Baptiste-Clément. **L. De Fais.** 1911.

"Versailles stone" *(meulière)* clads a picturesque house and garden. Tile and bracketed timber eaves join to make an architecture *sub-*urban.

**★[18b-8.] Logements, 2, place Jean-Baptiste-Clément,** corner rue Gabrielle. **J. Boucher** and **M. Bouriquet.** 1932.

Exuberant Classical/Art Moderne. The bellied balconies crown this in a rich crescendo, a sophisticated syncopation of paired and multiple forms.

---

"At the summit of rue Tholozé is the Moulin de la Galette, a somewhat prudish museum of dances despite its 'legs in the air' reputation. Not so long ago, *galettes* were still sold there. Together with the Moulin Rouge—before they were colonized by Negroes without exoticism, Russians without Russia, painters without talent, palette, or easel, politicians without party, and voyeurs without opportunity—it was inhabited by artists of the first rank, among whom one must put Lautrec and Maurice Utrillo. One of the true visualists of Montmartre, the historical painter of the Butte, Utrillo now appears in the astonished brains of our future bachelors (of fine arts) with all the charm and mystery of Egypt of the Pharoahs."

---

**[18b-9.] Moulin du Radet/Restaurant Graziano.** 77, rue Lepic, corner rue Girardon.

Fantasy or reality? This miniature mill remembers the thirty that crowned this **butte** early in the 19th century, wind catchers that ground the flour of Paris. The real mill remaining could be reached through a simple gate to one side of the restaurant. The **Moulin de la Galette** still sits up there, part of a private, gated compound of houses, but visible from afar as a silhouette.

---

### Les Moulins de la Butte

According to a study published by **André Maillard** in the *Bulletin du Vieux Montmartre,* the first mills appeared in the 16th century, not the 13th century of popular tradition.

The first verified mention of a mill dates from 1529 . . . the **moulin du Palais,** from the name of its location. It was situated to the west of the present **Moulin de la Galette** on the passage between the rue Lepic and No. 11, avenue Junot. . . . The ninth, erected in 1717 on land corresponding to **24, rue Norvins,** was the **Moulin Chapon,** known as **le Radet;** it was moved in 1834 by **Nicolas-Charles Debray,** next to the **Moulin Blute**

**Fin,** which he owned. He added a tavern and a dance hall and called the ensemble Moulin de la Galette.

---

**[18b-10.] Maisons, 4–10, rue de l'Armée-d'Orient,** a loop off rue Lepic. No. 4 remodeled by **Auguste Perret.** 1913.

Perret's exterior traces are mild, perhaps only remnants of good Perret Frères contracting. No. 6 is a studio building with eclectic class: glazed, balconies, greenhouses, the trappings of a comfortable artist. Its adjoining garden, together with Nos. 8–10, makes it all an urbane *pas de quatre.*

**[18b-11.] Logements, 64, rue Lepic,** corner rue Garreau.

Guarding a garden of this mini-*hôtel particulier,* now apartments, are four tiers of variations on a theme of the Venus de Milo (except that the third floor's guardian is a boy). In their niches they survey the street life.

★**[18b-12.] Maison/Atelier, 5, rue Tourlaque,** corner rue Caulaincourt. **Gérard.** 1881.

The corner bay window is, in fact, flush; the great *pan coupé's* geometry gives it the posture of a bay. Polychromatic brick, stucco, tile, slate, glass. **Viollet-le-Duc,** roll over.

**[18b-13.] Foyer pour les personnes âgées, 4, rue Eugène-Carrière,** corner rue Steinlen. **Yves Jenkins** and **B. Coutellier.** 1982.

The aged have glazed tile surfacing their lair. Boring.

**[18b-14.] Logements, 21, rue Eugène-Carrière,** at place Nattier and rue Félix-Ziem. **Yves Jenkins.** 1983.

A modest PoMo *immeuble,* its pseudo-mansard happily the brow of a fifth-floor terrace; here again urbanism wins. The architecture is a bit fragile, a throwaway.

**[18b-15.] Logements, 49, avenue Junot,** between rue Caulaincourt and rue Simon-Dereure.

What a stair! A sober Haussmannian pile of stone gives vent to a glassy modern incision, but the stair behind that translucence is a clunk. There have been bow windows and bay windows; and here is a bow stair.

★**[18b-16.] Ateliers/apartments, 36, avenue Junot,** between rue Caulaincourt and rue Simon-Dereure. **Adolphe Thiers.** 1929.

The broken form gives these studio apartments an appropriate scale in response to its uphill neighbors and the steeply sloping street. Look through to the court within: more light and studios. In fact, the building reappears at last, around the corner on rue Simon-Dereure.

★**[18b-17.] Hôtels particuliers, 26 and 28, avenue Junot,** corner rue Simon-Dereure. **Adolphe Thiers.** 1925.

A rather graceless cubism by Thiers, who seems more practical as a constructor of ateliers than as a creator of urban form. See also his building, **Montmartre aux Artistes** at 187, rue Ordener **[17b-7.]**.

**[18b-18.] Atelier, 22, rue Simon-Dereure,** off avenue Junot. **Adolphe Thiers.** 1925.

The behind of 36, avenue Junot **[18b-16.]**

**[18b-19.] Immeuble/ateliers, 15, rue Simon-Dereure,** off avenue Junot. circa 1930s.

Double-scaled studios, stacked, their skylights to the north. Crude and bold, a bit pseudo-futuristic in the style of Alexander Korda's 1936 film *Things to Come.*

★**[18b-20.] Villa Léandre,** off 23 bis, avenue Junot, just uphill and opposite rue Simon-Dereure. 1926.

Just when you thought you'd escaped the comfy villas of the 1920s, here is another charming cul-de-sac. Walk in. The less radical citizens of Montmartre (or artists disguised as bourgeois) live here, and both groups seem to think that this is really England.

★★**[18b-21.] Maison Tristan Tzara,** 15, avenue Junot, between villa Léandre and rue Girardon. **Adolf Loos.** 1926.

This Viennese purist, whose obsession with the removal of all ornament was his greatest creative act, created an impurity for the surrealist poet Tristan Tzara. Forms are confused by the use of two materials: stucco, which had promised crisp white purity in his Viennese essays at denuding; and rubble stone, the dreaded material of suburbia. Perhaps this was a form of perverse surrealism—which Loos is the real Loos?

Loos, in *Ornament and Crime* (1908) had said: "I made the following discovery and offered it to the world: cultural evolution is synonymous with the disappearance of ornament from utensils. I thought I was bringing new joy to the world, which did not thank me. People were gloomy and hung their heads. What depressed one man was the realization that no new ornament can be created. . . . Then I said, 'Don't shed any tears. See, that's what makes for greatness in our own time: that it is incapable of generating any new ornament. We have conquered ornament, we have finally made our way to the absence of ornamentation. Look, the day is at hand, our fulfillment is waiting. Soon the city streets will gleam like white walls. Like Zion, the holy city, the capital of heaven. Then we will be fulfilled.' "

**[18b-22.] Logements, 12, avenue Junot,** between rue Simon-Dereure and rue Girardon. **Fernand-Camille Chevalier.** 1935.

Polygonal bay windows and limestone serve this late neo-Classic/Art Moderne block. The bay windows also serve as symbolic columns (cf. Bofill), the cantilevered penthouse (there's even more above) as cornice, and the portal as base.

**[18b-23.] Casadesus House**/originally **Château des Brouillards,** rue Girardon at place des Quatre-Frères-Casadesus. 1772. Altered, 1920s.

An 18th-century *folie,* later a Napoléon I château, engardened at the shoulder of Montmartre. The levels and walks around ensure privacy for this family of musicians.

**[18b-24.] Logements, 7, rue Darwin,** between rue de la Fontaine-du-But and rue des Saules.

Bay windows but with solid reveals—then why have a bay? Or is this a badge of style?

**[18b-25.] Logements, 38, rue des Saules** at rue Darwin. 1930s.

Art Moderne strip balconies in perforated brick. This would be at home on New York's Upper East Side.

★[18b-26.] Musée d'Art Juif, in le Merkaz de Montmartre, 42, rue des Saules, between rue Darwin and rue Custine.

*Meulière* and terra-cotta in an exotic but hardly Middle Eastern pile—like crumbled cookies and icing.

★[18b-27.] Cimetière Saint-Vincent, rue Lucien-Gaulard, rue Saint-Vincent, and rue des Saules. Enter rue Lucien-Gaulard.

Here is a bizarre view of Sacré-Coeur up the butte. And here lies the French actor Harry Baur; the French painter Maurice Utrillo, and a host of French others. Like most Parisian cemeteries, it is a collection of miniature architecture.

[18b-28.] Logements, 17, rue des Saules, between rue Saint-Vincent and rue de l'Abreuvoir. 1930s.

Neo-Classical/Art Moderne. White and monolithic, the forms step out as the building rises.

★★[18b-29.] Château d'Eau, 9 bis, rue Norvins, at rue Lepic. 1835.

An octagonal temple to water, in Greek Revival dress, centered in a modest but enveloping garden. The 1927 *château d'eau* on rue du Mont-Cenis, next to Saint-Pierre, waters the quarter well.

---

**Feu Montmartre**

"I've discovered, an Englishman was telling me recently, why Parisians don't travel: they have Montmartre. You travel by going to Montmartre. Canadians, displaced South Americans, Germans, or Slavs buy suitcases and apply for passports in order to come to Montmartre, the homeland of the night world. A great novelist once said that the four fortresses of the western world were the Vatican, the English Parliament, German General Staff headquarters, and the Académie Française. He forgot Montmartre, the fifth fortress, which is more impregnable than the others and will survive all upheavals.

"Willette, one of the mandarins of the Butte, or breast of Paris, . . . never failed to point out to journalists interviewing him about his art, that, 'Like Jesus between the two thieves, Sacré-Coeur stands between the Moulin de la Galette and the Moulin Rouge.' " **Léon-Paul Fargue** in *Le piéton de Paris.*

---

★★★[18b-30.] Eglise Saint-Pierre-de-Montmartre. Rue du Mont-Cenis, off place du Tertre. Choir, transepts, and nave (excluding vaults west of bay adjacent to choir), 1147. Western vaults, 15th century. Facade, 18th century. Restored, **Louis Sauvageot.** 1908. Stained glass. 1954.

Romanesque on its way to Gothic, this is one of the great churches of Paris and one of the city's oldest. The cool, dark Romanesque nave is in moral and sophisticated contrast to the cacophony of tourism outside and to the exploitative symbolism of Sacré-Coeur. Perhaps the latter should be stuffed, like a fuzzy elephant won at a rifle range or amusement park.

At the choir are four Roman columns, seemingly from the temple that preceded this church, the oldest things here. The apse is one of three early ribbed vaults of the Paris region, of which the others are **Saint-Denis** (the precocious product under Abbot Suger) and **Saint-Martin des Champs,** where they now shelter not an altar but the "ancient" automobiles of the Conservatoire des Arts et Métiers.

**St. Thomas à Becket** prayed here, and in 1534 **St. Ignatius of Loyola** made his vow here to found the Jesuit order.

But for us today, this is a special place, the redeeming grace of the Butte.

It should be taken in small doses and frequently, as vaccination and booster shot against the banality all around. And then go out and wallow in glorious *fast-food* and *fast-art.*

★[18b-31.] **Place du Calvaire,** off place du Tertre, toward the view and around the corner.

A placid cul-de-sac and point of view aside the frantic place du Tertre, the latter filled with non- and pseudo-artists in shorts and pink polyester pantsuits. Place du Tertre is both the apogee and perigee of tourism, the first in quantity, the latter in quality. Americans in groups usually love it.

★★[18b-32.] **Basilique du Sacré-Coeur.** at the summit of the Butte. **Paul Abadie,** architect. **Daumet, Laisné, Rauline, Magne,** masters of the work. 1876–1919.

If, as suggested, it were inspired by **Saint-Front** in Périgueux, that wouldn't be surprising, as Abadie had already "restored" that church with a vigor that even his master **Viollet-le-Duc** could not match. Saint-Front is an almost new building built in the same general profiles as its predecessor, but of a cold gray stone, with hard and harsh profiles that belie its ancient beginnings.

Sacré-Coeur is so notorious that it is scarcely seen as a building—let alone as a church. It is an obvious symbol of Paris, sitting atop its mountain, like the radiator cap of an entire city. Shown to those whose brain has been incessantly imprinted with its eyed image, it evokes nostalgia for freshly baked bread, Gauloises, red wine, and old Gene Kelly movies. So this grand bit of white, this white pastry crowning an invisible wedding cake (supplied by the mind's eye this time), is the ultimate kitsch, a logo for Paris.

You can ascend the dome, but the view from the parvis is already superb, and a walk around the crest of the Butte will offer vistas of charm in every direction.

The stone is of a remarkable self-cleaning variety, the chemistry of which combines with rain to flush clinging pollution. In theory the whole building will eventually dissolve—gracefully, of course. If energy pushes you on, walk down the great flight of steps to **place Saint-Pierre,** at the foot of the Butte. Look back at Sacré-Coeur's profile, particularly appropriate in concert with the gaudy merry-go-round at the bottom. Then turn left to the corner to find:

★[18b-33,] **Musée d'Art Naïf and Musée en Herbe**/originally **Halle Saint-Pierre,** place Saint-Pierre at rue Paul-Albert. 1868.

What was an iron-and-glass market in the Baltard era is now shuttered and glazed and bricked, neutralizing its detail and form. If the arcades had been allowed to survive articulately (brick wall freestanding behind), shade, shadow, and form would have vastly increased the extant value.

# 51
# EIGHTEENTH ARRONDISSEMENT
## CLICHY

### PLACE DE CLICHY TO CINEMA LOUXOR

Place de Clichy; 2, rue Biot: **Michel Roux-Spitz;** Cinéma Wepler-Pathé: **Vladimir Scob;** square Berlioz; Moulin Rouge; Le Pigalle: **Gridaine;** La Cigale: **Philippe Starck;** Elysée Montmartre; Cinéma Louxor: **Ripey**

Métro: **Place de Clichy**

**[18c-11a.] Villa des Platanes.** circa 1900.

The night life of Montmartre tumbled out of place Clichy, then along boulevard Clichy and boulevard Rochechouart to boulevard de Magenta and boulevard Barbès. Here were the Moulin Rouge, the Elysée-Montmartre, and much later, the wondrous Cinéma Louxor. These were places of fantasies, of strange adventure and sensuality, now overtly catering to those searching for the reality, or just voyeurism of raw sex. Cinemas provide vicarious heterosexual or homosexual orgies, and there is paraphernalia aplenty for the black-leather-and-studs gang. But something of a renaissance may be in the wings. The Elysée-Montmartre is a symbol, and some of the tawdriness may return to good, not so clean, fun.

★[18c-1.] **Place de Clichy,** gathering boulevard de Clichy, avenue de Clichy, boulevard des Batignolles, rue de Léningrad, rue d'Amsterdam, and rue de Clichy.

Here is the knuckle of four arrondissements, a noisy tourist center that offers a broad range of seafood restaurants (oysters, oysters, oysters), movie theaters, and other profane activities, some innocent, some aesthetic, some banal. Here stood the Barrière de Clichy by Ledoux in the wall of the Fermiers-Généraux, which followed the path of the two boulevards.

The monument at the center (1869. **Doublemard**) remembers the defense of Paris on March 30, 1814, against the armies of the allies. The *barrière* was held, but the armistice intervened. Three weeks later, with Napoléon dethroned, Louis XVIII entered Paris here, only to exit at the same point a year later on Napoléon's return from Elba.

[18c-1a.] **Charlot (restaurant),** 12, place Clichy.

Reputedly Art Deco with fish. Now the remodeled interiors are redecorated in a somewhat flashy fifties pastiche. Forget it for architecture. Stick with the fish.

★[18c-2.] **Logements, 2, rue Biot,** at place de Clichy. **Michel Roux-Spitz.** 1930.

A blocky Roux-Spitz reminiscent of 115, avenue Henri-Martin **[16h-41.].** There is a "modern" character here not only in the building's form and detail but also in the frenetic activity at its street level—not unlike a proper Park Avenue-ite on the shores of Times Square or a Mayfair-ite on the shores of Trafalgar.

★[18c-3.] **Cinéma Wepler-Pathé,** 140, boulevard de Clichy, at place de Clichy. **Vladimir Scob.** 1956.

This movie palace anchors boulevard de Clichy, as that of Louxor anchors the other end of these boulevards. Signs and posters are the architecture of the base and place. Above, however, some late-blooming Art Moderne architecture, vintage 1930s–1940s prevails, but it is slowly being crushed by the pressures of advertising.

[18c-4.] **Hôtel Mercure** and **Hôtel Ibis,** 1, rue Caulaincourt, at boulevard de Clichy and rue Cavallotti. **Dominique Hertenberger** and **Jacques Vitry.** 1982.

The architects aver that this is "at the scale of the Haussmannian *immeubles* that surround it." The size, perhaps; but not the syncopation of forms and windows—particularly the histrionics at the sidewalk. Clichy may be a gaudy place, but the gaud of **Wepler Pathé** is far more urbane than this rock and roll architecture.

★[18c-5.] **PTT, 61, rue de Douai,** between boulevard de Clichy and place Adolphe-Max. **Dumont.** 1975.

Serrated, polished aluminum mini-bay windows attempt a postal renaissance: a bit of architectural jazz next to the garish space of the place de Clichy. The PTTs of the 1920s and 1930s were, with Citroën garages, the radical leaders of their times.

### ★[18c-6.] Place Adolphe-Max/Square Berlioz.

Here the horse-chestnut and plane trees intermingle around a saccharin statue of Hector Berlioz, looking love-sick and plaintive. This park is certainly not a *Symphonie Fantastique* but a lovely *fantaisie impromptu,* near the cacophony of Clichy. Rest here.

### ★[18c-7.] Hôtel particulier, 10, place Adolphe-Max, between rue de Douai and rue de Bruxelles. 18th century.

This will help you remember pre-Haussmannian Paris both in terms of the street and the adjoining private gardens.

### [18c-8.] Cité Véron, 94, boulevard de Clichy, between avenue Rachel and rue Lepic.

The Théâtre Ouvert for young authors and the Foundation Boris-Vian, where contemporary painters are exposed, sprouted here.

### ★[18c-9.] Moulin Rouge, 82, boulevard de Clichy, between rue Lepic and avenue Rachel. 1889. Burned and reconstructed, 1915.

Robert Venturi (in his 1972 book, *Learning from Las Vegas*) would count this as architecture of the people, a symbol as powerful as that of Sacré-Coeur. But the question is, which is more valid?

Mills, of course, covered the slopes of the Butte Montmartre in the 19th century. This fake mill (and real nightclub) remembers them, just as José Ferrer sketching the cancan there "remembers" Toulouse-Lautrec.

### [18c-10.] Hôtel particulier, 7, impasse Marie-Blanche, off rue Cauchois and, in turn, rue des Abbesses. d'Eymonnaud. 1880.

Gothic Revival of the corny sort that is just right for these precincts. The parties that once reigned here were succeeded by galleries and art.

### [18c-11.] 2 and 4, rue Coustou, between boulevard de Clichy and rue Lepic. 1930s.

Sex shops downstairs, Art Moderne upstairs, fluted with elegant garde-corps. Perhaps this might be termed *Cubo-Grec.*

### ★[18c-11a.] Villa des Platanes, 58–60, boulevard de Clichy, just east of rue Coustou. circa 1900.

The boulevard entry building is an elegant tunneled guardhouse to a Beaux Arts block behind, and villas in turn behind that.

### [18c-12.] Le Pigalle (bar), 23, boulevard de Clichy, at place Pigalle. Alfred-Maurice Gridaine. 1954.

"Witness of the sixties." *Classé* as a *monument historique* for the record, not for the eyes. Perhaps drink will soften the hard 1950s design.

### ★[18c-13.] La Cigale (discothèque), 120, boulevard Rochechouart, between rue des Martyrs and villa Dancourt. 1830s. Restored, interior seating, etc. Philippe Starck. 1988.

In this "polyvalent" hall (like **Bercy** and **Le Zénith**) fifteen hundred rockers can groove to the beat. The neo-Baroque interior is a *monument classé.*

★★**[18c-14.] Elysée-Montmartre (cabaret),** 72, boulevard de Rouche-chouart, between rue des Trois-Frères and rue de Steinkerque. 1889. Remodeled, 1988.

Fountainhead of the cancan built for the Exposition of 1889 (the Moulin Rouge was a later follower). ROCK LIVES and will perhaps be the savior of this wondrous strip of Toulouse-Lautrecian reminiscences. Who will the great rock painter be?

★★**[18c-15.] Cinéma Louxor,** 170, boulevard de Magenta, corner boulevard de la Chapelle. **Ripey.** 1921.

Egypt has been a French friend ever since Champollion translated the Rosetta Stone and Napoléon's troops marched around in a way not seen since Alexander the Great. The romance for the masses remained, and where better to exploit its allure than in a cinéma? The Luxorian parts are scattered, although the whole is hardly even Ptolemaic. It is Cecil B. DeMille's Egypt here, rather than Champollion's.

# 52
# EIGHTEENTH ARRONDISSEMENT
## CLIGNANCOURT-CHAPELLE
### MAIRIE XIIIE ARRONDISSEMENT TO PORTE DE
### LA CHAPELLE

Eglise Norte-Dame-de-Clignancourt; Mairie: **Marcellin Varcollier;** 7, rue Tretaigne: **Henri Sauvage;** HBM; rue Duc: **Léon Besnard;** HBMs; boulevard Ney: **Léon Besnard** and **Henri Provensal** and **Alexandre Maistrasse;** Immeuble à gradins: **Henri Sauvage;** Square de Clignancourt; Conservatoire de Musique XVIIIe: **Claude Charpentier;** 21, rue de Laghouat: **André Bertin** and **Abro Kandjian;** former Magasins Dufayel: **Gustave Rivès;** Eglise Saint-Denis-de-la-Chapelle; Marché de la Chapelle: **Auguste Magne**

Métro: **Jules-Joffrin**

**[18ci-33.] Eglise Saint-Denis-de-La-Chapelle.** Early 13th century. Facade, 18th century.

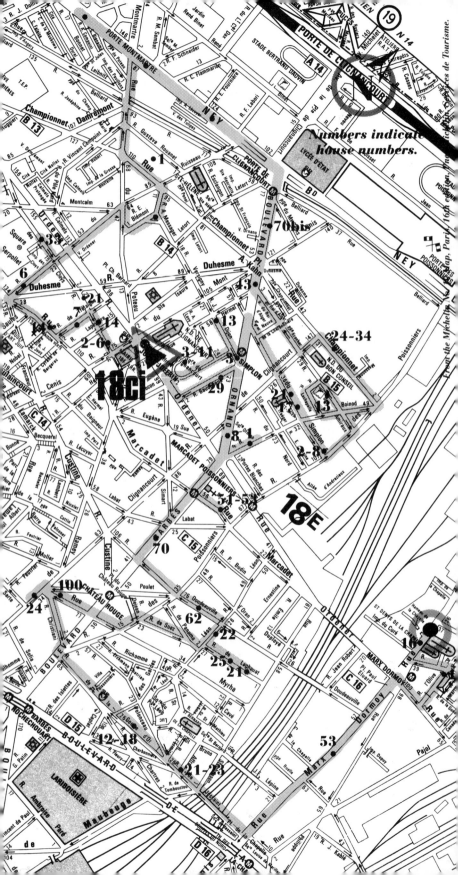

★[18ci-1.] **Eglise Notre-Dame-de-Clignancourt,** place Jules-Joffrin, at intersection of rue Ordener and rue du Mont-Cenis. **Eugène Lequeux.** 1863. Later modifications.

A "Roman" basilican facade fronts a neo-Gothic nave and side aisles.

★★[18ci-2.] **Mairie,** place Jules-Joffrin, at intersection of rue Ordener and rue du Mont-Cenis. **Marcelin Varcollier.** 1892. Interior remodeling, **Jean-Pierre Heim.** 1988.

The facades are the usual late 19th-century fussing with a neo-Renaissance vocabulary, but the courtyard within is a choir of light, under one of those *parapluies* of iron and glass. Enter and blossom.

★[18ci-3.] **HBM, 2, 3,** and **6, rue Duc,** corner rue du Mont-Cenis. **Léon Besnard.** 1925.

A concrete frame, inlaid tile, with bricks infilling create a small-scale *logement social* of considerable charm. The palette is modest but rich and articulate.

[18ci-4.] **Logements, 14, rue Duc,** between rue de Trétaigne and rue Lapeyrère. **C. de l'Oeil.** 1912.

A rich limestone ornation, with handsome bay windows and the exuberance of the Belle Epoque.

★[18ci-5.] **Logements, 7, rue de Trétaigne,** between rue Duc and rue Marcadet. **Henri Sauvage** and **Charles Sarrazin.** 1904.

A modest *logement social,* with prowed bay windows in an exposed concrete frame. Here the première of concrete for the masses vies with Perret's rue Franklin concrete grid for the classes.

★[18ci-6.] **PTT, 21, rue Duc,** through to **14, rue Marcadet,** between rue de Trétaigne and rue Duhesme. **Georges Labro.** Rue Marcadet side, 1932. Rue Duc side, 1936.

Along rue Duc, triple-hung windows in a rare instance of this Anglo-Saxon system in Paris. The iron grille is exceptional, the lettering wonderful for its time.

★★[18ci-6a.] **Ecole, 6, rue du Ruisseau,** corner of rue Duhesme. **Georges Pancréac'h** 1989.

A strong grid on Ruisseau ends with a modern *poivrière* at the acute intersection: a distinguished new building, powerful, yet serene.

[18ci-7.] **Ecole Maternelle, 33, rue des Cloÿs,** between rue du Ruisseau and rue Montcalm. **Fabrice Dusapin** and **François Leclerq.** 1988.

Smooth stone on the streetfronts for a "railroad car" sequence streaming in metal to the heart of the block.

★★[18ci-7a.] **Lycée, 1, rue Gustave Rouanet,** between rue du Poteau and rue du Ruisseau. **Emile Bois.** 1934–1950.

Some more monumental *Classical-Moderne* brickwork with entries that could put many Post Modernists, playing with columns, to shame.

★[18ci-8.] **HBM,** rue Emile-Blémont at rue André-Messager. **Agence d'Architecture de l'Office HBM.** 1928–1933.

One of the best of these complexes, futuristic to the population of the early 1930s. Atop the bow windows are a plethora of balconies, artists' *ateliers*, and trellised pergolas; but it all fits comfortably into the context of the quarter.

★[18ci-9.] HBMs, boulevard Ney, between avenue de la Porte-de-Clignancourt and rue Arthur-Ranc (Hôpital Bichat). **Agence de l'Office d'HBM.** Avenue de la Porte-de-Clignancourt to rue Camille-Flammarion, **Léon Besnard.** Rue Camille-Flammarion to Porte de Montmartre, **Henri Provensal.** Porte de Montmartre to rue Arthur-Ranc, **Alexandre Maistrasse.** 1926–1930.

The blocks closest to the Porte Clignancourt are the earliest: concrete-framed but with red tile roofs in a Stick Style that recalls the wood chalets of the 19th century and their imitators in romantic villas of the 20th, such as Hameau de Danube [19v-27.] This merits some strolling, for the ensemble brought to the truly poor of Paris substantial housing that is not only charming, handsome, and well groomed but also at a civilized urban scale. The 2,730 units run from studios to four rooms.

★[18ci-10.] Titania Hotel, 70 bis, boulevard Ornano, between boulevard Ney and rue Championnet. **Remoissonet Frères.** 1919.

A crisply detailed and bayed concrete frame, tiled à la Bigot, in an industrial aesthetic brought to travelers via 25 bis, rue Franklin and Perret [16c-22.].

★[18ci-11.] Ed l'Epicier/ formerly **Cinéma Ornano,** 43, boulevard Ornano, corner rue Hermel. **Alfred-Maurice Gridaine.** 1933.

Ed l'Epicier strikes again; see also [19r-26]. A grocer with such good taste in 1930s architecture must have something going for him (his prices are the cheapest in Paris for staples). The lettering above (★★), in concrete, is bold and elegant.

[18ci-12.] RATP Offices (Réseau Autonomne des Transports Parisiens), 24–34 rue Championnet, at end of rue Clignancourt. 1950s.

A *retardataire* Art Moderne complex for the Métro.

★★★[18ci-13.] Immeuble à gradins, 13, rue des Amiraux, at rue Herman-Lachapelle. **Henri Sauvage.** Designed, 1909. Opened, 1922.

For workers afflicted with tuberculosis and other chest diseases, these stepped terraces form what might be accurately termed a *vertical garden city.* The innards shelter common services and, in particular, a great swimming pool open to the public for a fee (bring your swimsuit). The white tile was an appropriate symbol for those seeking the hygienic route to full health: sun, sanity, sanitariness, and swimming.
Aside from its restorative intentions, this brought light and air to the street and gardens to the inmates. Why are such wondrous ideas rarely followed?

[18ci-14.] Logements, 2–8, rue du Simplon, corner rue des Poissonniers, **Jean-Marie Charpentier.** 1986.

Post Modern blah. But note the torii (repopularized in America by Philip Johnson) and the bulging facias: are they fasces?

★[18ci-15.] Logements, 21, rue du Simplon, between rue Boinod and rue de Clignancourt. **F. C. Laboux.** 1912.

Bracketed in two technologies, concrete and wood, and railed in iron, this is eclectic engineering as well as architecture. Well worn, it is an imposing specialty in this mixed neighborhood.

**[18ci-16.] Logements, 17, rue du Simplon,** between rue Boinod and rue de Clignancourt. **F. C. Laboux.** 1910.

Stick Style at the sky, strong brick neo-Romanesque arches below. The play of stone forms, and the incisions, enliven a dour facade.

★**[18ci-17.] Logements, 3, rue Joseph-Dijon,** corner square de Clignancourt.

Stream-liner, those corner apartments must be spectacular spaces from which to eye the street.

**[18ci-18.] Logements, 13, rue Joseph-Dijon,** between square de Clignancourt and rue Hermel. **Pierre Antoine Bled.** 1903.

Bay-bow windows with extravagant supporting brackets. The perforated metal hoods shielding them are like grandma's antimacassars.

★★**[18ci-19.] Square de Clignancourt** between rue Joseph-Dijon, rue Hermel, and rue Ordener. 1914.

Here new buildings of 1913–1914 created the square, another in the style of London's Bloomsbury: **Paul Morice** was responsible for **Nos. 3, 4, 5, 6, 7, 8,** and **11,** allowing short shrift for **Pavy** at **No. 9.** and **Martinaud** at **No. 10.** Such architectural unity has given a consistent tone to this piano-shaped plan.

**[18ci-20.] Conservatoire de Musique,** 29, rue Baudelique, between boulevard Ornano and rue Ordener. **Claude Charpentier.** 1985.

A glazed and high sculptural relief in ocher, brown, blue, and white is the mysterious decoration of this ponderously detailed, bay-windowed conservatory. Perhaps musicians' aural senses inhibit their vision; but probably such vision was only blurred in ranks of bureaucrats judging the *concours.*

★**[18ci-21.] Logements, 8, boulevard Ornano,** corner rue Boinod. 1930s.

Social housing that seems more bourgeois than usual. Its serrated bowed-brick windows are rich with toothy spandrels. That flat fluted ironwork is stylish—and with style.

**[18ci-22.] Logements, 1, rue Boinod,** through to square Ornano, off boulevard Ornano. 1980s.

PoMo *logements* that also open on the cul-de-sac, square Ornano, behind; gray tile with white sash. The central cylinder is a popular mannerism, slashing a void. And oculi.

★**[18ci-23.] 51–53, rue Marcadet,** between rue des Poissonniers and boulevard Barbès. **Fau** and **Ayer.** 1984.

Neo–Art Deco massing in white glazed tile fits the street, making everything else seem dirty and dingy. How about a version of Post Modern architecture, now that historical forms are in vogue, with pre-patinaed stone, a bit of moss and lichen, a crack or two? See **[5s–19.]** for possibilities.

**[18ci-24.] Centre EDF-GDF, 70, boulevard Barbès,** between rue Marcadet and rue Custine. 1925.

An Art Deco (1925 was the year of the exposition) symbol of the creativity of electricity and gas. It is now partially degraded by a gross reglazing in brown solar glass, with fat aluminum frames, a 1960s debasement that replaced slender steel sash in the manner of the elegantly glazed ateliers of Paris. Shame on you, EDF-GDF!

**[18ci-25.] Logements, 62, rue Doudeauville,** between rue des Poissonniers and rue Léon. **A. Bird** and **Jean-Jacques Fernier.** 1981.

Neither creative nor original, this wants to be both. Perhaps it is more appropriate to the strivers of Passy than to this no-nonsense workers' neighborhood. But perhaps these are transitional tenants, on their way to life in Neuilly.

**[18ci-26.] Logements, 22, rue Léon,** between rue Doudeauville and rue de Laghouat. 1980s.

How culture becomes part of an architecture foreign to it. And that culture's solution to all that monochromaticism, is a rug, pendant from the windows. The PoMo souk.

★**[18ci-27.] Logements, 25, rue de Laghouat,** between rue Léon and rue Stephenson. 1980s.

Light gray tile and blue sash to cheer the less advantaged. The broken form is a positive modulation of the street.

★**[18ci-28.] Logements, 21, rue de Laghouat,** between rue Léon and rue Stephenson. 1980s. **André Bertin** and **Abro Kandjian.** 1934.

*Pierre de taille* was still de rigueur outside the chic precincts of Le Corbusier and Mallet-Stevens, although Kandjian refers to Mallet-Stevens as his fountainhead.

**[18ci-29.] Magasin Deloffre,** 100, rue Myrhha, at rue de Clignancourt. 1952.

If this really was the product of 1952, it seems more an artifact from the time capsule of the 1937 Exposition: Classical-Moderne. A little ratty today, it would be a smashing store in which to sell canoes.

★**[18ci-30.] BNP (Banque Nationale de Paris)**/originally **Magasins Dufayel,** 24, rue de Clignancourt, corner rue Myrrha. **Gustave Rivès.** 1895–1915.

A glorying exedra with somewhat out-of-place pomposity on this narrow street. It needs a *parvis, parterre*—space! The pediment sculpture is by **Jules Dalou,** and there are some *caryatids* by **Alexandre Falguière.**
    "When you go back up toward Montmartre through the streets that lead there from the center of Paris, two monuments attract glances even from the most indifferent: the basilica of Sacré-Coeur and the great Dufayel department store. And it is toward two destinations, one of faith and the other of commerce, that crowds push with equal curiosity.
    "This dome [now demolished], which made such a grandiose impression, is by the fashionable architect Rivès. Artistic celebrities including Dalou, Falguière, and Luc-Olivier Merson collaborated on the ornamentation." *Le Monde illustré.* January 12, 1910.

**[18ci-31.]Gymnase de la Goutte d'Or,** 12–18, rue de la Goutte-d'Or, between rue Polonceau and rue des Gardes. **Gérard Thurnauer** and **Antoine Aygalinc.** 1990.

The Parisian love and concern for health through sports, particularly solo, as in swimming, has burgeoned *piscines* everywhere, some distinguished, as that of **Sauvage:** see **[18ci-13.].**

**[18ci-32.] Immeuble, 21–23, rue de Jessaint,** between the rail lines and rue de la Charbonnière. **Antoine Stinco.** 1990.

Stinco is architect of the reincarnation of the **Jeu de Paume.** See **[1s-10.].**

A side trip of some distance to La Chapelle brings quality but not quantity; a wondrous 13th-century church and a 19th-century market are the stars. Your goal is the intersection of rue Ordener and rue de La Chapelle (extension of rue Marx-Dormoy).

Métro: **Marx Dormoy**

★★★★**[18ci-33.] Eglise Saint-Denis-de-La-Chapelle,** 16, rue de La Chapelle, between rue de Torcy and rue Marc-Séguin. Early 13th century. Facade, 18th century.

This late Romanesque church retains an unusual timber king-post truss, supporting a wood-plank pointed (ogee) barrel vault. It is an oasis of serenity, although the noise of traffic penetrates, and is similar in quality to Montmartre's **Eglise Saint-Pierre. Joan of Arc** prayed here during the evening of September 7, 1429. What she saw within is still largely intact, except for the 19th-century choir.

★★**[18ci-34.] Marché de La Chapelle,** 10 rue l'Olive, at place de Torcy. **Auguste Magne.** 1885.

The only extant 19th-century market that remains unsullied by exterior gentrification, although the interior is cluttered with canopies over the merchants' booths and bands of disgusting fluorescent lights. Both intrusions debase the wonderful space.

For modernists, a short walk down rue Marx Dormoy brings us to the architects' outpost in this quarter:

★**[18ci-35.] Ecole Maternelle** and **logements, 53, rue Marx-Dormoy,** between cour de La Chapelle and rue Doudeauville. **Jean-Claude Le Bail** and **Julien Penven.** 1980.

A play of large, small, and non-bay windows in stucco, wood, and glass, in a field of terra-cotta (natural color) tile. A good neighbor on this messy street, a leader to be followed.

Further outside, beyond the Porte de La Chapelle:

**[18ci-36.] Déchetterie, 17–25, avenue de la Porte-de-la-Chapelle.** 1980s.

A place for recycling waste that smacks of an earlier era of elegant concrete work.

# 53
# NINETEENTH ARRONDISSEMENT
## BELLEVILLE

### PORTE DES LILAS THROUGH BELLEVILLE TO
### HOPITAL SAINT-LOUIS

Archives de Paris: **Henri Gaudin;** Hôpital Robert-Debré: **Pierre Riboulet;** Eglise Sainte-Marie-Madeleine: **Henri Vidal;** Direction Régionale: **Claude Parent** and **André Remondet;** rue Paul-de-Kock; Bains-Douches Municipaux: **André Sill;** 61, rue Olivier-Métra: **Alex Weisengrün, et al.;** Eglise Saint-Jean-Baptiste-de-Belleville: **Lassus;** Parc de Belleville: **François Debulois;** passage Plantin; 100, boulevard de Belleville: **Frédéric Borel;** Odoul et Cie.: **Eugène Beaudouin** and **Marcel Lods;** Hôpital Saint-Louis: **Claude Vellefaux;** L'Egalitaire: **Raphaël Loiseau**

Métro: **Porte des Lilas**

[19b-3.] Hôpital Robert Debré. Pierre Riboulet. 1988.

**★★★[19b-1.] Archives de Paris,** Porte des Lilas. **Henri** and **Bruno Gaudin.** 1990.

Reminiscent of the formal functional volumetric articulations of **Louis Kahn** (Richards Medical Center, Philadelphia), it is not a pretty place, but it is a powerful one, an intellectual island at a point in Paris that can only be an island, contained by the Réservoirs des Lilas and the Périphérique.

**[19b-2.] Logements, 66, rue Romainville,** between rue de Belleville and rue Haxo. 1980s.

Here are with some of the serrated and/or cubistic balcony volumes that Vladimir Bodiansky, a Le Corbusier acolyte, brought to Morocco. The street, however, is still held in line, overseen by these pocket balconies.

**★★★[19b-3.] Hôpital Robert-Debré,** 48, boulevard Sérurier, at avenue de la Porte-du-Pré-Saint-Gervais. **Pierre Riboulet.** 1988.

This urbane edge to the city is interpenetrated by a glassy public gallery that traverses its myriad functions. White tile here (for a hospital: providing sanitary reality as well as thoughts) covers a complex multiplicity of functional forms. The whole volume edges the bluff of Belleville, where the old Butte de Beauregard drops precipitously to the modern Périphérique. For the periphering arriver it forms an *avant-porte* to that of *Lilas,* which should perhaps be renamed *Porte des Enfants* in honor of the hospital's many patients.

Riboulet has given hospital architecture a good name. On both sides of the Atlantic hospitals have been the province of specialists more concerned with the aggregation of separately functioning parts than with any coherent, articulate, or—dare one say—handsome whole. This could well be an aphorism for a small city, a way of creating an urban and urbane civilization, where the monument is as much the experience as it is the object.

**[19b-4.] Eglise Sainte-Marie-Madeleine,** 46, boulevard Sérurier, embraced within the arms of the Hôpital Robert-Debré. **Henri Vidal.** 1951–1954.

The happiest future for this turgid, rock-face, gross, and rusticated volume is demolition, for the sake of both abstract aesthetics and the wondrous new Hôpital Robert-Debré. The liberated land could then better embrace a park for the healthy children of the neighborhood, spiritual siblings of the patients within.

**[19b-5.] HBM Cité Orme/Sérurier.** 79, boulevard Sérurier, between rue des Bois and rue de l'Orme. 1930s. Renovation. **P. Lesage.** 1988.

A barrel-vaulted entry leads to a multileveled, tight, but pleasant, courtyard.

**★[19b-6.] Direction Régionale des Affaires Sanitaires et Sociales,** 58–62, rue de Mouzaïa, between rue de l'Inspecteur-Allès and rue des Lilas. **Claude Parent** and **André Remondet.** 1974.

Bulky concrete, infilled with a strip of aluminum and glass. It fails to fulfill the potential of a statement at the edge of neo-brutalism. A sturdy architectural attempt.

**★★[19b-7.] Rue Emile-Desvaux and rue Paul-de-Kock,** between rue des Bois and rue de Romainville. 1920s.

Villas and small apartment houses of a venerable scale line these streets in architecture that is variegated from Art Moderne to Hansel and Gretel.

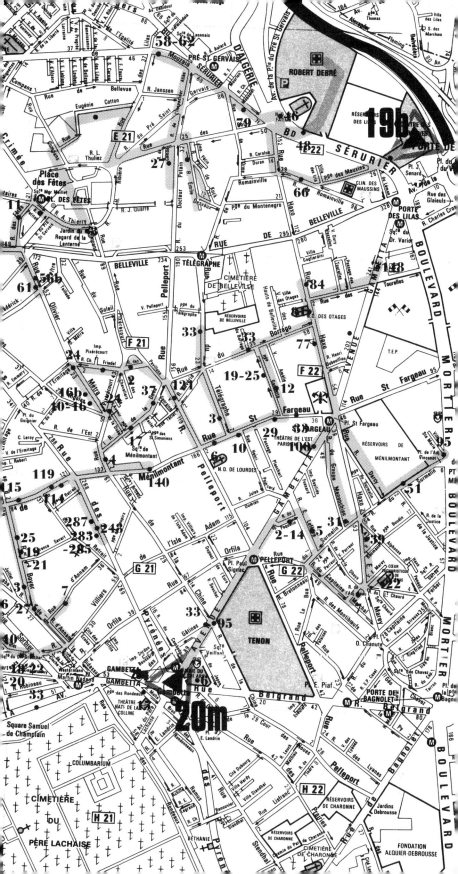

Note particularly the crisp white stucco Art Moderne at **22, rue Paul-de-Kock** and the rather awkward brick and glass Post Modernism of **No. 34.** The latter bears a rather pretentious tesserae frieze, IN ARTE VITA. Is this the revenge of the bourgeois Sunday artist?

★**[19b-8.] HBM, 27, rue du Docteur-Potain,** at rue des Bois. **Raoul and Daniel and Lionel Brandon.** 1927.

Whereas the "red belt" of the 1930s is rich with *moderne* HBMs, this and many sister complexes relish a late Stick Style—albeit in concrete. Thus its polychromatic brick, bay windows, and tiled-column balconies deliver a richly textured and modulated facade.

★**[19b-9.] Ecoles elémentaires,** rue Eugénie-Cotton, at rue des Lilas. **Jean Peccoux.** 1975.

One, two, and four levels ramble polygonally in brown-stained concrete. This stylish school has aged gracelessly—a bit of retardataire 1960s neo-brutalism.

**[19b-10.] Place des Fêtes.**

A sorry fate befell a once vital open space dedicated to the maneuvers of the local national guard and public festivities, all under orderly arranged lindens. The adjacent towers are bad enough, but the park proper has been degraded with parking and bad taste.

★**[19b-11.] Regard de la Lanterne,** 3, rue Augustin-Thierry at rue Compans. 17th century.

One last monument of the original Parisian system of aqueducts, this watergate of the Aqueduct of Belleville marks the beginning of its downhill plunge to Paris under the rue de Belleville. Within are inscriptions recording the upgrading of the aqueduct in 1457, 1583, and 1613.

★★**[19b-12.] Bains-Douches municipaux,** corner rue Petitot and rue des Fêtes. **André Sill.** 1936.

That rippling sea with a bronze boat under full sail is the delicate entrance canopy of these municipal baths from a time not so long ago when Parisian plumbing was scarce, particularly in these then-poor quarters.

**[19b-13.] Maison particulière, 11, rue des Fêtes,** off place des Fêtes. Late 19th century.

Grinning and scowling faces adorn the keystones. Set back in its own courtyard, like a minor *hôtel particulier* of the Marais, this is stuff for those who have—but in the wrong part of town. Perhaps the local factory owner lived here to keep an eye on his minions.

★**[19b-14.] Logements, 61, rue Olivier-Métra,** between rue de Belleville and rue Frédérick-Lemaître. **Alex Wiesengrün, P. Rocca,** and **A. Brauny.** 1982.

A foreigner in port, it gracefully violates the scale and texture of the street: white tile, amid brick and stone. This is an unnecessary statement, but Wiesengrün has some remarkable talent for the future.

**[19b-15.] Logements, 56 bis, rue Olivier-Métra,** between rue de Belleville and rue Frédérick-Lemaître. 1930s.

A play of balconies and spandrels in off-white stucco against pilasters in ocher stucco. Colonnettes are banded in tile, creating a lively facade against **No. 56,** next door, its "modern" parent.

★[19b-16.] **Eglise Saint-Jean-Baptiste-de-Belleville,** 139, rue de Belleville, at rue du Jourdain. **Lassus,** then **Truchy.** 1854–1859.

Gothic Revival with considerable care—a bit too neat, symmetric, and of one piece to be of the true Middle Ages, where architecture evolved in sequential styles. Baron Haussmann was present at its dedication (he loved Gothic for churches), although Belleville did not become part of Paris until the next year.

★[19b-17.] **Foyer de Célibataires, 1, rue des Solitaires,** corner rue de La Villette. **J. M. Hennin** and **N. Normier.** 1986.

The yellow-enameled ground-floor entryway and sash give this simple PoMo stucco building (tiled white entry) a bit of dash. Some more green tiles would have enlivened it even more.

[19b-18.] **Logements, 78, rue de La Villette,** between rue des Solitaires and rue Botzaris. **Louis Doco** and **François Spy.** 1976.

One of the worst offenders in the crazed Côte d'Azur flamboyance sweepstakes. The prismatic canted balconies give this a passing stylishness without style. Where did the Cadillac fins go? Aren't we glad that they were portable, disposable, and revered only as a bit of bizarre history?

★[19b-19.] **Ecole, 9, rue des Alouettes,** corner, rue Fessart. **Michel Birmant.** 1983.

Broken forms give this small neighborhood school the ancient scale of this quarter, unlike the looming apartment complex across rue Fessart to the south; tiled white with yellow trim. If only the detailing were more elegant—those awkward window frames and the edge against the sky!

[19b-20.] **Logements, 2, rue des Alouettes,** corner rue Fessart. **Adrien Rosner** and **A. C. Bernadac.** 1979.

A modest neighbor to the new school across the street.

★[19b-21.] **Logements, 1, rue Mélingue,** corner rue de Belleville. **D. Girardet.** 1984.

Anchored by a remodeled villa at Belleville, these five-level housing units embrace a handsome entrance courtyard. The architecture is decorative, the urban space within is elegant.

[19b-22.] **Logements, 102, rue de Belleville,** opposite rue Mélingue. **Charles Blanche.** 1901.

Savor the bay windows supported by cast-iron columns and brackets. Their brick spandrels complete an articulation in the spirit of Viollet-le-Duc.

★[19b-23.] **Logements, 15, rue Jouye-Rouve,** at the end of rue Lesage. **Jacques Bardet** assisted by **R. Reveau.** 1984.

Stucco, tile, and a couple of waiting angels. The axial continuation of rue Lesage is its most exciting role—stepped stairs leading into the newly reconstructed Parc de Belleville.

★★★[19b-24.] **Parc de Belleville,** entered atop from opposite 22, rue Piat, between rue de Belleville and rue du Transvaal. **François Debulois.** 1990.

A vast remodeling of this precipitous park, from the crest of which is a magnificent view of Paris to the west, made even more dramatic at sunset. The "street furniture," including plastic vaults over stumpy piers (the *belvé-dère*), is a bit facile and ungainly, but nothing can destroy the magnificence of the site. At your feet is a vast ZAC to which you can descend through the park after a walk down rue Transvaal and back. This is the highest point in Paris, some 8 meters above the butte Montmartre. From beneath the kiosk tumbles a cascade of water, and an amphitheater with five hundred seats makes a pseudo-Greek incision into the hillside (like Segesta?).

The water, of course, doesn't flow in the winter, and its absence produces a kind of bleakness. The materials of the steps and waterways are of poor concrete, wearing badly in their first year, like a Hollywood set meant to last only for the course of filming.

**[19b-25.] Immeuble, 13, rue du Transvaal,** between rue Piat and rue des Couronnes. circa 1890.

Left over from an earlier street alignment, and with a gated front garden, this wrought-iron festival sports a bit of New Orleans' ironwork.

**[19b-26.] Villa Castel,** 16, rue du Transvaal, between rue Piat and rue des Couronnes.

A private clutch of houses.

★**[19b-27.] Passage Plantin,** between 14, rue du Transvaal and 81, rue des Couronnes.

A steep alley flanked by the walls of private villas. This gives you another vintage vantage over Belleville.

★**[19b-27a.] Cité de Genes,** 1–11, rue Bisson, between rue des Couronnes and rue de Pali-Kao. 1989.

Sculptured white form in sinuous and mathematical ways. It is a lovely understatement among more aggressive architecture.

**[19b-28.] Ecole maternelle, rue de Pali-Kao and rue Bisson.** 1987.

This takes the role of "palace on the square," the latter the lap of the Parc de Belleville, in the reurbanization of old Belleville.

★**[19b-29.] Logements, rue de Tourtille,** between rue Bisson and rue de Pali-Kao. **Catherine Morgoulis** and **Pierre Coquet.** 1987.

A complex stucco volume surrounds a court open through arcades to the street. The corner cylindrical glazing should be forgotten (take it away), but the central courtyard is serene, a bit overwhelmed by those powerful open-balcony forms.

**[19b-30.] Logements, rue Bisson,** corner rue de Tourtille. **Jean-Paul Phillipon.** 1988.

★★**[19b-31.] Logements, 23, rue Bisson,** between rue de Tourtille and boulevard de Belleville. **Jacques Ripeault.** 1988.

Bold balconies front these simple, deeply sculpted apartments. Behind is a pleasant court with cylindrical balcony volumes, crisply prismatic.

**[19b-32.] Logements, 17, rue Bisson,** between rue de Tourtille and boulevard de Belleville. **Jean-Claude Delorme.** 1989.

**[19b-33.] Logements, 11, rue Bisson,** between rue de Tourtille and boulevard de Belleville.

A somewhat garbled set of PoMo forms with its ubiquitous stucco and tile and a neo-mansard roof. The entrance, however, seemingly of petrified candy, is something to write home about—in invisible ink.

★★**[19b-34.] Logements, 100, boulevard de Belleville,** between rue Bisson and rue Ramponeau. **Frédéric Borel.** 1988.

This complex of strong concrete and high-tech metal dominates the street, admittedly shoddy around here. The self-embraced cul-de-sac feeds, and is fed by, adjacent buildings, creating a wonderful urbanistic interlock. A former protégé of Portzamparc, Borel brings some of the same nervous, but brilliant, Japanese quality to his work.

★**[19b-35.] Logements, 6–12, rue Ramponeau,** between boulevard de Belleville and rue de Tourtille. **Jacques Ripeault.** 1988.

Sleek, stucco, neo-Modern—a *crudité* in the manner of the great Dutch architect of the 1930s, Willem Dudok; see the Dutch pavilion at the Cité Universitaire **[14s-6.]** for Dudok's work firsthand. The break in form modulates the street's flatness, without lessening its strength, reinforcing the neighborhood.

**[19b-35a.] Immeuble d'habitation, 20–28, rue Ramponneau,** between boulevard de Belleville and rue de Tourtille. **Fernando Montès.** 1989.

★**[19b-36.] Logements, 13-15, rue Dénoyez,** between rue Ramponeau and rue de Belleville.

A sober, understated pair of infill buildings in sandy stucco, with white stone frames. The latter make what might have been banal into a subtle and elegant presence on the street. Some of this self-effacement is a relief from endless architectural histrionics.

**[19b-37.] Bureaux, 2, boulevard de La Villette,** corner rue de Belleville. **A. and D. Sloan.** 1984.

Sandstone and metal panels in this modestly articulated office block. It would have been better if in all sandstone with a lower, stronger colonnade at the *rez-de-chaussée;* the scale is awkward.

**[19b-38.] Logements, 10-20, boulevard de La Villette,** corner rue de Belleville. **Pierre Sonrel, Jean Duthilleul,** and **A. and D. Sloan.** 1984.

Forming the granite-paved place Jean-Rostand with **No. 2,** this massive block holds the line of the boulevard, relieving its own bulk with balconies and bay windows.

**[19b-39.] Place Marcel-Achard,** behind 2-20, boulevard de La Villette. **Etienne Hajdu,** sculptor. 1984.

A generously paved and treed urban space, 1980s division. The rear of the apartment building seems more in spirit with the Sloans' No. 2, simplified from the boulevard facade of Nos. 10-20.

★★**[19b-40.] Logements, 19, rue de l'Atlas,** between boulevard de La Villette and avenue Simon-Bolivar. **Robert Parisot.** circa 1930.

Stepped, bold cubism, corner-windowed, with decorative vent tubes to the kitchen cold boxes *(garde-manger)*. With articulated brick at the *rez-de-chaussée*, it is a strong 60-year-old statement for Belleville.

★**[19b-41.] Odoul et Cie. (entrepôts),** 8, passage de l'Atlas, off rue de l'Atlas. **Eugène Beaudouin** and **Marcel Lods.** 1933.

Warehouses in concrete, brick, and glass block, stepped back to give light to the street in the manner of Sauvage's *Maisons à gradins* (rue Vavin **[6s-22.]** and rue des Amiraux **[18ci-13.]**). The brick volumes reek of early constructivism.

**[19b-42.] Logements, 54, boulevard de La Villette,** between rue Rébeval and rue Burnouf. 1987.

White on white, with half-cylindrical tiled balconies against a somber stucco background.

**[19b-43.] Transformateur Eléctrique,** 18, rue du Buisson-Saint-Louis, between boulevard de La Villette and rue Saint-Maur. **G. Darsonval** and **Michel Duplay.** 1983.

Stucco and mirror-glazed bay windows disguise this transformer substation, a technocratic intrusion. A casual glance might suggest studios for affluent artists.

**[19b-44.] Logements, 13–15, passage du Buisson-Saint-Louis,** off rue du Buisson-Saint-Louis. 1980s.

A potentially charming loop, this *passage* is less than blessed with this cylindrically bayed and balconied *logement* in orange-ocher stucco. The shingled false mansards are disgusting. Things banal are often acceptable; this is not.

**[19b-45.] Logements, 192, rue Saint-Maur,** corner rue du Buisson-Saint-Louis. **Michel Duplay.** 1988.

Vulgar and pretentious, with the sort of arbitrary styling and tasteless excess that should go out with the *poubelles.*

★**[19b-45a.] Ateliers, 36, rue Jacques-Louvel-Tessier,** between rue Saint-Maur and avenue Parmentier. 1890s.

A facade with both structure and sash of steel make this a strong variant on the street. Certainly, this is at least vigorous eclecticism.

**[19b-45b.] Lithographie Parisienne,** 27 bis, rue Jacques-Louvel-Tessier, between rue Saint-Maur and avenue Parmentier. 1890s.

More steel, brick infilled, for the printing trades "since 1866." Bones and bulk.

★★★★**[19b-46.] Hôpital Saint-Louis,** avenue Claude-Vellefaux and surrounded by rue Alibert, rue Bichat, rue de la Grange-aux-Belles, and rue Juliette-Dodu. **Claude de Châtillon,** architect for design. **Claude Vellefaux,** architect for construction. 1607–1611.

Henri IV's world of brick and stone, so magnificent and well known at the place des Vosges, is equalled but hardly known here. Originally an isolated place of rampant plagues, the hospital was built as an open quadrilateral of patients within a larger square of service, separated by a "moat" of open space. Within the central void is a lovely park, one of those wonderful and unexpected Parisian hidden delights, a fringe benefit of magnificent architecture. The central and corner pavilions articulate the mass eight times.

★[19b-47.] Annexe, Hôpital Saint-Louis, 1–19 rue Juliette-Dodu, between avenue Claude-Vellefaux and rue de la Grange-aux-Belles. **Daniel Badani** and **Pierre Roux-Dorlut**. 1984.

An awkward monument in the style of the 1960s, built in the 1980s. Why are most hospitals usually so afflicted with mediocre architecture, and then divorced from the urban design of the surrounding city? This is particularly galling at a site where the parent building is a 17th-century gem of both architecture and urbanism. Within, a soaring glass entry hall provides a monumental and skylit space for the entering patient.

★★[19b-48.] Originally **L'Egalitaire (coopérative),** 17, rue de Sambre-et-Meuse, between rue Claude-Vellefaux and boulevard de La Villette. **Raphaël Loiseau.** 1894.

A sturdy postclassic building with multicolored brick spandrels and bold steel lintels, atop sometimes ornate capitals; an early modern venture in the spirit of Bernard Maybeck's San Francisco Packard showroom (1926).

It was described by **Jean Gaumont** in 1921: "Bastion, fortress, or house of the people, what does it matter! The red flag, which expresses the socialist faith of its members, flies in its rooms and interior courtyards. The eye sees it, and the heart is comforted. The organization welcomes not only members of a cooperative but also union groups and electoral committees of the Socialist Workers' Party."

[19b-49.] Ecole, 19–21, rue de Sambre-et-Meuse, between rue Claude-Vellefaux and boulevard de La Villette. 1988.

A neo-brutalist school.

# 54
# NINETEENTH ARRONDISSEMENT
## BUTTES-CHAUMONT

### PARC DES BUTTES-CHAUMONT AND ENVIRONS

### TO THE NORTHWEST

Parc des Buttes-Chaumont: **Adolphe Alphand, Pierre Barillet-Deschamps,** and **Gabriel Davioud;** Eglise Saint-Serge: **Staletzky;** Mairie: **Gabriel Davioud;** Eglise Notre-Dame-des-Buttes-Chaumont: **D. Honegger;** Piscine Pailleron: **Lucien Pollet;** Marché Secrétan: **Victor Baltard;** PCF Headquarters: **Oscar Niemayer**

Métro: **Botzaris**

**[19bu-1.] Temple and Suspension Bridge/Parc des Buttes-Chaumont. Adolphe Alphand,** supervising engineer. **Gabriel Davioud,** architect. 1867.

★★★★[19bu-1.] **Parc des Buttes-Chaumont**, between rue Botzaris, rue Manin, and rue de Crimée. **Adolphe Alphand**, supervising engineer. **Pierre Barillet-Deschamps**, horticulturist. **Darcel**, engineer; **Gabriel Davioud**, architect. Park, 1867. Temple, 1869.

These ruins of ancient "plaster of Paris" gypsum quarries, barren and sometimes home to the homeless, surrounded by poverty and squatters, became a symbol of renovation of this forgotten northeast sector of Paris. The very chaos caused by the natural and forced collapse of underground chambers allowed a violent picturesqueness to devolve. The result is an extravagant topographical phantasmagoria (made even more extravagant by the addition and molding of artificial rock), accentuated by dramatic bridges, and crowned with Davioud's version of the **Temple de la Sybille** at Tivoli. This outclassed most of 18th- and 19th-century English parks and follies, the park's very inspiration. Napoléon III, instigator of this among other vast Parisian works (boulevards, markets, sewers, transit), was an avid devotee of the *English garden* while in resident exile in England.

**Pont des Suicides** (★★). Named for its obvious morbid and melodramatic use, it is now better utilized by those not inclined to jump, its visual role muted by screening.

**Temple** (★★). From this magnificent crow's nest you can almost be a stand-in for Montgolfier. But the Paris seen now is a far cry not only from his time but also from 1867, when the park opened.

**Suspension Bridge** (★★★). This owes much to Isaac Brunel, the British engineer of French ancestry, and to Thomas Telford, the British engineer of British ancestry. It was finished two years before the Brooklyn Bridge was started.

**Assorted guardhouses and restaurants.** Davioud supplied these as well as the temple in a style more endemic to the 1860s: brick and sticks. One now stands out gastronomically as well as architecturally: Le Pavillon du Lac.

**The lake.** The 2-hectare lake is fed from a reservoir on rue Botzaris and thence down a dramatic fall of artificial stone to be seen from the south walk.

---

"It is the baroque spirit of the Second Empire that one discovers at the Buttes-Chaumont, and it the spirit of Offenbach that carries you away."
Yvan Crist

---

★[19bu-2.] **Eglise Saint-Serge**, 93, rue de Crimée, between rue Manin and rue Meynadier. 1858–1865. Later frescoes, **Staletzky**, 1918.

A Russian chalet, originally built as a Lutheran church, brings more of the rural Buttes-Chaumont style to that neighborhood.

★[19bu-3.] **Mairie, place Armand-Carrel,** between avenue de Laumière and rue du Rhin. **Gabriel Davioud.** 1876.

Most of the mairies constructed after the annexation of the faubourgs beyond the wall of the Fermiers-Généraux were in this same Haussmannian *Hôtel de Ville* style. Davioud, however, brought one off one step higher in rank than many of his confrères.

This *hôtel*, if not precisely *de ville*, with an ornate entrance porch supported by stocky Tuscan columns, is a local public building that would make you proud to be local.

[19bu-4.] **Eglise Notre-Dame-des-Buttes-Chaumont**, 80, rue de Meaux, opposite rue de la Moselle. **Denis Honegger.** 1966.

Concrete in the spirit of Perret, crowded between high HLMs—an urbanistic insanity. Such a church must, by its very nature, be freestanding.

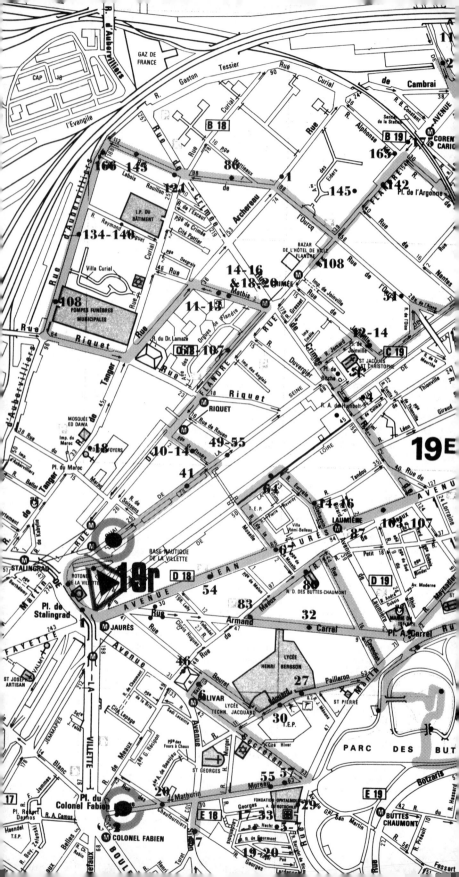

**[19bu-5.] HLM, 32, rue Armand-Carrel,** between rue de Meaux and rue Cavendish.

A grid of concrete and a grillage of perforated concrete block evoke more memories of Perret in this complex (one end of which surrounds Notre Dame above). Trees have grown here among Perret's happy progeny, giving the quality of the best of British buildings in a park.

**[19bu-6.] GM/OPEL Garage,** 83, rue de Meaux, corner rue Armand-Carrel. 1930s.

More crisp white concrete in one of the myriad garages that enliven the streets of Paris with the technocratic 1930s.

**[19bu-7.] Lycée Henri-Bergson,** 27, rue Edouard-Pailleron, between rue Main and rue Bouret. 1960s.

A campus of neat and well-groomed buildings in careful concrete. Pleasant landscaping and annexed buildings emblazoned with supergraphics give an exurban air to these teenaged grounds (kids arriving and departing in their own cars!).

**★[19bu-8.] Piscine Pailleron,** 30, rue Edouard-Pailleron, between rue Main and rue Bouret. **Lucien Pollet.** 1933.

A sturdy brick pavilion with a thrusting semicircular canopy, much in the spirit of Frank Lloyd Wright's **Francisco Terrace Apartments** in Chicago. Offbeat, unique, wonderful.

**★★[19bu-9.] Marché Secrétan,** 46, rue de Meaux, at avenue Secrétan. **Victor Baltard.** 1868.

The swan song of Baltard's Parisian markets, where the flavor but not the substance of his great work, Les Halles Centrales, can be relished. Unfortunately, it is now prettied up with external shutters, and a new infilling wall mutes the articulation of the cast- and wrought-iron facade elements.

**[19bu-10.] Bureaux, 6, rue Baste,** opposite Marché Secrétan.

A glassy crown atop a rubble peasant. The surelevation is so bizarre as to be acceptable: these precincts are eclectic.

**[19bu-11.] Fondation Ophtalmologique Adolphe-Rothschild,** 29, rue Manin. 1905.

A picturesque stone-and-brick pile that enhances the edge of the Parc des Buttes-Chaumont. Multifarious materials and forms make this a sort of intellectual "castle."

**★[19bu-12.] Maisons, 55** and **57, avenue Mathurin-Moreau,** between rue Manin and rue Murger. No. 55, **F. Crozet.** circa 1930. No. 57, **Remond** 1927.

A cubist No. 57 and a Classical-moderne No. 55 are gracious neighbors to two older villas opposite the Fondation Ophtalmologique.

**★★[19bu-12a.] Maisons. 5, 7** and **17–33, rue Philippe-Hecht, 19 and 20, rue Edgar-Poë,** an enclave off avenue Mathurin-Moreau and rue Manin. 1925–1935.

Styled rowhouses, ranging from the stucco and timber romanticism of the 1920s to the crisp cubism of the 1930s.

**★[19bu-13.] HBM, 97, avenue Simon-Bolivar** and **20, avenue Mathurin-Moreau,** bounded by rue Henri-Turot, boulevard de la Villette and rue des Chaufourmiers. **Charles Heubès.** 1924–1930.

Virtuoso polychromatic brickwork surrounds a formal central garden. The changes in level enliven the spatial modulation. As usual, this HBM is quality housing for those of moderate income and less. Little populist housing in the United States could match it.

**★★[19bu-14.] Parti Communiste Français** (PCF), 2, place du Colonel-Fabien. **Oscar Niemeyer,** with assistance of **Paul Chemetov, Jean Deroche, Jean-Maur Lyonnet,** and **Jean Prouvé.** 1980.

A schematic work from the hand of Oscar Niemeyer, Brazil's most renowned architect (most of Brasilia is from this hand). Ostensibly a devotee of Le Corbusier, with whom he associated for the Ministry of Education in Rio di Janeiro in 1937, Niemeyer had a slicker and more diagrammatic style. Corbu in the 1970s had already put behind him the powerful concrete works of **Ronchamp** and **La Tourette.**

What might be the Parisian headquarters of IBM perches on a green baize, the soul mate of the works of Harrison & Abramovitz: They were the ones who fulfilled the Le Corbusier–Niemeyer scheme for the United Nations in New York.

Métro: **Colonel Fabien**

# 55
# NINETEENTH ARRONDISSEMENT
## ROTONDE-BASSIN
### STALINGRAD TO STALINGRAD

Rotonde de la Villette: **Claude-Nicolas Ledoux;** Bassin de la Villette: **Bernard Huet;** Métro Aérien: **Fulgence Bienvenue** and **Jean-Camille Formigé;** Conservatoire de Musique XIXe: **Fernand Pouillon;** 64, quai de la Loire: **Edith Girard;** Collège Tandou: **Henri Gaudin;** Gymnase and bains-douches: **Charles Gauthier** and **Charles Narjoux;** pont Levant de la Villette: **Fives-Lilles;** Eglise Saint-Jacques-Saint Christophe: **Pierre-Eugène Lequeux;** 23, quai de l'Oise: **Claude Vasconi;** rue de Flandre, former Entrepôts/Galerie Barbès: **Christian Maisonhaute** and **Jacques Lévy;** Hôtel Industriel: **Jean-Paul Viguier** and **Jean-François Jodry;** Logements/rue Mathis: **Jean-Pierre Buffi;** Les Orgues de Flandre: **Martin van Treeck;** Ateliers/passage de Flandre: **Yves Lion** and **François Leclercq;** Eglise Notre-Dame-des-Foyers

Métro: **Stalingrad**

**[19r-30.] Logements**/originally **Entrepôts des Meubles des Galeries Barbès.** circa 1890. Reconstructed, **Christian Maisonhaute** and **Jacques Lévy.** 1980.

**★★★[19r-1.] Rotonde de la Villette,** place de Stalingrad, at the head of the Bassin de la Villette. **Claude-Nicolas Ledoux.** 1784.

One of the two remaining discrete pavilions (two more are altered pairs) of the fifty-two built by Ledoux as entry points and toll-collecting places *(barrières)* at the wall of the Fermiers Généraux. Here stood the administrative headquarters for revenues on wine and produce entering Paris. The neo-Palladian *rotonde* sits atop a squat and stocky octastyle base, lording it over the newly renewed surrounds of its axial Bassin de la Villette. Because of the wall, poor farmers were inspired to become smugglers, and urban revolutionaries were inspired (partly by the taxing tolls) to take action only five years later.

**★★[19r-2.] Bassin de la Villette,** stretching from place de Stalingrad to rue de Crimée, between quai de la Seine, and quai de la Loire. 1809. Reconstruction and environs, **Bernard Huet.** 1989.

This was a grand landing place for barges arriving from the canals (and hence rivers beyond) of the Marne and the Ourcq, and warehouses lined these banks (the basin is 80 by 800 meters). Sometimes whimsically referred to as the Champs-Elysées of the East (of Paris), it is considerably more charming, and Huet's renovations make it a grand mall for pedestrians and cyclists. The architecture along its banks is a bit spotty, but this should be rectified in the 1990s if the new urbanistic architectural attitudes of Paris continue.

**★★[19r-3.] Place de Stalingrad/Métro Aérien,** boulevard de la Chapelle, boulevard de la Villette. **Fulgence Bienvenue,** supervising engineer. **Jean-Camille Formigé,** architect. 1903.

Tuscan columns (with their own capitals), and neo-Assyrian surelevated supercapitals above, support this cast-iron and steel aerial Métro. Underneath you can see the small brick vaults that spring between supporting steel struts, the original construction method for this and the early "fireproof" multistoried *immeubles* of the period, up to the time of the victory of concrete. **Formigé** was architect for all of the Métro's overhead works, while **Hector Guimard** handled the underworld entrances.

**[19r-4.] Logements, 1 place de Stalingrad,** at rue La Fayette. **Martin Van Treeck.** 1982.

This facile architect brings back some "Mansart," complete with dormer windows, dressed in tile and stucco, creating a strangely uncomplicated decorative complexity. Would that serious architecture were that uncomplicated.

**★[19r-5.] Conservatoire de Musique du XIXe Arrondissement Jacques-Ibert,** avenue Jean-Jaurès, corner rue Armand-Carrel and rue Bouret. **Fernand Pouillon.** 1988.

Before his death in 1986 **Pouillon** had created sketches for the conservatory that no one dared to modify when converted into the present reality. Too bad. The result is heavy-handed, with a lot of ideas clustered (or is it cluttered?) on a small building; a bit of culling was the least one could have done for his memory. The fountain on a radial line of Ledoux's Rotonde is a Post Modern joke: stacked, truncated, quasi-Doric columns (they look like huge ramekins), with a bit of neo-baroque tomfoolery in the drooling stonework below. Try Pouillon's novel, *The Stones of the Abbey,* for a taste of *his* taste (12th-century Romanesque).

**★★[19r-5a.] Bureaux, corner avenue Jean-Jaurès and rue Armand-Carrel. D. Kahane.** 1990.

A flat glassy slab on the avenue is broken by articulated masonry and an open corner: a narrow **flat-iron** shop hovers over the pedestrian. Here a Haussmannian-style street (**Armand-Carrel**) is finally penetrated, fulfilled and contained by this, the **Conservatoire**, and the **Portzamparc** apartments opposite.

★[19r-5b.] **Immeuble de la Conservatoire,** between avenue Jean-Jaurès and rue Clovis-Hugues. **Christian de Portzamparc**. 1990.

Some curvilinear plasticity at the skyline marks this necessarily more sober work of **Portzamparc**. He earlier defied the orthogonal street and presented either spectacular sinuosity (Cité de la Musique) or a private but excellent urban world of its own (rue des Hautes-Formes).

[19r-6.] **Logements, 54, avenue Jean-Jaurès,** between rue Lally-Tollendal and passage de Melun.

Medium Post Modern, with a modulated (in depth) facade—one of the increasing pack of these half-baked PoMos. Why all that anodized aluminum curtain walling? It's wallpaper in bad taste.

[19r-7.] **Caisse d'Allocations Familiales,** 67, avenue Jean-Jaurès, corner rue de la Moselle. **Michel Herbert**. 1984.

The local social security dispensary. Herbert is quoted as saying "a solicitude for the public is manifested by the luminosity of the building, the careful finishing of the polished concrete, and the pleasant arcades, false vaults that invite one to enter." If words could create great architecture, Herbert would have succeeded here. The reality is an extravagant gesture to the modest local family. It would loom nicely as a bank in a lesser suburb of Miami.

★★★[19r-8.] **Logements, 64, quai de la Loire,** between rue de la Moselle and rue Euryale-Dehaynin. **Edith Girard**. 1985.

A modernist who needs no Post Modern excuses—or crutches, Girard makes the adjacent works (the rear of those facing avenue Jean-Jaurès) seem like trash. She would be a welcome Haussmannian, her interior graces (the court) fulfilling her exterior style. Savor the chromatic-tiled penthouses. This is the Queen of the Canals.

★★★[19r-9.] **Extension, Collège Tandou**, 14–16, rue Euryale-Dehaynin, between quai de la Loire and rue Tandou. **Henri Gaudin**. 1987.

Subtle, super, without the multiplicity of tricks so common among its peer buildings of the same date. The pregnant spaces belly the facade with the arc of so many French modernists (the greatest is that of Nouvel's Institut du Monde Arabe). This is a superb mannerist at work among Philistines. Gaudin's work in Paris to date is too limited. Here is a great architect, near at hand.

★[19r-10.] **Gymnase** and **bains-douches municipaux,** 87, avenue Jean-Jaurès, between rue Euryale-Dehaynin and rue Pierre-Girard. **Charles Gauthier**. 1914. Campanile reconstructed, **Charles Narjoux**. 1920.

Here is romantic brick for a gymnasium (the dimensions were originally set by rifle practice!) and public ablutions, complete with glazed tile friezes, lintels, and an articulated metal frame. Posters now advertise judo, a *cercle olympique*, and other healthy activities.

[19r-11.] **Logements, 103–107, avenue Jean-Jaurès,** between rue Pierre-Girard and rue de Crimée. **Jacques Lévy** and **Christian Maison-haute**. 1984.

Stucco—and more stucco. Mansards and *garde-fous*, with tile at the *rez-de-chaussée*.

**[19r-12.] Logements, 4, quai de la Marne,** at rue de Crimée. **Martin Van Treeck.** 1984.

A mostly Post Modern mansarded mass, with a play of openings. It is of the quality of mediocre HBMs of the 1930s.

★★**[19r-13.] Pont levant de la Villette,** rue de Crimée, crossing the Canal de l'Ourcq. **Fives-Lilles,** constructors. 1888.

At the exposition of 1889 **Fives-Lilles** presented a model of this lift bridge, commenting, "It comprises a hydraulic mechanism for its lifting, powered by the municipal water system. This same movement can also be activated by a crank in case of failure of the water supply or of damage."

For the passerby, this bridge, with its *Egypto-Ionic* capitals, offers great pulley disks that raise the auto street above the canal traffic. Super and monumental, cast iron here does heavy work.

★**[19r-14.] Entrepôt.** quai de la Loire, at rue de Crimée. **Emile Veugnier,** engineer. 1862.

A lusty vernacular warehouse, remnant of aquatic commerce, the original function of these waterways. The rubble stonework is articulated with cut-stone quoins and window frames. Within, cast-iron columns punctuate the space on a 3.8 by 3.8 meter (15 by 15 feet) grid, providing modular bays for the structure. A twin, symmetrically disposed on quai de la Seine, burned in 1989.

★**[19r-15.] Eglise Saint-Jacques/Saint-Christophe,** place de Bitche, off rue de Crimée. **Pierre-Eugène Lequeux.** 1844.

The *Jésuitique* facade brings a bit of Roman sentiment to these onetime industrial quarters. Inside is sheltered a neo–early Christian church, basilican, clerestoried, its nave with quasi-Tuscan columns, upper-fluted, echinus-decorated, and based.

The coffered timber ceiling is neo-Baroque. All together, this is a bit of simulated archaeology of Italian architecture from 400 to 1700.

**[19r-16.] Locaux Sociaux** and **crèche, 12–14, rue de Joinville,** behind Saint-Jacques/Saint-Christophe. **Comianos Agapitos.** 1980.

More space age architecture, with metal made to curve and harbor space—but without grace. A misfire in any *concours*, this is from an ego that displays facility rather than talent.

★**[19r-17.] HBM, 51, rue de l'Ourcq,** between quai de l'Oise and rue de Flandre. **Agence d'Architecture HBM.** 1920–1923.

Before the fortification of Thiers was demolished in the early 1930s, providing the future red belt of HBMs, this early pioneer settled on inexpensive industrial land. It has a graceful posture, in contrast to most public housing of the 1950s through 1970s, which ignored the street and isolated those imprisoned in their lonely towers. It's architectural heaven compared to the banalities of most of the new rue de Flandre.

★★**[19r-18.] Logements, 23, quai de l'Oise,** adjacent to railroad bridge. **Claude Vasconi.** 1986.

A sinuous play of white tile makes an appropriate gesture at the edge of the Canal de l'Ourcq. There are slender nautical *garde-fous* and elegant detailing (all those transoms over the windows proper). Inside (beyond the tower's lobby), are five-level ateliers facing a quiet garden: charming, light, and civilized.

**[19r-19.] Logements, 5, rue de l'Argonne,** at junction of Canal Saint-Denis, and Canal de l'Ourcq. **Yves Lion.** 1986.

Stylish, mansarded stucco, yet cool and understated. it makes the Hotel Arcade next door seem like the local prostitute—sleazy with its tricky shapes and forms.

★**[19r-20.] Logements, 26, rue Barbanègre,** at quai de la Gironde. circa 1930.

Sleek and stripped housing in the style of the 1930s, overlooking the canal and the Parc de La Villette beyond.

**[19r-21.] Logements, 14, rue Barbanègre,** at rue de l'Argonne. **Laurent Bourgois, Pierre Eidikins,** and **Patrick de Turenne.** 1984.

This pastiche of ideas fits the block but is Post Modern fancy dress applied to a dull body.

★**[19r-22.] Logements, 175, rue de Flandre** and **2–16, rue Alphone-Karr. Delaage/Tsaropoulos.** 1989.

Sleek white balconies overview rue de Flandre; separate entries interspersed with brown brick, smaller-balcony-dominated, line rue Alphonse-Karr.

★**[19r-23,] Logements, 165, rue de Flandre,** corner rue Alphonse-Karr. **Laurent Bourgois, Pierre Edeikins,** and **Patrick de Turenne.** 1989.

Here **Bourgois** and partners have created a successful cornering of the street, extending the spirit of the adjacent HBMs to rue de Flandre, which was raped to the south but maintained as an outpost of civility at rue Alphonse-Karr, a remembrance of what the whole streetfront could be.

**[19r-24.] Maisons, 142, rue de Flandre,** between rue de l'Argonne and rue de Nantes, behind the street front building. **Martin Van Treeck.** 1984.

Buzz yourself though the *porte cochère* to the courtyards behind. Here you will find a bit of Heritage Village (fancy housing for the elderly), crossbred with the *Forum des Halles*—all in brick and painted concrete block, with "cute" concrete vaults atop. Is this for retired assistant ministers of culture?

**[19r-25.] Logements, "Cité des Eiders,"** 145, rue de Flandre, between rue Alphonse-Karr and rue de l'Ourcq. **Mario Heymann** and **H. Jirou.** 1981.

The spaceships are back, here on an impoverished stretch of the rue de Flandre. This is from a particularly unfortunate period in French modern architecture, when bizarre building shapes and colors seemed the way to "enrichment" of popular environments. The whole of rue de Flandre is being widened, with a central mall to come, ostensibly to serve the vast auto traffic between the Parc de La Villette and Neuilly?

**Rue de Flandre** in its more gloried days was the *grande route,* a former Roman road that became one of royalty's entryways to the city and served as the main street of the village of La Villette. Henri IV entered Paris ceremonially along this way.

The street has changed a bit since then—and not necessarily for the best.

★★[19r-26.] Ed l'Epicier/formerly **Cinéma,** 108, rue de Flandre, between rue de Nantes and rue de l'Ourcq. **L. Thomas.** 1939.

Here in a symbolic minor monument of the 1930s, locals might reassemble to combat the degradation of rue de Flandre, first insulted architecturally, then raped urbanistically.

Streamlined, embalconied: Ed, you should announce the sales each morning from the balcony.

★[19r-27.] **Collège,** 1, rue de Cambrai, corner rue de l'Ourcq. **Wladimir Mitrofanoff.** 1986.

A pavilion at the corner of an *ilôt/grand ensemble* harboring high-rise "point blocks." Tiled in white, gray, and blue, its form is diminished by the awkward scale of its parts; the columns and floating screen wall would seem more real if the columns were not tiled. This is wishful neo-Corbu, but with the quality of cardboard.

[19r-28.] **Logements, 86, rue de l'Ourcq,** between rue de Cambrai and rue Curial. 1988.

A tricky street facade shelters a serene courtyard that is hard to enter in this era of real and paranoic insecurity (you must know the code).

[19r-29.] **Logements, 121, rue de l'Ourcq,** corner rue Curial and rue de Crimée. **Michel Duplay.** 1986.

Fancy, gabled, and balconied, with a grandly scaled *rez-de-chaussée* that gives it a Middle Eastern theatrical stance. Less clever would be nicer.

★★★[19r-30.] **Logements**/originally **Entrepôts des Meubles des Galeries Barbès,** 145, rue de l'Ourcq, between rue Curial and rue d'Aubervilliers. circa 1890. Reconstructed, **Christian Maisonhaute** and **Jacques Lévy.** 1980.

Steel columns and lintels articulate this late 19th-century warehouse, now elegantly converted into apartments. Rubble stone, cut stone, steel, and window sash—all in counterpoint.

The inner skylit steel-frame-encaged stairs and access balconies are a delight. It has the relaxed and pleasant ambience of Harvard Square or the best of renewed 19th-century warehouse architecture anywhere. It deserves to be repeated.

[19r-31.] **Logements, 166, rue d'Aubervilliers,** corner rue de l'Ourcq. **Michel Duplay.** 1982.

A flashy form, with smoked-glass balcony panels and bay windows without their spatial (three-way view) advantages. Pretentious.

★★[19r-32.] **Hôtel industriel, Metropole 19,** 134–140, rue d'Aubervilliers, between rue Labois-Rouillon and rue Riquet. **Jean-Paul Viguier** and **Jean-François Jodry.** 1989.

A bold and austere statement in the spirit of the late Eero Saarinen, whose relentless originality could be more than excused by his superb detailing. Here is a smooth skin with the panache of Saarinen's General Motors Technical Center (1948–1956) near Detroit. These sleek, light, and futuristic industrial quarters present style far from the vulgarity of La Défense. In these 14,000 square meters you have a sense of what greater Paris might still become, with an interwoven commercial and residential urban fabric of elegance.

Note the carefully cropped metal, framing the windows of the first two levels. It's a bit as if Perret had been reborn in 1980s steel (far from Prouvé). There is a conservative radicalism here, rather than the let-it-all-hang-out attitude at Beaubourg.

★★[19r-32a.] Ateliers de la Direction de la Propreté de Paris, rue Radiguet between rue d'Aubervilliers and rue Curial. **Renzo Piano.** 1989.

A sleek glass and metal place that houses shops to maintain and repair the street-cleaning machinery of Paris. Articulate and elegant.

[19r-33.] **Service Municipal des Pompes Funèbres de Paris,** 108, rue d'Aubervilliers, between rue Labois-Rouillon and rue Riquet. **Delebarre.** 1874.

All caskets are transported by the municipality (law of 1904), both to and from church, and to the cemetery. This vast metal-and-glass structure, shielded behind a Beaux Arts facade, was built by agents of the church but was later coopted by the City of Paris after formal separation of the church and state (1907). Here were sheltered horses and hearses, now motor hearses. Savor the iron-and-glass roof behind.

★★[19r-34.] **Logements, 14–16,** and **18–20, rue Mathis,** between rue Archereau and rue de Flandre. **Jean Pierre Buffi. Nos. 14–16,** 1985. **Nos. 18–20,** 1982.

At No. 14, a serpentine facade above plays with the straight street front below (a good lesson for Van Treeck opposite). No. 16 is a neo-1930s *logement,* with a mannered bay (Buffi says the facade "pivots around the column/bow window") of brown aluminum and glass. If he had forgotten that element, but kept his slots, ins, outs, and curves, the project would have been better.

[19r-35.] **Piscine/gymnase,** 11–13, rue Mathis, between rue Archereau and rue de Flandre. **Martin Van Treeck.** 1980s.

"All That Jazz" in white tile, deep reveals, aluminum, and glass. It's another flouncy teenager decked out in thrift-shop jewelry.

[19r-36.] **Les Orgues de Flandre,** 67–107, rue de Flandre, between rue de Crimée and rue Riquet, through to rue Archereau. **Martin Van Treeck.** 1973–1980.

The density of population was a mistake on the part of those programming authorities who gave this mission to the architect. But the authoritarian result is pretentious and couldn't be worse. Of course, the excuse might be "everyone loves a cheap apartment." Van Treeck said that it was "designed with attention to the pedestrian." What pedestrian—King Kong?

It does not even retain the scale and delicacy of a baroque organ. This is a Wurlitzer for a 6,000-seat 1920s movie house.

★★★[19r-37.] **Ateliers des artistes,** 10–14, **passage de Flandre,** corner quai de la Seine. **Yves Lion** and **François Leclercq.** 1986.

Subtle, elegant, and industrial with reflections, translucence, transparency, and the scale of a wonderful street. This is a loving and lovely place. Note the delicate attachments by screws of the panels and the gentle contrast of white window sash with the gray surface.

★[19r-38.] **Immeuble d'habitation** and **foyer pour les personnes âgées, 49–55, quai de la Seine,** between passage de Flandre and rue de Rouen. **Yves Lion** and **François Leclercq.** 1990.

A less elegant effort by Lion and Leclercq, but appropriately understated.

[19r-39.] **Logements, 41, quai de la Seine,** near passage de Flandre. **Michel Duplay.** 1985.

Provincial histrionics that defies the geometry of the basin and hopes to create a world of its own. Dreadful. If one qualifies as an architect, one does not necessarily become an urbane citizen.

[19r-40.] **Eglise Notre-Dame-des-Foyers,** 18, rue de Tanger, between rue Riquet and rue du Maroc.

A simplistic modern concrete church, more charming on the interior than outside. The street facade is brutal without the vigor of English brutalism. But go in anyway.

# 56
# NINETEENTH ARRONDISSEMENT
## VILLETTE

### PORTE DE LA VILLETTE

### TO PARC DES BUTTES-CHAUMONT

113, Boulevard MacDonald: **P. Enault;** Maison de la Villette; Villette Nord: **Gérard Thurnauer;** Cité des Sciences et de l'Industrie: **Adrian Fainsilber;** Les Folies: **Bernard Tschumi;** Le Jardin des Bambous: **Alexandre Chemetov;** La Grande Halle, **Jules de Mérindol, Bernard Reichen,** and **Philippe Robert;** Bureau de Poste: **Jacques Debat-Ponsan;** 190, avenue Jean-Jaurès: **Aldo Rossi;** Cité de la Musique: **Christian de Portzamparc;** ZAC Manin-Jaurès: **Grumbach, Bardon, Colboc, Briand, Cardin, Boursicot, Loth, Robert, Testas, Nunez-Tanowski, Vasconi, Hondelette, Maurios, Andren, Schlumberger, Sarfati, Jenkins, Aygalinc, Nordemann, Decq, PLI, Dollander, Gillet,** and **Portzamparc;** place de Rhin-et-Danube; Hameau de Danube: **Eugène Gonnot** and **Georges Albenque;** Villa Amalia; Immeubles d'habitation des Reservoirs des Buttes-Chaumont: **Denis Valode** and **Jean Pistre**

Métro: **Porte de la Villette**

**[19v-5.] Cité des Sciences et de l'Industrie. Adrian Fainsilber. 1987.**

## The conversion of Henri IV at La Villette

After preliminary negotiations at Suresnes, "the least ruined place in the environs of Paris," the representatives of the King and of the League assembled for their two last sessions at la Roquette, in the Faubourg Saint-Antoine, on June 5, 1593, and at La Villette on June 11, in the house of **Emeri de Thou.** At this ultimate conference it was announced that **Henri IV** would convert to Catholicism, as reported by **Pierre de l'Estoile:**

"On Friday the 11th, we went to the conference at La Villette, where Chomberg returned with definite news of the (imminent) conversion of the king."

On Sunday, July 25, Henri IV was converted with great pomp at Saint Denis and again on July 31 at La Villette. The general truce was signed between the members of the League led by Mayenne and partisans of the king. The text of this agreement concludes:

"Made and recorded at La Villette, between Paris and Saint-Denis, on the last day of July 1593, and published on the first day of the following August in the said cities of Paris and Saint-Denis, to the sound of trumpets and a public crier in the customary places."

★★[19v-1.] 113, Boulevard Macdonald (logements), between avenue Corentin-Cariou and Canal Saint-Denis. **P. Enault.** 1933.

Bay windows become peninsular in this gray *grès* tiled sleek moderne building (no Art Deco here), a precocious precursor of the later 1930s. The three "modern" (1960s style) buildings to the east can only be described as trash. No. 113's own *poubelle* is undoubtedly more studied.

This is an island of distinction on this barren stretch of the Boulevard Macdonald, but worth a side trip from La Villette.

★[19v-2.] Entrepôts, 27, quai de la Gironde, along Canal Saint-Denis, north of avenue Corentin-Cariou. circa 1870.

Stepped gables crown these brick-and-stone warehouses, newly cleaned and renovated, with new windows and encaged fire stairs. These comprise a dour and sturdy set of facades that remember La Villette's days before the glitz.

---

**Parc de la Villette:** This is another vast and recycled precinct of Paris, like the Hôpital Jussieu (Université de Paris VI, Pierre and Marie Curie) once **Les Halles aux Vins,** and the Forum shopping center with adjacent park, formerly Les Halles Centrales. Here were the **Marché aux Bestiaux** and the *abattoirs,* the former to the south of the Canal de l'Ourcq, the latter to the north. The unlucky beasts, after sale to a butcher, were led across the canal bridge to the appropriate abattoir (whether for cattle, calves, pigs, or sheep). The *grande halle* in the south section is one of the original market buildings.

---

[19v-3.] Maison de la Villette/originally **Rotonde de la Villette,** avenue Corentin-Cariou. 1883. Reconstruction, **Dubusset, Lyon, Morita.** 1987.

Originally the quarters of veterinarians attached to the *marché*/abattoirs. This stumpy octagon is crudely reminiscent of the *barrières* of Ledoux, now remodeled as a reception center and gallery of events, both past and present, of the park. Why do "modern" architects ruin historical scale by introducing fixed sheets of glass into openings where there were once windows with mullions, muntins, and frames?

★[19v-4.] Villette Nord, along avenue Corentin-Cariou and boulevard Macdonald. **Gérard Thurnauer.** 1990.

A giant hulk that forms a massive slab along boulevard Macdonald. Here are an intermix of residential and commercial uses. Some architectural tricks, such as the articulated stairs at the top, don't succeed in calming this Gargantua. On the Cité side complex, three-dimensional blue-painted steel grids offer both balconies and empty structural interplay to the plaza.

★★[19v-5.] Cité des Sciences et de l'Industrie, bounded by avenue Corentin-Cariou, Canal Saint-Denis, Canal de l'Ourcq, and boulevard Macdonald. **Adrian Fainsilber.** 1987.

Technological histrionics worthy of Paris's original and continuing role as a pioneer in the architecture and engineering of iron and glass: **Les Halles** (centrales), **Notre Dame du Travail,** the **Tour Eiffel, Jardin Fleuriste,** and others crossbred the economics of industrialization with a new aesthetic largely ignored in the "modern" of the 1920s through the 1970s, except for mavericks such as America's **Buckminster Fuller,** and France's **Jean Prouvé.** Now, England's **Norman Foster,** France's **Jean Nouvel,** and here, its **Adrian Fainsilber,** use this as their aesthetic cutting edge.

The **Géode** is exactly that: an industrial jewel mined from the mind of Buckminster Fuller, a dymaxion myriad of triangles that reflects in its unconscious fun house mirrors the museum and the city surrounding.

The moated museum block brings the commercial château (Azay-le-Rideau) up to the present. *And,* this is the era of the grass mansard, enough to drive professional lawn mowers mad.

★★★[19v-6.] Les Folies, throughout the Parc de la Villette on a geometric grid. **Bernard Tschumi.** 1988 and later.

These thirty red "follies" are scarcely foolish, acting as the geometric nodes (on a 100 by 100 meter grid) of these vast 120 acres. All are symbolic, and most have functions (brasserie, kindergarten, shop, information, etc.). All are fun, which is the least a folly can attempt. Like enormous chessmen, they imply a chessboard.

Each is constructed from a basic cube, ten meters on a side, each face divided into nine equal squares. To this schematic model, and in each case, Tschumi adds and subtracts structure, always leaving the memory of the twenty-seven cubes with which he began. Tschumi's checkmate occurred in 1988, when he became dean of the School of Architecture at Columbia University in New York.

★★[19v-7.] Jardin de Bambous, in the middle of the Parc de la Villette. **Alexandre Chemetov,** landscape architect. **Daniel Buren,** sculptor. 1987.

"A place that I love and that represents an ideal: mine. A manifesto made of leaves and concrete. My path as urban gardener has made me love concrete, the kind that is neither polished nor architectonic but rough, like certain works of art that also deal with territory, "low tech concrete," as my friend Marc Mimram would say, works that bear the marks of their fabrication and that retain memories of the construction site, which it is not acceptable to recall on the glossy paper of the journals for which I have the pleasure of writing.

"The hollow here is not dissimulation but multiplication . . . multiplication of atmospheres, viewpoints, and rediscovered sky. It is also silence, warmth, a climate favorable for growing plants, contemplation, perhaps reflection." Alexandre Chemetov in *L'architecture d'aujourd'hui* April 1989.

★[19v-8.] Le Zénith, in the middle of the Parc de la Villette, near the Canal de l'Ourcq. **Philippe Chaix** and **Jean-Paul Morel.** 1983.

Taut tent (certainly not for those uptight). Here 6,300 seated fans can rock to rock under a polyester skin stretched over a metal framework spanning 230 feet. Outside its silver-gray surface offers some vestigial shimmers: the inevitable pollution is dulling its sheen. The diving aircraft, symbol of the Zénith from afar, falls from a tower that was once the silo for the **Marché aux Bestiaux.** Within, raucous music sounds for youth and neo-youth, in hard rock, post rock, melted rock, crushed rock, and sand.

★★**[19v-9.] La Grande Halle,** originally **Halle aux Boeufs,** part of the **Marché aux Bestiaux,** 211, avenue Jean-Jaurès. Supervising architect, **Louis-Adolphe Janvier.** Architect of La Grande Halle, **Jules de Mérindol.** 1867. Restored, **Reichen and Robert.** 1985.

This great basilica is the glorious remnant of the beef, veal, and lamb market that, in three great *salles,* and later a fourth for pork, offered the wholesale butchers of Paris live animals to inspect before they were dispatched to the north, beyond the Canal de l'Ourcq. Cast and wrought iron and glass straddle a nave with three side aisles. Myriad expositions of a sophistication and sweetness that the hall has only recently enjoyed now give it a sanitary air: among those relating to this guide, the Salon International d'Architecture.

★**[19v-10.] Logements, 3, avenue Jean-Lolive,** outside Porte de Pantin. **Paul Chemetov, Christian Devillers, Valentin Fabré,** and **Jean Perrotet.** 1981.

The brickwork, in the words of Chemetov, is a "salute to the HBM of the red belt," on the inner side of the *Périphérique*—a happy thought, for most of those *habitations à bon marché* are the distinguished vernacular of Paris housing in the 1930s. Here, trapped by an existing and banal tower next door, and beholden to the overwhelming densities demanded by the municipality of Pantin, Chemetov et Cie. built a massive block difficult to defend. It is too big and too bulky, and the play of picture frame windows and curtain wall in contrast to simple punched openings is a futile exercise. Within the interior courtyard, However, there is a more playful game.

**[19v-11] Stade Gymnase Jules-Ladoumèque,** off place de la Porte-de-Pantin.

Here on a section of the *non aedificandi* before the 1845 Thiers wall, is one of the many activities that form a gymnastic and scholastic belt around Paris. Conoids shelter the spectator in forms reminiscent of the Spanish engineer **Eduardo Torroja.** It's a bit jazzy behind: why can't architects merely stop at the breathless purity of great engineering?

★**[19v-12.] Eglise Sainte-Claire,** 179, boulevard Sérurier, at place de la Porte-de-Pantin. **André Le Donné.** 1956.

From the days when a modern church seemed a holy mission to young architects, somehow redeeming the validity of the modern idea if it were accepted by the agents of God. It is more than austere on the exterior, but the quality of light within is delightful. Behind, a pregnant apse faces the retired railway *(petite ceinture),* now promoted to the promenade plantée Manin-Jaurès.

★**[19v-13.] Lycée Technique d'Alembert,** 20, rue Sente-des-Dorées, corner avenue Jean-Jaurès. **Pol Abraham** and **Pierre Tabon.** 1938. Extension and restructuring, **Alain Gillet.** 1990.

Brick à la hollandaise for the masses: a great pile of education in this heavy-handed Art Moderne brick block, aggressively dominating its students in a way that schools of the 19th century did not.

★★**[19v-14.] PTT, 207, avenue Jean-Jaurès,** opposite rue Eugène-Jumin. **Jacques Debat-Ponsan.** 1931.

A lonely object in search of neighbors that would make it a smashing street-corner event. The southwest corner presents some precocious concrete-grilled cubism.

★★★[19v-15.] Logements, 190, avenue Jean-Jaurès, between rue Eugène-Jumin and rue Adolph-Mille. Aldo Rossi, with Claude Zuber. 1989.

"The project was designed as a fragment of a larger composition and as part of the heritage of Paris; it emphasizes the importance of the street, homogeneous facades, great zinc roofs, arcades, and colorful and lively shops. Although it is also a new city block, it retains typical Parisian elements, notably the *passage*. . . .
"The main buildings are of stucco, since stucco makes possible the use of a traditional prefabricated structure (concrete, masonry . . .). The roofs are metallic, in zinc or galvanized metal, or even in metal painted with the gray of many Parisian roofs. The 'head' of the building is in stone, gray or light yellow, identical to that found in much French construction of the 18th century and later. . . .
"These are the principal characteristics of the project . . . a project that seeks not to be a unique monument in the city's interior but, rather, to be part of that city and, ultimately, to become a Parisian building." Aldo Rossi in *L'architecture d'aujourd'hui*, October 1987.

★[19v-16.] Le Jules Verne (immeuble), 2, rue Adolphe-Mille, corner avenue Jean-Jaurès. Philippe Dubois. 1989.

The not-so-fine line between quality and schlock is vividly demonstrated here. The banal *immeuble* to the east is the product of five architects who produced not the camel but its detritus. Though not brilliant, Dubois is good—and that is more than most of us can expect without the iron hand of Haussmann's entourage.

★★★[19v-17.] Cité de la Musique, 211, avenue Jean-Jaurès, opposite rue Eugène-Jumin. Christian de Portzamparc. 1989.

Two complexes flank the fountain-plaza centered before the *grande halle;* the one to the left, or west, is reserved for students and holds classrooms and practice rooms. The right, or east block houses the public places, ranging from a concert hall and museum, to shops and housing.
The schemes are highly complex, both in functions and in their architectural response, so visually complex that there is sufficient form-making for a whole city. Perhaps *that* is why it is termed the City of Music? Portzamparc, unfortunately, doesn't always know when to stop. Similar problems occur at a smaller scale in his other works such as the VII arrondissement Conservatoire de Musique [7w–14.]. But at Hautes-Formes [13se-10.] he maintained his serenity in a rich urban complex. As in the case of Louis Kahn, Portzamparc must await late middle age perhaps, to achieve his greatest works.

[19v-18.] Ecole, rue Delesseux, between rue Adolphe-Mille and rue des Ardennes. 1980s.

A bizarre spaceship has tucked itself into this back street. The avenue couldn't stand much more of this ego flaunting.

★[19v-19.] Logements and écoles, 160–162, avenue Jean-Jaurès, between rue du Hainaut and rue de Lunéville. Georges Pancreac'h. 1985.

Here Post Modernism allows the stepping of the volume to match buildings to each side and a stepping in depth to maintain the streetfront, while simultaneously allowing a deep play of light and shadow. An 80-meter-deep glass-roofed corridor leads to the cluster of schools behind.

**[19v-20.] Bâtiment industriel, 16, rue du Hainaut,** between avenue Jean-Jaurès and rue Petit. 1901.

A sophisticated remnant of vernacular service buildings that laced through this quarter at the turn of the century.

**[19v-21.] Logements, 83 bis, rue Petit,** corner rue Hainaut.

No. 83 bis is a heavy-handed work in brick and stucco, where tricks seem more important than serious architecture: the floating "picture frame" that corners the block, the triad of 1930s revival balconies, the dated "industrial brick" patterning. Unfortunately, built reality is not school (where you can at least throw away the cardboard model). This is a C-minus, whereas next door at **8–10, rue Hainaut** there is understated class (despite the millions of little white tiles), earning a B-plus.

★**[19v-22.] HBM, 108–110, boulevard Sérurier,** opposite rue des Carrières d'Amérique. **Agence d'Architecture HBM.** 1935.

A grand arch gives special entry meaning to this murky brick and concrete ensemble. Did H. H. Richardson pass by? The blocks around are filled with 1930s HBMs.

★★**[19v-23.] ZAC Manin-Jaurès,** between avenue Jean-Jaurès and rue de Crimée, mostly facing rue Manin but sometimes behind older streetfront buildings. **Alain Sarfati,** coordinating architect.

As part of the cut and roadway of the *petite ceinture* ring railroad of the Frères Pereire, this precedes many of the surrounding streets. The sinuous curve of new buildings along rue Manin follows the southeasterly embankment of this segment, but sometimes there were buildings of the 1950s (and earlier) along portions. Most of the nineteen sites designated for this ZAC are complete:

| | | |
|---|---|---|
| 1. Immeuble | **Antoine Grumbach** | 1991 |
| 2. Ateliers | **Renaud Bardon** and **Pierre Colboc** | 1990 |
| 3. Immeuble | **Jean-François Briand** and **Jean-Louis Cardin** | 1990 |
| 4. Immeuble | **Olivier Le Boursicot, Guillaume Loth, Yves Robert,** and **Guillaume Testas** | 1990 |
| 5. CES Manin-Jaurès | **Manolo Nunez-Tanowski** | 1990 |
| 6. Immeuble | **Claude Vasconi** | 1989 |
| 7. Immeuble | **Claude Vasconi** | 1989 |
| 8. École élémentaire | **Jacques Hondelette** | 1991 |
| 9. Immeuble | **Georges Maurios** | 1990 |
| 10. Immeuble | **Jacques Andren** and **Robert Schlumberger** | 1989 |
| 11. Ecole maternelle | **Alain Sarfati** | 1989 |
| 12. Immeuble | **Yves Jenkins** | 1990 |
| 13. Immeuble | **Antoine Aygalinc** and **Francis Nordemann** | 1990 |
| 14. Immeuble | **Odile Decq** | 1989 |
| 15. Immeuble | **PLI architecture** | 1990 |
| 16. Immeuble | **PLI architecture** | 1990 |
| 17. Immeuble and ateliers | **Serge Dollander** | 1990 |
| 18. Lycée Technique reconstruction | **Alain Gillet** | 1990 |
| 19. Immeuble and hôtel | **Christian de Portzamparc** | 1992 |

**[19v-24.] Logements, 137, boulevard Sérurier,** between rue des Car-rières-d'Amérique and rue de la Solidarité. 1988.

Stylish kitsch, complete with mansarded *combles* and a skin of brick and stucco in arbitrary juxtapositions. This is a fresh kid on the block opposite the regality of the HBM opposite at **No. 108.**

**[19v-25.] Logements, 8, place de Rhin-et-Danube.** circa 1930.

Chevron balconies, an Art Deco *comble,* and other stucco mannerisms festoon this lone *immeuble,* a high-rise at the edge of a sea of villas of lovely scale and architecture.

---

**Hôpital Hérold and the ancient Butte de Beauregard:** place de Rhin-et-Danube: This abandoned site, has ceded its work to its medical surrogate and successor, the new **Hôpital Robert-Debré,** near the Porte des Lilas. The future of this great block will apparently be divided between a new *lycée* and a hospice (housing) for the elderly. If the new hospital serves as inspiration, things might bode well for the future of architecture in this neighborhood. Too much jazz hereabouts would upset the tranquility of endless lovely private streets: villas, an *hameau,* an *impasse,* all lined with bourgeois town houses.

The Butte de Beauregard, cresting at the place de Rhin-et-Danube, housed one of the greatest gypsum quarries (plaster of Paris) in the Ile de France in its volume: the Carrières d'Amérique—so named because much of it was exported to the New World. After condemnation of all quarries in Paris, due to the collapse of several and loss of life, the Carrières d'Amé-rique were filled with 1.2 million cubic yards of earth!

**[19v-26.] HBM, 2–10, rue de la Solidarité,** between rue David-d'Angers and rue d'Alsace. **Paul Pelletier** and **Arthur Teisseire.** 1913–1925.

Tan and rose brick, with bracketed eaves and some stubby Tuscan-columned porches. Around the corner on rue de la Prévoyance you can see a contrasting housing system: brick houselike pavilions around a garden at a much lower density (**André Arfvidson, Joseph Bassompierre,** and **Paul de Rutté.** 1923–1926.)

★★**[19v-27.] Hameau du Danube,** 46, rue du Général-Brunet, off place de Rhin-et-Danube. **Eugène Gonnot** and **Georges Albenque.** 1924.

Stucco, brick, tile, vines, and flowered romanticism, entered through a trellised wood gate. This is a place for the song of sparrows, where the ghost of Haussmann might keep away. It is a planned garden-city wonder equal to New York's Forest Hills Gardens but tighter and smaller. Here the bucolic and the urban join together.

★**[19v-28.] Villa Amalia,** 36, rue du Général-Brunet, between place de Rhin-et-Danube and rue de Mouzaïa. 1892.

A sequence of walls and grills, festooned with ivy, gives a Mediterranean quality to these Italianate villas. The streets around the place de Rhin-et-Danube are laced with similar villas, pedestrian quietways that are charming and a more than pleasant place in which to live.

**[19v-29.] Maison, 5, villa d'Hauterive.**

Even these quiet alleys were invaded by 1930s fashion, bringing a concrete and stucco style amid the flowers, vines, and wrought ironwork of the period.

**[19v-30.] 33, rue Miguel-Hidalgo,** between place de Rhin-et-Danube, at Villa Maurice-Rollinat. 1930s.

A *maison particulière* in brick, its concrete wall crowned with tubular Art Deco rails and with a vine-clad roof garden against the sky.

Walk on to the villa de Cronstadt and the villa Claude-Monet, where more charm abounds.

**★[19v-31.] 23, rue Miguel-Hidalgo,** corner villa Claude-Monet. **Germain Debré.** 1932.

A once-stylish small *immeuble,* curved and cornered at the entrance to villa Claude-Monet. Such streamlining was more an act of Art Moderne than of Art Deco.

**★[19v-32.] Logements, 82, rue Botzaris,** off rue de Crimée, at the Parc des Buttes-Chaumont. **F. Nanquette.** circa 1930.

Bulky and bold early modern, the balconies ribbed with remembrances of Classical columns. The columns splitting the *rez-de-chaussée* service windows are prescient Post Modern.

**[19v-33.] Réservoirs des Buttes-Chaumont,** 72, rue Botzaris, corner rue de La Villette. **Diet.** 1887.

Here is where the successors of Napoléon III's henchmen placed the reservoir to feed the cascades and lake of the Buttes-Chaumont.

**[19v-34.] Immeubles d'habitation des Reservoirs des Buttes-Chaumont** between rue Botzaris, rue des Alouettes and rue de la Villette, **Denis Valode** and **Jean Pistre.** 1992.

On this glorious site, peaking over the park across the street, will rise apartments with spectacular views.

You are now at the eastern entrance of the Parc des Buttes-Chaumont, a convenient place to rest, or to contemplate the beginnings of the park, or to go home via the Métro stop Botzaris. If you feel adventurous (or indefatigable) and have comfortable walking shoes, you might continue on, entering the park at this corner. Turn to Chapter 54.

# 57
# TWENTIETH ARRONDISSEMENT
## CHARONNE AND SOUTH
### PLACE GAMBETTA TO PLACE AUGUSTE
### METIVIER VIA CHARONNE AND PERE LACHAISE

Place Gambetta; Cinéma Belgrand; **Henri Sauvage;** 5 bis, rue du
Capitaine-Ferber: **G. Imbert;** Campagne à Paris; Pavillon de
l'Ermitage: **Serin;** 21, rue Pelleport: **Alex Weisengrün** and **P.
Rocca;** 9–11, rue des Prairies: **A. Burel, et al.;** 1, chemin du
Parc-de-Charonne: **Yann Brunel** and **Sinikka Ropponeu;** Dispensaire
Jouye-Rouve: **Louis Bonnier;** Saint-Germain-de-Charonne; 26, rue
Saint-Blaise: **Jacques Bardet;** College Vitruve: **Jacques Bardet;**
Logements et Ateliers des Musiciens: **Yann Brunel** and **Sinikka
Ropponeu;** place de la Réunion; Eglise Saint-Jean-de-Bosco: **Rotter;**
rue de Fontarabie: **Charles** and **Henri Delacroix;** rue de la Réunion:
**Gérard Thurnauer;** Père Lachaise; place Auguste-Metivier

Side Trip. Ateliers Davout: **Jean-Marie Charpentier, et al.;**
Ministère des Finances: **Bernard Zehrfuss;** Lycée Hélène-Boucher: **L.
Sallez;** Ateliers Bricard: **Alexandre Borgeaud;** Barrières du Trone:
**Claude-Nicolas Ledoux**

Métro: **Gambetta** to Métro: **Père Lachaise**

[20s-4.] **Logements, 31, boulevard Davout. Pierre Parat** and **Michel
Andrault.** 1985.

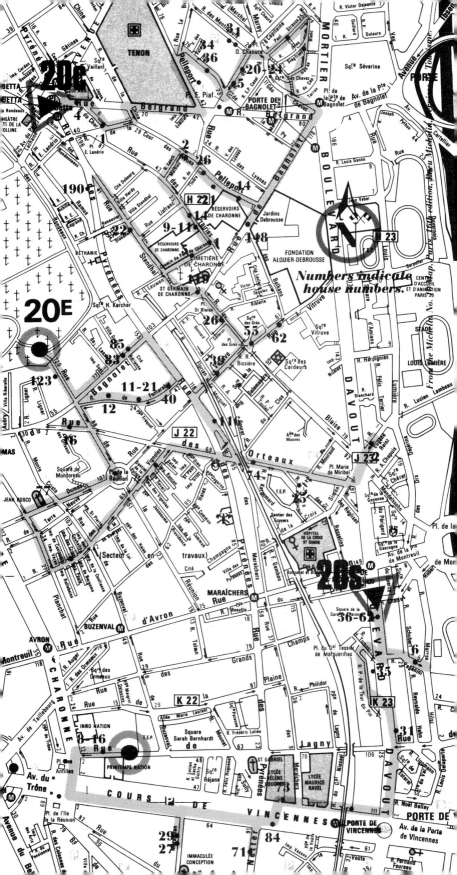

**Numbers indicate house numbers.**

★[20c-1.] Cinéma, 4, rue Belgrand, at rue du Cher. Henri Sauvage. 1930.

Poor Henri. His building's body has been decorated with obscene (but not pornographic) golden decor. The **Cinéma 3 Gambetta** leaves a curved facade as an early modern remembrance.

[20c-2.] Logements, 1, rue de la Chine, at rue de la Cour-des-Noues. Henri Sauvage and Charles Sarrazin. 1909.

Only the top remembers the creativity of Sauvage, here emporched in concrete.

[20c-3.] EDF (Electricité de France), place Edith-Piaf at rue Belgrand. circa 1914.

Polychromatic brick and tile clad even these sometimes "lowly" structures. Once the EDF, GDF, and PTT were all patrons of more graceful buildings and street furniture, such as this.

[20c-4.] HBM, rue de la Py, rue Pelleport, and place Edith-Piaf. 1930s.

The vernacular HBM of the "red belt," here closer in.

[20c-5.] Logements, 34–36, rue de la Py, between rue du Capitaine-Ferber and rue Le Bua. Michel Duplay. 1982.

A ragged serration of the street that attempts a sense of artists' ateliers, but the fussy scale and coarse detailing deflate the whole idea.

★[20c-6.] Logements, 5 bis, rue du Capitaine-Ferber, at rue de la Py. G. Imbert. 1931.

A clean, bay-windowed stucco prism, this is also 32, rue de la Py. Next door, at **Nos. 7** and **9**, neo-Classicism and modernism entwine in two *immeubles de rapport.*

[20c-7.] Ateliers (now Etablissements H. Dehayes), 20, rue du Capitaine-Ferber, between rue de la Py and rue des Montiboeufs. circa 1895.

It remembers Viollet-le-Duc in its brackets and polychromy, the architecture of the proto-technocratic 19th century.

[20c-8.] Bureaux, 22–24, rue du Capitaine-Feber, between rue de la Py and rue des Montiboeufs. A. Waser. 1906.

The early Beaux Arts extravagances (known in America as the "Second Empire" style) did not go far in Charonne or Ménilmontant. Here, in the land of the workers, there is more of a history of technology for the workplace (see **No. 20** next door.)

[20c-9.] Immeuble, 1, rue des Montiboeufs, off rue du Capitaine-Ferber. J. Curtz. 1930.

An awkward but valiant essay for an *immeuble* on a small site. The inevitable neo-Classical fluting and balcony balusters are present.

Next door, at **No. 3,** a more relaxed and traditional architecture has allowed some floral *grès à la Bigot* spandrels on the Haussmannian envelope, here basically in brick and stone.

★[20c-10.] Logements, 1, rue du Capitaine-Marchal, corner place Octave-Chanute.

Stonework of the 1930s is honored both in the corner carving at the first floor and at the sky, where a floral capitaled column and its exedra crown it all.

★★[20c-11.] Campagne à Paris (ilôt de 89 maisons), rue Irénée-Blanc, rue Jules-Siegfried, and rue Paul-Strauss. 1927.

These eighty-nine houses crown a hillcrest that rises above the place de la Porte-de-Bagnolet and the place Octave-Chanute. Stairs cascade downward in both directions, and atop are villas in sinuous private streets, mostly in dour *meulière*. Charming and peaceful, it is Lilliputian in contrast to, say, the avenue Gambetta or the HBMs of the boulevard Mortier. Campagne à Paris was incorporated as an HBM in 1907.

★★[20c-12.] Pavillon de l'Ermitage de Bagnolet, 148, rue de Bagnolet, on the grounds of the Hôspice Debrousse, corner rue des Balkans. Serin. 1734.

A remnant of the 18th century, an outbuilding of the Château de Bagnolet, once a residence of the Duchesse d'Orléans, daughter (by Mme. de Montespan) of Louis XIV and wife of Philippe d'Orléans, regent of France in the minority of Louis XV. The château was demolished to make way for the Fondation Alquier-Debrousse.

[20c-13.] Logements, 14, rue Pelleport, between rue de Bagnolet and rue Belgrand.

Bay windows and a bit of play in stucco, a bit of tile, a bit of glass block. The street facade is far more satisfactory than the ponderous flank.

★[20c-14.] Logements, 21, rue Pelleport, between rue de Bagnolet and rue Belgrand. Alex Weisengrün and P. Rocca. 1986.

Earthy brick and colored concrete, with maroon entrance *huisserie* and canopy. A somber but plastic entry on this eclectic street. Is brick coming back—a backlash against white tile?

★[20c-15.] Logements, 26, rue Pelleport, opposite rue de l'Indre. L. Sarret. 1931.

Little Tuscan columns from the long history of Classicism reappear as balcony members in this mini-HBM. Brick again for the lesser (but modern) bourgeois. A solid corner anchor to this and these blocks.

★[20c-16.] Logements, 2, rue de la Cour-des-Noues, off rue Pelleport. L. Sarret. 1920s.

The tenement exalted in corbeled brickwork and concrete cornices. Stepped up, stepped back, bay windowed without windows—a plastic play.

[20c-17.] Logements, 24–26, rue des Prairies, between rue de l'Indre and rue de Bagnolet. Jacques Lévy and Christian Maisonhaute. 1984.

★[20c-18.] Logements, 14, rue des Prairies, between rue Lisfranc and chemin du Parc-de-Charonne. P. Chavannes, Marcel Lambert, and M. F. Martin. 1986.

A sleek neighbor to Nos. 9–11 across the street. It offers more stucco and tile—and less richness of imagination and materials.

★★[20c-19.] Logements, 9–11 rue des Prairies, between rue Lisfranc and chemin du Parc-de-Charonne. Alain Burel, B. Lamy, and Daniel Vial. 1984.

Elegant bay windows articulated in blue sash with symbolic *garde-fous*, in a polychromatic palette of stucco, tile, sash, and ironwork. The courtyard within is unavailable to anonymous beggars and tourists. Here the "code" is almost always on, and these Parisian peeks are available only for official guests.

★[20c-20.] **Ateliers, 1, chemin du Parc-de-Charonne,** at rue des Prairies. **Yann Brunel** and **Sinikka Ropponeu.** 1982.

Block and timber from another culture make a strange corner *colombage* intruding on Paris. Or is it *pan de bois* again? This is a strange building, odd in this heterogeneous place. Creativity without urban propriety.

[20c-21.] **5, chemin du Parc-de-Charonne,** between rue des Prairies and rue Stendhal. **Michel Bourdeau.** 1989.

Chunky blocks, where a facade is the nine-square problem, with heavy-handed "picture frame" windows.

★[20c-22.] **Logements, 22, rue Stendhal,** at rue Lisfranc. **Jacques Starkier.** 1981.

The entryways are excised serrations along rue Lisfranc, in a nervy style of laminations, with planes lapping planes. Classy.

★[20c-23.] **Dispensaire Jouye-Rouve,** 190, rue des Pyrénées, at rue Stendhal. **Louis Bonnier.** circa 1910.

The *meulière* that supports the bourgeois of Versailles and **La Campagne à Paris** serves a more creative role for Bonnier. Not only rubble stone is presented, but also social and architectural engineering; and Bonnier's detailing includes an open stair along rue des Pyrénées that offers slated, stepping sills, with guardrails like iron tulips. Look carefully.

★[20c-24.] **Eglise Saint-Germain-de-Charonne,** 119, rue de Bagnolet, at place Saint-Blaise. 13th (bell tower)–19th centuries.

The church of a country village, now in the heart of urbanized Charonne. Sited on a stepped bluff, it dominates the old main street, rue Saint-Blaise. The interior is late Romanesque, with squat ribbed vaulting, and lusty vine-clad capitals. In the charming cemetery behind, you can discover the tomb of **François Bègue,** apocryphal "secretary of Robespierre and lover of roses."

---

**Promenade à Charonne**
"After lunch on Thursday, October 24, 1776, I followed the exterior boulevards as far as the rue du Chemin-Vert, by which I reached the heights of Ménil-montant; and from there, following footpaths across the vineyards and meadows as far as Charonne, I walked across the cheerful countryside that separates these two villages; then I made a detour in order to return over a different route across the same meadows. . . .

"It has been several days since the grape harvest; strollers from the city had already withdrawn. The farmers too were leaving the fields until their winter tasks. The countryside, still green and mellow, but partly defoliated and already deserted, was a picture of solitude and approaching winter. Its appearance evoked mixed feelings of sweetness and sadness too analogous to my age and destiny for me not to see a connection." **Jean-Jacques Rousseau** in *Les rêveries du promeneur solitaire, Deuxième promenade.*

---

★★[20c-25.] **Logements, 26, rue Saint-Blaise,** between place Saint-Blaise and rue Galleron. **Jacques Bardet.** 1985.

A wondrously sensitive huddling of old Charonne, in scale, color, texture, and detail. The alley and court behind are charming, something that central Paris harbors, even downtown, behind all that Haussmannian pomp.

**[20c-26.] Maison, 55, rue Vitruve**, between rue Saint-Blaise and rue des Balkans. Early 19th century.

**[20c-27.] Ecole maternelle,** 62, rue Vitruve, between rue Saint-Blaise and rue des Balkans. **Berdje Agopyan.** 1984.

More space age stuff, particularly galling in this serene old sector, where architects such as Jacques Bardet are fitting a vigorous new into the peaceful old.

★★**[20c-28.] Collège Saint-Blaise**, 39, rue Vitruve, at rue Florian. **Jacques Bardet.** 1982.

The trellis elevated to a streetfront screen (cf. the grilles at the Musée Carnavalet or the enveloping walls at the upper level of Le Corbusier's Villa Savoie). Low-rise, plastic in form, filled with sun and shadow, this is a lively modern monument for Charonne.

★**[20c-29.] Ilôt, rue Saint-Blaise, rue Vitruve, rue du Clos,** and **rue Courat.** 1988.

The central plaza (lid of a parking garage) is contained by bland and banal buildings, with a bit of concrete-balcony jazz. In spite of such thoughts, you may like it as mediocre architecture subordinate to a substantial urban space. If only Corbu had been given the space and designed the buildings.

★★**[20c-30.] Logements** and **ateliers de musique**, 116, rue des Pyrénées, between rue Vitruve and rue des Orteaux. **Yann Brunel** and **Sinikka Ropponeu.** 1986.

An alien presence, akin to those bizarre ideas of Japan's Metabolism Group, where objects and egos rule. This is "culture" served with a sledgehammer. Brunel says that "music is everywhere present on the facade . . . the great round openings like the bell of a trumpet, and the little round openings like notes on their scores"; he calls the construction "heavy and massive like a bunker." Serious architects are sometimes victims of their own hyperbole.

An aside down rue des Orteaux to boulevard Davout and back.

**[20c-31.] Logements, 74, rue des Orteaux,** between rue des Maraîchers and rue des Rasselins. **Pierre Giudicelli.** 1984.

The streetfront is an honorable urban element, straddling rue Pauline-Kergomard, that leads to a great space behind.

★**[20c-32.] Logements, 25, rue Mouraud,** along rue des Orteaux. 1980s.

Another street-spanner; the blue-tiled bay windows and balconies are done with grace. It seems so easy to be simple and elegant, as here, whereas the neighbors are awkward, morose, or overdone—or all three.

★**[20c-33.] Groupe scolaire, 2, rue Eugène-Reisz,** at boulevard Davout. **Abel** and **Mathieu.** 1931.

The encircling fortress of Thiers gave way to the brickwork of HBMs, schools, and other public amenities. Here the modern spirit recognizes light and scale, with some fanciful brickwork of the Art Deco, housing not only the **Collège Jean-Perrin** but also the **Ecole Elémentaire Mixte.**

**[20c-34.] Impasse Rançon,** off rue des Vignoles, between rue des Orteaux and rue de la Réunion.

An alley of the modest, off which entries seek tiny courtyards leading to stairs and flats behind. Another urban backwater that, with some slight style and restoration, could become a gracious, understated way to live.

**[20c-35.] Impasse des Crins,** off 23, rue des Vignoles, between rue de Buzenval and rue Planchat.

This narrow alley allows these blocks to be filled with less-than-modest houses, the lower-income answer to the villas of the arrondissement's more affluent sections. But here you can glimpse a "snapshot" of the tower of **Saint-Jean-Bosco.**

**[20c-36.] Place de la Réunion.**

This is space losing buildings, rather than buildings creating space: a *rond-point* plaza with two-thirds of its perimeter destroyed. With total demolition and an obelisk, it could become **place Louis XIX.** The conflict between urbanism, villagism, Charonne, and downtown continues.

★★**[20c-37.] Eglise Saint-Jean-Bosco**, 77, rue Vitruve, at rue Monte-Cristo. **René Rotter.** 1937.

Neo-Perret. Concrete is tickled into more elaboration than, say, Perret's church at Le Raincy (1925); but it is a vigorous avant-garde presence among the workers.

**[20c-38.] Logements, 16, rue des Orteaux,** at impasse des Orteaux. 1980s.

Such corner opportunities were one key to Haussmannian-*tardif;* here they are recreated in maroon tile and stucco. As usual, it is an entry into an inner world. Aside and around are uninteresting but well-groomed neighbors.

**[20c-39.] Ecole maternelle** and **logements, 12, rue de Fontarabie,** between rue de la Réunion and passage Fréquel. **Jacques Kalisz.** 1983.

Pretentious structuralism, without any sense of proportion or scale.

**[20c-40.] Passage Fréquel,** opposite 21, rue de Fontarabie.

Remnants of Charonne still inhabit back streets, overborne by their new neighbors.

★**[20c-41.] Logements, 11–21, rue de Fontarabie,** opposite passage Fréquel. **Georges Maurios.** 1985.

The great column, intended to be the symbol of a triumphal entry, merely detracts from the real quality of this complex: the pleasant courtyard beyond. The building penetrates the block to the rue de Bagnolet (**No. 74** there).

★★**[20c-42a.] Logements, 40, rue de Fontarabie,** just off rue des Pyrénées. **Charles and Henry Delacroix.** 1934.

A bit of Rietveld, a bit of cubism, but a lot of Delacroix. Where are you now that we need you?

★★[20c-42a.] **Villa Godin**, 85, rue de Bagnolet, between rue des Pyrénées and rue de la Réunion.

Against the south slopes of Père-Lachaise range a score of two-story "villas," holding on to a piece of Charonne.

[20c-43.] **Maison behind 83, rue de Bagnolet,** between rue des Pyrénées and rue de la Réunion.

A timber and tensile-rodded house, with great glazing and corrugated iron roofing, infills this, as do similar exclamation points, in endless backyards of Charonne.

★[20c-44.] **Logements, 123, rue de la Réunion,** at the south entry to Cimetière du Père-Lachaise. **Gérard Thurnauer.** 1984.

Those spiral Parisian stairs (of the 1980s) show a strong architectural hand. Here a little Mansart (in terne metal), a little green grillage, and some two-toned stucco give way to an entry to Père-Lachaise.

★★★[20c-45.] **Cimetière du Père-Lachaise,** bounded by avenue Gambetta, rue des Rondeaux (entrance), rue de Bagnolet (entrance on rue de la Réunion), and boulevard de Ménilmontant. **Alexandre Brongniart.** 1804.

Brogniart, to set the architectural tone, was the author of the tomb of the Abbé Delille as well as that of the Greffühle family. There are also tombs by **Percier, Fontaine, Viollet-le-Duc, Garnier, Visconti, Hittorf,** and **Davioud,**
Père La Chaise, confessor to Louis XIV, lived in Mont-Louis, a Jesuit convent at the crest of the hill, where the cemetery chapel now stands. In 1682 he requested Rome's authorization to reconstruct a collapsing building:
"Our school [teaching house] at Paris possesses in the suburbs very near the city a small house where our Fathers, once a month, habitually go to relax. It has long been riddled with cracks and is in danger of falling down. Would you permit me, with the aid of our Father and in these circumstances, to come to the aid of our school, which is in a state of extreme poverty, and rebuild this little house to accommodate its necessary functions, and to consecrate there, according to that which I will judge appropriate, the alms that I intend to request from my most excellent and very beloved king."
After its purchase in 1803 by the city, the administrators sought to publicize these new burial precincts by reinterring the bones of **Abélard** and **Héloïse** (1817).
Balzac, Molière, Sarah Bernhardt, Oscar Wilde, Chopin, Delacroix, Géricault, Jim Morrison, Ingres, and Brongniart, are here . . . inter alia.

---

"The cemetery of Père Lachaise, or Cemetery of the East, has already received a great number of tombs. Whether fashion, that frivolous passion that may be motivation even in the most grave and serious matters, shows here its power; or secret vanity which gives ambition to share the bed where rest so many illustrious people; or finally because of the natural majesty of this hill, where one can compare and wander through, successively, views of the city of the dead and that of the living, and seems itself to turn you to dolorous thoughts, it has been remarked that the cemetery of Père Lachaise is the object of sensitive preference on the part of the Parisians. Also, to avoid the inconvenience of inevitable encumbrances, the administration shows itself to be more and more severe on the maintenance of the allotment established for burials among the city's various cemeteries." *Le Magasin pittoresque.* 1850.

---

At the southeast corner of the 20th arrondissement, along boulevard Davout and the cours de Vincennes, starting at **Métro Porte de Montreuil** (or dropping off there from the PC autobus):

## PORTE DE MONTREUIL TO PLACE DE LA NATION

★[20s-1.] **Ateliers, 56-62, boulevard Davout,** between rue Charles-et-Robert and rue Paganini. **Jean-Marie Charpentier, Ros Borath, and B. Hubert.** 1983.

A multilevel industrial park with some architectural style equal to the myriad HBMs along this outside strip of the **Boulevards des Maréchaux.** Brick is dominant over an undulating, functionless, terra-cotta frieze that is just right. More would be vulgar; less would be boring.

[20s-2.] **Ministère de l'Economie et des Finances,** 6, rue Paganini, between rue Reynaldo-Hahn and rue Maryse-Hilsz. **Bernard Zehrfuss.** 1973.

Clichés collected in a pseudostucturalist, heavy-handed block. The HBM at **No. 5,** across the street, is solid, dour, functional, looking with disdain at this flashy parvenu.

★[20s-3.] **Logements, 35, boulevard Davout,** between rue d'Avron, and rue de Lagny. **Pierre Giudicelli.** 1984.

A new street (rue Patrice-de-la-Tour-du-Pin) created by this ensemble, is more important than the modest, multichromatic, but subtle stucco eight- and nine-level blocks that contain it. A pleasant way off the vigorous vagaries of boulevard Davout.

★[20s-4.] **Logements, 31, boulevard Davout,** at rue de Lagny. **Pierre Parat** and **Michel Andrault.** 1985.

Cylindrical concrete stair towers form the *rondelle* fortifications for these middle-class apartments. Mostly successful, they spoil a winning game with dinky bay windows at the top. There are too many ideas here, without follow-through or without elegant detailing. Best seen from afar.

[20s-5.] **Pont du chemin de fer,** at 101, cours de Vincennes. 1888.

Here the Petite Ceinture (the railroad that preceded the current bus) crossed. Supporting is some vintage cast-iron work, in the form of columns and capitals.

★[20s-6.] **Lycée Hélène-Boucher,** 73, cours de Vincennes, between rue des Pyrénées and rue des Maraïchers. **Lucien Sallez.** 1938.

A stylish entry pavilion gives presence—and modern details give substance—to a serious block. The detailing of the serrated window jambs, sloping sills, water tables, and basement grillages is all thoughtful and refined.

★[20s-7.] **Ateliers Bricard,** 84, cours de Vincennes, between passage de la Voûte and avenue du Docteur-Arnold-Netter. **Alexander Borgeaud.** 1904.

Brick and steel create a happy symbiosis, with polychromatic terra-cotta. The owners have maintained this super leftover of early technology with Tender Loving Care.

**★[20s-8.] Logements, 71, avenue du Docteur-Arnold-Netter,** between cours de Vincennes and avenue de Saint-Mandé. **Alain Ferrier** and **André Le Du.** 1985.

A bit of amateur neo-Gaudí, popping sinuous balconies in and out. It has an attractive confectionery character, despite the *retardataire* "mansard."

**[20s-9.] Logements, 27** and **29, rue Marsoulan,** south of cours de Vincennes. circa 1900.

Articulation sublime, where the column becomes an icon. Add wrought-iron lintels to show (No. 29) its guts exposed. Endangered by a permit for a *surélévation.*

**★★★[20s-10.] Barrière du Trône,** place de la Nation, at place des Antilles and place de l'Ile de la Réunion. **Claude-Nicolas Ledoux.** 1788. Sculpture atop, **Etex** and **Dumont.** 1845.

A pair of Ledoux's *barrières* and a pair of guardhouses for a single entrance through the wall of the Fermiers-Généraux. The impaling columns on the latter degrade them to superplinths. Study the former closely to relish the grand rusticated arches. See also **[11sw-28.]**

---

**Over the *Barrières***

"When night had fallen, the city (Paris within the *barrières*) was literally assaulted; the owners of suburban cabarets placed their ladders against the perimeter wall, and barrels of wine, bottles of eau-de-vie, beef, pork, vinegar, descended with the aid of ropes to accomplices who waited on the service road. If some poorly advised clerk attempted to reprimand this extravagant fraud, he was punched, and gagged, and the introduction of prohibited produce continued. What's more, tunnels were dug, passing under the exterior boulevards, under the encircling wall, under the service road, putting in communication the cabarets of the suburbs with those of the city." **Legrand d'Aussy** in *Vie publique et privée des Français,* 1826.

---

**[20s-11.] Logements** over shops, **8–16 rue de Lagny,** off boulevard de Charonne.

Television tubes or gross picture frames: here is an architectural dissonance, jazz surmounting slick shops below. Located near place de la Nation and behind Printemps, this is vendor's architecture. Although, if you lived atop among its trees, you wouldn't have to look at it—just the columns impaling poor Ledoux's pavilions.

# 58
# TWENTIETH ARRONDISSEMENT
## MENILMONTANT
### PLACE GAMBETTA TO PLACE AUGUSTE
### METIVIER

Place Gambetta; Mairie: **Claude-Augustin-Léon-Salleron;** Théâtre de
la Colline: **Valentin Fabré, Jean Perrotet,** and **Alberto Cattani;**
Logements/Fondation Lebaudy: **Auguste Labussière;** Eglise
Coeur-Euchariste-de-Jésus; Villa Sainte-Marie; Réservoirs du Dhuis:
**Eugène Belgrand;** Eglise Notre-Dame-des-Otages: **Julien Barbier;**
Piscine des Tournelles: **Roger Taillibert;** 12, passage Gambetta:
**Catherine Furet;** Crèche Laïque de Saint-Fargeau: **G. Marchand;**
Ateliers/rue de la Duée: **Florent L'Hernault;** HBM, 140, rue
Ménilmontant: **Louis Bonnier;** Hôtel de la Folie-Favart:
**Moreau-Desproux;** La Bellevilloise: **Emmanuel Chaine;**
Bains-Douches Municipaux: **Georges Planche;** Les Acacias: **Ionel
Schein;** Maison, 33, avenue Gambetta: **Louis-Löys Brachet;** place
Auguste Métivier

Métro: **Gambetta** to Métro: **Père-Lachaise**

[20m-48a.] Immeuble, 44, rue de Ménilmontant. Henri Gaudin.
1988.

**[20m-1.] Place Gambetta,** collecting the avenue Gambetta, avenue du Père-Lachaise, rue des Pyrénées, and rue Belgrand.

Here Léon Gambetta (1838–1882), republican, senator, minister of defense, and populist hero, is memorialized. Around the six-pointed *rond-point* are strung a series of cafés, brasseries, and restaurants and the bulky mairie of the 20th arrondissement.

**[20m-2.] Mairie,** 6, place Gambetta, between avenue Gambetta and rue Belgrand. **Claude-Augustin-Léon Salleron.** 1868–1878.

The embassy of Paris to the newly absorbed (1860) villages of Belleville (south) and Charonne, and including the precincts of Ménilmontant, this is somewhat pompous, as befits the emissaries of the Hôtel de Ville.

**★★[20m-3.] Théâtre National de la Colline,** 15, rue Malte-Brun, just off the place and avenue Gambetta. **Valentin Fabré, Jean Perrotet,** and **Alberto Cattani.** 1988.

A cultural outpost in the east, reinforcing the TEP (Théâtre de l'Est Parisien) up the avenue Gambetta near place Saint-Fargeau. The TEP was to have occupied this building, but it seems two theaters are better than one in a culturally starved precinct.

Its seductive facade, sheeted with glass à la Champs-Elysées showrooms, could be a place to sell BMWs. But no—happily, it shelters an auditorium.

**★[20m-4.] Logements, 95, avenue Gambetta,** at rue de la Chine. **Adolphe Bocage.** 1908.

Note the encrustations of green-purple-gray terra-cotta under the first floor—which is the third level here, over the *rez-de-chaussée* and *entresol*. An exuberant participant in Haussmannianism. The avenue Gambetta is a lone spine through Ménilmontant.

**[20m-5.] Logements, 33, rue des Gatines,** near avenue Gambetta. **Dody Coullard.** 1980.

Planned chaos amid Haussmanianism. The flamboyant balconies seem to wave a very vulgar flag. Would that this was of the same quality (1980 model).

**[20m-6.] Logements, 2–14 (except No. 6), rue du Docteur-Paquelin,** between avenue Gambetta and rue Ernest-Lefèvre. **G. Martin.** 1913.

A dour and comfortable curved short street, quiet and withdrawn from the hum of avenue Gambetta. This modest housing is in the spirit of the later HBMs, with a bit of patterned brick, wrought-iron balconies, and one more floor than Haussmann.

**★[20m-7.] Logements de la Fondation Lebaudy,** 5, rue Ernest-Lefèvre. **Auguste Labussière.** 1905.

A great stone arch leads to a many-staired courtyard. Here is housing with a little style at the entrance and a cool courtyard. Within, where "architecture" didn't count for so much, the lintels are steel rather than stone!

**[20m-8.] Logements, 10, rue de l'Adjudant-Réau,** between rue du Capitaine-Marchal and rue de la Dhuis. ca. 1930.

A bold building for the modest local population.

**[20m-9.] Eglise du Coeur-Euchariste-de-Jésus,** 22, rue du Lieutenant-Chauré, off rue Etienne-Mary. **Charles Venner.** 1938.

A country church between Charonne and Ménilmontant that offers a simple place of worship.

**[20m-10.] Square Chauré,** off 17, rue du Lieutenant-Chauré.

Near the Coeur-Euchariste-de-Jésus, it offers a pleasant mews of three-level town houses.

**[20m-11.] Logements, 39, rue Etienne-Marey,** between rue du Lieutenant-Chauré and rue du Surmelin. 1980s.

A serrated set of balconies ravages this quiet street with more Mediterranean-resort styling. From people obsessed with the idea that "modern" means merely something different. Pseudocreativity.

**[20m-12.] Logements, 31, rue du Surmelin and 1, rue du Groupe-Manouchian.** 1930s.

Raked brick-joints, some glass block, and stylish wrought-iron balconies make this a pocket of grace.

★**[20m-13.] Villa Sainte-Marie,** at 95, boulevard Mortier. 1980s.

In any such Parisian alley it is refreshing to find new works supporting the scale, here again with pregnant brick-faced balconies. But the success, as usual, is urbanism, with modest architecture—as opposed to Le Corbusier, Mies, and Wright, who provided magnificent architecture with, usually, non-urbanism.

**[20m-14.] Logements, 100, avenue Gambetta,** corner rue du Groupe-Manouchian. 1930s.

Sleek bay windows are the most "modern" feature on this Haussmannian corner building *(pan coupé)*. The black, filigreed railings are planar, voids severed from a solid sheet. Stylish.

★**[20m-15.] Réservoirs de Ménilmontant/du Dhuis,** 51, rue du Surmelin between rue Darcy and rue Saint-Fargeau. **Eugène Belgrand,** engineer. 1863–1865.

Belgrand, Haussmann's handpicked director of water supply and sewers, created a vast roofed reservoir, supported by a forest of concrete columns. Covered with earth and grass, it forms a greenspace ventilating this district.
"In those days the city was supplied only by water of doubtful quality, coming from the Seine or the Canal de l'Ourcq. These waters had had their own part in propagating epidemics of cholera. The great originality of Haussmann's plan had been to decide, against a body of opinion, to conduct water to Paris in subterranean aqueducts. It was thus determined to build here a two-story reservoir, the upper volume to receive the waters of the Dhuis, the lower that of the Marne, pumped by the works at Saint-Maur. The softness of the land that had to support 130,000 tons of water caused much anxiety among the engineers, as a rupture would have catastrophic consequences in a district as populated as that.
"The reservoir covers two hectares. To preserve the freshness of the spring water *sui generis* the whole is covered with a roof that has been sodded." **Simon Lacordaire.** *Vie et histoire XXe arrondissement.*

★**[20m-16.] Logements, 77, rue Haxo,** at rue du Borrégo. 1980s.

Unique for Paris, these cantilevered balconies, with a great trellised concrete canopy atop, are reminiscent of the work of Frank Lloyd Wright (and perhaps his Dutch disciples).

★[20m-17.] Eglise Notre-Dame-des-Otages, 81, rue Haxo, between rue du Borrégo and rue des Tourelles. Julien Barbier. 1939.

The hostages were those of the communards of 1871, although the building's costume reeks of much later wars (such as that in Spain). It presents a slightly rusticated Art Moderne facade, wishing it were all still Gothic. The timing is as if the Holocaust were remembered in a temple of 2013.

★[20m-18.] Piscine des Tourelles, 148, avenue Gambetta, at rue des Tourelles. Léopold Bevière. 1924. Reconstruction, Roger Taillibert. 1989.

A bold, no-nonsense concrete "fortress," with a new arched laminated timber roof, shelters a public swimming pool and its concomitant stadium seating. Deep blue tile now veneers the body, with openings styled as "eyebrows" and circles to update it all. Taillibert was also architect of the Parc des Princes [16s-20.]

[20m-19.] Logements, 84, rue Haxo, near rue de Belleville. L. E. Durand. 1988.

Bicolored stucco with tile accents and *garde-fous* in yellow-orange. A modest, understated PoMo, waiting for time and weather. The blue entrance doors articulate arrival.

★[20m-20.] Villa du Borrégo, off 33, rue du Borrégo.

A charming impasse with helter-skelter buildings. Look up to see polychromatic tile.

★[20m-21.] Logements, 19–25, passage Gambetta, between rue du Borrégo and rue Saint-Fargeau. 1980s.

To reinforce the street and give it the vent of a garden, this simple complex, understated and gracious, is the kind of neighbor, in a new vernacular, that one would want. Urbanism is victor here in this small-scaled back alley of Ménilmontant. If only some of those overpowered alleys of the 16th arrondissement savored the same charms.

★★[20m-22.] Logements, 12, passage Gambetta, between rue du Borrégo and rue Saint-Fargeau. Catherine Furet. 1988.

Wonderful in architecture, urbanism, and scale. Articulated terraces, columns single and paired, enrich this bit of neo-1920s cubism—updated, of course, with strains of PoMo. This is a complex and rich addition to the vitality of the *passage*.
Next door, at No. 14, is a 19th-century villa that serves as an object and garden foil to Furet's crisp work.

★[20m-23.] Logements, 29, rue Saint-Fargeau, and along passage Gambetta. Groupe Architecture Jean Castex, Philippe Panerai, and Alain Payeur. 1984.

The part along passage Gambetta (★★) is a winner in the race to rebuild the urbanity of this sector. New and old give a graceful scale to the *passage*, mixing new HLMs, *logements sociaux*, with elderly houses and workshops: a lovely fate for this offbeat alley.

The corner block at rue Saint-Fargeau is an unhappy part of this ensemble.

**[20m-24.] Logements, 33, rue Saint-Fargeau,** at passage Gambetta. **J. Audren, P. Lamude, D. Lenglart, R. Schlumberger,** and **F. Touitou.** 1984.

A PoMo neighbor to **No. 29** across passage Gambetta, in the right direction but without the latter's redeeming and brilliant "tail" along the passage. At least the street is honored here, as it was next door.

★**[20m-25.] HBM, 10, rue Saint-Fargeau,** opposite rue du Télégraphe. 1930s.

Brick and bay windows of the 1930s, the decade of most HBMs. The inner life of the block is, as usual, more interesting than the street. There is that HBM specialty, a grand entrance portal.

**[20m-26.] Logements, 3 rue du Télégraphe,** between rue Saint-Fargeau and rue du Borrégo. **G. Debrie.** 1903.

PROPRIETE DE LA SOCIETE ANONYME DES LOGEMENTS POUR FAMILLES NOMBREUSES NO. 1! Louis Kahn would have liked the T-shaped windows of this early experiment in social housing.

★**[20m-27.] Crèche Laïque de Saint-Fargeau,** 33, rue du Télégraphe, between rue du Borrégo and rue de Belleville. **G. Marchand.** 1914.

The cavetto cornice in mosaic tile crowns this large "villa" for the neighborhood's infants.

**[20m-28.] Ateliers, 6, rue Saint-Fargeau,** between rue Pelleport and rue Henri Poincaré. 19th century.

A smiling entrance archway leads to a court, and then another, in "modern" *colombage* of timber and brick. This brings back some of the three-dimensional urbanity of the old Ménilmontant.

★**[20m-29.] Ecole, 121, rue Pelleport,** at rue Taclet. **René Dubos.** 1947.

Because of the war, 1947 sometimes seems like only a continuation of the mid-1930s. The stucco cubism seems somewhat schizophrenic—between glass and moldings. Naturally *retardataire*, it creates a sort of architectural nostalgia.

The iron railings are a special treat, as is the lettering on the facade. It abuts some charming villas.

★**[20m-30.] Logements, 2, rue des Pavillons,** at rue Pixérécourt. **Florent L'Hernault.** 1982.

An ice cream block, somewhat sooty, with metal cagework suspended in front to provide balconies for the not-so-French windows (too wide). Here tile makes it only to the recessed entry: PARIS—PAVILLONS MCMLXXXII. It will soon be a suitably patinaed neighbor.

**[20m-31.] Logements, rue Charles-Friedel and rue Pixérécourt. Cabinet Imagine.** 1989.

**[20m-32.] Ecole de Garçons, 24, rue Olivier-Métra,** at rue de l'Ermitage. 1901.

Tile *(grès)* in the spirit of the Bigots enriches both the spandrels and frieze of this two-level school. The boys are here, the girls across the street. Take a stroll to the end of the building to see the **villa Olivier-Métra,** a charming impasse at **No. 28.**

**★[20m-33.] Maison, 16 bis, rue Olivier-Métra,** between rue Pixérécourt and rue Charles-Friedel. **Louis Thore.** 1926.

This has a bit of the 19th-century English architect Richard Norman Shaw.

**★[20m-34.] Logements, 10–16, rue Olivier-Métra** and **10, rue Charles-Friedel. Cabinet Imagine: R. Belluge, P. Guibert, and Francis Soler.** 1985.

Broken brick, tile, and stucco give an appropriate fractionalization to this relatively bulky building in a field of minor structures. Look through the entrance void to the graceful silhouette of spiral stairs, although the ironwork and window detailing are hopeless. But it's a nice neighbor.

**[20m-35.] Logements, 24, rue Pixérécourt,** opposite rue Olivier-Métra. **Florent L'Hernault.** 1984.

A stucco-and-tile multifamily residence for four. Brutal outside, this is an intellectual's decoration of a barren cube.

**★[20m-36.] Ateliers des Artistes, 17, rue de la Duée,** along passage de la Duée. **Florent L'Hernault.** 1983.

Three simple two-level stucco studio buildings face the beginnings of an ultranarrow roofless *passage.* Their charm comes from sharing the alley with wandering and ancient stones, adding a friendly scale and multicolored sash.

**[20m-37.] Villa Georgina,** 37, rue de la Duée, between passage de la Duée and rue des Pavillons. **Florent L'Hernault.** 1983.

A tiled facade infills this eclectic street; formal and pseudopedimented, it reeks of the quick sketch and ill proportions. Are windows a neo-Renaissance game, or do they also serve? Even Haussmann's strict facades had more logic. Go behind: it is as in the aphorism, "Queen Anne front, Mary Ann behind."

**★[20m-38.] Logements, 4, rue Pixérécourt,** off rue de Ménilmontant. **Christian Enjolras.** 1988.

The Italians were here (in spirit) and left a door handle. Above is understatement worthy of **Ignazio Gardella.**

**★[20m-39.] HBM, 140, rue de Ménilmontant,** at rue de la Chine. **Louis Bonnier.** 1925.

Great interlocking masses of brickwork shelter an inner world of pedestrian space, while maintaining the street facade; one of the solemn *îlots* of social housing pioneered in the 1920s, and here by the great Louis Bonnier (he was 69).

To be demolished as a social cancer, it is in the same rank as the experimental housing of **Minoru Yamasaki** in St. Louis, which won prizes and publication and was finally destroyed by dynamiting. Social deterioration resulted despite architectural qualities at a grand scale.

It is also host to one of the great bakeries of Paris, **Ganachaud,** at **No. 150,** worth a pit stop on the route for bread or more exotic goodies. You will be refueled for more vigorous wanderings thereafter.

**[20m-40.] Maison particulière, 287, rue des Pyrénées,** south of rue de Ménilmontant. circa 1860.

A three-level brick house with front garden left from an earlier Ménilmontant street geometry.

**[20m-41.] Logements, 283–285, rue des Pyrénées,** south of rue de Ménilmontant. **Roger Anger, Mario Heymann, and Pierre Puccinelli.** 1969.

Tiny gray-green tiles clad this serrated cousin of the rue de Romainville. Neocubistic jigs and jags leave their arris at the edge of the street. Barred windows also reek of "safety"—a safety that is in fact an excuse for decoration.

★**[20m-42.] PTT, 248, rue des Pyrénées. Paul Bessine.** 1930s.

The incised graphics on this brick-and-stone PTT are a welcome enrichment. Some slight and delicate iron grillages and tile spandrels give it an elegant boost.

Rusticated stone, gesturing at the base, participates in this classical-*moderne* equivocal equation.

★★**[20m-43.] Pavillon de l'Asile des Petits-Orphelins**/originally **Hôtel de la Folie Favart,** 119, rue de Ménilmontant, corner rue des Pyrénées. **Moreau-Desproux.** circa 1771.

This and the Pavillon de l'Ermitage **[20c-12.]** are Belleville's and Charonne's respective 18th-century monuments. Here is a neo-Classical villa fronting a walled garden.

**[20m-44.] Gymnase, 114, rue de Ménilmontant,** west of rue des Pyrénées. 1988.

Is there a neo-neo-Classical? This cool limestone and travertine athletic center sports a frieze similar to a running fret at the classical position: an appropriately understated background building.

★**[20m-45.] Logements, 115, rue de Ménilmontant,** between rue des Pyrénées and rue de l'Ermitage. 1988.

Concrete that seems almost travertine clads and supports this 11-unit apartment house—a graceful neighbor. From the green bay windows one can glimpse central Paris and Beaubourg down the hill.

★**[20m-46.] Logements, 7–23, rue des Cascades,** between rue de Ménilmontant and rue de Savies. **Antoine Grumbach.** 1980s.

Where water once cascaded down the slopes, Grumbach cascades his buildings, complex and handsome. Walk through and behind to see architecture more sculptured than that of the quiet streetfront.

★★**[20m-47.] Logements, 43–45, rue des Cascades,** between rue de Ménilmontant and rue de Savies. **R. Belluge, P. Guibert,** and **Francis Soler.** 1984.

A simple play of articulated stucco, tile, and bay windows—the ins and outs along this narrow, ancient street hanging along topography's edge. French windows and their *garde-fous* are the detail here. Crisp and well-proportioned.

**[20m-48.] Maison, 3, rue Henri-Chevreau,** along the tracks of the old Petite Ceinture. **T. Claude.** 1980.

Timber framed and skylit, this is redolent of America's Pacific Northwest. A free spirit must live here. The stained shingles add that Portland, Oregon, touch . . . but those flagrant green garage doors!

★★★[20m-48a.] **Immeuble, 44, rue de Ménilmontant,** corner rue Delaitre. **Henri Gaudin.** 1988.

A superb moment of infill, the best in Paris, that brings glory to this bedraggled neighborhood. Within the courtyard are articulations and elegances that sing. Thank God and hurray!

★★[20m-49.] **La Bellevilloise,** 19–21, and 25, rue Boyer, between rue de Ménilmontant and rue Laurence-Savart. Nos. 19–21. **Emmanuel Chaine.** 1910. No. 25. **F. Guillouet.** 1927.

The lower floors of No. 19 have been smoothed and "modernized," but the tile-soffited cavetto cornice and its crowning brick parapet are in turn topped by an elegance of ironwork; note particularly the triumphant corners. Some bastard has incised his mark as well at the entry, but the old frame remembers: early reinforced concrete with the sinuousity of the steel-framed 124, rue Réaumur.

La Bellevilloise was a workers' association, bringing shops to the outer quarters and suburbs of Paris. No. 19 was its headquarters. No. 25 is rich but ponderous, near its suave ancestor.

[20m-50.] **HBM, 3, rue Boyer,** near rue de la Bidassoa. **André Berry** and **Mallot.** 1922.

Access galleries in red grillage enliven this venerable HBM.

★★[20m-51.] **HBM/Fondation Mme. Jules Lebaudy,** 7, rue d'Annam, between rue de la Bidassoa and rue du Retrait. **Auguste Labussière.** 1913.

Built when ornament was in fashion for the poor. Sculpture embraces a tiled barrel-vaulted entry, and iron and rubble stonework enrich the facade. Steel lintels cry progress in the new century, just before World War I. This is a luxurious remembrance of how the less privileged were once honored, as well as housed.

The foundation was instrumental in the construction of several Parisian *logements sociaux.*

★[20m-52.] **Bains-Douches Municipaux, 27, rue de la Bidassoa,** opposite rue Boyer. **Georges Planche.** 1934.

The 1930s brick (symbol of modernity of municipal housing, schools, and swimming pools) here veneers a modest public bath, where even the chimney becomes a major form, a tower signaling *hot water* here, in a modern bathing place.

[20m-53.] **Ateliers, 22, rue Soleillet,** off rue Sorbier. **Ernest Bertrand.** 1911.

Another early iron-and-glass industrial remnant. Look into the courtyard.

★[20m-54.] **Hotel d'Activités Les Lilas,** 18–20, rue Soleillet, between rue des Partants and place Henri-Matisse. **Ayméric Zublena.** 1985.

Tan tile and green sash make these ateliers handsome neighbors to **Nos. 8–10** across the alley.

★★[20m-55.] **Logements, 10, rue Soleillet,** at place Henri-Matisse. **Ayméric Zublena.** 1985.

Yellow sash and green balcony railings enliven this handsome precast-concrete housing. Surrounding a central courtyard, it spills down a flight of stairs to the place Henri-Matisse. One of the most urbane and successful projects in the ZAC des Amandiers.

[20m-56.] **PTT, 26, rue Sorbier,** at rue Elisa-Borey, and place Henri-Matisse. **Georges Planche.** 1933.

The second *T* (for telephone) of PTT perforates the sky with microwave finials. Once upon a time, the PTT was an architectural leader. This lusty concrete building retains traces of the Art Nouveau in form, plus a frank industrial modernism.

[20m-57.] **Conservatoire Municipal due Vingtième Arrondissement Georges-Bizet,** 54, rue des Cendriers between rue des Amandiers and rue Duris. **Jean-Claude Jallat** and **Guy de Nayer.** 1985.

This unfortunate architectural atrocity cannot even claim the mantle of kitsch. The false fronts that punctuate the facade are gross. Blow it up.

★★[20m-58.] **Les Coudriers (logements),** 24, rue de Tlemcen, between rue Duris and rue des Amandiers. **Pierre Parat** and **Michel Andrault.** 1985.

Brick and bay windows surround a central courtyard that displays sculpture and planting but is devoid of activity. How about less mineralization and more planting—there are *four* trees! Something more should happen here: open a café.

★[20m-59.] **Les Acacias (logements),** 9–17 rue Duris, between passage Duris and rue Jacques-Prévert. **Ionel Schein.** 1984.

Though pretentious at its "bow," this has engaging interior spaces. Sadly for the public, much of the charm of Paris is now locked within private center blocks, formerly accessible to a friendly buzz but now secured against all but residents and friends who know the code.

★★[20m-60.] **Logements, 15, rue des Amandiers,** between rue Houdart and rue Jacques-Prévert. **Renaud Bardon, Pierre Colboc,** and **Jean-Paul Philippon.** 1988.

Post Modern here matures in a subtle interplay of form (in stucco and tile, of course), with accents of color, white, grays, and nile green. A whole city like this would seem to reek of Alexander Korda's futuristic film *Things to Come* (1936), where the sets of Korda's brother, Vincent, created an elegant protomodern world.

★[20m-61.] **Maison, 33, avenue Gambetta,** between rue Désirée and rue Sorbier. **Louis-Loÿs Brachet.** 1907.

Art Nouveau manners (in *béton armé*) with a corner oriel, a roof terrace overlooking the Jardin Samuel de Champlain, and other romantic, picturesque postures. This is a lone sheep in wolf's clothing among Haussmanian progeny. It is abandoned and needs love. Buy it.

# INDEX

# NOTES

# NOTES

# NOTES

# NOTES

# NOTES

# NOTES